Movies

**CineBooks Home Library Series
No. 6**

War Movies

A guide
to more than 500 films
on videocassette

CineBooks

CineBooks
Evanston, Illinois, 1989

President: Anita L. Werling; **Editorial Director:** William Leahy; **Editors:** James J. Mulay, Daniel Curran, Jeffrey H. Wallenfeldt, Jenny Mueller; **Research Director:** William C. Clogston; **Associate Editors:** Jeannette Hori, Jennifer Howe, Michaela Tuohy.

Business Manager: Jack Medor; **Assistant:** Bernie Gregoryk; **Advertising Manager:** Craig Carter.

Published by CineBooks, a division of News America Publishing Incorporated

Copyright © 1989, News America Publishing Incorporated

All rights reserved; no part of this book may be reproduced or utilized in any form or means, electronic or mechanical, including photocopying, recording or by any information retrieval system, without permission in writing from CINEBOOKS, 990 Grove Street, Evanston, Illinois 60201.

ISBN: 0-933997-25-6

Printed in the United States

First Edition

1   2   3   4   5   6   7   8   9   10

Table of Contents

Introduction vii

Films by Star Rating ix

Films by Parental Recommendation xii

Films by Year xvi

Film Reviews 1

Alternate Title Index 171

Name Index 173

Introduction

Because of its inherent conflict war is easy to dramatize and hence has long been a favorite subject of filmmakers, who have both glorified and deplored it—though some critics have argued that it is impossible to make an antiwar movie because the very nature of the film spectacle glamorizes the subject. Whatever one's reactions to war, however, it is difficult to deny the exhilaration that a good war film elicits in the viewer, hard to imagine anyone who isn't moved by the raising of the American flag in the finale of THE SANDS OF IWO JIMA, or overcome with sadness by the cold-blooded murder of the German soldier by partisans at the end of A TIME TO LOVE AND A TIME TO DIE.

Within the pages of this book, there are reviews of hundreds of films about war, many of which—those propaganda efforts produced to entice men to enlist—are inseparable from war itself. Films such as AIR FORCE; BOMBARDIER; or WAKE ISLAND were as much a part of the war effort as any military offensive, and with few exceptions, the war films made between 1930 and the mid-1960s generally present a view of war that is romantic, exciting, and heroic. The war in Vietnam, the first fought on television, began to alter the public's perception, however. Instead of watching a wounded lookout fall bloodlessly from a tree in BATAAN, Americans saw geysers of real blood spurt from combatants on the nightly news. After television's Vietnam, Hollywood's WW II looked like child's play. Only John Wayne had the audacity in his GREEN BERETS to contradict the images that television brought into our homes. It was not until some time after US involvement in the war ended that American audiences began to see other films on the subject. COMING HOME and THE DEER HUNTER examined the aftershock of Vietnam; Stallone's "Rambo" films distanced audiences by turning their Vietnam veteran hero into a comic book character; PLATOON practically put the viewer in combat boots and a rice paddy. And after taking a hyperrealistic journey into the war's heart of darkness in APOCALYPSE NOW, Francis Coppola drove what may be viewed as the final nail into the coffin of Vietnam with GARDENS OF STONE—a film that manages to be pro-military *and* antiwar without depicting combat.

Because the nature of battle has changed, the war film as a genre has also developed and been redefined. When one thinks of a war film, the Civil War may come to mind, with its visions of cannons exploding and raised bayonets, or one may picture German tanks rumbling through a devastated French village. Instead of cataloging only these films, we have taken a broad look at film's treatment of war. While a majority of the entries deal specifically with battle (from Alexander's invasion of India to Nicaraguan border skirmishes) others consider the psychological effects of war or civilian life during wartime. Alfred Hitchcock never made a war film per se, but his LIFEBOAT is one of the greatest pictures ever made about human nature during wartime. Francois Truffaut, known for his films about obsessive love, stretched this theme to include THE GREEN ROOM, a dark story of a WW I veteran who builds a shrine to the dead. Charlie Chaplin used satire in THE GREAT DICTATOR to create one of the most astute commentaries on the evils of tyranny, and Ernst Lubitsch, perhaps film's greatest director of comedies, also dealt with the war humorously in TO BE OR NOT TO BE, the outrageous tale of a theater director who helps foil a Nazi plan. On the same page as THE DESERT FOX, the biography of the brilliant WW II German field commander Erwin Rommel, you can find the 1986 action picture THE DELTA FORCE, the story of a war waged on terms dictated by the modern warrior known as a terrorist or freedom fighter. Although the French Resistance was prominently featured in number of films, terrorism is relatively new to film, and while several films have taken on the subject, Gillo Pontecorvo's THE BATTLE OF ALGIERS is still the best. Recent developments in military technology have also brought the threat of nuclear obliteration, a possibility the cinema has dealt with as spectacular drama (FAIL SAFE), personal tragedy (TESTAMENT), black comedy (DR. STRANGELOVE), and even as a love story (HIROSHIMA MON AMOUR).

Instead of rekindling the flames of war by championing a film like RAMBO: FIRST BLOOD PART II, we have chosen in this book to look at war from all sides. We have also included a selection of foreign pictures that offer a variety of perspectives on world military history, films from Argentina (A FUNNY, DIRTY LITTLE WAR), Australia (GALLIPOLI) Czechoslovakia (TRANSPORT FROM PARADISE), France (BLACK AND WHITE IN COLOR), Nazi Germany (KOLBERG), Japan (FIRES ON THE PLAIN), Libya (LION OF THE DESERT), Poland (ASHES AND DIAMONDS), or the Soviet Union (THE BALLAD OF A SOLDIER). We can only hope that this guide will help video buyers and renters choose from a growing market that appeals to hawks and doves alike.

FILMS BY STAR RATING

Listed below are all films included in this volume by Star rating. The ratings indicate: *****: masterpiece; ****: excellent; ***: good; **: fair; *: poor; zero: without merit

5 Stars
AFRICAN QUEEN, THE
AIR FORCE
ALEXANDER NEVSKY
ALL QUIET ON THE WESTERN FRONT
APOCALYPSE NOW
BATTLE OF ALGIERS, THE
BEAU GESTE
BEST YEARS OF OUR LIVES, THE
BRIDGE ON THE RIVER KWAI, THE
CABARET
CASABLANCA
CHARGE OF THE LIGHT BRIGADE, THE
DRUMS ALONG THE MOHAWK
FOREIGN CORRESPONDENT
FORT APACHE
49TH PARALLEL
FOUR FEATHERS, THE
GONE WITH THE WIND
GRAND ILLUSION
GREAT DICTATOR, THE
HENRY V
HIROSHIMA, MON AMOUR
HOPE AND GLORY
LAWRENCE OF ARABIA
LIFEBOAT
MRS. MINIVER
NIGHT TRAIN TO MUNICH
OPEN CITY
PAISAN
PATHS OF GLORY
PATTON
RAN
RED BADGE OF COURAGE, THE
RICHARD III
RIO GRANDE
SEA HAWK, THE
SERGEANT YORK
STALAG 17
TO BE OR NOT TO BE
TWELVE O'CLOCK HIGH
ZULU

4 Stars
ALAMO, THE
ASHES AND DIAMONDS
ASSAULT, THE
BACK TO BATAAN
BALLAD OF A SOLDIER
BATAAN
BIG RED ONE, THE
BIRDY
BOAT, THE
BREAKER MORANT
BRIDGES AT TOKO-RI, THE
BURN
CHIMES AT MIDNIGHT
COURT-MARTIAL OF BILLY MITCHELL, THE
CROSS OF IRON
CRUEL SEA, THE
DAM BUSTERS, THE
DAMNED, THE
DANTON
DAWN PATROL, THE
DEER HUNTER, THE
DESERT FOX, THE
DESTINATION TOKYO
DIARY OF ANNE FRANK, THE
DIRTY DOZEN, THE
DR. STRANGELOVE: OR HOW I LEARNED TO STOP WORRYING AND LOVE THE BOMB
DRUMS
DUCK SOUP
84 CHARLIE MOPIC
EMPIRE OF THE SUN
FAREWELL TO ARMS, A
FIRE OVER ENGLAND
FIRES ON THE PLAIN
FROM HERE TO ETERNITY
FULL METAL JACKET
GALLIPOLI
GARDEN OF THE FINZI-CONTINIS, THE
GARDENS OF STONE
GATE OF HELL
GENERALE DELLA ROVERE
GERMANY, YEAR ZERO
GOOD, THE BAD, AND THE UGLY, THE
GREAT ESCAPE, THE
GREAT SANTINI, THE
GUADALCANAL DIARY
GUY NAMED JOE, A
HEARTBREAK RIDGE
IN WHICH WE SERVE
IVAN THE TERRIBLE, PARTS I & II
KAGEMUSHA
KAMERADSCHAFT
KANAL
LAST OF THE MOHICANS, THE
LIFE AND DEATH OF COLONEL BLIMP, THE
LIVES OF A BENGAL LANCER
LONGEST DAY, THE
MARATHON MAN
MARRIAGE OF MARIA BRAUN, THE
M*A*S*H
MEN IN WAR
MEPHISTO
MERRY CHRISTMAS, MR. LAWRENCE
MISSING
MOROCCO
MOUSE THAT ROARED, THE
MY NAME IS IVAN
OBJECTIVE, BURMA!
PAWNBROKER, THE
PLATOON
PORK CHOP HILL
RAZOR'S EDGE, THE
SABOTEUR
SAHARA
SALVADOR
SAND PEBBLES, THE
SANDS OF IWO JIMA
SAYONARA
SEVEN DAYS IN MAY
SHE WORE A YELLOW RIBBON
SHOP ON MAIN STREET, THE
SOUTHERN COMFORT
SPARTACUS
STAGE DOOR CANTEEN
STRANGER, THE
THEY DIED WITH THEIR BOOTS ON
THEY WERE EXPENDABLE
THRONE OF BLOOD
TIME TO LOVE AND A TIME TO DIE, A
TRAIN, THE
TWO WOMEN
ULZANA'S RAID
UP IN ARMS
WAKE ISLAND
WATCH ON THE RHINE
WHAT PRICE GLORY?

3.5 Stars
BANANAS
BATTLE OF THE BULGE
BEAST, THE
BEHOLD A PALE HORSE
BILOXI BLUES
BLOOD ON THE SUN

BRIDGE AT REMAGEN, THE
BURMESE HARP
CAST A GIANT SHADOW
CATCH-22
COMMANDOS STRIKE AT DAWN, THE
CORNERED
COUP DE GRACE
COURT MARTIAL
CRANES ARE FLYING, THE
DARK JOURNEY
DESERT RATS, THE
DIAMONDS OF THE NIGHT
DISTANT DRUMS
EDGE OF DARKNESS
EL CID
EYE OF THE NEEDLE
FATHER GOOSE
FORCE 10 FROM NAVARONE
FUNNY, DIRTY LITTLE WAR, A
GO TELL THE SPARTANS
GOOD MORNING, VIETNAM
GREEN ROOM, THE
GUNGA DIN
GUNS OF NAVARONE, THE
HAMBURGER HILL
IMMORTAL BATTALION, THE
IMMORTAL SERGEANT, THE
INN OF THE SIXTH HAPPINESS, THE
JUDGMENT AT NUREMBERG
KILLING FIELDS, THE
KING OF HEARTS
LA MARSEILLAISE
LAST METRO, THE
LES CARABINIERS
LOST PATROL, THE
LOVE AND DEATH
MAC ARTHUR
MEN, THE
MISTER ROBERTS
NICHOLAS AND ALEXANDRA
ODESSA FILE, THE
ONE OF OUR AIRCRAFT IS MISSING
OPERATION PETTICOAT
PASSAGE TO MARSEILLE
PEDESTRIAN, THE
PIMPERNEL SMITH
REDS
RETURN OF THE SOLDIER, THE
REVOLT OF JOB, THE
SHENANDOAH
SOLDIER OF ORANGE
SPITFIRE
THIRTY SECONDS OVER TOKYO
THIS LAND IS MINE
TIN DRUM, THE
TUNES OF GLORY
TWILIGHT'S LAST GLEAMING
UNDER FIRE

VON RYAN'S EXPRESS
WALK IN THE SUN, A
WE DIVE AT DAWN
WHERE EAGLES DARE
WHO'LL STOP THE RAIN?
WIND AND THE LION, THE
WOODEN HORSE, THE
YEAR OF LIVING DANGEROUSLY, THE
YOUNG LIONS, THE

3 Stars

ADVENTURES OF TARTU, THE
ALEXANDER THE GREAT
ASSISI UNDERGROUND, THE
BAT 21
BATTLE OF BRITAIN, THE
BATTLE OF NERETVA
BLACK AND WHITE IN COLOR
BLUE MAX, THE
BOMBARDIER
BOYS FROM BRAZIL, THE
BRIDGE TOO FAR, A
CAL
CARNIVAL IN FLANDERS
CLOAK AND DAGGER
COCKLESHELL HEROES, THE
COLDITZ STORY, THE
COLONEL REDL
COMING HOME
CRIMSON ROMANCE
CUBA
D-DAY, THE SIXTH OF JUNE
DAMN THE DEFIANT!
DAVID
DESIREE
DESTINATION GOBI
D.I., THE
DOCTOR ZHIVAGO
DOGS OF WAR, THE
DON'T CRY, IT'S ONLY THUNDER
DRAGON SEED
DRUMS IN THE DEEP SOUTH
DUELLISTS, THE
EAGLE HAS LANDED, THE
ELUSIVE CORPORAL, THE
EVERY TIME WE SAY GOODBYE
FAIL SAFE
55 DAYS AT PEKING
FIGHTING SEABEES, THE
FIREFOX
FLAT TOP
FLESH AND BLOOD
FLYING LEATHERNECKS
FLYING TIGERS
FOUR IN A JEEP
FRIEDA
GO FOR BROKE
GUNG HO!
HELL TO ETERNITY
HIDING PLACE, THE

HILL 24 DOESN'T ANSWER
HOME OF THE BRAVE
HORSE SOLDIERS, THE
HOW I WON THE WAR
HUMAN CONDITION, THE
IN HARM'S WAY
KELLY'S HEROES
KIM
KOLBERG
LION OF THE DESERT
LITTLE BIG MAN
LORDS OF DISCIPLINE, THE
LOVE AND ANARCHY
MAC ARTHUR'S CHILDREN
MALTA STORY
MARCH OR DIE
MASSACRE IN ROME
MORITURI
NAPOLEON
NIGHT OF THE GENERALS, THE
NIGHT OF THE SHOOTING STARS, THE
NORTHERN PURSUIT
NURSE EDITH CAVELL
OFFICER AND A GENTLEMAN, AN
ONLY WAY, THE
PLENTY
PT 109
PURPLE HEART, THE
PURSUIT OF THE GRAF SPEE, THE
RAZOR'S EDGE, THE
ROLLING THUNDER
RUN SILENT, RUN DEEP
SALUTE JOHN CITIZEN
SEA SHALL NOT HAVE THEM, THE
SEA WOLVES, THE
SHERLOCK HOLMES AND THE SECRET WEAPON
SOME KIND OF HERO
SPY IN BLACK, THE
START THE REVOLUTION WITHOUT ME
TAPS
TESTAMENT
THIS ABOVE ALL
THIS IS THE ARMY
TOO LATE THE HERO
TRANSPORT FROM PARADISE
WALKER
WANNSEE CONFERENCE, THE
WAR AND PEACE
WAR AND PEACE
WAR LOVER, THE
WARGAMES
YANK IN THE R.A.F., A
ZULU DAWN

2.5 Stars
AGAINST ALL FLAGS
ALVAREZ KELLY
ANZIO
AU REVOIR LES ENFANTS
BATTLE CRY
BATTLE OF AUSTERLITZ, THE
BERLIN EXPRESS
BOYS IN COMPANY C, THE
BRADY'S ESCAPE
BUCK PRIVATES
CLAY PIGEON, THE
CODE NAME: EMERALD
DARBY'S RANGERS
DAYS OF GLORY
DEEP SIX, THE
DESPERATE JOURNEY
FIRST BLOOD
GLORY AT SEA
GREAT GUNS
HANNA'S WAR
HEROES
HITLER'S CHILDREN
HOT BOX, THE
JOHNNY GOT HIS GUN
JUNGLE PATROL
KING RAT
LOST COMMAND, THE
LOVE IN GERMANY, A
MASTER RACE, THE
MURPHY'S WAR
NIGHT PORTER, THE
1941
NO DRUMS, NO BUGLES
NORTH STAR, THE
ODD ANGRY SHOT, THE
ON THE BEACH
ONE THAT GOT AWAY, THE
PRIVATE BENJAMIN
SECRET WAR OF HARRY
  FRIGG, THE
SHOUT AT THE DEVIL
SLAUGHTERHOUSE-FIVE
STREAMERS
SUNDOWN
SWING SHIFT
THAT HAMILTON WOMAN
TO BE OR NOT TO BE
TO HELL AND BACK
TOBRUK
UGLY AMERICAN, THE
UNBEARABLE LIGHTNESS OF
  BEING, THE
WACKIEST SHIP IN THE ARMY,
  THE
WARKILL

2 Stars
ACTION IN ARABIA
AWAY ALL BOATS
BATTLE HELL
BEHIND THE RISING SUN
BLACK TENT, THE
BRASS TARGET
BUCCANEER, THE
CALL OUT THE MARINES
CAPTIVE HEARTS
CROMWELL
CRY OF BATTLE
DEADLINE
DEATH BEFORE DISHONOR
DELTA FORCE, THE
DIRTY HEROES
DISTANT THUNDER
ELENI
ENSIGN PULVER
ESCAPE TO ATHENA
FAREWELL TO THE KING
FINAL COUNTDOWN, THE
FIRST YANK INTO TOKYO
FORBIDDEN GAMES
FOUR HORSEMEN OF THE
  APOCALYPSE, THE
FRANCIS IN THE NAVY
FROM HELL TO VICTORY
GOING HOME
GREEN BERETS, THE
HANOI HILTON, THE
HELLCATS OF THE NAVY
HINDENBURG, THE
HITLER: THE LAST TEN DAYS
INVASION U.S.A.
KEEP, THE
LAST DAY OF THE WAR, THE
LATINO
MIDWAY
MIRACLE OF THE WHITE
  STALLIONS
MISFIT BRIGADE, THE
MISSING IN ACTION
MISSING IN ACTION 2—THE
  BEGINNING
MR. WINKLE GOES TO WAR
NIGHTWARS
OFF LIMITS
OPERATION AMSTERDAM
OUTPOST IN MOROCCO
PLATOON LEADER
P.O.W. THE ESCAPE
POWER PLAY
PRAYER FOR THE DYING, A
PURPLE HEARTS
REVOLUTION
RIDDLE OF THE SANDS, THE
SNOW TREASURE
STEEL CLAW, THE
SUPERNATURALS, THE
TOP GUN
TORA! TORA! TORA!
UNCOMMON VALOR
VICTORY
WHITE GHOST
WILD GEESE, THE

1.5 Stars
DRAGONFLY SQUADRON
HITLER
IRON EAGLE
LAST REMAKE OF BEAU
  GESTE, THE
LITTLE DRUMMER GIRL, THE
MISSION BATANGAS
NAKED AND THE DEAD, THE
OPERATION CIA
RAMBO III
REASON TO LIVE, A REASON
  TO DIE, A
REBEL
REBEL LOVE
SOLDIER'S REVENGE
TARAS BULBA
VOYAGE OF THE DAMNED
WHICH WAY TO THE FRONT?
WILD GEESE II

1 Star
ANGKOR-CAMBODIA EXPRESS
ASSAULT OF THE REBEL GIRLS
BATTLE TAXI
BEST DEFENSE
BRADDOCK: MISSING IN
  ACTION III
CONQUEROR, THE
FINAL OPTION, THE
FLYING DEUCES, THE
IRON EAGLE II
LAST HUNTER, THE
PRIVATES ON PARADE
RAID ON ROMMEL
RED DAWN
SALZBURG CONNECTION, THE
SKY BANDITS
SOLDIER BLUE
TASTE OF HELL, A
TIME OF DESTINY, A

Zero Stars
NO DEAD HEROES
RAMBO: FIRST BLOOD, PART II

FILMS BY PARENTAL RECOMMENDATION (PR)

Listed below are films by their Parental Recommendation (PR). The recommendations indicate: AA—good for children; A—acceptable for children; C—cautionary, some scenes may be objectionable; O—objectionable for children

AA
AFRICAN QUEEN, THE, 1951
ALAMO, THE, 1960
DUCK SOUP, 1933
FRANCIS IN THE NAVY, 1955
INN OF THE SIXTH HAPPINESS, THE, 1958
KIM, 1950
MIRACLE OF THE WHITE STALLIONS, 1963
THIS IS THE ARMY, 1943
UP IN ARMS, 1944

A
ACTION IN ARABIA, 1944
ADVENTURES OF TARTU, THE, 1943
AGAINST ALL FLAGS, 1952
AIR FORCE, 1943
ALEXANDER THE GREAT, 1956
ALVAREZ KELLY, 1966
ANZIO, 1968
AUSTERLITZ, 1960
AWAY ALL BOATS, 1956
BACK TO BATAAN, 1945
BALLAD OF A SOLDIER, 1960
BATTLE CRY, 1955
BATTLE HELL, 1957
BATTLE OF BRITAIN, THE, 1969
BATTLE OF NERETVA, 1969
BATTLE OF THE BULGE, 1965
BATTLE TAXI, 1955
BEAU GESTE, 1939
BEST YEARS OF OUR LIVES, THE, 1946
BLACK TENT, THE, 1956
BOMBARDIER, 1943
BRIDGES AT TOKO-RI, THE, 1954
BUCCANEER, THE, 1958
CALL OUT THE MARINES, 1942
CARNIVAL IN FLANDERS, 1936
CASABLANCA, 1942
CHARGE OF THE LIGHT BRIGADE, THE, 1936
CLAY PIGEON, THE, 1949
CLOAK AND DAGGER, 1946
COCKLESHELL HEROES, THE, 1955
COLDITZ STORY, THE, 1955
COMMANDOS STRIKE AT DAWN, THE, 1942
COURT MARTIAL, 1954
COURT-MARTIAL OF BILLY MITCHELL, THE, 1955
CRANES ARE FLYING, THE, 1960
CROMWELL, 1970
CRUEL SEA, THE, 1953
CRY OF BATTLE, 1963
D-DAY, THE SIXTH OF JUNE, 1956
DAM BUSTERS, THE, 1955
DAMN THE DEFIANT!, 1962
DARBY'S RANGERS, 1958
DARK JOURNEY, 1937
DAYS OF GLORY, 1944
DEEP SIX, THE, 1958
DESERT FOX, THE, 1951
DESERT RATS, THE, 1953
DESIREE, 1954
DESPERATE JOURNEY, 1942
DESTINATION GOBI, 1953
DESTINATION TOKYO, 1944
D.I., THE, 1957
DIARY OF ANNE FRANK, THE, 1959
DIRTY HEROES, 1971
DISTANT DRUMS, 1951
DOCTOR ZHIVAGO, 1965
DRAGON SEED, 1944
DRAGONFLY SQUADRON, 1953
DRUMS, 1938
DRUMS IN THE DEEP SOUTH, 1951
EDGE OF DARKNESS, 1943
EL CID, 1961
ELUSIVE CORPORAL, THE, 1963
EMPIRE OF THE SUN, 1987
ENSIGN PULVER, 1964
FAREWELL TO ARMS, A, 1932
55 DAYS AT PEKING, 1963
FIRE OVER ENGLAND, 1937
FLAT TOP, 1952
FOREIGN CORRESPONDENT, 1940
FORT APACHE, 1948
49TH PARALLEL, 1941
FOUR FEATHERS, THE, 1939
FOUR HORSEMEN OF THE APOCALYPSE, THE, 1962
FOUR IN A JEEP, 1951
FRIEDA, 1947
GLORY AT SEA, 1952
GO FOR BROKE, 1951
GONE WITH THE WIND, 1939
GRAND ILLUSION, 1937
GREAT DICTATOR, THE, 1940
GREAT ESCAPE, THE, 1963
GUY NAMED JOE, A, 1943
HELL TO ETERNITY, 1960
HELLCATS OF THE NAVY, 1957
HENRY V, 1944
HEROES, 1977
HILL 24 DOESN'T ANSWER, 1955
IMMORTAL BATTALION, THE, 1944
IMMORTAL SERGEANT, THE, 1943
IN HARM'S WAY, 1965
IN WHICH WE SERVE, 1942
IVAN THE TERRIBLE, PARTS I & II, 1945
JUNGLE PATROL, 1948
LA MARSEILLAISE, 1938
LAST DAY OF THE WAR, THE, 1969
LAST OF THE MOHICANS, THE, 1936
LIFE AND DEATH OF COLONEL BLIMP, THE, 1945
LIFEBOAT, 1944
LIVES OF A BENGAL LANCER, 1935
MAC ARTHUR, 1977
MASTER RACE, THE, 1944
MIDWAY, 1976
MISSION BATANGAS, 1968
MISTER ROBERTS, 1955
MR. WINKLE GOES TO WAR, 1944
MRS. MINIVER, 1942
NAPOLEON, 1955
NIGHT TRAIN TO MUNICH, 1940
NO DRUMS, NO BUGLES, 1971
NORTHERN PURSUIT, 1943
NURSE EDITH CAVELL, 1939
OBJECTIVE, BURMA!, 1945
ONE OF OUR AIRCRAFT IS MISSING, 1942
ONE THAT GOT AWAY, THE, 1958
ONLY WAY, THE, 1970
OPERATION AMSTERDAM, 1960
OPERATION CIA, 1965
OPERATION PETTICOAT, 1959
OUTPOST IN MOROCCO, 1949
PASSAGE TO MARSEILLE, 1944
PIMPERNEL SMITH, 1942
PT 109, 1963
PURPLE HEART, THE, 1944

PURSUIT OF THE GRAF SPEE, 1957
REASON TO LIVE, A REASON TO DIE, 1974
RIO GRANDE, 1950
SABOTEUR, 1942
SAHARA, 1943
SALUTE JOHN CITIZEN, 1942
SAYONARA, 1957
SEA HAWK, THE, 1940
SEA WOLVES, THE, 1980
SERGEANT YORK, 1941
SHE WORE A YELLOW RIBBON, 1949
SHERLOCK HOLMES AND THE SECRET WEAPON, 1942
SNOW TREASURE, 1968
SPITFIRE, 1943
SPY IN BLACK, THE, 1939
STAGE DOOR CANTEEN, 1943
STEEL CLAW, THE, 1961
SUNDOWN, 1941
TARAS BULBA, 1962
TESTAMENT, 1983
THAT HAMILTON WOMAN, 1941
THEY DIED WITH THEIR BOOTS ON, 1942
THEY WERE EXPENDABLE, 1945
THIRTY SECONDS OVER TOKYO, 1944
THIS ABOVE ALL, 1942
THIS LAND IS MINE, 1943
TO BE OR NOT TO BE, 1942
TOBRUK, 1966
TRANSPORT FROM PARADISE, 1967
WACKIEST SHIP IN THE ARMY, THE, 1961
WAKE ISLAND, 1942
WALK IN THE SUN, A, 1945
WARGAMES, 1983
WATCH ON THE RHINE, 1943
WE DIVE AT DAWN, 1943
WHICH WAY TO THE FRONT?, 1970
WOODEN HORSE, THE, 1951
YANK IN THE R.A.F., A, 1941

A-C

AU REVOIR LES ENFANTS, 1988
BRASS TARGET, 1978
BREAKER MORANT, 1980
CAST A GIANT SHADOW, 1966
ELENI, 1985
FORCE 10 FROM NAVARONE, 1978
GALLIPOLI, 1981
KAMERADSCHAFT, 1931
LOST COMMAND, THE, 1966
LOVE AND DEATH, 1975
MALTA STORY, 1954
MEN IN WAR, 1957
MISSING, 1982
NORTH STAR, THE, 1943
RICHARD III, 1956
RUN SILENT, RUN DEEP, 1958
SEA SHALL NOT HAVE THEM, THE, 1955
SECRET WAR OF HARRY FRIGG, THE, 1968
SKY BANDITS, 1986
SWING SHIFT, 1984
TIME TO LOVE AND A TIME TO DIE, A, 1958
TO HELL AND BACK, 1955
TOP GUN, 1986
UGLY AMERICAN, THE, 1963
VICTORY, 1981
VOYAGE OF THE DAMNED, 1976
WANNSEE CONFERENCE, THE, 1987
WAR AND PEACE, 1956
WAR AND PEACE, 1967

C

ALEXANDER NEVSKY, 1939
ALL QUIET ON THE WESTERN FRONT, 1930
ASHES AND DIAMONDS, 1961
ASSAULT, THE, 1986
ASSAULT OF THE REBEL GIRLS, 1960
ASSISI UNDERGROUND, THE, 1985
BANANAS, 1971
BATAAN, 1943
BATTLE OF ALGIERS, THE, 1967
BEHIND THE RISING SUN, 1943
BEHOLD A PALE HORSE, 1964
BERLIN EXPRESS, 1948
BIG RED ONE, THE, 1980
BLACK AND WHITE IN COLOR, 1976
BLOOD ON THE SUN, 1945
BLUE MAX, THE, 1966
BRADY'S ESCAPE, 1984
BRIDGE AT REMAGEN, THE, 1969
BRIDGE ON THE RIVER KWAI, THE, 1957
BRIDGE TOO FAR, A, 1977
CABARET, 1972
CAPTIVE HEARTS, 1988
CHIMES AT MIDNIGHT, 1967
CODE NAME: EMERALD, 1985
CORNERED, 1945
COUP DE GRACE, 1978
CRIMSON ROMANCE, 1934
CUBA, 1979
DAVID, 1979
DAWN PATROL, THE, 1938
DEATH BEFORE DISHONOR, 1987
DIAMONDS OF THE NIGHT, 1964
DR. STRANGELOVE: OR HOW I LEARNED TO STOP WORRYING AND LOVE THE BOMB, 1964
DUELLISTS, THE, 1977
EAGLE HAS LANDED, THE, 1976
ESCAPE TO ATHENA, 1979
EVERY TIME WE SAY GOODBYE, 1986
FAIL SAFE, 1964
FAREWELL TO THE KING, 1989
FIGHTING SEABEES, THE, 1944
FINAL COUNTDOWN, THE, 1980
FIREFOX, 1982
FIRST YANK INTO TOKYO, 1945
FLYING LEATHERNECKS, 1951
FLYING TIGERS, 1942
FORBIDDEN GAMES, 1953
FROM HELL TO VICTORY, 1979
FROM HERE TO ETERNITY, 1953
GARDEN OF THE FINZI-CONTINIS, THE, 1971
GENERALE DELLA ROVERE, 1959
GERMANY, YEAR ZERO, 1947
GOING HOME, 1988
GREAT SANTINI, THE, 1979
GREEN BERETS, THE, 1968
GUADALCANAL DIARY, 1943
GUNG HO!, 1943
GUNGA DIN, 1939
GUNS OF NAVARONE, THE, 1961
HINDENBURG, THE, 1975
HITLER, 1962
HITLER: THE LAST TEN DAYS, 1973
HITLER'S CHILDREN, 1942
HOME OF THE BRAVE, 1949
HOPE AND GLORY, 1987
HORSE SOLDIERS, THE, 1959
HOW I WON THE WAR, 1967
IRON EAGLE, 1986
IRON EAGLE II, 1988
JUDGMENT AT NUREMBERG, 1961
KAGEMUSHA, 1980
KANAL, 1957
KING OF HEARTS, 1967
LAST REMAKE OF BEAU GESTE, THE, 1977
LAWRENCE OF ARABIA, 1962
LONGEST DAY, THE, 1962
LOST PATROL, THE, 1934
MAC ARTHUR'S CHILDREN, 1985
MASSACRE IN ROME, 1973
MEN, THE, 1950
MORITURI, 1965
MOROCCO, 1930

xiii

NICHOLAS AND ALEXANDRA, 1971
ODD ANGRY SHOT, THE, 1979
ODESSA FILE, THE, 1974
PAISAN, 1948
PATHS OF GLORY, 1957
PATTON, 1970
PAWNBROKER, THE, 1965
PEDESTRIAN, THE, 1974
PORK CHOP HILL, 1959
POWER PLAY, 1978
RAID ON ROMMEL, 1971
RAZOR'S EDGE, THE, 1946
RED BADGE OF COURAGE, THE, 1951
RETURN OF THE SOLDIER, THE, 1983
REVOLUTION, 1985
RIDDLE OF THE SANDS, THE, 1979
SALZBURG CONNECTION, THE, 1972
SANDS OF IWO JIMA, 1949
SEVEN DAYS IN MAY, 1964
SHENANDOAH, 1965
SHOUT AT THE DEVIL, 1976
SOLDIER'S REVENGE, 1986
SPARTACUS, 1960
STALAG 17, 1953
STRANGER, THE, 1946
TAPS, 1981
TASTE OF HELL, A, 1973
TIME OF DESTINY, A, 1988
TO BE OR NOT TO BE, 1983
TOO LATE THE HERO, 1970
TORA! TORA! TORA!, 1970
TRAIN, THE, 1965
TUNES OF GLORY, 1960
TWELVE O'CLOCK HIGH, 1949
VON RYAN'S EXPRESS, 1965
WAR LOVER, THE, 1962
WHAT PRICE GLORY?, 1952
WHERE EAGLES DARE, 1968
WHITE GHOST, 1988
WHO'LL STOP THE RAIN?, 1978
WIND AND THE LION, THE, 1975
YEAR OF LIVING DANGEROUSLY, THE, 1982
YOUNG LIONS, THE, 1958
ZULU, 1964

C-O

BILOXI BLUES, 1988
BOAT, THE, 1982
BOYS FROM BRAZIL, THE, 1978
COMING HOME, 1978
DIRTY DOZEN, THE, 1967
EYE OF THE NEEDLE, 1981
GATE OF HELL, 1953
GREEN ROOM, THE, 1978
HANNA'S WAR, 1988

HARP OF BURMA, 1967
HIDING PLACE, THE, 1975
HIROSHIMA, MON AMOUR, 1959
KELLY'S HEROES, 1970
LAST METRO, THE, 1980
LATINO, 1985
LITTLE BIG MAN, 1970
LITTLE DRUMMER GIRL, THE, 1984
MARCH OR DIE, 1977
M*A*S*H, 1970
MURPHY'S WAR, 1971
1941, 1979
PRAYER FOR THE DYING, A, 1987
PURPLE HEARTS, 1984
RAZOR'S EDGE, THE, 1984
REBEL LOVE, 1986
REDS, 1981
SAND PEBBLES, THE, 1966
SHOP ON MAIN STREET, THE, 1966
START THE REVOLUTION WITHOUT ME, 1970
TWO WOMEN, 1960
ZULU DAWN, 1980

O

ANGKOR-CAMBODIA EXPRESS, 1986
APOCALYPSE NOW, 1979
BAT 21, 1988
BEAST, THE, 1988
BEST DEFENSE, 1984
BIRDY, 1984
BOYS IN COMPANY C, THE, 1978
BRADDOCK: MISSING IN ACTION III, 1988
BURN, 1970
CAL, 1984
CATCH-22, 1970
COLONEL REDL, 1985
CROSS OF IRON, 1977
DAMNED, THE, 1969
DANTON, 1983
DEADLINE, 1987
DEER HUNTER, THE, 1978
DELTA FORCE, THE, 1986
DISTANT THUNDER, 1988
DOGS OF WAR, THE, 1980
DON'T CRY, IT'S ONLY THUNDER, 1982
84 CHARLIE MOPIC, 1989
FINAL OPTION, THE, 1982
FIRES ON THE PLAIN, 1962
FIRST BLOOD, 1982
FLESH AND BLOOD, 1985
FULL METAL JACKET, 1987
FUNNY, DIRTY LITTLE WAR, A, 1983
GARDENS OF STONE, 1987

GO TELL THE SPARTANS, 1978
GOOD MORNING, VIETNAM, 1987
GOOD, THE BAD, AND THE UGLY, THE, 1967
HAMBURGER HILL, 1987
HANOI HILTON, THE, 1987
HEARTBREAK RIDGE, 1986
HOT BOX, THE, 1972
HUMAN CONDITION, THE, 1958/1961
INVASION U.S.A., 1985
JOHNNY GOT HIS GUN, 1971
KEEP, THE, 1983
KILLING FIELDS, THE, 1984
KING RAT, 1965
KOLBERG, 1945
LAST HUNTER, THE, 1984
LES CARABINIERS, 1963
LION OF THE DESERT, 1981
LORDS OF DISCIPLINE, THE, 1983
LOVE AND ANARCHY, 1973
LOVE IN GERMANY, A, 1984
MARATHON MAN, 1976
MARRIAGE OF MARIA BRAUN, THE, 1979
MEPHISTO, 1981
MERRY CHRISTMAS, MR. LAWRENCE, 1983
MISFIT BRIGADE, THE, 1988
MISSING IN ACTION, 1984
MISSING IN ACTION 2—THE BEGINNING, 1985
MY NAME IS IVAN, 1962
NAKED AND THE DEAD, THE, 1958
NIGHT OF THE GENERALS, THE, 1967
NIGHT OF THE SHOOTING STARS, THE, 1982
NIGHT PORTER, THE, 1974
NIGHTWARS, 1988
NO DEAD HEROES, 1987
OFF LIMITS, 1988
OFFICER AND A GENTLEMAN, AN, 1982
ON THE BEACH, 1959
OPEN CITY, 1945
PLATOON, 1986
PLATOON LEADER, 1988
PLENTY, 1985
P.O.W. THE ESCAPE, 1986
PRIVATE BENJAMIN, 1980
PRIVATES ON PARADE, 1984
RAMBO: FIRST BLOOD, PART II, 1985
RAMBO III, 1988
RAN, 1985
REBEL, 1985
RED DAWN, 1984

REVOLT OF JOB, THE, 1984
ROLLING THUNDER, 1977
SALVADOR, 1986
SLAUGHTERHOUSE-FIVE, 1972
SOLDIER BLUE, 1970
SOLDIER OF ORANGE, 1979
SOME KIND OF HERO, 1982
SOUTHERN COMFORT, 1981
STREAMERS, 1983
SUPERNATURALS, THE, 1987
THRONE OF BLOOD, 1961
TIN DRUM, THE, 1979
TWILIGHT'S LAST GLEAMING, 1977
ULZANA'S RAID, 1972
UNBEARABLE LIGHTNESS OF BEING, THE, 1988
UNCOMMON VALOR, 1983
UNDER FIRE, 1983
WALKER, 1987
WARKILL, 1968
WILD GEESE, THE, 1978
WILD GEESE II, 1985

FILMS BY YEAR

Listed below are films included in this volume by their year of release.

1930
ALL QUIET ON THE WESTERN FRONT
MOROCCO

1931
KAMERADSCHAFT

1932
FAREWELL TO ARMS, A

1933
DUCK SOUP

1934
CRIMSON ROMANCE
LOST PATROL, THE

1935
LIVES OF A BENGAL LANCER

1936
CARNIVAL IN FLANDERS
CHARGE OF THE LIGHT BRIGADE, THE
LAST OF THE MOHICANS, THE

1937
DARK JOURNEY
FIRE OVER ENGLAND
GRAND ILLUSION

1938
DAWN PATROL, THE
DRUMS
LA MARSEILLAISE

1939
ALEXANDER NEVSKY
BEAU GESTE
DRUMS ALONG THE MOHAWK
FLYING DEUCES, THE
FOUR FEATHERS, THE
GONE WITH THE WIND
GUNGA DIN
NURSE EDITH CAVELL
SPY IN BLACK, THE

1940
FOREIGN CORRESPONDENT
GREAT DICTATOR, THE
NIGHT TRAIN TO MUNICH
SEA HAWK, THE

1941
BUCK PRIVATES
49TH PARALLEL
GREAT GUNS
SERGEANT YORK
SUNDOWN
THAT HAMILTON WOMAN
YANK IN THE R.A.F., A

1942
CALL OUT THE MARINES
CASABLANCA
COMMANDOS STRIKE AT DAWN, THE
DESPERATE JOURNEY
FLYING TIGERS
HITLER'S CHILDREN
IN WHICH WE SERVE
MRS. MINIVER
ONE OF OUR AIRCRAFT IS MISSING
PIMPERNEL SMITH
SABOTEUR
SALUTE JOHN CITIZEN
SHERLOCK HOLMES AND THE SECRET WEAPON
THEY DIED WITH THEIR BOOTS ON
THIS ABOVE ALL
TO BE OR NOT TO BE
WAKE ISLAND

1943
ADVENTURES OF TARTU, THE
AIR FORCE
BATAAN
BEHIND THE RISING SUN
BOMBARDIER
EDGE OF DARKNESS
GUADALCANAL DIARY
GUNG HO!
GUY NAMED JOE, A
IMMORTAL SERGEANT, THE
NORTH STAR, THE
NORTHERN PURSUIT
SAHARA
SPITFIRE
STAGE DOOR CANTEEN
THIS IS THE ARMY
THIS LAND IS MINE
WATCH ON THE RHINE
WE DIVE AT DAWN

1944
ACTION IN ARABIA
DAYS OF GLORY
DESTINATION TOKYO
DRAGON SEED
FIGHTING SEABEES, THE
HENRY V
IMMORTAL BATTALION, THE
LIFEBOAT
MASTER RACE, THE
MR. WINKLE GOES TO WAR
PASSAGE TO MARSEILLE
PURPLE HEART, THE
THIRTY SECONDS OVER TOKYO
UP IN ARMS

1945
BACK TO BATAAN
BLOOD ON THE SUN
CORNERED
FIRST YANK INTO TOKYO
IVAN THE TERRIBLE, PARTS I & II
KOLBERG
LIFE AND DEATH OF COLONEL BLIMP, THE
OBJECTIVE, BURMA!
OPEN CITY
THEY WERE EXPENDABLE
WALK IN THE SUN, A

1946
BEST YEARS OF OUR LIVES, THE
CLOAK AND DAGGER
RAZOR'S EDGE, THE
STRANGER, THE

1947
FRIEDA
GERMANY, YEAR ZERO

1948
BERLIN EXPRESS
FORT APACHE
JUNGLE PATROL
PAISAN

1949
CLAY PIGEON, THE
HOME OF THE BRAVE
OUTPOST IN MOROCCO
SANDS OF IWO JIMA
SHE WORE A YELLOW RIBBON
TWELVE O'CLOCK HIGH

1950
KIM
MEN, THE
RIO GRANDE

1951
AFRICAN QUEEN, THE
DESERT FOX, THE
DISTANT DRUMS
DRUMS IN THE DEEP SOUTH
FLYING LEATHERNECKS

FOUR IN A JEEP
GO FOR BROKE
RED BADGE OF COURAGE, THE
WOODEN HORSE, THE

1952
AGAINST ALL FLAGS
FLAT TOP
GLORY AT SEA
WHAT PRICE GLORY?

1953
CRUEL SEA, THE
DESERT RATS, THE
DESTINATION GOBI
DRAGONFLY SQUADRON
FORBIDDEN GAMES
FROM HERE TO ETERNITY
GATE OF HELL
STALAG 17

1954
BRIDGES AT TOKO-RI, THE
COURT MARTIAL
DESIREE
MALTA STORY

1955
BATTLE CRY
BATTLE TAXI
COCKLESHELL HEROES, THE
COLDITZ STORY, THE
COURT-MARTIAL OF BILLY MITCHELL, THE
DAM BUSTERS, THE
FRANCIS IN THE NAVY
HILL 24 DOESN'T ANSWER
MISTER ROBERTS
NAPOLEON
SEA SHALL NOT HAVE THEM, THE
TO HELL AND BACK

1956
ALEXANDER THE GREAT
AWAY ALL BOATS
BLACK TENT, THE
CONQUEROR, THE
D-DAY, THE SIXTH OF JUNE
RICHARD III
WAR AND PEACE

1957
BATTLE HELL
BRIDGE ON THE RIVER KWAI, THE
D.I., THE
HELLCATS OF THE NAVY
KANAL
MEN IN WAR
PATHS OF GLORY
PURSUIT OF THE GRAF SPEE
SAYONARA

1958
BUCCANEER, THE
DARBY'S RANGERS
DEEP SIX, THE
INN OF THE SIXTH HAPPINESS, THE
NAKED AND THE DEAD, THE
ONE THAT GOT AWAY, THE
RUN SILENT, RUN DEEP
TIME TO LOVE AND A TIME TO DIE, A
YOUNG LIONS, THE
HUMAN CONDITION, THE

1959
DIARY OF ANNE FRANK, THE
GENERALE DELLA ROVERE
HIROSHIMA, MON AMOUR
HORSE SOLDIERS, THE
MOUSE THAT ROARED, THE
ON THE BEACH
OPERATION PETTICOAT
PORK CHOP HILL

1960
ALAMO, THE
ASSAULT OF THE REBEL GIRLS
AUSTERLITZ
BALLAD OF A SOLDIER
CRANES ARE FLYING, THE
HELL TO ETERNITY
OPERATION AMSTERDAM
SPARTACUS
TUNES OF GLORY
TWO WOMEN

1961
ASHES AND DIAMONDS
EL CID
GUNS OF NAVARONE, THE
JUDGMENT AT NUREMBERG
STEEL CLAW, THE
THRONE OF BLOOD
WACKIEST SHIP IN THE ARMY, THE

1962
DAMN THE DEFIANT!
FIRES ON THE PLAIN
FOUR HORSEMEN OF THE APOCALYPSE, THE
HITLER
LAWRENCE OF ARABIA
LONGEST DAY, THE
MY NAME IS IVAN
TARAS BULBA
WAR LOVER, THE

1963
CRY OF BATTLE
ELUSIVE CORPORAL, THE
55 DAYS AT PEKING
GREAT ESCAPE, THE

LES CARABINIERS
MIRACLE OF THE WHITE STALLIONS
PT 109
UGLY AMERICAN, THE

1964
BEHOLD A PALE HORSE
DIAMONDS OF THE NIGHT
DR. STRANGELOVE: OR HOW I LEARNED TO STOP WORRYING AND LOVE THE BOMB
ENSIGN PULVER
FAIL SAFE
FATHER GOOSE
SEVEN DAYS IN MAY
ZULU

1965
BATTLE OF THE BULGE
DOCTOR ZHIVAGO
IN HARM'S WAY
KING RAT
MORITURI
OPERATION CIA
PAWNBROKER, THE
SHENANDOAH
TRAIN, THE
VON RYAN'S EXPRESS

1966
ALVAREZ KELLY
BLUE MAX, THE
CAST A GIANT SHADOW
LOST COMMAND, THE
SAND PEBBLES, THE
SHOP ON MAIN STREET, THE
TOBRUK

1967
BATTLE OF ALGIERS, THE
CHIMES AT MIDNIGHT
DIRTY DOZEN, THE
GOOD, THE BAD, AND THE UGLY, THE
HARP OF BURMA
HOW I WON THE WAR
KING OF HEARTS
NIGHT OF THE GENERALS, THE
TRANSPORT FROM PARADISE
WAR AND PEACE

1968
ANZIO
GREEN BERETS, THE
MISSION BATANGAS
SECRET WAR OF HARRY FRIGG, THE
SNOW TREASURE
WARKILL
WHERE EAGLES DARE

1969
BATTLE OF BRITAIN, THE
BATTLE OF NERETVA
BRIDGE AT REMAGEN, THE
DAMNED, THE
LAST DAY OF THE WAR, THE

1970
BURN
CATCH-22
CROMWELL
KELLY'S HEROES
LITTLE BIG MAN
M*A*S*H
ONLY WAY, THE
PATTON
SOLDIER BLUE
START THE REVOLUTION
   WITHOUT ME
TOO LATE THE HERO
TORA! TORA! TORA!
WHICH WAY TO THE FRONT?

1971
BANANAS
DIRTY HEROES
GARDEN OF THE
   FINZI-CONTINIS, THE
JOHNNY GOT HIS GUN
MURPHY'S WAR
NICHOLAS AND ALEXANDRA
NO DRUMS, NO BUGLES
RAID ON ROMMEL

1972
CABARET
HOT BOX, THE
SALZBURG CONNECTION, THE
SLAUGHTERHOUSE-FIVE
ULZANA'S RAID

1973
HITLER: THE LAST TEN DAYS
LOVE AND ANARCHY
MASSACRE IN ROME
TASTE OF HELL, A

1974
NIGHT PORTER, THE
ODESSA FILE, THE
PEDESTRIAN, THE
REASON TO LIVE, A REASON
   TO DIE, A

1975
HIDING PLACE, THE
HINDENBURG, THE
LOVE AND DEATH
WIND AND THE LION, THE

1976
BLACK AND WHITE IN COLOR
EAGLE HAS LANDED, THE
MARATHON MAN
MIDWAY
SHOUT AT THE DEVIL
VOYAGE OF THE DAMNED

1977
BRIDGE TOO FAR, A
CROSS OF IRON
DUELLISTS, THE
HEROES
LAST REMAKE OF BEAU
   GESTE, THE
MAC ARTHUR
MARCH OR DIE
ROLLING THUNDER
TWILIGHT'S LAST GLEAMING

1978
BOYS FROM BRAZIL, THE
BOYS IN COMPANY C, THE
BRASS TARGET
COMING HOME
COUP DE GRACE
DEER HUNTER, THE
FORCE 10 FROM NAVARONE
GO TELL THE SPARTANS
GREEN ROOM, THE
POWER PLAY
WHO'LL STOP THE RAIN?
WILD GEESE, THE

1979
APOCALYPSE NOW
CUBA
DAVID
ESCAPE TO ATHENA
FROM HELL TO VICTORY
GREAT SANTINI, THE
MARRIAGE OF MARIA BRAUN,
   THE
1941
ODD ANGRY SHOT, THE
RIDDLE OF THE SANDS, THE
SOLDIER OF ORANGE
TIN DRUM, THE

1980
BIG RED ONE, THE
BREAKER MORANT
DOGS OF WAR, THE
FINAL COUNTDOWN, THE
KAGEMUSHA
LAST METRO, THE
PRIVATE BENJAMIN
SEA WOLVES, THE
ZULU DAWN

1981
EYE OF THE NEEDLE
GALLIPOLI
LION OF THE DESERT
MEPHISTO
REDS
SOUTHERN COMFORT
TAPS
VICTORY

1982
BOAT, THE
DON'T CRY, IT'S ONLY THUNDER
FINAL OPTION, THE
FIREFOX
FIRST BLOOD
MISSING
NIGHT OF THE SHOOTING
   STARS, THE
OFFICER AND A GENTLEMAN,
   AN
SOME KIND OF HERO
YEAR OF LIVING
   DANGEROUSLY, THE

1983
DANTON
FUNNY, DIRTY LITTLE WAR, A
KEEP, THE
LORDS OF DISCIPLINE, THE
MERRY CHRISTMAS, MR.
   LAWRENCE
RETURN OF THE SOLDIER, THE
STREAMERS
TESTAMENT
TO BE OR NOT TO BE
UNCOMMON VALOR
UNDER FIRE
WARGAMES

1984
BEST DEFENSE
BIRDY
BRADY'S ESCAPE
CAL
KILLING FIELDS, THE
LAST HUNTER, THE
LITTLE DRUMMER GIRL, THE
LOVE IN GERMANY, A
MISSING IN ACTION
PRIVATES ON PARADE
PURPLE HEARTS
RAZOR'S EDGE, THE
RED DAWN
REVOLT OF JOB, THE
SWING SHIFT

1985
ASSISI UNDERGROUND, THE
CODE NAME: EMERALD
COLONEL REDL
ELENI
FLESH AND BLOOD
INVASION U.S.A.
LATINO
MAC ARTHUR'S CHILDREN
MISSING IN ACTION 2—THE
   BEGINNING

PLENTY
RAMBO: FIRST BLOOD, PART II
RAN
REBEL
REVOLUTION
WILD GEESE II

1986
ANGKOR-CAMBODIA EXPRESS
ASSAULT, THE
DELTA FORCE, THE
EVERY TIME WE SAY GOODBYE
HEARTBREAK RIDGE
IRON EAGLE
PLATOON
P.O.W. THE ESCAPE
REBEL LOVE
SALVADOR
SKY BANDITS
SOLDIER'S REVENGE
TOP GUN

1987
DEADLINE
DEATH BEFORE DISHONOR
EMPIRE OF THE SUN
FULL METAL JACKET
GARDENS OF STONE
GOOD MORNING, VIETNAM
HAMBURGER HILL
HANOI HILTON, THE
HOPE AND GLORY
NO DEAD HEROES
PRAYER FOR THE DYING, A
SUPERNATURALS, THE
WALKER
WANNSEE CONFERENCE, THE

1988
AU REVOIR LES ENFANTS
BAT 21
BEAST, THE
BILOXI BLUES
BRADDOCK: MISSING IN ACTION III
CAPTIVE HEARTS
DISTANT THUNDER
GOING HOME
HANNA'S WAR
IRON EAGLE II
MISFIT BRIGADE, THE
NIGHTWARS
OFF LIMITS
PLATOON LEADER
RAMBO III
TIME OF DESTINY, A
UNBEARABLE LIGHTNESS OF BEING, THE
WHITE GHOST

1989
84 CHARLIE MOPIC
FAREWELL TO THE KING

War Movies

Film Reviews

ACTION IN ARABIA**
(1944) 75m RKO bw

George Sanders *(Gordon)*, Virginia Bruce *(Yvonne)*, Lenore Aubert *(Mouniran)*, Gene Lockhart *(Danesco)*, Robert Armstrong *(Reed)*, H.B. Warner *(Rashid)*, Alan Napier *(Latimer)*, Andre Charlot *(Leroux)*, Marcel Dalio *(Chakka)*, Robert Anderson *(Chalmers)*, Jamiel Hasson *(Kareem)*, John Hamilton *(Hamilton)*, Rafael Storm *(Hotel Clerk)*, Michael Ansara *(Hamid)*.

An American newspaper correspondent, Gordon (George Sanders), courts intrigue in 1941 Damascus, where Free French and German spies attempt to involve the Arab tribes in the war. Gordon falls in love with the mysterious Yvonne (Virginia Bruce), then suspects her of being a Nazi agent before learning she is working with the French underground. The duo follows German agents to a desert castle where they meet with Arab sheiks who intend to deliver their tribesmen to the Axis side in return for heavy pay. Much of the excellent desert footage for this pic was culled from the many reels shot by Merian C. Cooper and Ernest B. Schoedsack (creators of KING KONG) when they journeyed to Damascus years earlier to make an epic on Lawrence of Arabia that never materialized. That footage is cleverly incorporated into this production in which highly polished Sanders exercises wry wit and boisterous banter.

p, Maurice Geraghty; d, Leonide Moguy; w, Philip MacDonald and Herbert Biberman; ed, Robert Swink; ph, J. Roy Hunt.

(PR:A MPAA:NR)

ADVENTURES OF TARTU, THE***
(1943, Brit.) 103m MGM bw (AKA: TARTU)

Robert Donat *(Capt. Terence Stevenson)*, Valerie Hobson *(Maruschka)*, Walter Rilla *(Inspector Otto Vogel)*, Glynis Johns *(Paula Palacek)*, Phyllis Morris *(Anna Palacek)*, Martin Miller *(Dr. Novothy)*, Anthony Eustrel *(Officer)*, Percy Walsh *(Dr. Willendorf)*, Frederic Richter *(Nestor)*, John Penrose *(Lt. Krantz)*, Mabel Terry Lewis *(Mrs. Stevenson)*.

This far-fetched but involving wartime espionage picture opens in London in 1940 as a British officer, Capt. Terence Stevenson (Robert Donat), is assigned to sneak behind enemy lines, infiltrate a Nazi-run poison gas factory in Czechoslovakia, obtain a secret formula, and destroy the plant. Stevenson poses as chemical engineer Jan Tartu, a member of the Rumanian Iron Guard, and is provided with papers that will secure his safe passage to the Hungarian border. Believed to be a refugee, "Tartu" is given a job in the factory as an assembly line foreman and lodging in the house that has been commandeered by Inspector Otto Vogel (Walter Rilla). Living under the same roof are the Czech proprietress, Anna Palacek (Phyllis Morris); her daughter, Paula (Glynis Johns); and the attractive and fiercely independent Maruschka (Valerie Hobson), the mistress of a Nazi commandant. It's not long before "Tartu" discovers that Paula is a member of the underground and Maruschka an Allied agent. Donat turns in one of his most playful and entertaining performances, though today, in light of his great work in THE 39 STEPS and THE GHOST GOES WEST, it is barely remembered.

p, Irving Asher; d, Harold S. Bucquet; w, Emmet Rogers, John Lee Mahin, and Miles Malleson, based on a story by John C. Higgins; ph, John J. Cox; m, Hubert Bath.

(PR:A MPAA:NR)

AFRICAN QUEEN, THE*****
(1951, US/Brit.) 105m Horizon-Romulus/UA c

Humphrey Bogart *(Charlie Allnut)*, Katharine Hepburn *(Rose Sayer)*, Robert Morley *(Rev. Samuel Sayer)*, Peter Bull *(Captain of "Louisa")*, Theodore Bikel *(1st Officer)*, Walter Gotell *(2nd Officer)*, Gerald Onn *(Petty Officer)*, Peter Swanwick, Richard Marner *(Officers at Shona)*.

Here is a film that has everything—adventure, humor, spectacular photography, and superb acting. In his only Oscar-winning performance, Humphrey Bogart stars as Charlie Allnut, a roustabout who uses his little battered steamer, *The African Queen*, to run supplies to small villages in East Africa at the onset of WW I. At one stop he meets Rose (Katharine Hepburn), the devoted spinster sister of Rev. Samuel Sayer (Robert Morley). When Charlie returns to the village later, he finds that German troops have invaded, torched its buildings, herded off the natives, and killed the reverend. He offers to take the distraught Rose back to civilization on the *Queen* and they start off downriver, Charlie swilling from an ample supply of gin, resentful of Rose's chiding. After a perilous journey through the jungle, they reach the lake commanded by the *Louisa*, a huge German warship that Rose is determined to blow sky-high, using the explosives still on board the *Queen*. THE AFRICAN QUEEN's marvelous script—featuring unforgettable exchanges between Bogart and Hepburn—was written as a straight drama by James Agee but director John Huston and his stars give it a punchy tongue-in-cheek treatment that fills the screen with hilarious humanity. Early scenes on this elaborate on-location production were shot near Ponthierville on the Lualaba River, then Huston moved the entire cast and the *Queen* 1,500 miles to the confluence of the Albert and Victoria Nile Rivers at Lake Mobutu, bringing great hardship to the crew and actors. Everyone got deathly sick (including Lauren Bacall, traveling with husband Bogart), except Huston and Bogie, who consistently downed large quantities of booze. A Hollywood film of the first order.

p, S.P. Eagle [Sam Spiegel]; d, John Huston; w, James Agee and John Huston, based on the novel by C.S. Forester; ed, Ralph Kemplen; ph, Jack Cardiff, Technicolor; m, Alan Gray.

(PR:AA MPAA:NR)

AGAINST ALL FLAGS**½
(1952) 83m UNIV c

Errol Flynn *(Brian Hawke)*, Maureen O'Hara *(Spitfire Stevens)*, Anthony Quinn *(Roc Brasiliano)*, Alice Kelley *(Princess Patma)*, Mildred Natwick *(Molvina MacGregor)*, Robert Warwick *(Capt. Kidd)*, Harry Cording *(Gow)*, John Alderson *(Harris)*, Phil Tully *(Jones)*, Lester Matthews *(Sir Cloudsley)*, Tudor Owen *(Williams)*, Maurice Marsac *(Capt. Moisson)*, James Craven *(Capt. Hornsby)*, Olaf Hytten *(King William)*.

AGAINST ALL FLAGS opens in 1700 as Brian Hawke (Errol Flynn), a British naval officer, is being whipped before his shipmates. Shortly thereafter, he jumps overboard and swims to the shore of Madagascar. The flogging has been a ruse; Hawke is actually posing as a renegade so that he can infiltrate a pirate stronghold. Dragged before a pirate tribunal, he is challenged by Roc Brasiliano (Anthony Quinn), who demands that Hawke be put to death, but Spitfire Stevens (Maureen O'Hara), a fierce female buccaneer, comes to his defense. Hawke then joins Brasiliano's crew and takes part in a bloody raid against a ship sailing under the flag of the emperor of India, whose daughter, Princess Patma (Alice Kelley), and harem are kidnaped, though only Hawke recognizes the princess. Spitfire's jealousy flares, but she continues to aid Hawke, eventually helping him escape Brasiliano's evil clutches and defeat the pirates. Although best classified as a swashbuckler, this fast-paced hybrid actioner has more than enough espionage and war-related elements to be characterized as a war film. Russell Metty's Technicolor photography, Bernard Herzbrun and Alexander Golitzen's art direction, and the set design of Russell A. Gausman and Oliver Emert make the film a visual treat. AGAINST ALL FLAGS was remade in 1967 as THE KING'S PIRATE with Doug McClure in Flynn's role and Guy Stockwell in Quinn's.

p, Howard Christie; d, George Sherman; w, Aeneas MacKenzie and Joseph Hoffman, based on a story by MacKenzie; ed, Frank Gross; ph, Russell Metty, Technicolor; m, Hans J. Salter.

(PR:A MPAA:NR)

AIR FORCE*****
(1943) 124m WB bw

John Ridgely *(Capt. Mike Quincannon)*, Gig Young *(Lt. Bill Williams)*, Arthur Kennedy *(Lt. Tommy McMartin)*, Charles Drake *(Lt. Munchauser)*, Harry Carey *(Sgt. Robby White)*, George Tobias *(Cpl. Weinberg)*, Ward Wood *(Cpl. Peterson)*, Ray Montgomery *(Pvt. Chester)*, John Garfield *(Sgt. Joe Winocki)*, James Brown *(Lt. Tex Rader)*, Stanley Ridges *(Maj. Mallory)*, Willard Robertson *(Colonel)*, Moroni Olsen *(Col. Blake)*, Edward Brophy *(Sgt. J.J. Callahan)*, Richard Lane *(Maj. W.G. Roberts)*, Faye Emerson *(Susan McMartin)*.

One of the finest (if not the finest) American war propaganda films produced during WW II, AIR FORCE fits perfectly into the canon of its director, Howard Hawks. A filmmaker who excels at portraying group action (as opposed to John Ford, whose films depict individual stances), Hawks tells the story of the *Mary Ann*, a B-17 bomber, and its crew. The film begins with the Japanese attack on Pearl Harbor and ends with a retaliatory US strike on Tokyo; in the interim, Hawks shows us the crew fighting as a unified group. While there is much here the viewer may find offensive (notably the predictable anti-"Jap" rhetoric), Hawks' mesmerizing direction is so assured and emotional that one cannot but help be drawn into the characters' world. Made with the full cooperation of the Army Air Corps, the film is a mosaic of the essential elements of war propaganda: sense of loss, vengeance (the midair machine-gunning of a young paratrooper by an enemy fighter and John Garfield's retaliation are harrowing and unforgettable), pride, nationalism, and above all for Hawks, survival of the group.

p, Hal B. Wallis; d, Howard Hawks; w, Dudley Nichols and William Faulkner (uncredited); ed, George Amy; ph, James Wong Howe and Elmer Dyer; m, Franz Waxman.

(PR:A MPAA:NR)

ALAMO, THE****
(1960) 161m Batjac/UA c

John Wayne *(Col. David Crockett)*, Richard Widmark *(Col. James Bowie)*, Laurence Harvey *(Col. William Travis)*, Frankie Avalon *(Smitty)*, Patrick Wayne *(Capt. James Butler Bonham)*, Linda Cristal *(Flaca)*, Joan O'Brien *(Mrs. Dickinson)*, Chill Wills *(Beekeeper)*, Joseph Calleia *(Juan Sequin)*, Ken Curtis *(Capt. Almeron Dickinson)*, Carlos Arruza *(Lt. Reyes)*, Jester Hairston *(Jethro)*, Veda Ann Borg *(Blind Nell)*, John Dierkes *(Jocko Robertson)*, Denver Pyle *(Gambler)*, Aissa Wayne *(Angelina Dickinson)*, Hank Worden *(Parson)*, Richard Boone *(Gen. Sam Houston)*.

An inspiring history lesson, this film is an excellent re-creation of the defense of the Alamo in 1836 Texas, when 187 Americans and Texicans held off Santa Anna's army of 7,000 men for 13 days. It depicts how those men came to be inside the tiny mission-cum-fort in the dusty village of San Antonio, concentrating on colonels William Travis (Laurence Harvey), Davy Crockett (John Wayne) and Jim Bowie (Richard Widmark). Wayne, whose Batjac Productions spent some $15 million mounting this superb epic (shot in 91 days, with $1.5 million spent re-creating the fort), produced, starred, and directed, with uncredited second-unit assistance from good friend John Ford. The result is an old-fashioned patriotic movie *and* a rousing epic that, nonetheless, performed poorly at the box office, perhaps because it chronicled one of America's most famous military *losses*. Wayne and friends do go on a bit about the joys of freedom and the sacrifice necessary to maintain it, but presumably that is exactly the kind of talk that went on at the Alamo. Moreover, James Edward Grant's excellent screenplay crackles with wit and humor. High drama well played, THE ALAMO should be seen by anyone who wonders why men give up their lives for an ideal and their fellow man. Originally released at 192 minutes, it was later edited down to 140 minutes, reportedly cutting out much of the Ford-directed footage. The videocassette runs 161 minutes, but fails to recapture the sumptuous Todd-AO widescreen photography.

p, John Wayne; d, John Wayne; w, James Edward Grant; ed, Stuart Gilmore; ph, William Clothier, Todd-AO, Technicolor; m, Dmitri Tiomkin.

(PR:AA MPAA:NR)

ALEXANDER NEVSKY*****

(1939) 107m Mosfilm/AMKINO bw

Nikolai Cherkassov (*Prince Alexander Yaroslavich Nevsky*), N.P. Okhlopkov (*Vassily Buslai*), A.L. Abrikossov (*Gavrilo Olexich*), D.N. Orlov (*Ignat. Master Armourer*), V.K. Novikov (*Pavsha*), N.N. Arski (*Domash*), V.O. Massalitinova (*Amefa Timofeyevna*), S.K. Blinnikov (*Tverdillo*).

Sergei Eisenstein's classic tale of 13th-century Russia is as magnificent today as it must have been in 1938. One of the greatest achievements of Soviet (and world) cinema, this epic concerns the trying period when Russia was invaded by Teutonic knights on one front and Tartars on the other. As a result, the motherland is plundered and the morale of the people crumbles. Finally, the moody, volatile Prince Nevsky (Nikolai Cherkassov) is summoned to lead his people in their struggle against the oppressors. A valiant and intelligent nobleman, Nevsky forms his army (an undertaking that consumes half the film), then wins a decisive battle at frozen Lake Peipus in 1242. Eisenstein had the Russian army at his disposal, and the battle scenes, populated with thousands of men, are overwhelming. Wearing terrifying helmets fashioned after gargoyles, ogres, and fierce animals, the Teutonic knights engage the Russian army of peasants and nobles, hacking with sword, spear, and axe until the armor-burdened invaders fall victim to the lake's cracking ice. Eisenstein's attention to detail is meticulous down to every horse blanket and homemade shoe, and the mounting of his monument to Russia's ancient hero is nothing less than superb. Eisenstein, whose career was on the verge of collapse, was rewarded for his work (a thinly veiled piece of Stalinist propaganda with the heroic Nevsky as Stalin and the savage Teutons as the Nazis) by being named head of Mosfilm Studios. (In Russian; English subtitles.)

d, Sergei Eisenstein and D.I. Vassillev; w, Sergei Eisenstein and Peter Pavlenko; ph, Edward Tisse; m, Sergei Prokofiev.

(PR:C MPAA:NR)

ALEXANDER THE GREAT***

(1956) 143m UA c

Richard Burton (*Alexander the Great*), Fredric March (*Philip of Macedonia*), Claire Bloom (*Barsine*), Danielle Darrieux (*Olympias*), Harry Andrews (*Darius*), Stanley Baker (*Attalus*), Niall MacGinnis (*Parmenio*), Peter Cushing (*Memnon*), Michael Hordern (*Demosthenes*), Barry Jones (*Aristotle*), Marisa De Leza (*Eurydice*), Gustavo Rojo (*Cleitus*), Ruben Rojo (*Philotas*), William Squire (*Aeschines*), Helmut Dantine (*Nectanebus*), Friedrich Ledebur (*Antipater*).

This engrossing spectacle from director Robert Rossen chronicles Alexander of Greece's conquest of the world in the fourth century, B.C. In the early scenes, King Philip of Macedonia (Fredric March), a ruthless, slightly mad but powerful ruler, is plotted against by his wife, Olympias (Danielle Darrieux), and shown to be hated by his son, Alexander (Richard Burton). Philip, on the other hand, loves Alexander but distrusts his teachers, including Aristotle (Barry Jones), feeling that his son is engaging in lofty intellectual pursuits unbefitting a warrior prince. Father and son quarrel over philosophy and Philip's flagrant mistreatment of Olympias, but she gains her revenge by arranging for the king's assassination so that Alexander gains the throne. Alexander and his armies then win the battle of Granicus, defeat the King of Prussia in the battle of Issus, consolidate Asia Minor, and invade India, before this King of Kings finally dies, at age 32, in 323 B.C. Although Rossen was blessed with a superb cast, he chose to concentrate on the CinemaScope spectacle of the innumerable battles and Alexander's philosophizing about fate and destiny.

p, Robert Rossen; d, Robert Rossen; w, Robert Rossen; ed, Ralph Kempler; ph, Robert Krasker, CinemaScope, Technicolor; m, Mario Nascimbene.

(PR:A MPAA:NR)

ALL QUIET ON THE WESTERN FRONT*****

(1930) 140m UNIV bw

Louis Wolheim (*Katczinsky*), Lew Ayres (*Paul Baumer*), John Wray (*Himmelstoss*), George "Slim" Summerville (*Tjaden*), Russell Gleason (*Muller*), William Bakewell (*Albert*), Scott Kolk (*Leer*), Walter Browne Rogers (*Behm*), Ben Alexander (*Kemmerick*), Owen Davis, Jr. (*Peter*), Harold Goodwin (*Detering*), G. Pat Collins (*Lt. Berlenck*), Richard Alexander (*Westhus*), Arnold Lucy (*Prof. Kantorek*), Heinie Conklin (*Hammacher*), Edmund Breese (*Herr Mayer*), Bodil Rosing (*Wachter*), Bill Irving (*Ginger*).

A remarkably faithful adaptation of Erich Maria Remarque's classic pacifist novel, ALL QUIET ON THE WESTERN FRONT remains one of the great antiwar films and holds considerable power to this day, mainly due to Lewis Milestone's inventive direction. Set during WW I and told from the German point of view, the story centers on Paul Baumer (Lew Ayres), an energetic, sensitive youth who is recruited, along with his entire class, by a war-mongering professor (Arnold Lucy) advocating "glory for the Fatherland." Paul and his friends enlist and are trained by Himmelstoss (John Wray), a kindly postmaster turned brutal corporal, then sent to the front lines to taste battle, blood, and death. Paul comes under the protective wing of an old veteran, Katczinsky (Louis Wolheim), who teaches him how to survive the horrors of war. The film is devastating, emotionally draining, and so riveting and realistic that it will be forever etched in the mind of any viewer. Milestone's magnificent direction is frequently inspired, most notably during the battle scenes. In one such scene,

ALVAREZ KELLY—

the camera serves as a kind of machine gun, shooting down the oncoming troops as it glides along the trenches. Universal spared no expense in its production, converting more than 20 acres of a large California ranch into "battlefields" occupied by more than 2,000 ex-servicemen extras. After its initial release, some foreign countries refused to run the film. Poland banned it for being pro-German, while the Nazis labeled it anti-German, with Joseph Goebbels, later propaganda minister, publicly denouncing the film. The movie took heat in America as well, with Maj. Frank Pease, who headed the Hollywood Technical Directors Institute, labeling the film brazen "propaganda," adding that it was created to "undermine belief in the Army and in authority." Pease even tried to have the film banned in the US. ALL QUIET ON THE WESTERN FRONT received an Academy Award as Best Picture and Milestone was honored as Best Director. Originally released with a running time of 140 minutes, the film has suffered many cuts over the years, with some prints running as short as 90 minutes. The most recent videotape release, however, restores the film to its full 140-minute running time. An interesting, but now-forgotten, sequel titled THE ROAD BACK and directed by James Whale (THE BRIDE OF FRANKENSTEIN) was made in 1937, and the original was remade as a television movie in 1979.

p, Carl Laemmle, Jr.; d, Lewis Milestone; w, Del Andrews, Maxwell Anderson, George Abbott, and Lewis Milstone, based on the novel by Erich Maria Remarque; ed, Edgar Adams and Milton Carruth; ph, Arthur Edeson and Karl Freund; m, David Broekman.

(PR:C MPAA:NR)

ALVAREZ KELLY**½

(1966) 116m COL c

William Holden *(Alvarez Kelly)*, Richard Widmark *(Col. Tom Rossiter)*, Janice Rule *(Liz Pickering)*, Patrick O'Neal *(Maj. Albert Stedman)*, Victoria Shaw *(Charity Warwick)*, Roger C. Carmel *(Capt. Angus Ferguson)*, Richard Rust *(Sgt. Hatcher)*, Arthur Franz *(Capt. Towers)*, Donald Barry *(Lt. Farrow)*, Duke Hobbie *(John Beaurider)*, Harry Carey, Jr. *(Cpl. Peterson)*.

William Holden plays the title character, an avaricious cattleman of Irish-Mexican ancestry, in this uneven, offbeat Civil War drama. En route to delivering the 5,000 head of prime beef cattle he has promised Union officer Albert Stedman (Patrick O'Neal), Kelly is waylaid by a contingent of tough Confederate troopers lead by Col. Tom Rossiter (Richard Widmark), who orders Kelly to drive the herd into Rebel territory. Everyone wants the prized beef, it seems, and the journey is filled with action—from Indian attacks to battles with Union troops. Nonetheless, ALVAREZ KELLY lags until the thrilling climactic stampede. Widmark is particularly menacing as a ruthless cutthroat who will do anything for the grand Lost Cause, including shooting off one of Kelly's fingers to show he means business. Janice Rule plays the temptress who "belongs" to Rossiter but dallies with Kelly, incurring the wrath of the Confederate colonel. Regrettably, Holden's performance lacks his usual inten-

sity; returning to the screen after a two-year absence, he is dominated in scene after scene by Widmark, who steals the movie.

p, Sol C. Siegel; d, Edward Dmytryk; w, Franklin Coen and Elliott Arnold, based on a story by Franklin Coen; ed, Harold F. Kress; ph, Joseph MacDonald, Panavision, Eastmancolor; m, John Green.

(PR:A MPAA:NR)

ANGKOR-CAMBODIA EXPRESS*

(1986, Thai./It.) 96m Network-Spectacular Trading/Monarex c

Robert Walker, Jr. *(Andy Cameron)*, Christopher George *(MacArthur)*, Woody Strode *(Woody)*, Nancy Kwan *(Sue)*.

Filmed in 1981, but unavailable to American viewers until its 1986 videocassette release, ANGKOR-CAMBODIA EXPRESS would have been better left unseen. Set in Thailand and Cambodia two years after the US withdrawal from Vietnam, the film follows American journalist Andy Cameron (Robert Walker, Jr.) as he returns to Cambodia to cover a press conference held by vicious Khmer Rouge warlord Mitr Saren (Lui Leung Wai). Feigning illness, Cameron leaves the gathering and sneaks off to meet Mieng (Nit Alisa), his Cambodian girl friend, who refused to flee her homeland with him two years previously. Now a member of the Khmer Rouge, and Mitr Saren's lover (both against her will), Mieng regrets remaining behind, but Cameron vows to help her escape. Eventually he bumps into another old friend, photographer Montiri (Suchao Pongwilai), who gives the journalist negatives of a Khmer Rouge slaughter of civilians to smuggle out of the country. Undaunted by capture and torture, Cameron slogs through the jungles of Thailand to meet with a renegade American general, "Mad Mac" MacArthur (Christopher George), who is now fighting the war on his own terms with a makeshift army. Tedious, poorly filmed, and badly scripted, ANGKOR-CAMBODIA EXPRESS manages to drag out nearly every war movie cliche known. The frequently laughable dialog features such classically hackneyed lines as "There are many ways to make you talk," offered during the torture scene, and the old standby "So we meet again," which prefaces the climactic hand-to-hand contest.

p, Lek Kitiparaporn and Richard Randall; d, Lek Kitiparaporn; w, Roger Crutchley and Kailan; ed, Morris Goodyear; ph, Roberto Forges Davanzati, Technicolor; m, Stelvio Cipriani.

(PR:O MPAA:NR)

ANZIO**½

(1968, It.) 117m COL c (GB: BATTLE FOR ANZIO, THE)

Robert Mitchum *(Dick Ennis)*, Peter Falk *(Cpl. Rabinoff)*, Robert Ryan *(Gen. Carson)*, Earl Holliman *(Sgt. Stimler)*, Mark Damon *(Richardson)*, Arthur Kennedy *(Gen. Lesly)*, Reni Santoni *(Movie)*, Joseph Walsh *(Doyle)*, Thomas Hunter *(Andy)*, Giancarlo Giannini *(Cellini)*, Anthony Steel

(Gen. Marsh), Patrick Magee (Gen. Starkey), Arthur Franz (Gen. Howard), Tonio Selwart (Gen. Von Mackensen).

This disappointing WW II film stars Robert Mitchum as Dick Ennis, a cynical American reporter who lands at Anzio with the Allied invasion forces on June 22, 1944. Accompanied by two soldiers, Movie (Reni Santoni) and Rabinoff (Peter Falk), Ennis drives a jeep all the way to Rome without encountering a single German soldier. When this is reported to Gen. Lesly (Arthur Kennedy), he decides not to advance, suspecting a trap; however, the Germans capitalize on this delay by reinforcing their positions. The fighting is slow and bloody, with the Nazis managing to stifle the Allied advance. After four months of horrible fighting, the Allies finally break through the enemy lines and roll into Rome, although Gen. Lesly is relieved of his command. With a great cast and a veteran director, ANZIO should be a solid war film, but the picture seems to go wrong right from the beginning, opening with an awful and inappropriate theme song sung by Jack Jones. From this point on the film is mostly a dull and feeble affair, plodding through what should be a gripping campaign. When soldiers aren't being picked off one-by-one by a Nazi sniper, they engage in overwritten philosophical discussions on the meaning of war, leadership, and heroism. While many aspects of the battle for Anzio seem tailor-made for compelling drama—especially the headline-grabbing, incompetent top brass who seem to have no concern for their men—the screenwriters and director Edward Dmytryk squander the potential.

p, Dino De Laurentiis; d, Edward Dmytryk; w, Hal Craig, based on the book by Wynford Vaughan-Thomas; ed, Alberto Gallitti and Peter Taylor; ph, Giuseppe Rotunno; m, Riz Ortolani.

(PR:A MPAA:NR)

APOCALYPSE NOW*****

(1979) 139m UA c

Marlon Brando (Col. Kurtz), Robert Duvall (Lt. Col. Kilgore), Martin Sheen (Capt. Willard), Frederic Forrest (Chef), Albert Hall (Chief), Sam Bottoms (Lance), Larry Fishburne (Clean), Dennis Hopper (Photo-journalist), G.D. Spradlin (General), Harrison Ford (Colonel), Scott Glenn (Civilian), Bill Graham (Agent).

Francis Ford Coppola's notorious and controversial contribution to the Vietnam movie subgenre remains, despite its flaws, one of the most powerful, complex, fascinating, and unforgettable war movies ever made. With a plot structure inspired by Joseph Conrad's classic 19th-century novella Heart of Darkness, APOCALYPSE NOW follows Willard (Martin Sheen), a cold and amoral Army captain, as he journeys upriver into Cambodia to assassinate Col. Kurtz (Marlon Brando), a renegade Green Beret who has broken from the American military and set himself up as a god among a tribe of Montagnard warriors, using them to wage his own private war. Told by the CIA to terminate the colonel with "extreme prejudice," Willard is given a small gunboat and a four-man crew—who know nothing of the mission—to take him to Kurtz. What follows is a hallucinatory look at the madness of the American involvement in Vietnam, a trip that somehow manages to seem both intensely real and surreal at the same time. Some of the stops along the way include a run-in with Lt. Col. Kilgore (Robert Duvall in a brilliant performance), an unbelievably gung-ho Air Cavalry commander who blares Wagner's "Ride of the Valkyries" from his helicopters while attacking Vietnamese villages; the inadvertent slaughter of an innocent Vietnamese family by Willard's men; a bizarre USO show held in the middle of the jungle in which a trio of Playboy bunnies are trotted out to tease the sex-starved soldiers; a hallucinatory nighttime siege on a bridge held by the Americans; and finally the primordial Montagnard compound and the mad Col. Kurtz himself—a completely bald demon poking his head from the darkness. More than five years in the making, APOCALYPSE NOW became a *cause celebre* even before it opened. As documented by numerous press accounts and the book *Notes*, a collection of journal entries written by Coppola's wife, Eleanor, the filming in the Philippines was hellish, disaster-plagued, and decadent, beginning with a $12 million budget and going over $31 million before the 238-day shooting schedule ended, with Coppola's own money making up the difference. The result of such madness is an extraordinary film experience—especially in its 70mm Dolby stereo incarnation—that succeeds in transporting the viewer into the "heart of darkness." While many have expressed annoyance or disappointment with the film once Willard comes face-to-face with Kurtz (the last part of the movie is basically a pseudo-philosophical monolog by Brando), the conclusion cannot diminish the power of what comes before. With an invasion by an American crew into an Asian country, the haphazard approach of the production, the indecision on the set, the massive amounts of money and technology invested, the harsh weather, disasters, and costly set-backs, the very making of APOCALYPSE NOW served as an ironically appropriate metaphor for America's involvement in Vietnam and adds yet another layer of fascination to this remarkable film.

p, Francis Ford Coppola; d, Francis Ford Coppola; w, John Milius and Francis Ford Coppola, based on the novella *Heart of Darkness* by Joseph Conrad; ed, Richard Marks; ph, Vittorio Storaro, Technovision, Technicolor; m, Carmine Coppola and Francis Ford Coppola.

(PR:O MPAA:R)

ASHES AND DIAMONDS****

(1961, Pol.) 105m Janus bw (POPIOL Y DIAMENT)

Zbigniew Cybulski (Maciek), Eva Krzyzewska (Christine), Adam Pawlikowski (Andrzej), Waclaw Zastrzezynski (Szczuka), Bogumil Kobiela (Drewnowski), Jan Ciecierski (Porter), Stanislaw Milski (Pienionzek), Arthur Mlodnicki (Kotowicz), Halina Kwiatkoska (Mrs. Staniewicz), Ignancy Machowski (Waga), Zbigniew Skowronski (Slomka), Barbara Krafft (Stefka), Alexander Sewruk (Swiencki).

Set on the first day of peace after the end of WW II, this disturbing film concentrates on the conflicts that remained between Polish political factions at the end of their struggle

ASSAULT, THE—

against the Germans. Unwilling to submit to Communist rule, the Armii krajowej refuse to lay down their arms and send two men—young, rebellious Maciek (wonderfully acted by bespectacled Zbigniew Cybulski) and older, professional Andrzej (Adam Pawlikowski)—to assassinate Szczuka (Waclaw Zastrzezynski), a Communist official. The pair, however, mistake two men returning from a German labor camp for their prey, and gun them down. During the next day and evening, Maciek, who is still under orders to kill Szczuka, battles his conscience, questioning the morality of Poles killing Poles. Director Andrzej Wajda's brilliance is evident from the film's opening ambush scene, wherein he establishes the moral dilemma facing Maciek and his fellow Poles as they begin the internecine struggle to determine who will shape their country's future. Outside of a peaceful country church, the Pole brutally murders an innocent countryman, who falls face first into the chapel as the sorrowful Christ looks down from his cross. A film of great power, ASHES AND DIAMONDS (Wajda's third feature) is the final chapter in Wajda's "war trilogy," preceded in 1954 by A GENERATION and in 1957 by KANAL. Available on videocassette in both dubbed and subtitled (Polish into English) versions.

d, Andrzej Wajda; w, Andrzej Wajda and Jerzy Andrzejewski, based on his novel; ed, Halina Nawrocka; ph, Jerzy Wojcik; m, Aroclaw Radio Quintet.

(PR:C MPAA:NR)

ASSAULT, THE****

(1986, Neth.) 155m Cannon c

Derek De Lint *(Anton Steenwijk)*, Marc van Uchelen *(Anton as a Boy)*, Monique van de Ven *(Truus Coster/Saskia de Graaff)*, John Kraaykamp *(Cor Takes)*, Huub van der Lubbe *(Fake Ploeg/His Father)*, Elly Weller *(Mrs. Beumer)*, Ina van der Molen *(Karin Korteweg)*, Frans Vorstman *(Father Steenwijk)*, Edda Barends *(Mother Steenwijk)*, Caspar De Boer *(Peter Steenwijk)*.

A powerful motion picture that asks more questions than it answers, THE ASSAULT will haunt anyone who lived through WW II. Spanning a 40-year period, it begins in Holland as the war is waning, and the Germans realize they will be beaten. One night while dining by candlelight during curfew, a Dutch family sees a local collaborator killed by a sniper. Fearing that they will be blamed, the family watches in horror as their neighbors pull the dead body in front of their home. Soon Germans are everywhere, the family is arrested and shot, their house is burned, and the son, Anton (Marc van Uchelen), is taken away to prison. Years later, he becomes a physician, marries, and has his own family, but the memory of that bleak night continues to haunt him. Winner of the 1986 Academy Award for Best Foreign Film, THE ASSAULT is a powerful indictment of the Nazi horror, though it seldom editorializes. Much more than the war picture it begins as, this documentary-like Dutch film explores lives that have been torn apart by German occupation. (Dubbed into English.)

p, Fons Rademakers; d, Fons Rademakers; w, Gerard Soeteman, based on the novel by Harry Mulisch; ed, Kees Linthorst; ph, Theo van de Sande, Fujicolor; m, Jurriaan Andriessen.

(PR:C MPAA:PG)

ASSAULT OF THE REBEL GIRLS*

(1960) 68m Exploit/Brenner bw (AKA: CUBAN REBEL GIRLS)

Errol Flynn *(Himself/Narrator)*, Beverly Aadland *(Beverly)*, John MacKay *(Johnny)*, Jackie Jackler *(Jacqueline)*, Marie Edmund *(Maria)*, Ben Ostrovsky *(Raoul)*, Regnier Sanchez, Esther Oliva, Todd Brody, Al Brown, Clelle Mahon.

The withering Errol Flynn tried desperately to recast himself in the role of a heroic modern-day swashbuckler, but only revealed his own dissipation, in this sad semidocumentary of the overthrow of the Batista dictatorship in Cuba by Castro's guerrilla forces. The film boasts "actual footage shot during the star's real-life adventures with the Castro rebels"; it's actually nothing more than a sorry exit for a once-great film star. Flynn also chose to cast his 16-year-old girl friend, Beverly Aadland, as Beverly, a young American girl who travels to Havana before the fall of Batista's regime in order to find her boy friend, Johnny (John MacKay). The star plays himself—a war correspondent who was writing a day-to-day account for the Hearst syndicate (a task Flynn actually was engaged in). Essentially a home movie about a pathetic old reactionary (Flynn's ties to the Nazi party are well documented; his involvement in Cuba was pro-Batista), ASSAULT OF THE REBEL GIRLS is interesting only as an autobiographical footnote. Flynn reportedly tried to stop its release, but it hit the big screen after his death in 1959.

p, Barry Mahon; d, Barry Mahon; w, Errol Flynn.

(PR:C MPAA:NR)

ASSISI UNDERGROUND, THE***

(1985) 115m Golan-Globus c

Ben Cross *(Padre Rufino)*, James Mason *(Bishop Nicolini)*, Irene Papas *(Mother Giuseppina)*, Maximilian Schell *(Col. Mueller)*, Karl-Heinz Hackl *(Capt. Von Velden)*, Riccardo Cucciolla *(Luigi Brizzi)*, Angelo Infanti *(Giorgio Kropf)*, Paolo Malco *(Paolo Josza)*, Tom Felleghy *(Gen. Bremer)*, Delia Boccardo *(Countess Cristina)*, Edmund Purdom *(Cardinal Della Costa)*, Geoffrey Copleston *(Police Chief Bertolucci)*.

It's 1943 and Hitler's forces are in Italy crushing a rebellion against Mussolini's fascist rule; meanwhile, the Allies have landed in Sicily and are now advancing up the Boot. The story takes place in the tranquil village of Assisi, where Padre Rufino (Ben Cross) runs the Franciscan mission of San Damiano. From Bishop Nicolini (James Mason in one of his final assignments) the priest learns that Rome's Jews are racing away from the German invaders, trying to get to the port of Genoa to board ships from neutral countries. Naturally, the brave and capable father is chosen by Bishop Nicolini to help the fleeing Jews. Soon, Rufino is in charge of protecting hundreds of Jews, hiding them in various places in and around Assisi—churches, convents, and monasteries. Director-screenwriter Alexander Ramati, a Polish Jew, adapted this true story from his own "documentary novel," engaging in extensive research and conducting many interviews. Cross, best remembered for his work in CHARIOTS OF FIRE, prepared for his role by checking into the San Damiano monastery, and having his head tonsured in friar fashion. Despite the honest efforts that went into the picture (Giuseppe Rotunno's photography in particular), one wishes it were as poignant as its subject matter. Originally released at 178 minutes.

p, Menahem Golan and Yoram Globus; d, Alexander Ramati; w, Alexander Ramati, based on his novel; ed, Michael Duthie; ph, Giuseppe Rotunno, Starvision, Technicolor; m, Dov Seltzer.

(PR:C MPAA:PG)

AU REVOIR LES ENFANTS**½

(1988, Fr.) 104m Nouvelles Editions de Films-MK2-Stella/Orion Classics c (Trans: Goodbye, Children)

Gaspard Manesse (Julien Quentin), Raphael Fejto (Jean Bonnet), Francine Racette (Mme. Quentin), Stanislas Carre de Malberg (Francois Quentin), Philippe Morier-Genoud (Fr. Jean), Francois Berleand (Fr. Michel), Francois Negret (Joseph), Peter Fitz (Muller), Benoit Henriet (Ciron), Irene Jacob (Mlle. Davenne), Jacqueline Paris (Mme. Perrin).

This sincere but curiously unemotional quasi-autobiography from Louis Malle is set in January 1944 during the German Occupation of France. After spending the holidays with his mother, 12-year-old Julien (Gaspard Manesse) is sent to a provincial Catholic boarding school, where he is brighter than all of his classmates except one—Bonnet (Raphael Fejto), a new arrival who, like Julien, has a great love of books. Their friendship grows and eventually Julien learns Bonnet's secret: he is one of three Jews being hidden from the Gestapo by the school's gutsy cleric, Fr. Jean (Philippe Morier-Genoud). Based on a childhood trauma experienced by producer-director-writer Malle, AU REVOIR LES ENFANTS is a deeply personal project that he has long wanted to make. Unfortunately, the film fails to generate the emotional power one would expect from a film dealing with Holocaust-related personal tragedy. Still, the film hit home with many audiences, winning the Golden Lion at the 1987 Venice Film Festival, and earning two Oscar nominations—Best Foreign Film and Best Screenplay. The videotape is available in dubbed and subtitled (French into English) versions.

p, Louis Malle; d, Louis Malle; w, Louis Malle; ed, Emmanuelle Castro; ph, Renato Berta, Eastmancolor; m, Franz Schubert and Camille Saint-Saens.

(PR:A-C MPAA:PG)

AWAY ALL BOATS**

(1956) 114m UNIV c

Jeff Chandler (Capt. Jeb Hawks), George Nader (Lt. Dave MacDougall), Julie Adams (Nadine MacDougall), Lex Barker (Comdr. Quigley), Keith Andes (Dr. Bell), Richard Boone (Lt. Fraser), William Reynolds (Ens. Kruger), Charles McGraw (Lt. Mike O'Bannion), Jock Mahoney (Alvick), John McIntire (Old Man), Frank Faylen (Chief "Pappy" Moran), Grant Williams (Lt. Sherwood), Floyd Simmons (Lt. Robinson), Don Keefer (Ens. Twitchell), Sam Gilman (Lt. Randall).

In the South Pacific during WW II, hardened Navy captain Jeb Hawks (Jeff Chandler) trains a bunch of green sailors on the attack transport USS Belinda. To keep his men from fighting among themselves, Hawks plays the role of self-centered elitist snob, prompting the sailors to direct their anger at him. Former Merchant Marine Dave MacDougall (George Nader) picks up on Hawks' game, however, and clues in his shipmates, who grow to understand and respect their captain. Then, under attack, the crew pulls together in the great tradition of the US Navy. More or less a wide-screen advertisement for the seafaring branch of the armed forces (as TO HELL AND BACK was for the Army), AWAY ALL BOATS becomes overly involved in heavy-handed melodrama, detracting from the thrills provided by some of the battle scenes.

p, Howard Christie; d, Joseph Pevney; w, Ted Sherdeman, based on the novel by Kenneth M. Dodson; ed, Ted J. Kent; ph, William Daniels, VistaVision, Technicolor; m, Frank Skinner.

(PR:A MPAA:NR)

B

BACK TO BATAAN****

(1945) 97m RKO bw

John Wayne (Col. Joe Madden), Anthony Quinn (Capt. Andres Bonifacio), Beulah Bondi (Bertha Barnes), Fely Franquelli (Dalisay Delgado), Richard Loo (Maj. Hasko), Philip Ahn (Col. Kuroki), J. Alex Havier (Sgt. Biernesa), "Ducky" Louie (Maximo), Lawrence Tierney (Lt. Comdr. Waite), Leonard Strong (Gen. Homma), Paul Fix (Spindle Jackson), Abner Biberman (Japanese Captain/Japanese Diplomat).

This stirring WW II film combines a documentary approach and dramatic incidents in the defense, fall, and retaking of the Philippines. Opening with the freeing of American prisoners at Cabanatuan in central Luzon by American Rangers, director Edward Dmytryk then moves in flashback to the dark days of the war during the defense of the Bataan Peninsula and the island fortress of Corregidor. On Bataan, Col. Joe Madden (John Wayne) commands a company of

BALLAD OF A SOLDIER—

Philippine Scouts. His friend and second-in-command is Capt. Andres Bonifacio (Anthony Quinn), who is embittered because his Filipino sweetheart, Dalisay Delgado (Fely Franquelli), is broadcasting over the radio for Japanese commanders in Manila, urging her countrymen to surrender. Only Madden and his commander know that Dalisay is really not a traitor, but an American sympathizer who has been slipping coded signals into her speeches, warning the American and Filipino forces of impending Japanese attacks. Devastating battle action is shown when Madden visits his front-line troops, who are under heavy bombardment, the Japanese attacking in human waves, bridging barbed wire with their bodies. Madden, leaving Bonifacio in command, is assigned to leave the battle line and organize resistance among Filipino partisan bands, taking charge of a small group of underground fighters. Though there is a great deal of flag-waving here, it was only natural in a film designed to keep spirits high until the war ended. This is the only film in which Dmytryk and Wayne were both involved—a none-too-surprising fact considering Wayne's strong right-wing stance and Dmytryk's association with the Communist Party. Paralleling international configurations, however, the two enemies joined forces here in battle against the Axis powers.

p, Robert Fellows; d, Edward Dmytryk; w, Ben Barzman and Richard Landau, based on a story by Aeneas MacKenzie, William Gordon; ed, Marston Fay; ph, Nicholas Musuraca; m, Roy Webb.

(PR:A MPAA:NR)

BALLAD OF A SOLDIER****
(1960, USSR) 89m Mosfilm/Kingsley bw

Vladimir Ivashov *(Alyosha)*, Shanna Prokhorenko *(Shura)*, Antonina Maximova *(Alyosha's Mother)*, Nikolai Kruchkov *(General)*, Evgeni Urbanski *(Invalid)*.

BALLAD OF A SOLDIER is the heart-tearing profile of Alyosha (Vladimir Ivashov), a young soldier fighting on the front during WW II, who performs the heroic act of disabling two German tanks and is rewarded with a six-day leave. As Alyosha makes the long journey home to see his mother (Antonina Maximova), he meets a variety of people—both friendly and antagonistic. More than a ballad of the soldier Alyosha, this startlingly realistic picture is the ballad of all the USSR's people. An episodic and hauntingly visual film, BALLAD OF A SOLDIER is a fine example of the Soviet Realist tradition—a style of filmmaking paralleled by the more cinematically innovative techniques of such Soviet directors as Sergei Paradzhanov (SHADOWS OF FORGOTTEN ANCESTORS) and Andrei Tarkovsky (MY NAME IS IVAN). Although the film is nationalistic, its appeal crossed all boundaries, taking not only the Lenin Prize at the Moscow Film Festival, but also a Gold Palm at the Cannes Film Festival and an Oscar nomination for Best Original Screenplay. (In Russian; English subtitles.)

d, Grigori Chukhrai; w, Valentin Yoshow and Grigori Chukhrai; m, Michael Siv.

(PR:A MPAA:NR)

BANANAS***½
(1971) 82m UA c

Woody Allen *(Fielding Mellish)*, Louise Lasser *(Nancy)*, Carlos Montalban *(Gen. Vargas)*, Natividad Abascal *(Yolanda)*, Jacob Morales *(Esposito)*, Miguel Suarez *(Luis)*, David Ortiz *(Sanchez)*, Rene Enriquez *(Diaz)*, Jack Axelrod *(Arroyo)*, Howard Cosell, Roger Grimsby, Don Dunphy *(Themselves)*, Charlotte Rae *(Mrs. Mellish)*, Stanley Ackerman *(Dr. Mellish)*.

In BANANAS, Woody Allen is his usual neurotic New Yorker, this time called Fielding Mellish, and is trying to make it with a political activist, Nancy (Louise Lasser, Allen's wife at the time), who'll have nothing to do with him, since she's totally immersed in the revolution taking place in the fictional Latin American country San Marcos. As fate would have it, Mellish, wearing a false red beard, winds up president of San Marcos. He returns to the US, is unmasked as a fraud, tried for subversion, and winds up marrying Nancy. Although some of the humor falls flat in this early Allen comedy, his satire of revolutions and revolutionaries is at times wickedly funny. Seeing Allen, the actor, as the Chaplinesque not-so-GREAT DICTATOR is worth the price of admission.

p, Charles H. Joffe and Jack Grossberg; d, Woody Allen; w, Woody Allen and Mickey Rose; ed, Ron Kalish; ph, Andrew M. Costikyan, Deluxe Color; m, Marvin Hamlisch.

(PR:C MPAA:NR)

BAT 21***
(1988) 105m Eagle/Tri-Star c

Gene Hackman *(Lt. Col. Iceal Hambleton)*, Danny Glover *(Capt. Bartholomew Clark)*, Jerry Reed *(Col. George Walker)*, David Marshall Grant *(Ross Carver)*, Clayton Rohner *(Sgt. Harley Rumbaugh)*, Erich Anderson *(Maj. Jake Scott)*, Joe Dorsey *(Col. Douglass)*, Rev. Michael Ng *(Vietnamese Man)*, Theodore Chan Woei-Shyong *(Boy on Bridge)*.

A welcome change from RAMBO-style Vietnam films, BAT 21 concentrates on developing its American characters and puts a complicated face on the enemy. Based on a true story, the film stars Gene Hackman as Lt. Col. Iceal Hambleton, a military strategist who has spent his entire career in the air or behind a desk. Acting on reports that a major North Vietnamese offensive is being mobilized, Hambleton goes up in a bomber to take a look, but the plane is hit over enemy territory and Hambleton is the only survivor. Alone in the jungle, with no infantry training and only a minimum of survival gear, he waits for the military to pick him up. A spotter pilot, Capt. Clark (Danny Glover), code-named "Birddog," is dispatched to locate Hambleton, "Bat 21," for a helicopter rescue. Although the two men are able to communicate by radio, the area is still too hot for Hambleton to be picked up immediately, and he spends the night in the jungle, buoyed by the pilot's radioed pep talks (monitored by the enemy). Witnessing war from ground level for the first time, Hambleton is horrified by the effects of his own strategies; he must even kill a man for the first time before his ordeal ends. With time running out before a scheduled US air strike and after one rescue attempt fails tragically, the rescue mission is called off. Clark, obsessed with rescuing Hambleton, defies orders and steals a helicopter he barely knows how to fly in one last attempt to save him. Directed by Peter Markle with an eye for military detail, BAT 21 manages to be compelling without extended battle scenes; more important, what violence there is shows *people* getting killed, not faceless commie hordes. The film tends to belabor its points and is overly melodramatic, but its lack of partisan, macho warmongering remains refreshing, and its refusal to takes sides allows it to concentrate on the humanity of the combatants. Moreover, BAT 21 works well as a traditional male adventure story. Hackman turns in his usual solid performance, and Glover is strong as the pilot who develops a deep empathy for the officer, although the device of having the men interact almost entirely by radio limits development of their relationship. The film was shot in Malaysia.

p, David Fisher, Gary A. Neill, and Michael Balson; d, Peter Markle; w, William C. Anderson and George Gordon, based on the novel by William C. Anderson; ed, Stephen E. Rivkin; ph, Mark Irwin, Deluxe Color; m, Christopher Young.

(PR:O   MPAA:R)

BATAAN****

(1943) 113m MGM bw

Robert Taylor *(Sgt. Bill Dane)*, George Murphy *(Lt. Steve Bentley)*, Thomas Mitchell *(Cpl. Jake Feingold)*, Lloyd Nolan *(Cpl. Barney Todd/Danny Burns)*, Lee Bowman *(Capt. Henry Lassiter)*, Robert Walker *(Leonard Purckett)*, Desi Arnaz *(Felix Ramirez)*, Barry Nelson *(F.X. Matowski)*, Phillip Terry *(Matthew Hardy)*, Roque Espiritu *(Cpl. Juan Katigbak)*, Kenneth Spencer *(Wesley Epps)*, J. Alex Havier *(Yankee Salazar)*.

This tough, uncompromising film tells the story of a group of determined soldiers fighting on Bataan, knowing they must delay the advancing Japanese troops and that they will be doomed in their attempt. Based on the heroic defense of the Philippines in early 1942, the film shows soldiers from all points of America, as well as Filipinos fighting for their own soil. Robert Taylor gives a rugged and inspiring performance as the grim but kind-hearted Sgt. Bill Dane, who commands the small group in a rear-guard action, protecting MacArthur's ragged army as it limps away down the narrow peninsula, where it would make its stand for three harrowing months. Capt. Lassiter (Lee Bowman) originally leads the group, but is killed, leaving Sgt. Dane to take over with an approving nod from Lt. Steve Bentley (George Murphy), a pilot trying to repair his crippled plane. Cpl. Jake Feingold (Thomas Mitchell) and Cpl. Barney Todd (Lloyd Nolan) are old troopers, the latter using a phony name because he is wanted for shooting another soldier. Robert Walker, in his screen debut, is Leonard Purckett, a naive, all-American, gum-chewing boy, who in his youthful optimism refuses to the last to believe that none of the men will get out alive. Also making an impression is a young Desi Arnaz, whose most memorable scene has him mesmerized by a radio broadcast of Tommy Dorsey. One by one, the soldiers are brutally picked off (not unlike the forlorn members of John Ford's 1934 film THE LOST PATROL) until only a handful are left. While the hand-to-hand combat is startling and brutal, and the use of miniatures is rather effective, BATAAN obviously occurs within the confines of a studio set. For a more realistic look at the fighting that occurred at Bataan, watch 1945's BACK TO BATAAN.

p, Irving Starr; d, Tay Garnett; w, Robert D. Andrews; ed, George White; ph, Sidney Wagner; m, Bronislau Kaper.

(PR:C   MPAA:NR)

BATTLE CRY**½

(1955) 147m WB c

Van Heflin *(Maj. Huxley)*, Aldo Ray *(Andy)*, Mona Freeman *(Kathy)*, Nancy Olson *(Pat)*, James Whitmore *(Sgt. Mac/Narrator)*, Raymond Massey *(Gen. Snipes)*, Tab Hunter *(Danny)*, Dorothy Malone *(Elaine)*, Anne Francis *(Rae)*, William Campbell *(Ski)*, John Lupton *(Marion)*, Justus E. McQueen [L.Q. Jones] *(L.Q. Jones)*, Perry Lopez *(Joe Gomez)*, Fess Parker *(Speedy)*, Carleton Young *(Maj. Wellman)*, Rhys Williams *(Enoch Rogers)*, Chick Chandler *(Chaplain)*.

Based on the novel by Leon Uris, this huge, sprawling, and essentially disappointing movie focuses more on the romantic relationships of a group of Marines and their sweethearts than it does on the story—of a Marines communications battalion sent to New Zealand, where they jump to glory or death. Huxley (Van Heflin) is the tough major who combines gentleness with necessary discipline to mold his youthful charges into fighting machines. In the love department, Andy (Aldo Ray) falls for Pat (Nancy Olsen), a New Zealander whose husband and brother were both war casualties; Danny (Tab Hunter) finds himself involved with two ladies, hometown sweetheart Kathy (Mona Freeman) and the married Elaine (Dorothy Malone); and the reserved Marion (John Lupton) is paired with good-time girl Rae (Anne Francis). Raoul Walsh, who spent much of his career making action films (OBJECTIVE BURMA; WHITE HEAT; WHAT PRICE GLORY?) is hampered somewhat by the Uris script, but the Max Steiner score and the use of actual combat footage help to sustain the excessive two-and-a-half-hour length.

p, Raoul Walsh; d, Raoul Walsh; w, Leon W. Uris, based on his novel; ed, William Zeigler; ph, Sid Hickox, CinemaScope, Warnercolor; m, Max Steiner.

(PR:A   MPAA:NR)

BATTLE HELL—

BATTLE HELL**
(1957, Brit.) 113m Herbert Wilcox/Brit. Lion bw (GB: YANGTSE INCIDENT; ESCAPE OF THE AMETHYST)

Richard Todd *(Lt. Comdr. Kerans)*, William Hartnell *(Leading Seaman Frank)*, Akim Tamiroff *(Col. Peng)*, Keye Luke *(Capt. Kuo Tai)*, Donald Houston *(Lt. Weston)*, Robert Urquhart *(Flight Lt. Fearnley)*, Sophie Stewart *(Nurse Dunlap)*, James Kenney *(Lt. Hett)*.

This film tells the true story of the British H.M.S. *Amethyst*, which became stranded on the Communist-dominated Yangtse River in 1949. Directed by craftsman Michael Anderson, BATTLE HELL is a factual, rather dry recounting of events on the ship as it lay crippled in the water, unable to escape from the heavy shellfire that was bursting around it in the midst of Chinese civil war. Under the lead of the ship's new captain, Lt. Comdr. Kerans (Richard Todd), the ship and crew travel 140 miles downriver in the dark of night to break the Communist blockade and rejoin the rest of the British fleet. Akim Tamiroff is stereotypically evil as the Chinese colonel who throws obstacles into the negotiations with the British.

p, Herbert Wilcox; d, Michael Anderson; w, Eric Ambler, based on the book *Escape of the Amethyst* by Laurence Earl.

(PR:A MPAA:NR)

BATTLE OF ALGIERS, THE*****
(1967, It./Algeria) 120m Magna/Rizzoli bw

Yacef Saadi *(Kader)*, Jean Martin *(Col. Mathieu)*, Brahim Haggiag *(Ali La Pointe)*, Tommaso Neri *(Captain)*.

A frightening and powerful battle cry for Marxist revolutionaries, THE BATTLE OF ALGIERS details the struggle for Algerian independence from France. The film begins in Algiers in 1957, as a tortured Arab prisoner informs against Ali la Pointe (Brahim Haggiag), the last surviving member of the FLN (Algerian Liberation Front). As French soldiers surround Ali's apartment, Col. Mathieu (Jean Martin) issues a final warning to Ali and his family: surrender or be blown to pieces. With the sides clearly laid out—revolutionary vs. counterrevolutionary—the film shifts to 1954, as the Algerian conflict develops. Photographed in grainy black and white to suggest the style of documentaries and television news reports, THE BATTLE OF ALGIERS most closely resembles the Neo-Realism of Roberto Rossellini and the revolutionary technique of Sergei Eisenstein. Like Eisenstein, director Gillo Pontecorvo took his camera to the actual locations of the revolution, re-created certain events, and cast local nonprofessionals. Only Martin is a professional actor, while Yacef Saadi, the film's coproducer, plays an FLN leader—a character based on his real-life role as the organizer of the resistance and the military commander of the FLN. What makes THE BATTLE OF ALGIERS' power creditable (its content has been attacked as being too inflammatory, and it was reportedly used as a terrorist primer in the late 1960s) is Pontecorvo's ability to present combatants on both sides as multidimensional, nonheroic human beings, even though it's obvious where the director's own sentiments lie. The film received the Golden Lion at Venice in 1966, and secured Oscar nominations for Best Foreign Film, Best Screenplay, and Best Director. (Dubbed in English.)

p, Antonio Musu and Yacef Saadi; d, Gillo Pontecorvo; w, Gillo Pontecorvo and Franco Solinas; ed, Mario Serandrei and Mario Morra; ph, Marcello Gatti; m, Gillo Pontecorvo and Ennio Morricone.

(PR:C MPAA:NR)

BATTLE OF AUSTERLITZ, THE**½
(1960, Fr./It./Yugo.) 180m CFPI-Lyre-GalateaDubrava/LUX c (AKA: AUSTERLITZ)

Rossano Brazzi *(Lucien Bonaparte)*, Claudia Cardinale *(Pauline)*, Martine Carol *(Josephine)*, Maria Ferrero *(Elise)*, Ettore Manni *(Murat)*, Jean Marais *(Carnot)*, Georges Marchal *(Lannes)*, Jack Palance *(Weirother)*, Vittorio De Sica *(Pope)*, Michel Simon *(Grognard)*, Orson Welles *(Robert Fulton)*, Pierre Mondy *(Napoleon Bonaparte)*.

This ambitious effort from Abel Gance deals with the same period in French history as his brilliant silent epic NAPOLEON, focusing on the titanic battle between the "emperors'" armies and their overwhelming opposition. Although there is an undeniable grandeur to THE BATTLE OF AUSTERLITZ, it is nearly impossible to judge Gance's original intent in its radically edited (read shred to ribbons) videocassette format. Even the battle scenes (which were so stunning in NAPOLEON) are disjointed and meaningless here. The $4-million price tag for this opus was staggering at the time, nearly bankrupting its producers, yet today one can pick up a public domain copy of the videocassette for as little as $5.99. Unfortunately, these tapes are far inferior to the nicely packaged version from U.S.A. Home Video. If the name of Abel Gance isn't reason enough to rent the film, then how about a cast that includes Orson Welles, Claudia Cardinale, Michel Simon, Vittorio De Sica, Jean Marais, Jack Palance, and Leslie Caron? The original script for the film was written in 1924 as part of an unrealized cycle of films about Napoleon's career.

p, Alexander Salkind; d, Abel Gance; w, Abel Gance; ed, Leonide Azar and Yvonne Martin; ph, Henri Alekan, Dyaliscope, Eastmancolor.

(PR:A MPAA:NR)

BATTLE OF BRITAIN, THE***
(1969, Brit.) 133m Spitfire/UA c

Harry Andrews *(Senior Civil Servant)*, Michael Caine *(Squadron Leader Canfield)*, Trevor Howard *(Air Vice Marshal Keith Park)*, Curt Jurgens *(Baron von Richter)*, Ian McShane *(Sgt. Pilot Andy)*, Kenneth More *(Group Capt. Baker)*, Laurence Olivier *(Air Chief Marshal Sir Hugh Dowding)*, Nigel Patrick *(Group Capt. Hope)*, Christopher Plummer *(Squadron Leader Harvey)*, Michael Redgrave *(Air Vice Marshal Evill)*, Ralph Richardson *(British Minister in Switzerland)*, Robert Shaw *(Squadron Leader Skipper)*,

Patrick Wymark (Air Vice Marshal Trafford Leigh-Mallory), Susannah York (Section Officer Maggie Harvey), Michael Bates (W.O. Warrick).

This great, stirring saga of England's WW II defense of its homeland features a staggering, star-studded cast, who compensate for the film's lengthy docudrama style with excellent portrayals down the line, despite their restricted roles. Michael Caine, Christopher Plummer, and Kenneth More have the meatier parts, with love interest provided by Susannah York as Plummer's WAAF wife who hates the war and craves affection. Laurence Olivier is in top form as Sir Hugh Dowding, whose crafty tactics with his limited fighter command induced the Luftwaffe to make fatal errors that led to its destruction, and Robert Shaw is superb as an exhausted but relentlessly tough fighter commander who orders his men again and again into the air. While the film is a fitting paean of praise for the noble RAF in its "finest hour," nodding recognition is also given to the Czech and Polish flyers who fought alongside their British comrades. Except for Curt Jurgens, however, the German actors are mere caricatures of the Nazi high command (Rulf Stiefel is ludicrous as a berserk Hitler). The aerial photography of the German bombing and the dogfights between the British and German fighters are spectacular and fascinating; it was the high production value of these segments that cost the producers the bulk of their $12 million investment. Ironically, Adolf Galland, one of the sharpest German aces to vex the British during WW II, was employed as a technical advisor on the film.

p, Harry Saltzman and S. Benjamin Fisz; d, Guy Hamilton; w, James Kennaway, S. Benjamin Fisz, and Wilfred Greatorex; ed, Bert Bates; ph, Freddie Young and Bob Huke, Panavision, Technicolor; m, Sir William Walton and Ron Goodwin.

(PR:A MPAA:G)

BATTLE OF NERETVA***

(1969, Yugo./It./Ger.) 106m Jadran Film-Bosna Film Commonwealth-United-Eichberg/AIP c (BITKA NA NERETVI)

Yul Brynner (Vlado), Hardy Kruger (Col. Kranzer), Franco Nero (Capt. Riva), Sylva Koscina (Danica), Orson Welles (Senator), Curt Jurgens (Gen. Lohring), Anthony Dawson (Gen. Morelli), Milena Dravic (Nada), Sergei Bondarchuk (Martin), Liubisa Samardjic (Novak), Bata Zivojinovic (Partisan Captain), Boris Dvornik (Stipe), Oleg Vidov (Nicola).

The most expensive Yugoslavian production of its day ($12 million) and an Oscar nominee for Best Foreign-Language Film, THE BATTLE OF NERETVA is an international war epic that was originally to have run 240 minutes, was cut to 175 minutes for its (successful) Yugoslavian run, and emerged at 106 minutes on videocassette. Set in early 1943, as the Yugoslavian partisans are battling the onslaught of German and Italian troops, the film focuses on a group of local resistance fighters who struggle to cross the Neretva River and reach a mountain stronghold. Determined to destroy this resistance movement is German general Lohring (Curt Jurgens) and his aide, Col. Kranzer (Hardy Kruger). After intense battling and severe losses, the partisans make it to the Neretva, only to learn from demolitions expert Vlado (Yul Brynner) that Marshal Tito has ordered the Neretva Valley bridge blown up in order to halt an advancing Panzer division. The star-studded cast also includes Franco Nero as an Italian officer, Soviet actor-director Sergei Bondarchuk (WAR AND PEACE) as a partisan commander, and the epical Orson Welles as a senator of the royalist Chetniks who urges his countrymen to lay down their weapons and is then shot as a traitor.

p, Veljko Bulajic; d, Veljko Bulajic; w, Veljko Bulajic, Ratko Durovic, Ugo Pirro, and Stevo Bulajic; ed, Vojislav Bjenjas; ph, Tomislav Pinter, Technicolor; m, Vladimir Rajteric-Kraus.

(PR:A MPAA:NR)

BATTLE OF THE BULGE***½

(1965) 141m Cinerama/WB c

Henry Fonda (Lt. Col. Kiley), Robert Shaw (Col. Hessler), Robert Ryan (Gen. Grey), Dana Andrews (Col. Pritchard), George Montgomery (Sgt. Duquesne), Ty Hardin (Schumacher), Pier Angeli (Louise), Barbara Werle (Elena), Charles Bronson (Wolenski), Werner Peters (Col. Kohler), Hans Christian Blech (Conrad), James MacArthur (Lt. Weaver), Telly Savalas (Guffy), Karl Otto Alberty (Von Diepel), William Conrad (Narrator).

Overlong at 141 minutes, almost completely devoid of any plot, and as historically incorrect as one could imagine, BATTLE OF THE BULGE still manages to be a fairly entertaining war picture that glorifies and mythicizes battle through the Hollywood fetish of filming with the high-tech camera processes Ultra-Panavision, CinemaScope, and Technicolor. Col. Hessler (Robert Shaw), a master tactician in the German tank corps, is planning a full-scale attack on US troops. His Allied counterparts across the Bastogne are Gen. Grey (Robert Ryan), Col. Pritchard (Dana Andrews), and Lt. Col. Kiley (Henry Fonda), the last of whom feels keenly that the Germans are preparing an offensive. Kiley keeps after his superiors about the suspected pending attack, but they won't hear of it. Once the lieutenant colonel is vindicated, the rest of the film comprises an inch-by-inch (fictionalized) account of the battle. The movie is very inaccurate and any veteran of the real battle will laugh at the climax, which takes place on a butte, with squadrons of tanks in a militarized showdown a la HIGH NOON.

p, Milton Sperling and Philip Yordan; d, Ken Annakin; w, Philip Yordan, Milton Sperling, and John Melson; ed, Derek Parsons; ph, Jack Hildyard, Ultra-Panavision, Technicolor; m, Benjamin Frankel.

(PR:A MPAA:NR)

BATTLE TAXI*

(1955) 82m UA bw

Sterling Hayden (Capt. Russ Edwards), Arthur Franz (Lt.

BEAST, THE—

Pete Stacy), Marshall Thompson (2d Lt. Tim Vernon), Leo Needham (Sgt. Slats Klein), Jay Barney (Lt. Col. Stoneham), John Goddard (Wounded G.I.), Robert Sherman (Lt. Joe Kirk), Joel Marston (Lt. Marty Staple), John Dennis (Sgt. Joe Murdock), Dale Hutchinson (Blue Boy Three-Gene), Andy Andrews (Lazy Joker Two), Vance Skarstedt (Lt. Smiley Jackson), Michael Colgan (Medic, Capt. Larsen), Capt. Vincent McGovern (Copilot Harry).

This uninteresting and standard war tale stars Sterling Hayden as Capt. Russ Edwards, leader of a Korean War helicopter air rescue group. His major task appears to be convincing his pilots that they should listen to the maxim, "there are old pilots and there are bold pilots but there are no old, bold pilots." BATTLE TAXI was made with the cooperation of the Department of Defense, making it seem more a piece of propaganda than anything else and resulting in a film that's all rescues and heroics with very little story in between. It is worthwhile only for the stock footage, courtesy of the 42d Air Rescue Squadron.

p, Ivan Tors and Art Arthur; d, Herbert L. Strock; w, Malvin Wald, based on a story by Malvin Wald, Art Arthur; ed, Jodie Copelan; ph, Lothrop B. Worth; m, Harry Sukman.

(PR:A MPAA:NR)

BEAST, THE***½

(1988) 109m A&M/COL c

George Dzundza (Daskal), Jason Patric (Koverchenko), Steven Bauer (Taj), Stephen Baldwin (Golikov), Don Harvey (Kaminski), Kabir Bedi (Akbar), Erick Avari (Samad), Shosh Marciano (Moustafa).

An intelligent look at the Soviet-Afghan war from the participants' point of view, stylishly directed by Kevin Reynolds, THE BEAST is set in 1981, the second year of the Soviet occupation. Having decimated a small Afghan village, a Soviet tank—called "The Beast" by the natives—is separated from its unit and trapped in a valley. Daskal (George Dzundza), the brutal commander, wrongly blames his men for the mistake and keeps them in line through intimidation; only the driver, Koverchenko (Jason Patric), dares to speak up to him. Meanwhile, aided by a battlefield-scrounged anti-tank device, two bickering Afghan factions join forces and, led by Taj (Steven Bauer), launch a small-scale jihad, making Daskal so paranoid that he executes his Afghan navigator, whom he suspects is a collaborator. Koverchenko, who had befriended the Afghan and learned about his culture, fails in an attempt at mutiny and is left by Daskal to die. Just as the driver is about to be stoned to death, however, Taj and his men appear. When the Soviet speaks their word for "asylum" (tradition stipulates that an Afghan must shelter even his sworn enemy if he asks for asylum), he is spared and joins the attack on "the Beast," which is eventually tamed. Dramatic and moving, THE BEAST both delivers its genre goods and explores the nature of the Soviet-Afghan conflict without polarizing rhetoric. The film, fairly even-handed in its portrayal of the two sides, is more concerned with the human tragedy of war than its politics. The invaders' perspective is juxtaposed with that of the mujahadeen, and, as a result, THE BEAST yields an insightful look at Afghan culture. Reynolds, shooting in Israel, makes good use of both the vast, dry landscape and the cramped quarters of the tank, and the acting is excellent. Working against the film, however, is the unrealistic portrayal of the Soviets. Pains were taken to make the Afghans seem authentic, including having the actors speak in (subtitled) dialect, but the Soviets all look, act, and speak like Americans, as if the rebels were fighting a bunch of Californians who took a wrong turn at Zuma Beach. That, however, may be the point; Reynolds may want viewers to see parallels between the USSR's behavior in Afghanistan and US involvement in Vietnam. (In Pushtu and English; English subtitles.)

p, John Fiedler; d, Kevin Reynolds; w, William Mastrosimone, based on his play Nanawatai; ed, Peter Boyle; ph, Douglas Milsome, Rank Color; m, Mark Isham.

(PR:O MPAA:R)

BEAU GESTE*****

(1939) 114m PAR bw

Gary Cooper (Michael "Beau" Geste), Ray Milland (John Geste), Robert Preston (Digby Geste), Brian Donlevy (Sgt. Markoff), Susan Hayward (Isobel Rivers), J. Carrol Naish (Rasinoff), Albert Dekker (Schwartz), Broderick Crawford (Hank Miller), Charles Barton (Buddy McMonigal), James Stephenson (Maj. Henri de Beaujolais), Heather Thatcher (Lady Patricia Brandon), G.P. Huntley, Jr. (Augustus Brandon).

Gary Cooper essays the title role with quiet magnificence in this superb adventure tale loaded with drama, action, and mystery. Presented in an intricate flashback structure, the film tells the story of the three Geste brothers—Beau (Cooper), Digby (Robert Preston), and John (Ray Milland). As youths (a young Donald O'Connor plays young Beau) they are obsessed with valor; then, as men, they test their ideals in the French Foreign Legion. Interwoven with their story is the financial hardship of their aunt, Lady Patricia Brandon (Heather Thatcher); the theft of her family heirloom; the death of the vicious Sgt. Markoff (Brian Donlevy) during the defense of a desert fort; and Beau's childhood wish for a "Viking burial." Cooper's great performance is backed up solidly by Milland and Preston, with Susan Hayward appearing briefly as John's love interest, Isobel. Donlevy, however, steals almost every scene he's in with a squinty-eyed, snarling performance that will scare the blazes out of anyone, while J. Carrol Naish's hyenalike Rasinoff is unforgettable. P.C. Wren, author of the novel on which the film is based, spent his Foreign Legion hitch fighting in North Africa and penning the Geste saga, which became a worldwide best-seller and was made into a great Paramount silent in 1926 with Ronald Colman as Beau. When William Wellman was brought in to remake the silent version, he was instructed to follow the original to the letter, which he did, even using the same locale, the dunes of Yuma, Arizona, where a new Fort Zinderneuf was completely rebuilt. A third version followed in 1966, and in 1977, a comic version of the story was released, titled THE LAST REMAKE OF BEAU GESTE.

p, William A. Wellman; d, William A. Wellman; w, Robert Carson, based on the novel by Percival Christopher Wren; ed, Thomas Scott; ph, Theodor Sparkuhl and Archie Stout; m, Alfred Newman.

(PR:A MPAA:NR)

BEHIND THE RISING SUN**
(1943) 88m RKO bw

Margo (Tama), Tom Neal (Taro), J. Carrol Naish (Publisher), Robert Ryan (Lefty), Gloria Holden (Sara), Donald Douglas (O'Hara), George Givot (Boris), Adeline de Walt Reynolds (Grandmother), Leonard Strong (Tama's Father), Iris Wong (Secretary), Wolfgang Zilzer (Max), Mike Mazurki (Japanese Wrestler).

A slam-bang, flag-waving, anti-Japanese movie released at the nadir of WW II, BEHIND THE RISING SUN served to rally moviegoers to the War Bond effort that was promoted in every theater. Director Edward Dmytryk and screenwriter Emmet Lavery (who teamed earlier on RKO's highly successful HITLER'S CHILDREN) tell the story of a Japanese publisher (J. Carrol Naish) who becomes Minister of Propaganda and forces his Cornell-educated son, Taro (Tom Neal), to join the Japanese Army against his will. Taro is brainwashed by Japanese ideology, and eventually becomes a devoted nationalist whose naming of names disgusts even his own father. The picture today seems pure and simple US nationalism, but at the time of its making it stirred a lot of hearts and minds. There's also the ludicrous casting of Margo, Neal, Naish, and Mike Mazurki as Asians, but that's the way it was back then.

d, Edward Dmytryk; w, Emmett Lavery, based on the book by James R. Young; ed, Joseph Noriega; ph, Russell Metty; m, Roy Webb.

(PR:C MPAA:NR)

BEHOLD A PALE HORSE***½
(1964) 118m COL bw

Gregory Peck (Manuel Artiguez), Anthony Quinn (Capt. Vinolas), Omar Sharif (Fr. Francisco), Mildred Dunnock (Pilar), Raymond Pellegrin (Carlos), Paolo Stoppa (Pedro), Daniela Rocca (Rosanna), Christian Marquand (Lt. Zaganar), Marietto Angeletti (Paco Degas), Perette Pradier (Maria), Zia Mohyeddin (Luis), Rosalie Crutchley (Teresa).

Reportedly based on the real-life exploits of Francisco Sabater, BEHOLD A PALE HORSE tells the story of a Spanish guerrilla named Manuel Artiguez (an oddly cast Gregory Peck) who lives in exile in France and still leads raids on Spain from Pau, continuing a nearly one-man effort after the end of the Spanish Civil War. Twenty years later, Artiguez is told that his mother, Pilar (Mildred Dunnock), is dying in Spain. What he doesn't realize is that this is a trap set by Capt. Vinolas (Anthony Quinn), the vicious Spanish police chief who has been after Artiguez for years. Pilar, aware that her son has been set up, pleads with a priest, Fr. Francisco (Omar Sharif), to inform her son of the danger, and since Fr. Francisco sees himself more as Artiguez's fellow human being than as his enemy, he agrees. Artiguez, however, is determined to visit his mother. Lots of preachy moralizing and allegory mark this artistic film directed by Fred Zinnemann (HIGH NOON) from a novel by British filmmaker Emeric Pressburger (longtime collaborator of Michael Powell), which never found its expected great commercial success. Nonetheless, Peck is very good, Quinn is superb, and everyone involved with this powerful movie should take a bow.

p, Fred Zinnemann; d, Fred Zinnemann; w, J.P. Miller, from the novel Killing a Mouse on Sunday by Emeric Pressburger; ed, Walter Thompson; ph, Jean Badal; m, Maurice Jarre.

(PR:C MPAA:NR)

BERLIN EXPRESS**½
(1948) 86m RKO bw

Merle Oberon (Lucienne), Robert Ryan (Robert Lindley), Charles Korvin (Perrot), Paul Lukas (Dr. Bernhardt), Robert Coote (Sterling), Reinhold Schunzel (Walther), Roman Toporow (Lt. Maxim), Peter Von Zerneck (Hans Schmidt), Otto Waldis (Kessler), Fritz Kortner (Franzen), Michael Harvey (Sgt. Barnes), Tom Keene (Major), Jim Nolan (Train Captain).

It's three years after Adolf and Eva died in the bunker and there are still Nazis roaming Germany, trying their best to disrupt the peace. On board the Berlin Express from Paris, a famed leader of the international peace movement, Dr. Bernhardt (Paul Lukas) is kidnaped by members of this Nazi underground. Yank Robert Lindley (Robert Ryan), Brit Sterling (Robert Coote), and Russky Lt. Maxim (Roman Toporow) are a trio of officers assigned to find Bernhardt, root out the underground vermin, and set the country back on the right track. Along the way, Bernhardt's secretary, Lucienne (Merle Oberon), lends Lindley a hand in locating the hidden Nazi headquarters. The bombed-out backgrounds of Frankfurt and Berlin lend a great deal of credibility to the movie, as do the combined talents of director Jacques Tourneur and cinematographer Lucien Ballard.

p, Bert Granet; d, Jacques Tourneur; w, Harold Medford, based on a story by Curt Siodmak; ed, Sherman Todd; ph, Lucien Ballard; m, Frederick Hollander.

(PR:C MPAA:NR)

BEST DEFENSE*
(1984) 94m PAR c

Dudley Moore (Wylie Cooper), Eddie Murphy (Landry), Kate Capshaw (Laura), George Dzundza (Loparino), Helen Shaver (Claire Lewis), Mark Arnott (Brank), Peter Michael Goetz (Frank Joyner), Tom Noonan (Holtzman), David Rasche (Jeff), Darryl Henriques (Col. Zayas).

This wholly unfunny comedy intercuts between two characters, in two different parts of the world, at two different times. 1982: Wylie Cooper (Dudley Moore), an Army officer and beleaguered engineer, struggles to perfect a gyro

BEST YEARS OF OUR LIVES, THE—

that will be the core component in the missile system for a new tank. 1984: Landry (Eddie Murphy), a soldier on duty in an Arabian desert, vainly attempts to keep his new tank under control, but the gyro is malfunctioning. These scenes are played one after the other as the picture switches from 1982 to 1984, leaving the audience bewildered as to whether they are watching flashbacks or premonitions. When Wylie accidentally comes upon the plans for a gyro that will work, he is in danger of being killed by a nutso industrial spy (David Rasche) who has also been seeking the plans. The film continues to cut back and forth, Wylie struggling to perfect the gyro while, in the other time frame, Landry finds himself involved in a situation that calls for a reliable weapon. Try as they might, neither the cast nor the filmmakers can cover up the fact that this movie, like Wylie's prototype, is a dud.

p, Gloria Katz; d, Willard Huyck; w, Gloria Katz and Willard Huyck, based on the novel *Easy and Hard Ways Out* by Robert Grossbach; ed, Sidney Wolinsky and Michael A. Stevenson; ph, Don Peterman, Movielab Color; m, Patrick Williams.

(PR:O   MPAA:R)

BEST YEARS OF OUR LIVES, THE*****
(1946) 172m Goldwyn/RKO bw

Myrna Loy *(Milly Stephenson)*, Fredric March *(Al Stephenson)*, Dana Andrews *(Fred Derry)*, Teresa Wright *(Peggy Stephenson)*, Virginia Mayo *(Marie Derry)*, Cathy O'Donnell *(Wilma Cameron)*, Hoagy Carmichael *(Butch Engle)*, Harold Russell *(Homer Parrish)*, Gladys George *(Hortense Derry)*, Roman Bohnen *(Pat Derry)*, Ray Collins *(Mr. Milton)*, Steve Cochran *(Cliff)*, Minna Gombell *(Mrs. Parrish)*, Walter Baldwin *(Mr. Parrish)*, Dorothy Adams *(Mrs. Cameron)*, Don Beddoe *(Mr. Cameron)*, Erskine Sanford *(Bullard)*, Marlene Aames *(Luella Parrish)*, Michael Hall *(Rob Stephenson)*, Charles Halton *(Prew)*, Ray Teal *(Mr. Mollett)*, Dean White *(Novak)*, Howland Chamberlin *(Thorpe)*, Victor Cutler *(Woody Merrill)*.

"I don't care if it doesn't make a nickel," Sam Goldwyn reportedly stated in a famous *oxymoron* regarding this film, "I just want every man, woman, and child in America to see it." The colorful producer got the idea for the film after reading a *Life* article about WW II veterans and their difficulties in adjusting to civilian life. With a brilliant script by Robert E. Sherwood, effective direction by William Wyler, masterful photography by Gregg Toland, and excellent performances by the entire cast, this film about returning American servicemen is justifiably considered a classic. Three servicemen—Al Stephenson (Fredric March), Fred Derry (Dana Andrews), and Homer Parrish (Harold Russell)—are shown returning to their hometown, full of awful memories of war and doubts about their future in a country they have difficulty remembering. After sharing space on board the bomber that flies them home, the three take a cab to their separate addresses. The sailor Homer comes home to his girl with a pair of hooks where his hands once were (Russell, the only nonprofessional in the cast, lost his hands in a training accident while in the service); middle-aged Al returns to his loving wife (Myrna Loy), children, and old job as a banker; Fred finds a spouse who has more or less abandoned him, and no prospects for a job. The delicate and painful process of readjustment is the subject of this sensitive film, which succeeds splendidly. Although everyone in Hollywood thought Goldwyn would lose his shirt on THE BEST YEARS OF OUR LIVES, it was a massive hit and won Academy Awards for Best Picture, Best Actor (March), Best Supporting Actor (Russell), Best Direction, Best Original Screenplay, Best Score, and Best Editing.

p, Samuel Goldwyn; d, William Wyler; w, Robert E. Sherwood, based on the novella *Glory for Me* by MacKinlay Kantor; ed, Daniel Mandell; ph, Gregg Toland; m, Hugo Friedhofer.

(PR:A   MPAA:NR)

BIG RED ONE, THE****
(1980) 113m Lorimar/UA c

Lee Marvin *(Sergeant)*, Mark Hamill *(Griff)*, Robert Carradine *(Zab)*, Bobby DiCicco *(Vinci)*, Kelly Ward *(Johnson)*, Siegfried Rauch *(Schroeder)*, Stephane Audran *(Walloon)*, Serge Marquand *(Rensonnet)*, Charles Macaulay *(General/Captain)*, Alain Doutey *(Broban)*, Maurice Marsac *(Vichy Colonel)*, Joseph Clark *(Shep)*, Ken Campbell *(Lemchek)*, Doug Werner *(Switolski)*, Perry Lang *(Kaiser)*.

Veteran writer-director Samuel Fuller (THE STEEL HELMET; FIXED BAYONETS; VERBOTEN!; MERRILL'S MARAUDERS) waited more than 35 years to make this dream project, a WW II picture that follows the exploits of his unit, the First Infantry Division, nicknamed "the Big Red One" because of the big red number one on the division arm patch. Instead of staging huge battle scenes with hundreds of soldiers and dozens of vehicles, Fuller chose to make a more intimate film, concentrating on a small squad of soldiers as they battle the Germans from Northern Africa and into Europe during the years 1942-45. The squad is made up of four green recruits: Griff (Mark Hamill), Vinci (Bobby DiCicco), Johnson (Kelly Ward), and the cigar-chomping Zab (Robert Carradine), an aspiring writer obviously patterned after Fuller. These young men are led by a grizzled, tough, no-nonsense sergeant (Lee Marvin), a WW I veteran determined to teach his charges how to survive the rigors of battle. Episodic in structure, the film shows a skirmish here and a battle there, but focuses mainly on the small details of survival taught by the Sarge. Some of the highlights include the sergeant instructing his soldiers to put condoms over the barrels of their rifles to keep out water when landing on a beachhead, an eerie skirmish in a misty forest, the squad stumbling across an abandoned mental hospital where the patients have been left to fend for themselves, the birth of a baby in a tank, and the discovery of a concentration camp abandoned by the Germans. Fuller injects much humor into his narrative, constantly balancing the horrible and violent with the sardonic, most notably in a scene in which Johnson steps on a mine and has a testicle blown off. The Sarge rushes to the boy's side and fishes around in the dirt until he finds

— BLACK AND WHITE IN COLOR

the severed part, shows it to the soldier, tosses it over his shoulder, and reassuringly says, "That's why God gave you two." In THE BIG RED ONE, Fuller refuses to indulge in melodramatics or Hollywood-style heroics and instead concentrates on a group of men determined to survive the war and go home in one piece. Filled with memorable scenes, plenty of humor, and excellent performances, especially from Marvin, THE BIG RED ONE is a remarkable film and one of the best ever made about WW II.

p, Gene Corman; d, Samuel Fuller; w, Samuel Fuller; ed, Morton Tubor; ph, Adam Greenberg, Metrocolor; m, Dana Koproff.

(PR:C   MPAA:PG)

BILOXI BLUES***½
(1988) 107m Rastar/UNIV c

Matthew Broderick (Eugene Morris Jerome), Christopher Walken (Sgt. Merwin J. Toomey), Matt Mulhern (Joseph Wykowski), Corey Parker (Arnold Epstein), Markus Flanagan (Roy Selridge), Casey Siemaszko (Donald Carney), Michael Dolan (James J. Hennessey), Penelope Ann Miller (Daisy Hannigan), Park Overall (Rowena), Alan Pottinger (Peek), Mark Evan Jacobs (Pinelli).

BILOXI BLUES works better than it has any right to, thanks to the skillful direction of Mike Nichols and excellent performances from Matthew Broderick and Christopher Walken. An adaptation of Neil Simon's autobiographical play, the film follows New Yorker Eugene Morris Jerome (Broderick) through his Army basic training in Biloxi, Mississippi, in the last days of WW II. Eugene is bemused by his fellow draftees—including vulgar roughnecks Wykowski (Matt Mulhern) and Selridge (Markus Flanagan), hanger-on Carney (Casey Siemaszko), and likable farm boy Hennessey (Michael Dolan)—and writes about them in his notebook. The Biloxi heat gets him down, as does his strange DI, Sgt. Toomey (Walken), whose sadism works in quiet, mysterious ways, sowing dissent among his troops. The weeks of bad food, long marches, and humiliation are somewhat relieved, however, when Eugene falls in love with Daisy (Penelope Ann Miller) on a weekend pass. When his buddies find Eugene's notes and read his hurtful remarks about them—including his musings as to whether or not Epstein (Corey Parker) is homosexual—the aspiring writer discovers just how powerful words can be. This lesson is further enforced when two recruits are caught in a homosexual act and one of them escapes, his face unseen. The Army is determined to ferret out the homosexual, and because of Eugene's notes suspicion falls on Epstein, though it isn't he who is the culprit. Later, Toomey flips out completely, holds a gun to Eugene's head, and has to be talked into giving up the weapon. By the time training ends, the war is over. BILOXI BLUES is a very cinematic adaptation of Simon's popular play. Nichols avoids presenting the jokes in the set-up-to-big-punchline formula typical of Simon, the dialog flows naturally, and the jokes come in an almost off-hand manner, a naturalistic approach that helps make Simon's basically cliched service comedy fresh. Broderick brings appealing nuance to

the role he created onstage, and Walken makes his sergeant a quietly chilling, ambiguous character. Nichols and cinematographer Bill Butler's complex visual style opens up the stagebound original material beautifully, and the entire film is intelligently directed and tightly constructed, without a dull scene or wasted moment, transforming what might have been routine material into entertaining art.

p, Ray Stark; d, Mike Nichols; w, Neil Simon, based on his play; ed, Sam O'Steen; ph, Bill Butler; m, Georges Delerue.

(PR:C-O   MPAA:PG-13)

BIRDY****
(1984) 120m Malton/Tri-Star c

Matthew Modine (Birdy), Nicolas Cage (Al Columbato), John Harkins (Dr. Weiss), Sandy Baron (Mr. Columbato), Karen Young (Hannah Rourke), Bruno Kirby (Renaldi), Nancy Fish (Mrs. Prevost), George Buck (Birdy's Father), Delores Sage (Birdy's Mother), Robert L. Ryan (Joe Sagessa), James Santini (Mario Columbato), Maude Winchester (Doris Robinson), Marshall Bell (Ronsky), Elizabeth Whitcraft (Rosanne), Sandra Beall (Shirley).

BIRDY is one of those rare movies that successfully bring a psychological novel to the screen without sacrificing its saliency or complexity. Though the book by William Wharton is set in the days after WW II, the film has been updated to the post-Vietnam era to tell the story of the deep friendship between Birdy (Matthew Modine) and Al Columbato (Nicolas Cage), a pair of young men whose lives have been scarred by the Vietnam experience. Birdy has had an obsessive affinity for birds since he was a lad (his youth is shown in flashback), but in the period after his wartime service he believes he has actually transformed into a bird and, as a result, is confined to a military asylum. His best friend, Al, whose war wounds are only physical, is now determined to bring Birdy out of his fantasy. One of the most bizarre accounts of postwar trauma, BIRDY succeeds because of the outstanding performances of both Cage and Modine. Modine's sensitive portrayal of the young man who transcends species boundaries is spellbinding; Cage is at once affable, concerned, and frustrated. The story presents a fresh alternative to such "realistic" postwar films as COMING HOME; WHO'LL STOP THE RAIN; or ROLLING THUNDER.

p, Alan Marshall; d, Alan Parker; w, Sandy Kroopf and Jack Behr, based on the novel by William Wharton; ed, Gerry Hambling; ph, Michael Seresin, Metrocolor; m, Peter Gabriel.

(PR:O   MPAA:R)

BLACK AND WHITE IN COLOR***
(1976, Fr.) 100m AA c (LA VICTOIRE EN CHANTANT)

Jean Carmet (Sgt. Bosselet), Jaques Dufilho (Paul Rechampot), Catherine Rouvel (Marinette), Jacques Spiesser (Hubert Fresnoy), Dora Doll (Maryvonne), Maurice Barrier (Caprice), Claude Legros (Jacques

BLACK TENT, THE—

Rechampot), Jacques Monnet *(Pere Simon)*, Peter Berling *(Pere Jean De La Croix)*.

The winner of the 1976 Oscar for Best Foreign Film, this first feature from Jean-Jacques Annaud (THE NAME OF THE ROSE) is set in a French colonial outpost in 1915. When Hubert Fresnoy (Jacques Spiesser), a conscientious young geologist, writes home to Paris to lament the "dangers" of Africa (chief among which is boredom), he begs that newspapers and books be sent. Some time later the papers arrive, bringing the news—six months late—that France is at war with Germany. This poses a bit of a problem at the outpost for a number of reasons—the colonists are friendly with a group of neighboring Germans; their commander, Sgt. Bosselet (Jean Carmet), has never been in battle; and they have no trained army. Rising to the challenge, Bosselet conscripts all the healthy male natives that live near the outpost and teaches them to speak French, operate bayonets, wear shoes, and sing "La Marseillaise." Ultimately, the natives are even honored with French names. A biting satire on war, colonialism, and French patriotism, BLACK AND WHITE IN COLOR juxtaposes scenes of gaiety and humor with the brutalities of racism and war. The result is something of a combination of Philippe de Broca's superb antiwar satire, KING OF HEARTS, and Jamie Uys' THE GODS MUST BE CRAZY. Deserving of special mention is the playful score by Pierre Bachelet. (In French; English subtitles.)

p, Arthur Cohn, Jacques Perrin, and Giorgio Silagni; d, Jean-Jacques Annaud; w, Jean-Jacques Annaud and Georges Conchon; ed, Francoise Bonnot; ph, Claude Agostini, Eastmancolor; m, Pierre Bachelet.

(PR:C MPAA:PG)

BLACK TENT, THE**

(1956, Brit.) 93m RANK c

Anthony Steel *(David Holland)*, Donald Sinden *(Charles Holland)*, Anna Maria Sandri *(Mabrouka)*, Andre Morell *(Sheik Salem)*, Ralph Truman *(Croft)*, Donald Pleasence *(Ali)*, Anthony Bushell *(Baring)*, Michael Craig *(Faris)*, Anton Diffring, Frederick Jaeger *(German Officers)*.

Set in the desert, this unspectacular British film follows Charles Holland (Donald Sinden) as he travels to Libya to tidy up the affairs of his soldier brother David (Anthony Steel), killed there during WW II. In flashback, David is wounded in a tank battle and taken in by Bedouin tribesmen. The British soldier and a sheik's daughter, Mabrouka (Anna Maria Sandri), then fall in love and are permitted to marry, and when he is left behind by his division, David decides to make his life among the nomads. Still full of hatred for the Germans, David persuades the sheik to help him wage guerrilla war behind their lines. Although the campaign is a success, David is killed saving the life of his father-in-law during an ambush off a German convoy. Later, Daoud (Terence Sharkey), Mobrouka and David's half-British, half-Libyan son, must decide whether remain in his homeland or start a new life in Britain. Shot in Vista-Vision (which is lost on videocassette) and Technicolor in the expansive deserts of North Africa, THE BLACK TENT is visually interesting, but its relatively unconventional story isn't particularly compelling.

p, William MacQuitty; d, Brian Desmond Hurst; w, Robin Maugham and Bryan Forbes; ed, Alfred Roome; ph, Desmond Dickinson, Technicolor, Vista-Vision; m, William Alwyn.

(PR:A MPAA:NR)

BLOOD ON THE SUN***½

(1945) 98m UA bw

James Cagney *(Nick Condon)*, Sylvia Sidney *(Iris Hilliard)*, Wallace Ford *(Ollie Miller)*, Rosemary De Camp *(Edith Miller)*, Robert Armstrong *(Col. Tojo)*, John Emery *(Premier Tanaka)*, Leonard Strong *(Hijikata)*, Frank Puglia *(Prince Tatsugi)*, Jack Halloran *(Capt. Oshima)*, Hugh Ho *(Kajioka)*, Philip Ahn *(Yamamoto)*, Joseph Kim *(Hayashi)*, Marvin Miller *(Yamada)*, Rhys Williams *(Joseph Cassell)*.

This tough flag-waver set in the late 1920s focuses on worldly newspaper editor Nick Condon (James Cagney) of the American-owned *Tokyo Chronicle*, who prints a controversial story by reporter Ollie Miller (Wallace Ford) and his wife, Edith (Rosemary De Camp). Japanese authorities demand a retraction but Condon refuses, learning later that the Millers have been murdered while trying to get out of the country with the "Tanaka Plan," a secret document that outlines Japan's plan to invade Manchuria. When Cagney tries to investigate, he is accused of murdering the couple during a drunken brawl, and jailed. Coming to his assistance is the beautiful Iris Hilliard (Sylvia Sidney), an Anglo-Chinese double agent trying to settle an old score with the Japanese. There's a lot of action here as Cagney demonstrates his proficiency in jujitsu and wins a slambang fight with a brutish Japanese secret service captain (Jack Halloran). The sets, atmospheric lighting, and quick-paced direction by Frank Lloyd are commendable and enhance Cagney's electrifying performance. Most fascinating, though, are the details relating to the "Tanaka Plan," a real document stolen in 1927 and exposed in the international press.

p, William Cagney; d, Frank Lloyd; w, Lester Cole, based on a story by Garrett Fort; ed, Truman Wood and Walter Hannemann; ph, Theodor Sparkuhl; m, Miklos Rozsa.

(PR:C MPAA:NR)

BLUE MAX, THE***

(1966) 155m FOX c

George Peppard *(Bruno Stachel)*, James Mason *(Count von Klugermann)*, Ursula Andress *(Countess Kaeti)*, Jeremy Kemp *(Willi von Klugermann)*, Carl Schell *(Richthofen)*, Karl Michael Vogler *(Heidemann)*, Loni Von Friedl *(Elfi Heidemann)*, Anton Diffring *(Holbach)*, Peter Woodthorpe *(Rupp)*, Harry Towb *(Kettering)*, Derek Newark *(Ziegel)*, Derren Nesbitt *(Fabian)*, Friedrich Ledebur *(Field Marshal Von Lenndorf)*, Roger Ostime *(Crown Prince)*, Hugo Schuster *(Hans)*.

Offering some of the best WW I aerial footage ever committed to film, THE BLUE MAX stars George Peppard as Bruno Stachel, an ambitious German infantryman who escapes the trenches to become a fighter pilot. Like every other German flyboy, Bruno dreams of winning the "Blue Max" (named for ace Max Immelman), the highest honor his country can bestow upon a pilot. Utterly ruthless, he soon becomes an ace, but is never accepted by the other pilots, most of whom are members of the old Prussian aristocracy. Determined to overtake ace Willi Von Klugermann (Jeremy Kemp), he becomes increasingly more daring, and when not adding "kills" to his tally, Bruno scores with Countess Kaeti (Ursula Andress), the wife of Willi's uncle and commander (James Mason). Strange and overlong, THE BLUE MAX impressively captures the reality of war in the trenches and in the air, but is less interesting when the focus shifts to its relatively steamy bedroom affairs. Where THE BLUE MAX differs from so many war films is in its portrayal of German war heroes not as the usual stereotypes but as ruthless opportunists more concerned with personal gain than patriotism.

p, Christian Ferry; d, John Guillermin; w, David Pursall, Jack Seddon, and Gerald Hanley, based on the novel by Jack D. Hunter; ed, Max Benedict; ph, Douglas Slocombe, CinemaScope, Deluxe Color; m, Jerry Goldsmith.

(PR:C MPAA:NR)

BOAT, THE****

(1982) 150m Bavaria Atelier/COL c (DAS BOOT)

Jurgen Prochnow *(The Captain)*, Herbert Gronemeyer *(Lt. Werner/Correspondent)*, Klaus Wennemann *(Chief Engineer)*, Hubertus Bengsch *(1st Lt./Number One)*, Martin Semmelrogge *(2nd Lieutenant)*, Bernd Tauber *(Chief Quartermaster)*, Erwin Leder *(Johann)*, Martin May *(Ullmann)*, Heinz Honig *(Hinrich)*, U.A. Ochsen *(Chief Bosun)*, Claude Oliver Rudolph *(Ario)*, Jan Fedder *(Pilgrim)*.

Based on the wartime experiences of photographer Lothar-Guenther Buchheim, this superbly filmed action movie chronicles a U-boat voyage in 1941, detailing above- and below-the-surface horrors as well as the mundane hours that characterize much of the time spent at sea. Although most of the footage concentrates on the intense, noble Captain (Jurgen Prochnow), the only fully developed character in the film is the boat as it undergoes numerous attacks. Decidedly anti-Nazi in tone, THE BOAT presents the crew as individual warriors upholding their own brand of honor and sneering at Hitler's Reich. The chief attraction of this film, however, is the incredible camerawork; racing through the sub, squeezing through tiny openings, director Wolfgang Petersen's camera brilliantly evokes the claustrophobia and clamor of undersea battle. A technical marvel, THE BOAT is a breathtaking and powerful portrait of war and death. Although the film was originally released on videocassette as the subtitled DAS BOOT, most copies now available are dubbed into English.

p, Gunter Rohrbach and Michael Bittins; d, Wolfgang Petersen; w, Wolfgang Petersen, based on the novel by Lothar-Guenther Buchheim; ed, Hannes Nikel; ph, Jost Vacano, Fujicolor; m, Klaus Doldinger.

(PR:C-O MPAA:R)

BOMBARDIER***

(1943) 97m RKO bw

Pat O'Brien *(Maj. Chick Davis)*, Randolph Scott *(Capt. Buck Oliver)*, Anne Shirley *(Burt Hughes)*, Eddie Albert *(Tom Hughes)*, Walter Reed *(Jim Carter)*, Robert Ryan *(Joe Connors)*, Barton MacLane *(Sgt. Dixon)*, Leonard Strong *(Japanese Officer)*, Richard Martin *(Chito Rafferty)*, Russell Wade *(Paul Harris)*, James Newill *(Capt. Rand)*, John Miljan *(Chaplain Craig)*.

Chick Davis (Pat O'Brien) and Buck Oliver (Randolph Scott) are officers at a bombardier training school, each arguing his own methods of hitting targets. Buck believes that dive-bombing with skilled pilots is the best means; Chick argues for precision bombing and the use of a new bombsight, the "Golden Goose." Chick and Buck agree to a bombing showdown for the top brass and, when Chick's methods prove most effective, a group of cadets are trained in precision bombing. Complicating matters is Burt Hughes (Anne Shirley), who has turned over her father's bombing school to the government as a training grounds. Naturally, neither Chick nor Buck can keep his eyes off of the comely Burt. Oddly, the action is kept mostly on the ground, with the movie proceeding like a training film for a bombardier school, building up to the attack on Pearl Harbor. Interesting mostly as an artifact of a nation at war, the blatantly propagandistic BOMBADIER was begun before Pearl Harbor and underwent several revisions over the next couple of years, finally appearing three years after production commenced. O'Brien's Chick Davis reminds us that "the three greatest things in a bombardier's existence are: Hit the target, hit the target, hit the target."

p, Robert Fellows; d, Richard Wallace; w, John Twist, based on a story by John Twist, Martin Rackin; ed, Robert Wise; ph, Nicholas Musuraca; m, Roy Webb.

(PR:A MPAA:NR)

BOYS FROM BRAZIL, THE***

(1978) 123m FOX c

Gregory Peck *(Josef Mengele)*, Laurence Olivier *(Ezra Lieberman)*, James Mason *(Eduard Seibert)*, Lilli Palmer *(Esther Lieberman)*, Uta Hagen *(Frieda Maloney)*, Rosemary Harris *(Mrs. Doring)*, John Dehner *(Henry Wheelock)*, John Rubinstein *(David Bennett)*, Anne Meara *(Mrs. Curry)*, Steve Guttenberg *(Barry Kohler)*, Denholm Elliott *(Sidney Beynon)*, Jeremy Black *(Jack Curry/Simon Harrington/ Erich Doring/Bobby Wheelock)*, David Hurst *(Strasser)*, Bruno Ganz *(Prof. Bruckner)*, Walter Gotell *(Mundt)*, Prunella Scales *(Mrs. Harrington)*.

This fast-moving picture features a battle of wits between "The Angel of Death," Nazi war criminal Josef Mengele (Gregory Peck), and fictional Nazi hunter Ezra Lieberman (Laurence Olivier, his character seemingly based on real-

BOYS IN COMPANY C, THE—

life Nazi hunter Simon Wiesenthal), placed against a somewhat far-fetched plot having to do with the cloning of Hitler. Mengele's plan is to harvest hundreds of young men (all of whom have been raised in environments nearly identical to that Hitler grew up in) in an attempt to re-create the Fuhrer's upbringing as well as his genetic structure. The picture barrels along for about 115 minutes, then falls apart in a wildly ludicrous finale. The cast is great—including Peck, Olivier, James Mason, Denholm Elliott, and even Steve Guttenberg, in one of his first roles—and the film is compelling, albeit pretty silly, in its elaborate "What if?" plot mechanics.

p, Martin Richards and Stanley O'Toole; d, Franklin J. Schaffner; w, Heywood Gould, based on the novel by Ira Levin; ed, Robert E. Swink; ph, Henri Decae, Deluxe Color; m, Jerry Goldsmith.

(PR:C-O MPAA:R)

BOYS IN COMPANY C, THE**½
(1978, US/Hong Kong) 125m COL c

Stan Shaw *(Tyrone Washington)*, Andrew Stevens *(Billy Ray Pike)*, James Canning *(Alvin Foster)*, Michael Lembeck *(Vinnie Fazio)*, Craig Wasson *(Dave Bisbee)*, Scott Hylands *(Capt. Collins)*, James Whitmore, Jr. *(Lt. Archer)*, Noble Willingham *(Sgt. Curry)*, Lee Ermey *(Sgt. Loyce)*, Santos Morales *(Sgt. Aquilla)*.

This was one of the first Hollywood films since John Wayne's embarrassing THE GREEN BERETS (1968) to show Americans in battle in Vietnam, and while it's definitely a lesser effort than THE DEER HUNTER (1978) or APOCALYPSE NOW (1979), it is not without interest. Structured like a traditional WW II movie, the film follows five young men as they go through rigorous basic training (led by drill sergeant Lee Ermey, who would perform similar duty 10 years later in Stanley Kubrick's FULL METAL JACKET) and into combat. Tyrone Washington (Stan Shaw) is a streetwise dope dealer who sees service in Vietnam as a good way to expand his business. Of course, his character conforms to the time-honored notion that the Army makes men of such delinquents and he becomes the leader of his squad. The rest of the soldiers are stereotypes as well: Billy Ray Pike (Andrew Stevens) is an athlete from the South who turns to drugs in Vietnam, Dave Bisbee (Craig Wasson) is an unrepentant hippie who tries to retain his pacifism while blasting away at the VC, Vinnie Fazio (Michael Lembeck) is a macho, perpetually horny GI who gets himself into trouble by pursuing a commander's daughter, and Alvin Foster (James Canning) is the aspiring writer eager to chronicle the horrors of war. This is a rather schizophrenic movie, attempting to extol traditional notions of honor and virtue in war while highlighting the confused nature of America's involvement in Vietnam. Most of the commanders—American and South Vietnamese—are shown to be incompetent, crazy, corrupt, or evil, while the soldiers steadily develop into a crack fighting unit loyal to the cause and each other. Writer Richard Natkin and director Sidney Furie seem to want the film to be all things to all people—to say that yes, there was incompetence and corruption by the American government and military, but those brave boys did their best and came out better for it. This oversimplification—ignoring as it does what such a corrupt system really did to the psyches of the soldiers who came home—cripples the film and prevents it from rising above the status of B-picture entertainment.

p, Andrew Morgan; d, Sidney J. Furie; w, Rick Natkin and Sidney J. Furie; ed, Michael Berman, Frank J. Urioste, Allan Pattillo, and James Benson; ph, Godfrey A. Godar, Panavision, Technicolor; m, Jaime Mendoza-Nava.

(PR:O MPAA:R)

BRADDOCK: MISSING IN ACTION III*
(1988) 103m Golan-Globus/Cannon c

Chuck Norris *(Col. James Braddock)*, Aki Aleong *(Gen. Quoc)*, Roland Harrah III *(Van Tan Cang)*, Miki Kim *(Lin Tan Cang)*, Yehuda Efroni *(Rev. Polanski)*, Ron Barker *(Mik)*, Jack Rader *(Littlejohn)*, Floyd Levine *(Gen. Duncan)*, Melinda Betron *(Thuy)*.

Chuck Norris returns to Southeast Asia again here, single-handedly avenging American defeat and rescuing a bunch of children in the bargain. During the fall of Saigon, Col. James Braddock (Norris) searches the chaotic streets for his Vietnamese wife, Lin (Miki Kim), then mistakenly believes she is dead. She, meanwhile, has her passport stolen en route to the US embassy and cannot leave. Braddock, however, is evacuated. Thirteen years later in the US, he learns from a missionary that Lin is alive and has a son. At first Braddock can't believe him, but when the CIA officially tells him to disregard this information, he knows it's all true and, sooner than you can say "one-man army," is back in Vietnam, where the priest leads him to his wife and son, Van (Roland Harrah III). Attempting to flee the country, they are caught by soldiers commanded by Gen. Quoc (Aki Aleong), who shoot Lin on the spot and take Van and Braddock to dungeons to be tortured. Braddock, however, overpowers his guards, frees his son, and heads for the mission. Quoc anticipates the move and takes all the mission children into captivity, along with Van and the priest. Eventually, Braddock stages a single-handed attack to free them, killing dozens of soldiers, and a long chase through the jungle ensues, until, at the Thai border—notwithstanding the fact that Vietnam and Thailand share no border—another battle takes place as American soldiers look on, itching to be involved. It's useless to try to relate BRADDOCK: MISSING IN ACTION III to any sort of reality concerning Vietnam (other than that of American revenge fantasies), so one can only appraise it in the context of war films in general, and as such it fails miserably. Norris is woodenly invincible, Harrah is annoying in the way that only child actors can be, and the only performance of note is that of Aleong, who seems to have stepped right out of the most xenophobic, anti-Japanese WW II films. He appears to appreciate the irony of his role, however, and hams it up to the hilt, puncturing the incredible sense of self-importance that otherwise pervades the film—which concludes with a title stating that 15,000 children of American servicemen are still in Vietnam, a real issue that the movie fails to address in offering only invasion as a solution.

p, Menahem Golan and Yoram Globus; d, Aaron Norris; w, James Bruner and Chuck Norris, based on characters created by Arthur Silver, Larry Levinson, Steve Bing; ed, Michael J. Duthie and Ken Bornstein; ph, Joao Fernandes, Rank Color; m, Jay Chattaway.

(PR:O MPAA:R)

BRADY'S ESCAPE**½
(1984, US/Hung.) 96m Robert Halmi-Brady's Run Associates/Satori c (GB: LONG RIDE, THE)

John Savage *(Brady)*, Kelly Reno *(Miki)*, Ildiko Bansagi *(Klara)*, Laszlo Mensaros *(Dr. Dussek)*, Ferenc Bacs *(Wortman)*, Dzsoko Rosic *(Csorba)*, Laszlo Horvath *(Moro)*, Matyas Usztics *(Sweede)*.

Brady (John Savage) is a US bomber pilot in WW II forced to bail out over Nazi-occupied Hungary. He and his wounded navigator, Sweede (Matyas Usztics), are found by a group of hard-living nomads who initially want to kill Brady for bombing their country, then decide to hide him from the Germans. Sweede later dies of his wounds; Brady falls in love with Klara (Ildiko Bansagi), who is teaching him Hungarian; and little orphan Miki (Kelly Reno) comes to idolize Brady. Eventually the flier makes a break for freedom, riding fast across the Hortobagy plain for Yugoslavia, where he can join up with Tito's partisans. The kind of war film no one makes anymore, BRADY'S ESCAPE is surprisingly good—an exciting story well told. Only the villains (cardboard Nazis indistinguishable from the thousands of other Nazi villains throughout film history) are weak enough to damage the picture, but the camerawork, quick pace, and competent performances by Savage and the supporting cast make the film well worth checking out for simple entertainment.

p, Robert Halmi, Jr.; d, Pal Gabor; w, William W. Lewis, based on a story by Pal Gabor; ed, Norman Gay and Eva Karmento; ph, Elemer Ragayli; m, Charles Gross.

(PR:C MPAA:NR)

BRASS TARGET**
(1978) 111m UA c

Sophia Loren *(Mara)*, John Cassavetes *(Maj. Joe DeLuca)*, George Kennedy *(Gen. George S. Patton, Jr.)*, Robert Vaughn *(Col. Donald Rogers)*, Patrick McGoohan *(Col. Mike McCauley)*, Bruce Davison *(Col. Robert Dawson)*, Edward Herrmann *(Col. Walter Gilchrist)*, Max Von Sydow *(Shelley/Webber)*, Ed Bishop *(Col. Elton F. Stewart)*, Lee Montague *(Lucky Luciano)*.

Another "What if?" movie, BRASS TARGET asks us to believe that Gen. George S. Patton (George Kennedy) did not die in a car accident, but at the hands of assassins, as part of a gold robbery scheme. Adapted from Frederick Nolan's *The Algonquin Project*, this ludicrously plotted film boasts a big-name cast and a competent technical crew, but still manages to be terribly boring. As if international intrigue and a far-fetched conspiracy theory aren't enough to sustain viewer interest (and they're not in this film), there is a love triangle between John Cassavetes, Sophia Loren, and Max Von Sydow. Even crime figure Lucky Luciano (Lee Montague) becomes part of the story.

p, Arthur Lewis; d, John Hough; w, Alvin Boretz, based on the novel *The Algonquin Project* by Frederick Nolan; ed, David Lane; ph, Tony Imi, Metrocolor; m, Laurence Rosenthal.

(PR:A-C MPAA:PG)

BREAKER MORANT****
(1980, Aus.) 107m South Australian Film/NW c

Edward Woodward *(Lt. Harry Morant)*, Jack Thompson *(Maj. J.F. Thomas)*, John Waters *(Capt. Alfred Taylor)*, Bryan Brown *(Lt. Peter Handcock)*, Rod Mullinar *(Maj. Charles Bolton)*, Lewis Fitz-Gerald *(Lt. George Witton)*, Charles Tingwell *(Lt. Col. Denny)*, Vincent Ball *(Lt. Ian Hamilton)*, Frank Wilson *(Dr. Johnson)*, Terence Donovan *(Capt. Simon Hunt)*, Russell Kiefel *(Christian Botha)*, Alan Cassell *(Lord Kitchener)*, Judy Dick *(Mrs. Shiels)*, Barbara West *(Mrs. Bristow)*.

Set during the Boer War, fought in South Africa between the descendants of Dutch colonists (the Boers) and the British during the years 1899-1902, BREAKER MORANT chronicles an obscure incident in 1901, when three Australian soldiers who came to South Africa to assist the British were court martialed for executing enemy prisoners. Fighting what was, in essence, a guerrilla war, Lt. Harry "Breaker" Morant (Edward Woodward) ordered the executions because he was acting under orders of the British command. As it turned out, one of the prisoners was a German citizen fighting alongside the Boers and, eager to maintain a good relationship with Germany, the British made scapegoats of the Australians. After a bitter trial, Morant and Lt. Peter Handcock (Bryan Brown) were sentenced to death, while Lt. George Witton (Lewis Fitz-Gerald) received life imprisonment. Powerfully directed by Australian Bruce Beresford and brilliantly acted, especially by Woodward, BREAKER MORANT is a fascinating and draining experience. Unfolding his film in flashback during testimony at the trial, Beresford does a masterful job in translating Kenneth Ross' play to the screen. With an eye for historical accuracy, Beresford briskly interweaves the events before and after the execution of the prisoners—which he does not attempt to justify—with the political machinations taking place during the trial. As staged by Beresford, the execution scene is tragic and deeply affecting.

p, Matt Carroll; d, Bruce Beresford; w, Bruce Beresford, Jonathan Hardy, and David Stevens, based on the play by Kenneth Ross; ed, William Anderson; ph, Don McAlpine, Panavision, Eastmancolor; m, Phil Cunneen.

(PR:A-C MPAA:PG)

BRIDGE AT REMAGEN, THE***½
(1969) 116m UA c

George Segal *(Lt. Phil Hartman)*, Robert Vaughn *(Maj. Paul Kreuger)*, Ben Gazzara *(Sgt. Angelo)*, Bradford Dillman *(Maj. Barnes)*, E.G. Marshall *(Brig. Gen. Shinner)*, Peter Van Eyck *(Gen. Von Brock)*, Matt Clark *(Col. Jellicoe)*, Fritz Ford *(Col. Dent)*, Tom Heaton *(Lt. Pattison)*, Bo Hopkins *(Cpl. Grebs)*, Robert Logan *(Pvt. Bissell)*, Paul Prokop *(Capt. Colt)*, Steve Sandor *(Pvt. Slavek)*, Frank Webb *(Pvt. Glover)*, Hans Christian Blech *(Capt. Carl Schmidt)*, Joachim Hansen *(Capt. Otto Baumann)*, Gunter Meisner *(SS Gen. Gerlach)*.

As US forces move toward Germany, the Nazi high command orders the Remagen bridge destroyed. Realizing that this will cut off thousands of troops from safety in their homeland, German officer Paul Kreuger (Robert Vaughn) delays action on the bridge's demolition. Meanwhile, the American offensive, spearheaded by a platoon led by Lt. Phil Hartman (George Segal), closes in on Kreuger and the bridge. Deftly capturing the confusion and intensity of a single wartime moment, this underrated WW II film contains a number of tense battle scenes (with stuntwork supervised by Hal Needham) and balances visceral excitement with an understanding of the harsh realities of war. Segal contributes an excellent portrayal of a simple man who has difficulty sending men into a no-win situation, Vaughn is good as the equally scrupulous German commander, and, in a smaller role, Ben Gazzara is a treasure as an especially sleazy GI. Veteran cinematographer Stanley Cortez's photography of the battle scenes is breathtaking, and he succeeds brilliantly in using the German countryside to create a particularly dark, haunting atmosphere. Though some of the film was shot in Czechoslovakia during the days before the Prague Spring, the production moved to Italy when Soviet tanks rolled in.

p, David L. Wolper; d, John Guillermin; w, Richard Yates and William Roberts, based on a story by Roger Hirson; ed, William Cartwright; ph, Stanley Cortez, Deluxe Color; m, Elmer Bernstein.

(PR:C MPAA:M)

BRIDGE ON THE RIVER KWAI, THE*****
(1957) 161m COL c

William Holden *(Shears)*, Alec Guinness *(Col. Nicholson)*, Jack Hawkins *(Maj. Warden)*, Sessue Hayakawa *(Col. Saito)*, James Donald *(Maj. Clipton)*, Geoffrey Horne *(Lt. Joyce)*, Andre Morell *(Col. Green)*, Peter Williams *(Capt. Reeves)*, John Boxer *(Maj. Hughes)*, Percy Herbert *(Grogan)*, Harold Goodwin *(Baker)*, Ann Sears *(Nurse)*, Henry Okawa *(Capt. Kanematsu)*, K. Katsumoto *(Lt. Miura)*, M.R.B. Chakrabandhu *(Yai)*.

Directed by David Lean, this intelligent and exciting WW II tale features a gripping performance from the great Alec Guinness as Col. Nicholson, a British officer who has surrendered with his regiment to the Japanese in Burma (photographed in Ceylon) in 1943. Martinet Nicholson insists that his men conduct themselves by the book and flatly refuses to cooperate with the equally dutiful Japanese commander, Col. Saito (Sessue Hayakawa). When Saito insists that the British prisoners construct an elaborate bridge over the gorge of the River Kwai, Nicholson refuses to permit his officers to work side-by-side with the enlisted men, citing the Geneva Convention. After realizing that he can no longer refuse Saito's orders, Nicholson becomes determined to build the best bridge possible, thereby restoring his men's morale *and* providing a shining example of British rectitude. Meanwhile, Shears (William Holden), an American, escapes from the prison camp and makes his way to Australia, where he impersonates an officer to obtain the privileges of rank. Maj. Warden (Jack Hawkins), the British officer in charge of guerrilla operations, then sends Shears back to the jungle prison as the guide for a small team of British soldiers assigned to destroy the bridge that Nicholson and his men are so frantically attempting to complete. Lean's direction is masterful as he juxtaposes action sequences with a psychological examination of war, pointing out the folly of it all. In adapting his own novel, Pierre Boule retained the terse, tough dialog and black humor of the original—both of which find their most obvious expression in Holden's cowardly wise-guy character. Based on fact, the story was inspired by the Bangkok-to-Rangoon "Death Railway" that was constructed by Allied prisoners in 1942. One of the finest war films ever, THE BRIDGE ON THE RIVER KWAI won seven Oscars, including Best Picture, Best Actor (Guinness), and Best Director (Lean), as well as the awards for writing, editing, cinematography, and music.

p, Sam Spiegel; d, David Lean; w, Pierre Boule, based on his novel, Michael Wilson and Carl Foreman uncredited scenarists; ed, Peter Taylor; ph, Jack Hildyard, CinemaScope, Technicolor; m, Malcolm Arnold.

(PR:C MPAA:NR)

BRIDGE TOO FAR, A***
(1977, Brit.) 176m UA c

Dirk Bogarde *(Lt. Gen. Browning)*, James Caan *(Sgt. Dohun)*, Michael Caine *(Lt. Col. Vandeleur)*, Sean Connery *(Maj. Gen. Urquhart)*, Edward Fox *(Lt. Gen. Horrocks)*, Elliott Gould *(Col. Stout)*, Gene Hackman *(Maj. Gen. Sosabowski)*, Anthony Hopkins *(Lt. Col. John Frost)*, Hardy Kruger *(Gen. Ludwig)*, Laurence Olivier *(Dr. Spaander)*, Ryan O'Neal *(Brig. Gen. Gavin)*, Robert Redford *(Maj. Cook)*, Maximilian Schell *(Lt. Gen. Bittrich)*, Liv Ullmann *(Kate ter Horst)*, Wolfgang Preiss *(Field Marshal Von Rundstedt)*, Siem Vroom *(Underground Leader)*, Denholm Elliott, Jeremy Kemp *(RAF Meteorological Officers)*, Ben Cross *(Trooper Binns)*.

A BRIDGE TOO FAR is the true story of a WW II military blunder that cost many lives and, in the end, meant little to the war effort. Field Marshal Montgomery and Gen. Eisenhower planned to drop 35,000 Allied troops into Holland to secure the six bridges leading to Germany, after which a British force was to speed through Belgium to the last bridge at Arnhem. From there, the two groups were to smash into the Ruhr area and crush the already damaged factories of the German war effort. Everything went wrong; bad weather, bad judgement, panic, and bad luck all took their toll, and the operation (code-named "Market Garden") was a total disaster. A BRIDGE TOO FAR is *not* a disaster, but it is a thoroughly disappointing picture, promising much (three hours of film and one of the most impressive casts ever assembled) and delivering little. Nonetheless, this overproduced, overstarred, and overlong endeavor should not be missed by any serious fan of war movies, just for its sheer scope. In addition, among all the huge exercises and troop advances, screenwriter William Goldman has added many little touches to the characters and dialog that add a level of intimacy and humanity to this otherwise gargantuan production.

p, Joseph E. Levine, Richard Levine, and Michael Stanley-Evans; d, Richard Attenborough; w, William Goldman, based on the book by Cornelius Ryan; ed, Anthony Gibbs; ph, Geoffrey Unsworth, Panavision, Technicolor; m, John Addison.

(PR:C MPAA:PG)

BRIDGES AT TOKO-RI, THE****

(1954) 102m PAR c

William Holden *(Lt. Harry Brubaker, USNR)*, Fredric March *(Rear Adm. George Tarrant)*, Grace Kelly *(Nancy Brubaker)*, Mickey Rooney *(Mike Forney)*, Robert Strauss *(Beer Barrel)*, Charles McGraw *(Comdr. Wayne Lee)*, Keiko Awaji *(Kimiko)*, Earl Holliman *(Nestor Gamidge)*, Richard Shannon *(Lt. Olds)*, Willis Bouchey *(Capt. Evans)*, Nadene Ashdown *(Kathy Brubaker)*, Cheryl Lynn Calloway *(Susie)*, Teru Shimada *(Japanese Father)*.

This psychological study of war's effects stars William Holden as Lt. Harry Brubaker, a family man called back to active duty who feels he already did enough for his country in WW II and resents the Korean War's intrusion on his life with wife Nancy (Grace Kelly) and their kids. Still a military man, Brubaker doggedly goes about his duty as a bomber pilot, spending long stretches on a flat top. The narrative drives toward the climactic bombing of the five bridges of Toko-Ri, which span a strategic pass in Korea's interior. Along the way Brubaker has some intimate scenes with Nancy, who waits for him in Tokyo, and some buddy scenes with pilots Mike Forney (Mickey Rooney) and Nestor Gamidge (Earl Holliman). The film is based on the novel by James Michener, made very visual thanks to some explosively exciting naval and aerial action.

p, William Perlberg; d, Mark Robson; w, Valentine Davies, based on the novel by James Michener; ed, Alma Macrorie; ph, Loyal Griggs; m, Lyn Murray.

(PR:A MPAA:NR)

BUCCANEER, THE**

(1958) 121m PAR c

Yul Brynner *(Jean Lafitte)*, Charlton Heston *(Andrew Jackson)*, Claire Bloom *(Bonnie Brown)*, Charles Boyer *(Dominique You)*, Inger Stevens *(Annette Claiborne)*, Henry Hull *(Ezra Peavey)*, E.G. Marshall *(Gov. Claiborne)*, Lorne Greene *(Mercier)*, Ted de Corsia *(Capt. Rumbo)*, Douglas Dumbrille *(Collector of Port)*, Robert F. Simon *(Capt. Brown)*, Sir Lancelot *(Scipio)*, Fran Jeffries *(Cariba)*.

THE BUCCANEER is a lackluster remake of the 1938 Cecil B. De Mille film of the same name, this time starring Yul Brynner (with a full head of hair) as the pirate Jean Lafitte, who comes to the aid of Gen. Andrew Jackson (Charlton Heston) when the British attack New Orleans during the War of 1812. In the process, Lafitte falls toupee over heels in love with Annette Claiborne (Inger Stevens), the daughter of William Claiborne, first governor of Louisiana. Brynner, dashing and powerful as the pirate Lafitte, plays his character with a fair amount of historical accuracy—not as a wild swashbuckler but as a debonair patriot who staunchly denied all charges of piracy. This film was Anthony Quinn's first and only directing job; in a prime example of nepotism, Quinn was handed the reins to the $6 million epic when his then father-in-law, De Mille, became ill. The specter of the great epic director is very much present amidst the incredibly gaudy costumes, sets, and trappings, as well as in the editing process, which De Mille supervised.

p, Henry Wilcoxon; d, Anthony Quinn; w, Jesse L. Lasky, Jr. and Bernice Mosk, based on a screenplay by Harold Lamb, Edwin Justus Mayer, C. Gardner Sullivan and Jeanie Macpherson's adaptation of *Lafitte the Pirate* by Lyle Saxon; ed, Archie Marshek; ph, Loyal Griggs, VistaVision, Technicolor; m, Elmer Bernstein.

(PR:A MPAA:NR)

BUCK PRIVATES**½

(1941) 82m UNIV bw (GB: ROOKIES)

Lee Bowman *(Randolph Parker III)*, Alan Curtis *(Bob Martin)*, Bud Abbott *(Slicker Smith)*, Lou Costello *(Herbie Brown)*, The Andrews Sisters *(Themselves)*, Jane Frazee *(Judy Gray)*, Nat Pendleton *(Sgt. Michael Collins)*, Samuel S. Hinds *(Maj. Gen. Emerson)*, Harry Strang *(Sgt. Callahan)*, Nella Walker *(Mrs. Parker II)*, Leonard Elliott *(Henry)*.

The comic duo of Abbott and Costello had their first big success with this enjoyable Army comedy, which became one of the top grossing films of 1941. Slicker (Abbott) and Herbie (Costello) accidentally wander into an Army recruitment office and, before they know it, are enlisted in the US Army. Naturally, they wreak havoc in their boot camp and create a variety of headaches for their superiors. In the meantime, recent draftees Randolph Parker III (Lee Bowman) and Alan Curtis (Bob Martin) vie for the affections of pretty camp hostess Judy Gray (Jane Frazee). Adding to the appeal of BUCK PRIVATES is the appearance of the Andrews Sisters, who deliver a number of tunes, including "Boogie Woogie Bugle Boy from Company B," "Bounce Me Brother with a Solid Four," and "I'll Be with You in Apple Blossom Time." Abbott and Costello reteamed in 1947 for a sequel, BUCK PRIVATES COME HOME.

BURMESE HARP—

p, Alex Gottlieb; d, Arthur Lubin; w, Arthur T. Horman and John Grant; ed, Philip Cahn; ph, Milton Krasner.

(PR:AA   MPAA:NR)

BURMESE HARP***½

(1967, Jap.) 120m Nikkatsu/Brandon bw (BIRUMANO TATEGOTO; AKA: HARP OF BURMA)

Shoji Yasui *(Private Mizushima)*, Rentaro Mikuni *(Capt. Inouye)*, Taniye Kitabayashi *(Old Woman)*, Tatsuya Mihashi *(Defense Commander)*, Yunosuke Ito

One of Kon Ichikawa's greatest films (ranking with his fine WW II drama FIRES ON THE PLAIN), this lyrical antiwar film is the picture that brought the brilliant Japanese director international renown. Private Mizushima (Shoji Yasui) is assigned to convince a Burmese unit of Japanese soldiers to surrender during the final days of WW II. When he is unsuccessful, the unit is attacked and wiped out with the exception of Mizushima, who is injured but nursed back to health by a Buddhist monk. Wearing a monk's robe, Mizushima then proceeds to bury the dead, honoring their dignity as he is transformed from a soldier into a holy man. This outstanding film was remade in color by Kon Ichikawa in 1985. (In Japanese; English subtitles.)

p, Masayuki Takagi; d, Kon Ichikawa; w, Natto Wada, based on the novel by Michio Takeyama; ed, Masanori Tsujii; ph, Minoru Yokoyama; m, Akira Ifukube.

(PR:C-O   MPAA:NR)

BURN****

(1970, Fr./It.) 112m Produzioni Europee Associates/Les Productions Artistes Associes/UA c (AKA: QUEIMADA!)

Marlon Brando *(Sir William Walker)*, Evaristo Marquez *(Jose Dolores)*, Renato Salvatori *(Teddy Sanchez)*, Norman Hill *(Shelton)*, Tom Lyons *(Gen. Prada)*, Wanani *(Guarina)*, Joseph Persuad *(Juanito)*, Gianpiero Albertini *(Henry)*, Carlo Pammucci *(Jack)*, Cecily Browne *(Lady Bella)*, Dana Ghia *(Francesca)*, Maurice Rodriguez *(Ramon)*, Alejandro Obregon *(English Major)*.

Aristocratic Englishman William Walker (Marlon Brando) is sent on a secret mission to the Caribbean island of Queimada, where the Portuguese have established a highly profitable sugar cane plantation worked by thousands of black slaves. Once on Queimada, Walker befriends Jose Dolores (Evaristo Marquez), a powerful black stevedore, instills him with revolutionary fervor, prompts him to rob a bank, and transforms him into an outlaw hero. After enlisting the aid of Teddy Sanchez (Renato Salvatori), a hotel clerk with political aspirations, Walker ensures that Dolores and his guerrilla followers overthrow the Portuguese. Under Walker's guidance, Sanchez assassinates the governor and takes control of the government with Dolores' blessing, permitting Walker to return to England secure in the knowledge that, with Sanchez in control, Queimada will accede to the wishes of Walker's British merchant bosses. Ten years later, a drunken, disillusioned Walker is hired to return to the island to halt a Dolores-led revolution that has erupted in response to corruption in the Sanchez government. Determined to work on a strong political film, Brando contacted Italian director Gillo Pontecorvo, whose brilliant BATTLE OF ALGIERS is one of the most powerful depictions of revolution ever filmed. The two men, eager to work with each other, chose as their subject matter the Spanish intervention on the island of Queimada in the 1520s, when a slave uprising threatened sugar production. When the Spanish government protested the idea, the director simply changed the country in question to Portugal, enabling him to make a film that showed the purity of revolution, the cruelty of colonialism, and the inhumanity of slavery. In 1988's WALKER, director Alex Cox took a revisionist look at a somewhat similar situation in 19th-century Nicaragua, basing his story on a real-life American adventurer whose name also happened to be William Walker.

p, Alberto Grimaldi; d, Gillo Pontecorvo; w, Franco Solinas, Giorgio Arlorio, based on a story by Gillo Pontecorvo, and Giorgio Arlorio; ed, Mario Morra; ph, Marcello Gatti, Deluxe Color; m, Ennio Morricone.

(PR:O   MPAA:NR)

C

CABARET*****

(1972) 124m AA c

Liza Minnelli *(Sally Bowles)*, Michael York *(Brian Roberts)*, Helmut Griem *(Maximilian von Heune)*, Joel Grey *(Master of Ceremonies)*, Fritz Wepper *(Fritz Wendel)*, Marisa Berenson *(Natalia Landauer)*, Elisabeth Neumann-Viertel *(Fraulein Schneider)*, Sigrid Von Richthofen *(Fraulein Maur)*, Helen Vita *(Fraulein Kost)*, Gerd Vespermann *(Bobby)*, Ralf Wolter *(Herr Ludwig)*, Georg Hartmann *(Willi)*, Ricky Renee *(Elke)*, Estrongo Nachama *(Cantor)*.

Along with Luchino Visconti's THE DAMNED, CABARET ranks as one of the most compelling visions of pre-Third Reich Germany and the general decadence that characterized Weimar Berlin. Unlike Visconti, however, CABARET director Bob Fosse has used this subject as the backdrop to a breathtakingly original musical in the Brecht-Weill vein. The setting is Berlin, 1931, as the Weimar Republic nears its end and the Nazi tide rises. Sally Bowles (Liza Minnelli) is an American cabaret performer at the Kit-Kat Club who falls in love with young Brit Brian Roberts (Michael York), a repressed homosexual who, until meeting Sally, has had a history of problematic relationships with women. They become lovers and eventually both have an affair with the bisexual Baron Maximilian von Heune (Helmut Griem). In addition to a great performance by Minnelli, CABARET contains the role for which Joel Grey will forever be remembered—the frightening, heavily greasepainted Master of Ceremonies at the cabaret. To Fosse's credit, the film has an underlying feeling of danger; no matter how happy the songs and dances, you can't help feeling there's a Brownshirt lurking in the wings, ready to bring his club down on any one of the characters. Among the more memorable musical numbers are Minnelli's rendition of the title song and the Minnelli-Grey duet "Money, Money, Money."

p, Cy Feuer; d, Bob Fosse; w, Jay Presson Allen, based on the play by Joe Masteroff, the play "I Am A Camera" by John Van Druten, and the writings of Christopher Isherwood; ed, David Bretherton; ph, Geoffrey Unsworth, Technicolor; m, Ralph Burns.

(PR:C MPAA:PG)

CAL***

(1984, Ireland) 102m Enigma/WB c

Helen Mirren *(Marcella)*, John Lynch *(Cal)*, Donal McCann *(Shamie)*, John Kavanagh *(Skeffington)*, Ray McAnally *(Cyril Dunlop)*, Stevan Rimkus *(Crilly)*, Kitty Gibson *(Mrs. Morton)*, Louis Rolston *(Dermot Ryan)*, Tom Hickey *(Preacher)*, Gerard Mannix Flynn *(Arty)*, Seamus Ford *(Old Man Morton)*, Edward Byrne *(Skeffington Senior)*.

This bleak but beautiful love story, set amidst Northern Ireland's Catholic-Protestant conflict, follows Cal (John Lynch), a confused, 19-year-old Catholic who is more interested in blues music than in joining the Irish Republican Army. He lives with his genteel, widowed father, Shamie (Donal McCann), in a quiet Protestant neighborhood, where he meets Marcella (Helen Mirren), the widow of a policeman murdered a year earlier in an IRA bombing. Cal and Marcella fall in love, but Cal keeps a terrible secret from her regarding her husband's murder. Meanwhile, Cal and his father are the victims of Protestant threats and must stay up nights to defend their home. CAL succeeds in painting a realistic picture of "the Troubles" because it avoids simplification, presenting the motives of love and war as full of complications and contradictions, just as they are in life. Of his debut film, director Pat O'Connor said: "What I would like is to allow people to see Northern Ireland for the tragedy it is, through the love affair in which these two people are trapped by what goes on around them." Mirren received some much-deserved recognition when she was named Best Actress at the 1984 Cannes Film Festival.

p, Stuart Craig and David Puttnam; d, Pat O'Connor; w, Bernard McLaverty, based on his novel; ed, Michael Bradsell; ph, Jerzy Zielinski, Rank Color; m, Mark Knopfler.

(PR:O MPAA:R)

CALL OUT THE MARINES**

(1942) 66m RKO bw

Victor McLaglen *(McGinnis)*, Edmund Lowe *(Harry Curtis)*, Binnie Barnes *(Vi)*, Paul Kelly *(Jim Blake)*, Robert Smith *(Billy Harrison)*, Dorothy Lovett *(Mitzi)*, Franklin Pangborn *(Wilbur)*, Corinna Mura *(Rita)*, George Cleveland *(Bartender)*, The King's Men Six Hits and a Miss

CALL OUT THE MARINES is a dull military comedy concerning a pair of Marine sergeants—McGinnis (Victor McLaglen) and Curtis (Edmund Lowe)—stationed in San Diego, who concentrate most of their time on chasing women and competing against each other—both physically and mentally—in order to prove who is the better man. Both fall in love with a cafe girl (Binnie Barnes) who plays up their rivalry to the hilt—until the boys discover that their lady love is an enemy spy. McLaglen and Lowe previously played a similar military duo named Flagg and Quirt in a series of WW I comedies. CALL OUT THE MARINES marked their short-lived reunion.

p, Howard Benedict; d, Frank Ryan and William Hamilton; w, Frank Ryan and William Hamilton; ed, Theron Warth; ph, Nicholas Musuraca and J. Roy Hunt.

(PR:A MPAA:NR)

CAPTIVE HEARTS**

(1988) 97m MGM/UA c

Noriyuki [Pat] Morita *(Fukushima)*, Chris Makepeace *(Robert)*, Mari Sato *(Miyoko)*, Michael Sarrazin *(Sgt. McManus)*, Seth Sakai *(Takayama)*, Denis Akiyama *(Masato)*.

This tale of cross-cultural love and loyalties is set in WW II Japan, where US airmen Sgt. McManus (Michael Sarrazin) and Robert (Chris Makepeace), a young lieutenant, are shot down and parachute into a remote northern village. The men are spared execution when respected elder Fukushima (Pat Morita) intercedes on their behalf, commuting their sentence from death to labor in the village. McManus cannot shake his intense hatred of the Japanese, however, and ultimately dies in an escape attempt; Robert becomes friends with Fukushima and so absorbed in village life that he falls in love with his mentor's widowed daughter-in-law, Miyoko (Mari Sato). Problems arise when a local old-timer (Seth Sakai) appears determined to make Miyoko his own bride, but this difficulty is surmounted by the predictable—at least by the logic of this film, which plays down its potential cultural conflicts—happy ending.

p, John A. Kuri; d, Paul Almond; w, Pat Morita and John A. Kuri, based on a story by Sargon Tamimi; ed, Yurij Luhovy; ph, Thomas Vamos, Metrocolor; m, Osamu Kitajima.

(PR:C MPAA:PG)

CARNIVAL IN FLANDERS***

(1936, Fr.) 95m Film Sonoris Tobis/American Tobis bw
(LA KERMESSE HEROIQUE)

Francoise Rosay *(Cornelia, the Burgomaster's Wife)*, Jean Murat *(Duke d'Olivares)*, Andre Alerme *(Burgomaster)*, Louis Jouvet *(Friar)*, Lyne Clevers *(Fishwife)*, Micheline Cheirel *(Siska)*, Maryse Wendling *(Baker's Wife)*, Ginette Gaubert *(Innkeeper's Wife)*, Marguerite Ducouret *(Brewer's Wife)*, Bernard Lancret *(Jan Brueghel)*.

This well-made French comedy, which was extremely popular upon its release but has dated poorly, details the temporary occupation of a small Flanders village by Spanish troops. Fearing the brutal treatment received by other towns at the hands of the Spanish, the male citizens decide to "play dead." The townspeople pretend to be in a state of mourning for their mayor, while the rest of the men remain hidden. Hoping that the Spanish interlopers, led by the Duke (Jean Murat) and including a friar (Louis Jouvet), will soon be on their way, the women of the town treat them to an outpouring of hospitality that even leads to the bedroom. A pleasant enough farce, the film is today best remembered for its superb acting, especially that of director Jacques Feyder's wife, Francoise Rosay. Set in 1616, the film does a fine job re-creating the visual style of Flemish painters, namely Jan Brueghel, whose character figures into the plot. Credit for the art direction goes to Alexandre Trauner, Lazare Meerson, and Georges Wakhevitch. (In French; English subtitles.)

d, Jacques Feyder; w, Charles Spaak, Jacques Feyder, and Bernard Zimmer, based on a story by Charles Spaak; ed, Jacques Brillouin; ph, Harry Stradling; m, Louis Beydts.

(PR:A MPAA:NR)

CASABLANCA*****

(1942) 102m WB bw

Humphrey Bogart *(Rick Blaine)*, Ingrid Bergman *(Ilsa Lund Laszlo)*, Paul Henreid *(Victor Laszlo)*, Claude Rains *(Capt. Louis Renault)*, Conrad Veidt *(Maj. Heinrich Strasser)*, Sydney Greenstreet *(Senor Ferrari)*, Peter Lorre *(Ugarte)*, S.Z. Sakall *(Carl)*, Madeleine LeBeau *(Yvonne)*, Dooley Wilson *(Sam)*, Joy Page *(Annina Brandel)*, John Qualen *(Berger)*, Leonid Kinskey *(Sascha)*, Helmut Dantine *(Jan Brandel)*, Marcel Dalio *(Emil)*, Corinna Mura *(Singer)*, Ludwig Stossel *(Mr. Leuchtag)*, Ilka Gruning *(Mrs. Leuchtag)*, Charles La Torre *(Senor Martinez)*.

More an icon of American popular culture than a true work of art, CASABLANCA is the epitome of slick Hollywood product where all the elements—script, casting, technique—operate flawlessly to create a satisfying and memorable entertainment. The plot, on the odd chance that some readers have not seen the film, concerns expatriate American Rick Blaine (Humphrey Bogart), a cynical nightclub owner in Casablanca who discovers that his ex-lover, Ilsa (Ingrid Bergman), who abandoned him years before, has arrived in Casablanca with her husband, Resistance leader Victor Lazlo (Paul Henreid). With the Germans on Victor's trail, Ilsa comes to Casablanca to beg Rick for the precious letters of transit that have come into his possession. The documents would allow Victor to escape Casablanca and continue the fight against fascism. Handed a golden opportunity either to get his revenge on Ilsa or force her back into his arms, Rick struggles with his conscience, while Vichy police captain Louis Renault (Claude Rains) keeps a wary eye on him. Since its November 1942 release, CASABLANCA has been *the* movie, one that perfectly blends a turbulent love story with harrowing intrigue, heroic and evil characters, believable melodrama, and the kind of genuine sentiment that makes the heart grow fonder with each viewing. Even at its initial release, the film appealed to nostalgia for the vanishing, romanticized world between the two great wars, a cafe society crushed by fascism, a civilized, urbane generation in white linen suits, spectator shoes, and wide-brimmed sunhats desperately clinging to values no longer cherished. Given its turbulent production history—the script was being rewritten almost on a daily basis—CASABLANCA was also a *lucky* film on all levels. It opened on Thanksgiving Day, 1942, at the Hollywood Theater in New York, three weeks after the Allies had landed at Casablanca, and further enjoyed widespread publicity generated by the Casablanca Conference two months later, when the eyes of the free world focused upon its leaders' meeting in the Moroccan city. The film received eight Academy Award nominations and won three: Best Picture, Best Screenplay, and Best Director. It propelled Bogart's star to new heights, and made Bergman one of the most popular actresses in the world. Thirty years later, Woody Allen paid tribute to the lasting effect CASABLANCA has had on its legion of fans in his play and movie PLAY IT AGAIN, SAM (1972).

p, Hal B. Wallis; d, Michael Curtiz; w, Julius J. Epstein, Phillip G. Epstein, and Howard Koch, based on the play "Everybody Goes to Rick's" by Murray Burnett, Joan Alison; ed, Owen Marks; ph, Arthur Edeson; m, Max Steiner.

(PR:A MPAA:NR)

CAST A GIANT SHADOW***½

(1966) 144m Mirisch-Llenroc-Batjac/UA c

Kirk Douglas *(Col. David "Mickey" Marcus)*, Senta Berger *(Magda Simon)*, Angie Dickinson *(Emma Marcus)*, James Donald *(Maj. Safir)*, Stathis Giallelis *(Ram Oren)*, Luther Adler *(Jacob Zion)*, Gary Merrill *(Pentagon Chief of Staff)*, Haym Topol *(Abou Ibn Kader)*, Frank Sinatra *(Vince)*, Yul Brynner *(Asher Gonen)*, John Wayne *(Gen. Mike Randolph)*, Ruth White *(Mrs. Chaison)*, Gordon Jackson *(James McAfee)*, Michael Hordern *(British Ambassador)*, Allan Cuthbertson *(British Immigration Officer)*.

CAST A GIANT SHADOW is the interesting film biography of the virtually unknown Col. Mickey Marcus, an American WW II hero and military advisor to Franklin Roosevelt who was recruited by the Israeli government to organize Israel's army into a military force that could withstand Arab attacks after the British pulled out of the region in 1949. Marcus (Kirk Douglas) is asked by Maj. Safir (James Donald) to get the dispirited and undisciplined Israeli army into condition, and accepts the assignment despite objections from his wife, Emma (Angie Dickinson). The objections are echoed by his superior, Pentagon resident Gen. Mike Randolph (John Wayne, whose Batjac Productions coproduced the film). Refusing to be deterred, Marcus resigns from the Army and leaves for Israel to work closely with Jacob Zion (Luther Adler, whose character is obviously modeled on Ben-Gurion) and Asher Gonen (Yul Brynner) to combine the potential military might of the *Haganah* (the underground) and *Palmach* (a youth commando squad). Despite the draw of Douglas, Wayne, and Frank Sinatra (in an absurd caricature of a mercenary pilot), CAST A GIANT SHADOW made little impact at the box office. Producer-director-writer Melville Shavelson's struggles to get the film made resulted in his writing a book about the experience, titled *How to Make a Jewish Movie*.

p, Melville Shavelson and Michael Wayne; d, Melville Shavelson; w, Melville Shavelson, based on the book by Ted Berkman; ed, Bert Bates and Gene Ruggiero; ph, Aldo Tonti, Panavision, Deluxe Color; m, Elmer Bernstein.

(PR:A-C MPAA:NR)

CATCH-22***½
(1970) 121m PAR/FILMWAYS c

Alan Arkin *(Capt. Yossarian)*, Martin Balsam *(Col. Cathcart)*, Richard Benjamin *(Maj. Danby)*, Art Garfunkel *(Capt. Nately)*, Jack Gilford *(Doc Daneeka)*, Bob Newhart *(Maj. Major)*, Anthony Perkins *(Chaplain Tappman)*, Paula Prentiss *(Nurse Duckett)*, Martin Sheen *(Lt. Dobbs)*, Jon Voight *(Milo Minderbinder)*, Orson Welles *(Gen. Dreedle)*, Seth Allen *(Hungry Joe)*, Robert Balaban *(Capt. Orr)*, Peter Bonerz *(Capt. McWatt)*, Charles Grodin *(Aardvark)*, Buck Henry *(Lt. Col.Korn)*, Marcel Dalio *(Old Man)*.

A flawed but nonetheless fascinating adaptation of Joseph Heller's caustic novel *Catch 22*, this big-budget, all-star effort was a notorious flop in its day, but has held up rather well over the years and deserves some serious reassessment. Set on a small island just off Italy, circa 1944, the film follows Capt. Yossarian (Alan Arkin), an American bombardier who attempts to have himself grounded by claiming insanity. Unfortunately, as Doc Daneeka (Jack Gilford) informs him, the paradoxical rule of "catch-22" prevents this, since anyone who voluntarily flies on air raids must be crazy, so asking to be grounded indicates that one is sane. As Yossarian becomes increasingly desperate, the inherent madness of the war intensifies. The ambitious Col. Cathcart (Martin Balsam) orders an absurd number of bombing missions in the hopes that he will be featured in *The Saturday Evening Post*; the perpetually puzzled laundry officer Maj. Major (Bob Newhart) is inexplicably promoted to Capt. Major and made squadron leader; Gen. Dreedle (Orson Welles) visits the base to hand out medals to men who dropped their bombs into the sea and then shouts, "Take him out and shoot him!" of anyone who annoys him; and Milo Minderbinder (Jon Voight) uses the war to create a major black-market corporation that deals in everything from morphine to prostitution and eventually cuts a deal with Cathcart to bomb their own base and sell surplus supplies to the Germans. Bleak, nihilistic, and darkly hilarious throughout, CATCH-22 can be a frustrating experience for those unprepared for Mike Nichols' episodic, detached, and sometimes surreal treatment of the novel. Like a nightmare, the film shifts from one bizarre episode to another, with Alan Arkin's dazed Yossarian reacting to the madness that surrounds him. Although Nichols and screenwriter Buck Henry occasionally falter, CATCH-22 remains one of the most effective and scathing condemnations of war ever filmed.

p, Martin Ransohoff and John Calley; d, Mike Nichols; w, Buck Henry, based on the novel by Joseph Heller; ed, Sam O'Steen; ph, David Watkin, Panavision, Technicolor;

(PR:O MPAA:R)

CHARGE OF THE LIGHT BRIGADE, THE*****
(1936) 115m WB bw

Errol Flynn *(Maj. Geoffrey Vickers)*, Olivia de Havilland *(Elsa Campbell)*, Patric Knowles *(Capt. Perry Vickers)*, Donald Crisp *(Col. Campbell)*, Henry Stephenson *(Sir Charles Macefield)*, Nigel Bruce *(Sir Benjamin Warrenton)*, David Niven *(Capt. James Randall)*, G.P. Huntley, Jr. *(Maj. Jowett)*, Spring Byington *(Lady Octavia Warrenton)*, C. Henry Gordon *(Surat Khan)*, E.E. Clive *(Sir Humphrey Harcourt)*, Lumsden Hare *(Col. Woodward)*, Robert Barrat *(Count Igor Zvolonoff)*, Walter Holbrook *(Cornet Barclay)*, Charles Sedgwick *(Cornet Pearson)*, J. Carrol Naish *(Subahdar Major Puran Singh)*.

THE CHARGE OF THE LIGHT BRIGADE is one of the finest epics ever put on film, with some of the most dynamic and thrilling action sequences in the history of the medium. Great pains were taken to re-create the 1850s milieu, from exact replicas of uniforms down to the last brass button and even postage stamps of the era, although Warner Bros. typically discarded the real facts surrounding the magnificent military blunder, retaining instead the era's pomp and the stirring lines of Tennyson's famous poem. The story begins in northwest India, 1850, in the years leading up to the Crimean War, as Maj. Geoffrey Vickers (Errol Flynn), a dashing British officer of the 27th Lancers, crosses paths with a scheming Indian potentate, Surat Khan (C. Henry Gordon), who is severing ties with the British and allying himself with the Russians in preparation for a revolt. After Surat Khan leads a massacre at a British fort at Chukoti, Vickers finally gets revenge during the foolish but heroic charge on the Russian forces at the Balaclava heights in the Crimea where Surat Khan has fled. In throwing his lance at Khan, Vickers loses his own life. Meanwhile, Elsa Campbell (Olivia de Havilland), the woman Vickers loves, has secretly fallen in love with his brother, Capt. Perry Vickers (Patric Knowles). As a history lesson, THE CHARGE OF THE LIGHT BRIGADE couldn't be more wrong if it tried, but as entertainment it rarely gets better than this. The facts were set straight in 1968 with Tony Richardson's remake, which put forward the truth about the military idiocy that led to the slaughter, but movie audiences didn't seem to care.

p, Samuel Bischoff; d, Michael Curtiz; w, Michel Jacoby and Rowland Leigh, based on a story by Jacoby inspired by the poem by Alfred, Lord Tennyson; ed, George Amy; ph, Sol Polito; m, Max Steiner.

(PR:A MPAA:NR)

CHIMES AT MIDNIGHT****

(1967, Sp./Switz.) 115m Internacional Films Espanola-Alpine/Peppercorn-Wormser-U-M bw (CAMPANADAS A MEDIANOCHE; AKA: FALSTAFF)

Orson Welles *(Sir John "Jack" Falstaff)*, Jeanne Moreau *(Doll Tearsheet)*, Margaret Rutherford *(Hostess Quickly)*, John Gielgud *(King Henry IV)*, Keith Baxter *(Prince Hal, later King Henry V)*, Marina Vlady *(Kate Percy)*, Norman Rodway *(Henry Percy, "Hotspur")*, Alan Webb *(Justice Shallow)*, Walter Chiari *(Mr Silence)*, Michael Aldridge *(Pistol)*, Tony Beckley *(Poins)*, Fernando Rey *(Worcester)*, Beatrice Welles *(Falstaff's Page)*, Andrew Faulds *(Westmoreland)*, Jose Nieto *(Northumberland)*, Jeremy Rowe *(Prince John)*, Paddy Bedford *(Bardolph)*, Ralph Richardson *(Narrator)*.

Although CITIZEN KANE and THE MAGNIFICENT AMBERSONS still have their staunch defenders, Orson Welles scholars seem to agree that the greatest of Welles' screen achievements is CHIMES AT MIDNIGHT, a brilliant film that takes a tragic look at one of Shakespeare's most famous comic characters. Combining portions of Shakespeare's "Richard II," "Henry IV" (parts I and II), "Henry V," and "The Merry Wives of Windsor" along with (in the narration) Raphael Holinshed's *The Chronicles of England*, CHIMES AT MIDNIGHT tells the story of Sir John "Jack" Falstaff (Welles), the massive companion to Prince Hal (Keith Baxter), heir to the besieged British throne. Rather than come to the defense of his royal father, Hal passes his time drinking and carousing with Falstaff. Finally, however, he does go into battle, slaying the honorable, doomed challenger to the crown, Hotspur (Norman Rodway). After the battle, Falstaff claims to have killed Hotspur, when in fact he spent most of its duration quivering with fear. The old king (John Gielgud) dies and Hal becomes King Henry V. Falstaff attends the coronation, sure that a high title is forthcoming; instead, he is banished. While not as technically dazzling as CITIZEN KANE, CHIMES AT MIDNIGHT is the work of a mature artist, vastly more intelligent in middle age than as a 25-year-old director of bravura. In addition to the perfect performances (from Welles down to the last coronation guard), the film contains one of the best battle scenes in cinema—a grim, brutal affair fought on a mud-soaked field as the waddling knight Falstaff makes every attempt to escape death.

p, Emiliano Piedra; d, Orson Welles; w, Orson Welles, based on the plays "Henry IV Part I" "Henry IV, Part II," "Henry V," "Richard II," "The Merry Wives of Windsor" all by William Shakespeare, and the book *The Chronicles of England* by Raphael Holinshed; ed, Fritz Muller; ph, Edmond Richard; m, Angelo Francesco Lavagnino.

(PR:C MPAA:NR)

CLAY PIGEON, THE**½

(1949) 63m RKO bw

Bill Williams *(Jim Fletcher)*, Barbara Hale *(Martha Gregory)*, Richard Quine *(Ted Niles)*, Richard Loo *(Tokoyama)*, Frank Fenton *(Lt. Comdr. Prentice)*, Frank Wilcox *(Hospital Doctor)*, Marya Marco *(Helen Minoto)*, Robert Bray *(Blake)*, Martha Hyer *(Receptionist)*, Harold Landon *(Blind Veteran)*, James Craven *(John Wheeler)*, Grandon Rhodes *(Clark)*.

A short, taut, and uninventive low-budget picture, THE CLAY PIGEON concerns a sailor, Jim Fletcher (Bill Williams), who regains consciousness in a Navy hospital after having been comatose for months. Upon coming to, he is informed that he is about to be court-martialed on charges of treason and for having caused the death of a friend in a Japanese prison camp. Fletcher turns to his friend, Ted (Richard Quine), for help, but Ted is conspiring with the Japanese guard (Richard Loo) who actually killed Fletcher's pal. This was the first RKO film produced with Howard Hughes at the studio helm.

p, Herman Schlom; d, Richard Fleischer; w, Carl Foreman; ed, Samuel E. Beetley; ph, Robert de Grasse.

(PR:A MPAA:NR)

CLOAK AND DAGGER***

(1946) 106m United States Pictures/WB bw

Gary Cooper *(Prof. Alvah Jesper)*, Lilli Palmer *(Gina)*, Robert Alda *(Pinkie)*, Vladimir Sokoloff *(Dr. Polda)*, J. Edward Bromberg *(Trenk)*, Marjorie Hoshelle *(Ann Dawson)*, Ludwig Stossel *(German)*, Helene Thimig *(Katerin Loder)*, Dan Seymour *(Marsoli)*, Marc Lawrence *(Luigi)*, James Flavin *(Col. Walsh)*, Patrick O'Moore *(Englishman)*, Charles Marsh *(Erich)*, Don Turner *(Lingg)*, Robert Coote *(Cronin)*.

This improbable but exciting story concerns physics professor Alvah Jesper (Gary Cooper), recruited by the OSS because of his far-reaching knowledge of atomic weaponry and sent to Italy at the end of WW II to locate Dr. Polda (Vladimir Sokoloff), an atomic scientist being held by the Germans. En route, he meets in Switzerland with Austrian scientist Katerin Loder (Helene Thimig), who is killed, whereupon Jesper moves on to Italy, followed by Nazi agent Ann Dawson (Marjorie Hoshelle). Once in Italy, Jesper and his associates—local partisan Gina (Lilli Palmer, in her first US film role) and Allied agent Pinkie (Robert Alda)—combine their talents to find the scientist and assure his safe passage to the US. The action is brisk under Fritz Lang's expert direction, but the film is nowhere near what he envisioned. In fact, Warner Bros. cut most of the fourth reel, an appeal against the use of nuclear weapons. At one point, Cooper (by this time an American icon) states: "This is the first time I am sorry that I am a scientist. Society is not ready for atomic energy. I'm scared stiff." Lang, however, was able to present realistically the dirty side of espionage and total war, although much of the picture is taken up with standard Hollywood romancing. Producer Milton Sperling had been an OSS operative during wartime, and the story was based on the actual experiences of technical advisor Michael Burke, who, as an OSS agent, was assigned to smuggle Adm. Eugenio Minisi out of Italy. By successfully completing the mission, Burke prevented the Nazis from getting hold of an electronic torpedo mechanism Minisi developed.

p, Milton Sperling; d, Fritz Lang; w, Albert Maltz and Ring Lardner, Jr., based on a story by Boris Ingster and John Larkin, suggested by the book by Corey Ford and Alastair MacBain; ed, Christian Nyby; ph, Sol Polito; m, Max Steiner.

(PR:A MPAA:NR)

COCKLESHELL HEROES, THE***
(1955, Brit.) 97m Warwick/COL c

Jose Ferrer *(Maj. Stringer)*, Trevor Howard *(Capt. Thompson)*, Victor Maddern *(Sgt. Craig)*, Anthony Newley *(Clarke)*, David Lodge *(Ruddock)*, Peter Arne *(Stevens)*, Percy Herbert *(Loman)*, Graham Stewart *(Booth)*, John Fabian *(Cooney)*, John Van Eyssen *(Bradley)*, Robert Desmond *(Todd)*, William Fitzgerald *(Gestapo Commandant)*, Christopher Lee *(Submarine Commander)*.

Maj. Stringer (Jose Ferrer, who also directed) leads a small group of Royal Marines on a secret raid in which they travel downriver by kayak (two men per) to the docks of Bordeaux to plant mines on Nazi vessels. During the assault, all but two of the men are killed. THE COCKLESHELL HEROES is an intense, exciting war drama with a core of tragedy. Ferrer and Trevor Howard, who plays Stringer's second-in-command, are superb as feuding mission leaders whose mutual respect forms a deep bond. The film was coproduced by Albert Broccoli, the man behind the James Bond series.

p, Irving Allen and Albert R. Broccoli; d, Jose Ferrer; w, Bryan Forbes and Richard Maibaum; ed, Alan Osbiston; ph, John Wilcox, CinemaScope, Technicolor and Ted Moore; m, John Addison.

(PR:A MPAA:NR)

CODE NAME: EMERALD**½
(1985) 93m NBC/MGM-UA c

Ed Harris *(Gus Lang)*, Max Von Sydow *(Jurgen Brausch)*, Horst Buchholz *(Walter Hoffman)*, Helmut Berger *(Ernst Ritter)*, Cyrielle Claire *(Claire Jouvet)*, Eric Stoltz *(Andy Wheeler)*, Patrick Stewart *(Col. Peters)*, Graham Crowden *(Sir Geoffrey Macklin)*.

This odd WW II espionage item harks back to the 1960s and films like THE COUNTERFEIT TRAITOR and ORDERS TO KILL. Capt. Gus Lang (Ed Harris) is an American agent sent from Britain to occupied Paris, charged with making sure that Andy Wheeler (Eric Stoltz), a captured American officer with secret information about the upcoming Normandy invasion, doesn't talk. Horst Buchholz, Helmut Berger, and Max von Sydow play the Germans Lang must fool as he impersonates a German officer, trying to get close enough to Wheeler to ensure his silence by whatever means necessary. This routine WW II spy drama has almost no action, which makes one wonder why anyone ever wanted to bring it to the screen. It was the first and only directorial effort from Jonathan Sanger, the multi-Oscar winning producing force behind THE ELEPHANT MAN and FRANCES.

p, Martin Starger; d, Jonathan Sanger; w, Ronald Bass, based on the novel *The Emerald Illusion* by Ronald Bass; ed, Stewart Linder; ph, Freddie Francis, Metrocolor; m, John Addison.

(PR:C MPAA:PG)

COLDITZ STORY, THE***
(1955, Brit.) 97m BL bw

John Mills *(Maj. Pat Reid)*, Eric Portman *(Col. Richmond)*, Christopher Rhodes *(Mac)*, Lionel Jeffries *(Harry)*, Bryan Forbes *(Jimmy)*, Ian Carmichael *(Robin)*, Richard Wattis *(Richard)*, David Yates *(Dick)*, Frederick Valk *(Commandant)*, Denis Shaw *(Priem)*, Anton Diffring *(Fischer)*, Ludwig Lawinski *(Franz Josef)*, Carl Duering *(German Officer)*, Keith Pyott *(French Colonel)*, Eugene Deckers *(La Tour)*, Rudolf Offenbach *(Dutch Colonel)*, Theodore Bikel *(Vandy)*, Arthur Butcher *(Polish Colonel)*.

During WW II at Colditz castle, the Germans' escape-proof war prison, Maj. Pat Reid (John Mills) and other "problem" POWs from the British, Dutch, French, and Polish armies try to figure out various ways of escape. After their tunnel is discovered with the help of a Polish spy planted by the Germans and several men are machine-gunned to death trying to bridge the sea of barbed wire that surrounds the fortress, Reid and three others manage to engineer a successful escape in this suspenseful, often humorous war drama that portrays the compelling drive to break out of captivity. The imposing, frightening qualities of Colditz are well presented, lending credence to the "impossible task" premises of the script. The story was reportedly based on the personal experiences of its author, Maj. P.R. Reid.

p, Ivan Foxwell; d, Guy Hamilton; w, Guy Hamilton and Ivan Foxwell, based on the book by P.R. Reid; ed, Peter Mayhew; ph, Gordon Dines; m, Francis Chagrin.

(PR:A MPAA:NR)

COLONEL REDL***
(1985, Hung./Aust./Ger.) 144m Mafilm-Objectiv-Manfred Durniok-ORF-ZDF/Orion Classics c (REDL EZREDES; OBERST REDL)

Klaus Maria Brandauer *(Alfred Redl)*, Armin Mueller-Stahl *(Crown Prince Archduke Franz-Josef)*, Gudrun Landgrebe *(Katalin Kubinyi)*, Jan Niklas *(Kristof Kubinyi)*, Hans Christian Blech *(Col. von Roden)*, Laszlo Mensaros *(Col. Ruzitska)*, Andras Balint *(Dr. Gustav Sonnenschein)*, Karoly Eperjes *(Lt. Jaromil Schorm)*, Dorottya Udvaros *(Clarissa, Redl's Wife)*, Laszlo Galffi *(Alfredo Velocchio)*, Robert Ratonyi *(Baron Ullmann)*, Gabor Svidrony *(Alfred Redl as a Child)*.

Istvan Szabo's follow-up to MEPHISTO again stars Klaus Maria Brandauer, here as Col. Alfred Redl, who became head of the Austro-Hungarian military intelligence bureau in the early 1900s, despite his impoverished origins. His Gatsby-like strivings for upper-class acceptance prove, however, to be his downfall when a czarist agent threatens to expose Redl's homosexual double life. Rather than sac-

COMING HOME—

rifice the status he has achieved, Redl reveals top secret information and eventually takes his own life. While not as richly textured or urgent as MEPHISTO, COLONEL REDL is an expertly made historical drama that, while fictionalizing some events, truthfully examines the desire for power and the catalysts of war. The film boasts yet another tour de force performance by Brandauer, as well as an equally strong portrayal by Armin Mueller-Stahl as the ruthless, power-hungry Archduke. The film won the Jury Prize at the Cannes Film Festival. (In German; English subtitles.)

p, Manfred Durniok and Joszef Marx; d, Istvan Szabo; w, Istvan Szabo and Peter Dobai, based on the play "A Patriot for Me" by John Osborne; ed, Zsuzsa Csakany; ph, Lajos Koltai, Eastmancolor; m, Robert Schumann, Johann Strauss, Frederic Chopin, and Franz Liszt.

(PR:O MPAA:R)

COMING HOME***

(1978) 126m UA c

Jane Fonda (Sally Hyde), Jon Voight (Luke Martin), Bruce Dern (Capt. Bob Hyde), Robert Ginty (Sgt. Dink Mobley), Penelope Milford (Viola Munson), Robert Carradine (Bill Munson), Charles Cyphers (Pee Wee), Mary Jackson (Fleta Wilson), Kenneth Augustine (Ken), Tresa Hughes (Nurse De Groot), Willie Tyler (Virgil), David Glennon (Tim), Olivia Cole (Corrine), Ron Amador (Beany), Cornelius H. Austin, Jr. (Corny), Richard Blanchard (Rick).

Nominated for eight Academy Awards and winning Best Actress (Jane Fonda), Best Actor (Jon Voight), and Best Original Screenplay (THE DEER HUNTER won Best Picture and Best Director), COMING HOME was one of the first films to deal seriously with the plight of returning Vietnam veterans. Unfortunately, it is marred by some cloying melodramatics and overly preachy politics—both of which may cause unintentional laughter. It opens circa 1968, when Bob Hyde (Bruce Dern) is a gung-ho Marine captain finally going off to Nam on active duty. His dutiful wife, Sally (Fonda), wants to do her share and begins volunteer work at a local veterans' hospital, where she meets Luke (Jon Voight), a bitter paraplegic. In the next month, Sally and Luke learn that they went to the same high school, had many of the same friends, and have much more in common than most people at the hospital. Luke's anger begins to subside and he starts speaking out publicly against the war. Sally's friendship with him begins to radicalize her, too, and soon she is becoming more politicized, feminist, and independent of her husband. Eventually, Luke and Sally become lovers (in a notorious lovemaking scene). Their relationship is jeopardized, however, when Bob is wounded in the leg and comes home from the war a changed man—taciturn but potentially violent. While COMING HOME has its heart in the right place, the script by Waldo Salt and Robert C. Jones is too pat, and Hal Ashby's direction is simply too self-satisfied to be wholly effective. The climax—in which Dern's character conveniently walks off into the ocean to a cliched presumed suicide—is simply ridiculous. What does work in COMING HOME are the small moments and the performances, which are undeniably appealing and deservedly praised.

p, Jerome Hellman; d, Hal Ashby; w, Waldo Salt and Robert C. Jones, based on a story by Nancy Dowd; ed, Don Zimmerman; ph, Haskell Wexler, Deluxe Color.

(PR:C-O MPAA:R)

COMMANDOS STRIKE AT DAWN, THE***½

(1942) 100m COL bw

Paul Muni (Erik Toresen), Anna Lee (Judith Bowen), Lillian Gish (Mrs. Bergesen), Sir Cedric Hardwicke (Adm. Bowen), Robert Coote (Robert Bowen), Ray Collins (Bergesen), Rosemary De Camp (Hilma Arnesen), Richard Derr (Gunner Korstad), Alexander Knox (German Captain), Rod Cameron (Pastor), Louis Jean Heydt (Lars Amesen), Elizabeth Fraser (Anna Korstad), Erville Alderson (Johan Garmo), Lloyd Bridges (Young Soldier).

Paul Muni is dynamic and compelling as Erik Toresen, a simple fisherman living with his daughter (Ann Carter) on the coast of Norway. A widower, he falls in love with Judith Bowen (Anna Lee), whose father (Sir Cedric Hardwicke) is a British admiral. Shortly after Judith and her father return to England, Hitler's forces invade Norway, occupying Toresen's small village. When the situation worsens, he and others escape in a small boat and sail to England. There, the fisherman agrees to lead British troops in a commando raid against the village to knock out a German airfield, on the condition that the British help rescue his daughter, who, along with others, is being held hostage. A sensitive portrait of life under occupation, THE COMMANDOS STRIKE AT DAWN forgoes action in favor of characterization. The final battle for the airfield and village, however, is spectacular, staged by veteran action director John Farrow, who did such a splendid job with WAKE ISLAND. The rugged Norwegian coast was duplicated for this film by the coast of Vancouver Island in British Columbia, Canada, where the film was photographed.

p, Lester Cowan; d, John Farrow; w, Irwin Shaw, based on a story by C. S. Forester; ed, Anne Bauchens; ph, William C. Mellor; m, Louise Gruenberg.

(PR:A MPAA:NR)

CONQUEROR, THE*

(1956) 111m Hughes/RKO c

John Wayne (Temujin), Susan Hayward (Bortai), Pedro Armendariz (Jamuga), Agnes Moorehead (Hunlun), Thomas Gomez (Wang Kahn), John Hoyt (Shaman), William Conrad (Kasar), Ted de Corsia (Kumlek), Leslie Bradley (Targutai), Lee Van Cleef (Chepei), Peter Mamakos (Bogurchi), Leo Gordon (Tartar Captain), Richard Loo (Captain of Wang's Guard), Billy Curtis (Midget Tumbler).

A notoriously awful John Wayne effort, THE CONQUEROR has been written about and discussed continually since its disastrous premiere for a variety of reasons, including its remarkably atrocious dialog, ridiculous casting, producer Howard Hughes' bizarre obsession with the film in his later years, and, most importantly, the fact that the film was shot in Utah, only 136 miles from a huge atomic test site. Of the 220 people who worked on the film, more than 90 later contracted cancer, and half of those died from the disease. The deaths included director Dick Powell and stars John Wayne, Susan Hayward, Pedro Armendariz, and Agnes Moorehead. This terrible sacrifice was made for a truly bad film, which has little or nothing to do with the historical Genghis Khan. Temujin (Wayne), later to be known as Genghis Khan, and Jamuga (Armendariz) are Mongols who love nothing better than raping and pillaging. They attack a caravan and capture Bortai (Hayward), daughter of Kumlek (Ted de Corsia), the Tartar ruler. Although she is resistant at first, the fiery redhead eventually comes to love the brutal Mongol and becomes his loyal wife, despite the fact that he's waging war against her people. RKO chief Hughes sank $6 million into this Cinemascope production, and while it didn't flop outright, it was a disappointment at the box office. Oddly, Hughes was to become obsessed with the film, and a year after selling RKO he bought back the rights to THE CONQUEROR and the almost-as-bad JET PILOT (1957) for $12 million, an unheard-of sum. Hughes pulled all prints of both from the market and had them screened privately, night after night, for his own edification. But since THE CONQUEROR is now widely available on videocassette, you don't have to be an eccentric multimillionaire to gawk at this true oddity of Hollywood history in the privacy of your very own home.

p, Dick Powell; d, Dick Powell; w, Oscar Millard; ed, Robert Ford and Kenneth Marstella; ph, Joseph LaShelle, Leo Tover, Harry J. Wild, and William Snyder, CinemaScope, Technicolor; m, Victor Young.

(PR:C-A MPAA:NR)

CORNERED***½

(1945) 102m RKO bw

Dick Powell *(Laurence Gerard)*, Walter Slezak *(Incza)*, Micheline Cheirel *(Mme. Jarnac)*, Nina Vale *(Senora Camargo)*, Morris Carnovsky *(Santana)*, Edgar Barrier *(DuBois)*, Steven Geray *(Senor Camargo)*, Jack La Rue *(Diego)*, Luther Adler *(Marcel Jarnac)*, Gregory Gay *(Perchon)*, Jean Del Val *(1st Prefect)*, Louis Mercier *(Rougon)*, Martin Cichy *(Jopo)*, Georges Renavent *(2nd Prefect)*, Nelson Leigh *(Dominion Official)*, Leslie Dennison *(Finance Officer)*.

Canadian flier Laurence Gerard (Dick Powell) gets out of a POW camp with his mind set on avenging the death of his French war bride, caused by Vichy officer Marcel Jarnac (Luther Adler). Although by all reports Jarnac is dead, Gerard refuses to believe the war criminal is under the sod. He pursues leads through Switzerland and then to Buenos Aires, where he encounters an underground group of Nazi hunters, Santana (Morris Carnovsky), DuBois (Edgar Barrier), and Diego (Jack La Rue). His quest is further complicated when he finds himself drawn to the attractive Mme. Jarnac (Micheline Cheirel), who married the vicious Jarnac, without ever having met him, in order to emigrate safely. Tightly directed by the talented Edward Dmytryk, CORNERED is a superb thriller, with Powell turning in another tough-talking, hardboiled performance as the man seeking vengeance with cold-blooded determination. The script was based on the title of a 20-page Ben Hecht treatment that was, according to Dmytryk, "such poor stuff" that they kept only the title and brought in new writers to shape the film.

p, Adrian Scott; d, Edward Dmytryk; w, John Paxton, based on a story by John Wexley and a title by Ben Hecht; ed, Joseph Noriega; ph, Harry J. Wild; m, Roy Webb.

(PR:C MPAA:NR)

COUP DE GRACE***½

(1978, Ger./Fr.) 96m Argos-Bioskop/Cinema V bw (DER FANGSCHUSS)

Margarethe von Trotta *(Sophie von Reval)*, Matthias Habich *(Erich von Lhomond)*, Rudiger Kirschstein *(Conrad von Reval)*, Matthieu Carriere *(Volkmar von Plessen)*, Valeska Gert *(Aunt Praskovia)*, Marc Eyraud *(Dr. Paul Rugen)*, Frederik Zichy *(Franz von Aland)*, Bruno Thost *(Chopin)*, Henry van Lyck *(Borschikoff)*, Franz Morek

Set in the Baltic states during the winter of 1919 just after WW I's end, this historical fiction follows the lives of three aristocrats who, along with servants and a haunting, heavily made-up old aunt (Valeska Gert), attempt to maintain their day-to-day existence despite the bombings and fighting that disrupt their lives. Erich (Matthias Habich) is a Prussian officer who commands a garrison at the aristocratic estate of fellow soldier Konrad (Rudiger Kirchstein). Sophie (Margarethe von Trotta), Konrad's strong and independent sister, also lives there, and is in love with the detached Erich, who does not reciprocate her affection but does seem attracted to Konrad. Despite her love for Erich, however, she does not share his determination to crush the Bolshevik cause and execute its supporters. Shot in a cold, wintry black and white, this is an eerie, sometimes dreamlike picture whose political and historical references may be obscure for most viewers, although its creation of atmosphere is strong. This was the final professional collaboration for husband-and-wife filmmaking team Volker Schlondorff and von Trotta, both subsequently directing films of their own. (In German and French; English subtitles.)

p, Eberhard Junkersdorf; d, Volker Schlondorff; w, Genevieve Dormann, Margarethe von Trotta, and Jutta Bruckner, based on the novel by Marguerite Yourcenar; ed, Jane Sperr, Anette Dorn, and Henri Colpi; ph, Igor Luther and Peter Arnold; m, Stanley Myers.

(PR:C MPAA:NR)

COURT MARTIAL***½

(1954, Brit.) 105m IF/BL bw (GB: CARRINGTON V.C.)

David Niven *(Maj. Carrington V.C.)*, Margaret Leighton *(Valerie Carrington)*, Noelle Middleton *(Capt. Alison Graham)*,

COURT-MARTIAL OF BILLY MITCHELL, THE—

Laurence Naismith *(Maj. Panton)*, Clive Morton *(Lt. Col. Huxford)*, Mark Dignam *(Prosecutor)*, Allan Cuthbertson *(Lt. Col. Henniker)*, Victor Maddern *(Sgt. Owen)*, John Glyn-Jones *(Evans)*, Raymond Francis *(Maj. Mitchell)*, Newton Blick *(Judge Advocate)*, John Chandos *(Adjutant Rawlinson)*, Geoffrey Keen *(President)*, Maurice Denham *(Lt. Col. Reeve)*.

David Niven stars in this taut courtroom drama as Maj. Carrington, a celebrated war hero shoved into a nowhere position during peacetime. Plagued by financial troubles and a nagging wife (Margaret Leighton), Carrington tries without success to get the War Office to reimburse him for his expense account. When the pencil-pushing commanding officer, Lt. Col. Henniker (Allan Cuthbertson), refuses to process Carrington's request, the major is forced to "borrow" from the till. Henniker is outraged and orders a court martial, during which it is revealed that Carrington had an affair with a young female officer, Capt. Alison Graham (Noelle Middleton), who tried to cover up her lover's theft. When this is disclosed, Carrington's wife gets her revenge by falsely testifying against her husband. The compelling courtroom drama is augmented by a healthy cynicism concerning the treatment of war veterans.

d, Anthony Asquith; w, John Hunter, based on a play by Dorothy Christie, Campbell Christie; ed, Ralph Kemplen; ph, Desmond Dickinson.

(PR:A   MPAA:NR)

COURT-MARTIAL OF BILLY MITCHELL, THE****

(1955) 100m United States/WB c (GB: ONE-MAN MUTINY)

Gary Cooper *(Gen. Billy Mitchell)*, Charles Bickford *(Gen. Guthrie)*, Ralph Bellamy *(Congressman Frank Reid)*, Rod Steiger *(Maj. Allan Guillion)*, Elizabeth Montgomery *(Margaret Lansdowne)*, Fred Clark *(Col. Moreland)*, James Daly *(Col. Herbert White)*, Jack Lord *(Comdr. Zachary Lansdowne)*, Peter Graves *(Capt. Elliott)*, Darren McGavin *(Russ Peters)*, Robert F. Simon *(Adm. Gage)*, Charles Dingle *(Senator Fullerton)*, Dayton Lummis *(Gen. Douglas MacArthur)*, Tom McKee *(Capt. Eddie Rickenbacker)*, Steve Roberts *(Maj. Carl Spaatz)*, Herbert Heyes *(Gen. John J. Pershing)*, Robert Brubaker *(Maj. H.H. Arnold)*, Ian Wolfe *(President Calvin Coolidge)*, Phil Arnold *(Fiorello LaGuardia)*, Will Wright *(Adm. William S. Sims)*.

This fine courtroom drama features Gary Cooper as the visionary and much-maligned Billy Mitchell, who, in 1925, was placed on secret military trial for bucking the Army and fighting for a separate Air Force, and who also predicted that the US would some day have to fight Japan. Mitchell, as Assistant Chief of the Army Air Service following WW I, unsuccessfully tries to convince superiors of the necessity of a strong air force. Since he persists in annoying his bosses, he is demoted from general to colonel, relieved of his post, and sent to a remote Texas command. The dogged Mitchell launches a letter-writing campaign to convince superiors and politicians that air power must be America's first line of defense, but fails to gain support. After several air disasters, including the crash of an unsafe Navy dirigible, Mitchell goes public with his complaints, condemning the War and Navy departments for "incompetence and criminal negligence." The top brass retaliates by putting him on trial in a Washington, DC, warehouse, intending to railroad him as soon as possible, but Frank Reid (Ralph Bellamy), a sympathetic congressman, comes to Mitchell's aide and defends him before a military tribunal. There's not much action outside the courtroom antics, but Otto Preminger's direction, the Oscar-nominated Milton Sperling-Emmet Lavery script, and the powerful and dignified performance of Cooper provide all the action needed (unfortunately, the many real-life figures—Gen. Douglas MacArthur, Fiorello LaGuardia, Adm. William S. Sims, Maj. Carl Spaatz, President Calvin Coolidge, Maj. Hap Arnold, Gen. John J. Pershing—are portrayed rather stiffly, as if these movers and shakers were marble statues). Curiously, the film was photographed in CinemaScope, presumably to make the static visuals somehow more cinematic.

p, Milton Sperling; d, Otto Preminger; w, Milton Sperling and Emmett Lavery, based on the story by Milton Sperling, Emmett Lavery; ed, Folmar Blangsted; ph, Sam Leavitt, CinemaScope, WarnerColor; m, Dimitri Tiomkin.

(PR:A   MPAA:NR)

CRANES ARE FLYING, THE***½

(1960, USSR) 97m Mosfilm/WB bw (LETYAT ZHURAVLI)

Tatyana Samoilova *(Veronica)*, Alexei Batalov *(Boris)*, Vasily Merkuryev *(Fyodor Ivanovich)*, Alexander Shvorin *(Mark)*, Svetlana Kharitonova *(Irina)*, Konstantine Niktin *(Volodya)*, Valentin Zubkov *(Stepan)*, Alla Bogdanova *(Grandmother)*, B. Kokobkin *(Tyernov)*, E. Kupriyanova *(Anna Mikhailovna)*.

Generally free of the party line one usually associates with Soviet films of its period, THE CRANES ARE FLYING is an antiwar love story, set during WW II, which centers on the romance between pretty young Veronica (Tatyana Samoilova) and sensitive factory worker Boris (Alexei Batalov). Boris, like hordes of other patriotic Soviet men, marches off to war, leaving behind the woman he loves. She is eventually told of his death, but refuses to accept the horrible news. Finally, however, she resigns herself to a loveless marriage with Boris' draft-dodger brother, Fyodor (Vasily Merkuryev), despite the fact that he raped her during an air raid and although she still loves Boris. The film gained international attention and was one of the first postwar Soviet features to be seen in the West. A beautiful performance is given by the gorgeous Samoilova, the great-niece of Stanislavsky and daughter of an actor father, Yevgeni Samoilov. The Cannes Film Festival awarded Samoilova the Golden Palm for her electrifying performance, and named the film as Best Picture. (In Russian; English subtitles.)

p, Mikhail Kalatozov; d, Mikhail Kalatozov; w, Victor Rozov, based on his play; ed, M. Timofeyeva; ph, Sergei Urussevsky; m, Moisei Vaynberg.

(PR:A   MPAA:NR)

CRIMSON ROMANCE***

(1934) 70m Mascot bw

Ben Lyon *(Bob Wilson)*, Sari Maritza *(Alida Hoffman)*, Erich von Stroheim *(Wolters)*, Hardie Albright *(Hugo)*, James Bush *(Fred von Bergen)*, William Bakewell *(Adolph)*, Herman Bing *(Himmelbaum)*, Bodil Rosing *(Mama von Bergen)*, Arthur Clayton *(Baron von Eisenlohr)*, Oscar Apfel *(John Fleming)*, Purnell Pratt *(Franklyn Pierce)*, Jason Robards, Jr. *(Pierre)*.

This interesting film about the German army regrettably suffers from preachiness and anachronistic content (its release was contemporaneous with the rise of the Nazis and corresponding anti-German sentiment). Primarily an opus of loyalty and pacifism, it has no real winners or heroes. Two enthusiastic American lads join the German air force, only to learn that they will soon be battling against the boys from their homeland. Bob Wilson (Ben Lyon) decides to remain loyal to America and fight on its side; Fred von Bergen (James Bush), however, remains loyal to his German ancestry and continues flying with the Luftwaffe. Before long he is shot down and killed, leaving Bob to move in on his dead pal's *fraulein*, Alida (Sari Maritza). Back in the States, Fred's mother (Bodil Rosing) delivers an antiwar eulogy that still rings true today. Eric von Stroheim is awesome in the granite-hard role of a sadistic captain.

p, Nat Levine; d, David Howard; w, Mildred Krims and Doris Schroeder, based on a story by Al Martin, Sherman Lowe; ed, Doris Drought; ph, Ernest Miller.

(PR:C MPAA:NR)

CROMWELL**

(1970, Brit.) 139m COL c

Richard Harris *(Oliver Cromwell)*, Alec Guinness *(King Charles I)*, Robert Morley *(Earl of Manchester)*, Dorothy Tutin *(Queen Henrietta Maria)*, Frank Finlay *(John Carter)*, Timothy Dalton *(Prince Rupert)*, Patrick Wymark *(Earl of Stafford)*, Patrick Magee *(Hugh Peters)*, Nigel Stock *(Sir Edward Hyde)*, Charles Gray *(Lord Essex)*, Michael Jayston *(Henry Ireton)*, Richard Cornish *(Oliver Cromwell II)*, Anna Cropper *(Ruth Carter)*, Michael Goodliffe *(Solicitor General)*.

This long, tedious costume epic *did* win the Oscar for Best Costume Design—but that's about all one notices. The indefatigable Richard Harris plays Oliver Cromwell, the 17th-century English statesman who trained and led the Puritan "Roundheads" in a civil war against the Cavaliers, the royalist allies of Parliament and the increasingly unjust King Charles I (Alec Guinness). Fearing that King Charles' French Catholic wife, Henrietta Maria (Dorothy Tutin), is polluting her husband's Anglican religious ideology, Cromwell vows to keep England from slipping under the influence of Catholicism. Far from being a history lesson, the blatantly erroneous CROMWELL is also rather far from being entertaining. Guinness does some of his usual fine work as the weak Charles I, Tutin is fine as the queen, Robert Morley is exciting as the nasty Earl of Manchester, a young Timothy Dalton has some fun with his role, and cinematographer Geoffrey Unsworth makes it all look very lovely; Harris, however, is a tough sell in just about any movie, and CROMWELL is no exception. Costing $9 million, CROMWELL justifiably went belly-up at the box office, raking in only about a third of that figure.

p, Irving Allen; d, Ken Hughes; w, Ken Hughes and Ronald Harwood; ed, Bill Lenny; ph, Geoffrey Unsworth, Panavision, Technicolor; m, Frank Cordell.

(PR:A MPAA:NR)

CROSS OF IRON****

(1977, Brit./Ger.) 133m AE c

James Coburn *(Cpl. Steiner)*, Maximilian Schell *(Capt. Stransky)*, James Mason *(Brandt)*, David Warner *(Kiesel)*, Klaus Lowitsch *(Kruger)*, Vadim Glowna *(Kem)*, Roger Fritz *(Triebig)*, Dieter Schidor *(Anselm)*, Burkhardt Driest *(Maag)*, Fred Stillkraut *(Schnurrbart)*, Senta Berger *(Eva)*.

One of director Sam Peckinpah's most underrated films, CROSS OF IRON is a bleak, unpleasant, and ugly look at men in combat that was almost universally panned by the mainstream press upon its initial release. Its complex and vivid portrayal of the absurdity of war, however, prompted none other than Orson Welles to write Peckinpah and proclaim it the finest antiwar film he had ever seen. Based on a celebrated novel by German author Willi Heinrich, the film is set at the Russian front circa 1943, as the Germans are retreating before the Soviet army. We follow Cpl. Steiner (James Coburn, giving what may be his best performance), a German soldier—not a Nazi—who "hates this uniform and everything it stands for." Loyal only to his men, a tight-knit group of soldiers fighting for their survival, Steiner finds his nemesis in his new commander, Capt. Stransky (Maximilian Schell), an arrogant, narcissistic Prussian aristocrat who desperately wants to come home with an Iron Cross, Germany's highest honor for bravery, but who is terrified of battle. Since Steiner comes highly recommended by other commanders and has already been awarded the Iron Cross himself, Stransky promotes him to sergeant in the hope of winning an ally. After a seige on their compound in which many brave men die while Stransky cowers in his bunker, Steiner learns that the captain has filed a false report claiming that he led the counterattack—a deed certain to earn an Iron Cross. When Steiner refuses to confirm Stransky's claims (he also refuses to call him a liar, which would indicate reverence for a medal Steiner considers worthless), the captain plots to dispose of the troublesome Steiner and his men. CROSS OF IRON, which was plagued with production problems (producer Wolf C. Hartwig ran out of money before the final sequence was filmed) and was cut extensively by its American distributor before its US release, is yet another mutilated Peckinpah film, but one that holds up exceedingly well despite such blows (the uncut version was restored for home video). From its opening, a brilliant montage of WW II stock footage intercutting Hitler and his armies with shots of Hitler Youth raising a flag on a mountain while a chorus of German children sing a tune, to its

CRUEL SEA, THE—

bizarre—almost surreal—climax, CROSS OF IRON is anything but a standard WW II movie, especially compared to its mythicizing contemporaries like A BRIDGE TOO FAR (1977), MIDWAY (1976), or MACARTHUR (1977). Shot superbly by cinematographer John Coquillon, the film shows war as hideously brutal, inglorious, and insane. With its focus on the corruption of moral values and the betrayal of the innocence of children, CROSS OF IRON is an angry film that ends in bitter weariness with a quote from Bertolt Brecht: "Do not rejoice in his defeat you men. For though the world has stood up and stopped the bastard, the bitch that bore him is in heat again." Followed by an absurd sequel titled BREAKTHROUGH, in which the Sgt. Steiner character (now played by Richard Burton) becomes involved in a plot to kill Hitler. None of the original cast or crew were involved and the film was never released in the US.

p, Wolf C. Hartwig; d, Sam Peckinpah; w, Herbert Asmodi and Julius J. Epstein, based on the book *Cross of Iron* by Willi Heinrich; ed, Mike Ellis, Tony Lawson, and Herbert Taschner; ph, John Coquillon, Technicolor; m, Ernest Gold.

(PR:O   MPAA:R)

CRUEL SEA, THE****

(1953, Brit.) 120m Ealing/Balcon/GFD bw

Jack Hawkins *(Capt. Ericson)*, Donald Sinden *(Lockhart)*, John Stratton *(Ferraby)*, Denholm Elliott *(Morrell)*, Stanley Baker *(Bennett)*, John Warner *(Baker)*, Bruce Seton *(Tallow)*, Liam Redmond *(Watts)*, Virginia McKenna *(Julie Hallam)*, Moira Lister *(Elaine Morell)*, June Thorburn *(Doris Ferraby)*, Megs Jenkins *(Tallow's Sister)*.

THE CRUEL SEA is the tough, often gruesome account of British corvette life on the Atlantic during WW II as seen through the tormented consciousness of Lt. Comdr. Ericson (Jack Hawkins). After losing one ship to a U-boat while protecting a convoy, Ericson's ship, *Compass Rose*, is itself torpedoed; only Ericson and a handful of his men barely survive, adrift on a raft. Given a new command on the frigate *Saltash Castle*, Ericson is again at the mercy of the "cruel sea" and must face an impossible choice in risking the lives of his men. The film is shot in documentary style, with harsh black-and-white images. and is based on the actual wartime exploits of author Nicholas Monsarrat, whose novel was here adapted by suspense writer Eric Ambler. The supporting cast members appear marginally as crew members in the Royal Navy and in brief flashback and furlough sequences. A top-notch film from Britain's Ealing Studios, with Hawkins turning in an intense, fascinating performance.

p, Leslie Norman; d, Charles Frend; w, Eric Ambler, based on the novel by Nicholas Monsarrat; ed, Peter Tanner; ph, Gordon Dines; m, Alan Rawsthorne.

(PR:A   MPAA:NR)

CRY OF BATTLE**

(1963, US/Phil.) 99m AA bw (AKA: TO BE A MAN)

Van Heflin *(Joe Trent)*, Rita Moreno *(Sisa)*, James MacArthur *(David McVey)*, Leopoldo Salcedo *(Manuel Careo)*, Sidney Clute *(Col. Ryker)*, Marilou Munoz *(Pinang)*, Oscar Roncal *(Atong)*, Liza Moreno *(Vera)*, Michael Parsons *(Capt. Davis)*, Claude Wilson *(Matchek)*, Vic Solyin *(Capt. Garcia)*.

This WW II actioner follows the exploits of David McVey (James MacArthur), the son of a wealthy businessman, who arrives in the Philippines on December 8, 1941, after the Japanese have attacked Pearl Harbor and turned their attention to the Philippines. McVey hooks up with the hardened fighter Joe Trent (Van Heflin), who keeps a watchful eye over his inexperienced new friend. Trent, however, is less concerned than McVey with the Filipino people or their resistance movement—he rapes a young local woman; shoots a Filipino fighter; attempts to seduce Sisa (Rita Moreno), a guerrilla fighter; and plots to murder Careo (Leopoldo Salcedo), the leader of the resistance. As the savage Trent becomes increasingly brutish, McVey's allegiance to him is pushed to the breaking point.

p, Joe Steinberg; d, Irving Lerner; w, Bernard Gordon, based on the novel *Fortress in the Rice* by Benjamin Appel; ed, Verna Fields; ph, Felipe Sacdalan; m, Richard Markowitz.

(PR:A   MPAA:NR)

CUBA***

(1979) 122m UA c

Brooke Adams *(Alexandra Pulido)*, Sean Connery *(Maj. Robert Dapes)*, Jack Weston *(Gutman)*, Hector Elizondo *(Ramirez)*, Denholm Elliott *(Skinner)*, Martin Balsam *(Gen. Bello)*, Chris Sarandon *(Juan Pulido)*, Alejandro Rey *(Faustino)*, Lonette McKee *(Therese)*, Danny De La Paz *(Julio)*, Louisa Moritz *(Miss Wonderly)*, Walter Gotell *(Don Palido)*, Earl Cameron *(Col. Rosell Y. Leyva)*.

This is an intelligent, zany satire of Cuban military dictatorships and revolutions from director Richard Lester and screenwriter Charles Wood, who previously collaborated on a number of projects, including HOW I WON THE WAR and the 1968 CHARGE OF THE LIGHT BRIGADE. Robert Dapes (Sean Connery) is a British mercenary enlisted by the Batista regime to come to Havana and help crush Castro's guerrillas. In addition to encountering various scoundrels—including a nasty Batista general (Martin Balsam), an angry young guerrilla (Danny De La Paz), and a grotesque American businessman (Jack Weston)—Dapes meets former flame Alexandra Pulido (Brooke Adams), a Cuban tobacco factory manager with a philandering husband (Chris Sarandon). As the rekindled romance between Dapes and Alexandra heats up, so too does the revolution. Instead of taking sides politically by painting either Batista or Castro as a hero, Lester and Wood concentrate on how revolutions don't necessarily mean change for a country's people: the characters in CUBA are all drunk, corrupt, lazy, and cynical under Batista and show no signs of changing under Castro's rule. This old-fashioned, entertaining romance set against a backdrop of political turmoil intentionally recalls such classics as CASABLANCA.

p, Arlene Sellers and Alex Winitsky; d, Richard Lester; w, Charles Wood; ed, John Victor Smith; ph, David Watkin, Technicolor; m, Patrick Williams.

(PR:C MPAA:R)

D

D-DAY, THE SIXTH OF JUNE***

(1956) 106m FOX c (AKA: SIXTH OF JUNE, THE)

Robert Taylor *(Brad Parker)*, Richard Todd *(John Wynter)*, Dana Wynter *(Valerie)*, Edmond O'Brien *(Col. Timmer)*, John Williams *(Brigadier Russell)*, Jerry Paris *(Raymond Boyce)*, Robert Gist *(Dan Stenick)*, Richard Stapley *(David Archer)*, Ross Elliott *(Maj. Mills)*, Alex Finlayson *(Col. Harkens)*, Marie Brown *(Georgina)*, Rama Bai *(Mala)*, Dabbs Greer *(Arkinson)*, Boyd "Red" Morgan *(Sgt. Brooks)*, Queenie Leonard *(Corporal)*, Geoffrey Steel *(Maj. McEwen)*, George Pelling *(Capt. Waller)*.

D-DAY, THE SIXTH OF JUNE sets a love triangle amidst the havoc of WW II. Robert Taylor is Brad Parker, an officer assigned to London and working for an egocentric colonel (Edmond O'Brien, in a revealing, often grating performance), who longs to make a name for himself in combat. Parker's story is told in flashback as he awaits the sailing of the invasion armada to Normandy. He thinks back to his first meeting with Valerie (Dana Wynter), an English enlisted woman whose fiance, John (Richard Todd), is fighting in Africa. Valerie tries unsuccessfully to resist falling in love with Parker, who has a wife in the States. Their tryst is interrupted when John is furloughed after being seriously wounded and Valerie returns to him. When both men later participate in the D-Day landings, only one survives. This standard, well-made tale bogs down in spots, but is enlivened by O'Brien's unmilitary, often bizarre conduct.

p, Charles Brackett; d, Henry Koster; w, Ivan Moffat and Harry Brown, based on the novel by Lionel Shapiro; ed, William Mace; ph, Lee Garmes, CinemaScope, Deluxe Color; m, Lyn Murray.

(PR:A MPAA:NR)

DAM BUSTERS, THE****

(1955, Brit.) 125m ABF/WB bw

Richard Todd *(Wing Comdr. Guy Gibson)*, Michael Redgrave *(Dr. Barnes N. Wallis)*, Ursula Jeans *(Mrs. Wallis)*, Basil Sydney *(Sir Arthur Harris)*, Derek Farr *(Group Capt. J.N.H. Whitworth)*, Patrick Barr *(Capt. Joseph Summers)*, Charles Carson *(Doctor)*, Stanley Van Beers *(Sir David Pye)*, Colin Tapley *(Dr. W.H. Glanville)*, Raymond Huntley *(Laboratory Official)*, Ernest Clark *(AVM Ralph Cochrane)*, John Fraser *(Flight Lt. Hopgood)*, Nigel Stock *(Flight Lt. Spafford)*, Bill Kerr *(Flight Lt. Martin)*, George Baker *(Flight Lt. Maltby)*, Robert Shaw *(Flight Sgt. Pulford)*.

This exciting war story is based on two books about the RAF's destruction of the Ruhr dams that supplied industrial Germany with the power to run huge factories in WW II. Scientist Barnes N. Wallis (Michael Redgrave) comes up with an idea of how to demolish the German war machine. The dams are built in such a fashion that they could not be done in by the bombs of 1943, but Wallis conceives of a bomb that would be delivered low, skip along the water like a stone, and hit the dams in the middle. He tests his theory with golf and ping-pong balls, but no one can be certain of the weapon's effectiveness until its use is attempted. It must be dropped from a height of 60 feet by a plane traveling exactly 240 miles per hour and precisely 1,800 feet from the target. The job of training a crew to do so is taken on by Wing Comdr. Guy Gibson (Richard Todd); much of this absorbing film has to do with that instruction. Since the story is based on real events, we know that Wallis' plan did work, and marked an important turning point in the war effort.

p, Robert Clark and W.A. Whittaker; d, Michael Anderson; w, R.C. Sherriff, based on the books *Enemy Coast Ahead* by Wing Comdr. Guy Gibson and *The Dam Busters* by Paul Brickhill; ed, Richard Best; ph, Erwin Hillier; m, Eric Coates and Leighton Lucas.

(PR:A MPAA:NR)

DAMN THE DEFIANT!***

(1962, Brit.) 101m G.W. Films/COL c (GB: HMS DEFIANT)

Alec Guinness *(Capt. Crawford)*, Dirk Bogarde *(Lt. Scott-Padget)*, Maurice Denham *(Surgeon Goss)*, Nigel Stock *(Senior Midshipman Kilpatrick)*, Richard Carpenter *(Lt. Ponsonby)*, Peter Gill *(Lt. D'Arblay)*, David Robinson *(Harvey Crawford)*, Robin Stewart *(Pardoe)*, Ray Brooks *(Hayes)*, Peter Greenspan *(Johnson)*, Anthony Quayle *(Vizard)*, Tom Bell *(Evans)*, Murray Melvin *(Wagstaffe)*, Victor Maddern *(Dawlish)*.

Alec Guinness stars in this British sea adventure set during the Napoleonic wars as Capt. Crawford, of the HMS *Defiant*. Dirk Bogarde is the brutal Lt. Scott-Padget, whose cruel treatment of the crew has added fuel to their plan to participate in a fleet-wide mutiny against the British Navy. Crawford is unaware of Scott-Padget's behavior, but when the lieutenant inflicts a vicious punishment upon Crawford's midshipman son he begins to take notice. Because the ship is needed to battle the French, the sailors are torn between their desire to mutiny and their duty to defend England. Anthony Quayle turns in a strong performance as Vizard, the chief mutineer.

p, John Brabourne; d, Lewis Gilbert; w, Nigel Kneale and Edmund H. North, based on the novel *Mutiny* by Frank

DAMNED, THE—

Tilsley; ed, Peter Hunt; ph, Christopher Challis, CinemaScope, Eastmancolor; m, Clifton Parker.

(PR:A   MPAA:NR)

DAMNED, THE****

(1969, It./Ger.) 155m
Pegaso-Praesidens-Eichberg/WB-Seven Arts c (LA CADUTA DEGLI DEI; GOTTERDAMMERUNG)

Dirk Bogarde *(Friedrich Bruckmann)*, Ingrid Thulin *(Baroness Sophie von Essenbeck)*, Helmut Griem *(Aschenbach)*, Helmut Berger *(Martin von Essenbeck)*, Renaud Verley *(Gunther von Essenbeck)*, Umberto Orsini *(Herbert Thallman)*, Rene Kolldehoff *(Baron Konstantin von Essenbeck)*, Albrecht Schoenhals *(Baron Joachim von Essenbeck)*, Charlotte Rampling *(Elisabeth Thallman)*, Florinda Bolkan *(Olga)*, Nora Ricci *(Governess)*, Wolfgang Hillinger *(Yanek)*, Bill Vanders *(Commissar)*, Irina Vanka *(Lisa Keller)*, Karin Mittendorf *(Thilde Thallman)*.

Luchino Visconti's epic of decadence, set in Germany during 1933 and 1934, parallels the end of a family of industrialists with the rise of Naziism. The films opens with an extravagant dinner celebrating the retirement of the family patriarch, Baron Joachim von Essenbeck, the magnate of a huge steel enterprise, and his appointment of an outsider, Friedrich Bruckmann (Dirk Bogarde) as temporary head. While at first all seems very respectable and bourgeois, the gathering turns strange when Joachim's grandson, Martin (Helmut Berger) delivers his rendition of Marlene Dietrich's "Falling in Love Again" dressed in drag. Before the party is over, it is announced that the Reichstag has been burned, symbolizing the end of German democracy. Later, as the highly organized SS plots to annihilate the SA (the populist Fascist front), Martin, a bisexual, sadistic, pedophilic drug addict who even rapes his own mother, engineers his plot to stop a takeover attempt by Friedrich and Sophie (Ingrid Thulin), Friedrich's lover and Martin's mother. THE DAMNED is Visconti at his most operatic (the German title is GOTTERDAMMERUNG, after Wagner), containing baroque sets and costumes, highly melodramatic acting, and orgiastic scenes of violence and sex. While it has been criticized on a number of levels (the equating of perverts and pedophiles with fascists has been done before; its English dialog is often poor; it indulges in its own distastefulness; it's too long; etc.), the film is a spectacular, meticulously crafted work that cannot fail to elicit some response, be it disgust or appreciation, from its audience. (In English.)

p, Alfredo Levy and Ever Haggiag; d, Luchino Visconti; w, Luchino Visconti, Nicola Badalucco, and Enrico Medioli; ed, Ruggero Mastroianni; ph, Armando Nannuzzi and Pasquale De Santis; m, Maurice Jarre.

(PR:O   MPAA:X)

DANTON****

(1983, Fr./Pol.) 136m GAU-TF1-S.F.P.C.-Film Polski-Les Film du Losange/Triumph c

Gerard Depardieu *(Georges Danton)*, Wojciech Pszoniak *(Maximillian de Robespierre)*, Patrice Chereau *(Camille Desmoulins)*, Angela Winkler *(Lucile Desmoulins)*, Boguslaw Linda *(Saint Just)*, Roland Blanche *(Lacroix)*, Anne Alvaro *(Eleonore Duplay)*, Roger Planchon *(Fouquier Tinville)*, Serge Merlin *(Philippeaux)*, Lucien Melki *(Fabre d'Eglantine)*, Andrzej Seweryn *(Bourdon)*, Franciszek Starowieyski *(Jacques Louis David)*, Emmanuelle Debever *(Louison Danton)*.

DANTON is a powerful drama of revolution set in France, 1794, during the second year of the Republic, centering on the rivalry between the humanist Georges Danton (Gerard Depardieu) and the ideologue Maximillian de Robespierre (Wojciech Pszoniak), "The Incorruptible." After temporarily retiring from politics and retreating to the countryside, Danton, the most popular of the French revolutionaries, returns to Paris to stop the Reign of Terror led by Robespierre, his former compatriot in the Revolution whose efforts to keep the "pure patriots" in power have turned tyrannical. Although a great freedom fighter and proponent of political, religious, and human rights, Robespierre, with his Committee of Public Safety, has become just as oppressive as the monarchs he fought against. Despite the fact that Danton is a people's hero, Robespierre convinces himself that Danton, who hopes for an end to the bloodshed, must be executed in order to save the Republic. A stirring film on freedom from Andrzej Wajda, in his first directing effort outside of Poland, DANTON takes place in the eye of a hurricane. Criticized by some for being too static and theatrical, the film takes care to show only the center of the Revolution and its aftermath: the battle between Danton and Robespierre and the unseen fight for liberty that takes place behind closed doors. Wajda disregards the rebellion in the streets in favor of showing us the power in the hands of government—those chosen few who are supposed to be representatives of the people. (In French; English subtitles.)

p, Margaret Menegoz; d, Andrzej Wajda; w, Jean-Claude Carriere, Andrzej Wajda, Agnieszka Holland, Boleslaw Michalek, and Jacek Gasiorowski, based on the play "The Danton Affair" by Stanislawa Przybyszewska; ed, Halina Prugar-Ketling; ph, Igor Luther; m, Jean Prodromides.

(PR:O   MPAA:PG)

DARBY'S RANGERS**½

(1958) 120m WB bw (GB: YOUNG INVADERS)

James Garner *(Maj. William Darby)*, Etchika Choureau *(Angelina De Lotta)*, Jack Warden *(Master Sgt. Saul Rosen)*, Edward Byrnes *(Lt. Arnold Dittman)*, Venetia Stevenson *(Peggy McTavish)*, Torin Thatcher *(Sgt. McTavish)*, Peter Brown *(Rollo Burns)*, Joan Elan *(Wendy Hollister)*, Corey Allen *(Tony Sutherland)*, Stuart Whitman *(Hank Bishop)*, Murray Hamilton *(Sims Delancey)*, William Wellman, Jr. *(Eli Clatworthy)*, Andrea King *(Sheilah*

Andrews), Adam Williams (Heavy Hall), Frieda Inescort (Lady Hollister), Reginald Owen (Sir Arthur).

Here is the saga of Maj. William Darby (James Garner), who organized a group of American rangers into a covert operations force for use in North Africa and southern Italy during WW II. Running two hours, the film is divided into halves: the opening hour devoted to the genesis of the Rangers and their subsequent training exercises, and the latter half concentrating on their enormous success as they establish beachheads and penetrate enemy lines. When not involved in battle, Darby's Rangers spend time charming the ladies. While the romantic angle gives the film a supposedly more realistic touch, it deflates much of the excitement created in the well-crafted battle scenes. Garner, fresh from the success of his television series "Maverick," makes an energetic and likable Darby.

p, Martin Rackin; d, William A. Wellman; w, Guy Trosper, based on a book by Maj. James Altieri; ed, Owen Marks; ph, William Clothier; m, Max Steiner.

(PR:A MPAA:NR)

DARK JOURNEY***½

(1937, Brit.) 77m Korda/LF/UA bw (AKA: ANXIOUS YEARS, THE)

Conrad Veidt (Baron Karl von Marwitz), Vivien Leigh (Madeleine Godard), Joan Gardner (Lupita), Anthony Bushell (Bob Carter), Ursula Jeans (Gertrude), Eliot Makeham (Anatole Bergen), Margery Pickard (Colette), Austin Trevor (Dr. Muller), Sam Livesey (Maj. Schaffer), Cecil Parker (Captain), Edmund Willard (German Intelligence Officer), Charles Carson (Fifth Bureau Man), William Dewhurst (Killer), Robert Newton (Officer of U-boat).

This clever and engrossing espionage drama is set in neutral Sweden during WW I. Madeleine Godard (Vivien Leigh) runs a smart dress shop in Stockholm while secretly working as a double agent for both the German and French governments. Her method of passing information is an ingenious one—encoding messages and coordinates in the sheer fabrics of her pricy designs. She begins to arouse suspicions, however, after making numerous trips to Paris. When a German baron, Karl von Marwitz (Conrad Veidt), arrives in Stockholm, he takes a liking to Madeleine. The pair fall deeply in love, and Madeleine, fearing that she will like some of her fellow agents be executed, begs to be relieved of her duties, but she is given one final mission—to learn the identity of a German operative in Sweden. Naturally, Marwitz is the man. DARK JOURNEY is superbly acted, from Leigh and Veidt on down to some well-defined supporting performances by Eliot Makeham, Ursula Jeans, and Margery Pickard as Madeleine's shop employees. Also worthy of mention is the excellent photography by Georges Perinal and Harry Stradling, employing some beautiful deep-focus compositions.

p, Alexander Korda; d, Victor Saville; w, Arthur Wimperis, based on a story by Lajos Biro; ed, William Hornbeck,

Hugh Stewart, and Lionel Hoare; ph, Georges Perinal and Harry Stradling; m, Richard Addinsell.

(PR:A MPAA:NR)

DAVID***

(1979, Ger.) 125m von Vietinghoff-Pro-ject-Filmverlag-ZDF-F.F.A.T.-Dedra/Kino International c

Walter Taub (Rabbi Singer), Irena Vrkljan (Wife), Eva Mattes (Toni), Mario Fischel (David), Dominique Horwitz (Leo), Torsten Henties (David as Child), Rudolph Sellner (Krell).

Peter Lilienthal's German-made entry focuses on the plight of David (Mario Fischel), a teenage Jewish boy whose family is caught in the midst of the Nazi atrocities. His rabbi father (Walter Taub) sees his synagogue burned down by the Nazis, whose further desecrations include carving a swastika on top of his bald head. After his parents are forced to pay a shoemaker to hide their daughter (Eva Mattes) in his shop, David separates from his family, hides out, makes money doing odd jobs, and eventually is able to escape to Israel. This powerful film from Lilienthal is of interest to American audiences chiefly because of its German origins. Lilienthal, a German Jew, is part of a generation of German filmmakers who were children during the war years and are not afraid to look back at the inhumanity of the previous generation. Although DAVID is relatively unknown in America, it received a measure of success abroad in being named the best film of the 1979 Berlin Film Festival, beating out such better-known German pictures as Werner Herzog's NOSFERATU and Rainer Werner Fassbinder's THE MARRIAGE OF MARIA BRAUN. (In German; English subtitles.)

p, Joachim von Vietinghoff; d, Peter Lilienthal; w, Peter Lilienthal, Jurek Becker, and Ulla Zieman, based on the novel by Joel Konig; ed, Siegrun Jager; ph, Al Ruban, Eastmancolor; m, Wojciech Kilar.

(PR:C MPAA:NR)

DAWN PATROL, THE****

(1938) 103m WB bw

Errol Flynn (Capt. Courtney), David Niven (Lt. Scott), Basil Rathbone (Maj. Brand), Donald Crisp (Phills), Melville Cooper (Watkins), Barry Fitzgerald (Bott), Carl Esmond (Von Mueller), Peter Willes (Hollister), Morton Lowry (Johnnie Scott), Michael Brooke (Squires).

A superbly cast remake of Howard Hawks' 1930 picture of the same name, THE DAWN PATROL concerns a dashing, conscience-haunted flight commander, Capt. Courtney (Errol Flynn), of the 59th Squadron in France during WW I. He and his men fly the most dangerous aircraft, rickety crates that almost fall apart before they are off the ground—one source of Courtney's seething anger, which he tries to cover with carefree banter and cynical humor—creating unsafe odds for the fliers and contributing to their untimely deaths. The fatalities mount so drastically that

DAYS OF GLORY—

raw recruits with little flying experience are sent into the skies to battle without much chance of survival. Between the daily dawn patrols that decimate the command, the fliers face death with stiff upper lips and scotch and sodas at the club bar, where a battered gramophone continually grinds out the plaintive "Poor Butterfly." ("So stand by your glasses steady / This world is a world of lies / Here's to the dead already— / Hurrah for the next man who dies!") In another room sits Maj. Brand (Basil Rathbone), the deskbound commander whose job it is to assign fliers to each dawn patrol, mechanically writing their names on a blackboard and methodically erasing those killed each day. Later, when Brand is reassigned, Courtney is called on to replace him; now it is he who must decide which flier will take off to face a certain death. Though the original story of Hawks' film was retained, the dialog was rewritten and polished to great improvement, chiefly in the relationship between Courtney and his best pal, Lt. Scott (David Niven). As in the original (or in Hawks' AIR FORCE), the remake is very much concerned with fraternity, loyalty, and courage in the face of death.

p, Hal B. Wallis and Robert Lord; d, Edmund Goulding; w, Seton I. Miller and Dan Totheroh, based on the story "The Flight Commander" by John Monk Saunders; ed, Ralph Dawson; ph, Tony Gaudio; m, Max Steiner.

(PR:C   MPAA:NR)

DAYS OF GLORY**½
(1944) 86m RKO bw

Tamara Toumanova *(Nina)*, Gregory Peck *(Vladimir)*, Alan Reed *(Sasha)*, Maria Palmer *(Yelena)*, Lowell Gilmore *(Semyon)*, Hugo Haas *(Fedor)*, Dena Penn *(Olga)*, Glenn Vernon *(Mitya)*, Igor Dolgoruki *(Dimitri)*, Edward L. Durst *(Petrov)*, Lou Crosby *(Johann Staub)*, William Challee *(Ducrenko)*, Joseph Vitale *(Seminov)*, Erford Gage *(Col. Prilenko)*.

Gregory Peck, in his first motion picture performance (after having been seen on the Broadway stage by producer Casey Robinson), stars here as Vladimir, the leader of a Soviet resistance group fighting the Germans during WW II. Caught behind enemy lines is Nina (Tamara Toumanova), a famous dancer who eventually falls in love with Vladimir. Producer Robinson had hoped to achieve a sense of realism and, to that end, cast performers who were unknown to movie audiences, including Peck and Toumanova (the latter a prima ballerina with the Ballet Russe de Monte Carlo). It wasn't long before Peck was an Oscar nominee (for his lead role in THE KEYS OF THE KINGDOM, his second film) and Toumanova was Mrs. Casey Robinson. As for the rest of the "unknowns," most remained that way, though Alan Reed did go on to become the voice of Fred Flintstone and Hugo Haas became one of the most curious of Hollywood's independent film directors. Director Jacques Tourneur had just come off the successes of his classic horror films CAT PEOPLE; I WALKED WITH A ZOMBIE; and THE LEOPARD MAN; this was his first bigbudget production for RKO, but the film quickly disappeared from theaters.

p, Casey Robinson; d, Jacques Tourneur; w, Casey Robinson, based on a story by Melchior Lengyel; ed, Joseph Noriega; ph, Tony Gaudio; m, Constantin Bakaleinikoff.

(PR:A   MPAA:NR)

DEADLINE**
(1987, Brit./Ger./Israel) 99m Creative-Caro-Norddeutcher Rundfunk GPMS Intl./Skouras c

Christopher Walken *(Don Stevens)*, Marita Marschall *(Linda Larson)*, Hywel Bennett *(Mike Jessop)*, Arnon Zadok *(Hamdi Abu-Yussuf)*, Amos Lavie *(Yessin Abu-Riadd)*, Ette Ankri *(Samira)*, Martin Umbach *(Bernard)*, Moshe Ivgi *(Abdul)*, Sason Gabay *(Bassam)*.

DEADLINE is yet another "enlightening" political drama that takes one of the world's hot spots and throws a detached American journalist into the abyss, allowing him to undergo a change of character and sort out the complicated mess for the moviegoing public. Like Volker Schlondorff's CIRCLE OF DECEIT (1982), DEADLINE is set in war-torn Beirut, where the PLO and the Christian Phalangists battle as the Israeli army acts as referee. Enter lazy, cynical American TV correspondent Don Stevens (Christopher Walken), fresh from covering a fashion show in Paris. Sent by his fictional network, ABS, to act as a temporary replacement for a reporter who has fallen ill, Stevens is content to stay far away from the action and piece together his reports from outtakes filmed by other correspondents. Things change, however, when he is given a shot at an exclusive interview with a disgruntled PLO leader. This man tells Stevens that he feels it is time to abandon terrorism and look for a negotiated settlement with the Israelis. This news sends shock waves around the world and draws immediate denials from the PLO, who claim that the man was an impostor. As it turns out, he was a charlatan, and Stevens becomes determined to get to the bottom of this mystery—a search that finally awakens him to the plight of the people he is there to cover. DEADLINE is set in one of the world's most violent, chaotic places, yet somehow manages to be deathly dull and hopelessly middle-of-the-road. The filmmakers pretend to approach the material objectively and to present confusing complexities with an even hand, but merely turn all the players into meaningless caricatures. The Phalangists are a bunch of psychotic murderers, the PLO a band of vicious-but-misunderstood killers, and the Israelis an overworked police force. Not that a filmmaker can sort out the turbulence of the Middle East in less than two hours, but DEADLINE tells us nothing.

p, Elisabeth Wolters-Alfs; d, Nathaniel Gutman; w, Hanan Peled; ed, Peter Przygodda; ph, Amnon Salomon and Thomas Mauch, Geyer-Werhe Color; m, Jacques Zwart and Hans Jansen.

(PR:O   MPAA:R)

DEATH BEFORE DISHONOR**
(1987) 95m Lawrence Kubik-M.P.I.-Bima/NW-Balcor c

Fred Dryer *(Sgt. Jack Burns)*, Joey Gian *(Ramirez)*, Sasha Mitchell *(Ruggieri)*, Peter Parros *(James)*, Brian Keith *(Col. Halloran)*, Paul Winfield *(Ambassador)*, Joanna Pacula *(Elli)*, Kasey Walker *(Maude)*, Rockne Tarkington *(Jihad)*, Dan Chodos *(Amin)*.

Fred Dryer (TV's "Hunter") is Sgt. Jack Burns, a tough-as-nails Marine sent to the Middle Eastern country of Jamal (Lebanon by another name). A short-of-fuse man of action with no time for by-the-book types, Burns is commissioned by his old pal Col. Halloran (Brian Keith) to run security at the US embassy. Burns stews as Arabs burn the US flag in front of the embassy, but can't do anything about it, hamstrung by his orders. Although technically a security person, his real job is to act as an ally and observer for the local military forces, who are constantly besieged by terrorists. After Halloran is kidnaped by a small band of terrorists, Burns fears for his buddy's life and wants to go after them right away, but the US ambassador (Paul Winfield) insists on "playing this by the book." Now them's fightin' words to Burns—his best friend has been kidnaped, an Israeli diplomat and his family have been killed, the flag has been burned, and the bureaucrats want to try diplomacy! Burns knows of a photographer, Elli (Joanna Pacula), who is in contact with the terrorists, and through her manages to find their hideout. Director Terry J. Leonard spent most of his career helming second units and handling stunts; this was his directorial debut. He can stage an action scene, but his work with actors is less than steady, with veteran performer Keith contributing the only memorable work. Israeli locations stand in for the thinly veiled Lebanon, with much of the action taking place at Nebbi Mussa, a 12th-century Moslem fort. Strangely, Moslem authorities allowed the filmmakers to shoot at the holy place where thousands pray annually, only to have themselves and their religion insulted by yet another simpleminded, jingoistic American fantasy-fulfillment picture.

p, Lawrence Kubik; d, Terry J. Leonard; w, John Gatliff and Lawrence Kubik, based on a story by John Gatliff, Lawrence Kubik; ed, Steve Mirkovich; ph, Don Burgess, Deluxe Color; m, Brian May.

(PR:C MPAA:R)

DEEP SIX, THE**½
(1958) 105m Jaguar/WB c

Alan Ladd *(Alec Austen)*, Dianne Foster *(Susan Cahill)*, William Bendix *(Frenchy Shapiro)*, Keenan Wynn *(Lt. Comdr. Edge)*, James Whitmore *(Comdr. Meredith)*, Efrem Zimbalist, Jr. *(Lt. Blanchard)*, Joey Bishop *(Ski Krakowski)*, Barbara Eiler *(Clair Innes)*, Ross Bagdasarian *(Slobodjian)*, Jeanette Nolan *(Mrs. Austen)*, Walter Reed *(Paul Clemson)*, Peter Hansen *(Lt. Dooley)*, Perry Lopez *(Al Mendoza)*, Nestor Paiva *(Pappa Tatos)*, Carol Lee Ladd *(Ann)*, Ann Doran *(Elsie)*, Jerry Mathers *(Steve)*.

Alec Austen (Alan Ladd), a Quaker working for an advertising agency, and its chief art director, Susan Cahill (Dianne Foster), are about to marry when the Japanese attack Pearl Harbor and he is drafted. Assigned to the USS *Poe* as a gunnery officer, Alec immediately becomes friendly with Frenchy Shapiro (William Bendix), a tough-talking sailor whose vulnerability is visible only to his best pals. Lt. Comdr. Edge (Keenan Wynn), a hard-bitten patriot who hates the world and is secretly hooked on morphine, finds out about Austen's pacifist beliefs and chides him about them, loudly predicting that when the chips are down, Austen will fail to come through. Austen does seemingly fail his first test as a gunner when he refuses to fire upon an approaching plane; however, he is vindicated when the plane turns out to be piloted by an American. Nonetheless, the crew doesn't trust him and Austen has to go to great lengths to earn their confidence. This is a hell of a theme, and one wishes that more had been done with it here; unfortunately, to receive the cooperation of the Navy the hard-hitting book on which the film was based had to be toned down.

p, Martin Rackin; d, Rudolph Mate; w, John Twist, Harry Brown, and Martin Rackin, based on the novel by Martin Dibner; ed, Roland Gross; ph, John Seitz, Warner Color; m, David Buttolph.

(PR:A MPAA:NR)

DEER HUNTER, THE****
(1978) 183m EMI/COL/WB c

Robert De Niro *(Michael)*, John Cazale *(Stan)*, John Savage *(Steven)*, Christopher Walken *(Nick)*, Meryl Streep *(Linda)*, George Dzundza *(John)*, Chuck Aspegren *(Axel)*, Shirley Stoler *(Steven's Mother)*, Rutanya Alda *(Angela)*, Pierre Segui *(Julien)*, Mady Kaplan *(Axel's Girl)*, Amy Wright *(Bridesmaid)*, Mary Ann Haenel *(Stan's Girl)*, Richard Kuss *(Linda's Father)*.

THE DEER HUNTER, director Michael Cimino's epic look at how the Vietnam War affected a small Pennsylvania steel community, was a huge hit at the box office and garnered several awards, including a Best Picture Oscar, but despite its undeniable power, Cimino's film still remains controversial in its wanton distortion of the war and implicitly racist view of the Vietnamese. Lasting three hours and neatly divided into three acts, the film follows a trio of close friends, Michael (Robert De Niro), Nick (Christopher Walken), and Steven (John Savage), who are about to undergo a tour of duty in Vietnam. Just before their departure, the steelworkers attend Steven's wedding to Angela (Rutanya Alda); later, Michael and Nick go deer hunting with friends Axel (Chuck Aspegren), Stan (John Cazale), and John (George Dzundza). After the hunt, the film rudely cuts to the heat of battle in Vietnam. Michael, Nick, and Steven are all taken prisoner by the Viet Cong, and are forced to play Russian roulette while their captors make bets on the outcome. After several hours of torture, Michael is able to help his friends escape, but they are separated for the duration of the war. When Michael returns to Pennsylvania, he finds Steven in a VA hospital with both his legs gone. Ashamed and embittered, Steven refuses to make contact with his young bride. Michael also

DELTA FORCE, THE—

learns that Nick has chosen to remain in Vietnam and has been sending hundreds of dollars to Steven without explanation. Determined to bring his friend back, Michael returns to Vietnam just as Saigon is about to fall. Moving, dynamic, traumatic, and wholly memorable, THE DEER HUNTER is an emotionally draining production, which skillfully draws a vivid portrait of its characters and their milieu and succeeds in showing the devastating effect the war has on their lives, as well as their brave attempts at renewal. Unfortunately, the film falters when it comes to the larger questions of America's involvement in Vietnam, preferring to show Southeast Asia as a surreal state of mind than to present a realistic portrayal of complex events. Although many critics expressed dismay over the characters' (and, by implication, Cimino's) failure to question the legitimacy of the war or their part in it, it seems completely consistent in the context of the film that these small-town Americans are patriotic enough to go overseas and risk life and limb without ever doubting the justness of the cause. Indeed, the film's memorable closing scene, while ambiguous, is deeply ironic and more than a little sad.

p, Barry Spikings, Michael Deeley, Michael Cimino, and John Peverall; d, Michael Cimino; w, Deric Washburn, based on a story by Michael Cimino, Deric Washburn, Louis Garfinkle, and Quinn K. Redeker; ed, Peter Zinner; ph, Vilmos Zsigmond, Panavision, Technicolor; m, Stanley Myers.

(PR:O MPAA:R)

DELTA FORCE, THE**

(1986) 129m Golan-Globus/Cannon c

Chuck Norris (Maj. Scott McKay), Lee Marvin (Col. Nick Alexander), Martin Balsam (Ben Kaplan), Joey Bishop (Harry Goldman), Robert Forster (Abdul), Lainie Kazan (Sylvia Goldman), George Kennedy (Father O'Malley), Hanna Schygulla (Ingrid), Susan Strasberg (Debra Levine), Bo Svenson (Capt. Campbell), Robert Vaughn (Gen. Woolbridge), Shelley Winters (Edie Kaplan).

This is an old-time action film that employs all the war cliches without a real war to depict, except for the one invented by producers Menahem Golan and Yoram Globus. Maj. Scott McKay (Chuck Norris), backed up by Col. Nick Alexander (Lee Marvin), is a one-man army who dispatches bloodthirsty terrorists with the same calm precision Norris brought to his martial-arts films. Golan, who directs without much imagination, manipulates contemporary headlines to get the public into the theaters for another "fantasy through firepower," RAMBO-style. In this case, a TWA airliner was actually hijacked by terrorists in Athens, then flown to Beirut, after which followed several trips back and forth to Algiers until the terror ended back in Beirut. The terrorists killed a US Marine and had several passengers removed and held hostage in Beirut. In the film, the terrorist operation is headed by Abdul (Robert Forster), who, once he instructs the plane to head for Beirut, separates the Jewish males from the rest of the passengers. Also picked out are three young Navy recruits whom the terrorists insist on labeling Marines. While the plane is in the air, Alexander and McKay join the exclusive anti-terrorist military team—the "Delta Force"—ordered to Lebanon by the President to free the passengers. THE DELTA FORCE is yet another action film that seeks to satisfy popular frustrations by creating a fictitious situation in which it is possible to win a decisive victory against an elusive foe. While producers Golan and Globus tell us that this makes for a healthy release of tension, one must wonder: Is it really better to oversimplify a complex situation to the point of absurdity, offering false solutions, than it is to deal with reality? The film discards any semblance of logic as it shows the Pentagon and an unseen president brashly ordering troops into full-scale combat, risking a wide-open war in Lebanon. Golan barely touches on the fundamental conflicts that created the situation there and simply offers a pack of wild-eyed, swarthy Arabs preying on passive, middle-aged Jews represented by the likes of Shelley Winters, Martin Balsam, Joey Bishop, and Lainie Kazan. Such horrors do happen, but they do not have to be presented as a cartoon.

p, Menahem Golan and Yoram Globus; d, Menahem Golan; w, James Bruner and Menahem Golan; ed, Alain Jakubowicz; ph, David Gurfinkel; m, Alan Silvestri.

(PR:O MPAA:R)

DESERT FOX, THE****

(1951) 88m FOX bw (GB: ROMMEL—DESERT FOX)

James Mason (Erwin Rommel), Sir Cedric Hardwicke (Dr. Karl Strolin), Jessica Tandy (Frau Rommel), Luther Adler (Hitler), Everett Sloane (Gen. Burgdorf), Leo G. Carroll (Field Marshal Von Rundstedt), George Macready (Gen. Fritz Bayerlein), Richard Boone (Aldinger), Eduard Franz (Col. Von Stauffenberg), Desmond Young (Himself), William Reynolds (Manfred Rommel), Charles Evans (Gen. Schultz), Walter Kingsford (Admiral Ruge), John Hoyt (Keitel), Don De Leo (Gen. Maisel), Dan O'Herlihy (Commando Captain), Michael Rennie (Desmond Young's Voice).

The first film that attempted to humanize a WW II German military leader, THE DESERT FOX features a magnetic performance by James Mason as Hitler's greatest field commander, Field Marshal Erwin Rommel—grudgingly respected by his opponents, loyally followed by men of the Afrika Korps. Opening with a British commando raid on Rommel's headquarters, the film traces the general's remarkable career from his early success in North Africa to his defeat at El Alamein (where he disregarded Hitler's "victory or death" command and retreated), on to his illness, command of the French coastal defenses, and role in a failed attempt to assassinate Hitler, leading to his high command-mandated, face-saving suicide. Though Mason is properly the whole show in this fragmentary biography done in semi-documentary style, the supporting cast is excellent (particularly Luther Adler's unforgettable cameo as Hitler), Henry Hathaway's direction is as brisk as a panzer attack, and Nunnally Johnson's script is literate and penetrating. Mason's sympathetic portrait of Rommel is in marked contrast with other cinematic treatments of the general: Erich Von Stroheim in FIVE GRAVES TO CAIRO, Albert Lieven in FOXHOLE IN CAIRO, Werner Hinz in THE LONGEST DAY, Gregory Gay in HITLER, Christopher Plummer in THE NIGHT OF THE GENERALS, Wolfgang Preiss in RAID ON ROMMEL, Karl Michael Vogler in PATTON, and Mason, once more, in THE DESERT RATS.

p, Nunnally Johnson; d, Henry Hathaway; w, Nunnally Johnson, based on the biography by Desmond Young; ed, James B. Clark; ph, Norbert Brodine; m, Daniele Amfitheatrof.

(PR:A MPAA:NR)

DESERT RATS, THE***½

(1953) 88m FOX bw

Richard Burton (Capt. MacRoberts), Robert Newton (Bartlett), Robert Douglas (General), Torin Thatcher (Barney), Chips Rafferty (Smith), Charles Tingwell (Lt. Carstairs), James Mason (Rommel), Charles Davis (Pete), Ben Wright (Mick), James Lilburn (Communications), John O'Malley (Riley), Ray Harden (Hugh), Richard Peel (Rusty), John Wengraf (German Doctor).

A follow-up to THE DESERT FOX, THE DESERT RATS concentrates on the Australian side of the first film's events. Capt. MacRoberts (Richard Burton) is a tough British officer who takes over command of the 9th Australian Division at Tobruk in 1941, at a desert fortress surrounded and hard pressed by the *Afrika Korps* led by Field Marshall Rommel (James Mason, in a reprise of his role in THE DESERT FOX). MacRoberts looks down on his men, viewing them as inferior to the British regulars. Attempting to change that view is Bartlett (Robert Newton), MacRoberts' former college professor, a lowly volunteer and a raving alcoholic. Burton is his usual forceful self, but it's Newton who steals every scene he's in, playing a floppy, roaring, and weepy drunk spouting philosophy and sentiment. Robert Wise's direction is another element in the film's success, as is Lucien Ballard's excellent and realistic photography.

p, Robert L. Jacks; d, Robert Wise; w, Richard Murphy; ed, Barbara McLean; ph, Lucien Ballard; m, Leigh Harline.

(PR:A MPAA:NR)

DESIREE***

(1954) 110m FOX c

Marlon Brando (Napoleon Bonaparte), Jean Simmons (Desiree Clary), Merle Oberon (Josephine), Michael Rennie (Gen. Jean-Baptiste Bernadotte), Cameron Mitchell (Joseph Bonaparte), Elizabeth Sellars (Julie), Charlotte Austin (Paulette), Cathleen Nesbitt (Mme. Bonaparte), Evelyn Varden (Marie), Isobel Elsom (Madame Clary), John Hoyt (Talleyrand), Alan Napier (Despereaux), Nicolas Koster (Oscar), Richard Deacon (Etienne), Edith Evanson (Queen Hedwig), Carolyn Jones (Mme. Tallien), Sam Gilman (Fouche), Larry Craine (Louis Bonaparte).

A lavish but disappointing period piece whose most significant element is the appearance of Marlon Brando in the role of Napoleon Bonaparte, this Jean Simmons vehicle presents historical soap opera on a grand scale. Desiree Clary (Simmons) is the daughter of a wealthy Marseilles silk merchant who meets the young Corsican general Napoleon and falls in love with him. He leaves for Paris, where he hopes to be placed in charge of the Italian campaign. Months later, Desiree follows. The increasingly powerful and famous Napoleon has announced his plans to marry the influential Josephine (Merle Oberon); a crushed Desiree eventually weds Gen. Jean-Baptiste Bernadotte (Michael Rennie) and moves with him to Stockholm, where he is named as an heir to the throne. Napoleon's invasion of Russia fails, his plan to conquer England never materializes, and he is exiled (through the efforts of Bernadotte, among others) to Elba. Later, when he makes plans to form a new army and a new empire, the United States of Europe, it is Desiree who persuades him to lay down his sword. Though not even remotely factual (Napoleon did wed one woman named Josephine and love another named Desiree, but that's about as close as this film gets to accuracy), DESIREE is an entertaining romance. Simmons is completely convincing in the title role, realistically transforming from merchant's daughter to influential woman behind the scenes of history, and Brando is exciting, as always, in a part he took reluctantly.

p, Julian Blaustein; d, Henry Koster; w, Daniel Taradash, based on the novel by Annemarie Selinko; ed, William Reynolds; ph, Milton Krasner, CinemaScope, Deluxe Color; m, Alex North.

(PR:A MPAA:NR)

DESPERATE JOURNEY**½

(1942) 107m WB bw

Errol Flynn (Flight Lt. Terrence Forbes), Ronald Reagan (Flying Officer Johnny Hammond), Raymond Massey (Maj. Otto Baumeister), Nancy Coleman (Kaethe Brahms), Alan Hale (Flight Sgt. Kirk Edwards), Arthur Kennedy (Flying Officer Jed Forrest), Sig Rumann (Preuss), Patrick O'Moore (Squadron Leader Lane-Ferris), Ronald Sinclair (Flight Sgt. Lloyd Hollis), Louis Arco (Feldwebel Gertz), Charles Irwin (Capt. Coswick), Richard Fraser (S/L Clark), Lester Matthews (Wing Commander), Helmut Dantine (German Copilot), William Hopper (Aircraftsman).

If the Germans had been as stupid and silly as they are in this film WW II would have been over in weeks, but DESPERATE JOURNEY was lensed in 1942, when Propaganda was the word. The film tells of an RAF bomber crew shot down over German-occupied Poland; eight men are in the plane, but only five survive the crash and subsequent travails. Flight Lt. Terrence Forbes (Errol Flynn) and his men—Johnny Hammond (Ronald Reagan), Kirk Edwards (Alan Hale), Jed Forrest (Arthur Kennedy), and Lloyd Hollis (Ronald Sinclair)—have no other choice but to sneak through Axis territory to make it back to Merry Olde. In the course of the picture, they are chased relentlessly by Nazi major Otto Baumeister (Raymond Massey), destroy a chemical factory, knock off several Germans, steal Ger-

DESTINATION GOBI—

man uniforms, and masquerade as officers by pilfering Goering's car and taking it to an area near Berlin. A bomber is being prepared to attack London's water works and Forbes and Hammond, the remaining members of the crew, steal the plane and fly across the channel. As he's about to land, Forbes says, "Now for Australia and a crack at those Japs!" DESPERATE JOURNEY was viewed at the time of its release as a ludicrous, comic-strip war adventure. That view has only been strengthened over the years.

p, Hal B. Wallis; d, Raoul Walsh; w, Arthur T. Horman, based on the story "Forced Landing" by Horman; ed, Rudi Fehr; ph, Bert Glennon; m, Max Steiner.

(PR:A MPAA:NR)

DESTINATION GOBI***

(1953) 89m FOX c

Richard Widmark *(CPO Sam McHale)*, Don Taylor *(Jenkins)*, Casey Adams *(Walter Landers)*, Murvyn Vye *(Kengtu)*, Darryl Hickman *(Wilbur Cohen)*, Martin Milner *(Elwood Halsey)*, Ross Bagdasarian *(Paul Sabatello)*, Judy Dann *(Nura-Satu)*, Rodolfo Acosta *(Tomec)*, Russell Collins *(Comdr. Wyatt)*, Leonard Strong *(Wali Akham)*, Anthony Earl Numkena [Earl Holliman] *(Son of Kengtu)*.

Set in Inner Mongolia during WW II, DESTINATION GOBI is a rather peculiar war tale, based in fact but heavy on the fiction, about a crack meteorological team sent to the desert to monitor weather conditions. When their commanding officer is killed during a Japanese attack, Chief Petty Officer Sam McHale (Richard Widmark) takes the reins and leads the men on an 800-mile trek to safety. Along the way, they receive assistance from the First Mongolian Cavalry of the US Navy, a group of Mongol tribesmen who demand 60 US Cavalry saddles as their only recompense. The film features excellent action sequences from Robert Wise, great desert locations, and an enjoyable performance from Widmark, who, through the entire film, looks completely disgusted with the sand, sun, and desert heat.

p, Stanley Rubin; d, Robert Wise; w, Everett Freeman, based on an unpublished story by Edmund G. Love; ed, Robert Fritch; ph, Charles Clarke, Technicolor; m, Sol Kaplan.

(PR:A MPAA:NR)

DESTINATION TOKYO****

(1944) 135m WB bw

Cary Grant *(Capt. Cassidy)*, John Garfield *(Wolf)*, Alan Hale *(Cookie)*, John Ridgely *(Reserve)*, Dane Clark *(Tin Can)*, Warner Anderson *(Executive)*, William Prince *(Pills)*, Bob Hutton *(Tommy)*, Tom Tully *(Mike)*, Faye Emerson *(Mrs. Cassidy)*, Peter Whitney *(Dakota)*, John Forsythe *(Sparks)*, Whit Bissell *(Yo Yo)*.

One of the most rousing, action-filled WW II films ever produced, with a powerful cast and a terrific story, DESTINATION TOKYO remains a classic war drama to this day. Though there are many cameo stories within the framework of the film, the actual protagonist is the submarine in which its characters serve, the USS *Copperfin*. Leaving a West Coast port on Christmas Eve, the sub heads out into the Pacific. Sub commander Capt. Cassidy (Cary Grant) has his secret orders: the destination is Tokyo, where Cassidy is to put ashore a meteorologist (John Ridgely) who will obtain vital data for future air raids over the Japanese metropolis. More than an action film, DESTINATION TOKYO, under the honest direction of Delmer Daves, is a study of the lives of those brave (and some not-so-brave) individuals who serve as submarine crewmen. The story is a human one, with Grant turning in a touching performance as the likable captain. The intimate feel of submarine life is ever-present in the film, from the claustrophobic confinement to the wonderful camaraderie of the shipmates.

p, Jerry Wald; d, Delmer Daves; w, Albert Maltz and Delmer Daves, based on a story by Steve Fisher; ed, Christian Nyby; ph, Bert Glennon; m, Franz Waxman.

(PR:A MPAA:NR)

D.I., THE***

(1957) 104m WB bw

Jack Webb *(T/Sgt. Jim Moore)*, Don Dubbins *(Pvt. Owens)*, Jackie Loughery *(Anne)*, Lin McCarthy *(Capt. Anderson)*, Monica Lewis *(Burt)*, Virginia Gregg *(Mrs. Owens)*, Jeannie Beacham *(Hostess)*, Lu Tobin *(Bartender)*, Earle Hodgins *(Guard)*, Jeanne Baird *(Mother)*, Barbara Pepper *(Customer)*, Melody Gale *(Little Girl)*.

This uncompromising portrait of Marine training on Parris Island features "Dragnet" star Jack Webb as the tough DI (drill instructor) Jim Moore, who runs the would-be shock troops through one shock after another, from night hikes to barracks scrub-downs. Aside from a minor romance with an off-base cutie, Moore spends most of his time trying to make a man out of sniveling, whining Pvt. Owens (Don Dubbins), who has only joined up to please his mother. (It's a family tradition: his father and two brothers were also Marines, all three of them killed during WW II.) Instead of coddling or reasoning with the youth, Moore lays on the double-duty, almost breaking his spirit. But the lad's courage seeps out of sweating pores and he finally earns his place in the Corps. Webb is the whole show, producing and directing the taut film with furious pace and articulating his orders like a battleship firing salvos. He's mean, but he's no Lee Ermey (see FULL METAL JACKET).

p, Jack Webb; d, Jack Webb; w, James Lee Barrett, based on the teleplay "Murder of a Sandflea" by James Lee Barrett; ed, Robert M. Leeds; ph, Edward Colman; m, David Buttolph.

(PR:A MPAA:NR)

DIAMONDS OF THE NIGHT***½

(1964, Czech.) 70m Ceskoslovensky/Impact bw
(DEMANTY NOCI)

Ladislav Jansky *(1st Boy)*, Antonin Kumbera *(2nd Boy)*, Ilse Bischofova *(The Woman)*.

Another outstanding example of Czech New Wave cinema, DIAMONDS OF THE NIGHT was directed in 1964 by the 27-year-old Jan Nemec and based on the writings of Holocaust survivor Arnost Lustig. Running just over an hour, the film compresses four days in the lives of two Jewish boys (Ladislav Jansky and Antonin Kumbera) who, while being transferred to a concentration camp, jump from the transport and escape into the woods. Physically and mentally exhausted, hungry, lost, and desperate, they scrounge for food and shelter and are later chased and caught by a group of old men, only to be released. As their fatigue increases, the boys begin to hallucinate, imagining that the trees are falling down on them or that swarms of ants are crawling on their bodies. Perhaps even more impressive than the startling visual style—there is much hand-held camerawork, and a sense of realism or, as Nemec would call it, "dream realism"—is the sound, or the lack thereof. DIAMONDS OF THE NIGHT is practically without dialog, and there are long stretches in which nothing is heard but the ticking of a clock or the sound of breathing. Available on videotape with Nemec's first short, 1959's LOAF OF BREAD, also based on an Arnost Lustig story. The videocassette is subtitled (Czech into English).

d, Jan Nemec; w, Arnost Lustig and Jan Nemec; ed, Miroslav Hajek; ph, Jaroslav Kucera.

(PR:C MPAA:NR)

DIARY OF ANNE FRANK, THE****

(1959) 170m FOX bw

Millie Perkins *(Anne Frank)*, Joseph Schildkraut *(Otto Frank)*, Shelley Winters *(Mrs. Van Daan)*, Richard Beymer *(Peter Van Daan)*, Gusti Huber *(Edith Frank)*, Lou Jacobi *(Mr. Van Daan)*, Diane Baker *(Margot Frank)*, Douglas Spencer *(Kraler)*, Dody Heath *(Miep)*, Ed Wynn *(Albert Dussell)*, Charles Wagenheim *(Sneak Thief)*, Frank Tweddell *(Night Watchman)*.

This touching and inspirational film is based on the famous WW II diary of the young Anne Frank. Running a lengthy three hours, directed by George Stevens (who photographed much of the famous concentration camp footage after Germany's defeat), the film is told in flashback, as Otto Frank (Joseph Schildkraut), a camp survivor, returns to the warehouse attic in Amsterdam where his Jewish family hid from the "Green Police" (the Dutch Gestapo) for two years. Cramped in uncomfortable quarters, Otto; his wife, Edith (Gusti Huber); and their two daughters, Margot (Diane Baker) and the 13-year-old Anne (Millie Perkins), are sheltered through the kindness and courage of two Gentile shop owners. Also sharing the tiny living space are Mr. and Mrs. Van Daan (Lou Jacobi and Shelley Winters); their teenage son, Peter (Richard Beymer); and the aging dentist Albert Dussell (Ed Wynn). As the atrocities rage outside their hideaway, Anne concerns herself with many of the usual teenage problems—parental relationships, her affection for Peter, her jealousy towards her older sister—and records them in her diary. There are a number of close calls, surprise searches, and suspenseful moments that terrify the hidden inhabitants, who, when they are finally discovered, are carted off to a concentration camp. Only Otto survives, returning to the attic to find Anne's written reflections. He is moved to tears and shamed when he reads Anne's famous line: "In spite of everything, I still believe that people are really good at heart."

p, George Stevens; d, George Stevens; w, Frances Goodrich and Albert Hackett, based on the play by Frances Goodrich, Albert Hackett and the autobiography, *Anne Frank, Diary of A Young Girl*; ed, Robert Swink, William Mace, and David Brotherton; ph, William C. Mellor and Jack Cardiff; m, Alfred Newman.

(PR:A MPAA:NR)

DIRTY DOZEN, THE****

(1967, Brit.) 149m MGM c

Lee Marvin *(Maj. Reisman)*, Ernest Borgnine *(Gen. Worden)*, Charles Bronson *(Joseph Wladislaw)*, Jim Brown *(Robert Jefferson)*, John Cassavetes *(Victor Franko)*, Richard Jaeckel *(Sgt. Bowren)*, George Kennedy *(Maj. Max Armbruster)*, Trini Lopez *(Pedro Jiminez)*, Ralph Meeker *(Capt. Stuart Kinder)*, Robert Ryan *(Col. Everett Dasher-Breed)*, Telly Savalas *(Archer Maggott)*, Donald Sutherland *(Vernon Pinkley)*, Clint Walker *(Samson Posey)*.

One of the most popular of all WW II movies, THE DIRTY DOZEN is also one of the most unusual, for it presents the viewer with a distinctly unpleasant cast of characters who might make the Nazis look positively civilized by comparison. Expertly directed by the forever underrated Robert Aldrich, the film follows nonconformist Maj. Reisman (Lee Marvin) in his assigned task of assembling a suicide squad of military felons (murderers, rapists, thieves) to infiltrate and destroy a chateau in occupied France at which the Nazi top brass congregates. Reisman, aided by his assistant, Sgt. Bowren (Richard Jaeckel), selects 12 men (John Cassavetes, Telly Savalas, Charles Bronson, Donald Sutherland, Jim Brown, Clint Walker, Trini Lopez, Al Mancini, Stuart Cooper, Ben Carruthers, Tom Busby, and Colin Maitland), ranging from the merely dim-witted to the overtly psychotic, to form his "dirty dozen," then subjects them to brutal training designed to mold them into an efficient fighting force. While Reisman's men are obviously the dregs of society, many of his commanding officers (Robert Ryan, Robert Webber) are morally corrupt misfits of a different sort, treating war as just a game, their soldiers nothing more than pawns. After the lengthy, wholly entertaining training session, which climaxes in a war game pitting Reisman's troops against Gen. Worden's (Ernest Borgnine) crack squad, the dirty dozen and their leaders parachute into France to begin a mission that most of them will not survive. Action-packed, funny, and extremely violent for its time, THE DIRTY DOZEN was a box-office smash that continues to be popular to this day, despite hundreds of showings on television (indeed, two made-for-TV sequels appeared in the 1980s). Boasting excellent performances from a stellar cast, this is the ultimate macho action movie—but one that is slyly subversive in calling into question the morals of the *Americans*, not the Germans. Director Aldrich, working from a script by indus-

DIRTY HEROES—

try veterans Lukas Heller and Nunnally Johnson, draws the audience in for the film's first half, which climaxes in the amusing war-game sequence, then turns the tables on the viewer by presenting the actual mission—whose reality is brutal, sadistic, horrible, and insane. Certainly, there are moments of individual honor and heroism, but in the end there is nothing but death—and for what? So that a bunch of fat-cat commanders can smugly sip sherry and smoke cigars, content that the mission was accomplished and that some of their most troublesome recruits died in carrying it out. Aldrich was a master at presenting his distinctly cynical outlook in the context of crowd-pleasing entertainment, and THE DIRTY DOZEN is one of his most effective and lasting efforts.

p, Kenneth Hyman; d, Robert Aldrich; w, Lukas Heller and Nunnally Johnson, based on the novel by E.M. Nathanson; ed, Michael Luciano; ph, Edward Scaife, Metrocolor; m, Frank DeVol.

(PR:C-O   MPAA:NR)

DIRTY HEROES**

(1971, It./Fr./Ger.) 117m Fida Cinematografica-Productions Jacques Roitfeld-Gloria/Golden Eagle c (DALLE ARDENNE ALL' INFERNO, LA)

Frederick Stafford *(Sesamo)*, Daniela Bianchi *(Kristina von Keist)*, Curt Jurgens *(Gen. von Keist)*, John Ireland *(Capt. O'Connor)*, Adolfo Celi *(Rollman)*, Helmut Schneider *(Gen. Hassler)*, Michael Constantine *(Pertowsky)*, Faida Nicols *(Marta/Magda)*.

A blatant attempt to capitalize on the success of THE DIRTY DOZEN, this European coproduction teams a bunch of ex-cons turned US soldiers and some Dutch partisans to recover a cache of stolen diamonds from German-occupied territory. The locations are nice to look at and the Ennio Morricone score is passable, but Frederick Stafford, John Ireland, and Curt Jurgens are a far cry from the tough luminaries of THE DIRTY DOZEN. Originally released in 1967 at 120 minutes, DIRTY HEROES was chopped down to 105 minutes for its US theatrical release in 1971; some precious footage was apparently put back for the videocassette, which runs 117 minutes.

p, Edmundo Amati; d, Alberto De Martino; w, Dino Verde, Vincenzo Flamini, Alberto Verucci, Alberto De Martino, Franco Silvestri, and Louis Agotay, based on their story; ed, Otello Colangeli; ph, Gianni Bergamini, Technicolor; m, Ennio Morricone and Bruno Nicolai.

(PR:A   MPAA:G)

DISTANT DRUMS***½

(1951) 100m United States Pictures/WB c

Gary Cooper *(Capt. Quincy Wyatt)*, Mari Aldon *(Judy Beckett)*, Richard Webb *(Richard Tufits)*, Ray Teal *(Pvt. Mohair)*, Arthur Hunnicutt *(Monk)*, Robert Barrat *(Gen. Zachary Taylor)*, Clancy Cooper *(Sgt. Shane)*, Larry Carper *(Chief Oscala)*, Dan White *(Cpl. Peachtree)*, Mel Archer *(Pvt. Jeremiah Hiff)*, Angelita McCall *(Amelia)*, Lee Roberts *(Pvt. Tibbett)*, Gregg Barton *(Pvt. James Tasher)*, Sheb Wooley *(Pvt. Jessup)*.

During the Seminole Indian War in 1840, a US Army captain, Quincy Wyatt (Gary Cooper), leads a military expedition against a ring of gun runners. He is surrounded by hordes of hostile Seminoles, who drive Wyatt and his men ever deeper into the Everglades, taking love interest Judy Beckett (Mari Aldon) with them. Capt. Wyatt is stoic and heroic as he leads his men to the supposed safety of his own island, and at the end of the trail fights an underwater knife duel with Seminole chief Oscala (Larry Carper), just barely surviving. His bedraggled soldiers, or what's left of them, are saved at the last moment by US troops, who drive off the Indians. Director Raoul Walsh provides plenty of quick-paced thrills in this remake of his own WW II film, OBJECTIVE BURMA, which starred Errol Flynn; Max Steiner's score is as lush as the Everglades that almost swallow up Cooper and company.

p, Milton Sperling; d, Raoul Walsh; w, Niven Busch and Martin Rackin, based on a story by Niven Busch; ed, Folmar Blangsted; ph, Sid Hickox, Technicolor; m, Max Steiner.

(PR:A   MPAA:NR)

DISTANT THUNDER**

(1988, US/Can.) 114m PAR c

John Lithgow *(Mark Lambert)*, Ralph Macchio *(Jack Lambert)*, Kerrie Keane *(Char)*, Reb Brown *(Harvey Nitz)*, Janet Margolin *(Barbara Lambert)*, Dennis Arndt *(Larry)*, Jamey Sheridan *(Moss)*.

Mark Lambert (John Lithgow) is a Vietnam veteran who withdrew from society after his 1970 Army discharge, deserting his wife and son in Illinois. Now living in the woods of Washington state along with other disaffected vets, Mark decides to rejoin civilization after one of his buddies kills himself by walking in front of a train ("kissing a train," the vets call it). Encouraged by his friend Char (Kerrie Keane), Mark takes a job with a logging company and writes to his 18-year-old son, Jack (Ralph Macchio), saying he wants to get together. While Jack travels cross-country to meet him, Mark gets in a fight with Char's jealous boy friend, Moss (Jamey Sheridan), which traumatizes him back into seclusion. Jack and Char, followed by Moss, head into the woods to find him, but Moss' intrusion on the small veterans' community provokes a violent reaction from one of Mark's disturbed comrades and forces Mark to face an especially painful memory. During the arduous journey down the mountains with the badly injured Moss, Mark and Jack try to reconcile their differences. It isn't easy, and Mark almost kisses a train himself before it's over, but finally the two make peace. Lithgow talked with Vietnam veterans who were receiving counseling for post-traumatic stress syndrome to prepare for his role here, and scriptwriter Robert Stitzel has also obviously done his homework on the subject. Yet DISTANT THUNDER trivializes the problems it wants to explore, for when the chips are down and the movie really needs some action to break things open, it brings on a stereotypical psychotic Vietnam vet to explode on a rampage of violence. The film is also slow and predictable, its father-son confrontations stagy and cliched despite Lithgow's typically solid work (Macchio is stuck with the worst dialog and barely struggles through). Filmed in British Columbia, which stands in for Washington.

p, Robert Schaffel; d, Rick Rosenthal; w, Robert L. Stitzel, based on a story by Robert L. Stitzel, Deedee Wehle; ed, Dennis Virkler; ph, Ralf D. Bode, Technicolor; m, Maurice Jarre.

(PR:O   MPAA:R)

DR. STRANGELOVE: OR HOW I LEARNED TO STOP WORRYING AND LOVE THE BOMB****

(1964, Brit.) 93m COL bw

Peter Sellers *(Group Capt. Lionel Mandrake/President Merkin Muffley/Dr. Strangelove)*, George C. Scott *(Gen. "Buck" Turgidson)*, Sterling Hayden *(Gen. Jack D. Ripper)*, Keenan Wynn *(Col. "Bat" Guano)*, Slim Pickens *(Maj. T.J. "King" Kong)*, Peter Bull *(Ambassador de Sadesky)*, Tracy Reed *(Miss Scott)*, James Earl Jones *(Lt. Lothar Zogg)*, Jack Creley *(Mr. Staines)*, Frank Berry *(Lt. H.R. Dietrich)*, Glenn Beck *(Lt. W.D. Kivel)*, Shane Rimmer *(Capt. G.A. "Ace" Owens)*, Paul Tamarin *(Lt. B. Goldberg)*, Gordon Tanner *(Gen. Faceman)*, Robert O'Neil *(Admiral Randolph)*.

Easily the funniest movie ever made about global thermonuclear holocaust, DR. STRANGELOVE seems to grow more relevant with each passing year. Obsessed with the idea that communists are trying to rob Americans of their "precious bodily fluids," Gen. Jack D. Ripper (Sterling Hayden), the commander of Burpelson Air Force Base, goes completely mad, seals off the base, and sends his bomber wing to attack the USSR. United States president Merkin Muffley (Peter Sellers) meets desperately with his advisors, including the blustery Gen. "Buck" Turgidson (George C. Scott) and a mysterious, wheelchair-bound, ex-Nazi scientist named Dr. Strangelove (again Sellers). Left with little choice, the powers that be formulate a plan to have the Russians shoot down the American bombers. However, the Soviet ambassador (Peter Bull), informs the president and those assembled that Russia has constructed a "Doomsday Device," which will automatically trigger buried nuclear weapons if their country is hit. Meanwhile, British officer Lionel Mandrake (once more Sellers) busies himself with trying to trick Gen. Ripper into revealing the code that will recall the bombers. Eventually, all of them are shot down or recalled, except for one flown by Maj. T.J. "King" Kong (Slim Pickens), a crafty pilot who manages to evade Russian fighters and missiles as he heads for his target deep inside the Soviet Union. Written by Terry Southern, Stanley Kubrick, and Peter George (and based on George's book *Red Alert*), DR. STRANGELOVE is the ultimate black comedy, one that makes unthinkable horror unbearably funny. Expertly directed by Kubrick, who deftly intercuts the events at Burpelson with the conference in the War Room and the action on Kong's B-52, the film is a model of barely controlled hysteria in which the very real absurdity of Cold War posturing becomes devastatingly funny—and at the same time nightmarishly frightening. While at times Kubrick seems to strive a bit too hard for laughs (Keenan Wynn's being sprayed in the face after shooting a Coca-Cola machine comes to mind), the film contains some truly remarkable comedic performances—especially from Sellers in his triple role and Hayden as the mad general—and genuinely priceless dialog. Twenty-five years after its release, DR. STRANGELOVE continues to be a prophetic look at the insanity of superpower politics and, like George Orwell's *1984*, has entered the lexicon of modern political discourse.

p, Stanley Kubrick; d, Stanley Kubrick; w, Stanley Kubrick, Terry Southern, and Peter George, based on the novel *Red Alert* by Peter George; ed, Anthony Harvey; ph, Melvin Pike; m, Laurie Johnson.

(PR:C   MPAA:NR)

DOCTOR ZHIVAGO***

(1965) 197m MGM c

Geraldine Chaplin *(Tonya Gromeko)*, Julie Christie *(Lara)*, Tom Courtenay *(Pasha/Strelnikoff)*, Alec Guinness *(Yevgraf)*, Siobban McKenna *(Anna)*, Ralph Richardson *(Alexander)*, Omar Sharif *(Yuri Zhivago)*, Rod Steiger *(Komarovsky)*, Rita Tushingham *(The Girl)*, Adrienne Corri *(Amelia)*, Geoffrey Keen *(Prof. Kurt)*, Jeffrey Rockland *(Sasha)*, Lucy Westmore *(Katya)*, Noel Willman *(Razin)*, Gerard Tichy *(Liberius)*, Klaus Kinski *(Kostoyed)*, Jack MacGowran *(Petya)*.

This sprawling adaptation of Boris Pasternak's epic novel of the Russian Revolution was director David Lean's follow-up to his masterful LAWRENCE OF ARABIA (1962). Told in flashback, the film follows Yuri Zhivago (Omar Sharif) and Tonya Gromeko (Geraldine Chaplin), who meet as youths when the orphaned Yuri is taken in by Tonya's parents. Eventually Yuri becomes a physician and marries Tonya, but several times during WW I he crosses paths with Lara (Julie Christie), the beautiful daughter of a dressmaker, and the two fall into a passionate affair that is disrupted by the Bolshevik Revolution. Although engaging throughout its lengthy running time, this epic film is not as exciting or powerful as LAWRENCE OF ARABIA, due partly to Robert Bolt's screenplay, which leaves out great chunks of Pasternak's novel, making the narrative somewhat awkward in the last half. More regrettable is the miscasting of Sharif, a capable performer who isn't very persuasive in a role better suited to a star of greater stature. The supporting cast is excellent, however; and Christie, Alec Guinness, and Rod Steiger are all impressive. As always, Lean's handling of the purely physical aspects of the material is spectacular, with the scenes of revolution, the harsh Russian winters, and Zhivago's trek across the steppes simply unforgettable. Maurice Jarre's score, much praised at the time, now seems somewhat repetitive and grating. Despite its flaws, DR. ZHIVAGO became one of the all-time box-office champions (grossing nearly $100 million on its initial release) and was nominated for eight

DOGS OF WAR, THE—

Academy Awards, winning Best Screenplay, Music, Cinematography, Art Direction, and Costumes.

p, Carlo Ponti; d, David Lean; w, Robert Bolt, based on the novel by Boris Pasternak; ed, Norman Savage; ph, Freddie Young, Panavision, Metrocolor; m, Maurice Jarre.

(PR:A MPAA:NR)

DOGS OF WAR, THE***
(1980, Brit.) 122m UA c

Christopher Walken *(Shannon)*, Tom Berenger *(Drew)*, Colin Blakely *(North)*, Hugh Millais *(Endean)*, Paul Freeman *(Derek)*, Jean-Francois Stevenin *(Michel)*, JoBeth Williams *(Jessie)*, Robert Urquhart *(Capt. Lockhart)*, Winston Ntshona *(Dr. Okoye)*, Pedro Armendariz, Jr. *(Major)*, Harlan Cary Poe *(Richard)*, Ed O'Neill *(Terry)*, Isabel Grandin *(Evelyn)*, Ernest Graves *(Warner)*, Shane Rimmer *(Dr. Oaks)*, Victoria Tennant

Based on the gripping Frederick Forsyth novel, THE DOGS OF WAR is a slickly made actioner about a cold-blooded mercenary whose political conscience is heightened somewhat by a particularly nasty little war in Africa. The story centers on Shannon (Christopher Walken), an American soldier of fortune who, in the exciting opening scene, is shown with some of his mercenary buddies, fighting to catch the last plane out of a war-torn country. Looking for more work, Shannon accepts a job from a powerful American businessman (Hugh Millais)—to overthrow a small government in Africa. To prepare for the coup, Shannon visits the country in the guise of a nature photographer. The government, however, becomes suspicious and throws him in jail. Between torture sessions, Shannon meets an imprisoned dissident political leader, from whom he learns more about the country's political struggles. Eventually Shannon is deported, but he returns with a group of mercenaries and, with some Africans hired by his employer, makes an impressive raid on a military outpost that is also the headquarters of the country's dictator. While competently directed by John Irvin, who knows how to deliver a well-crafted action film (RAW DEAL; HAMBURGER HILL), THE DOGS OF WAR suffers from a lack of character development that may leave some viewers cold. No new light is shed on those men who choose to be soldiers of fortune in this exceedingly well-shot (by Jack Cardiff) action film that will evaporate from memory shortly after the end credits roll.

p, Larry DeWaay; d, John Irvin; w, Gary DeVore and George Malko, based on the novel by Frederick Forsyth; ed, Antony Gibbs; ph, Jack Cardiff, Technicolor; m, Geoffrey Burgon.

(PR:O MPAA:R)

DON'T CRY, IT'S ONLY THUNDER***
(1982) 108m Sanrio Communications c

Dennis Christopher *(Brian)*, Susan Saint James *(Katherine)*, Roger Aaron Brown *(Moses)*, Robert Englund *(Tripper)*, James Whitmore, Jr. *(Maj. Flaherty)*, Lisa Lu *(Sr. Marie)*, Thu Thuy *(Sr. Hoa)*, Travis Swords *(Allen)*.

An honest, unfairly overlooked film, DON'T CRY, IT'S ONLY THUNDER concerns Brian, a cynical, drug-dealing medic in Vietnam who spends all his time trying to turn a profit. He meets Army doctor Katherine (Susan Saint James), who tries to get him to assist a group of Vietnamese war orphans, first through guilt and then through blackmail. They are opposed in their efforts, not only by the US government, but also by the constant bombardment of enemy shells. The film gets a bit too dramatic at points, but refuses to reduce its complex situation to easy answers or a tidy denouement. This is one of a handful of movies Dennis Christopher appeared in after his fine performance in BREAKING AWAY; in a supporting role is Robert Englund, who would later find fame as Freddy Krueger in the "Nightmare on Elm Street" films.

p, Walt deFarla; d, Peter Werner; w, Paul Hensler; ed, Jack Woods and Barbara Pokras; ph, Don McAlpine, Deluxe Color; m, Maurice Jarre.

(PR:O MPAA:PG)

DRAGON SEED***
(1944) 145m MGM bw

Katharine Hepburn *(Jade)*, Walter Huston *(Ling Tan)*, Aline MacMahon *(Mrs. Ling Tan)*, Akim Tamiroff *(Wu Lien)*, Turhan Bey *(Lao Er)*, Hurd Hatfield *(Lao San)*, Frances Rafferty *(Orchid)*, Agnes Moorehead *(3rd Cousin's Wife)*, Henry Travers *(3rd Cousin)*, Robert Lewis *(Capt. Sato)*, J. Carrol Naish *(Kitchen Overseer)*, Jacqueline De Wit *(Mrs. Wu Lien)*, Anna Demetrio *(Wu Soo)*, Ted Hecht *(Maj. Yohagi)*, Abner Biberman *(Capt. Yasuda)*, Benson Fong *(Student)*, Lionel Barrymore *(Narrator)*.

A strong cast (with taped eyelids) render good performances in this lengthy film, which is based on Pearl Buck's best-seller about the wartime atrocities leveled by the Japanese against the Chinese. Jade (Katharine Hepburn) is the aggressive and idealistic wife of Lao Er (Turhan Bey) whose practical outlook and aggressive behavior confuse her husband. Fearing imminent Japanese invasion, Jade persuades her husband to escape to the mountains to work in a munitions factory, although her father-in-law, Ling Tan (Walter Huston), refuses to believe that the Japanese will attack. En route they stay with Ling Tan's son-in-law, Wu Lien (Akim Tamiroff), a well-to-do merchant who slavishly collaborates with local Japanese troops. When Jade learns that Wu Lien is preparing a banquet for Japanese officers, she poisons the food; as a result, Wu Lien is executed. Jade and Lao Er later return to find Ling Tan's farm looted and the old man's opinion of the Japanese drastically changed. Together with his neighbors, Ling Tan organizes a revolt to prevent the Japanese from further humiliating his people. DRAGON SEED dramatizes the plight of the Chinese farmer in sensitive and human terms. As was fashionable in post-Pearl Harbor wartime Hollywood, the filmmakers carefully funneled their patriotic audience's hatred of the Japanese into the storyline. At a time in American history when all were lumped together, this film at least made the effort to differentiate between two very dissimilar nations.

p, Pandro S. Berman; d, Jack Conway and Harold S. Bucquet; w, Marguerite Roberts and Jane Murfin, based on the novel by Pearl S. Buck; ed, Harold F. Kress; ph, Sidney Wagner; m, Herbert Stothart.

(PR:A MPAA:NR)

DRAGONFLY SQUADRON*½
(1953) 82m AA bw

John Hodiak (Maj. Mathew Brady), Barbara Britton (Donna Cottrell), Bruce Bennett [Herman Brix] (Dr. Cottrell), Jess Barker (Dixon), Gerald Mohr (Capt. MacIntyre), Chuck Connors (Capt. Warnowski), Harry Lauter (Capt. Vedders), Pamela Duncan (Anne Taylor), Adam Williams (Capt. Wyler), John Lupton (Capt. Taylor), Benson Fong (Capt. Liehtse), John Hedloe (Capt. Wycoff), Fess Parker (Texas Lieutenant).

Mathew Brady (John Hodiak), a major in the USAF, is stationed in South Korea, trying to get the local air force ready for battle. While he pushes the Korean airmen at a sadistic pace, he finds time to continue the romance he and Donna Cottrell (Barbara Britton) began in Hawaii, until Donna's husband, who she thought was dead, turns up alive and complicates matters. When the North Koreans attack with tanks, the aerial squadron predictably wipes them out. The story line and cliched characters have been worn to shreds by previous use in countless other, better war entries.

p, John Champion; d, Lesley Selander; w, John Champion; ed, Walter Hannemann; ph, Harry Neumann.

(PR:A MPAA:NR)

DRUMS****
(1938, Brit.) 96m LFP-Korda/UA c (GB: DRUM, THE)

Sabu (Prince Azim), Raymond Massey (Prince Ghul), Valerie Hobson (Mrs. Carruthers), Roger Livesey (Capt. Carruthers), Desmond Tester (Bill Holder), Martin Walker (Herrick), David Tree (Lt. Escott), Francis L. Sullivan (Governor), Roy Emerton (Wafadar), Edward Lexy (Sgt. Maj. Kernel).

Set in northwest India at the height of the British presence there, DRUMS finds the treacherous Indian Prince Ghul (Raymond Massey) usurping his brother's kingdom by murdering his sibling and forcing his nephew and the heir apparent, Prince Azim (Sabu), into hiding. The boy finds refuge at the British garrison, whose commander, Capt. Carruthers (Roger Livesey), and his wife (Valerie Hobson) treat him with kindness. Azim learns the regulations of the British Army and how to beat military cadence on a drum, a skill he uses later to warn the garrison that it is about to be attacked by Ghul and his evil followers. The spectacle is excellent, the direction and beautiful color cinematography superb. Sabu is wonderful as the innocent, wide-eyed royal youth, a role that earned him 100 fan letters a day, and Livesey is a great match for the wily Massey, who seems not to have a decent bone in his body.

p, Alexander Korda; d, Zoltan Korda; w, Arthur Wimperis, Patric Kirwan, and Hugh Gray, based on Lajos Biro's adaptation of the novel by A.E.W. Mason; ed, William Hornbeck and Henry Cornelius; ph, Georges Perinal, Osmond Borradaile, Robert Krasker, Christopher Challis, and Geoffrey Unsworth, Technicolor; m, John Greenwood and Miklos Rozsa.

(PR:A MPAA:NR)

DRUMS ALONG THE MOHAWK*****
(1939) 103m FOX c

Claudette Colbert (Lana "Magdelena" Martin), Henry Fonda (Gil Martin), Edna May Oliver (Mrs. Sarah McKlennar), Eddie Collins (Christian Reall), John Carradine (Caldwell), Dorris Bowdon (Mary Reall), Jessie Ralph (Mrs. Weaver), Arthur Shields (Rev. Rosenkrantz), Robert Lowery (John Weaver), Roger Imhof (Gen. Nicholas Herkimer), Francis Ford (Joe Boleo), Ward Bond (Adam Helmer), Kay Linaker (Mrs. DeMooth), Russell Simpson (Dr. Petry), Si Jenks (Jacob Small), Jack Pennick (Amos Hartman), Chief Big Tree (Blue Back), Mae Mars (Pioneer).

This richly directed and acted colonial epic concerns Gil (Henry Fonda) and Lana (Claudette Colbert) Martin, young newlyweds starting out on the frontier of the Mohawk Valley just before the outbreak of the Revolutionary War. The transition from a life of privilege to that of the rugged frontier is difficult, especially for Lana. To help fend off Indian attacks engineered by the British, Gil joins the militia and goes off to fight; finally, after many battles and hardships, the future of the new Americans begins to look bright. This historical chronicle directed by John Ford is made believable through its attention to small details, presenting a mosaic of frontier life. One of Ford's biggest problems in making the spectacular film was the unavailability of necessary props and costumes; Fox had not specialized in costume or historical films, particularly those with 18th-century settings, and almost everything had to be made from scratch at great cost. The ancient flintlock muskets brandished by scores of extras were the real weapons of the era, however, not reproductions. A Fox prop man chased the flintlocks down in Ethiopia—where they had actually seen combat in the mid-1930s, when they were used by Ethiopian soldiers against Mussolini's armies. This was Ford's first color film and he made the most of it, his cameras recording the lush forests and valleys of northern Utah. So rich and verdant is the color in this film that it later provided stock footage for several Fox productions, including BUFFALO BILL (1944) and MOHAWK (1956).

p, Raymond Griffith; d, John Ford; w, Lamar Trotti and Sonya Levien, based on the novel by Walter D. Edmonds; ed, Robert Simpson; ph, Bert Glennon and Ray Rennahan, Technicolor; m, Alfred Newman.

(PR:AAA MPAA:NR)

DRUMS IN THE DEEP SOUTH***

(1951) 87m RKO c

James Craig (Clay), Barbara Payton (Kathy), Guy Madison (Will Denning), Barton MacLane (McCardle), Craig Stevens (Braxton Summers), Tom Fadden (Purdy), Robert Osterloh (Harper), Taylor Holmes (Albert Monroe), Robert Easton (Jerry), Lewis Martin (Gen. Johnston), Peter Brocco (Union Corporal), Dan White (Cpl. Jennings), Louis Jean Heydt (Col. House).

This above-average Civil War drama, with unusual twists provided by talented director-production designer William Cameron Menzies, follows cadets Clay (James Craig), Will (Guy Madison), and Braxton (Craig Stevens) as they graduate from West Point and later meet in Atlanta just before shots are fired at Fort Sumter. Will fights for the North, Clay and Braxton for the South, and they meet again three years later when Sherman makes his march to the sea through Georgia. The Union advance is halted by a mountaintop battery, manned by Clay and 20 Confederate soldiers, while on a nearby plantation, Clay's wife, Kathy (Barbara Payton), spies on the Yankees, including Will, and delivers information to her husband. Espionage, romance, and battle action are combined to produce a unique and exciting picture, and Menzies, who had won an Oscar for art direction for GONE WITH THE WIND, does a fine job in bringing it all together.

p, Maurice King and Frank King; d, William Cameron Menzies; w, Philip Yordan and Sidney Harmon, based on a story by Hollister Noble; ed, Richard Heermance; ph, Lionel Linden, Supercinecolor; m, Dimitri Tiomkin.

(PR:A MPAA:NR)

DUCK SOUP****

(1933) 70m PAR bw

Groucho Marx (Rufus T. Firefly), Chico Marx (Chicolini), Harpo Marx (Brownie), Zeppo Marx (Bob Rolland), Raquel Torres (Vera Marcal), Louis Calhern (Ambassador Trentino), Margaret Dumont (Mrs. Teasdale), Verna Hillie (Secretary), Leonid Kinskey (Agitator), Edmund Breese (Zander), Edwin Maxwell (Secretary of War).

Fast-moving, irreverent, almost anarchistic in style, DUCK SOUP is considered by many to be the Marx Brothers' greatest achievement. The story, if one can call it that, concerns Mrs. Teasdale (Margaret Dumont), a dowager millionairess who will donate $20 million to the destitute duchy of Freedonia if it will agree to make Rufus T. Firefly (Groucho) its dictator. Firefly woos Mrs. Teasdale and spends his spare time insulting Trentino (Louis Calhern), the ambassador from neighboring Sylvania; Trentino hires the sultry Vera Marcal (Raquel Torres) to vamp Firefly so that Trentino can move in on Mrs. Teasdale, marry her, and get control of Freedonia. To aid his chicanery, Trentino hires Chicolini (Chico), a peanut salesman, and his friend Brownie (Harpo) as spies. Eventually war breaks out and, after much manic double-crossing and side-switching, Freedonia emerges victorious. Perhaps the best, and funniest, depiction of the absurdities of war ever committed to celluloid, DUCK SOUP today remains a masterpiece of film comedy. The Marxes' depiction of two-bit dictators destroying their own countries was a slap at the rising fascists, so much so that Mussolini considered it a direct insult and banned the film in Italy. Naturally, the Marx Brothers were thrilled to hear that.

p, Herman Mankiewicz; d, Leo McCarey; w, Bert Kalmar, Harry Ruby, Arthur Sheekman, and Nat Perrin; ed, LeRoy Stone; ph, Henry Sharpe.

(PR:AA MPAA:NR)

DUELLISTS, THE***

(1977, Brit.) 95m PAR c

Keith Carradine (D'Hubert), Harvey Keitel (Feraud), Albert Finney (Fouche), Edward Fox (Col. Reynard), Cristina Raines (Adele), Robert Stephens (Gen. Treillard), Tom Conti (Jacquin), Diana Quick (Laura), Alun Armstrong (Lacourbe).

The feature debut of director Ridley Scott, who would go on to make the popular science-fiction films ALIEN and BLADE RUNNER, THE DUELLISTS is a beautifully photographed adaptation of a Joseph Conrad story in which two officers in Napoleon's army, D'Hubert (Keith Carradine) and Feraud (Harvey Keitel), fall out and proceed to engage in an obsessive series of duels for the next 30 years. While there really isn't much of a story, the film is a sumptuous visual feast in which the Napoleonic Wars are merely the backdrop to the duellists' insane obsession with military codes of conduct and personal honor. Pretty pictures alone do not a good film make, but the remarkable performances of Keitel, as the more deranged of the duellists, and Carradine, as the fairly rational officer who is pushed almost to the point of abandoning his principles by his rival's persistence, add another level of interest to this basically monotonous tale. Scott is a problematic filmmaker: his choice of subject matter and eye for casting are always compelling, but his rather slick stylistic approach seems more imposed on the material than derived from it. Nevertheless, his films are not without interest and deserve some attention.

p, David Puttnam; d, Ridley Scott; w, Gerald Vaughn-Hughes, based on the story "The Duel" [or "The Point of Honour"] by Joseph Conrad; ed, Pamela Powers; ph, Frank Tidy; m, Howard Blake.

(PR:C MPAA:PG)

E

EAGLE HAS LANDED, THE***

(1976, Brit.) 123m ITC Ent.-Assoc. General Films-Filmways Australasian/COL c

Michael Caine (Col. Kurt Steiner), Donald Sutherland (Liam

Devlin), Robert Duvall (Col. Max Radl), Jenny Agutter (Molly Prior), Donald Pleasence (Heinrich Himmler), Anthony Quayle (Adm. Wilhelm Canaris), Jean Marsh (Joanna Grey), Sven Bertil Taube (Capt. Ritter Neumann), John Standing (Fr. Philip Verecker), Judy Geeson (Pamela Verecker), Treat Williams (Capt. Harry Clark), Larry Hagman (Col. Clarence E. Pitts), Siegfried Rauch (Sgt. Brandt), John Barrett (Laker Armsby), Leigh Dilley (Winston Churchill/George Foster).

Silly but exciting, this WW II espionage drama concerns a German colonel, Max Radl (Robert Duvall), who, under direct orders from Heinrich Himmler (Donald Pleasence), plots to kidnap Winston Churchill. To do this, Radl hires an Irishman, Liam Devlin (Donald Sutherland), who holds a grudge against the English. Together with a 16-man task force led by Col. Kurt Steiner (Michael Caine), Devlin parachutes into England and receives the secret information he needs to set the plan in motion. Matters are complicated, however, when Devlin falls in love with local girl Molly Prior (Jenny Agutter). It's all a great deal of fun, especially if one doesn't mind suspending disbelief for a couple of hours. Anyone with even the slightest knowledge of history knows that Churchill was never kidnaped, which destroys much of the film's suspense. Director John Sturges, however, is an excellent craftsman and, with the help of a very good cast, manages to make the proceedings entertaining.

p, Jack Winer and David Niven, Jr.; d, John Sturges; w, Tom Mankiewicz, based on a novel by Jack Higgins; ed, Irene Lamb and Anne V. Coates; ph, Tony Richmond and Peter Allwork, Panavision, Eastmancolor; m, Lalo Schifrin.

(PR:C MPAA:PG)

EDGE OF DARKNESS***½

(1943) 120m WB bw

Errol Flynn (Gunnar Brogge), Ann Sheridan (Karen Stensgard), Walter Huston (Dr. Martin Stensgard), Nancy Coleman (Katja), Helmut Dantine (Capt. Koenig), Judith Anderson (Gerd Bjarnesen), Ruth Gordon (Anna Stensgard), John Beal (Johann Stensgard), Morris Carnovsky (Sixtus Andresen), Charles Dingle (Kaspar Torgerson), Roman Bohnen (Lars Malken), Richard Fraser (Pastor Aalesen), Art Smith (Knut Osterholm), Tom Fadden (Hammer), Henry Brandon (Maj. Ruck), Tonio Selwart (Paul), Helene Thimig (Frida), Frank Wilcox (Jensen).

A WW II German patrol boat sails into a Norwegian port to discover that the whole German occupation force and the citizens of the town lie dead, apparently killed in a bloody battle that ended with the Norwegian flag flying over the invaders' garrison. In flashback, we see the events leading up to the slaughter. Gunnar Brogge (Errol Flynn) is a Norwegian fisherman who leads the local underground movement; Karen Stensgard (Ann Sheridan) is his brave and loyal fiancee; Gerd Bjarnesen (Judith Anderson) is a fiery innkeeper who becomes enraged when Nazis murder her husband; and Dr. Martin Stensgard (Walter Huston) is a highly respected man who hesitates to join the resistance movement. The brave Karen is his daughter, but his wife, Anna (Ruth Gordon), is a shy, frightened woman, and his son, Johann (John Beal), is a collaborator. All of this goes on under the watchful eye of Koenig (Helmut Dantine), the brutal German captain determined to retain control of the town. The underground continues on a course of passive resistance until it is finally forced into a violent rebellion, aided by British fighters. An insightful look at the mechanics of a resistance movement, EDGE OF DARKNESS calls to mind Jean Renoir's superior picture THIS LAND IS MINE, released the same year. See also COMMANDOS STRIKE AT DAWN, which takes place in occupied Norway.

p, Henry Blanke; d, Lewis Milestone; w, Robert Rossen, based on the novel by William Woods; ed, David Weisbart; ph, Sid Hickox; m, Franz Waxman.

(PR:A MPAA:NR)

84 CHARLIE MOPIC****

(1989) 95m Charlie Mopic/New Century-Vista c

Jonathan Emerson (LT), Nicholas Cascone (Easy), Jason Tomlins (Pretty Boy), Christopher Burgard (Hammer), Glenn Morshower (Cracker), Richard Brooks (OD), Byron Thames (Mopic), Russ Thurman, Joseph Hieu, Don Schiff

Another attempt to convey the harsh experiences of men in battle without moralizing on the cause of the conflict, 84 CHARLIE MOPIC presents a single reconnaissance mission performed by a six-man team as seen through the eyes of an Army Motion Picture (MoPic) Unit cameraman given the task of filming a documentary to be shown to recruits during their training so they will know what to expect from combat. Shot entirely in hand-held documentary style (an experiment tried before in the Vietnam segment of the now-forgotten MORE AMERICAN GRAFFITI, 1979), the film follows a close-knit group of soldiers led by a taciturn black sergeant (Richard Brooks) as they "hump" through the brush in the Central Highlands of Vietnam. After years of trying to convince producers that a Vietnam film could be made *without* a cast of brat packers or a nonstop rock'n'roll soundtrack, writer-director Patrick Duncan, a Vietnam veteran who served as an infantryman for 13 months during 1968-69, finally landed a $1 million budget—minuscule by Hollywood standards—and shot the film in the hills outside Los Angeles using Super 16mm film stock, which was later blown up to 35mm for theatrical release. The gimmick here—an entire movie seen through the eyes of an Army cameraman—works better than it has any right to. While other mainstream movies have occasionally experimented with extensive use of a subjective camera—most notably in Robert Montgomery's THE LADY IN THE LAKE (1947)—the trick usually comes off as forced, stilted, annoying, or simply silly. In 84 CHARLIE MOPIC, however, the device works because Duncan creates a viable, realistic situation for its use. This method is fraught with peril for both director and actors, but when it works the sense of realism—characters seemingly caught off-guard, meaningful glances or muffled comments captured—lends an air of spontaneity and excitement to familiar material. While some may find the first half of the film boring, 84 CHARLIE MOPIC presents a fascinating and

EL CID—

detailed account of what common infantrymen faced on a daily basis. From jungle rot to booby traps to burying chewing gum wrappers so the enemy won't find them, the film offers a wealth of heretofore unseen details of the life of a foot-soldier in Vietnam. As a result, Duncan establishes a sense of intimacy with his soldiers that few other war films have achieved. Indeed, the most effective passages of the film come when soldiers are killed and we watch as the emotional sergeant carefully prepares their bodies for transport out of the jungle. Just when it appeared that the Vietnam film had become a cliche or, worse yet, a vehicle for jingoistic fantasies, 84 CHARLIE MOPIC came along to remind us of the reality and tremendous cost of war.

p, Michael Nolin and Jill Griffith; d, Patrick Duncan; w, Patrick Duncan; ed, Stephen Purvis; ph, Alan Caso, Duart color; m, Donovan.

(PR:O MPAA:R)

EL CID***½

(1961, US/It.) 180m Bronston-Rank/AA c

Sophia Loren *(Chimene)*, Charlton Heston *(Rodrigo Diaz de Bivar/El Cid)*, John Fraser *(King Alfonso)*, Raf Vallone *(Count Ordonez)*, Genevieve Page *(Queen Urraca)*, Gary Raymond *(King Sancho)*, Herbert Lom *(Ben Yussef)*, Massimo Serato *(Fanez)*, Douglas Wilmer *(Moutamin)*, Frank Thring *(Al Kadir)*, Hurd Hatfield *(Count Arias)*.

After making several superb westerns featuring Jimmy Stewart (WINCHESTER 73; BEND OF THE RIVER; THE NAKED SPUR; THE FAR COUNTRY; THE MAN FROM LARAMIE) marked by their psychological force and powerful use of landscape, director Anthony Mann graduated into the realm of big-budget historical epic filmmaking, of which EL CID is his first and finest attempt. Impressively mounted by producer Samuel Bronston, the film recounts the legendary exploits of 11th-century Spain's heroic Rodrigo Diaz de Bivar (Charlton Heston), dubbed El Cid (The Lord) because of his nobility, courage, and spirituality. Chimene (Sophia Loren), his fiancee, is estranged from him early on, after he kills her father (Andrew Cruickshank), who has unjustly accused the knight of treason at court. El Cid and Chimene are married, but never enjoy a wedding night; she plots against him and, when her intrigues come to naught, enters a convent. Upon the death of King Ferdinand (Ralph Truman), Spain—which is continually besieged by the Islamic Moors—is further divided by the deceased ruler's warring offspring. Meanwhile, Chimene realizes that her husband is an honorable man and they reconcile, eventually having children. The family retreats to a monastery while El Cid lays siege to Valencia, the last outpost of the Moorish usurpers. The spectacle and grandeur of 11th-century Spain are fully on display here; the photography by Robert Krasker is spectacular, as are the battle scenes, filmed with the help of veteran stuntman Yakima Canutt as second-unit director. Canutt staged the siege of Valencia brilliantly, employing the ancient walled city of Pensacola, 5,000 Spanish army troops, and a Moorish battle fleet of 35 perfectly reconstructed lifesize ships. Bronston spent untold millions on EL CID, including $150,000 for medieval art objects and $40,000 for jewelry. When the production was not allowed to shoot at the site of an ancient cathedral at Burgos, he ordered an exact reproduction built on the back lot of Sevilla studios in Madrid. While the film is impressive visually, director Mann's trademark exploration of the psychologically torn hero is almost nonexistent due to the immense size of the production and the legendary stature of El Cid. Moreover, Heston is no Jimmy Stewart, and is simply incapable of conveying anything remotely resembling vulnerability or moral doubt. Nonetheless, Mann does ponder the nature of national heroes and the way events conspire to force them to become infallible, invincible beings—especially in the film's remarkable climax, when El Cid's stiffening corpse is strapped to a horse and sent out to lead the final charge.

p, Samuel Bronston and Anthony Mann; d, Anthony Mann; w, Philip Yordan and Fredric M. Frank; ed, Robert Lawrence; ph, Robert Krasker, Super Technirama, Technicolor; m, Miklos Rozsa.

(PR:A MPAA:NR)

ELENI**

(1985) 114m CBS/WB c

Kate Nelligan *(Eleni)*, John Malkovich *(Nick)*, Linda Hunt *(Katina)*, Oliver Cotton *(Katis)*, Ronald Pickup *(Spiro)*, Rosalie Crutchley *(Grandmother)*, Glenne Headly *(Joan)*, Dimitra Arliss *(Ana)*, Steve Plytas *(Christos)*, Peter Woodthorpe *(Grandfather)*, John Rumney *(Lukas)*, Alison King *(Lukas' Wife)*, Leon Lissek *(Antoni)*.

Based on Nicholas Gage's much-respected, best-selling nonfiction book, this powerful film follows journalist Gage (well played by John Malkovich) as he uses his assignment as the head of the *New York Times'* Athens bureau to investigate his mother's execution during the Greek Civil War. Alternating between Gage's present-day pursuit of the facts, including his return to the small Greek village that he fled as a nine-year-old, and a flashback re-creation of the turmoil that gripped the village during the war, the film slowly peels away the truth of the death of his mother, Eleni (Kate Nelligan, under seemingly layers of makeup). When it becomes clear that the Communists who have taken control of the village are going to send the children off to "safety" in Eastern Europe, Eleni helps organize a mass escape, but coincidence prevents her from joining her children's flight to rejoin their father in the US. She is then convicted by a kangaroo court and sentenced to death by Katis (Oliver Cotton), a brutal rebel leader whom Gage eventually confronts and nearly kills. Though some critics felt that Peter Yates' film failed to convey the intensity of Gage's book, ELENI is nonetheless intriguing, carefully paced, and full of moments of high drama, well acted by Malkovich, Nelligan, and Linda Hunt (THE YEAR OF LIVING DANGEROUSLY) as Eleni's friend.

p, Nick Vanoff, Mark Pick, and Nicholas Gage; d, Peter Yates; w, Steve Tesich, based on the book by Nicholas

Gage; ed, Raymond Lovejoy; ph, Billy Williams; m, Bruce Smeaton.

(PR:A-C MPAA:PG)

ELUSIVE CORPORAL, THE***

(1963, Fr.) 108m Films du Cyclope/Pathe Cinema-Union bw (LE CAPORAL EPINGLE)

Jean-Pierre Cassel *(The Corporal)*, Claude Brasseur *(Pater)*, Claude Rich *(Ballochet)*, Jean Carmet *(Emile)*, Mario David *(Caruso)*, Philippe Castelli *(Electrician)*, Jacques Jouanneau *(Penche-a-Gauche)*, Conny Froboess *(Erika)*, Raymond Jourdan *(Dupieu)*.

Where Jean Renoir's THE GRAND ILLUSION addressed life in POW camps during WW I, this effortlessly crafted (or so it appears) Renoir tale takes place during WW II, after the fall of France. The Corporal (Jean-Pierre Cassel) and two friends, Pater and Ballochet (Claude Brasseur and Claude Rich), try repeatedly to escape from their prison, but each time their efforts prove fruitless. They are separated but, in time, reunited, only to continue their attempts to gain freedom, although it is not long before they realize that there is no liberty and that the prison walls are not the only ones confining them. Not by accident was this Renoir's first black-and-white film in over a decade. In filming thus, Renoir draws a connection both to his past as a filmmaker and to Paris' past—emphasizing the senseless repetition of war and the timeless universality of man's fight for liberty. (In French; English subtitles.)

p, Rene G. Vuattoux; d, Jean Renoir; w, Jean Renoir and Guy Lefranc, based on a novel by Jacques Perret; ed, Renee Lichtig; ph, Georges Leclerc; m, Joseph Kosma.

(PR:A MPAA:NR)

EMPIRE OF THE SUN****

(1987) 152m Amblin Ent./WB c

Christian Bale *(Jim Graham)*, John Malkovich *(Basie)*, Miranda Richardson *(Mrs. Victor)*, Nigel Havers *(Dr. Rawlins)*, Joe Pantoliano *(Frank Demerest)*, Leslie Phillips *(Maxton)*, Masato Ibu *(Sgt. Nagata)*, Emily Richard *(Jim's Mother)*, Rupert Frazer *(Jim's Father)*, Peter Gale *(Mr. Victor)*, Takatoro Kataoka *(Kamikaze Boy Pilot)*, Ben Stiller *(Dainty)*, David Neidorf *(Tiptree)*, Ralph Seymour *(Cohen)*, Robert Stephens *(Mr. Lockwood)*, Guts Ishimatsu *(Sgt. Uchida)*, J.G. Ballard *(Guest at Costume Party)*.

The most emotionally complex film of Steven Spielberg's career, this adaptation of J.G. Ballard's 1984 quasi-autobiographical novel witnesses WW II through an adolescent's eyes, and does so almost entirely through a visual storytelling more akin to silent than to modern filmmaking. Spielberg's vision is no longer one of innocent wonderment; instead, the film concerns the end of innocence—a young boy thrown into adulthood and an entire generation thrown into an atomic age. The film opens in the 1940s just before the Japanese attack on Pearl Harbor. Jim Graham (Christian Bale) is a nine-year-old English brat who has lived all his life in Shanghai with his aristocratic parents. Although adventurous, he is also wholly dependent on his parents and servants. Later, as the Japanese conquer Shanghai and the war intensifies, he is separated from his parents and meets Basie (John Malkovich), an opportunistic merchant seaman reminiscent of Dickens' Fagin who somewhat reluctantly takes Jim under his wing and teaches him the most Darwinian methods of survival—lessons that help Jim survive a lengthy stay in a Japanese prison camp. Surprisingly, EMPIRE OF THE SUN, with its $35 million budget, is not a traditional Hollywood blockbuster. In fact, it breaks Hollywood's rules with its unknown lead, barely known supporting cast, and near-plotlessness. Further, Spielberg adapts a little-read novel, set it in far-off Shanghai, and makes his lead character a Briton who idolizes the Japanese. It should come as no surprise, then, that EMPIRE OF THE SUN grossed little at the box office compared to the usual tallies for Spielberg-directed films. Originally the film was conceived as a project for the master of the epic genre, David Lean, with Spielberg serving as producer.

p, Steven Spielberg, Kathleen Kennedy, and Frank Marshall; d, Steven Spielberg; w, Tom Stoppard and (uncredited) Menno Meyjes, (based on the novel by J.G. Ballard); ed, Michael Kahn; ph, Allen Daviau, Technicolor; m, John Williams.

(PR:A MPAA:PG)

ENSIGN PULVER**

(1964) 104m WB c

Robert Walker, Jr. *(Ens. Pulver)*, Burl Ives *(Captain)*, Walter Matthau *(Doc)*, Tommy Sands *(Bruno)*, Millie Perkins *(Scotty)*, Kay Medford *(Head Nurse)*, Larry Hagman *(Billings)*, Gerald S. O'Loughlin *(LaSueur)*, Sal Papa *(Gabrowski)*, Al Freeman, Jr. *(Taru)*, James Farentino *(Insigna)*, James Coco *(Skouras)*, Peter L. Marshall *(Carney)*, Jack Nicholson *(Dolan)*.

Robert Walker, Jr. takes the title Jack Lemmon role in this lame sequel to MISTER ROBERTS. The USS *Reluctant* roams the South Pacific in the waning days of World War II, dropping cargo at obscure island bases. The ship is ruled over by a tyrannical captain (played by the unlikely Burl Ives), and most of the comedy revolves around his excesses and the men's dissatisfaction. Pulver entertains ambitions of becoming a medical man and the ship's doctor (Walter Matthau) is his mentor. When a storm washes the captain overboard, Pulver goes out to rescue him, but it's not until morning that they are missed, and the pair drift in a rubber raft until they wash up on an island. There, the captain gets an attack of appendicitis and Pulver has to operate, getting his instructions over the radio from Doc back on the ship. Vastly inferior to its predecessor and terribly contrived, ENSIGN PULVER suffers most from its casting, with Walker no Lemmon and Ives no James Cagney. The best reason to see the film is to catch a number of future stars (Larry Hagman, James Farentino, James Coco, Jack Nicholson, et al.) at the beginning of their careers.

p, Joshua Logan; d, Joshua Logan; w, Joshua Logan and

ESCAPE TO ATHENA—

Peter S. Feibleman, based on characters in a play by Joshua Logan and Thomas Heggen and the novel by Heggen; ed, William Reynolds; ph, Charles Lawton, Panavision, Technicolor; m, George Duning.

(PR:A   MPAA:NR)

ESCAPE TO ATHENA**

(1979, Brit.) 125m Grade/Associated Film Dist. c

Roger Moore *(Maj. Otto Hecht)*, Telly Savalas *(Zeno)*, David Niven *(Prof. Blake)*, Claudia Cardinale *(Eleana)*, Richard Roundtree *(Nat)*, Stefanie Powers *(Dottie)*, Sonny Bono *(Rotelli)*, Elliott Gould *(Charlie)*, Anthony Valentine *(Volkmann)*.

Before director George Pan Cosmatos graced us with his RAMBO: FIRST BLOOD PART II, he collected a bunch of big name actors to appear in this lame WW II escape adventure. With a cast list that reads more like a "Love Boat" episode than a film, the story follows a group of inmates in a Greek POW camp run by Maj. Otto Hecht (Roger Moore), a good-guy German who helps the movie stars/POWs escape. They hitch up with a partisan group led by Zeno (Telly Savalas) and attempt to save some ancient Greek treasures from the Nazis. If nothing else, ESCAPE TO ATHENA has a certain—unintentional—camp value.

p, David Niven, Jr. and Jack Wiener; d, George Pan Cosmatos; w, Richard S. Lochte and Edward Anhalt, based on a story by Richard S. Lochte, George Pan Cosmatos; ed, Ralph Kemplen; ph, Gil Taylor, Panavision, Eastmancolor; m, Lalo Schifrin.

(PR:C   MPAA:PG)

EVERY TIME WE SAY GOODBYE***

(1986) 95m Tri-Star c

Tom Hanks *(David)*, Cristina Marsillach *(Sarah)*, Benedict Taylor *(Peter)*, Anat Atzmon *(Victoria)*, Gila Almagor *(Lea)*, Moni Moshanov *(Nessin)*.

It is 1942, and David (Tom Hanks), an American flier serving with the British Royal Air Force, is in Jerusalem, where he is recuperating from an injury. His squadron leader is about to marry, and David falls in love with Sarah (Cristina Marsillach), best friend of the bride-to-be. Though Sarah is initially hesitant, their romance blossoms, much to the dismay of her family, Sephardic Jews who strongly disapprove of David, the son of a Christian minister. Finally, in an outlandish attempt at extracting obedience from their daughter, Sarah's parents hold her captive in her room. Hanks, as usual, is extremely likable in this well-written romantic role for the comic actor, his performance giving an extra spark to the otherwise routine Romeo and Juliet story. Marsillach, a Spanish actress who has found more success in Europe than in the States, stars here in her first American picture. Director Moshe Mizrahi (best known for his 1977 Oscar-winning feature, MADAME ROSA) doesn't really capitalize on the film's time and place, other than to make a few token statements about British colonial rule.

p, Jacob Kotzky and Sharon Harel; d, Moshe Mizrahi; w, Moshe Mizrahi, Rachel Fabien, and Leah Appet, based on a story by Mizrahi; ed, Mark Burns; ph, Giuseppe Lanci; m, Philippe Sarde.

(PR:C   MPAA:PG-13)

EYE OF THE NEEDLE***½

(1981, Brit.) 111m Kings Road/UA c

Donald Sutherland *(Faber)*, Stephen MacKenna *(Lieutenant)*, Philip Martin Brown *(Billy Parkin)*, Kate Nelligan *(Lucy)*, Christopher Cazenove *(David)*, George Belbin *(Lucy's Father)*, Faith Brook *(Lucy's Mother)*, Barbara Graley *(Constable)*, Arthur Lovegrove *(Peterson)*, Colin Rix *(Oliphant)*, Barbara Ewing *(Mrs. Garden)*, Chris Jenkinson *(German SS Officer)*, William Merrow *(German Radio Operator)*, Patrick Connor *(Inspector Harris)*, David Hayman *(Canter)*, Ian Bannen *(Godliman)*.

A gripping, old-fashioned, WW II spy thriller, EYE OF THE NEEDLE features Donald Sutherland as Faber, a murderous Nazi spy stationed in Britain who uncovers the Allies' plans to invade Normandy. En route to a rendezvous with a U-boat at a remote island, Faber is stranded by a violent storm and forced to seek shelter with Lucy (Kate Nelligan), a sexually frustrated housewife, and her husband, a paraplegic ex-fighter pilot (Christopher Cazenove). Romance soon develops between Lucy and the spy, but Lucy's husband begins to suspect Faber's true identity. Directed with considerable flair by Richard Marquand, this adaptation of Ken Follett's best-selling novel boasts one of Sutherland's best performances. As the cold-blooded spy who thinks nothing of plunging a stiletto into anyone who gets in his way, he is positively chilling. Nelligan, a fine actress who has yet to find the screen success that she deserves, is excellent as well. Underrated at the time it was released, EYE OF THE NEEDLE is worthy viewing for anyone fond of classic Hollywood wartime thrillers.

p, Stephen Friedman; d, Richard Marquand; w, Stanley Mann, based on the novel by Ken Follett; ed, Sean Barton; ph, Alan Hume, Technicolor; m, Miklos Rozsa.

(PR:C-O   MPAA:R)

F

FAIL SAFE***

(1964) 111m COL bw

Dan O'Herlihy *(Gen. Black)*, Walter Matthau *(Groeteschele)*, Frank Overton *(Gen. Bogan)*, Edward Binns *(Col. Grady)*, Fritz Weaver *(Col. Cascio)*, Henry Fonda *(The President)*, Larry Hagman *(Buck)*, William Hansen *(Secretary Swenson)*, Russell Hardie *(Gen. Stark)*, Russell Collins *(Knapp)*, Sorrell Booke *(Congressman*

Raskob), Nancy Berg *(Ilsa Wolfe)*, Dom DeLuise *(Sgt. Collins)*.

Released only seven months after DR. STRANGELOVE by the very same studio, Columbia, the virtually identical, albeit totally serious, FAIL SAFE was a relative failure at the box office compared to Stanley Kubrick's wicked black comedy. In fact, Kubrick went to Columbia's top brass and threatened a plagiarism lawsuit (his own film was based on Peter George's almost unknown novel *Red Alert*). Since Columbia was distributing both DR. STRANGELOVE and FAIL SAFE, it appeesed Kubrick by releasing his film first, and, of course, that cult classic captured the lion's share of viewers, leaving FAIL SAFE to appear as a serious, almost dreary replay of the same story some months later. In it, a squadron of SAC bombers flies off to drop nuclear bombs on Moscow after a faulty transmission of orders that cannot be reversed through normal channels. The US military tries everything to stop them, but the bombers fly beyond "fail safe" and the president (Henry Fonda) is alerted. He goes to his bomb-proof bunker deep beneath the White House, where, in a simple, sterile room, he tries to inform Soviet leaders of the terrible blunder. Meanwhile, his cabinet and advisers meet in the War Room, keeping him informed of fast-developing events and channeling messages from the Omaha command center. After several attempts to recall or shoot down the planes, it becomes obvious that one of the bombers will deliver its load on Moscow. In a desperate effort to prevent a retaliatory attack by the Soviets that would result in all-out nuclear war, the president orders the Air Force to drop a nuclear device on New York City to atone for the accidental bombing of Moscow. Grim, bleak, and highly claustrophobic, FAIL SAFE is very much like director Sidney Lumet's previous film, 12 ANGRY MEN, in that it concentrates almost exclusively on the actors' performances and is shot mainly in tight close-up. While this is a wonderful showcase for some fine acting—notably by Fonda—it is not great filmmaking, and one may be left wishing for the biting, off-the-wall satire of DR. STRANGELOVE.

p, Max E. Youngstein; d, Sidney Lumet; w, Walter Bernstein, based on the novel by Eugene Burdick, Harvey Wheeler; ed, Ralph Rosenblum; ph, Gerald Hirschfeld.

(PR:C   MPAA:NR)

FAREWELL TO THE KING**

(1989) 117m Vestron/Orion c

Nick Nolte *(Learoyd)*, Nigel Havers *(Capt. Fairbourne)*, Frank McRae *(Sgt. Tenga)*, Gerry Lopez *(Gwai)*, Marilyn Tokuda *(Yoo)*, Choy Chang Wing *(Lian)*, Aki Aleong *(Col. Mitamura)*, Marius Weyers *(Sgt. Conklin)*, William Wise *(Dynamite Dave)*, Wayne Pygram *(Bren Armstrong)*, Richard Morgan *(Stretch Lewis)*, Elan Oberon *(Vivienne)*, James Fox *(Col. Ferguson)*, Michael Nissman *(Gen. Sutherland)*, John Bennett Perry *(Gen. MacArthur)*.

Once again writer-director John Milius attempts to re-create the sort of epic romantic adventure typical of 19th-century literature, only to fail miserably due to his basic ineptness as a writer and filmmaker. While he strives to emulate Conrad and Kipling, his work is really much closer to the daydreams of a lonely 10-year-old boy—and about as insightful. Nick Nolte stars as Sgt. Learoyd, a war-weary American soldier who deserts in Borneo at the height of WW II. Two years later, British army captain Fairbourne (Nigel Havers) and his sergeant, Tenga (Frank McRae), parachute into Borneo to enlist the help of Learoyd, who has become the leader of a tribe of Dayak headhunters, in fighting the Japanese. At first Learoyd refuses, but after much talk of the inevitability of history, the "king" agrees to help, with the stipulation that he receive a document signed by Gen. Douglas MacArthur recognizing Learoyd's sovereignty and the Dayaks' right to remain autonomous after the defeat of the Japanese. After the treaty is signed, Learoyd assembles a group of warriors, joins a small group of crack Allied commandos, and launches a series of guerilla attacks against the Japanese. Milius' typically muddled and pernicious right-wing politics aside, FAREWELL TO THE KING simply isn't a very good movie. As was the case with CONAN THE BARBARIAN and RED DAWN, FAREWELL TO THE KING boasts a scenario bursting with opportunities to showcase stunning action sequences, only to have that potential squandered by a director who doesn't know how to stage them. Even worse are his basic narrative skills; stitched together with such unwieldy cinematic devices as poorly deployed flashbacks and awkward narration, the film lurches along like a car with a broken clutch. Luckily, the film does boast a remarkably physical performance from Nolte, who toughs it out and is fairly memorable in a role fraught with potentially humiliating pitfalls.

p, Albert S. Ruddy and Andre Morgan; d, John Milius; w, John Milius, based on the novel *L'Adieu Au Roi* by Pierre Schoendoerffer; ed, Anne V. Coates and C. Timothy O'Meara; ph, Dean Semler, Deluxe color; m, Basil Poledouris.

(PR:C   MPAA:PG-13)

FAREWELL TO ARMS, A****

(1932) 90m PAR bw

Helen Hayes *(Catherine Barkley)*, Gary Cooper *(Lt. Frederic Henry)*, Adolphe Menjou *(Maj. Rinaldi)*, Mary Philips *(Helen Ferguson)*, Jack LaRue *(The Priest)*, Blanche Frederici *(Head Nurse)*, Henry Armetta *(Bonello)*.

Frank Borzage's masterful adaptation of Ernest Hemingway's celebrated novel stars Gary Cooper as Lt. Frederic Henry, an American adventurer serving in the Italian ambulance corps during WW I (as did Hemingway), and Helen Hayes as Catherine Barkley, the beautiful English nurse with whom he falls in love. When Lt. Henry returns to the front, his jealous friend and superior, Maj. Rinaldi (Adolphe Menjou), transfers Catherine to a hospital in Milan. When Henry is badly wounded, however, Rinaldi sends him to Milan so that he can be with his beloved, and the two share a blissful period before Henry returns to the war and Catherine travels to Switzerland to have their baby. Tragically, his letters never reach her and hers are intercepted by Rinaldi, but, after a major retreat, Henry

FATHER GOOSE—

learns of Catherine's whereabouts and rows across a storm-tossed lake to be with her as she fights for her life after their baby is born dead. Despite Hemingway's reported disgust with the film's happy ending (the alternative version, shown in Europe, had Catherine dying rather than left with the possibility of pulling through), A FAREWELL TO ARMS is generally faithful to his novel. Director Borzage is firmly in control of the film's emotions, and though by today's standards they are a bit overblown, the performances are so extraordinary that the film is still extremely moving. Hayes was never more appealing, Menjou is at his manipulative best, Cooper displays tremendous depth of feeling, and the supporting work is equally accomplished. Borzage's focus is on the love story, but his sweeping battles scenes, loaded with armies of extras, smack of war-torn reality, especially the famous retreat from Caporetto, brilliantly captured in montage by cinematographer Charles Lang. The story itself is drawn from Hemingway's WW I experiences, his battlefield injury, and his love affair with Agnes von Kurowsky. The story was brought to the screen twice more: in 1950 as FORCE OF ARMS with William Holden and Nancy Olsen, and under the original title in 1957 with Rock Hudson and Jennifer Jones.

d, Frank Borzage; w, Benjamin Glazer and Oliver H.P. Garrett, based on the novel by Ernest Hemingway; ed, Otho Lovering; ph, Charles Lang; m, Ralph Rainger, John Leipold, Bernhard Kaun, Paul Marquardt, Herman Hand, and W. Franke Harling.

(PR:A MPAA:NR)

FATHER GOOSE***½

(1964) 115m UNIV c

Cary Grant *(Walter Eckland)*, Leslie Caron *(Catherine Freneau)*, Trevor Howard *(Commodore Frank Houghton)*, Jack Good *(Lt. Stebbins)*, Verina Greenlaw *(Christine)*, Pip Sparke *(Anne)*, Jennifer Berrington *(Harriet)*, Stephanie Berrington *(Elizabeth)*, Laurelle Felsette *(Angelique)*, Nicole Felsette *(Dominique)*.

Playing against his sophisticated image, Cary Grant here essays the role of Walter Eckland, a drunken beach bum who sits out WW II on a South Seas island until he is coerced by an Australian naval officer (Trevor Howard) into monitoring Japanese air activity. When Eckland travels to a nearby island to rescue another plane watcher, he finds the observer dead, but schoolteacher Catherine Freneau (Leslie Caron) and her seven young female charges are very much alive after being marooned when their plane went down. They return with Eckland and clean up his act while he and Caron fall in love. Danger looms, however, as the Japanese forces close in. Grant's penultimate film (WALK, DON'T RUN was his last), this romantic comedy won Best Screenplay Oscars for Frank Tarloff and Peter Stone, who worked on the script separately but were awarded a shared credit by a Writers Guild arbitration.

p, Robert Arthur; d, Ralph Nelson; w, Frank Tarloff and Peter Stone, based on the story "A Place of Dragons" by S.H. Barnett; ed, Ted J. Kent; ph, Charles Lang, Jr., Technicolor; m, Cy Coleman.

(PR:AAA MPAA:NR)

55 DAYS AT PEKING***

(1963) 150m Bronston Prod./AA c

Charlton Heston *(Maj. Matt Lewis)*, Ava Gardner *(Baroness Natalie Ivanoff)*, David Niven *(Sir Arthur Robertson)*, Flora Robson *(Dowager Empress Tzu Hsi)*, John Ireland *(Sgt. Harry)*, Harry Andrews *(Fr. de Bearn)*, Leo Genn *(Gen. Jung-Lu)*, Robert Helpmann *(Prince Tuan)*, Kurt Kasznar *(Baron Sergei Ivanoff)*, Paul Lukas *(Dr. Steinfeldt)*, Jacques Sernas *(Maj. Bobrinski)*, Nicholas Ray *(American Minister)*.

This Samuel Bronston-produced historical epic (preceded by KING OF KINGS and EL CID), directed by Nicholas Ray, is set during China's Boxer Rebellion of 1900. After the foreign legations in Peking are besieged by the Society of the Righteous and Harmonious Fists, better known as the Boxers, hundreds of missionaries are murdered in a xenophobic and anti-Christian campaign. Maj. Matt Lewis (Charlton Heston) is placed in charge of a small multinational unit of foreign soldiers who take a stand against the Boxers from inside their international compound. For 55 days, Maj. Lewis, British ambassador Sir Arthur Robertson (David Niven), Russian baroness Natalie Ivanoff (Ava Gardner), and a host of others must defend themselves against the Boxers, running low on food and supplies while awaiting the arrival of reinforcements. Meanwhile, the sinister dowager empress Tzu Hsi (Flora Robson) secretly supports the Boxers, augmenting their siege of the international settlement with imperial troops. This massive, two-and-a-half-hour epic is not as compelling as it should be, director Nicholas Ray's talents being better suited to smaller, darker dramas than this huge historical tale. Heston is his usual forceful self and Gardner is effective, but Niven quietly steals the show as the witty British ambassador. Though ponderous, the film yields plenty of thrills (many of the action sequences were directed by Andrew Marton, who took over for the "ill"—disinterested—Ray) and the reconstructed 1900 Peking sets by Veniero Colasanti and John Moore are marvels to behold.

p, Samuel Bronston; d, Nicholas Ray; w, Philip Yordan, Bernard Gordon, and Robert Hamer; ed, Robert Lawrence; ph, Jack Hildyard and Manuel Berenger, Super Technirama 70, Technicolor; m, Dimitri Tiomkin.

(PR:A MPAA:NR)

FIGHTING SEABEES, THE***

(1944) 100m REP bw

John Wayne *(Wedge Donovan)*, Susan Hayward *(Constance Chesley)*, Dennis O'Keefe *(Lt. Comdr. Robert Yarrow)*, William Frawley *(Eddie Powers)*, Leonid Kinskey *(Johnny Novasky)*, J.M. Kerrigan *(Sawyer Collins)*, Grant Withers *(Whanger Spreckles)*, Paul Fix *(Ding Jacobs)*, Ben Welden *(Yump Lumkin)*, Duncan Renaldo *(Juan)*.

One of the most popular propaganda movies to come out

of WW II, THE FIGHTING SEABEES stars the swaggering John Wayne as Wedge Donovan, the head of a construction company working for the Navy on a remote Pacific island, building fortifications and an airstrip. Constance Chesley (Susan Hayward) is a news correspondent who falls in love with Donovan, who will have nothing to do with her; Navy commander Robert Yarrow (Dennis O'Keefe) is in love with Constance and at odds with Donovan over his unorthodox ways. When the Japanese invade the island, Donovan ignores Yarrow's orders to have his men take cover, then is enraged when some of his workers are machine-gunned by strafing Zeros. He orders his men armed and they attack the Japanese shock troops, resulting in slaughter as the construction workers are mowed down by the professional enemy. Eager to prevent another massacre, Donovan and Yarrow journey to Washington, where it is agreed to establish a new Navy unit, the Seabees, with Donovan and Yarrow at its head. All of Donovan's workers—along with the phalanxes of construction men he recruits—are enlisted, quickly but rigorously trained, and sent to another island. As they build their airstrip, the Japanese pick them off from hiding. Donovan can stand it no longer and, again, disobeys orders and leads his men in a sweep of the island. It's all very hokey—and racist—but it's as action-packed as the best of the serials, and Wayne's macho banter with the feisty Hayward is wholly enjoyable. At the risk of spoiling the ending, THE FIGHTING SEABEES is one of the very few films in which Wayne actually dies—and his death scene here is pretty spectacular. Director Edward Ludwig handles the action well and Walter Scharf's exceptional score earned him an Oscar nomination.

p, Albert J. Cohen; d, Edward Ludwig and Howard Lydecker; w, Borden Chase and Aeneas MacKenzie, based on a story by Chase; ed, Richard Van Enger; ph, William Bradford; m, Walter Scharf.

(PR:C   MPAA:NR)

FINAL COUNTDOWN, THE**

(1980) 104m UA c

Kirk Douglas *(Capt. Matthew Yelland)*, Martin Sheen *(Warren Lasky)*, Katharine Ross *(Laurel Scott)*, James Farentino *(Comdr. Richard Owens)*, Ron O'Neal *(Comdr. Dan Thurman)*, Charles Durning *(Sen. Chapman)*, Victor Mohica *(Black Cloud)*, James C. Lawrence *(Lt. Perry)*, Soon-Teck Oh *(Kimura)*, Joe Lowry *(Comdr. Damon)*, Dan Fitzgerald *(Navy Doctor)*.

America's finest nuclear-powered aircraft carrier, the USS *Nimitz*, is thrown through a time warp from 1980 to Pearl Harbor, December 7, 1941. Will the crew intervene? Will the course of history be changed forever? Martin Sheen is a hapless observer aboard ship, Charles Durning is a senator who sees the political implications in the situation, and Kirk Douglas goes on and on about ethics, history, and other biggies. The result is little more than a lengthy "Twilight Zone" episode. The *Nimitz* is actually used throughout the film, adding a minor air of authenticity.

p, Peter Vincent Douglas; d, Don Taylor; w, David Ambrose, Gerry Davis, Thomas Hunter, and Peter Powell; ed, Robert K. Lambert; ph, Victor J. Kemper, Panavision, Technicolor; m, John Scott.

(PR:C   MPAA:PG)

FINAL OPTION, THE*

(1982, Brit.) 125m Richmond Light Horse/MGM c (GB: WHO DARES WIN)

Lewis Collins *(Capt. Skellen)*, Judy Davis *(Frankie)*, Richard Widmark *(Secretary of State)*, Robert Webber *(Gen. Potter)*, Edward Woodward *(Comdr. Powell)*, Tony Doyle *(Col. Hadley)*, John Duttine *(Rod)*, Kenneth Griffith *(Bishop Crick)*, Rosalind Lloyd *(Jenny)*, Ingrid Pitt *(Helga)*.

This violent, ludicrous tale of antiwar sentiments, nuclear disarmament, commando squads, and hostages features Judy Davis as Frankie, the leader of a militant antinuclear group that resorts to terrorism in its fears that the world will end in a violent unilateral nuclear attack. She and her cohorts storm the US government building in London, take the visiting secretary of state (Richard Widmark) hostage, and demand the destruction of nuclear weapons. Capt. Skellen (Lewis Collins) is a Special Air Services man who goes undercover to infiltrate the gang, while Scotland Yard chief Cmdr. Powell (Edward Woodward) organizes his men. The politically skewed THE FINAL OPTION portrays the antinuclear movement as a militant, radical organization bent on violence; by the end of the film, however, the SAS, Scotland Yard, and US Air Force combine forces to wipe out this "enemy."

p, Euan Lloyd; d, Ian Sharp; w, Reginald Rose, based on the novel *The Tiptoe Boys* by George Markstein; ed, John Grover; ph, Phil Meheux.

(PR:O   MPAA:R)

FIRE OVER ENGLAND****

(1937, Brit.) 92m Mayflower-Pendennis-Korda-LFP/UA bw

Laurence Olivier *(Michael Ingolby)*, Flora Robson *(Queen Elizabeth)*, Leslie Banks *(Earl of Leicester)*, Raymond Massey *(Philip of Spain)*, Vivien Leigh *(Cynthia)*, Tamara Desni *(Elena)*, Morton Selten *(Burleigh)*, Lyn Harding *(Sir Richard)*, George Thirlwell *(Gregory)*, Henry Oscar *(Spanish Ambassador)*, Robert Rendel *(Don Miguel)*, Robert Newton *(Don Pedro)*, James Mason *(Hillary Vane)*.

FIRE OVER ENGLAND is a rare example of a film that succeeds superbly in two genres, as a swashbuckling epic and as a historical drama. Michael Ingolby (Laurence Olivier) is a young British naval officer whose father is burned to death for heresy by the Spanish Inquisition. He seeks revenge and finds his opportunity in the court of the tempestuous Queen Elizabeth I (Flora Robson). Elizabeth knows she is surrounded by traitors in league with her arch enemy, Philip of Spain (Raymond Massey), who plans to invade England, and when Michael offers to go to Spain, infiltrate Philip's court, and learn the identity of the English informants and the date of the invasion, she seizes the chance. Elizabeth is also romantically inclined toward the handsome and dashing officer, and a little vexed at the attentions he shows his childhood sweetheart and her lady-in-waiting, Cynthia (Vivien Leigh). Michael soon learns of Philip's plans, escapes to England, exposes the traitors, and helps lead the British ships into battle against the Spanish Armada. Typically glossy in its treatment of details (its spirit, however, seems relatively accurate), FIRE OVER ENGLAND succeeds through the combined talents of many great names—from Alexander Korda's sponsorship to Erich Pommer's production, James Wong Howe's superb photography, Lazare Meerson's grand sets, and the acting of Olivier, Robson, and Leigh. This was the first film collaboration for Oliver and Leigh (they would make only three films together) and it resulted in an affair that, four years later, would become a marriage. A host of versatile supporting players add to the depth of FIRE OVER ENGLAND, not the least of whom is Massey as the darkly brooding, expansionist King Philip. In a very small role as an envoy is a bearded, costumed James Mason.

p, Erich Pommer; d, William K. Howard; w, Clemence Dane and Sergei Nolbandov, based on the novel by A.E.W. Mason; ed, John Dennis; ph, James Wong Howe; m, Richard Addinsell.

(PR:A MPAA:NR)

FIREFOX***

(1982) 137m WB c

Clint Eastwood *(Mitchell Gant)*, Freddie Jones *(Kenneth Aubrey)*, David Huffman *(Buckholz)*, Warren Clarke *(Pavel Upenskoy)*, Ronald Lacey *(Semelovsky)*, Kenneth Colley *(Col. Kontarsky)*, Klaus Lowitsch *(Gen. Vladimirov)*.

Mitchell Gant (Clint Eastwood) is a top American fighter pilot called out of retirement and sent to the USSR to steal a new super-fighter that can run rings around anything the US has, and whose weapon systems are thought-controlled—but only if you're thinking in Russian. Gant goes off to England for training and is eventually smuggled into the Soviet Union. Narrowly avoiding hordes of suspicious bureaucrats and too-inept-to-be-real KGB men, he steals the plane and flies it back home, with two similar fighters in hot pursuit. Apart from the flying sequences, which are spectacular (though largely derivative of STAR WARS), this is one of Eastwood's least satisfying films. Overlong—it's more than an hour before Eastwood's character even starts on his mission—and hard to take seriously, FIREFOX nevertheless struck a nerve among Americans who wanted to see the Russians beaten by a real American hero. This same audience would make RED DAWN (1984), INVASION USA (1985), and the "Rambo" series great successes a couple of years later. For the more intelligent Eastwood fan, the film offers an interesting exploration of the actor-director's screen persona. Throughout, he experiments with a number of different disguises, finally embracing total dehumanization when he steps into the Firefox, dons the special mind-reading helmet, and literally becomes one with the sleek, gleaming, high-tech killing machine.

p, Clint Eastwood; d, Clint Eastwood; w, Alex Lasker and Wendell Wellman, based on the novel by Craig Thomas; ed, Ferris Webster and Ron Spang; ph, Bruce Surtees, Panavision, Deluxe Color; m, Maurice Jarre.

(PR:C MPAA:PG)

FIRES ON THE PLAIN****

(1962, Jap.) 105m Daiei/Harrison bw (NOBI)

Eiji Funakoshi *(Tamura)*, Osamu Takizawa *(Yasuda)*, Mickey Curtis *(Nagamatsu)*, Mantaro Ushio *(Sergeant)*.

A grim, intense Japanese war drama, FIRES ON THE PLAIN follows Tamura (Eiji Funakoshi), a tubercular soldier condemned to wander a battle-scarred landscape in the closing days of WW II. Separated from his unit and rejected by the hospital because he must have his own food in order to gain admittance, Tamura flees the advancing Americans and is forced to hide in the jungle, where he encounters all manner of death, disease, and horror. Stunningly composed in black and white on a widescreen DaieiScope canvas, FIRES ON THE PLAIN is beautiful to look at (its magnificent Philippine vistas swallowing the insignificant Tamura), though it is philosophically horrible to contemplate. The world director Kon Ichikawa brings to the screen (based on the 1951 novel by Shohei Ooka) is difficult to bear, a world of brutality, pain, death, destruction, and cannibalism—in short, a world of war. In it Ichikawa has created one of the great indictments of war and one of the most painful examinations of humanity. Unfortunately, the videocassette is not letterboxed (except for the opening credit tease), destroying the power and beauty of the visual composition. (In Japanese; English subtitles.)

p, Masaichi Nagata; d, Kon Ichikawa; w, Natto Wada, based on the novel by Shohei Ooka; ed, Hiroaki Fujii and Kon Ichikawa; ph, Setsuo Kobayashi, DaieiScope; m, Yasushi Akutagawa.

(PR:O MPAA:NR)

FIRST BLOOD**½

(1982) 97m Orion c

Sylvester Stallone *(John Rambo)*, Richard Crenna *(Trautman)*, Brian Dennehy *(Teasle)*, David Caruso *(Mitch)*, Jack Starrett *(Galt)*, Michael Talbott *(Balford)*, David Crowley *(Shingleton)*, Chris Mulkey *(Ward)*.

Back before he became a slobbering jingoist, John Rambo (Sylvester Stallone) was a somewhat interesting—albeit inarticulate—character who merely wanted to be left alone to sulk. In FIRST BLOOD, he is a vagabond Vietnam vet wandering the Pacific Northwest who is run out of a small town by a bullyboy sheriff (Brian Dennehy). When Rambo returns, he is arrested, roughed up, and otherwise maltreated by the local cops. Fed up with this persecution, he goes berserk, escapes, and causes the death of a pursuing officer. Hiding in the dense woodland and mountainous terrain, Rambo fends off the local posse using guerilla methods learned in Vietnam. Described by Trautman (Richard Crenna), his former commanding officer, as "a killing machine," one of the last indefatigable Green Berets who slew whole armies of the Viet Cong, the superhuman Rambo easily defeats the cops, who are then forced to turn to the National Guard for help. Platoons of men assault Rambo's mountain stronghold, and when they think they've blown him up in an old mining shaft where he has taken refuge, the hunt is called off. Trautman doesn't believe he's dead, however, and indeed, Rambo lives to vent his wrath on the small town that shunned him by destroying it single-handedly. Yes, it's all extremely silly, but director Ted Kotcheff knows how to stage an action scene with flair and keeps the film moving along at a rapid clip. Boasting some of the best use of rugged landscape since the westerns of Anthony Mann, FIRST BLOOD is an effective, if outlandish, picture that exists merely for its big-screen thrills. Stallone barely says a word in the entire film, save for one long and laughably pat speech about how the Vietnam War has affected him—a monolog that comes tumbling out in the last five minutes. What makes FIRST BLOOD less odious than its sequels is that it's more or less a straight action film, and mostly avoids right-wing sermonizing—although it does pin the blame for US failure in Vietnam on bureaucrats and a military who "didn't let us win." In the subsequent "Rambo" films, this aspect of the Rambo character takes precedence, and he becomes the fantasy vehicle for frustrated American warmongers who want to go back and "win" Vietnam, then kick the commies out of Afghanistan.

p, Buzz Feitshans; d, Ted Kotcheff; w, Michael Kozoll, William Sackheim, and Q. Moonblood, based on the novel by David Morrell; ed, Thom Noble and Joan Chapman; ph, Andrew Laszlo, Panavision, Technicolor; m, Jerry Goldsmith.

(PR:O   MPAA:R)

FIRST YANK INTO TOKYO**

(1945) 82m RKO bw (GB: MASK OF FURY)

Tom Neal *(Maj. Ross)*, Barbara Hale *(Abby Drake)*, Marc Cramer *(Jardine)*, Richard Loo *(Col. Okanura)*, Keye Luke *(Haan-soo)*, Leonard Strong *(Maj. Nogira)*, Benson Fong *(Capt. Tanahe)*, Clarence Lung *(Maj. Ichibo)*, Keye Chang *(Capt. Sato)*, Michael St. Angel *(Capt. Andrew Kent)*, Wallis Clark *(Dr. Langley)*, John Hamilton *(Dr. Stacey)*, Selmer Jackson *(Col. Blaine)*.

Maj. Ross (Tom Neal) is a super-patriotic WW II American pilot, raised in Japan, who agrees to return to the East to obtain weaponry information from captive scientist Jardine (Marc Cramer). The suicide mission doesn't frighten Ross; his sweetheart, Abby Drake (Barbara Hale), has died and he now only wishes to perish serving his country. After plastic surgeons remodel his features, Ross parachutes into Japan and heads for the camp where Jardine is confined. There, Ross discovers that Abby is a very much alive nurse who has also been taken prisoner, and who is now in love with another prisoner, American serviceman Capt. Andrew Kent (Michael St. Angel). Ross nevertheless follows his orders and obtains the vital information, in the process encountering and outwitting several unsavory Japanese, including the insidious Maj. Nogira (Leonard Strong). His true adversary, however, is Col. Okanura (Richard Loo), a wily intelligence agent with whom Ross actually went to college and who remembers every quirk of his school chum. Luckily for the producers, this film was finished just as the A-bomb was dropped on Japan. They therefore went back to the cameras and changed Ross' assignment from obtaining plans for a secret gun to obtaining vital A-bomb information. In a new and unlikely ending, a narrator explains how Ross gave up his life so that the bomb could be perfected. Pathe newsreel footage was then tacked on, showing nuclear explosions, thus making this the first Hollywood feature to deal with the atomic attack on Japan.

p, J. Robert Bren; d, Gordon Douglas; w, J. Robert Bren, based on a story by J. Robert Bren, Gladys Atwater; ed, Philip Martin, Jr.; ph, Harry J. Wild; m, Leigh Harline.

(PR:C   MPAA:NR)

FLAT TOP***

(1952) 83m MON/AA c

Sterling Hayden *(Dan Collier)*, Richard Carlson *(Joe Rodgers)*, William Phipps *(Red Kelley)*, John Bromfield *("Snakehips" MacKay)*, Keith Larsen *(Barney Smith)*.

Dan Collier (Sterling Hayden) is the hard-as-nails commanding officer of a carrier air group aboard the aircraft carrier USS *Princeton*. It is 1944, and the *Princeton* is traveling through the explosive Pacific. In addition to the Japanese Zeros attacking from above, Collier must battle Joe Rodgers (Richard Carlson), the commander of a new air group on the carrier. Rodgers is a friendly commander who never pushes his men too far, a philosophy directly at odds with Collier's rough edge. Collier runs a tight group because he wants to keep his men alive; the men don't like it but by the war's end they realize he was right. An entertaining picture, FLAT TOP has plenty of actual combat scenes intercut with the fiction, and many of the carrier's real personnel appear in the film.

p, Walter Mirisch; d, Lesley Selander; w, Steve Fisher; ed, William Austin; ph, Harry Neumann, Cinecolor; m, Marlin Skiles.

(PR:A   MPAA:NR)

FLESH AND BLOOD***

(1985) 126m Orion/Riverside c

Rutger Hauer *(Martin)*, Jennifer Jason Leigh *(Agnes)*, Tom Burlinson *(Steven)*, Susan Tyrrell *(Celine)*, Ronald Lacey *(Cardinal)*, Jack Thompson *(Hawkwood)*, Fernando Hillbeck *(Arnolfini)*, Brion James *(Karthans)*, John Dennis Johnston *(Summer)*.

A brutal and unremittingly grim look at the year 1501, FLESH AND BLOOD opens with the siege of a city somewhere in Western Europe, presumably northern Italy. Arnolfini (Fernando Hillbeck) is the former lord of the city, thrown out in a revolt, but now back to reclaim what's his with the help of a mercenary army organized by Hawk-

FLYING DEUCES, THE—

wood (Jack Thompson). Arnolfini tells the motley but dangerous professional soldiers that they may loot the city for 24 hours, but once it has been taken and the pillaging has commenced, he changes his mind and has Hawkwood order his men to lay down their arms and leave. The disgruntled mercenaries are forced to depart empty-handed, but one small band, led by Martin (Rutger Hauer), manages to slip out a sword under the robe of a priest. Later, when the men dig up a statue of St. Martin while burying a camp follower's stillborn baby, the priest takes it as a divine revelation that the saint's mercenary namesake will lead them to riches, chiefly by stealing from Arnolfini, with the spoils to include the lord's virginal daughter, Agnes (Jennifer Jason Leigh). Directed by Paul Verhoeven (ROBOCOP), FLESH AND BLOOD presents probably the least romanticized cinematic picture of the Middle Ages ever made. Cruelty, violence, filth, and pestilence are the order of the day; Verhoeven does not blink at his characters' awful day-to-day reality. The battle scenes are impressive, though underpopulated; the camerawork is fluid but not annoying. FLESH AND BLOOD came and went almost unnoticed in its US release, lost amid a welter of inferior European sword-and-sorcery films, but it deserved a better fate. A more appalling view of the turmoil and misery of the late Middle Ages may never be seen.

p, Gys Versluys; d, Paul Verhoeven; w, Gerard Soeteman and Paul Verhoeven, based on a story by Soeteman; ed, Ine Schenkkan; ph, Jan De Bont, Technovision, Deluxe Color; m, Basil Poledouris.

(PR:O MPAA:R)

FLYING DEUCES, THE*

(1939) 67m RKO bw

Stan Laurel (Stan), Oliver Hardy (Ollie), Jean Parker (Georgette), Reginald Gardiner (Francois), Charles Middleton (Commandant), Jean Del Val (Sergeant), Clem Wilenchick [Crane Whitley] (Corporal), James Finlayson (Jailer).

Based loosely on the French film THE TWO ACES, this amusing Laurel and Hardy comedy casts the boys as Iowa fishmongers who travel to Paris and join the French Foreign Legion after Ollie is jilted by a waitress. Once in the famous fighting force, the boys become the victims of a series of comic mishaps, and when they attempt to desert, they are captured and condemned to death. They escape in an airplane and go on a mad ride through the skies, until the plane crashes. Hardy dies and is reincarnated as a horse, while Laurel emerges totally unscathed. One of the film's cowriters was baby-faced Harry Langdon, who was in between pictures as an actor. Another silent film veteran, James Finlayson—who could get more laughs with a squint than most actors could get with a full page of dialog—has a small role as a prison jailer.

p, Boris Morros; d, A. Edward Sutherland; w, Ralph Spence, Alfred Schiller, Charles Rogers, and Harry Langdon; ed, Jack Dennis; ph, Art Lloyd; m, John Leopold and Leo Shuken.

(PR:AAA MPAA:NR)

FLYING LEATHERNECKS***

(1951) 102m Hughes/RKO c

John Wayne (Maj. Dan Kirby), Robert Ryan (Capt. Carl Griffin), Don Taylor (Lt. "Cowboy" Blithe), William Harrigan (Lt. Comdr. Joe Curan), Janis Carter (Joan Kirby), Jay C. Flippen (Master Sgt. Clancy), Carleton Young (Capt. McAllister), Brett King (Lt. Stark).

This overlong but action-filled WW II film offers John Wayne in a familiar role, that of Maj. Dan Kirby, the martinet commander of a fighter squadron on Guadalcanal in 1942, a man whose rigid discipline gets the job done but alienates the pilots flying under his orders. Capt. Carl Griffin (Robert Ryan), his easygoing, poetry-reciting second-in-command, thinks Kirby is a fine officer and leader of men but begins to criticize his uncompromising ways, believing that a freer hand should be taken with the men—that they should, as flying specialists who risk their lives more openly and frequently than the average infantryman, receive special consideration. Of course, this is all nonsense to Kirby, who must order up every man he considers fit for duty and able to stare death in the eye. Although a passable war film, FLYING LEATHERNECKS must be considered something of a disappointment for fans of Wayne, Ryan, and director Nick Ray. From its dogfight scenes, which attempt (not very successfully) to integrate studio footage with color newsreel shots of actual combat, to the endless debates between Kirby and Griffin on how to handle the men, this is very familiar material and merely rehashes the stress-of-command theme found in so many other WW II air movies—among them COMMAND DECISION (1949), FIGHTER SQUADRON (1948), TWELVE O'CLOCK HIGH (1950), and Wayne's own FLYING TIGERS (1942) and (regarding the infantry) SANDS OF IWO JIMA (1949).

p, Edmund Grainger; d, Nicholas Ray; w, James Edward Grant, based on a story by Kenneth Gamet; ed, Sherman Todd; ph, William Snyder, Technicolor; m, Roy Webb.

(PR:C MPAA:NR)

FLYING TIGERS***

(1942) 102m REP bw

John Wayne (Jim Gordon), John Carroll (Woody Jason), Anna Lee (Brooke Elliott), Paul Kelly (Hap Davis), Gordon Jones (Alabama Smith), Mae Clarke (Verna Bales), Addison Richards (Col. Lindsay), Edmund MacDonald (Blackie Bales), Bill Shirley (Dale).

This was Republic's salute to the all-American Volunteer Group flying for China and Chiang Kai-Shek, under the command of Gen. Claire Chennault, long before Pearl Harbor. These men were both patriotic and mercenary, receiving $500 for every Japanese plane shot down. John Wayne is Jim Gordon, the leader of one squadron of carefree pilots, backed up by Hap Davis (Paul Kelly), his tireless second-in-command, a weary veteran whose eyesight is failing. New recruit Woody Jason (John Carroll), a wisecracking nonconformist, arrives on the scene, disobeys orders, and creates dissension among the men. In the air, Woody relentlessly cuts in on the "kill" of other pilots to glean the $500 payoff, disregarding orders and jeopardizing his fellow pilots. Gordon is disgusted by Woody's behavior and eventually grounds him, but the disliked pilot is finally given a chance to redeem himself on a mission to bomb a bridge deep inside Japanese-held territory. FLYING TIGERS is wholesale propaganda, with a narrative structure blatantly cribbed from Howard Hawks' ONLY ANGELS HAVE WINGS (1939) (Kelly takes Thomas Mitchell's role and Carroll assumes the part of the disgraced pilot played by Richard Barthelmess). This was Wayne's first war film, one that set the pattern for him as a two-fisted—but soft-hearted—combat leader. Director David Miller provides plenty of action and all the standard WW II film cliches.

p, Edmund Grainger; d, David Miller; w, Kenneth Gamet and Barry Trivers, based on a story by Gamet; ed, Ernest Nims; ph, Jack Marta; m, Victor Young.

(PR:C   MPAA:NR)

FORBIDDEN GAMES**

(1953, Fr.) 90m Silver/Times Film bw (LES JEUX INTERDIT)

Brigitte Fossey (Paulette), Georges Poujouly (Michel Dolle), Lucien Hubert (Mons. Dolle), Suzanne Courtal (Mme. Dolle), Jacques Marin (Georges Dolle), Laurence Badie (Berthe Dolle), Andre Wasley (Mons. Gouard), Amedee (Francis Gouard).

Once one of the most highly esteemed films ever made about war and its effects, FORBIDDEN GAMES is a classic example of traditional, superficial filmmaking that today is little more than a museum piece. Disguising the artificiality of the Jean Aurenche-Pierre Bost script under the realism of Rene Clement's direction, FORBIDDEN GAMES begins with a harrowing sequence. As hundreds of refugees flee WW II Paris in the face of the German attack, the parents and dog of little Paulette (Brigitte Fossey, in the role that launched her to stardom) are killed, leaving the orphan to be befriended by Michel (Georges Poujouly), the 11-year-old son of peasant parents (Lucien Hubert and Suzanne Courtal). The constant wartime specter of death so greatly affects the children that they become obsessed with it, stealing crosses and constructing their own secret animal cemetery for moles, chickens, and insects—all of which are given elaborate memorial services. While Clement received resounding praise for his supposedly brilliant direction of children, the entire picture today seems forced, the young actors clearly "acting" instead of showing any real emotions or feelings. The film was a great critical success, and earned an Honorary Oscar for Best Foreign Film released in 1952. Originally released at 102 minutes. (In French; English subtitles.)

p, Robert Dorfman; d, Rene Clement; w, Rene Clement, Jean Aurenche, and Pierre Bost, based on the novel *Les Jeux Inconnus* by Francois Boyer; ed, Roger Dwyre; ph, Robert Juillard; m, Narciso Yepes.

(PR:C   MPAA:NR)

FORCE 10 FROM NAVARONE***½

(1978, Brit.) 118m AIP c

Robert Shaw (Maj.Mallory), Harrison Ford (Barnsby), Edward Fox (Miller), Barbara Bach (Maritza), Franco Nero (Lescovar), Carl Weathers (Weaver), Richard Kiel (Drazac), Angus MacInnes (Reynolds), Michael Byrne (Schroeder).

This is not quite a sequel to 1961's THE GUNS OF NAVARONE, but comes close. This time the squad is sent to Yugoslavia, to blow up a bridge that is vital to the German war effort. Harrison Ford (fresh from a different "Force" in STAR WARS) is the American member of the team, paired with Carl Weathers as a black soldier who has no more patience for racial hatred; Edward Fox is a demolitions expert; the exotic-looking Barbara Bach is a partisan who helps their cause; the gigantic Richard Kiel is a Nazi conspirator; and Franco Nero is a Nazi double agent. Heading the group is Maj. Mallory (Robert Shaw), a Briton who survived the Force's previous attack at Navarone. Filled with action, intrigue, and double-crosses, FORCE 10 FROM NAVARONE is worthwhile for war movie fans, although, apart from the great cast (Shaw, who is superb, died just before the film's release) and the notable action scenes, there isn't much that's praiseworthy in the film. Like THE GUNS OF NAVARONE, this one was based on a novel by Alistair MacLean.

p, Oliver A. Unger, John R. Sloan, and Anthony B. Unger; d, Guy Hamilton; w, Robin Chapman, based on a story by Carl Foreman and the novel by Alistair MacLean; ed, Ray Poulton; ph, Christopher Challis, Panavision, Technicolor; m, Ron Goodwin.

(PR:A-C   MPAA:PG)

FOREIGN CORRESPONDENT*****

(1940) 120m UA bw

Joel McCrea (Johnny Jones/Huntley Haverstock), Laraine Day (Carol Fisher), Herbert Marshall (Stephen Fisher), George Sanders (Scott Ffolliott), Albert Basserman (Van Meer), Robert Benchley (Stebbins), Edmund Gwenn (Rowley), Eduardo Ciannelli (Krug), Martin Kosleck (Tramp), Harry Davenport (Mr. Powers), Barbara Pepper (Doreen), Eddy Conrad (Latvian Diplomat), Charles Wagenheim (Assassin), Crauford Kent (Toastmaster), Alfred Hitchcock (Man with Newspaper).

One of the truly great espionage films, delivered with taut mastery by the stellar Alfred Hitchcock, FOREIGN CORRESPONDENT is packed with suspense, great atmosphere, and brilliant dialog. Johnny Jones (Joel McCrea) is a top American crime reporter reassigned as a foreign correspondent to Western Europe. Ordered to find the most provocative stories swirling in the cauldron of European politics just prior to WW II, he soon meets Stephen Fisher (Herbert Marshall), who heads a peace organization, and Fisher's attractive daughter, Carol (Laraine Day). Before long, Johnny gets entangled in an international intrigue involving the kidnaping and murder of Van Meer (Albert Basserman), an important Dutch diplomat who has memorized vital information. One of Hitchcock's greatest enter-

FORT APACHE—

tainments, FOREIGN CORRESPONDENT is also a stirring propaganda piece, which clearly indicts the Nazi regime, a fact recognized by Nazi propaganda minister Josef Goebbels, who nonetheless hailed the Hitchcock film as a masterpiece when he first saw it, calling it "a first-class production, a criminological bang-up hit, which no doubt will make a certain impression upon the broad masses of the people in enemy countries." The project was begun by producer Walter Wanger, who had purchased the rights to Vincent Sheean's autobiography, *Personal History*, which was then adapted for the screen, but canned in favor of a completely new script under Hitchcock's direction. (Wanger originally signed William Dieterle to direct and wanted the film to be a vehicle for Charles Boyer and Claudette Colbert, though Hitchcock had tried to cast Gary Cooper.) FOREIGN CORRESPONDENT also boasts some of the finest production design of its time—a huge windmill set was built to simulate a Dutch location, and a square in Amsterdam was reconstructed on a 10-acre set—a testament of the talents of Alexander Golitzen and William Cameron Menzies. One of the most spectacular scenes shows the crashing of a huge trans-Atlantic jet into the ocean, an example of the director's perfect mastery of technique.

p, Walter Wanger; d, Alfred Hitchcock; w, Charles Bennett, Joan Harrison, James Hilton, and Robert Benchley; ed, Otho Lovering and Dorothy Spencer; ph, Rudolph Mate; m, Alfred Newman.

(PR:A   MPAA:NR)

FORT APACHE*****

(1948) 127m Argosy/RKO bw

Henry Fonda *(Lt. Col. Owen Thursday)*, John Wayne *(Capt. Kirby York)*, Shirley Temple *(Philadelphia Thursday)*, Ward Bond *(Sgt. Maj. Michael O'Rourke)*, John Agar *(Lt. Mickey O'Rourke)*, George O'Brien *(Capt. Sam Collingwood)*, Irene Rich *(Mrs. Mary O'Rourke)*, Victor McLaglen *(Sgt. Festus Mulcahy)*, Anna Lee *(Mrs. Emily Collingwood)*, Pedro Armendariz *(Sgt. Beaufort)*, Guy Kibbee *(Dr. Wilkens)*, Grant Withers *(Silas Meacham)*, Jack Pennick *(Sgt. Shattuck)*, Dick Foran *(Sgt. Quincannon)*.

FORT APACHE is a superb epic western, the first of director John Ford's US Cavalry trilogy (the others are SHE WORE A YELLOW RIBBON and RIO GRANDE), with awesome exterior scenes that reflect Ford's early training as a painter. Lt. Col. Owen Thursday (Henry Fonda) is a martinet commander bitter over having been sent to fight "digger" Indians instead of being assigned a glory post. He leads his men to disaster, but is later presented by the press as a hero. FORT APACHE is rich beyond its wonderful action scenes and the outdoor panoramas so dear to Ford's heart. The film expertly depicts the social affairs of a far-flung military outpost, the struggle of the women to maintain civilized living conditions, and the routines of the men in their day-to-day military duties. The rich characterization and humor of the Irish cavalrymen is unforgettable; it's a supporting players' field day, with Victor McLaglen, Ward Bond, Dick Foran, Pedro Armendariz, and Jack Pen-

nick allowing caprice to conquer boredom in training raw recruits to march and ride. Of course, Fonda's character and the doomed route he takes with his heroic regiment are based wholly on the massacre of George Armstrong Custer's 7th Cavalry at Little Big Horn. Fonda is superb as the unyielding commander and John Wayne, in one of his best roles as an officer concerned for the lives of his men, is the perfect counterpoint to Fonda's tyrant. Ford filmed FORT APACHE in his beloved Monument Valley (a Navaho tribal park at the Arizona-Utah border, 2,000 square miles of desert and towering sandstone buttes), his favorite location, inaccessible in all but the summer months because of weather conditions. Though the film ends with a defeat, as did Ford's masterful THEY WERE EXPENDABLE (1945), its strong domestic scenes, colorful coterie of actors, and romantic portrait of an Old West no more leave a decidedly optimistic feeling, positive and sure as a strong horse beneath the saddle, that makes the far horizon appear reachable.

p, John Ford and Merian C. Cooper; d, John Ford; w, Frank S. Nugent, based on the story "Massacre" by James Warner Bellah; ed, Jack Murray; ph, Archie Stout; m, Richard Hageman.

(PR:A   MPAA:NR)

49TH PARALLEL*****

(1941, Brit.) 105m GFD/ORTUS/COL bw (AKA: INVADERS, THE)

Leslie Howard *(Philip Armstrong Scott)*, Raymond Massey *(Andy Brock)*, Laurence Olivier *(Johnnie)*, Anton Walbrook *(Peter)*, Eric Portman *(Lt. Hirth)*, Glynis Johns *(Anna)*, Niall MacGinnis *(Vogel)*, Finlay Currie *(Factor)*, Raymond Lovell *(Lt. Kuhnecke)*, John Chandos *(Lohrmann)*, Basil Appleby *(Jahner)*, Eric Clavering *(Art)*.

THE 49TH PARALLEL is an excellent war drama from British director Michael Powell, coscripted by his longtime collaborator, Emeric Pressburger. Filmed mostly in Canada, THE 49TH PARALLEL opens as the U-37, a German submarine, surfaces in the Gulf of St. Lawrence. It is obliterated by RCAF bombers, but six Germans survive and march to a Hudson Bay trading post. Constructed in an episodic fashion, the story shows them wandering through Canada to avoid detection. Along the way, they meet Johnnie (Laurence Olivier), a French-Canadian trapper who is filled with contempt for the Nazis, whom he finds foolish; a group of German Hutterites living on a Christian community headed by Peter (Anton Walbrook); and Philip Armstrong Scott (Leslie Howard), a decadent novelist living in a tepee while preparing a manuscript on the Blackfoot Indians. With each meeting, the "invaders'" number diminishes; some are captured, others killed, a decent one (Niall MacGinnis) tries to remain with the Hutterites. Finally, the last to elude death or capture (a hero to Nazis back home) meets Andy Brock (Raymond Massey), an AWOL Canadian soldier who complains about his country and the notion of democracy while stowing away on a freight train bound for the US. The anti-Fascist message is honest and eloquent, the performances uniformly superb, the Oscar-winning script witty and intelligent, and the photography handsome and atypical of a war film. Powell ties it all together in a directorial style that is part war adventure, part Robert Flaherty-influenced documentary, taking just as much time with action sequences as he does with Hutterite communal living, Eskimo culture, or Indian rituals. Unfortunately, much was cut from the British release, which runs nearly 20 minutes longer.

p, Michael Powell and John Sutro; d, Michael Powell; w, Rodney Ackland and Emeric Pressburger, based on a story by Pressburger; ed, David Lean; ph, Freddie Young; m, Ralph Vaughn Williams.

(PR:A MPAA:NR)

FOUR FEATHERS, THE*****

(1939, Brit.) 115m Korda-LFP/UA c

John Clements *(Harry Faversham)*, Ralph Richardson *(Capt. John Durrance)*, C. Aubrey Smith *(Gen. Burroughs)*, June Duprez *(Ethne Burroughs)*, Allan Jeayes *(Gen. Faversham)*, Jack Allen *(Lt. Willoughby)*, Donald Gray *(Peter Burroughs)*.

One of the all-time great adventure films, THE FOUR FEATHERS is based on the 1902 tale of cowardice and courage by A.E.W. Mason, many times filmed but never as marvelously as in this masterpiece of a production. The tale of empire, battle, and redemption begins when Harry Faversham (John Clements), the son of a brigadier general, refuses to follow family tradition and join the army, choosing instead to settle down and wed Ethne Burroughs (June Duprez). He resigns his commission just before his regiment leaves for the 1898 Sudan campaign conducted by Lord Kitchener, and his friends—John Durrance (Ralph Richardson), Peter Burroughs (Donald Gray), and Tom Willoughby (Jack Allen)—present him three white feathers symbolizing cowardice. Also disgusted by his actions is Ethne, who gives him the fourth feather. Determined to prove his courage, Faversham leaves for Egypt alone, eventually saving the lives of all three of his friends by disguising himself as a native, with his skin stained and the letter "S" branded on his forehead to indicate that he is of the Sangali tribe, whose ostracized members have had their tongues cut out by their enemies. One of the great British films of the 1930s and one of producer Alexander Korda's finest achievements, THE FOUR FEATHERS is directed by Alexander's brother Zoltan with the elan demanded by the action-packed story. His talent is particularly evident in the magnificent battle scenes, particularly the awesome attack of the "Fuzzi Wuzzies" against the British lines, shown in wide panorama by cameras mounted high on hilltops overlooking the battlefield.

p, Alexander Korda; d, Zoltan Korda; w, R.C. Sherriff, Lajos Biro, and Arthur Wimperis, based on the novel by A.E.W. Mason; ed, William Hornbeck and Henry Cornelius; ph, Georges Perinal, Osmond Borradaile, and Jack Cardiff, Technicolor; m, Miklos Rozsa.

(PR:A MPAA:NR)

FOUR HORSEMEN OF THE APOCALYPSE, THE**

(1962) 153m Blaustein-Montezuma/MGM c

Glenn Ford *(Julio Desnoyers)*, Ingrid Thulin *(Marguerite Laurier)*, Charles Boyer *(Marcelo Desnoyers)*, Lee J. Cobb *(Julio Madariaga)*, Paul Henreid *(Etienne Laurier)*, Paul Lukas *(Karl Von Hartrott)*, Yvette Mimieux *(Chi-Chi Desnoyers)*, Karl Boehm *(Heinrich Von Hartrott)*, Harriet MacGibbon *(Dona Luisa Desnoyers)*, Kathryn Givney *(Elena Von Hartrott)*.

A dismal remake of the 1921 silent classic starring Rudolph Valentino, this Vincente Minnelli-directed picture stars Glenn Ford as the Argentine playboy-turned-WW II resistance hero Julio Desnoyers. Patriarch Julio Madariaga (Lee J. Cobb), who has built a vast estate in the Argentine Pampas as a refuge against the ravages of war, holds a family reunion during the 1930s. When Madariaga discovers that his German-born nephew, Heinrich (Karlheinz Boehm), and Heinrich's father, Karl (Paul Lukas), have become Nazis, he rages against them, predicting that they will bring down upon the world the Four Horsemen of the Apocalypse: Conquest, Pestilence, War, and Death. After Madariaga's death, Desnoyers, Madariaga's playboy grandson, wanders to Paris with his French father, Marcelo (Charles Boyer). He plans to live a life of wealth and luxury, but becomes increasingly involved with the Resistance through his activist sister, Chi-Chi (Yvette Mimieux), and Marguerite Laurier (Ingrid Thulin, her voice dubbed by Angela Lansbury), the wife of an imprisoned underground leader. This overlong remake is ponderous and disjointed, with none of the roles fully developed. The film most notably lacks a compelling lead—Glenn Ford is a fine actor, but he's simply no Valentino and it appears that both he and Minnelli were aware of that fact.

d, Vincente Minnelli; w, Robert Ardrey and John Gay, based on the novel by Vicente Blasco Ibanez; ed, Adrienne Fazan and Ben Lewis; ph, Milton Krasner, CinemaScope, Metrocolor; m, Andre Previn.

(PR:A MPAA:NR)

FOUR IN A JEEP***

(1951, Switz.) 100m Praesens Film Zurich bw (DIE VIER IM JEEP)

Viveca Lindfors *(Franziska Idinger)*, Ralph Meeker *(Sgt. William Long)*, Joseph Yadin *(Sgt. Vassily Voroschenko)*, Michael Medwin *(Sgt. Harry Stuart)*, Dinan *(Sgt. Marcel Pasture)*, Paulette Dubost *(Mme. Pasture)*, Hans Putz *(Karl Idinger)*.

This Swiss-made post-WW II saga details the efforts of a multinational occupation force to keep the peace in Austria, following four MPs (Ralph Meeker is the American, Michael Medwin the Briton, Dinan the Frenchman, Joseph Yadin the Russian) whose duty to their respective countries, and to one another, often clouds their decision-making. Franziska Idinger (Viveca Lindfors) is an Austrian woman whose husband, Karl (Hans Putz), has escaped from a Russian prison camp and resurfaced in Vienna. The Russian is afraid he'll be shot if he doesn't turn the fugitive

FRANCIS IN THE NAVY—

in, despite the American's angry attempts to convince him to do otherwise. There is very little plot or action, but FOUR IN A JEEP is a well-written, humanistic depiction of four soldiers from different countries.

p, Lazar Wechsler; d, Leopold Lindtberg; w, Richard Schweizer; ed, Robert Blum; ph, Emil Berna; m, Hermann Haller.

(PR:A MPAA:NR)

FRANCIS IN THE NAVY**

(1955) 80m UNIV bw

Donald O'Connor (Lt. Peter Stirling/Slicker Donovan), Martha Hyer (Betsy Donovan), Richard Erdman (Murph), Jim Backus (Comdr. Hutch), Clint Eastwood (Jonesy), David Janssen (Lt. Anders), Leigh Snowden (Appleby), Martin Milner (Rick), Paul Burke (Tate).

After some previous military experience (FRANCIS GOES TO WEST POINT, 1952, and FRANCIS JOINS THE WACS, 1954), Francis, the jabbering ass, telephones his Army pal Lt. Peter Stirling (Donald O'Connor) to inform him that he, Francis, has been drafted into the Navy. Lt. Stirling comes to the aid of the muttering mule (who is about to be auctioned off as surplus), but is mistaken for Slicker Donovan, a bosun's mate (also played by O'Connor) who looks just like him. Slicker's pals think he's gone nuts and is impersonating an Army lieutenant. Of course, Pvt. Francis eventually straightens everything out. FRANCIS IN THE NAVY isn't all that funny and is unnecessarily complicated, but it does have a stellar cast of supporting players who, like Francis' small-screen relative "Mister Ed," have earned a place in television history—Jim Backus ("I Married Joan," "Gilligan's Island," and "Mr. Magoo"), David Janssen ("The Fugitive"), Martin Milner ("Route 66" and "Adam-12"), and, in only his second motion picture appearance, Clint Eastwood, who would first gain notoriety on "Rawhide."

p, Stanley Rubin; d, Arthur Lubin; w, Devery Freeman, based on the "Francis" character created by David Stern; ed, Milton Carruth and Ray Snyder; ph, Carl Guthrie;

(PR:AA MPAA:NR)

FRIEDA***

(1947, Brit.) 97m RANK/EAL-UNIV bw

David Farrar (Robert Dawson), Glynis Johns (Judy Dawson), Mai Zetterling (Frieda Dawson), Flora Robson (Nell Dawson), Albert Lieven (Richard Mannsfeld), Barbara Everest (Mrs. Dawson), Gladys Henson (Edith), Ray Jackson (Tony Dawson), Patrick Holt (Alan Dawson), Milton Rosmer (Tom Merrick), Barry Letts (Jim Merrick).

This postwar drama concerns a German nurse, Frieda (Mai Zetterling) who saves the life of RAF officer Robert Dawson (David Farrar) by helping him escape from a prison camp. To return the favor and get Frieda out of Germany, Robert marries her and brings her to his small hometown in England at the close of WW II. She is rejected by her husband's family and the townsfolk, whose view of Germans is understandably bitter and distrustful. To make things worse, her Nazi brother (Albert Lieven) arrives in town, spouting Fascist slogans and implicating Frieda. The film is surprisingly progressive in its understanding of postwar prejudice, considering it was made so soon after the war.

p, Michael Relph; d, Basil Dearden; w, Ronald Millar and Angus MacPhail, based on the play by Millar; ed, Leslie Norman; ph, Gordon Dines; m, John Greenwood.

(PR:A MPAA:NR)

FROM HELL TO VICTORY**

(1979, Fr./It./Sp.) 100m New Film-Princess Films-Jose Frade c (DA DUNKERQUE ALLA VITTORIA)

George Peppard (Bret), George Hamilton (Maurice), Horst Buchholz (Jurgen), Capucine (Nicole), Sam Wanamaker (Ray), Jean-Pierre Cassel (Bick), Annie Duperey (Fabienne).

Close friends of different nationalities (American, German, French, English) find themselves torn apart when WW II erupts. Before they go their separate ways, they vow to meet each year at the same cafe. During the war, most find themselves fighting for the Allies, but the German must reluctantly battle on the opposing side. Though some of the friends lose their lives, most survive to meet on the day Paris is liberated. This big-budget war picture is punctuated with some fairly exciting battle scenes, but the "same time, next year" angle is more than a little unbelievable.

d, Hank Milestone [Umberto Lenzi]; w, Umberto Lenzi, Jose Luis Martinez Molls, and Gianfranco Clerici; ed, Vincenzo Tomasi; ph, Jose Luis Alcaine, Eastmancolor; m, Riz Ortolani.

(PR:C MPAA:NR)

FROM HERE TO ETERNITY****

(1953) 118m COL bw

Burt Lancaster (Sgt. Milton Warden), Deborah Kerr (Karen Holmes), Montgomery Clift (Robert E. Lee Prewitt), Frank Sinatra (Angelo Maggio), Donna Reed (Alma Lorene), Ernest Borgnine (Sgt. "Fatso" Judson), Philip Ober (Capt. Dana Holmes), Jack Warden (Cpl. Buckley), Mickey Shaughnessy (Sgt. Leva), Harry Bellaver (Mazzioli), George Reeves (Sgt. Maylon Stark), John Dennis (Sgt. Ike Galovitch), Tim Ryan (Sgt. Pete Karelsen).

The massive James Jones novel, thought to be impossible to convert to the screen because of its frank portrayal of sex and vulgar language, is brought forth in this powerful, unforgettable portrait of pre-WW II enlisted men, their women, and the grim destiny that overtook them all. The film opens as Robert E. Lee Prewitt (Montgomery Clift) arrives at Schofield Barracks, the army base at Pearl Harbor, transferring after he refused to continue as a company boxer at his previous post. His new commander, Capt. Holmes (Philip Ober), a brutal, insecure officer, promises Prewitt that if he boxes on the company team he will be given the post of bugler, a job he very much wants. But Prewitt refuses, haunted by previous ugly experiences in the ring. For Prewitt's obstinacy, Holmes orders Sgt. Warden (Burt Lancaster) to give the soldier every dirty detail in the company. As it turns out, Warden is also involved with Holmes' wife, Karen (Deborah Kerr), and he secretly meets with her in what becomes a torrid affair. Meanwhile, Prewitt's suffering is eased by his newly established relationship with Alma Lorene (Donna Reed), a hostess at the New Congress Club, a dance hall frequented by enlisted men. Prewitt's only other friend, Maggio (Frank Sinatra), a wise-cracking, tough enlisted man, commits several small offenses and draws repeated company punishment—especially from a sadistic sergeant named Fatso (Ernest Borgnine) who hates Maggio because he's Italian. FROM HERE TO ETERNITY was an uphill battle all the way for its director, Fred Zinnemann. Most of his war was with Columbia's dictator, Harry Cohn, who had purchased the novel for $82,000 and was determined to retain its seamy story, raw language, and violence, rejecting one adaptation after another. The Army was not happy with Jones' fierce indictment of its system and refused to allow the use of Schofield Barracks unless some major concessions were made. One chief point involved the role of Capt. Holmes. In the novel he gets away with everything and is even promoted to major, but in the film he is cashiered for his cruelty and malfeasance. The feature roles were also difficult to cast under Cohn's whimsical supervision. Zinnemann had to fight to cast Clift; Sinatra, whose career was on the downswing, had to beg Cohn for the part of Maggio (exaggerated and fictionalized by Mario Puzo in The Godfather). The film won Academy Awards for Best Picture, Best Direction, and Best Screenplay and for Sinatra and Reed in best supporting roles, earning eight Oscars in all. Clift was utterly depressed at not winning for Best Actor; he considered this his superlative effort. Zinnemann gave him a consolation prize he kept all his life, a miniature gold trumpet mounted like an Oscar.

p, Buddy Adler; d, Fred Zinnemann; w, Daniel Taradash, based on the novel by James Jones; ed, William Lyon; ph, Burnett Guffey; m, George Duning.

(PR:C MPAA:NR)

FULL METAL JACKET****

(1987) 116m Natant/WB c

Matthew Modine *(Pvt. Joker)*, Adam Baldwin *(Animal Mother)*, Vincent D'Onofrio *(Leonard Lawrence, Pvt. Gomer Pyle)*, Lee Ermey *(Gunnery Sgt. Hartman)*, Dorian Harewood *(Eightball)*, Arliss Howard *(Pvt. Cowboy)*, Kevyn Major Howard *(Rafterman)*, Ed O'Ross *(Walter J. Schinoski, Lt. Touchdown)*, John Stafford *(Doc Jay)*, John Terry *(Lt. Lockhart)*, Kirk Taylor *(Payback)*, Ian Tyler *(Lt. Cleves)*, Keiron Jecchinis *(Crazy Earl)*.

An uncompromisingly bleak film, as cold and distant as they come, Stanley Kubrick's FULL METAL JACKET is a perversely fascinating movie—one that answers no questions, offers no hope, and has no meaning. Highly structured, the film is presented in two parts: the first details the training of a group of Marines at the hands of the sadistic and foul-mouthed DI, Gunnery Sgt. Hartman (Lee Ermey); and the second follows one of the recruits, Pvt. Joker (Matthew Modine), a reporter for *Stars and Stripes* who finds himself in combat at the height of the Tet Offensive. There is no characterization, no heroics, no drama in FULL METAL JACKET; instead, Kubrick coolly shows the systematic dehumanization required to turn men into killing machines, then sits back and watches as they perform their assigned task. From the shaving of the recruits' heads, the assignment of generic nicknames, and the profane bellowing that replaces conversation to the orderly, ritualized existence of the camp, the training period is designed to drain all traces of individuality and basic humanity from the soldier and to replace them with a cold hatred that can be directed at the enemy and used without hesitation. With his sarcastic humor and contradictory nature, Joker is the only character who retains a modicum of personality (indeed, one annoyed commander tells him to "get with the program and join up for the big win"). Kubrick, however, dangles him before the viewer and then pulls him away slowly until Joker, too, is drained of his humanity. Technically, FULL METAL JACKET is as flawless as any other meticulously designed Kubrick work and boasts superb cinematography by Douglas Milsome. Filming entirely in England, Kubrick scouted locations and chose a military barracks outside London that doubles for Parris Island in the film. He also used a vast, deserted gasworks in London's East End, a plant area that had been bombed to ruination during WW II, and further destroyed the area to great effectiveness. Kubrick's savvy and eclectic choice of music includes the songs "Hello Vietnam," "These Boots Are Made for Walking," "Chapel of Love," "Wooly Bully," "Surfin' Bird," "The Marines Hymn," and a particularly effective use of the Rolling Stones' "Paint It Black."

p, Stanley Kubrick; d, Stanley Kubrick; w, Stanley Kubrick, Michael Herr, and Gustav Hasford, based on the novel *The Short-Timers* by Gustav Hasford; ed, Martin Hunter; ph, Douglas Milsome, Rank Color; m, Abigail Mead.

(PR:O MPAA:R)

FUNNY, DIRTY LITTLE WAR, A***½

(1983, Arg.) 80m Aries c (NO HABRA MAS PENAS NI OLVIDO)

Federico Luppi *(Ignacio Fuentes)*, Hector Bidonde *(Suprino)*, Victor Laplace *(Reinaldo)*, Rodolfo Ranni *(Llanos)*, Miguel Angel Sola *(Juan)*, Julio De Grazia *(Cpl. Garcia)*, Lautaro Murua *(Mayor Gugliemini)*, Jose Maria Lopez *(Mateo Guastavino)*.

This powerful black comedy takes place in 1974 in the rural Argentine town of Colonia Vela, where Peronist factions are split into two forces—the Marxist ultraleft and the Fascist ultraright. Although all shout "Viva Peron," they have different views on how he should govern—each group believing their impression of Juan Peron (who died in 1974) is the true one. When the town mayor (Lautaro Murua), the local union organizer (Victor Laplace), the Per-

GALLIPOLI—

onist boss (Hector Bidonde), and the local police chief (Rodolfo Ranni) conspire to oust the supposedly Marxist assistant (Jose Maria Lopez) to the town's deputy mayor, Ignacio Fuentes (Federico Luppi), Fuentes takes matters into his own hands. He barricades himself in City Hall along with some opportunistic supporters, one of whom (Julio De Grazia) is a likable but dopey patrolman who is instantly promoted to corporal and later sergeant. When Fuentes refuses to surrender, a battle breaks out and the little village of Colonia Vela becomes a microcosm of the country's political situation. The result is a shockingly potent film, paralleling violence and torture with some brilliant comedy. Scenes of cold and brutal violence are placed directly next to scenes of broad, slapstick humor—making the viewer more than a little ill at ease. Unfortunately, many of the political references will lose viewers who lack prior knowledge of Peronist politics. The film won the Silver Bear at the 1984 Berlin Film Festival, after which director Hector Olivera, curiously, followed up with three Roger Corman cheapies—BARBARIAN QUEEN; WIZARDS OF THE LOST KINGDOM; and COCAINE WARS. (In Spanish; English subtitles.)

p, Fernando Ayala and Luis Osvaldo Repetto; d, Hector Olivera; w, Hector Olivera and Roberto Cossa, based on the novel by Osvaldo Soriano; ed, Eduardo Lopez; ph, Leonardo Solis; m, Oscar Cardoza Ocampo.

(PR:O   MPAA:NR)

G

GALLIPOLI****
(1981, Aus.) 110m PAR c

Mark Lee *(Archy)*, Bill Kerr *(Jack)*, Mel Gibson *(Frank Dunne)*, Ron Graham *(Wallace Hamilton)*, Harold Hopkins *(Les McCann)*, Charles Yunupingu *(Zac)*, Heath Harris *(Stockman)*, Gerda Nicolson *(Rose Hamilton)*.

Focusing on two fleet-footed young Australians, Peter Weir's extraordinarily moving antiwar film examines the disastrous WW I invasion of Gallipoli by the Australian-New Zealand Army Corps (ANZAC). Archy (Mark Lee) and Frank (Mel Gibson) come from different backgrounds, but share a love of king, country, and life—never more apparent than when the two speedsters race each other. Together, they join the army and become part of the ill-fated campaign to wrest control of the Dardanelles from the Ottoman Turks. Meeting heavy resistance from the well-entrenched Turks and their German allies, the ANZAC offensive bogs down on the beachhead, and poor generalship and worse communication eventually lead to a suicidal assault and a tremendous waste of young lives. Director Weir (PICNIC AT HANGING ROCK; THE YEAR OF LIVING DANGEROUSLY) and cinematographer Russell Boyd's recreation of the invasion and battle action is stunning, but what makes GALLIPOLI such an affecting film is its intimate presentation of the friendship between Archy and Frank (wonderfully essayed by Lee and Gibson). Weir uses the first part of the film to establish the vibrant optimism of their lives Down Under, then demonstrates how quickly and pointlessly such young lives can be snuffed out. Not always easy to watch, GALLIPOLI is both a fitting testimony to the courage of the thousands of Australians and New Zealanders who died fighting for their country and one of the most powerful filmic examinations of the futility and tragic cost of war.

p, Robert Stigwood and Patricia Lovell; d, Peter Weir; w, David Williamson, based on a story by Weir; ed, William Anderson; ph, Russell Boyd, Panavision, Eastmancolor; m, Brian May.

(PR:A-C   MPAA:PG)

GARDEN OF THE FINZI-CONTINIS, THE****
(1971, It./Ger.) 103m Documento Film-CCC Filmkunst/Titanus c (IL GIARDINO DEL FINZI-CONTINI)

Dominique Sanda *(Micol)*, Lino Capolicchio *(Giorgio)*, Helmut Berger *(Alberto)*, Fabio Testi *(Malnate)*, Romolo Valli *(Giorgio's Father)*, Raffaele Curi *(Ernesto)*, Camillo Angelini-Rota *(Micol's Father)*, Katina Viglietti *(Micol's Mother)*, Inna Alexeiff *(Micol's Grandmother)*.

Although Vittorio De Sica, who has made some of the great Neo-Realist films (SHOESHINE; THE BICYCLE THIEF; and UMBERTO D), spent much of the latter half of his career acting in other director's works (Roberto Rossellini's GENERAL DELLA ROVERE, for example), THE GARDEN OF THE FINZI-CONTINIS is proof that the great director had not lost his touch. Set in Ferrara, Italy, during WW II, this story of love and culture unfurls effortlessly, albeit a trifle slowly. The Finzi-Continis are a wealthy Jewish-Italian family who cannot believe that the war will ever invade their hallowed garden walls. Rather than flee, they stay on in the false hope that they will not be betrayed, but as they sit, posteriors barely touching their exquisite furniture, they come to realize that Fascism is not going to go away and that they must join the fight against it. While this film bears very little resemblance to De Sica's early works (like all previously state-funded filmmakers, he needed to concern himself more with his films' commercial potential), it is still directed with the same De Sica skill. Constructed with a heavy emphasis on flashbacks, THE GARDEN OF THE FINZI-CONTINIS is one of those few pictures in which the flashbacks not only work, but are absolutely necessary, giving the viewer a historical perspective the characters lack. De Sica's handling of the unknowns in the cast is exceptional, as is his direction of the wonderful Dominique Sanda. (Available on videocassette in Italian with English subtitles and in a poorly dubbed version.)

p, Arthur Cohn and Gianni Hecht Lucari; d, Vittorio De Sica; w, Cesare Zavattini, Vittorio Bonicelli, and Ugo Pirro, based on the novel by Giorgio Bassani; ed, Adriana Novelli; ph, Ennio Guarnieri, Eastmancolor; m, Manuel De Sica.

(PR:C   MPAA:R)

GARDENS OF STONE****

(1987) 111m Tri-Star-ML Delphi Premier/Tri-Star c

James Caan *(Sgt. Clell Hazard)*, Anjelica Huston *(Samantha Davis)*, James Earl Jones *(Sgt. Maj. "Goody" Nelson)*, D.B. Sweeney *(Pvt. Jackie Willow)*, Dean Stockwell *(Capt. Homer Thomas)*, Mary Stuart Masterson *(Rachel Feld)*, Dick Anthony Williams *(First Sgt. "Slasher" Williams)*, Lonette McKee *(Betty Rae)*, Sam Bottoms *(Lt. Webber)*, Elias Koteas *(Pete Deveber)*, Larry Fishburne *(Cpl. Flanagan)*, Casey Siemaszko *(Pvt. Albert Wildman)*, Peter Masterson *(Col. Feld)*, Carlin Glynn *(Mrs. Feld)*.

After more than a decade of films that examined the war in Vietnam from many different angles, Francis Ford Coppola concentrated not on the heroics, battles, bravery, or camaraderie of the war, but simply on the burial of the dead, in GARDENS OF STONE. From the vantage point of Arlington National Cemetery—"The Gardens of Stone," its landscape of white crosses a somber battlefield of dead soldiers—war appears most senseless. Sgt. Clell Hazard (James Caan) is a military man through and through, a hard-bitten veteran who, in 1968, hates the Vietnam War but loves the service. His job is to oversee the men assigned to the Old Guard at Arlington, that elite corps of soldiers who stand watch over the Tomb of the Unknown Soldier, escort the many bodies to their final resting places, and engage in various drill exercises as a public relations function for the government. Assigned to Hazard's unit is Pvt. Jackie Willow (D.B. Sweeney), the son of a slain veteran who had been Hazard's pal and a gung-ho soldier frustrated over being stationed at Fort Myer, Virginia, when he wants to be at the front. Jackie grows close to a number of people at Arlington, including surrogate father Hazard; Hazard's girl friend, Samantha (Anjelica Huston); and Rachel (Mary Stuart Masterson), the young woman with whom he falls in love. Nevertheless, Jackie's fatal desire is to serve his country in Vietnam. Unjustly underrated upon its release, GARDENS OF STONE is a quiet, respectful film filled with emotional power, exceptional acting (especially by Caan), and technical virtuosity. Coppola was directing from the heart on this one: his son Giancarlo died in a boating accident during production. The film is dedicated to the Third US Infantry.

p, Michael I. Levy and Francis Ford Coppola; d, Francis Ford Coppola; w, Ronald Bass, based on the novel by Nicholas Proffitt; ed, Barry Malkin; ph, Jordan Cronenweth, Deluxe Color; m, Carmine Coppola.

(PR:O MPAA:R)

GATE OF HELL****

(1953, Jap.) 89m Daiei c (JIGOKUMEN)

Machiko Kyo *(Lady Kesa)*, Kazuo Hasegawa *(Moritoh)*, Isao Yamagata *(Wataru)*, Koreya Senda *(Kiyomori)*, Yataro Kurokawa *(Shigemori)*, Kikue Mohri *(Sawa)*, Kotaro Bando *(Rokuroh)*.

GATE OF HELL is the dazzlingly beautiful and simple Japanese tale, set in the 12th century, of a heroic samurai, Moritoh (matinee idol Kazuo Hasegawa), who is to be rewarded for his bravery with anything he desires by his country's ruler. What he most desires is the beautiful Lady Kesa (Machiko Kyo), though she is already married. Attempts are made to persuade Kesa to leave her husband (Isao Yamagata), but her devotion to him is great, and Moritoh is left with no other choice than to murder his rival. Less revered today than RASHOMON or UGETSU (both of which also starred the gorgeous Kyo), GATE OF HELL was the first Japanese color film to reach US shores and one of the pivotal Japanese releases of its day (premiering in the US in 1954). All three films helped to pave the way for a succession of Japanese releases in the US and to build an international reputation for Japanese cinema. Although it was not widely appreciated in Japan, it did receive two Academy Awards and the Grand Prize at Cannes. (In Japanese; English subtitles.)

p, Masaichi Nagata; d, Teinosuke Kinugasa; w, Teinosuke Kinugasa, based on a play by Kan Kikuchi; ph, Kohei Sugiyama, Eastmancolor; m, Yasushi Akutagawa.

(PR:C-O MPAA:NR)

GENERALE DELLA ROVERE****

(1959, It./Fr.) 130m Zebra-GAU/Continental bw (IL GENERALE DELLA ROVERE)

Vittorio De Sica *(Bardone/Grimaldi)*, Hannes Messemer *(Col. Mueller)*, Vittorio Caprioli *(Banchelli)*, Guiseppe Rossetti *(Fabrizio/Pietro Valeri)*, Sandra Milo *(Olga)*, Giovanna Ralli *(Valeria)*, Anne Vernon *(Chiara Fassio)*, Baronessa Barzani *(Contessa della Rovere)*.

GENERAL DELLA ROVERE was the film that returned director Roberto Rossellini to international favor after he ended his filmmaking collaboration with Ingrid Bergman (FEAR, 1954, was their final work together) and embarked on the documentary course of INDIA. Although Rossellini, who took on the project in order to survive, looked upon this film with shame, it is one of his great achievements, the story of a man who discovers his own morality by imitating another's. With this essentially Christian underlying theme, the film is set during the German occupation of Genoa during the winter of 1943-44. After Resistance leader Gen. della Rovere is accidentally murdered by Gestapo troops, the local Nazi commandant makes an offer to Bardone (Vittorio De Sica), an amoral, low-life swindler, to impersonate the general. In this guise, Bardone is sent to Milan jail, where he is supposed to find and identify a partisan leader whom della Rovere had planned to meet before his death. Bardone, however, gradually begins to identify with his fellow prisoners and assumes the moral stance, if not the full being, of the Resistance leader. Recalling Rossellini's great early achievements (OPEN CITY and PAISAN), GENERAL DELLA ROVERE is a powerful, beautifully acted picture, which—and this is the source of Rossellini's discontent with the work—retreads the ideas and forms of his past successes. While it may have been a step backwards in the development of this great filmmaker, this cannot diminish the film's undeniable strength. (In Italian; English subtitles.)

GERMANY, YEAR ZERO—

p, Morris Ergas; d, Roberto Rossellini; w, Sergio Amidei, Diego Fabbri, and Indro Montanelli, based on a novel by Montanelli; ed, Anna Maria Montanari and Cesare Cavagna; ph, Carlo Carlini; m, Renzo Rossellini.

(PR:C   MPAA:NR)

GERMANY, YEAR ZERO****

(1947, It./Fr./Ger.) 75m Tevere-Salvo D'Angelo-Sadfilm/Superfilm bw (GERMANIA, ANNO ZERO)

Edmund Moeschke (Edmund Koehler), Franz Kruger (Herr Koehler), Barbara Hintz (Eva Koehler), Werner Pittschau (Karlheinz Koehler), Erich Guhne (Prof. Enning).

One of cinema's most frightening films, GERMANY, YEAR ZERO concerns one of the most frightening periods of history. Directed by Roberto Rossellini on the streets of Berlin, the film takes place at a point between two eras—the "year zero" between the awful violence of Hitler's fascism and the Holocaust and the German people's subsequent realization of these horrors and their implication in them. It is a film about the limbo between past and future—that interminable present when history must start anew. The film follows Edmund (Edmund Moeschke), a 12-year-old who lives with nine adults in miserable conditions, just barely surviving on their meager ration cards, living with daily fear that their heat or gas will be cut off. The boy's father is on his deathbed, while his brother, a former Nazi, must live in hiding (and therefore gets no ration card) to keep his past from catching up with him, leaving it up to Edmund to take care of his family. He has no opportunity to live as a child or even attend school; too young to work, he spends his days trying to find food, barter on the black market, or do occasional jobs (such as selling records of Hitler's speeches to Allied soldiers). When he meets a former teacher (Erich Guhne), a homosexual Fascist who procures young boys for a Nazi general, Edmund gets it into his head that the strong must have the courage to kill the weak. Since everything in his life revolves around the number of mouths he must feed, Edmund decides to poison his father, believing it is right to kill the sickly old man. At this point, Year Zero begins for the boy, who finds the moral weight of his actions too much to bear. This is the third part of Rossellini's "War Trilogy," preceded by OPEN CITY and PAISAN. The videocassette is in German with English subtitles, but is one of the least legible examples of subtitling you're likely to find.

p, Roberto Rossellini; d, Roberto Rossellini; w, Roberto Rossellini, Carlo Lizzani, and Max Kolpet, based on a story by Rossellini; ed, Eraldo Da Roma; ph, Robert Juillard; m, Renzo Rossellini.

(PR:C   MPAA:NR)

GLORY AT SEA**½

(1952, Brit.) 100m Molton-BL/IF bw (GB: GIFT HORSE, THE)

Trevor Howard (Lt. Comdr. Hugh Fraser), Richard Attenborough (Dripper Daniels), Sonny Tufts (Yank Flanagan), James Donald (Lt. Richard Jennings), Joan Rice (June Mallory), Bernard Lee (Stripey Wood), Dora Bryan (Glad), Hugh Williams (Captain), Robin Bailey (Lt. Michael Grant).

An antiquated, formerly mothballed destroyer flying under the Union Jack as part of the US wartime lend-lease agreement with Britain is the star of this well-paced WW II drama. Hugh Fraser (Trevor Howard), the by-the-book captain of The Gift Horse, court-martialed eight years earlier and trying to salvage his career, is vilified by his crew, but eventually earns their respect in battle. The old warship and its crew (including Richard Attenborough and Sonny Tufts) also prove their mettle during an assault on the German docks and submarine pens at St. Nazaire, during which they are captured, but not before spearheading the successful mission. Liberties are taken with the facts of the actual spectacular navy commando operation.

p, George Pitcher; d, Compton Bennett; w, William Fairchild, William Rose, and Hugh Hastings, based on a story by Ivan Goff, Ben Roberts; ph, Harry Waxman.

(PR:A   MPAA:NR)

GO FOR BROKE***

(1951) 92m MGM bw

Van Johnson (Lt. Michael Grayson), Lane Nakano (Sam), George Miki (Chick), Akira Fukunaga (Frank), Ken K. Okamoto (Kaz), Henry Oyasato (O'Hara), Harry Hamada (Masami), Henry Nakamura (Tommy), Warner Anderson (Col. Charles W. Pence), Don Haggerty (Sgt. Wilson I. Culley), Gianna-Maria Canale (Rosina), Dan Riss (Capt. Solari).

When inexperienced Army lieutenant Michael Grayson (Van Johnson) receives his first WW II command, he is anything but happy to learn that his troops are all Japanese-Americans. After surviving basic training together, however, Grayson and the men of the 442nd Regimental Combat Team distinguish themselves in battle in Italy, overcoming their prejudices and growing closer in the process. Finally, in France, they perform a heroic action that saves a threatened battalion of Texas good old boys, proving themselves to be just as damn American as anyone and earning commendation from President Truman and Gen. Mark W. Clark. Johnson gives a solid performance, as do the Asian-American actors who play his charges, in this effective message film from writer-director Robert Pirosh and producer Dore Schary, who had earlier collaborated on BATTLEGROUND (1949).

p, Dore Schary; d, Robert Pirosh; w, Robert Pirosh; ed, James E. Newcom; ph, Paul C. Vogel; m, Alberto Colombo.

(PR:A   MPAA:NR)

GO TELL THE SPARTANS***½

(1978) 114m Spartan/AE c

Burt Lancaster *(Maj. Asa Barker)*, Craig Wasson *(Cpl. Stephen Courcey)*, Jonathan Goldsmith *(Sgt. Oleonowski)*, Marc Singer *(Capt. Al Olivetti)*, Joe Unger *(Lt. Raymond Hamilton)*, Dennis Howard *(Cpl. Abraham Lincoln)*, David Clennon *(Lt. Finley Wattsberg)*, Evan Kim *(Cowboy)*, John Megna *(Cpl. Ackley)*, Hilly Hicks *(Signalman Coffee)*, Dolph Sweet *(Gen. Hamitz)*, Clyde Kusatsu *(Col. Minh)*, James Hong *(Cpl. Oldman)*, Denice Kumagai *(Butterfly)*, Tad Horino *(One-Eyed Charlie)*, Phong Diep *(Minh's Interpreter)*, Ralph Brannen *(Minh's Aide-de-Camp)*, Mark Carlton *(Capt. Schlitz)*.

Lost in the shuffle between THE DEER HUNTER and APOCALYPSE NOW was this small Vietnam movie, set early in the war (1964), concerning Maj. Asa Barker (Burt Lancaster), commander of a small group of combat advisors. Ordered to send a platoon of Vietnamese militia (old men with shotguns commanded by a Communist-hating mercenary played by Evan Kim) and a squad of American advisors under the green Lt. Hamilton (Joe Unger) to garrison an old French stronghold, Barker, a veteran of three wars, argues that the site is of no value and that the only effect in putting troops there will be to mass the Viet Cong for an attack. He is overruled on the grounds that the French abandoned the spot and lost the war—"and we don't want to make the same mistake the French did." Barker is proved right, though, and before long the Viet Cong have besieged the isolated outpost. A helicopter arrives to evacuate the men, but is only big enough for the Americans. Heroically, Barker and Cpl. Courcey (Craig Wasson), who volunteered to serve in Vietnam, refuse to leave the old militiamen to the enemy's mercy, and make plans to lead the evacuation. Featuring a typically fine performance from Lancaster, GO TELL THE SPARTANS received good notices upon its release but never found an audience, perhaps because of its low budget (less than $1 million) and lack of spectacular battle scenes. While there are scenes of combat, the film deals more with the moral ambiguities of the war and the American military's inability—represented by Lancaster—to understand what they had gotten themselves into. Even at this point in the war, it is obvious that the US doesn't belong in Southeast Asia; the Army command is seen as greedy and stupid, the South Vietnamese as thoroughly corrupt (Lancaster has to bribe the local warlord to give the battle some air support). The title derives from the inscription above the French cemetery, quoting the doomed Spartans at Thermopylae: "Stranger, go tell the Spartans how we lie, loyal to their laws, here we die." This is an excellent war movie, one that puts the Vietnam War in a historical context and points up the futility of the whole thing.

p, Allan F. Boddoh and Mitchell Cannold; d, Ted Post; w, Wendell Mayes, based on the novel *Incident at Muc Wa* by Daniel Ford; ed, Millie Moore; ph, Harry Stradling, Jr.; m, Dick Halligan.

(PR:O MPAA:R)

GOING HOME**

(1988, Brit./Can.) 100m Opix-Primedia-BBC-CBS-Telefilm Canada-Ontario Film Development c

Nicholas Campbell *(Cpl. Brill)*, Milan Cheylov *(Pvt. Yashin)*, Albert Schultz *(Lance Cpl. Millen)*, Eugene Lipinski *(Maj. Bannerman)*, William Hope *(Lt. Anson)*, Sioned Mair *(Vember)*, Bradley Lavelle *(Pvt. Franklin)*, Peter Banks *(Sgt. Maj. Wagner)*, Peter Whitman *(Pvt. Corti)*, Ian Morton *(Pvt. Bates)*.

Breaking down "the wall of secrecy imposed by two governments to reveal a story so violent, so sinister, it has taken over 60 years for the truth to be told," as GOING HOME's advertising put it, this British-Canadian coproduction delves into the mystery behind the presence of 80 Canadian graves in a Welsh churchyard. After WW I, some 20,000 Canadian troops ready to be shipped home are placed in transit camps in Wales, among them Cpl. Brill (Nicholas Campbell), who struggles to put the trauma of war behind him while carrying on a torrid affair with a local schoolmistress (Sioned Mair). The soldiers, practically imprisoned by their allies as they await transport across the Atlantic and suffering from overcrowding, bad weather, and the general humiliation of their state, grow increasingly tense, precipitating an explosion of violence that results in several casualties and a senseless continuation of the horrors of war. The film takes a damning look at the way societies treat the men that fight for them in what, for Americans at least, is a particularly fresh context.

p, Ray Marshall; d, Terry Ryan; ed, Tim Kruydenburg; ph, Paul Reed;

(PR:C MPAA:NR)

GONE WITH THE WIND*****

(1939) 220m SELZ/MGM c

Vivien Leigh *(Scarlett O'Hara)*, Clark Gable *(Rhett Butler)*, Leslie Howard *(Ashley Wilkes)*, Olivia de Havilland *(Melanie Hamilton)*, Butterfly McQueen *(Prissy)*, Hattie McDaniel *(Mammy)*, Everett Brown *(Big Sam)*, Zack Williams *(Elijah)*, Thomas Mitchell *(Gerald O'Hara)*, Barbara O'Neil *(Ellen O'Hara)*, Victor Jory *(Jonas Wilkerson)*, Evelyn Keyes *(Suellen O'Hara)*, Ann Rutherford *(Careen O'Hara)*, Alicia Rhett *(India Wilkes)*, Jane Darwell *(Dolly Merriwether)*, Eddie "Rochester" Anderson *(Uncle Peter)*, Ward Bond *(Yankee Captain, Tom)*, Cammie King *(Bonnie Blue Butler)*, Mickey Kuhn *(Beau Wilkes)*.

The best-remembered and most publicized film in Hollywood's colorful history, this star-studded Civil War epic based on Margaret Mitchell's immensely popular novel is as powerful and moving today as it was when first released in 1939. Shot in magnificent Technicolor and lavishly mounted by producer David O. Selznick, GONE WITH THE WIND presents its familiar story of the South at war with a minimum of actual battle scenes, showing the war's toll through corpse-strewn battlefields and, more importantly, through its impact on the lives of Scarlett O'Hara (Vivien Leigh), Rhett Butler (Clark Gable), Ashley Wilkes (Leslie Howard), and Melanie Hamilton (Olivia de Havil-

GOOD MORNING, VIETNAM—

land). Many Americans are more familiar with the story of these characters than they are with the actual history of the War Between the States, but for those who *don't* know the tale, Scarlett is the achingly beautiful daughter of Gerald O'Hara (Thomas Mitchell), lord of Tara, the plantation Scarlett comes to have faith in when all else fails her. Capable of winning any man but the one she loves—Ashley, who marries her eternally understanding cousin Melanie—Scarlett is widowed (by a young man she has wed on a whim) almost before the war has begun. She and Melanie pass much of the war in Atlanta (both anxiously awaiting the return of Ashley, who has gone off to fight), where Scarlett is pursued by Rhett, a suave blockade-runner who sees through her manipulative ways but loves her anyway. With Sherman's troops approaching an Atlanta littered with Confederate wounded and dead (shown in one of Hollywood's most memorable scenes, accomplished with an army of extras, shot from a 125-foot crane), Scarlett delivers Melanie's baby. Rhett then helps them flee the city as it is engulfed in fire (an incredible conflagration that sent flames high into the skies over Culver City as Selznick torched more than 30 acres of the old Pathe backlot, with every Technicolor camera in Hollywood rolling while firemen from three communities stood by). The film's focus then shifts back to Tara; the war winds to a close; Scarlet, still very much in love with the unattainable Ashley, weds another to save the plantation from financial ruin and is again widowed. Eventually, she and Rhett begin a tempestuous marriage and have a little girl who dies in a riding accident. By the film's end, Scarlett realizes that it is Rhett and not Ashley that she loves, but it's too late (or is it?), as Scarlett leaves the audience with her famous line, ". . . tomorrow is another day." Everything about GONE WITH THE WIND is superlative, from the direction by Victor Fleming (who, along with Selznick and production designer William Cameron Menzies, was primarily responsible for the film's brilliance) through the extraordinary lead performances by Gable, Howard, de Havilland, and Leigh—who won the role of Scarlett, the most sought after in film history, from a field that included Paulette Goddard, Norma Shearer, Miriam Hopkins, Jean Harlow, Carole Lombard, Tallulah Bankhead, Claudette Colbert, Jean Arthur, Joan Bennett, and Irene Dunne, among some 2,000 women tested in a much-ballyhooed two-year talent search. Moreover, all the supporting players, from Mitchell to Hattie McDaniel, are equally outstanding. Noted "woman's" director George Cukor began at the film's helm, but was replaced by Fleming (whose WIZARD OF OZ was also released in 1939), reportedly because Cukor had shifted the focus of the film too much to Scarlett and Melanie. During the course of the production Fleming suffered a nervous breakdown and Sam Wood stepped in until he was well enough to return. Though only Sidney Howard, who won an Oscar for Best Screenplay, is credited, a number of well-known writers also contributed to the script, including Ben Hecht, F. Scott Fitzgerald, and Jo Swerling. A big winner at the box office—where worldwide receipts totaled $50 million by 1959—and at the 1939 Academy Awards, where it took nine major Oscars and two "special" ones, GONE WITH THE WIND has been given several re-releases. Most notably, in 1967 it was released by MGM in a wide-screen format that greatly altered the original visuals (cutting off a significant portion of the frame); then, in 1989, for the film's 50th anniversary, Ted Turner (who bought MGM in 1986) distributed a restored version that brought its color back to its original glory—his penchant for colorizing finally put to good use.

p, David O. Selznick; d, Victor Fleming, George Cukor, and Sam Wood; w, Sidney Howard, Jo Swerling, Charles MacArthur, Ben Hecht, John Lee Mahin, John Van Druten, Oliver H.P. Garrett, Winston Miller, John Balderston, Michael Foster, Edwin Justus Mayer, F. Scott Fitzgerald, and David O. Selznick, based on the novel by Margaret Mitchell; ed, Hal C. Kern and James E. Newcom; ph, Ernest Haller and Lee Garmes, Technicolor; m, Max Steiner.

(PR:A MPAA:NR)

GOOD MORNING, VIETNAM***½
(1987) 119m Touchstone-Silver Partners III/BV c

Robin Williams *(Adrian Cronauer)*, Forest Whitaker *(Edward Garlick)*, Tung Thanh Tran *(Tuan)*, Chintara Sukapatana *(Trinh)*, Bruno Kirby *(Lt. Steven Hauk)*, Robert Wuhl *(Marty Lee Dreiwitz)*, J.T. Walsh *(Sgt. Major Dickerson)*, Noble Willingham *(Gen. Taylor)*, Richard Edson *(Pvt. Abersold)*, Juney Smith *(Phil McPherson)*, Richard Portnow *(Dan "The Man" Levitan)*.

Robin Williams was finally given a showcase for his rapid-fire improvisational wit in this, the first comedy set in Vietnam. Based on the story of real-life Armed Forces Radio disc jockey Adrian Cronauer, GOOD MORNING, VIETNAM begins in 1965, as Cronauer (Williams) arrives in Saigon, imported because his comedic broadcasts have proven a huge morale-booster elsewhere. At the AFR's Saigon station, Cronauer incurs the wrath of superiors who resent his intrusion in their programming, with its dull announcers, health and safety tips, censored news, and geriatric playlist. Cronauer changes all that, knocking listening troops out of their stupor with his howling salutation—"Gooood morning, Vietnammmm!"—hip song selection, and comedic improvisation, poking wild fun at any and all sacred cows. Outside the studio, he grows infatuated with a beautiful Vietnamese (Chintara Sukapatana), teaches her English class, and befriends her young brother (Tung Thanh Tran)—who, unbeknownst to Cronauer, is also a Viet Cong sympathizer, leading eventually to Cronauer's dis3charge for fraternizing with the enemy. Cronauer departs sobered by the reality of the escalating conflict, leaving his loyal aide (Forest Whitaker) to carry on his legacy at the microphone. GOOD MORNING, VIETNAM stumbles whenever Williams isn't behind the mike, placing him in melodramatic, hackneyed situations that become increasingly predictable and preposterous, and director Barry Levinson's seemingly endless reaction shots of listeners grooving to the DJ's antics become irritating. Levinson manages, however, to be one of the few filmmakers to show the Vietnamese as complex, cultured people, rather than helpless victims or the faceless enemy. Whitaker (BIRD) does wonders with a thankless part, Sukapatana is impressive, and Bruno Kirby, as Cronauer's nemesis, comes as close as any actor could to walking off with a film dominated by Williams at his best.

p, Mark Johnson, Larry Brezner, Ben Moses, and Harry Benn; d, Barry Levinson; w, Mitch Markowitz; ed, Stu Linder; ph, Peter Sova, Deluxe Color; m, Alex North.

(PR:O MPAA:R)

GOOD, THE BAD, AND THE UGLY, THE****

(1967, It./Sp.) 161m Produzioni Europee/UA c (IL BUONO, IL BRUTTO, IL CATTIVO)

Clint Eastwood *(Joe)*, Eli Wallach *(Tuco)*, Lee Van Cleef *(Setenza)*, Aldo Giuffre, Chelo Alonso, Mario Brega

Director Sergio Leone's epic end to the Clint Eastwood "Dollars" trilogy is a stunning, panoramic view of the West during the Civil War. THE GOOD, THE BAD, AND THE UGLY is a deceptively simple story detailing the efforts of three drifters, the "Good" (Eastwood), the "Bad" (Lee Van Cleef), and the "Ugly" (Eli Wallach), to find a fortune hidden in the unmarked grave of a man named Bill Carson. Leone's narrative structure is incredibly complex, with the characters' paths intersecting and sometimes intertwining (at various points in the story two of them may appear to team up against the other, but all of them ultimately want the treasure for themselves), and, as their personal brutality increases (toward themselves and others), the Civil War begins to enter their lives and dwarf their petty crimes. The war, a minor disturbance at first, slowly intrudes into their territory and eventually involves Eastwood and Wallach in a massive battle for an unimportant bridge, in which hundreds of soldiers go to their pointless doom. The scale of violence shocks these two violent men; Eastwood (whose character begins to show a humanity only hinted at in the previous two films) states that he has never "seen so many men wasted so badly." This is Leone's most violent film— necessarily showing the amount of brutality men can perform against each other—but also one of his most compassionate. One of its most memorable scenes shows the Union troops organizing an orchestra of Confederate prisoners-musicians to play an idyllic, beautiful tune (this is one of Ennio Morricone's finest musical scores) to cover the noise as Van Cleef, posing as a Union officer, tortures his prisoners. The effect is haunting, and recalls stories of similar incidents in Nazi death camps. Another touching moment occurs when Eastwood comes across a dying young soldier, covers the shivering man with his duster, and helps him smoke his final cigarette. Unlike the previous two entries in the trilogy, this was a big-budget effort; Leone expended more than $1 million on the film, more than the first two put together. Nearly one-fourth of that sum went to Eastwood, suddenly one of the high-ticket actors of the world. Though not Leone's masterpiece (which would be ONCE UPON A TIME IN THE WEST, 1969, in which the director synthesizes scale, narrative, casting, and style), THE GOOD, THE BAD, AND THE UGLY is a massive, many-faceted film that continues to hold up, viewing after viewing.

p, Alberto Grimaldi; d, Sergio Leone; w, Luciano Vincenzoni and Sergio Leone, based on a story by Age-Scarpelli, Vincenzoni, Leone; ed, Nino Baragli and Eugenio Alabiso; ph, Tonino Delli Colli, Techniscope, Technicolor; m, Ennio Morricone.

(PR:O MPAA:NR)

GRAND ILLUSION*****

(1937, Fr.) 95m R.A.C./World Pictures bw (LA GRANDE ILLUSION)

Jean Gabin *(Marechal)*, Pierre Fresnay *(Capt. de Boeldieu)*, Erich von Stroheim *(Von Rauffenstein)*, Marcel Dalio *(Rosenthal)*, Dita Parlo *(Elsa)*, Julien Carette *(Cartier)*, Gaston Modot *(Surveyor)*, Georges Peclet *(Soldier)*, Edouard Daste *(Teacher)*, Sylvain Itkine *(Demolder)*, Jacques Becker *(English Officer)*.

One of the undeniably great films in the history of cinema, Jean Renoir's GRAND ILLUSION is a comment on the borders that divide people, classes, armies, and countries. The film opens during WW I, as Marechal (Jean Gabin) and Boeldieu (Pierre Fresnay) are shot down by German ace Von Rauffenstein (Erich von Stroheim). The two survive the crash and are invited to lunch by Rauffenstein before ground troops arrive to cart the French officers off to a POW camp. Although Marechal and Boeldieu are compatriots, the latter has more in common with Von Rauffenstein, both of them being members of the white-gloved aristocracy. After lunch the Frenchmen are placed in barracks, where French officer Rosenthal (Marcel Dalio), a Jew, befriends them, along with several British officers who have also been taken prisoner. The newcomers join the others in working on an escape tunnel beneath the barracks, but a French victory on the Western Front is a sign that the war is turning against the Germans, and Marechal, Boeldieu, and the rest of the French prisoners are transferred to another prison, where they are reunited with Von Rauffenstein. Now confined to a neck brace after sustaining an injury in combat, the Commandant warmly welcomes the Frenchmen, pointing out that his prison, Wintersborn, is escape-proof. He treats his prisoners with great deference, having them to dinner and extending what meager courtesies he can, talking with Boeildieu about how this war will bring to an end the gentlemanly class of officers, dispensing with the honor and dignity of their rank and bloodlines. Caught someplace in between his loyalty to a member of his class (Von Rauffenstein) and to his country, Boeldieu once again agrees to assist his fellow prisoners in their escape attempts. Directed with patience and care by Renoir, the film was banned in Germany by Nazi Propaganda Minister Josef Goebbels, who labeled it "Cinematographic Enemy No. 1" and compelled his Italian counterpart to have the film banned in that country, although the 1937 Venice Film Festival gave the film a "Best Artistic Ensemble" award. It was thought that all European prints of the film were destroyed by the Nazis, but American troops uncovered a negative in Munich in 1945 (preserved, strangely, by the Germans themselves), leading to the edited film's reconstruction. Gabin, Fresnay, Dalio, and Stroheim all give impressive performances in this beautifully directed and written film. (In French; English subtitles.)

GREAT DICTATOR, THE—

p, Raymond Blondy; d, Jean Renoir; w, Jean Renoir and Charles Spaak; ed, Marguerite Renoir; ph, Christian Matras; m, Joseph Kosma.

(PR:A MPAA:NR)

GREAT DICTATOR, THE*****

(1940) 127m UA bw

Charles Chaplin (Adenoid Hynkel, Dictator of Ptomania/A Jewish Barber), Paulette Goddard (Hannah), Jack Oakie (Napaloni, Dictator of Bacteria), Reginald Gardiner (Schultz), Henry Daniell (Garbitsch), Billy Gilbert (Herring), Maurice Moscovich (Mr. Jaeckel), Emma Dunn (Mrs. Jaeckel), Grace Hayle (Mme. Napaloni), Carter de Haven (Bacterian Ambassador), Bernard Gorcey (Mr. Mann), Paul Weigel (Mr. Agar).

THE GREAT DICTATOR is Charlie Chaplin's brilliant and heartfelt plea for world peace and humanity in an era of atomic weaponry, mass annihilation, and the spread of fascism. Chaplin, well aware of the ironic physical similarity between his sweet Little Tramp and Adolf Hitler (curiously, Chaplin and Hitler were born within four days of one another in 1889), casts himself in a dual role as a nameless Jewish barber (looking much like the Little Tramp) and as Adenoid Hynkel, Dictator of Ptomania. The barber, a soldier for the German Army in WW I, awakens from a state of amnesia to learn that Hynkel, the country's new dictator, is calling for the persecution of all Jews. The barber's friend, Hannah (Paulette Goddard), is forced to flee the country; his barber shop is defaced and burned; finally, he is arrested and sent to a concentration camp for sheltering an old friend, Schultz (Reginald Gardiner). He escapes from the camp, is mistaken for Hynkel, and is ushered to a grandstand to make a victorious pro-Fascist speech to the citizens of a recently invaded country; instead, the clownish barber finds the courage to make an impassioned, prophetic plea for world peace. Filled with equal parts of humanity, outrage, and comedy, THE GREAT DICTATOR contains some of Chaplin's finest moments, including the famous upside-down flying sequence in which the barber doesn't even realize that he is not flying upright; Hynkel's fiery speech, delivered in an unintelligible German-English gibberish; and the film's scene of great genius, Hynkel's "ballet" with an air-filled globe of the world-tossing it, kicking it, adoring it, and, finally, destroying it as only a dictator dreaming of world domination could. The power of this strangely haunting film is augmented in the realization of how the extremes of human nature in the first half of this century were personified by these two mustached figures—Hitler and the Little Tramp.

p, Charles Chaplin; d, Charles Chaplin; w, Charles Chaplin; ed, Willard Nico; ph, Roland Totheroh and Karl Struss; m, Meredith Willson.

(PR:A MPAA:NR)

GREAT ESCAPE, THE****

(1963) 169m UA c

Steve McQueen ("Cooler King" Hilts), James Garner ("The Scrounger" Hendley), Richard Attenborough ("Big X" Bartlett), James Donald (Senior Officer Ramsey), Charles Bronson (Danny Velinski), Donald Pleasence ("The Forger" Blythe), James Coburn ("The Manufacturer" Sedgwick), David McCallum (Ashley-Pitt), Gordon Jackson (MacDonald), John Leyton (Willie), Angus Lennie ("The Mole" Ives), Nigel Stock (Cavendish), Jud Taylor (Goff), William Russell (Sorren), Robert Desmond ("The Tailor" Griffith), Tom Adams (Nimmo).

Masterfully directed and written, with an infectious undercurrent of wry humor, this classic WW II POW escape picture presents an all-star cast as the most hardened Allied prisoners with whom the Germans have to contend. These prisoners, who have all repeatedly attempted to get beyond the barbed wire, are brought together in a special, "escape-proof" camp. Naturally, the first thing they set about doing is planning another escape—not just any escape, but one so massive that thousands of German troops will be kept away from the front in the effort to track them down. The prime instigators include: "Big X" (Richard Attenborough), the British master planner; a Polish tunnel-digging expert (Charles Bronson); a forger of passports and papers (Donald Pleasence); and two Americans, "The Scrounger" (James Garner), in charge of assembling needed supplies, and Hilts (Steve McQueen), "The Cooler King," who has his own ideas about how to get out and who uses a baseball and mitt to wile away his days in solitary confinement when they fail. The prisoners ingeniously go about digging three tunnels, and though one of them is discovered, the big breakout still takes place and the film follows the principals as they try to make their way to safety—some successfully, others meeting tragic ends, but all providing great excitement. Based on a book detailing a real-life mass escape of Allied troops in 1942, producer-director John Sturges' film is involving throughout, due mainly to the universally excellent performances of its stellar cast. Also notable is Elmer Bernstein's exhilarating score, which is perfectly suited to the film's nonstop tension. A hit with the critics and at the box office, THE GREAT ESCAPE is for many the great "escape" film.

p, John Sturges; d, John Sturges; w, James Clavell and W.R. Burnett, based on the book by Paul Brickhill; ed, Ferris Webster; ph, Daniel L. Fapp, Deluxe Color; m, Elmer Bernstein.

(PR:A MPAA:NR)

GREAT GUNS**½

(1941) 73m FOX bw

Stan Laurel (Stan), Oliver Hardy (Oliver), Sheila Ryan (Ginger Hammond), Dick Nelson (Dan Forrester), Edmund MacDonald (Hippo), Charles Trowbridge (Col. Ridley), Ludwig Stossel (Dr. Hugo Schickel), Kane Richmond (Capt. Baker), Mae Marsh (Aunt Martha), Ethel Griffies (Aunt Agatha), Paul Harvey (Gen. Essick).

Stan and Ollie (Laurel and Hardy) are the chauffeur and gardener for Dan Forrester (Dick Nelson), a silver-spoon-in-the-mouth millionaire's son. He's drafted into the service, and Stan and Ollie join the Army to be near him, accompanied by Penelope, the pair's pet crow (an obviously mechanical bird), which hides in Ollie's trousers during inspections. Dan would much prefer to make it on his own without these mother hens, who drive Hippo (Edmund MacDonald), their sergeant at the cavalry camp in Texas, into several tantrums of frustration in his attempts to train them. The young scion falls for postal worker Ginger (Sheila Ryan), while Stan and Ollie conclude their careers by helping win a maneuvers campaign with some of the weirdest planning ever seen. This isn't one of Laurel and Hardy's funniest, but there's enough to keep you smiling. Look for Alan Ladd in a small part as a soldier in a photography store. On a par with BUCK PRIVATES, the Abbott and Costello feature made the same year.

p, Sol M. Wurtzel; d, Monty Banks; w, Lou Breslow; ed, Al DeGaetano; ph, Glen MacWilliams.

(PR:AAA MPAA:NR)

GREAT SANTINI, THE****

(1979) 115m Orion/WB c

Robert Duvall (Bull Meechum), Blythe Danner (Lillian Meechum), Michael O'Keefe (Ben Meechum), Lisa Jane Persky (Mary Anne Meechum), Julie Anne Haddock (Karen Meechum), Brian Andrews (Matthew Meechum), Stan Shaw (Toomer Smalls), Theresa Merritt (Arrabelle Smalls), David Keith (Red Pettus).

Robert Duvall received an Academy Award nomination for his forceful performance as a warrior without a war in this touching, well-crafted drama based on a novel by Pat Conroy (THE LORDS OF DISCIPLINE). As Marine pilot Bull Meechum, he rules his family with military discipline, setting impossibly high standards for his four children (Julie Ann Haddock, Brian Andrews, Lisa Jane Persky, and Michael O'Keefe). When Bull's harsh manner becomes too oppressive for his offspring, they know that their mother, Lillian (Blythe Danner), is there to provide an understanding shoulder to cry on, especially the sensitive Ben (O'Keefe), whose battle to earn his father's respect is most tellingly played out in one-on-one basketball games that force Bull to play dirty to win. Although Bull's kids are never able to reach their father (or he them), they do offer him the kind of stoic tribute that would have made him proud when tragedy strikes. Deftly scripted, beautifully shot—making good use of its South Carolina locations—and magnificently acted, THE GREAT SANTINI was deservedly nominated for an Academy Award as Best Picture. Though its emotions are big, the performances are so nicely nuanced that sentiment never overwhelms the story's emotional realism. In addition to Duvall's tour-de-force performance, Danner is outstanding as the nurturing mother, and O'Keefe's heartfelt portrayal of the tortured Ben earned him an Oscar nomination as Best Supporting Actor.

p, Charles A. Pratt; d, Lewis John Carlino; w, Lewis John Carlino, based on the novel by Pat Conroy; ed, Houseley Stevenson; ph, Ralph Woolsey, Technicolor; m, Elmer Bernstein.

(PR:C MPAA:PG)

GREEN BERETS, THE**

(1968) 141m Batjac/WB c

John Wayne (Col. Mike Kirby), David Janssen (George Beckworth), Jim Hutton (Sgt. Petersen), Aldo Ray (Sgt. Muldoon), Raymond St. Jacques (Doc McGee), Bruce Cabot (Col. Morgan), Jack Soo (Col. Cai), George Takei (Capt. Nim), Patrick Wayne (Lt. Jamison).

Only John Wayne could have made a flag-waving film about the Vietnam War in which excitement and impressive battle scenes are the focus and moral ambiguity is nowhere to be found. Wayne—who codirected with Ray Kellogg, and whose Batjac Productions put the project together—stars as Col. Mike Kirby, the blood-and-guts commander of a regiment of battle-toughened Green Berets who courageously defend, lose, and then retake an important position. Later, Kirby leads a mission behind enemy lines to kidnap a Viet Cong general, educating reporter George Beckworth (David Janssen) in the importance of fighting communism along the way. Moreover, when Sgt. Petersen (Jim Hutton) is killed, the journalist takes over the care of the Vietnamese boy Petersen had taken under his wing. Seemingly oblivious to the tenuous nature of the American involvement in Vietnam and the complex historical reality that underlies the conflict, Wayne presents the story like a standard WW II film, playing the same sort of heroic fighting man he portrayed in so many of those movies. Critics of the day were quick to point this out, but those who are able to get past Wayne's jingoism may find some interest in the relatively well-staged battles; although, make no mistake, PLATOON this ain't. It's worth noting, however, that enough Americans were interested in Wayne's view of the war that the film made over $11 million at the box office.

p, Michael Wayne; d, John Wayne and Ray Kellogg; w, James Lee Barrett, based on the novel by Robin Moore; ed, Otho Lovering; ph, Winton C. Hoch, Panavision, Technicolor; m, Miklos Rozsa.

(PR:C MPAA:NR)

GREEN ROOM, THE***½

(1978, Fr.) 94m Les Films Du Carrosse-UA/NW c (LA CHAMBRE VERTE)

Francois Truffaut (Julien Davenne), Nathalie Baye (Cecilia Mandel), Jean Daste (Bernard Humbert), Jean-Pierre Moulin (Gerard Mazet), Antoine Vitez (Bishop's Secretary), Jane Lobre (Mazet's Second Wife), Monique Dury (Monique, Editorial Secretary), Laurence Ragon (Julie Davenne), Marcel Berbert (Dr. Jardine).

Francois Truffaut's testimony of obsession THE GREEN ROOM is perhaps the most unheralded film of his career, and surely one of his most personal. Truffaut himself plays

GUADALCANAL DIARY—

Julien Davenne, a secretive man who excels at writing obituaries for a fading journal and who is stubbornly obsessed with death, believing that the deceased are not given the love and attention they deserve. His reverence is inspired both by his guilt over returning from WW I unharmed, while everyone he knew was killed or injured, and by the sudden death of the woman who was briefly his wife. In her memory, he constructs a shrine, complete with a frightening, lifesize wax figurine. He meets a former acquaintance, Cecilia (Nathalie Baye), and begins running into her on a steady basis at the cemetery. There, he also discovers an old chapel in need of restoration and remodels it as an elaborate temple for the dead, filling it with photos of dead friends and acquaintances killed in the trenches. On the surface, THE GREEN ROOM is an excessively depressing and strange portrait of a man who values death over life, but underneath it runs the study of a man driven by his obsessions, overflowing with exalted energy. An interesting and atmospheric counterpoint to the numerous war films that pay tribute to those who died for their country, THE GREEN ROOM concerns a man who lived through war, is tormented by survivor's guilt, and is driven to actively remember the dead. (In French; English subtitles.)

d, Francois Truffaut; w, Francois Truffaut and Jean Gruault, based on themes in the writings of Henry James; ed, Martine Barraque-Curie; ph, Nestor Almendros, Eastmancolor; m, Maurice Jaubert.

(PR:C-O MPAA:PG)

GUADALCANAL DIARY****

(1943) 93m FOX bw

Preston Foster *(Fr. Donnelly)*, Lloyd Nolan *(Hook Malone)*, William Bendix *(Taxi Potts)*, Richard Conte *(Capt. Davis)*, Anthony Quinn *(Jesus "Soose" Alvarez)*, Richard Jaeckel *(Pvt. Johnny Anderson)*, Roy Roberts *(Capt. Cross)*, Minor Watson *(Col. Grayson)*, Ralph Byrd *(Ned Rowman)*, Lionel Stander *(Butch)*, Reed Hadley *(Correspondent)*, John Archer *(Lt. Thurmond)*, Eddie Acuff *(Tex)*, Robert Rose *(Sammy)*, Miles Mander *(Weatherby)*, Selmer Jackson *(Col. Thompson)*.

Made before the US had even been involved in the war for a year, this hard-hitting WW II action film drew its story from Richard Tregaskis' best-selling nonfiction book, and superbly documents the first significant US counterattacks in the Pacific—the Marine invasion of the Solomon Islands. One group of Marines, a cross-section of Americans from all walks of life, is shown as they hit the beaches in August 1942. William Bendix plays a tough, dim-witted ex-cab driver with a heart of gold; Richard Conte a courageous officer; Preston Foster the company chaplain; Lionel Stander the company clown; Lloyd Nolan the old pro sergeant who looks out for young recruits like Richard Jaeckel (in his film debut); and Anthony Quinn is the rugged Mexican-American hero who seeks revenge for the slaughter of his platoon. The film follows the recruits from camp, to their first engagement, and through the hell that was Guadalcanal. Not a pretty picture, GUADALCANAL DIARY captures in painful detail the day-to-day survival of the stout-hearted Marines, presenting their humor and the full force of their dedication in scene after scene. Powerfully effective as propaganda, the film was in keeping with Hollywood's early efforts to depict a treacherous enemy, joining the ranks of such stellar WW II films as WAKE ISLAND and BATAAN, but unlike those films it depicted a major American victory. Lewis Seiler's direction is as quick and relentless as the chatter of a machine gun and all the cast members render believable and telling portraits. Filmed at Camp Pendleton, California.

p, Bryan Foy; d, Lewis Seiler; w, Lamar Trotti and Jerry Cady, based on the novel by Richard Tregaskis; ed, Fred Allen; ph, Charles Clarke; m, David Buttolph.

(PR:C MPAA:NR)

GUNG HO!***

(1943) 88m UNIV bw

Randolph Scott *(Col. Thorwald)*, Grace McDonald *(Kathleen Corrigan)*, Alan Curtis *(John Harbison)*, Noah Beery, Jr. *(Kurt Richter)*, J. Carrol Naish *(Lt. Cristoforos)*, David Bruce *(Larry O'Ryan)*, Peter Coe *(Kozzarowski)*, Robert Mitchum *(Pig Iron)*, Richard Lane *(Capt. Dunphy)*, Rod Cameron *(Rube Tedrow)*, Sam Levene *(Transport)*, Milburn Stone *(Comdr. Blade)*, Harold Landon *(Frankie Montana)*, John James *(Buddy Andrews)*, Louis Jean Heydt *(Lt. Roland Browning)*, Walter Sande *(Gunner McBride)*, Chet Huntley *(Narrator)*.

"Makin Taken" was an important newspaper headline in August 1942, signifying the recapture of an essential Pacific island by a hardened group of Marines under the command of Col. Evans Carlson, renamed Col. Thorwald and played by Randolph Scott in this wartime Hollywoodization of the event. After undergoing rigorous training, the "Raiders" sail to their destination, then take the island over fierce and fanatical resistance. The action-filled final sequences of GUNG HO! are exceptional, though brisk, bloody, and not for the squeamish. Scott is forceful and often inspiring, and the supporting cast is outstanding, with J. Carrol Naish as a tough lieutenant (a role based on Capt. W.S. LeFrancois, who was on the Makin raid and wrote the book on which the film is based), Sam Levene as a wise old sergeant, Walter Sande as another veteran noncom, and Peter Coe, Rod Cameron, Alan Curtis, and Robert Mitchum as stalwart grunts. A minor and somewhat awkwardly presented romance between Grace McDonald and two half-brothers (Noah Beery, Jr., and David Bruce) who both seek her favors provides the only love interest in the early part of the film, which is otherwise dominated by males. The raid itself is spectacularly handled by director Ray Enright, and John P. Fulton's special effects are top notch.

p, Walter Wanger; d, Ray Enright; w, Lucien Hubbard, based on the story by Capt. W.S. LeFrancois; ed, Milton Carruth; ph, Milton Krasner; m, Frank Skinner.

(PR:C MPAA:NR)

GUNGA DIN***½

(1939) 117m RKO bw

Cary Grant *(Sgt. Cutter)*, Victor McLaglen *(Sgt. MacChesney)*, Douglas Fairbanks, Jr. *(Sgt. Ballantine)*, Sam Jaffe *(Gunga Din)*, Eduardo Ciannelli *(Guru)*, Joan Fontaine *(Emmy Stebbins)*, Montagu Love *(Col. Weed)*, Robert Coote *(Higginbotham)*, Abner Biberman *(Chota)*, Lumsden Hare *(Maj. Mitchell)*, Cecil Kellaway *(Mr. Stebbins)*, Reginald Sheffield *(Journalist)*.

One of the classic films of the 1930s, GUNGA DIN has a bit of everything—humor, suspense, spectacle, action, *and* a heavy dose of racism, imperialism, and xenophobia. Based on a story by Ben Hecht and Charles MacArthur and the moving Rudyard Kipling poem, this rousing adventure opens as a remote, mountainous British outpost in India is raided by a band of rebel natives. Three of the Army's most reliable frontier veterans—sergeants Cutter (Cary Grant), MacChesney (Victor McLaglen), and Ballantine (Douglas Fairbanks, Jr.)—are sent to the now-silent outpost. Accompanying them is a small contingent of Indian troops and water-carriers, or *bhistis*, including Gunga Din (Sam Jaffe), whose only ambition in life is to become a soldier. The sergeants then receive their orders—to annihilate the murderous Thugs, a violent and mystical sect previously thought extinct. By the film's end, Gunga Din has indeed become a brave soldier, earning the respect of his fellow fighters and of the British government. Over his dead body, the now-famous Kipling poem is read, ending with the line "You're a better man than I am, Gunga Din." A $2 million picture that wowed them at the box office, GUNGA DIN is an undeniably rousing adventure tale. The performances and direction are a great deal of fun—part Three Musketeers adventure, part Laurel and Hardy comedy (director George Stevens began his career directing the duo's comedy shorts)—but it is difficult to overlook the blatantly racist nature of the proceedings, which endorse British imperialism and the violence inflicted on the Indian people. It's all done in the name of entertainment, but it's a bit tough to find amusing today. At different points, William Faulkner was hired to write the script and Howard Hawks was set to direct.

p, Pandro S. Berman; d, George Stevens; w, Fred Guiol, based on the story by Ben Hecht, Charles MacArthur, from the poem by Rudyard Kipling and (uncredited) William Faulkner; ed, Henry Berman and John Lockert; ph, Joseph H. August; m, Alfred Newman.

(PR:C MPAA:NR)

GUNS OF NAVARONE, THE***½

(1961, Brit.) 157m Open Road Films/COL c

Gregory Peck *(Capt. Mallory)*, David Niven *(Cpl. Miller)*, Anthony Quinn *(Col. Andrea Stavros)*, Stanley Baker *(CPO Brown)*, Anthony Quayle *(Maj. Franklin)*, Irene Papas *(Maria)*, Gia Scala *(Anna)*, James Darren *(Pvt. Pappadimos)*, James Robertson Justice *(Jensen)*, Richard Harris *(Barnsby)*, Bryan Forbes *(Cohn)*.

This WW II spectacle, with its cliched story, hackneyed characters, and triumph-over-impossible-odds finale, could only have been born in a Hollywood dream tank; nevertheless, it's great adventure. British intelligence learns that two enormous guns have been installed on the Aegean island of Navarone. The long-range field pieces are capable of destroying any British fleet trying to sail to Kheros, near Turkey, where a large British force is facing annihilation unless it is evacuated. It is the job of Capt. Mallory (Gregory Peck) and a handful of men to land secretly on Navarone and dismantle the guns. The group includes killers Pvt. Pappadimos (James Darren) and CPO Brown (Stanley Baker), explosives expert Cpl. Miller (David Niven), and tough Greek patriot Andrea Stavros (Anthony Quinn). Meeting the men along the way are resistance leader Maria (Irene Papas) and Anna (Gia Scala), a beautiful Greek girl who was reportedly tortured by the Germans. There are a few subplots in this stirring spectacle—Miller's dislike for Mallory's dispassionate procedures, Stavros' grudge against Mallory for an old disservice—but the destruction of the guns is the constant theme and it's handled well by veteran director J. Lee Thompson, with strong cast support and excellent production values that make it all lavish, rich, and often breathtaking. A sequel, FORCE 10 FROM NAVARONE, appeared in 1978.

p, Carl Foreman; d, J. Lee Thompson; w, Carl Foreman, based on the novel *Guns of Navarone* by Alistair MacLean; ed, Alan Osbiston; ph, Oswald Morris, CinemaScope, Eastmancolor; m, Dimitri Tiomkin.

(PR:C MPAA:NR)

GUY NAMED JOE, A****

(1943) 120m MGM bw

Spencer Tracy *(Pete Sandidge)*, Irene Dunne *(Dorinda Durston)*, Van Johnson *(Ted Randall)*, Ward Bond *(Al Yackey)*, James Gleason *(Col. "Nails" Kilpatrick)*, Lionel Barrymore *(The General)*, Barry Nelson *(Dick Rumney)*, Esther Williams *(Ellen Bright)*, Henry O'Neill *(Col. Sykes)*, Don DeFore *("Powerhouse" James J. Rourke)*, Charles Smith *(Sanderson)*, Addison Richards *(Maj. Corbett)*, Earl Schenck *(Col. Hendricks)*, Maurice Murphy *(Capt. Robertson)*, Mark Daniels *(Lieutenant)*.

A delightful, tear-jerking fantasy, A GUY NAMED JOE was one of the most popular movies during WW II, combining the considerable talents of Spencer Tracy, Irene Dunne, and Van Johnson in a big-scale production. Pete Sandidge (Tracy), a daredevil bomber pilot, dies when he crashes his plane into a German aircraft carrier (though, in fact, there were none in WW II), leaving his devoted girl friend, Dorinda (Irene Dunne), who is also a pilot, heartbroken. In heaven, Pete receives a new assignment: he is to become the guardian angel for Ted Randall (Van Johnson), a young Army flyer. Invisibly, Pete guides Ted through flight school and into combat, but the ectoplasmic mentor's tolerance is tested when Ted falls for Dorinda. Ultimately, however, Pete not only comes to terms with their relationship but also acts as Dorinda's copilot when she undertakes a dangerous bombing raid, so that Ted won't have to. Entertaining, witty, sad, and funny, this film goes in many directions at

HAMBURGER HILL—

the same time, effectively combining its romantic fantasy line and a grim war outlook. Dalton Trumbo's script is wry—with the best lines going to wisecracking Tracy—Victor Fleming's direction is expert, and Arnold Gillespie's special effects are impressive for the time. Surprisingly, there is no character in the film named "Joe"; the title is derived from the Army Air Corps practice of calling a "right fellow" Joe.

p, Everett Riskin; d, Victor Fleming; w, Dalton Trumbo, based on a story by Chandler Sprague, David Boehm, Frederick H. Brennan; ed, Frank Sullivan; ph, George Folsey and Karl Freund; m, Herbert Stothart.

(PR:A MPAA:NR)

H

HAMBURGER HILL***½

(1987) 110m RKO/PAR c

Anthony Barrile (Langulli), Michael Patrick Boatman (Motown), Don Cheadle (Washburn), Michael Dolan (Murphy), Don James (McDaniel), Dylan McDermott (Sgt. Frantz), M.A. Nickles (Galvin), Harry O'Reilly (Duffy), Daniel O'Shea (Gaigin), Tim Quill (Beletsky), Tommy Swerdlow (Bienstock), Courtney Vance (Doc Johnson), Steven Weber (Sgt. Worcester), Tegan West (Lt. Eden).

Instead of trying to match the hallucinatory bombast of APOCALYPSE NOW, the surreal metaphysics of PLATOON, or the studied idiosyncrasy of FULL METAL JACKET, director John Irvin reaches back to such classic combat films as THE SANDS OF IWO JIMA and PORK CHOP HILL for his inspiration here. So straightforward as to be old-fashioned, HAMBURGER HILL becomes unique by virtue of its unwillingness to participate in the current cycle of war-as-philosophical-metaphor Vietnam films and instead goes for a more conventional approach. Realistic almost to a fault, Irvin's film is an account of the Third Squad, First Platoon, Bravo Company of the 101st Airborne Division and its battle to secure Hill 937 in the Ashau Valley, Vietnam, 1969. Led by sergeants Frantz (Dylan McDermott) and Worcester (Steven Weber), the interracial platoon must contend with little support on the homefront, a contentious news media, racial tensions, personality conflicts, questionable tactics, and friendly fire while facing well-entrenched North Vietnamese regulars who refuse to give up the hill. Short on plot, the film derives its power from isolated moments: letters from home, chats, arguments, visits to a brothel, and, of course, intense combat—all performed with vigor by an almost faceless ensemble of unknown actors spouting a nearly incomprehensible stream of GI lingo. Shot in an unfussy, realistic manner by cinematographer Peter MacDonald, the visuals emphasize wide angles and deep focus, bombarding the senses without resorting to the kind of hallucinatory imagery found in most Vietnam films. (Director Irvin was in Vietnam in 1969, filming a documentary, and has legitimate claims at first-hand experience.) The battle for the hill is exhausting to watch as the soldiers struggle upwards in the mud, clinging to exposed roots, tree stumps, and each other in a desperate effort to advance. Irvin rarely allows a glimpse of the top of the hill, further preventing the viewer from thinking ahead, instead forcing him to concentrate on climbing the few feet visible before him right along with the GIs. Although it was underrated at the time of its release, time will eventually reveal that HAMBURGER HILL is one of the best and most realistic films made about the Vietnam War.

p, Marcia Nasatir and Jim Carabatsos; d, John Irvin; w, Jim Carabatsos; ed, Peter Tanner; ph, Peter MacDonald, Rank Color; m, Philip Glass.

(PR:O MPAA:NR)

HANNA'S WAR**½

(1988) 148m Golan-Globus/Cannon c

Ellen Burstyn (Katalin Senesh), Maruschka Detmers (Hanna Senesh), Anthony Andrews (Squadron Leader McCormack), Donald Pleasence (Rosza Gabor), David Warner (Capt. Julian Simon), Vincenzo Ricotta (Yoel Palgi), Christopher Fairbank (Ruven Dafne), Rob Jacks (Peretz Goldstein), Serge El-Baz (Tony), Eli Gorenstein (Aba Berdichev), Josef El-Dror (Yonah Rosen), Rade Serbedzija (Capt. Ivan), Miodrag Krivokapic (Col. Illya), Dorota Stalinska (Maritza), George Dillon (Milenko), Teri Tordai (Baroness Hatvany).

One of Israel's great martyrs, Hanna Senesh, a Hungarian-born poet and daughter of a prominent playwright who emigrated to Palestine in 1938, is the subject of this well-intentioned film. Recruited into the British secret service in 1944, Senesh (played here by Maruschka Detmers) was parachuted into Yugoslavia with instructions to make her way into Hungary, where she was to help establish escape routes for downed Allied fliers. Promptly captured, she was taken to Budapest, tortured, tried, and finally executed even as Soviet tanks were entering the city, and today she lies in the martyr's cemetery on Mt. Herzl. That this fascinating story, the stuff of true heroes, deserves wider renown is almost certainly what prompted Israeli producers Menahem Golan and Yoram Globus to make HANNA'S WAR. This could have been a fine film in different hands, but under Golan's direction it all becomes utterly trivialized. The absolute nadir occurs as the Jewish fighters join with the Yugoslavian guerrillas to attack a German train they believe to be carrying weapons. To a thumping, Eurodisco, pseudo-CHARIOTS OF FIRE score, they charge, taking heavy casualties and killing scores of Germans before capturing the train, which turns out to hold half-dead Jews bound for the camps—in a scene with the potential for real power, but which ends up flat and banal, simply because of its music. The gorgeous Detmers' commitment to the part is obvious, but, with the exception of the torture scenes, she seems just too glamorous and single-mindedly devoted to her mission to ring true; Ellen Burstyn, despite top billing, is in only a few scenes and leaves little lasting impression. On the plus side, however, are the performances of David Warner and Donald Pleasence, two of the best bad guys in the business. Released in Israel on the 40th anniversary of independence, this is clearly Golan's heartfelt attempt to make a patriotic classic. Just as clearly, he has fallen short of the mark.

p, Menahem Golan and Yoram Globus; d, Menahem Golan; w, Menahem Golan, based on the books *The Diaries of Hanna Senesh* by Hanna Senesh and *A Great Wind Cometh* by Yoel Palgi; ed, Alain Jakubowicz; ph, Elemer Ragalyi; m, Dov Seltzer.

(PR:C-O MPAA:NR)

HANOI HILTON, THE**
(1987) 123m Golan-Globus/Cannon c

Michael Moriarty *(Lt. Comdr. Williamson)*, Jeffrey Jones *(Maj. Fischer)*, Paul Le Mat *(Hubman)*, Stephen Davies *(Capt. Robert Miles)*, Lawrence Pressman *(Col. Cathcart)*, Aki Aleong *(Maj. Ngo "Cat" Doc)*, Gloria Carlin *(Paula)*, John Diehl *(Murphy)*, Rick Fitts *(Capt. Turner)*, David Soul *(Maj. Oldham)*, David Anthony Smith *(Gregory)*.

Ostensibly an ode to the brave Americans who suffered torture at the hands of the North Vietnamese behind the walls of Hanoi's dreaded Hoa Lo Prison, better known as the Hanoi Hilton, this film is really blatant right-wing propaganda loaded with a stunning amount of racial and political stereotypes. Set in the prison from 1964 to 1975, the story concerns a group of mostly American officer pilots, a tough, resolute bunch headed by Col. Cathcart (Lawrence Pressman), a by-the-book type who insists that military order and protocol be maintained despite the humiliation and torture inflicted upon his men. The prison commandant, Maj. Ngo Doc (Aki Aleong, whose performance recalls the stereotyped vindictiveness of such Hollywood WW II villains as Philip Ahn and Richard Loo), resolves to break the colonel and puts him through excruciating torture. Cathcart is traumatized into a zombielike state, and leadership falls to Navy flier Lt. Comdr. Williamson (Michael Moriarty). He tries to continue with Cathcart's rigid code of honor, but others, such as the easygoing Hubman (Paul Le Mat), are more vulnerable, and begin to confess acts and information they consider of negligible interest to the North Vietnamese. The horror inflicted upon them is almost nonstop over many years, although it ceases briefly when an American, ultraliberal, political activist actress (Gloria Carlin, obviously doing Jane Fonda) comes to Hanoi convinced the Communists are correct in their tactics and tries to get the prisoners to cooperate with them. Aside from the erratic Moriarty—a study in and of himself—there is little character development among the prisoners, who are typecast in roles that have been seen many times over in scores of POW films, from THE PURPLE HEART to STALAG 17. There is no relief from their misery, until the surviving prisoners are finally packed aboard a plane at war's end and sent back home; director Lionel Chetwynd seems to be trying to impress upon the audience the shifts between boredom and terror that were a way of life for the POWs, but he is too mundane a filmmaker to do so without making his film repetitive and boring. This, combined with his decidedly one-sided views (as if South Vietnamese and American soldiers had not subjected North Vietnamese to the same brutality), which more or less blame the loss of the war on senseless idiots from Hollywood and liberals, makes HANOI HILTON hard to sit through.

p, Menahem Golan and Yoram Globus; d, Lionel Chetwynd; w, Lionel Chetwynd; ed, Penelope Shaw; ph, Mark Irwin, TVC Color; m, Jimmy Webb.

(PR:O MPAA:R)

HEARTBREAK RIDGE****
(1986) 130m Malpaso-Jay Weston/WB c

Clint Eastwood *(Tom Highway)*, Marsha Mason *(Aggie)*, Everett McGill *(Maj. Powers)*, Moses Gunn *(Sgt. Webster)*, Eileen Heckart *(Little Mary)*, Bo Svenson *(Roy Jennings)*, Boyd Gaines *(Lt. Ring)*, Mario Van Peebles *(Stitch)*, Arlen Dean Snyder *(Choozoo)*, Vincent Irizarry *(Fragetti)*, Ramon Franco *(Aponte)*.

Further exploring his screen persona, producer-director-actor Clint Eastwood stars here as Tom Highway, a gruff, foul-mouthed anachronism of the old Marine Corps who drinks too much and is constantly getting in trouble. Nearing retirement age, having alienated most of his superiors, Highway asks to end his career where it began and is transferred to perform gunnery sergeant duties in his old outfit. There, the small reconnaissance platoon he is to train proves to be a group of lazy malcontents who feel that they've been duped by the slick military advertising on television. Earning the admiration of these young hotshots by besting them physically and mentally at every turn, Highway proceeds to whip them into a self-respecting fighting unit that knows how to work as a team. He also tries to rekindle the love of his ex-wife, Aggie (Marsha Mason), who divorced him because she was tired of his insensitivity and love for the military. Highway hopes to impress her with his newfound awareness ("Did we mutually nurture each other?" he clumsily asks her), culled from women's magazines on the sly. Just as it seems that he is making progress with Aggie, however, Highway and his men are sent off to a small Caribbean island none of them has ever heard of—Grenada—to rescue American medical students from a hostile Marxist government backed by Cuban troops. HEARTBREAK RIDGE has drawn flak from those who think Eastwood somehow endorsed the Grenada invasion by refusing to overtly criticize it. But Eastwood isn't interested in the political meaning of the action; what concerns him is how it defines his characters, who only want to survive, not analyze, the conflict. The strengths and foibles of human beings are what this film—and all of Eastwood's directorial efforts—is all about, and his Tom Highway is one of the most vividly etched male characters seen on-screen in years. Eastwood makes no apologies for this man who knows only how to train men to kill, but he does understand him. Highway knows he is an anachronism and that he will soon have to leave the only role in which he feels confident; he has made the Marines his family, but now that family is rejecting him in favor of a

HELL TO ETERNITY—

much more glamorous image. He isn't the kind of man who is willing to wallow in his mistakes, however, and in the only way he knows how he makes an attempt to understand the woman he has taken for granted, who will be his salvation. (The beautifully played scenes between Eastwood and Mason are some of the most telling and realistic between a man and a woman to be found in any recent film.) Eastwood believes that people can change, that contact with others can enlighten, and that attempting to understand one another is extremely valuable, but his characters are close-mouthed, wary, and afraid of appearing vulnerable, simply because they are vulnerable. He proves that it is still possible to infuse "an entertainment" with greater relevance. Eastwood fans who choose to simply watch and root for the "good guys" will not be disappointed by HEARTBREAK RIDGE, but neither will those looking for insights into the human condition.

p, Clint Eastwood; d, Clint Eastwood; w, James Karabatsos; ed, Joel Cox; ph, Jack N. Green, Technicolor; m, Lennie Niehaus.

(PR:O MPAA:R)

HELL TO ETERNITY***

(1960) 132m Atlantic/AA bw

Jeffrey Hunter *(Guy Gabaldon)*, David Janssen *(Bill)*, Vic Damone *(Pete)*, Patricia Owens *(Sheila)*, Richard Eyer *(Guy as a Boy)*, John Larch *(Capt. Schwabe)*, Miiko Taka *(Ester)*, Sessue Hayakawa *(Gen. Matsui)*, Bill Williams *(Leonard)*, Tsuru Aoki Hayakawa *(Mother Une)*, Michi Kobi *(Sono)*, George Shibata *(Kaz)*.

HELL TO ETERNITY is based on the experiences of real-life Marine war hero Guy Gabaldon, who single-handedly captured some 2,000 Japanese during the Saipan and Tinian campaigns. As a young boy, Guy (Richard Eyer) is adopted by a Japanese family and exposed to their customs and language. When Pearl Harbor is attacked, the older Guy (Jeffrey Hunter) leaves the West Coast Japanese community in which he lives to join the Marines and, because he speaks Japanese, persuades Gen. Matsui (Sessue Hayakawa) to have his men lay down their weapons and surrender rather than face certain defeat. An honest, gritty war film with fine performances (including those of David Janssen and Vic Damone as Guy's buddies) and a moody jazz score.

p, Irving H. Levin; d, Phil Karlson; w, Ted Sherdeman and Walter Roeber Schmidt, based on a story by Gil Doud; ed, George White and Roy V. Livingston; ph, Burnett Guffey; m, Leith Stevens.

(PR:A MPAA:NR)

HELLCATS OF THE NAVY**

(1957) 81m Morningside/COL bw

Ronald Reagan *(Comdr. Casey Abbott)*, Nancy Davis *(Helen Blair)*, Arthur Franz *(Lt. Comdr. Don Landon)*, Robert Arthur *(Freddy Warren)*, William Leslie *(Lt. Paul Prentice)*, William Phillips *(Carroll)*, Harry Lauter *(Wes Barton)*, Joseph Turkel *(Chick)*, Michael Garth *(Charlie)*, Don Keefer *(Jug)*, Selmer Jackson *(Adm. Nimitz)*, Maurice Manson *(Adm. Lockwood)*.

After two terms of Ronald and Nancy Reagan (nee Nancy Davis) in the White House, it's nearly impossible to judge this film—their only costarring vehicle—with any kind of objectivity, no matter what your politics. Suffice to say that recent history has made this mundane B-picture a genuine Hollywood oddity and an inadvertent camp favorite. Reagan plays the ultraserious Casey Abbott, a WW II submarine commander sent to retrieve Japanese mines so that Navy experts can uncover why they aren't detectable by sonar. During the operation, an enemy ship bears down on Abbott and his crew, forcing the commander to leave frogman Wes Barton (Harry Lauter) behind to save the rest of the crew. Suspicious officer Don Landon (Arthur Franz) thinks Abbott left Barton because the frogman had been chasing after Helen Blair (Nancy Davis), Abbott's former girl friend. Of course, this charge is totally unfounded and Abbott must prove through his own acts of sacrifice and heroism that Landon's allegations are false. Producer Charles H. Schneer and director Nathan Juran are best-known for their collaborations with stop-motion animation wizard Ray Harryhausen (20 MILLION MILES TO EARTH; THE SEVENTH VOYAGE OF SINBAD; THE FIRST MEN IN THE MOON), but some of Juran's lesser works, such as ATTACK OF THE 50 FT. WOMAN and THE BRAIN FROM PLANET AROUS, have become campy cult classics over the years. HELLCATS OF THE NAVY falls perfectly into place alongside Juran's other memorably silly work.

p, Charles H. Schneer; d, Nathan Juran [Nathan Hertz]; w, David Lang and Raymond Marcus, based on the book by Charles A. Lockwood, Hans Christian Adamson; ed, Jerome Thoms; ph, Irving Lippman; m, Mischa Bakaleinikoff.

(PR:A MPAA:NR)

HENRY V*****

(1944, Brit.) 127m TC/UA c

Laurence Olivier *(King Henry V)*, Robert Newton *(Ancient Pistol)*, Leslie Banks *(Chorus)*, Renee Asherson *(Princess Katherine)*, Esmond Knight *(Fluellen)*, Leo Genn *(Constable of France)*, Felix Aylmer *(Archbishop of Canterbury)*, Ralph Truman *(Mountjoy)*, Harcourt Williams *(King Charles VI of France)*, Ernest Thesiger *(Duke of Berri)*, Max Adrian *(The Dauphin)*, Francis Lister *(Duke of Orleans)*, Valentine Dyall *(Duke of Burgundy)*, Russell Thorndike *(Duke of Bourbon)*, George Robey *(Sir John Falstaff)*.

Made at the height of the German blitz, this dazzling British adaptation of Shakespeare's classic tale of victory in the face of overwhelming odds brought new hope and resolve to embattled Britons who saw it in 1944 (it was released in the US in 1946). Filippo del Giudice, an Italian lawyer who had fled Mussolini's rule, persuaded Laurence Olivier to undertake the project, and when William Wyler, Carol Reed, and Terence Young were unable to helm the film, Olivier not only took on the title role but the director's mantle, performing both roles magnificently. Innovatively structured, the film begins with a 17th-century staging of

Shakespeare's play at the Globe Theatre; then, gradually, the proscenium disappears as the film moves toward a more realistic presentation of the story, with stylized sets giving way to the real-life scenery of the impressive re-creation of the Battle of Agincourt (shot in Ireland). Finally, Olivier brings the film full circle, back to the stage of the Globe. Set in 1415, HENRY V chronicles the invasion of France undertaken by the 28-year-old English king in an attempt to consolidate his power at home. After a number of costly victories drastically deplete Henry's army, it is besieged by French forces that outnumber it nearly five to one. Under the king's courageous leadership, however, the English triumph at Agincourt. Olivier, who was mustered out of the navy to make the film, collaborated with movie critic Alan Dent on the adaptation, and editor Reginald Beck helped with direction chores when Olivier the star was in front of the cameras. Though given a large budget considering the wartime circumstances, the production was continually forced to cut corners, and its wonderfully realized costumes and sets are testaments to the ingenuity of the film's designers.

p, Laurence Olivier and Filippo Del Giudice; d, Laurence Olivier and Reginald Beck; w, Alan Dent and Laurence Olivier, based on the play by William Shakespeare; ed, Reginald Beck; ph, Robert Krasker and Jack Hildyard, Technicolor; m, Sir William Walton.

(PR:A MPAA:NR)

HEROES**½

(1977) 113m UNIV c

Henry Winkler *(Jack)*, Sally Field *(Carol)*, Harrison Ford *(Ken)*, Val Avery *(Bus Driver)*, Olivia Cole *(Jane)*, Hector Elias *(Dr. Elias)*, Dennis Burkley *(Gus)*, Tony Burton *(Chef)*, Michael Cavanaugh *(Peanuts)*.

One of the first Hollywood films to deal with the plight of Vietnam veterans, HEROES is a quirky little comedy-drama that, although far from perfect, is not unlikable. Henry Winkler plays Jack, a troubled Vietnam vet who escapes from a mental hospital to start a worm farm with money collected from his fellow inmates. He hops a bus to California and meets Carol (Sally Field), convincing her to join him. They eventually hook up with Jack's war buddy Ken (Harrison Ford), who, it turns out, has had even more trouble adjusting to civilian life than Jack. Although the script by James Carabatsos (who would later pen HEARTBREAK RIDGE and HAMBURGER HILL) is more than a little contrived and the direction by Jeremy Paul Kagan is unimaginative and made-for-TVish, the appealing performances by Winkler, Field, and Ford nearly make up for the lack of inspiration behind the camera. Note: Because of copyright conflicts, the song that originally closed the film, "Carry on My Wayward Son" by the rock group Kansas, has been replaced by a meaningless and treacly generic tune.

p, David Foster and Lawrence Turman; d, Jeremy Paul Kagan; w, James Carabatsos; ed, Patrick Kennedy; ph,

Frank Stanley, Technicolor; m, Jack Nitzsche and Richard Hazard.

(PR:A MPAA:PG)

HIDING PLACE, THE***

(1975) 150m World Wide c

Julie Harris *(Betsie)*, Eileen Heckart *(Katje)*, Arthur O'Connell *(Papa)*, Jeannette Cliff *(Corrie)*, Robert Rietty *(Willem)*, Pamela Sholto *(Tine)*, Paul Henley *(Peter)*, Richard Wren *(Kik)*.

After the Germans invade Amsterdam in WW II, a Dutch watchmaker (Arthur O'Connell) and his daughters devote themselves to saving persecuted Jews, laboring to outwit the SS troops that patrol the area and recruit others to their cause. They are caught, however, and sent to a concentration camp. THE HIDING PLACE is based on an autobiographical novel by Corrie ten Boom, who was 80 when the film was made and delivers its epilog. An accurate and inspiring representation of a period in history that has been placed on film countless times, this version adds little that's new to the depiction, but is still a worthwhile and honorable picture. It was produced by World Wide Pictures, a branch of the Billy Graham Evangelical Association, hence its deeply Christian themes.

p, Frank R. Jacobson; d, James F. Collier; w, Allan Sloane and Lawrence Holben, based on the novel by Corrie ten Boom, John Sherill, Elizabeth Sherill; ed, Ann Chegwidden; ph, Michael Reed, Metrocolor.

(PR:C-O MPAA:PG)

HILL 24 DOESN'T ANSWER***

(1955, Israel) 100m Sikor/CD bw

Edward Mulhare *(James Finnegan)*, Haya Harareet *(Miriam Mizrachi)*, Michael Shillo *(Yehude Berger)*, Michael Wager *(Allan Goodman)*.

The first feature to be filmed and processed entirely in Israel, HILL 24 DOESN'T ANSWER depicts the 1948 war of attrition between the Jews and the Arabs, with special attention to each side's attempts to gain and hold the Holy Land. This 20th-century Crusade is recounted, in rather trite cinematic fashion, from the perspectives of four soldiers—an Irishman, an American, a Palestinian Jew, and a Yemenite girl—all involved in holding the title ground for the new state-to-be. Their stories are told in flashback by their corpses, having been found by a United Nations team—although the four did hold the hill—after the signing of the historic truce that fixed the boundaries of the new land. An often moving film, despite its obvious propaganda motives and cliches. (In English, Hebrew, and other languages; non-English languages subtitled).

p, Thorold Dickinson and Peter Frye; d, Thorold Dickinson; w, Zvi Kolitz and Peter Frye, based on the story by Zvi Kolitz; ed, Joanna Dickinson and Thorold Dickinson; ph, Gerald Gibbs; m, Paul Ben Haim.

(PR:A MPAA:NR)

HINDENBURG, THE—

HINDENBURG, THE**
(1975) 125m UNIV c

George C. Scott *(Col. Ritter)*, Anne Bancroft *(The Countess)*, William Atherton *(Boerth)*, Roy Thinnes *(Martin Vogel)*, Gig Young *(Edward Douglas)*, Burgess Meredith *(Emilio Pajetta)*, Charles Durning *(Capt. Pruss)*, Richard A. Dysart *(Lehmann)*, Robert Clary *(Joe Spah)*, Rene Auberjonois *(Maj. Napier)*, Peter Donat *(Reed Channing)*, Alan Oppenheimer *(Albert Breslau)*, Katherine Helmond *(Mrs. Mildred Breslau)*.

This insipid, boring, implausible, senseless, deliciously funny, and expensively mounted film puts forth the theory that the Hindenburg disaster at Lakehurst, New Jersey, on the evening of May 6, 1937, was the direct result of a prewar anti-Nazi conspiracy theory. (How this incredible disaster, recorded graphically on newsreel footage, really came about is still a matter of debate.) Under Robert Wise's direction, the scenario centers on Col. Ritter (George C. Scott), a dedicated German security officer put on board the dirigible as it sails for America, assisted by Nazi partisan Martin Vogel (Roy Thinnes). Ritter suspects crew and passengers alike of potential sabotage and his subtle investigations encompass a host of characters, including a reefer-puffing countess (Anne Bancroft), a pair of card sharps (Burgess Meredith and Rene Auberjonois), and a nervous American ad exec (Gig Young). Throughout the rather uneventful voyage, Ritter probes and pries, finding no answers until this floating Grand Hotel is about to dock, when he discovers a bomb planted by a crew member who wishes to discredit Hitler's regime. There's no tension whatsoever and none of the characters are remotely interesting, let alone sympathetic. THE HINDENBURG did, however, win two Oscars (Peter Berkos for Best Sound Effects; Albert Whitlock and Glen Robinson for Best Visual Effects) and was nominated for three more (Cinematography, Art Direction, and Sound).

d, Robert Wise; w, Nelson Gidding, Richard A. Levinson, and William Link, based on the book by Michael M. Mooney; ed, Donn Cambern; ph, Robert Surtees, Technicolor; m, David Shire.

(PR:C MPAA:PG)

HIROSHIMA, MON AMOUR*****
(1959, Fr./Jap.) 88m Argos-Como-Daiei-Pathe/Zenith bw

Emmanuelle Riva *(Elle)*, Eiji Okada *(Lui)*, Stella Dassas *(Mother)*, Pierre Barbaud *(Father)*, Bernard Fresson *(German Lover)*.

It has been often, and quite correctly, stated that HIROSHIMA, MON AMOUR has been as important in the development of film art as CITIZEN KANE. The first feature from Alain Resnais, previously well known for his incredibly moving documentaries, the film is adapted from a script by the French writer Marguerite Duras, one of the greatest writers of the 20th century, and the combination of Duras' text and Resnais' blend of sound and image makes for a film that is completely modern. The story, which manages to be both complex (in its manipulation of past and present) and simple (it focuses on a very brief love affair), concerns a married Japanese architect (Eiji Okada) and a married French actress (Emmanuelle Riva) who have a two-day affair in Hiroshima. The pain that "She" (their names are never used) feels for the dead of Hiroshima reminds her of a loss she suffered in the past, when the young German soldier whom she loved in Nevers was killed on the day that town was liberated. Castigated by her family, she was imprisoned in a dark cellar, in disgrace for having loved the enemy. Now, she projects the entire city—the bomb, the death, the suffering and physical mutilation—onto her Japanese lover, whom she calls "Hiroshima," but knows that someday she will forget him. Interweaving sound and image, brutal documentary footage and tender shots of lovemaking, past and present, past and remembered past, city and individual, passion and despair, Resnais creates a breathtaking picture that, like so many great works of art, can never be entirely appreciated or understood. HIROSHIMA MON AMOUR must be felt—combining the soft loving caresses of two intertwined bodies with the burnt, blistering, peeling flesh of a dying victim of atomic warfare—and the feelings it evokes defy understanding or explanation. (In French; English subtitles.)

p, Samy Halfon; d, Alain Resnais; w, Marguerite Duras; ed, Henri Colpi, Jasmine Chasney, and Anne Sarraute; ph, Sacha Vierny and Michio Takahashi; m, Georges Delerue and Giovanni Fusco.

(PR:C-O MPAA:NR)

HITLER*½
(1962) 107m Three Crown/AA bw

Richard Basehart *(Adolf Hitler)*, Cordula Trantow *(Geli Raubal)*, Maria Emo *(Eva Braun)*, Martin Kosleck *(Joseph Goebbels)*, William Sargent *(Lt. Col. Count von Stauffenberg)*, Gregory Gay *(Field Marshal Erwin Rommel)*, Rick Traeger *(Heinrich Himmler)*, John Mitchum *(Hermann Goering)*.

Richard Basehart offers a surprisingly interesting interpretation of the Fuhrer in this uneven, psychologically oriented biopic, which puts as much emphasis on Hitler's sexual confusion as it does on the world-shaking events he set in motion. Averring that Hitler suffered from impotence as a result of his fixation with his mother, the film deals with his early relationship with his young niece (Cordula Trantow) and his later coupling with Eva Braun (Maria Emo). Along the way, it also chronicles the more familiar story of his rise to power and the destruction his madness loosed on the world.

p, E. Charles Straus; d, Stuart Heisler; w, Sam Neuman and E. Charles Straus; ed, Walter Hannemann; ph, Joseph Biroc; m, Hans J. Salter.

(PR:C MPAA:NR)

HITLER: THE LAST TEN DAYS**
(1973, Brit./It.) 106m PAR-Tomorrow Ent. c

Alec Guinness *(Adolf Hitler)*, Simon Ward *(Hauptmann*

Hoffmann), Adolfo Celi *(Gen. Krebs)*, Diane Cilento *(Hanna Reitsch)*, Gabriele Ferzetti *(Fieldmarshal Keitel)*, Eric Porter *(Gen. von Greim)*, Doris Kunstmann *(Eva Braun)*, Joss Ackland *(Gen. Burgdorf)*, John Bennett *(Josef Goebbels)*.

Even though Alec Guinness was the finest actor ever to portray Adolf Hitler, HITLER: THE LAST TEN DAYS is yet another failed attempt to make the Fuhrer the subject of compelling drama. Set almost entirely in Hitler's bunker, the film details the final days of the Third Reich. Unfortunately, nothing much happens, and despite Guinness' decision to eschew the "raving maniac" portrayal that most actors saddled with the role have relied on, the lifeless alternative he offers is neither involving nor particularly insightful.

p, Wolfgang Reinhardt; d, Ennio De Concini; w, Ennio De Concini, Marie Pia Fusco, Wolfgang Reinhardt, and Ivan Moffat, based on the book, *Last Days of the Chancellery* by Gerhard Boldt; ed, Kevin Connor; ph, Ennio Guarnieri, Technicolor; m, Mischa Spoliansky.

(PR:C MPAA:PG)

HITLER'S CHILDREN**½

(1942) 80m RKO bw

Tim Holt *(Karl Bruner)*, Bonita Granville *(Anna Muller)*, Kent Smith *(Prof. Nichols)*, Otto Kruger *(Col. Henkel)*, H.B. Warner *(The Bishop)*, Lloyd Corrigan *(Franz Erhart)*, Erford Gage *(Dr. Schmidt)*, Hans Conried *(Dr. Graf)*, Anna Loos *(NSV Worker)*.

Released in 1943 to an American public hungry for anti-Nazi propaganda, this sensationalistic melodrama, which might have been titled "I Was a Teenage Nazi," offers a horrifying portrait of the Hitler Youth. Tim Holt plays Karl Bruner, a rabid young Nazi who loves Anna Muller (Bonita Granville), despite her hatred of the Fuhrer he worships. Because of Anna's nonconformist stance, she is slated for involuntary sterilization and is the object of physical abuse. In time, Karl comes to recognize the evil that has engulfed his people, but though he and Anna become even greater soul mates as a result, they meet a tragic, brutal end. Based on Gregor Ziemer's nonfiction book *Education for Death*, HITLER'S CHILDREN is far from an even-handed depiction of National Socialism's seduction of German young people, but at the height of the war the American movie-going public was less interested in art than Nazi-bashing, and the film was a big hit at the box office.

p, Edward A. Golden; d, Edward Dmytryk; w, Emmett Lavery, based on the book *Education for Death* by Gregor Ziemer; ed, Joseph Noriega; ph, Russell Metty; m, Roy Webb.

(PR:C MPAA:NR)

HOME OF THE BRAVE***

(1949) 88m Screen Plays/UA bw

Douglas Dick *(Maj. Robinson)*, Steve Brodie *(T.J.)*, Jeff Corey *(Doctor)*, Lloyd Bridges *(Finch)*, Frank Lovejoy *(Mingo)*, James Edwards *(Moss)*, Cliff Clark *(Colonel)*.

Set against the backdrop of the war in the Pacific, this provocative (for its time) Stanley Kramer-produced message film deals with a black GI's psychosomatic paralysis. Moss (James Edwards) and four white comrades—including his boyhood friend (Lloyd Bridges) and a bigoted corporal (Steve Brodie)—are sent on a reconnaissance mission to a Japanese-held island. In the wake of a terrifying experience on the island and in response to prejudice he has encountered throughout his life, Moss becomes paralyzed from the waist down and is sent to a hospital where a psychiatrist (Jeff Corey) helps him get to the root of his pain. Originally produced on Broadway as an exploration of anti-Semitism, HOME OF THE BRAVE is commendable for its examination of the WW II experience of a black soldier at a time when Hollywood was steadfastly ignoring the concerns of African-Americans. Edwards gives a sensitive performance, and Mark Robson's direction never condescends or makes him an object of bleeding-heart pity.

p, Stanley Kramer; d, Mark Robson; w, Carl Foreman, based on the play by Arthur Laurents; ed, Harry Gerstad; ph, Robert de Grasse; m, Dimitri Tiomkin.

(PR:C MPAA:NR)

HOPE AND GLORY*****

(1987, Brit.) 113m COL c

Sebastian Rice-Edwards *(Bill Rohan)*, Geraldine Muir *(Sue Rohan)*, Sarah Miles *(Grace Rohan)*, David Hayman *(Clive Rohan)*, Sammi Davis *(Dawn Rohan)*, Derrick O'Connor *(Mac)*, Susan Wooldridge *(Molly)*, Jean-Marc Barr *(Cpl. Bruce Carey)*, Ian Bannen *(George)*, Annie Leon *(Bill's Grandmother)*, Jill Baker *(Faith)*, Amelda Brown *(Hope)*, Katrine Boorman *(Charity)*, Charley Boorman *(Luftwaffe Pilot)*, John Boorman *(Narrator)*.

HOPE AND GLORY is a wonderful film, an intelligent, heartfelt, personal, and marvelously entertaining look at what it was like to grow up in WW II England. A semi-autobiographical project from British director John Boorman, the film concerns nine-year-old Bill (Sebastian Rice-Edwards) as he experiences the wonders of war from his suburban London home. While Americans may find it somewhat disconcerting to see the Blitz and its horrors made the setting for a nostalgic comedy, the fact is that for a young boy the war was a particularly exciting and vivid time, and a joyous feeling permeates the film. The total upheaval of the staid family order, the lack of normal restrictions and discipline, and the liberating effect the war had on women are all brilliantly conveyed by Boorman, because he views the war from a child's perspective. Told in a series of vignettes, HOPE AND GLORY unfolds in a surprisingly nonchalant manner, tossing out its vividly realized observations at every turn. Boorman skillfully combines nuggets of truth with moments of mirth and is always prepared to surprise and amuse without sentimentalizing.

HORSE SOLDIERS, THE—

p, John Boorman and Michael Dryhurst; d, John Boorman; w, John Boorman; ed, Ian Crafford; ph, Philippe Rousselot and John Harris, Eastmancolor; m, Peter Martin.

(PR:C MPAA:PG-13)

HORSE SOLDIERS, THE***

(1959) 119m Mirisch/UA c

John Wayne *(Col. John Marlowe)*, William Holden *(Maj. Henry Kendall)*, Constance Towers *(Hannah Hunter)*, Althea Gibson *(Lukey)*, Hoot Gibson *(Brown)*, Anna Lee *(Mrs. Buford)*, Russell Simpson *(Sheriff)*, Stan Jones *(Gen. U.S. Grant)*, Carleton Young *(Col. Jonathan Miles)*, Willis Bouchey *(Col. Phil Secord)*, Ken Curtis *(Wilkie)*, O.Z. Whitehead *("Hoppy" Hopkins)*, Judson Pratt *(Sgt. Maj. Kirby)*, Denver Pyle *(Jagger Jo)*, Strother Martin *(Virgil)*, Hank Worden *(Deacon)*.

With the exception of the Civil War segment in HOW THE WEST WAS WON, THE HORSE SOLDIERS was director John Ford's only film dealing with the War Between the States. The film is gorgeously photographed and contains many memorable images (the opening credits and breathtaking final shot) and moving scenes (such as that in which a Southern military school is forced to send its cadets—all children—into battle against the Union forces), but this is not one of Ford's best efforts, suffering from a weak script and an overwrought performance from its female lead, Constance Towers. Based on an actual mission known as Grierson's Raid, the film takes place in the spring of 1863 and finds Union general U.S. Grant (Stan Jones) frustrated by his inability to take Vicksburg. Taking drastic action, Grant decides to send a cavalry unit to Newton Station, Mississippi, deep in Confederate territory, to cut enemy supply lines to Vicksburg. The man selected to lead this daring raid is tough, no-nonsense Col. Marlowe (John Wayne), a citizen soldier who designed railroads before the war. With him goes a bevy of officers with mixed motives, including Col. Seacord (Willis Bouchey), whose political ambitions dictate his every action, and Maj. Kendall (William Holden), a conscientious physician who sees no glory in war—only suffering and death. En route to Newton Station, the cavalry bivouacs at a plantation owned by Hannah (Towers), a Southern belle devoted to the Confederate cause. Caught spying on Marlowe and his commanders as they plan strategy, Hannah and her slave, Lukey (Althea Gibson), are taken along on the mission, lest they reveal the top-secret plans to the rebels. Eventually, the Union cavalry lays seige to Newton Station and destroys the railway depot and supplies (a necessary act that eats at former railroad man Marlowe), but the Confederate army is in hot pursuit and the small brigade is forced to make a desperate dash for Union-held Baton Rouge, located even deeper in enemy territory. While minor Ford is still head-and-shoulders above the best of most others, THE HORSE SOLDIERS is a mostly workmanlike effort in which the great director struggles against a poorly written script, with sketchy characters and overly explicit dialog in which deep feelings and motivations come tumbling out in succinct speeches. Such pat character development invariably lends a rather superficial feel to the conflicts and relationships among the principals, and the viewer never really feels very deeply for the protagonists. Ford is such a master of his craft that he injects enough personal spark into the material to nearly override the script's deficiencies, but there's no denying that THE HORSE SOLDIERS is the work of a distracted, tired, and somewhat bored artist. Indeed, in his famous interview with Peter Bogdanovich, the director couldn't recall whether or not he had even seen the final cut.

p, John Lee Mahin and Martin Rackin; d, John Ford; w, John Lee Mahin and Martin Rackin, based on the novel by Harold Sinclair; ed, Jack Murray; ph, William Clothier, Deluxe Color; m, David Buttolph.

(PR:C MPAA:NR)

HOT BOX, THE**½

(1972, US/Phil.) 85m NW c

Andrea Cagan *(Bunny)*, Margaret Markov *(Lynn)*, Rickey Richardson *(Ellie)*, Laurie Rose *(Sue)*, Carmen Argenziano *(Flavio)*, Charles Dierkop *(Garcia/Maj. Dubay)*.

Shot in the Philippines but set in Latin America, this Jonathan Demme-penned and -produced film depicts the radicalization of four American nurses working for the Peace Corps (Andrea Cagan, Margaret Markov, Rickey Richardson, and Laurie Rose). After being kidnaped, the nurses refuse to provide medical assistance for a band of guerrillas led by Flavio (Carmen Argenziano). Though they eventually begin to sympathize with the rebels' cause, the women finally escape, only to be captured, tortured, and, in one case, raped by a sadistic government army officer. Again they escape, but this time they seek out the rebels and join their struggle.

p, Jonathan Demme; d, Joe Viola; w, Joe Viola and Jonathan Demme; ed, Ben Barcelon; ph, Felipe Sacdalan, Metrocolor; m, Resti Umali.

(PR:O MPAA:R)

HOW I WON THE WAR***

(1967, Brit.) 109m UA c

Michael Crawford *(Lt. Ernest Goodbody)*, John Lennon *(Gripweed)*, Roy Kinnear *(Clapper)*, Lee Montague *(Sgt. Transom)*, Jack MacGowran *(Juniper)*, Michael Hordern *(Grapple)*, Jack Hedley *(Melancholy Musketeer)*, Karl Michael Vogler *(Odlebog)*, Ronald Lacey *(Spool)*, James Cossins *(Drogue)*.

Richard Lester, director of the hit Beatles movies A HARD DAY'S NIGHT and HELP, intended this black comedy as a stinging condemnation of war, but occasionally he fails even as he succeeds, eliciting such plentiful laughs that he blunts the impact of his message. Revolving around the rose-colored reminiscences of a middle-aged British WW II veteran whose wartime career was actually a disaster, HOW I WON THE WAR follows the inept Lt. Goodbody (Michael Crawford) as he misleads his men from North Africa to France. Among his unfortunate misfit charges are the overweight Clapper (Roy Kinnear), who is obsessed with his wife's infidelity; Juniper (Jack MacGowran), a music-hall comic; and Gripweed (then-Beatle John Lennon, whose billing is considerably more prominent than his presence in the film). Transom (Lee Montague), the only competent military man in the bunch, tries in vain to correct his superior's command blunders, but so ill-prepared to lead is Goodbody that he eventually causes the deaths of all of his men save one, the Melancholy Musketeer (Jack Hedley). The battles in which they fall are each presented in a different color tint, and when the ghosts of these dead soldiers reappear to accompany their comrades on the rest of their campaign, they are bedecked in the color of the fray that claimed them. Based on a novel by Patrick Ryan, Lester's film offers both hilarious moments of satire (of war and war movies) and grim, bloody depictions of the awful reality of combat. This seemingly incongruous admixture will work for some viewers, but not for others, and though the seriousness of Lester's intent may not be appreciated by everyone, most should at least find something here to make them laugh.

p, Richard Lester; d, Richard Lester; w, Charles Wood, based on the novel by Patrick Ryan; ed, John Victor Smith; ph, David Watkin, Eastmancolor; m, Ken Thorne.

(PR:C MPAA:NR)

HUMAN CONDITION, THE***

(1958/1961, Jap.) 200m Shochiku bw (NINGEN NO JOKEN; AKA: NO GREATER LOVE; ROAD TO ETERNITY; SOLDIER'S PRAYER, A)

Tatsuya Nakadai *(Kaji)*, Michiyo Aratama *(Michiko)*, Taketoshi Naito *(Tange)*.

Based on a six-volume novel by Junpei Gomikawa, this three-part, 9 1/2 hour epic is a massive antiwar statement about a Japanese man who fights to retain his human dignity during the horrors of WW II. Director Masaki Kobayashi's camera follows Kaji (Tatsuya Nakadai), who is sent to administer a mining camp in occupied Manchuria. Despite the odds against him, Kaji tries to keep the volatile situation from exploding in an orgy of violence, but when the oppressed Chinese workers turn against the occupying Japanese, Kaji can do nothing to stop the bloodshed. When he objects to a mass beheading of Chinese workers, the military police *charge* Kaji with being humane to the enemy and torture him mercilessly. Ordered to the front, Kaji is confronted by indignity after indignity and fights to remember himself as a decent, caring man who is deeply in love with his wife (Michiyo Aratama). Released in three parts—NO GREATER LOVE (1958), ROAD TO ETERNITY (1959), and A SOLDIER'S PRAYER (1961)—this brutal portrait of a brutal war also reflects Kobayashi's own wartime experiences in Manchuria.

p, Masaki Kobayashi, Shigeru Wakatsuki, and Tatsuo Hasoya; d, Masaki Kobayashi; w, Koicji Inagaki, Zenzo Matsuyama, and Masaki Kobayashi, based on the novel by Junpei Gomikawa; ed, Keiichi Uraoka; ph, Yoshio Miyajima, Shochiku Grandscope; m, Chuji Kinoshita.

(PR:O MPAA:R)

IJK

IMMORTAL BATTALION, THE***½

(1944, Brit.) 106m TC/FOX bw (AKA: WAY AHEAD, THE)

David Niven *(Lt. Jim Perry)*, Raymond Huntley *(Davenport)*, Billy Hartnell *(Sgt. Fletcher)*, Stanley Holloway *(Brewer)*, James Donald *(Lloyd)*, John Laurie *(Luke)*, Leslie Dwyer *(Beck)*, Hugh Burden *(Parsons)*, Jimmy Hanley *(Stainer)*, Renee Asherson *(Marjorie Gillingham)*, Penelope Dudley-Ward *(Mrs. Perry)*, Reginald Tate *(Commanding Officer)*, Leo Genn *(Company Commander)*.

Carol Reed already had developed a reputation in Britain as an accomplished director by the time WW II broke out, so when he joined the Army it was no surprise that he was assigned to the film unit. His 1942 short instructional documentary THE NEW LOT and an idea by Lt. Col. David Niven provided the inspiration for THE IMMORTAL BATTALION (released in the UK as THE WAY AHEAD). Set in the aftermath of the Dunkirk evacuation, the story focuses on Lt. Jim Perry (Niven) as he whips a group of ordinary conscripts into soldiers and then leads them into battle against Rommel's Afrika Korps at El Alamein. This semi-documentary was a big success in Britain, earning Reed even greater respect and leading to ODD MAN OUT; THE FALLEN IDOL; and THE THIRD MAN (all in quick succession), and serving as a patriotic contribution to the war effort.

p, John Sutro and Norman Walker; d, Carol Reed; w, Eric Ambler and Peter Ustinov, based on a story by Eric Ambler; ed, Fergus McDonell; ph, Guy Green; m, William Alwyn.

(PR:A MPAA:NR)

IMMORTAL SERGEANT, THE***½

(1943) 90m FOX bw

Henry Fonda *(Cpl. Colin Spence)*, Maureen O'Hara *(Valentine)*, Thomas Mitchell *(Sgt. Kelly)*, Allyn Joslyn *(Cassidy)*, Reginald Gardiner *(Benedict)*, Melville Cooper *(Pilcher)*, Bramwell Fletcher *(Symes)*, Morton Lowry *(Cottrell)*.

This mediocre drama stars Henry Fonda as a Cpl. Colin Spence, a Canadian (hence his lack of a British accent) serving with the British Eighth Army in the Libyan desert. He and his comrades in arms, commanded by tough old Sgt. Kelly (Thomas Mitchell), are cut off from their lines and face annihilation. During a lonely night vigil with the dying Kelly, Colin contemplates his slim chance of leaving the desert alive, and in flashback, we see his prewar life. A

IN HARM'S WAY—

reporter and would-be novelist, he is deeply in love with Valentine (Maureen O'Hara), but because of his reluctance to tell her so, she seems destined to pair up with Colin's polished, assertive rival, Benedict (Reginald Gardiner). The story creeps toward the present until, after Kelly's death, Colin leads a desperate attack against a German position, destroying the enemy and their supplies. Spotting the burning stores, a British unit arrives to find only three men left alive, including the wounded Colin. After recuperating in a Cairo hospital, he summons the courage he has found on the battlefield and sends a wire to Valentine, proposing. Following their marriage, Colin delivers a prayer for the sergeant who inspired him to become a man of action. Basically a propaganda film, THE IMMORTAL SERGEANT had the distinction of being the first American film to portray British troops in action in North Africa—and there's action aplenty in this production. After its completion, Fonda joined the Navy, preferring not to discuss this patriotic role (which he reportedly despised). He spent the rest of the war in the Central Pacific as an air combat intelligence officer, receiving a Bronze Star and a Presidential Citation.

p, Lamar Trotti; d, John Stahl; w, Lamar Trotti, based on the novel by John Brophy; ed, James B. Clark; ph, Arthur Miller and Clyde De Vinna; m, David Buttolph.

(PR:A MPAA:NR)

IN HARM'S WAY***

(1965) 165m Sigma Productions/PAR bw

John Wayne *(Capt. Rockwell Torrey)*, Kirk Douglas *(Comdr. Paul Eddington)*, Patricia Neal *(Lt. Maggie Haynes)*, Tom Tryon *(Lt. William McConnel)*, Paula Prentiss *(Bev McConnel)*, Brandon De Wilde *(Ens. Jeremiah Torrey)*, Jill Haworth *(Ens. Annalee Dorne)*, Dana Andrews *(Adm. Broderick)*, Stanley Holloway *(Clayton Canfil)*, Burgess Meredith *(Comdr. Powell)*, Franchot Tone *(CINCPAC I Admiral)*, Patrick O'Neal *(Comdr. Neal O'Wynn)*, Carroll O'Connor *(Lt. Comdr. Burke)*, Slim Pickens *(CPO Culpepper)*, James Mitchum *(Ens. Griggs)*, George Kennedy *(Col. Gregory)*, Barbara Bouchet *(Liz Eddington)*.

This exciting WW II action film directed by Otto Preminger begins with the attack on Pearl Harbor, during which Capt. Rockwell Torrey (John Wayne) and his longtime pal Comdr. Paul Eddington (Kirk Douglas) are at sea with a small force of destroyers. After being advised of the attack, Torrey is sent on a fool's mission to seek and destroy the long-gone Japanese fleet. In the process, Torrey's little battle group is attacked, and because he has disregarded regulations, he is brought before a court of inquiry. Meanwhile, Eddington learns that his sluttish wife (Barbara Bouchet) has been killed during the attack. Torrey is demoted to a desk job; Eddington becomes embittered. As this 165-minute war epic progresses, a number of subplots are introduced: conflict between Torrey and his callous son, Jeremiah (Brandon De Wilde); Torrey's relationship with his ex-wife, Lt. Maggie Haynes (Patricia Neal), a WAVE officer; Eddington's interest in Jere's sweetheart, Annalee (Jill Haworth), and her eventual suicide; the romance of newlyweds Bev (Paula Prentiss) and Lt. (jg) William McConnel (Tom Tryon); and Torrey and Eddington's attempt to redeem themselves in battle. Much of the plot plays like a TV soap opera, but Preminger's artistry is evident in every frame. The attack on Pearl Harbor (with as many shells exploding in the harbor as on the streets) is inventively and realistically photographed and invested with a sense of danger. Regrettably, the naval battles are less convincing, as Preminger and crew used large models and shot these scenes in a lake in Mexico. Part of the picture was also shot aboard the USS *Braine*, *Capitaine*, *O'Bannon*, *Philip*, *Renshaw*, *Saint Paul*, and *Walker*.

p, Otto Preminger; d, Otto Preminger; w, Wendell Mayes, based on the novel by James Bassett; ed, George Tomasini and Hugh S. Fowler; ph, Loyal Griggs, Panavision; m, Jerry Goldsmith.

(PR:A MPAA:NR)

IN WHICH WE SERVE****

(1942, Brit.) 115m Two Cities/BL bw

Noel Coward *(Capt. Kinross)*, John Mills *(Shorty Blake)*, Bernard Miles *(Walter Hardy)*, Celia Johnson *(Alix Kinross)*, Kay Walsh *(Freda Lewis)*, Joyce Carey *(Kath Hardy)*, Michael Wilding *(Flags)*, Penelope Dudley Ward *(Maureen Fenwick)*, Philip Friend *(Torps)*, James Donald *(Doctor)*, Richard Attenborough *(Young Stoker)*.

Noel Coward, known for his sophisticated comedies, performed with unexpected brilliance here as codirector, writer, musical composer, and star of this stirring WW II drama. Presented in a series of poignant and revealing vignettes, the film tells the story of the British destroyer *Torrin* and its crew, commanded by Capt. Kinross (Coward), a father figure for his stalwart men. Constructed like a documentary, IN WHICH WE SERVE is also narrated by Coward, who recounts the ship's heroic actions: hit by torpedoes, it survives and is towed back to England, later participating in the Dunkirk evacuation and in naval battles off Crete, where it is dive-bombed and sinks. Kinross and his crew cling to a raft for hours, and while waiting for rescue, remember their loved ones in a series of flashbacks. Noble and full of understated passion, the film is expertly performed and handled on all levels. Coward wisely chose the most distinguished film editor in England at the time, David Lean, to assist with the production; and so impressive was Lean's work that, halfway through the picture, Coward handed him the directorial reins. Out of respect, David Lean's next three productions—THIS HAPPY BREED, BLITHE SPIRIT; BRIEF ENCOUNTER—were adaptations of Coward's writing.

p, Noel Coward; d, Noel Coward and David Lean; w, Noel Coward, based on the experiences of Lord Louis Mountbatten; ed, Thelma Myers and David Lean; ph, Ronald Neame; m, Noel Coward.

(PR:A MPAA:NR)

INN OF THE SIXTH HAPPINESS, THE***½

(1958, Brit.) 158m FOX c

Ingrid Bergman *(Gladys Aylward)*, Curt Jurgens *(Capt. Lin Nan)*, Robert Donat *(Mandarin)*, Ronald Squire *(Sir Francis Jamison)*, Noel Hood *(Miss Thompson)*, Joan Young *(Cook)*, Moultrie Kelsall *(Dr. Robinson)*, Edith Sharpe *(Secretary)*, Richard Wattis *(Mr. Murfin)*, Athene Seyler *(Mrs. Lawson)*, Peter Chong *(Yang)*, Michael David *(Ho Ka)*, Burt Kwouk *(Li)*, Frank Blaine *(Madman)*, Ronald Kyaing *(Young Lin)*.

Set in pre-WW II China and based on the true story of Gladys Aylward, THE INN OF THE SIXTH HAPPINESS is an inspiring film. Aylward (Ingrid Bergman), an English domestic, ventures to an inn high in the mountains of northern China, where she helps a British missionary (Athene Seyler) save souls. In the process, Aylward earns the grudging respect of an old mandarin (Robert Donat), who, however, does his best to see that she is occupied with do-gooding and out of his hair. When invasion by the Japanese becomes imminent, Capt. Lin Nan (Curt Jur-3gens), a Chinese army officer, appears and enlists Aylward's help in informing the locals of the coming danger. The captain and Aylward fall in love, but when the invasion begins, he rejoins his unit and she leads the villagers' children on an arduous journey to the safety of a mission located in the country's interior. A touching film with a lovely performance from Bergman, whose interaction with her young wards is unforgettable, THE INN OF THE SIXTH HAPPINESS also marked the last screen appearance for the great Donat, making his final line—"We shall not see each other again, I think. Farewell."—all the more memorable. He died before the film was released.

p, Buddy Adler; d, Mark Robson; w, Isobel Lennart, based on the novel *The Small Woman* by Alan Burgess; ed, Ernest Walter; ph, Freddie Young, CinemaScope, Deluxe Color; m, Malcolm Arnold.

(PR:AA   MPAA:NR)

INVASION U.S.A.**

(1985) 108m Cannon c

Chuck Norris *(Matt Hunter)*, Richard Lynch *(Rostov)*, Melissa Prophet *(McGuire)*, Alexander Zale *(Nikko)*, Alex Colon *(Tomas)*, Eddie Jones *(Cassidy)*, Jon DeVries *(Johnston)*, James O'Sullivan *(Harper)*, Billy Drago *(Mickey)*, Jaime Sanchez *(Castillo)*.

This was yet another of the cycle of patriotic chest-beating films that captured the public's Reagan-era jingoism and gave Americans the chance to kill terrorists and communists—if not in the real world, then at least in the safety and comfort of the movie theater. The story begins as waves of terrorists hit the beach in Florida in old WW II surplus landing craft, then pile into unmarked trucks bound for various destinations throughout the country. The terrorists are a motley bunch; some of them seem to be Vietnamese, some Arab, others Cuban or Nicaraguan. These polyglot killers are under the command of Rostov (Richard Lynch), who has a possibly Russian accent and surname, and who directs the invaders to attack churches, shopping malls, and suburban tract homes with Christmas trees in their yards, all calculated to make the US government crumble. The only man who can save civilization as we know it is Matt Hunter (Chuck Norris), a retired secret agent who lives in the Everglades, where he tools around in his air boat. When the terrorists kill his best friend by mistake, Hunter kicks into high gear and, almost as if he were psychic—because he certainly is never shown doing any kind of investigative work—Hunter, with a pair of submachine guns slung under each armpit, suddenly and consistently appears wherever the villains are preparing their latest outrage against law and order. A numbingly stupid actioner, INVASION U.S.A. has one of the most laughable villains ever committed to film. Bad guys need to be convinced they're going to succeed in their nefarious schemes; Rostov is so certain that Hunter is going to triumph over him that at several points in the film he wakes up in a cold sweat after dreaming that the hero is pummeling him. Norris, who has occasionally shown some interesting talent, reverts to his usual stolidity here, impassively gunning down terrorists like fish in a barrel.

p, Menahem Golan and Yoram Globus; d, Joseph Zito; w, James Bruner and Chuck Norris, based on a story by Aaron Norris, James Bruner; ed, Daniel Loewenthal and Scott Vickrey; ph, Joao Fernandes, TVC Color; m, Jay Chattaway.

(PR:O   MPAA:R)

IRON EAGLE*½

(1986) 116m Tri-Star c

Louis Gossett, Jr. *(Chappy)*, Jason Gedrick *(Doug)*, David Suchet *(Defense Minister)*, Tim Thomerson *(Ted)*, Larry B. Scott *(Reggie)*, Caroline Lagerfelt *(Elizabeth)*, Jerry Levine *(Tony)*, Robbie Rist *(Milo)*, Michael Bowen *(Knotcher)*, Bobby Jacoby *(Matthew)*, Melora Hardin *(Katie)*, David Greenlee *(Kingsley)*.

Yet another totally absurd bout of macho wish-fulfillment for those frustrated by the American government and military's inability to deal effectively with terrorism, IRON EAGLE is actually more outlandish than most. Doug (Jason Gedrick) is a teenager about to go to his high school prom when he learns that his father (Tim Thomerson) has been shot down over an unnamed Arab country for venturing too close to its borders. When the US government doesn't move fast enough to gain his father's release, Doug, who more or less has free rein around the base and spends a great deal of time in the flight simulator when it's not being used by pilots, decides to rescue his dad himself by stealing an F-16. Realizing that there is no way he will be able to pull this off on his own, Doug contacts Chappy (Louis Gossett, Jr.), a retired Air Force colonel who, although reluctant at first, whips Doug and his Air Force brat pals into shape in the same way that he harangued recruits in his Oscar-winning performance in AN OFFICER AND A GENTLEMAN. Later, Chappy and Doug steal a pair of F-16s, and off they go to the Middle East. It really didn't matter that the film was

IRON EAGLE II—

totally jingoistic, fantastical, and moronic: IRON EAGLE was a surprise hit at the box office and spawned an even dumber sequel. Director Sydney J. Furie is a workmanlike talent whose action scenes are competent but unremarkable. If you can believe that a young boy, whose only flight experience was in a simulator, could pull off what young Doug does here, you'll believe anything.

p, Ron Samuels and Joe Wizan; d, Sidney J. Furie; w, Kevin Elders and Sidney J. Furie; ed, George Grenville; ph, Adam Greenberg, Metrocolor; m, Basil Poledouris.

(PR:C   MPAA:PG-13)

IRON EAGLE II*

(1988) 105m Alliance-Harkot/Tri-Star c

Louis Gossett, Jr. *(Chappy)*, Mark Humphrey *(Cooper)*, Stuart Margolin *(Stillmore)*, Alan Scarfe *(Vardovsky)*, Sharon H. Brandon *(Valeri Zuyeniko)*, Maury Chaykin *(Downs)*, Colm Feore *(Yuri)*, Clark Johnson *(Graves)*.

In TOP GUN, American pilots blow a Soviet squadron out of the sky, but World War III doesn't begin because both sides decide to keep it a secret. Apparently this sort of thing goes on all the time, because here it is again at the beginning of IRON EAGLE II, as an aerial game of tag between two Americans and two Russkies gets out of hand, resulting in the downing of one of the American fighters. Once again, none of this is ever made public. Right. At any rate, it seems that the pilot who is shot down was the young hero of IRON EAGLE, in which he teamed with Gen. Charles "Chappy" Sinclair (Lou Gossett, Jr.) to free his imprisoned dad from some unnamed Arab hellhole. In IRON EAGLE II, Sinclair is pulled out of retirement, put in charge of a group of misfits—including Cooper (Mark Humphrey), the survivor of the opening showdown—and told to team up with a squad of Soviet misfits at a base in Israel, where they will train for a top-secret mission to destroy a nuclear missile site in yet another unnamed Arab state. Naturally, there are tensions between the two teams, leading to a big fight; and, of course, one of the Russian pilots is a beautiful woman with whom Cooper falls in love. After Sinclair discovers that his superior really plans to sabotage the whole thing, he whips everyone into shape and the combined teams manage to penetrate the Arab defenses, successfully completing the mission. The misfits-assembled-for-a-suicide-mission plot is one of the hoariest in the war genre, best done in THE DIRTY DOZEN, which had an excellent cast and director (Robert Aldrich). IRON EAGLE II has only Gossett and filmmaker Sidney J. Furie, whose successes (THE IPCRESS FILE; THE BOYS IN COMPANY C) are outweighed by his failures (GABLE AND LOMBARD; SUPERMAN IV: THE QUEST FOR PEACE). Only the aerial sequences are commendable, and even these pale in comparison to TOP GUN.

p, Jacob Kotzky, Sharon Harel, and John Kemeny; d, Sidney J. Furie; w, Kevin Elders and Sidney J. Furie; ed, Rit Wallis; ph, Alain Dostie, Bellevue Pathe color; m, Amin Bhatia.

(PR:C   MPAA:PG)

IVAN THE TERRIBLE, PARTS I & II****

(1945, USSR) 96m Central Cinema-Alma Ata-Sovexportfilm/Janus-Artkino bw/c (IVAN GROZNYI)

Nikolai Cherkassov *(Czar Ivan IV)*, Serafima Birma

These are the first two parts of Sergei Eisenstein's intended trilogy about the 16th-century Russian hero Czar Ivan IV. Part I, completed in 1945, chronicles the ruler's coronation, his marriage, his illness and sudden unexplained recovery, the poisoning of his wife, and his battles against conspirators. By the end, he declares his intention of returning from Alexandrov to Moscow at the will of his people. Part II (subtitled "The Boyar's Plot"), filmed shortly after Part I but not released until 1958, follows Czar Ivan on his return, his confrontations with his enemies, the poisoning of his mother, and his discovery of an assassination plot. The black-and-white film ends with a brilliantly colored banquet scene. Although the scenario for Part III ("The Battles of Ivan") was approved by Stalin (oddly enough, since Stalin censored Part II because of its negative portrayal of Ivan's secret police), Eisenstein, who died in 1948, never completed the project. Viewers familiar only with Eisenstein's BATTLESHIP POTEMKIN will find the shift from that film's revolutionary editing style to IVAN's emphasis on composition and lighting quite a surprise. A vast, important, and occasionally difficult historical effort that closed Eisenstein's legendary career, IVAN THE TERRIBLE includes a remarkable score by Sergei Prokofiev. Both videocassettes are in Russian with English subtitles.

p, Sergei Eisenstein; d, Sergei Eisenstein; w, Sergei Eisenstein; ph, Edward Tisse and Andrei Moskvin; m, Sergei Prokofiev.

(PR:A   MPAA:NR)

JOHNNY GOT HIS GUN**½

(1971) 111m Cinemation c

Timothy Bottoms *(Joe Bonham)*, Kathy Fields *(Kareen)*, Marsha Hunt *(Joe's Mother)*, Jason Robards, Jr. *(Joe's Father)*, Donald Sutherland *("Christ")*, Diane Varsi *(Nurse)*, Sandy Brown Wyeth *(Lucky)*, Donald Barry *(Jody Simmons)*, Eric Christmas *(Cpl. Timlon)*, Eduard Franz *(Col./Gen. Tillery)*.

Flawed but powerful, Dalton Trumbo's adaptation of his disturbing 1939 antiwar novel won three awards at the 1971 Cannes Film Festival but met with mixed reviews at home. The film centers on Joe Bonham (Timothy Bottoms, in his film debut), a young American soldier who loses his legs, arms, and face when a bomb explodes near him on the last day of WW I. Deaf, dumb, and blind, he is kept alive by doctors who assume he is a vegetable and keep him in a locked room, intending to use him for medical research. Joe, however, can think and, in time, feel. To maintain his sanity, he roams a vast mental landscape in which memories and dreams commingle with meditations on the brutality and senselessness of war—an interior life represented in color, while the hospital scenes are in black and white. Eventually, a compassionate nurse (Diane Varsi) comes to understand Joe's condition and communicates with him by writing on his chest with her finger, to which he responds by using his head to tap Morse Code. When Joe's request to be put on display as a reminder of the terrible cost of war is denied, he asks to be killed. A number of critics have found JOHNNY GOT HIS GUN heavy-handed; others consider it to be among the cinema's most powerful antiwar statements. To be sure, Trumbo, directing his first film, drives home his points in a somewhat obvious, often awkward fashion that is overly talky, but so disquieting is his story and the reality underlying it that it is difficult not to be moved by the film and Bottoms' fine performance. When a 1965 production of the story that was to have been directed by Luis Bunuel fell through, as did a subsequent deal with Warner Bros., Trumbo and producer Bruce Campbell came up with $750,000 and made the film themselves under the rubric of Robert Rich (the pseudonym the blacklisted Trumbo used for his Academy Award-winning screenplay for 1957's THE BRAVE ONE) Productions.

p, Bruce Campbell; d, Dalton Trumbo; w, Dalton Trumbo, based on his novel; ed, William P. Dornisch; ph, Jules Brenner, Eastmancolor; m, Jerry Fielding.

(PR:O   MPAA:GP)

JUDGMENT AT NUREMBERG***½

(1961) 178m Roxlom/UA bw

Spencer Tracy *(Judge Dan Haywood)*, Burt Lancaster *(Ernst Janning)*, Richard Widmark *(Col. Tad Lawson)*, Marlene Dietrich *(Mme. Bertholt)*, Maximilian Schell *(Hans Rolfe)*, Judy Garland *(Irene Hoffman)*, Montgomery Clift *(Rudolph Petersen)*, William Shatner *(Capt. Harrison Byers)*, Edward Binns *(Sen. Burkette)*, Kenneth MacKenna *(Judge Kenneth Norris)*, Werner Klemperer *(Emil Hahn)*.

As with most courtroom dramas, JUDGMENT AT NUREMBERG is overlong and static, but, in its day, it was sensational—the first film to deal seriously with the trials of Nazi war criminals. The chief Allied judge, Dan Haywood (Spencer Tracy), has been sent to Germany after failing to be reelected to the bench in New England, a political payoff that does not go unnoticed by his adversaries. Prosecuting attorney Tad Lawson (Richard Widmark), an Army colonel, indicts several Germans who have committed war crimes in enforcing Hitler's mad mandates. In his defense of them, Hans Rolfe (Maximilian Schell) roars that his clients were merely upholding Hitler's laws and that to place them on trial is to judge all of Germany. Meanwhile, Haywood, in his off hours, wanders the ancient city of Nuremberg trying to understand what went wrong with a whole people and a great culture. The rest of the cast in this three-hour-plus picture is equally distinguished: Marlene Dietrich is the widow of a German general who was executed for ordering the slaughter of captured American soldiers at Malmedy, Burt Lancaster is an intellectual German judge who unwillingly aided the Nazis, Montgomery Clift is a dimwitted victim of sterilization who testifies for the prosecution, and Judy Garland is a woman who "polluted the Aryan race" by having sex with a Jew. Absorbing from beginning to end, though unrelentingly bleak, JUDGMENT AT NUREMBERG was originally offered on TV as a 1959 Playhouse 90 production directed by George Roy Hill and starring Claude Rains as Haywood, Paul Lukas in the Lancaster role, and Maximilian Schell in the part he repeats in the film.

p, Stanley Kramer; d, Stanley Kramer; w, Abby Mann; ed, Frederic Knudtson; ph, Ernest Laszlo; m, Ernest Gold.

(PR:C   MPAA:NR)

JUNGLE PATROL**½

(1948) 71m FOX bw

Kristine Miller *(Jean)*, Arthur Franz *(Mace)*, Ross Ford *(Skipper)*, Tom Noonan *(Ham)*, Gene Reynolds *(Minor)*, Richard Jaeckel *(Dick)*, Mickey Knox *(Louie)*, Harry Lauter *(Derby)*, Bill Murphy *(Johnny)*, G. Pat Collins *(Sgt. Hanley)*.

Eight fliers stationed at a temporary airfield near Port Moresby, New Guinea, are given the task of holding off the Japanese until a permanent air base can be constructed in this gripping B picture filled with strong characterizations. After downing nearly 100 enemy planes without suffering a loss, they begin agonizing over which of them will be the first to go. However, the performance of a visiting USO entertainer (Kristine Miller) helps to take the fliers' minds off their grim business . . . for a while.

p, Frank N. Seltzer; d, Joe Newman; w, Francis Swan, based on the play by William Bowers; ed, Bert Jordan; ph, Mack Stengler; m, Emil Newman and Arthur Lange.

(PR:A   MPAA:NR)

KAGEMUSHA****

(1980, Jap.) 179m Toho-Kurosawa/FOX c (AKA: DOUBLE, THE; SHADOW WARRIOR, THE)

Tatsuya Nakadai *(Takeda Kagemusha)*, Tsutomu Yamazaki *(Katsuyori)*, Kenichi Hagiwara *(Son)*, Kota Yui *(Takemaru)*, Hideji Otaki *(Yamagata)*, Hideo Murata *(Baba)*, Daisuke Ryu *(Oda)*, Kaori Momoi *(Otsuyanokata)*.

After a long period of inactivity, Akira Kurosawa returned to the genre of which he is the unequivocal master, the samurai film, with KAGEMUSHA. Tatsuya Nakadai plays a 16th-century warlord, Shingen Takeda, who uses doubles for himself on the battlefield, instilling confidence and fear through his constant presence while his clan fights to establish dominance in Japan. When he is killed, his current "shadow warrior," or kagemusha—in actuality a petty thief (again powerfully played by Tatsuya Nakadai)—must take over so that the army's morale will not die. Trained in secret by Shingen's assistants, the man genuinely begins to acquire some of his master's attributes, but is eventually exposed as a fake and banished from court. In the final, climactic battle, however, the deposed kagemusha is unable to restrain himself and grabs the clan's standard, rushing into the fray. Kurosawa's epic is alive with color, the spectacular visuals overlying a somber exploration of traditionalism, loyalty, and identity, played out against a tapestry of political intrigue and the 16th-century clan warfare that came to an end with the Tokugawa shogunate. The

KAMERADSCHAFT—

massive battle scenes rank with the director's best, using brilliant color and contrasts of light amidst the enormous cast with great style. Made and distributed with the financial aid and clout of George Lucas and Francis Ford Coppola, KAGEMUSHA prefigured and paved the way for the great RAN (1985), Kurosawa's epic adaptation of "King Lear." (In Japanese; with English subtitles.)

p, Akira Kurosawa and Masato Ide; d, Akira Kurosawa; w, Akira Kurosawa and Masato Ide; ph, Takao Saito, Shoji Ueda, Kazuo Miyagawa, and Asaichi Nakai, Eastmancolor; m, Shinichiro Ikebe.

(PR:C   MPAA:PG)

KAMERADSCHAFT****

(1931, Ger.) 93m Nero-Gaumont-Franco-Film-Aubert bw (AKA: COMRADESHIP)

Fritz Kampers *(Wilderer)*, Gustav Puttjer *(Kaplan)*, Alexander Granach *(Kaspers)*, Andree Ducret *(Francoise)*, Georges Charlia *(Jean)*, Ernst Busch *(Wittkopp)*, Daniel Mandaille *(Emile)*, Pierre Louis *(Georges)*, Alex Bernard *(Grandfather)*.

A heartfelt plea for peace and internationalism, KAMERADSCHAFT is set in the Lorraine mining region on the French-German border in the aftermath of WW I, though it is based on a actual 1906 mining disaster that claimed 1,200 lives. Combining Expressionism and realism (pre-dating the Italian Neo-Realists), G.W. Pabst introduces the viewer to the German and French miners. Separated by mine walls and metal bars below, and by armed border patrols above, they have little contact with one another, but when a series of explosions causes a cave-in on the French side, German hearts bleed. Wittkopp (Ernst Busch) appeals to his bosses to send a rescue team, while underground a trio of German miners breaks through a set of steel bars that mark the 1919 border. Meanwhile, on the French side, an old, retired miner (Alex Bernard) sneaks into the shaft, hoping to rescue his young grandson (Pierre Louis). Although occasionally over-sentimental, Pabst's plea for a peaceful future is both noble and honest, his direction of the heartbreak and devastation enhanced by the brilliant photography by Fritz Arno Wagner and Robert Baberske, and the frighteningly real set design by Erno Metzner and Karl Vollbrecht. The videocassette is in German and French with easy-to-read yellow English subtitles.

p, Seymour Nebenzahl; d, G.W. Pabst; w, Karl Otten, Peter Martin Lampel, and Ladislaus Vajda; ed, Hans Oser; ph, Fritz Arno Wagner and Robert Baberske.

(PR:A-C   MPAA:NR)

KANAL****

(1957, Pol.) 96m Film Polski/M.J.P.-Kingsley-International bw (AKA: THEY LOVED LIFE)

Teresa Izewska *(Daisy Stokrotka)*, Tadeusz Janczar *(Cpl. Korab)*, Wienczyslaw Glinski *(Lt. Zadra)*, Tadeusz Gwiazdowski *(Sgt. Kula)*, Stanislaw Mikulski *(The Slim [Smukly])*, Wladyslaw Sheybal *(Composer)*, Emil Karewiez *(The Wise [Madry])*, Teresa Berezowska *(Halinka)*.

This second feature from Andrzej Wajda takes place during the final days of the Warsaw Uprising in 1944, as three groups of Poles, no longer able to hold off the enemy, retreat to the city's *kanaly*, or sewer system. The viewer is told from the very start to "watch them closely; these are the last hours of their lives," and with this pessimistic tone established we watch them both trying to escape and living an underground existence free from the oppression and lost ideals of their lives above ground. Although we know that death awaits them, we also know that freedom from the sewers is only a relative freedom. Wajda spares the viewer nothing, showing death, betrayal, suffering, suicide, capture, and despair. Still the Poles fight on in the hope that they will see sunlight pouring into the sewer, even if it is filtered through a metai grate. The videocassette is available in both dubbed (Polish into English) and subtitled versions.

p, Stanislaw Adler; d, Andrzej Wajda; w, Jerzy Stefan Stawinski, based on a short story by Jerzy Stefan Stawinski; ed, Halina Nawrocka; ph, Jerzy Lipman; m, Jan Krenz.

(PR:C   MPAA:NR)

KEEP, THE**

(1983) 96m Capital/PAR c

Scott Glenn *(Glaeken Trismegestus)*, Alberta Watson *(Eva)*, Jurgen Prochnow *(Woermann)*, Robert Prosky *(Fr. Fonescu)*, Gabriel Byrne *(Kempffer)*, Ian McKellen *(Dr. Cuza)*, Morgan Sheppard *(Alexandru)*, Royston Tickner *(Tomescu)*, Michael Carter *(Radu)*, Phillip Joseph *(Oster)*.

A minor disaster. Director Michael Mann (THIEF, television's "Miami Vice" and "Crime Story") presents a fantastic-looking movie, filled with great production values and lush cinematography. Unfortunately, these are combined with a totally incoherent narrative, punctuated by incredibly inept performances from usually fine actors (Robert Prosky, who was so good in THIEF, is an embarrassment here, as is Ian McKellen). The film is set in Eastern Europe during WW II, but just what is going on there is hard to say. The plot has something to do with a castle in the Carpathian Mountains that possesses a powerful, evil force that sucks up every Nazi it comes across and spits out their bloody entrails. Called by psychic impulses (or something like that), a mysterious traveler (Scott Glenn) arrives to do battle with the evil force. THE KEEP is one of the more visually interesting horror films of the 1980s, making its complete narrative weakness all the more frustrating.

p, Gene Kirkwood and Howard W. Koch, Jr.; d, Michael Mann; w, Michael Mann, based on a novel by F. Paul Wilson; ed, Dov Hoenig; ph, Alex Thomson, Metrocolor; m, Tangerine Dream.

(PR:O   MPAA:R)

KELLY'S HEROES***
(1970, US/Yugo.) 143m Katzka-Loeb/MGM c

Clint Eastwood *(Kelly)*, Telly Savalas *(Big Joe)*, Don Rickles *(Crapgame)*, Donald Sutherland *(Oddball)*, Carroll O'Connor *(Gen. Colt)*, Gavin MacLeod *(Moriarty)*, Hal Buckley *(Maitland)*, Stuart Margolin *(Little Joe)*, Jeff Morris *(Cowboy)*, Richard Davalos *(Gutowski)*, Perry Lopez *(Petuko)*, Tom Troupe *(Job)*, Dick Balduzzi *(Fisher)*, Gene Collins *(Babra)*, Len Lesser *(Bellamy)*, George Savalas *(Mulligan)*.

This humorous, lively, and entertaining picture could be described as a caper film set against a WW II backdrop. Lt. Kelly (Clint Eastwood) is an atypical army man who, while boozing with a captured German general, learns of $16 million worth of gold bars behind enemy lines. Kelly reveals a plan to his fellow soldiers: they will use their upcoming three-day passes to sneak into enemy territory, steal the gold, bury it, and return after the war to divide it among themselves. Kelly sets the heist in motion, blazing a trail of destruction en route, backed by a wonderfully colorful cast of characters that includes Donald Sutherland as the appropriately named Oddball, a hippie tank driver; Don Rickles as Crapgame, a hustler and arms supplier; Telly Savalas as the skeptical sergeant who goes along for the ride; and Carroll O'Connor as the egotistical Gen. Colt, who is glad to be mistaken for Gen. Eisenhower. Directed by Brian G. Hutton, whose previous film was the deadly serious war adventure WHERE EAGLES DARE, KELLY'S HEROES again features Eastwood in its cast and adds a light-hearted air to the proceedings. The film's most memorable moments are the destruction of the railroad station to the tune of "I've Been Working on the Railroad" and the spoof of the spaghetti western musical scores of Ennio Morricone as Kelly and cohorts prepare for a showdown with a Panzer tank. Also deserving of mention is the photography of Gabriel Figueroa, the veteran Mexican cinematographer who worked extensively with Luis Bunuel and Emilio Fernandez.

p, Gabriel Katzka and Sidney Beckerman; d, Brian G. Hutton; w, Troy Kennedy Martin; ed, John Jympson; ph, Gabriel Figueroa, Panavision, Metrocolor; m, Lalo Schifrin.

(PR:C-O   MPAA:GP)

KILLING FIELDS, THE***½
(1984, Brit.) 141m Enigma-Goldcrest/WB c

Sam Waterston *(Sydney Schanberg)*, Haing S. Ngor *(Dith Pran)*, John Malkovich *(Al Rockoff)*, Julian Sands *(Jon Swain)*, Craig T. Nelson *(Military Attache)*, Spalding Gray *(US Consul)*, Bill Paterson *(Dr. Macentire)*, Athol Fugard *(Dr. Sundesval)*, Graham Kennedy *(Dougal)*, Katherine Krapum Chey *(Ser Moeun)*, Oliver Pierpaoli *(Titonel)*, Edward Entero Chey *(Sarun)*, Tom Bird *(US Military Advisor)*, Monirak Sisowath *(Phat)*, Lambool Dtangpaibool *(Phat's Son)*, Ira Wheeler *(Ambassador Wade)*, David Henry *(France)*.

A deeply moving though flawed film, THE KILLING FIELDS is the somewhat fictionalized story of *New York Times* reporter Sydney Schanberg (Sam Waterston) and his efforts to find his friend Dith Pran (Dr. Haing S. Ngor) after the Cambodian translator falls into the brutal hands of the Khmer Rouge. Though Dith's family is evacuated with the last US personnel to leave Phnom Penh, Schanberg persuades his translator to remain behind with him, and when Khmer Rouge troops enter the city, Dith convinces them that Schanberg and his photographer (John Malkovich) are French. Regrettably, Schanberg is unable to return the favor later, and Dith is sent off to a rural re-education camp, which he barely survives and eventually escapes. While undertaking the arduous journey to safety, he comes across the horrible remains of some of the three million people who died at the hands of the Khmer Rouge. Meanwhile, racked with guilt, Schanberg, who has received a Pulitzer Prize for "international reporting at great risk," does everything he can to locate his friend. Finally, Dith is reunited with his family and Schanberg. THE KILLING FIELDS wisely emphasizes the human element of its story, concentrating on Schanberg and Dith's friendship and letting the political situation speak for itself (though the use of John Lennon's "Imagine" to close the film provides a ham-fisted shove in the politically correct direction). Haing S. Ngor, the Cambodian physician who actually went through an experience similar to the one he reenacts, won a Best Actor Oscar for his sincere, heartrending performance. Though Waterston is less effective, he, too, contributes a believable performance, as does Malkovich, making an impressive film debut. Aided by Chris Menges' spectacular photography, director Roland Joffe's first feature is an assured effort, its sequences unfolding with precision as the heartfelt emotions mount.

p, David Puttnam; d, Roland Joffe; w, Bruce Robinson, based on the magazine article "The Death and Life of Dith Pran" by Sydney Schanberg; ed, Jim Clark; ph, Chris Menges; m, Mike Oldfield.

(PR:O   MPAA:R)

KIM***
(1950) 113m MGM c

Errol Flynn *(Mahbub Ali, the Red Beard)*, Dean Stockwell *(Kim)*, Paul Lukas *(Lama)*, Robert Douglas *(Col. Creighton)*, Thomas Gomez *(Emissary)*, Cecil Kellaway *(Hurree Chunder)*, Arnold Moss *(Lurgan Sahib)*, Reginald Owen *(Fr. Victor)*, Laurette Luez *(Laluli)*, Richard Hale *(Hassan Bey)*, Roman Toporow, Ivan Triesault *(Russians)*, Hayden Rorke *(Maj. Ainsley)*, Walter Kingsford *(Dr. Bronson)*, Frank Lackteen *(Shadow)*.

This adaptation of the classic Rudyard Kipling novel features a young, bright-eyed Dean Stockwell as Kim, the rebellious, adventure-seeking son of an English envoy in the 1880s in India. Fed up with his school's rigid rules, Kim assumes the guise of a turbaned peasant boy and wanders through the Indian marketplace. He is befriended by a philosophical lama (Paul Lukas) who treats him with fatherly warmth and offers him invaluable advice, while from Mahbub Ali (Errol Flynn), a flamboyant horse thief who doubles as a British agent, Kim learns the finer points

KING OF HEARTS—

of espionage. The adventure and fun continue when the three get involved in an explosive political situation as the Russians prepare an invasion of the Khyber Pass. Luxuriously photographed in Technicolor, KIM offers countless panoramic views of India, even though a large portion of the film was shot in California and the 13-year-old Stockwell never set foot in India. The film kicked around MGM for some time before it finally went into production, with Freddie Bartholomew and Robert Taylor cast in 1938, before WW II halted the project. Later, Mickey Rooney, Conrad Veidt, and Basil Rathbone were to star, but the tenuous situation that came with the Indian struggle for independence led to another shutdown. When independence was achieved in 1948, MGM finally thought it safe to begin this version.

p, Leon Gordon; d, Victor Saville; w, Leon Gordon, Helen Deutsch, and Richard Schayer, based on the novel by Rudyard Kipling; ed, George Boemler; ph, William V. Skall, Technicolor; m, Andre Previn.

(PR:AA MPAA:G)

KING OF HEARTS***½

(1967, Fr./It.) 100m Artistes Associes-Cinematografica Montoro-Fildebroc/Lopert-UA c (LE ROI DE COEUR; TUTTI PAZZIO MENO LO)

Alan Bates *(Pvt. Charles Plumpick)*, Pierre Brasseur *(Gen. Geranium)*, Jean-Claude Brialy *(The Duke—Le Duc de Trefle)*, Genevieve Bujold *(Coquelicot)*, Adolfo Celi *(Col. Alexander MacBibenbrook)*, Micheline Presle *(Mme. Eglantine)*, Francoise Christophe *(The Duchess)*, Julien Guiomar *(Bishop Daisy—Monseigneur Marguerite)*, Michel Serrault *(The Crazy Barber)*, Marc Dudicourt *(Lt. Hamburger)*, Daniel Boulanger *(Col. Helmut von Krack)*, Jacques Balutin *(Mac Fish)*.

Breathing new life into old themes, Philippe de Broca's charming antiwar dramedy KING OF HEARTS has been a perennial favorite on college campuses since it first reached the screen in 1967, at the height of the Vietnam War. Set during WW I, the film begins as the occupying Germans retreat from the town of Marville, France, but not before leaving behind a time bomb. The fleeing townspeople tell the approaching British forces about the hidden explosives, and Pvt. Charles Plumpick (Alan Bates), a poetry-loving Scotsman, is dispatched to locate the bomb. To avoid the German rear guard, Plumpick ducks into Marville's insane asylum, and the inmates hail him as the "King of Hearts" before retaking the town and resuming their former lives, albeit in a decidedly loony fashion. While trying to find and defuse the bomb, Plumpick comes to love the crazy but gentle citizens, especially Coquelicot (Genevieve Bujold). In time, the Germans and British clash in Marville, littering the town with bodies, and when the "real" townspeople return, Plumpick is left with a choice: go back to soldiering or join the "crazy" folks in the asylum. In addition to its strong antiwar message, KING OF HEARTS ponders the old question of who's crazier, the people who accept life's brutality or those who reject it? Some have said that de Broca states his case with a heavy hand—and

he does—but for those willing to open themselves to a lighthearted treatment of this all-too-serious subject, KING OF HEARTS will be both touching and life-affirming. The videocassette is dubbed in English.

p, Philippe de Broca; d, Philippe de Broca; w, Daniel Boulanger, based on an idea by Maurice Bessy; ed, Francoise Javet; ph, Pierre L'Homme, Techniscope, Deluxe Color; m, Georges Delerue.

(PR:C MPAA:NR)

KING RAT**½

(1965) 134m Coleytown/COL bw

George Segal *(Cpl. King)*, Patrick O'Neal *(Max)*, Todd Armstrong *(Tex)*, Sammy Reese *(Kurt)*, Joseph Turkel *(Dino)*, Michael Stroka *(Miller)*, William Fawcett *(Steinmetz)*, Dick Johnson *(Pop)*, James Fox *(Flight Lt. Marlowe)*, Denholm Elliott *(Lt. Col. Denholm Larkin)*, Leonard Rossiter *(Maj. McCoy)*, Tom Courtenay *(Lt. Grey)*, John Mills *(Col. Smedley-Taylor)*, Gerald Sim *(Col. Jones)*, John Merivale *(Foster)*, John Warburton *(Commandant)*, James Donald *(Dr. Kennedy)*.

Set in a WW II Japanese POW camp, this nicely photographed adaptation of a James Clavell novel stars George Segal as King, an American corporal who operates a lucrative racket, selling rats to his sickly British, Australian, and American fellow prisoners to supplement their meager food rations. When King learns that British officer Marlowe (James Fox) speaks the language of their Malaysian guards, he enlists his help in expanding his operation outside the confines of the camp. Then, after Marlowe becomes gravely ill, King does some wheeling and dealing with their captors and secures a much-needed antibiotic. Segal is excellent as the title schemer and Fox and the rest of the cast, notably Tom Courtenay, provide strong support. However, at 134 minutes, KING RAT is not as consistently interesting as it might have been at a more concise length. If you're looking for another STALAG 17, forget it.

p, James Woolf; d, Bryan Forbes; w, Bryan Forbes, based on the novel by James Clavell; ed, Walter Thompson; ph, Burnett Guffey; m, John Barry.

(PR:O MPAA:NR)

KOLBERG***

(1945, Ger.) 84m UFA c (AKA: BURNING HEARTS)

Kristina Soderbaum *(Maria)*, Heinrich George *(Nettelbeck)*, Horst Caspar *(Gen. Gneisenau)*, Paul Wegener *(Col. von Loucadou)*, Gustav Diessl *(Maj. Schill)*.

KOLBERG is Joseph Goebbels' attempt to outdo GONE WITH THE WIND and reportedly the most expensive German film ever, with over 90 hours of footage and film stock designed by Nazi chemists specifically for the picture. This propaganda film tells the story of the heroic attempts of a Prussian town, Kolberg, to ward off advancing French troops during the Napoleonic Wars. Nettelbeck (Heinrich George, who was to die in a Russian prison camp in 1946), the town mayor, organizes civilians to fight the enemy; Maria (Kristina Soderbaum, the director's wife), a farmer's daughter, convinces her brothers and lover to die for the glory of Prussia. After a year in production, the film premiered at La Rochelle, with the advancing Allies just miles away; future showings were extremely limited because of the war. Although not credited, Goebbels was a major contributor to the script. A total of 187,000 Wehrmacht extras were reassigned from the various besieged war fronts to lend authenticity to the movie, a testament to Goebbels and Hitler's belief that the film was at least as important to morale as a military victory. Although its worth—as a product of Naziism, directed by a devout party man and anti-Semite—can be debated, the film is not without some astounding production values and a certain historical importance. (In German; English subtitles.)

d, Veit Harlan; w, Alfred Braun and Thea von Harbou; m, Norbert Schultze.

(PR:O   MPAA:NR)

L

LA MARSEILLAISE***½

(1938, Fr.) 130m La Marseillaise Society/World bw

Pierre Renoir *(Louis XVI)*, Lise Delamare *(Marie Antoinette)*, Leon Larive *(Picard)*, William Haguet *(La Rochefoucald-Liancourt)*, Louis Jouvet *(Roederer)*, Aime Clairond *(M. de Saint-Laurent)*, Maurice Escande *(Le Seigneur du Village)*, Andre Zibral *(M. de Saint Merri)*, Paul Dullac *(Javel)*, Fernand Flamant *(Ardisson)*, Jean-Louis Allibert *(Moissan)*, Nadia Siberskaia *(Louison)*.

Telling the story of the march on Paris by a battalion of 500 volunteers who arrive on time to capture the Tuilleries, leading to the publication of the Brunswick Manifesto and the overthrow of the monarchy of Louis XVI, LA MARSEILLAISE is itself essentially a grand march from Marseilles to Paris, contrasting the lives of the commoners with those of the aristocracy. With this march, of course, came the most patriotic of French songs, "La Marseillaise," sung energetically here by the peasants—first as a quiet melody and later as an anthem. Jean Renoir does what he does best in providing a naturalistic, nearly documentary portrayal of the characters. In one sense, LA MARSEILLAISE is something of a western, its march paralleling the progress of the wagon train. Released on the heels of the brilliant GRAND ILLUSION, it suffered from the belief that a director can't make two masterpieces in a row in its reception. A vastly inferior 79-minute version was released in the US in 1939. (In French; English subtitles.)

d, Jean Renoir; w, Jean Renoir, Carl Koch, N. Martel Dreyfus, and Mme. Jean-Paul Dreyfus; ed, Marguerite Renoir and Marthe Huguet; ph, Jean-Serge Bourgoin, Alain Douarinou, Jean-Marie Maillols, Jean-Paul Alphen, and J.

Louis; m, Lalande, Gretry, Jean Philippe Rameau, Johann Sebastian Bach, Wolfgang Amadeus Mozart, Rouget de l'Isle, Joseph Kosma, and Sauveplane.

(PR:A   MPAA:NR)

LAST DAY OF THE WAR, THE**

(1969, US/It./Sp.) 96m Prodi Cinematografica-Atlantida-Valencia/Sagittarius c (L'ULTIMO GIORNO DELLA GUERRA; EL ULTIMO DIA DE LA GUERRA)

George Maharis *(Sgt. Chips Slater)*, Maria Perschy *(Elena Truppe)*, John Clarke *(Hobbs)*, James Philbrook *(Lt. Poole)*, Gerard Herter *(Maj. Skorch)*, Gustavo Rojo *(Hawk)*, Jack Stuart [Giacomo Rossi-Stuart] *(Kendall)*.

As WW II winds to a close, an American sergeant (George Maharis) leads a search for a German scientist whose help will be invaluable in perfecting the atomic bomb. Meanwhile, an SS major (Gerard Herter) searches for the same man, though he intends to execute him. Before the scientist is finally safe and sound, his daughter is brought from the States to help identify him, the Germans and Americans pursuing him clash, and the SS major receives his just reward at the hands of a group of concentration camp escapees.

p, Sam X. Abarbanel; d, Juan Antonio Bardem; w, Sam X. Abarbanel, Juan Antonio Bardem, and Howard Berk, based on the story by Howard Berk; ed, Margarita Ochoa; ph, Romolo Garroni, Eastmancolor; m, Franco Pezzullo.

(PR:A   MPAA:NR)

LAST HUNTER, THE*

(1984, It.) 95m Flora-Gico Cinematografica/World Northal c (AKA: HUNTER OF THE APOCALYPSE, THE)

David Warbeck *(Capt. Harry Morris)*, Tisa Farrow *(Jane Foster)*, Tony King *(Sgt. George Washington)*, Bobby Rhodes *(Carlos)*, Margit Evelyn Newton *(Carol)*.

The alternative title of this Italian-made Vietnam War film, THE HUNTER OF THE APOCALYPSE, betrays its two most obvious influences—APOCALYPSE NOW and THE DEER HUNTER. However, borrowing bits and pieces of the plots, approaches, and titles of great films isn't the way to go about making another great war film, as this inept production demonstrates. The story follows Capt. Harry Morris (David Warbeck) as he and a team that includes a fetching war correspondent (Tisa Farrow, sister of Mia) cross into enemy territory to destroy a radio transmitter that is beaming propagandistic broadcasts. Much to Morris' surprise, he learns that the woman responsible for the broadcasts is none other than his best pal's girl friend.

p, Gianfranco Couyoumdjian; d, Anthony M. Dawson [Antonio Margheriti]; w, Dardano Sacchetti; ed, Alberto Moriani; ph, Riccardo Pallottini, Technicolor; m, Franco Micalizzi.

(PR:O   MPAA:NR)

LAST METRO, THE—

LAST METRO, THE***½
(1980, Fr.) 133m Les Films Du Carrosse-Sedif-T.F.1 Societe Francaise de Production/UA c (LE DERNIER METRO)

Catherine Deneuve *(Marion Steiner)*, Gerard Depardieu *(Bernard Granger)*, Jean Poiret *(Jean-Loup Cottins)*, Heinz Bennent *(Lucas Steiner)*, Andrea Ferreol *(Arlette Guillaume)*, Paulette Dubost *(Germaine Fabre)*, Sabine Haudepin *(Nadine Marsac)*, Jean-Louis Richard *(Daxiat)*.

This precise, oddly restrained picture set during the German Occupation of France takes place almost entirely in a theater building. Marion Steiner (Catherine Deneuve, in an arresting performance) is the wife of top stage director Lucas Steiner (Heinz Bennent), who is forced to go underground in order to avoid Nazi persecution. Instead of fleeing Paris, however, Lucas hides in the cellar of a theater, secretly listening to and watching the rehearsals of his new play, which costars Marion and Bernard Granger (Gerard Depardieu). As time passes, the lives of the theater personnel become more open and difficult, especially in the case of Marion and Bernard, who fight their attraction to each other. Politics and romance are placed on parallel tracks in the figure of Marion, who tries to remain as loyal to her husband as she is to her countrymen. Often scolded for not addressing political issues in his pictures, director Francois Truffaut finally found a suitable vehicle in THE LAST METRO, a film dealing with the Occupation in romantic terms and capturing 1940s Paris as it has been mythicized in the movies of that period. Not surprisingly, Truffaut's image of occupied France is formed more by the films he saw than by history itself. (In French; English subtitles.)

d, Francois Truffaut; w, Francois Truffaut, Suzanne Schiffman, and Jean-Claude Grumberg, based on a story by Francois Truffaut, Suzanne Schiffman; ed, Martine Barraque; ph, Nestor Almendros; m, Georges Delerue.

(PR:C-O   MPAA:R)

LAST OF THE MOHICANS, THE****
(1936) 91m Small/UA bw

Randolph Scott *(Hawkeye)*, Binnie Barnes *(Alice Munro)*, Heather Angel *(Cora Munro)*, Hugh Buckler *(Col. Munro Girls)*, Henry Wilcoxon *(Maj. Duncan Heyward)*, Bruce Cabot *(Magua)*, Robert Barrat *(Chingachgook)*, Philip Reed *(Uncas)*, Willard Robertson *(Capt. Winthrop)*, Frank McGlynn, Sr. *(David Gamut)*, Will Stanton *(Jenkins)*.

Undoubtedly the finest film version of James Fenimore Cooper's classic adventure tale, THE LAST OF THE MOHICANS benefits from superlative performances by Randolph Scott as Hawkeye, Henry Wilcoxon as Maj. Duncan Heyward, and Bruce Cabot as the vicious, lascivious Magua, one of the most hateful roles in film history. During the height of the French and Indian War, Hawkeye escorts Maj. Heyward and Alice (Binnie Barnes) and Cora Munro (Heather Angel), the daughters of the commander of Ft. William Henry, through hostile lines, accompanied by Chingachgook (Robert Barrat) and his son, Uncas (Philip Reed), who are the last survivors of the Mohican tribe, wiped out by the French-allied Hurons. During the course of their dangerous trek to the fort, Alice becomes enamored of Hawkeye, Cora and Uncas fall in love, and Magua makes life miserable for everyone. Before Chingachgook sends Magua to the happy hunting ground, the sadistic Huron brings about the deaths of both Cora and Uncas. What's more, the British are routed at Ft. William Henry and Hawkeye is taken prisoner and tied to a stake by the Hurons before Maj. Heyward comes to his rescue. Packed with excitement and well-staged battle scenes, this superbly crafted adventure film was masterfully directed by George B. Seitz and magnificently lensed in California's high Sierras by Robert Planck. Cooper's famous tale has been brought to the screen a number of times (including two 1911 one-reelers; Maurice Tourneur and Clarence Brown's smashing 1922 feature-length silent with Wallace Beery as Magua; a 10-chapter 1924 serial version called LEATHERSTOCKING; Mascot Films' 1932 12-chapter serial with Harry Carey; and a 1947 Columbia version, THE LAST OF THE REDMEN, starring Jon Hall, Evelyn Ankers, and Buster Crabbe as Uncas), but none of these other versions matches the scope and wonderful performances of this extraordinary film.

p, Edward Small and Harry M. Goetz; d, George B. Seitz; w, Philip Dunne, John Balderston, Paul Perez, and Daniel Moore, based on the novel by James Fenimore Cooper; ed, Jack Dennis; ph, Robert Planck.

(PR:A   MPAA:NR)

LAST REMAKE OF BEAU GESTE, THE*½
(1977) 84m UNIV c

Ann-Margret *(Lady Flavia Geste)*, Marty Feldman *(Digby Geste)*, Michael York *(Beau Geste)*, Peter Ustinov *(Sgt. Markov)*, James Earl Jones *(Sheikh Abdul)*, Trevor Howard *(Sir Hector Geste)*, Henry Gibson *(Gen. Pecheur)*, Terry-Thomas *(Prison Governor)*, Roy Kinnear *(Cpl. Boldini)*, Spike Milligan *(Crumble)*, Avery Schreiber *(Used Camel Salesman)*, Hugh Griffith *(Judge)*, Sinead Cusack *(Isabel Geste)*, Martin Snaric *(Valentino)*, Ed McMahon *(Arab Horseman)*.

Written and directed by funnyman Marty Feldman (best remembered for his appearances in Mel Brooks' spoofs YOUNG FRANKENSTEIN and SILENT MOVIE), THE LAST REMAKE OF BEAU GESTE puts a comic spin on the classic 1939 Foreign Legion adventure. Beau Geste (essayed by Gary Cooper in the original) is now played by Michael York; his brother Digby (originally Robert Preston) is played by Feldman. As in the 1939 version, the plot revolves around Beau's heroics in the desert and the disappearance of a priceless family gem, but into this plot Feldman tosses anything and everything—some of it funny, some not so funny. Perhaps the best aspect of this rather haphazard production is the cast, which includes James Earl Jones, Henry Gibson, Peter Ustinov, Roy Kinnear, Terry-Thomas, Trevor Howard, and Ann-Margret. Definitely more gags than guns.

p, William S. Gilmore; d, Marty Feldman; w, Marty Feldman

and Chris Allen, based on a story by Marty Feldman and Sam Bobrick; ed, Jim Clark and Arthur Schmidt; ph, Gerry Fisher, Panavision, Technicolor; m, John Morris.

(PR:C MPAA:PG)

LATINO**

(1985) 105m Lucasfilm-Latino/Cinecom Int. c

Robert Beltran *(Eddie Guerrero)*, Annette Cardona *(Marlena)*, Tony Plana *(Ruben)*, Julio Medina *(Edgar Salasar)*, Gavin McFadden *(Metcalf)*, Luis Torrentes *(Luis)*.

Academy Award-winning cinematographer Haskell Wexler waited 16 years after his critically acclaimed MEDIUM COOL to return to feature film directing with LATINO, another highly political picture, this time about the US sponsorship of the contra war against the Sandinista government of Nicaragua. Eddie (Robert Beltran) and Ruben (Tony Plana) are Hispanic US Army officers (Vietnam veterans) working with the contras in Honduras. While there, Eddie falls for Marlena (Annette Cardona), a Nicaraguan expatriate who eventually becomes a convert to the Sandinista cause after returning to her homeland. Eddie's relationship with Marlena, and his experiences with both the contras and the Nicaraguans he encounters on across-the-border actions, bring about a gradual moral awakening in him, a repugnance for what his country has called upon him to do, and by the film's end he symbolically renounces his not-so-secret role in the war. The problem here is Wexler's heavy-handed one-sidedness. While his shot composition is filled with the sort of nuances one expects from so accomplished a cinematographer, his characters and the issues he addresses are drawn in black and white: the Sandinistas are gallant innocents, the contras barbarians, Eddie's conversion a little too pat, the film's symbolism a bit obvious. But flawed though it is, LATINO is a noble undertaking by a filmmaker willing to put his heart and his politics before box-office expectations. As the end credits roll, Jackson Browne sings: "Can you hear me? / Wake up / Where's the Voice of America?" With LATINO, Wexler poses the same question; unfortunately, his plea has been more than a little muffled by his own heavy hand.

p, Benjamin Berg; d, Haskell Wexler; w, Haskell Wexler; ed, Robert Dalva; ph, Tom Sigel; m, Diane Louie.

(PR:C-O MPAA:NR)

LAWRENCE OF ARABIA*****

(1962, Brit.) 216m Horizon/COL c

Peter O'Toole *(T.E. Lawrence)*, Alec Guinness *(Prince Feisal)*, Anthony Quinn *(Auda Abu Tayi)*, Jack Hawkins *(Gen. Allenby)*, Jose Ferrer *(Turkish Bey)*, Anthony Quayle *(Col. Harry Brighton)*, Claude Rains *(Mr. Dryden)*, Arthur Kennedy *(Jackson Bentley)*, Donald Wolfit *(Gen. Murray)*, Omar Sharif *(Sherif Ali Ibn El Kharish)*.

One of the cinema's most awe-inspiring accomplishments, David Lean's splendid adventure biography of the enigmatic T.E. Lawrence paints its complex portrait of the desert-loving Englishman who united Arab tribes in battle against the Ottoman Turks in WW I on a sun-drenched 70mm canvas that often seems as large as the Arabian peninsula itself. At the center of Lean's stunning visuals is Peter O'Toole's eccentric but magnificent portrayal of the erudite, Oxford-educated lieutenant, who wangles an assignment as an observer with Prince Feisal (Alec Guinness), the leader of the Arab revolt against the Turks. Feisal is resigned to allowing his tribal army to become just another branch of the British forces, but the messianic Lawrence, determined to prevent the Arabs from falling under British colonial domination, undertakes a military miracle. He, Sherif Ali (Omar Sharif)—whom Lean introduces as a tiny dot on the desert horizon that steadily enlarges, in one of the film's most striking scenes—and 50 men traverse the "uncrossable" Nefud Desert; join forces with their traditional tribal enemies, led by Auda Abu Tayi (Anthony Quinn); and rout the Turks at the strategic port city of Aqaba. Given the go-ahead by Gen. Allenby (Jack Hawkins), worshiped by the Arabs he has brought together, and cloaked in their flowing white robes, "El Aurens" leads the Arabs in a brutal guerrilla war that is as much about establishing Arab sovereignty as it is about defeating the Turks, his thrilling exploits glorified by the Lowell Thomas-like American journalist Jackson Bentley (Arthur Kennedy). In time, however, Lawrence's legions dwindle, he begins to revel sadistically in violence, his grand attempt at overseeing the formation of a united Arab Council in Damascus collapses, and he returns to Britain exhausted. Although the grandeur of Lean's sumptuous imagery is horribly compromised on TV—only a portion of the original frame survives the transfer to the small screen—LAWRENCE OF ARABIA remains a wholly involving film in this format, primarily because of O'Toole's tour-de-force performance and the excellent support he receives from Sharif, Quinn, Hawkins, Anthony Quayle, and Claude Rains. The plot is fairly straightforward, but the film's delineation of character and culture make it a gem even without its breathtaking visuals. Obviously, however, Lean's film is best appreciated on the big screen, and in 1989 a carefully restored version of LAWRENCE was released that reinstated 20 minutes cut for the original roadshow release and another 15 minutes trimmed when it was rereleased in 1970. Moreover, Lean and his original editor, Anne V. Coates, were finally given the chance to do a "fine cut" on the film, now 216 memorable minutes long. Fortunately, the videocassette rerelease has been letterboxed, offering LAWRENCE in *all* its glory, though the incredible detail and resolution of the film's shot-on-70mm visuals (most 70mm films today are shot on 35mm and enlarged) cry out for the big screen.

p, Sam Spiegel and David Lean; d, David Lean; w, Robert Bolt and Michael Wilson, based on *The Seven Pillars of Wisdom* by T.E. Lawrence; ed, Anne V. Coates; ph, F.A. Young, Super Panavision 70, Technicolor; m, Maurice Jarre.

(PR:C MPAA:NR)

LES CARABINIERS—

LES CARABINIERS***½
(1963, Fr./It.) 80m Rome-Paris-Laetitia/New Yorker bw (GB: SOLDIERS, THE)

Marino Mase *(Ulysses)*, Albert Juross *(Michel Ange)*, Genevieve Galea *(Venus)*, Catherine Ribero *(Cleopatre)*, Gerard Poirot *(1st Carabinier)*, Jean Brassat *(2nd Carabinier)*, Alvaro Gheri *(3rd Carabinier)*, Barbet Schroeder *(Car Salesman)*, Odile Geoffroy *(Young Communist Girl)*, Catherine Durante *(Heroine of the Film-Within-the-Film)*, Jean Gruault *("Bebe's" Father)*.

Jean-Luc Godard's fifth film is an ultraimpersonal exercise on the subject of war. A pair of soldiers (Albert Juross and Marino Mase) are called up to fight for the King. Promised great riches in return for their soldiering, they leave their wives and set off, sending their spouses letters detailing their activities—saluting the Statue of Liberty, endlessly executing a woman, buying a Masarati, going to the cinema. Back home, they display their great conquests: a massive collection of postcards of various sites, including the Grand Canyon, the Eiffel Tower, the Empire State Building, and the Egyptian pyramids. But the men wind up on the wrong end of the war, go in search of the King to collect their booty, and are gunned down. LES CARABINIERS was a tremendous box-office and critical bomb, and for the first hour it *is* a difficult viewing experience, with Godard going to great lengths to develop unsympathetic characters and distance the audience from the onscreen proceedings. He purposely shot the film on a grainy film stock, then made it even grainier in the processing, yielding an old-newsreel effect and even incorporating actual stock footage into the final film. After the first hour, however, comes a remarkable Eisensteinian montage, consisting of 12 minutes of "conquests"—the postcard sequence. In LES CARABINIERS, Godard succeeded in portraying war as an ugly and ignoble atrocity, in a manner entirely different from what he has called "the beautiful Zanuck-ian style." If LES CARABINIERS cannot be called a compelling dramatic work, the film represents a liberating step beyond cinematic convention. (In French; English subtitles.)

p, Georges de Beauregard and Carlo Ponti; d, Jean-Luc Godard; w, Jean-Luc Godard, Jean Gruault, and Roberto Rossellini, based on the play "I Carabinieri" by Benjamino Joppolo; ed, Agnes Guillemot and Lila Lakshmanan; ph, Raoul Coutard; m, Philippe Arthuys.

(PR:O MPAA:NR)

LIFE AND DEATH OF COLONEL BLIMP, THE****
(1945, Brit.) 163m The Archers/GFD c (AKA: COLONEL BLIMP)

Roger Livesey *(Clive Candy)*, Deborah Kerr *(Edith Hunter/Barbara Wynne/Johnny Cannon)*, Anton Walbrook *(Theo Kretschmar-Schuldorff)*, Roland Culver *(Col. Betteridge)*, James McKechnie *(Spud Wilson)*, Albert Lieven *(Von Ritter)*, Arthur Wontner *(Embassy Counsellor)*, David Hutcheson *(Hoppy)*, Ursula Jeans *(Frau von Kalteneck)*, John Laurie *(Murdoch)*, Harry Welchman *(Maj. Davis)*, Reginald Tate *(Van Zijl)*, A.E. Matthews *(President of Tribunal)*.

One of Michael Powell and Emeric Pressburger's most highly praised films, THE LIFE AND DEATH OF COLONEL BLIMP tells the story of Clive Candy (Roger Livesey), a stuffy British soldier whose life is shown in episodes, ranging from 1902, when he had a dashing career as a young officer in the Boer War, to 1943, when he creaks crankily about in the London blitz, looking for his lost youth and loves. Deborah Kerr plays three different roles from separate eras; Anton Walbrook is Theo Kretschmar-Schuldorff, the charming Prussian officer whom Clive fights in a duel and who far exceeds the Briton in sensitivity and understanding. As a young man, Clive loses his girl, Edith (Kerr), to Theo during the Boer War, only to marry a nurse who resembles his lost love (again Kerr) later. Many years afterwards, during WW II, Clive relives his younger days when his pretty young driver, Johnny (Kerr's third role), stirs old memories. By this point, Clive is an out-of-touch brigadier on the brink of retirement, representing everything archaic in the waning British Empire. The title comes from the satiric character created by cartoonist David Low in the *London Evening Standard*, by which members of Britain's pompous and stiff military upper-crust came to be known as "Colonel Blimps." This was the third Powell-Pressburger collaboration (after THE 49TH PARALLEL and ONE OF OUR AIRCRAFT IS MISSING) and the first produced under the banner of The Archers. Prime Minister Winston Churchill illegally prohibited the film's exportation for two years, citing its portrayal of a Colonel Blimp as "detrimental to the morale of the Army." Refusing to heed to the advice of the Ministry of Information (which felt his position would do more harm than good), Churchill lifted the ban only after the film became such a smash commercial hit in England that its export could no longer be thwarted. Initially released in America in a butchered 93-minute version, the film was restored to its full length in 1986 by Britain's National Film Archive.

p, Michael Powell and Emeric Pressburger; d, Michael Powell; w, Michael Powell and Emeric Pressburger; ed, John Seabourne; ph, Jack Cardiff and Georges Perinal, Technicolor; m, Allan Gray.

(PR:A MPAA:NR)

LIFEBOAT*****
(1944) 96m FOX bw

Tallulah Bankhead *(Connie Porter)*, William Bendix *(Gus)*, Walter Slezak *(The German)*, Mary Anderson *(Alice)*, John Hodiak *(Kovak)*, Henry Hull *(Rittenhouse)*, Heather Angel *(Mrs. Higgins)*, Hume Cronyn *(Stanley Garrett)*, Canada Lee *(Joe)*, William Yetter, Jr. *(German Sailor)*, Alfred Hitchcock *(Man in "Before and After" Ad)*.

Alfred Hitchcock's taut wartime thriller concerns a handful of survivors who climb into a lifeboat after their ship is torpedoed by a German U-boat. The captain (Walter Slezak) of the U-boat, which has also sunk, swims to the already crowded boat and is taken aboard by the kind-hearted survivors. Since he is the only man capable of handling the craft in rough weather and navigating it to a safe harbor, he is elected helmsman. The survivors are an odd lot—fashion writer Connie Porter (Tallulah Bankhead), industrial tycoon Rittenhouse (Henry Hull), socially conscious seaman Kovak (John Hodiak), wounded stoker Gus (William Bendix), meek radio operator Stanley Garrett (Hume Cronyn), bewildered nurse Alice (Mary Anderson), a mother in shock (Heather Angel) who cradles her recently dead child, and black steward Joe (Canada Lee). Slowly, and with insidious cleverness, the German steers a course not for land, but to a secret rendezvous with a German mother ship. The entire cast is superb, but the standouts are Bankhead, as the spoiled, wealthy dilettante writer whose expensive furs and jewelry are worth more to her than the lives of her fellow survivors, and Bendix, as the compassionate but not-too-bright stoker whose gangrenous leg poses a threat to his dreams of returning home to dance with his sweetheart. John Steinbeck, on whose original story the film was based, was first assigned to pen the script, but reportedly felt too restricted by the film's single set (the lifeboat). Jo Swerling eventually wrote the script, but, as was customary with Hitchcock, the talented Ben Hecht was brought in at the last moment to tighten up scenes and sharpen dialog.

p, Kenneth Macgowan; d, Alfred Hitchcock; w, Jo Swerling, based on the story by John Steinbeck; ed, Dorothy Spencer; ph, Glen MacWilliams; m, Hugo Friedhofer.

(PR:A   MPAA:NR)

LION OF THE DESERT***

(1981, Libya/Brit.) 162m Falcon International/United Film Distribution c (AKA: OMAR MUKHTAR)

Anthony Quinn *(Omar Mukhtar)*, Oliver Reed *(Gen. Rodolfo Graziani)*, Rod Steiger *(Benito Mussolini)*, John Gielgud *(Sharif El Gariani)*, Irene Papas *(Mabrouka)*, Raf Vallone *(Diodiece)*, Gastone Moschin *(Maj. Tomelli)*, Stefano Patrizi *(Lt. Sandrini)*, Sky Dumont *(Prince Amadeo)*, Robert Brown *(Al-Fadeel)*.

With a running time of over two and one-half hours, featuring a heroic Libyan fighting Italian fascism, and sporting the financial backing of Muammar Qaddafi, it's not surprising that LION OF THE DESERT failed miserably at the box office. What is surprising is that LION OF THE DESERT is a quality historical epic a la LAWRENCE OF ARABIA. Starring Anthony Quinn (who costarred in the David Lean film), featuring a score by LAWRENCE composer Maurice Jarre, and filling the screen with just as much sand, LION OF THE DESERT tells the story of Omar Mukhtar (Quinn), a famed Arab hero who fought off the Italian advance of 1929-31. Leading the Italian troops is Gen. Rodolfo Graziani (Oliver Reed), who is attempting to invade Libya under the orders of Mussolini (Rod Steiger). While technically superior to most contemporary epics, LION OF THE DESERT unfortunately fails to provide the character complexity and directorial flair that made Lean's picture such a success. Directed in 1979 by Moustapha Akkad (who previously made MOHAMMAD: MESSENGER OF GOD, also with Quinn), the film was funded with a healthy chunk of Libyan leader Col. Qaddafi's money—a reported $35 million.

p, Moustapha Akkad; d, Moustapha Akkad; w, Hal Craig; ed, John Shirley; ph, Jack Hildyard, Panavision, Eastmancolor; m, Maurice Jarre.

(PR:O   MPAA:PG)

LITTLE BIG MAN***

(1970) 147m NG c

Dustin Hoffman *(Jack Crabb)*, Faye Dunaway *(Mrs. Pendrake)*, Martin Balsam *(Allardyce T. Merriweather)*, Richard Mulligan *(Gen. George A. Custer)*, Chief Dan George *(Old Lodge Skins)*, Jeff Corey *(Wild Bill Hickok)*, Aimee Eccles *(Sunshine)*, Kelly Jean Peters *(Olga)*, Carole Androsky *(Caroline)*, Robert Little Star *(Little Horse)*, Cal Bellini *(Younger Bear)*, Ruben Moreno *(Shadow that Comes at Night)*, Steve Shemayne *(Burns Red in the Sun)*, William Hickey *(Historian)*.

This strange tale of the Old West is recounted in flashback by 121-year-old Jack Crabb (Dustin Hoffman), who claims to be the only survivor of the massacre at the Little Big Horn. As a boy, Jack is taken in by Cheyenne Indians and raised by Old Lodge Skins (Chief Dan George), but later he protests that he is white when his tribe is attacked by the cavalry, beginning a pattern of cultural fence-hopping that dominates the rest of his life. Over the next century or so, Jack earns the name Little Big Man for his bravery in battle; is taken in by a preacher and his randy wife (Faye Dunaway); becomes both an assistant to a cure-all-peddling drummer (Martin Balsam) and a less-than-successful gunfighter; nearly dies when Custer (Richard Mulligan) and his troops attack his tribe at the Washita River; turns to alcohol; and guides the Seventh Cavalry into the Little Big Horn massacre. Based on a Thomas Berger novel, Arthur Penn's film wasn't the first movie to revise the cinematic history of the Old West with a sympathetic slant toward the native American point of view, but, given its oddly whimsical tone, it is one of the most unconventional westerns ever made. Unlike HOW THE WEST WAS WON, in which the characters' lives and the history of the West unfold with the certainty of Manifest Destiny, Jack's story is a series of seemingly random occurrences in which history acts *upon* him, almost always with tragic or tragicomic results. Aided by a strong supporting cast, Hoffman gives a fine performance as the bewildered man-in-the-middle in this odd but engaging film.

p, Stuart Millar; d, Arthur Penn; w, Calder Willingham, based on the novel by Thomas Berger; ed, Dede Allen; ph, Harry Stradling, Jr., Panavision, Technicolor; m, John Hammond.

(PR:C-O   MPAA:GP)

LITTLE DRUMMER GIRL, THE*½

(1984) 130m Pan Arts/WB c

Diane Keaton *(Charlie)*, Yorgo Voyagis *(Joseph)*, Klaus Kinski *(Kurtz)*, Sami Frey *(Khalil)*, David Suchet *(Mester-*

LIVES OF A BENGAL LANCER—

bein), Eli Danker (Litvak), Ben Levine (Dimitri), Jonathan Sagalle (Teddy), Shlomit Hagoel (Rose), Juliano Mer (Julio), Danni Roth (Oded), Anna Massey (Chairlady).

Based on a novel by John Le Carre, THE LITTLE DRUMMER GIRL depicts the radical political transformation of Charlie (Diane Keaton), a London-based American actress whose pro-Palestinian sympathies are world famous (shades of Vanessa Redgrave). Traveling to Greece to shoot a commercial, she falls for Joseph (Yorgo Voyagis), believing him to be a Palestinian terrorist. Actually he is an Israeli agent, and the commercial is a setup to get her into the hands of Israeli intelligence. Kurtz (Klaus Kinski), another Israeli agent, "persuades" Charlie not only to switch to the Israeli side in the struggle but to infiltrate the Palestinian terrorist organization. The locales change quickly, jumping from place to place as Kurtz and his minions search out terrorists and the repeatedly tested Charlie is put through the psychological wringer. The miscast Keaton delivers a flat performance, but Klaus Kinski is outstanding as the heavy-hitting Israeli agent. Crammed into 130 minutes of screen-time, Le Carre's story loses much in motivation, and though plenty of action and suspense remain, it often seems that things are happening in the wrong places to the wrong people. Moreover, while THE LITTLE DRUMMER GIRL purports to take no sides in the continuing struggle between its PLO types and the Israelis, the massacre scenes are deliberately staged in such a manner as to cause an audience to stand up and cheer when the Arabs are knocked off.

p, Robert L. Crawford; d, George Roy Hill; w, Loring Mandel, based on the novel by John Le Carre; ed, William Reynolds; ph, Wolfgang Treu, Technicolor; m, Dave Grusin.

(PR:C-O MPAA:R)

LIVES OF A BENGAL LANCER****

(1935) 109m PAR bw

Gary Cooper (Lt. Alan McGregor), Franchot Tone (Lt. John Forsythe), Richard Cromwell (Lt. Donald Stone), Sir Guy Standing (Col. Stone), C. Aubrey Smith (Maj. Hamilton), Monte Blue (Hamzulia Khan), Kathleen Burke (Tania Volkanskaya), Colin Tapley (Lt. Barrett), Douglas Dumbrille (Mohammed Khan), Akim Tamiroff (Emir), Jameson Thomas (Hendrickson), Noble Johnson (Ram Singh), Lumsden Hare (Maj. Gen. Woodley), J. Carrol Naish (Grand Vizier).

Set in northwest India, this rousing adventure film was hailed by some, at the time of its release, as the greatest war movie ever made. Under Henry Hathaway's adroit direction, Gary Cooper stars as 41st Bengal Lancers member Lt. McGregor, a seasoned frontier fighter who doesn't hesitate to speak his mind or violate orders—a man first and a soldier second. His commanding officer, Col. Stone (Sir Guy Standing), is his very opposite, a total military man who will soon be retiring. In order to keep alive the name of Stone in the regiment, a fellow officer, Maj. Hamilton (C. Aubrey Smith), has Stone's son (Richard Cromwell) transferred into the unit, along with another new officer, Lt. Forsythe (Franchot Tone). The two new arrivals get a quick initiation, as Col. Stone and British intelligence try to prevent a planned Indian uprising by blocking a local chieftain's attempt to steal two million rounds of ammunition from the friendly Emir of Gopal (Akim Tamiroff). The script is filled with plenty of humor and builds two strong, honest friendships—McGregor and Forsythe have a great buddy rapport, while the cold and stubborn Col. Stone opens up to his cub soldier son. The Indian atmosphere is lovingly captured by Hathaway's direction (his love of the exotic, heavily molded by his association with Josef von Sternberg, is clearly in the fore) and by Charles Lang and Ernest B. Schoedsack's photography (incorporating some stock footage previously shot by Schoedsack). While the glorification of British imperialism hangs over the picture, the portrayal of the Indians is fortunately less offensive than in other Hollywood films, such as 1939's GUNGA DIN.

p, Louis D. Lighton; d, Henry Hathaway; w, Waldemar Young, John Balderston, Achmed Abdullah, Grover Jones, and William Slavens McNutt, based on the novel by Maj. Francis Yeats-Brown; ed, Ellsworth Hoagland; ph, Charles Lang and Ernest Schoedsack; m, Milan Roder.

(PR:A MPAA:NR)

LONGEST DAY, THE****

(1962) 180m FOX bw

John Wayne (Col. Benjamin Vandervoort), Robert Mitchum (Brig. Gen. Norman Cota), Henry Fonda (Brig. Gen. Theodore Roosevelt, Jr.), Robert Ryan (Brig. Gen. James Gavin), Rod Steiger (Destroyer Commander), Robert Wagner Fabian, Paul Anka, Tommy Sands (US Rangers), Richard Beymer (Schultz), Mel Ferrer (Maj. Gen. Robert Haines), Jeffrey Hunter (Sgt. Fuller), Sal Mineo (Pvt. Martini), Roddy McDowall (Pvt. Morris), Stuart Whitman (Lt. Sheen), Eddie Albert (Col. Newton), Edmond O'Brien (Gen. Raymond O. Barton), Red Buttons (Pvt. Steele), Tom Tryon (Lt. Wilson), Peter Lawford (Lord Lovat), Richard Burton (RAF Pilot), Curt Jurgens (Maj. Gen. Gunther Blumentritt).

One of the most ambitious war films ever undertaken, this star-studded depiction of the D-Day invasion was long the pet project of Fox Studios boss Darryl Zanuck, who spared no expense in bringing THE LONGEST DAY breathtaking scope and authenticity, going so far as to insist that the shooting be done only in weather conditions that matched those of the actual event. Based on Cornelius Ryan's compilation of interviews with D-Day survivors, the film is presented in three segments, the first detailing the Allied preparation for the invasion and the wait for the weather to break; the second re-creating the movement of the massive armada across the English Channel and the preliminary, behind-the-lines sallies of paratroops and glider-transported commandos; and the last depicting the assaults on the Normandy beaches. Intercut with the portrayal of the Allied side of the momentous invasion is the German (subtitled) response, including the report to headquarters of the first German officer to spot the armada: "Those thousands of ships you say the Allies don't have—

well, they have them!" The work of three credited directors (reportedly, Zanuck helmed all the American and British interiors himself) and no less than eight cameramen, THE LONGEST DAY is visually stunning—its extraordinary camera movement and Cinemascope photography brilliantly augmenting the meticulously reenacted battle scenes. The only thing bigger than the film's scope are its stars, including John Wayne (who received $250,000 for four days' work) as Lt. Col. Benjamin Vandervoort of the 82nd Paratroop Division; Henry Fonda as Brig. Gen. Theodore Roosevelt, Jr.; Robert Mitchum as Brig. Gen. Norman Cota, who finally moves his hard-pressed men off bloody Omaha Beach, where they are being slaughtered by German crossfire; Red Buttons as a paratrooper; Rod Steiger as the captain of one of the armada ships; Peter Lawford as the flamboyant commando leader Lord Lovat (who was present at the shoot); Richard Burton as a wounded pilot; and Curt Jurgens as German general Blumentritt. Made for $10 million, this magnificent film was the most expensive black-and-white production to its date.

p, Darryl F. Zanuck; d, Andrew Marton, Ken Annakin, and Bernhard Wicki; w, Cornelius Ryan, Romain Gary, James Jones, David Pursall, and Jack Seddon, based on the book by Cornelius Ryan; ed, Samuel E. Beetley; ph, Jean Bourgoin, Henri Persin, Walter Wottitz, and Guy Tabary; m, Maurice Jarre.

(PR:C MPAA:G)

LORDS OF DISCIPLINE, THE***

(1983) 102m PAR c

David Keith *(Will)*, Robert Prosky *(Bear)*, G.D. Spradlin *(Gen. Durrell)*, Barbara Babcock *(Abigail)*, Michael Biehn *(Alexander)*, Rick Rossovich *(Pig)*, John Lavachielli *(Mark)*, Mitchell Lichtenstein *(Trado)*, Mark Breland *(Pearce)*, Malcolm Danare *(Poteete)*, Judge Reinhold *(Macabbee)*, Greg Webb *(Braselton)*, Bill Paxton *(Gilbreath)*.

Based on a Pat Conroy novel (see THE GREAT SANTINI), this underrated film stars David Keith as a cadet at the fictional Carolina Military Institute in 1964. CMI has just admitted its first black, and Will (Keith), a senior who believes deeply in the code of honor symbolized by the Institute's graduation ring, is asked by Bear (Robert Prosky), one of the school's ranking instructors, to look after the black cadet, Pearce (Mark Breland). Racism is rampant at CMI, and though neither Will nor Bear are civil rights activists, both believe Pearce deserves the same chance to prove himself as his classmates. When the sanctioned hazing of underclassmen begins, it becomes clear that Pearce is the target of special harassment by "the Ten," a secret organization of cadets determined to guarantee the purity of the Institute. After another "undesirable" student dies and Pearce is nearly castrated, Will, the reluctant champion of justice, unravels a conspiracy of hate that originates in CMI's loftiest towers of power. Thomas Pope and Lloyd Fonvielle's meticulously crafted screenplay is deftly directed by Franc Roddam (QUADROPHENIA), who effectively balances moments of reflection with action-filled tension, building his film to an arresting climax.

Keith—who had already made his mark as a warrior in training in AN OFFICER AND A GENTLEMAN—gives a fine performance as the courageous and conscientious Will, Prosky is excellent as the honorable old instructor, and G.D. Spradlin turns in his usual fine work as the heavy. Equally convincing in his film debut is Breland—later the WBA welterweight champion, but at the time the film was made an amateur of some renown whose newspaper photo was spotted by an impressed casting director.

p, Herb Jaffe and Gabriel Katzka; d, Franc Roddam; w, Thomas Pope and Lloyd Fonvielle, based on the novel by Pat Conroy; ed, Michael Ellis; ph, Brian Tufano, Eastmancolor; m, Howard Blake.

(PR:O MPAA:R)

LOST COMMAND, THE**½

(1966) 129m Red Lion/COL c

Anthony Quinn *(Lt. Col. Pierre Raspeguy)*, Alain Delon *(Capt. Philippe Esclavier)*, George Segal *(Lt. Ben Mahidi)*, Michele Morgan *(Countess de Clairefons)*, Maurice Ronet *(Capt. Boisfeuras)*, Claudia Cardinale *(Aicha)*, Gregoire Aslan *(Ben Saad)*, Jean Servais *(Gen. Melies)*, Maurice Sarfati *(Merle)*, Jean-Claude Bercq *(Orsini)*.

Set against the backdrop of the French-Algerian war of the late 1950s and early 1960s, this action film takes a considerably more commercial and entertaining look at the events covered (far more authentically) in the previous year's BATTLE OF ALGIERS. After France's defeat at Dienbienphu in Indochina in 1954, a unit of paratroopers led by Lt. Col. Pierre Raspeguy (Anthony Quinn) is sent to North Africa to quiet the Algerian freedom fighters. One of the unit's officers, Lt. Ben Mahidi (George Segal), joins forces with the rebels. Raspeguy, meanwhile, takes up with Countess de Clairefons (Michele Morgan), a wealthy beauty widowed when her husband, a general, was killed in Asia. Raspeguy is well below her socially, but her attraction to him is such that she gets him posted to Algeria, where she hopes he can quickly rise from lieutenant colonel to general. If he comes back a general, she will marry him. Raspeguy takes over a ragged unit and persuades his two wartime comrades, Capt. Philippe Esclavier (Alain Delon) and Capt. Boisfeuras (Maurice Ronet), to help get the ragtags into shape. The unit's plans misfire, however, when Esclavier become involved with Aicha (Claudia Cardinale). Unknown to Esclavier, Aicha is Lt. Mahidi's sister, and she is reporting Raspeguy's every move back to her brother. Quinn turns in a dynamic performance in his unsympathetic role, that of a quasi-mercenary who is fighting for personal glory *and* the hand of the woman he loves. Credit must go to director Mark Robson, who manages to balance the intimacy of romance with the violence of war.

p, Mark Robson; d, Mark Robson; w, Nelson Gidding, based on the novel *The Centurions* by Jean Larteguy; ed, Dorothy Spencer; ph, Robert Surtees, Panavision, Pathe Color; m, Franz Waxman.

(PR:A-C MPAA:NR)

LOST PATROL, THE***½

(1934) 74m RKO bw

Victor McLaglen (The Sergeant), Boris Karloff (Sanders), Wallace Ford (Morelli), Reginald Denny (George Brown), J.M. Kerrigan (Quincannon), Billy Bevan (Herbert Hale), Alan Hale (Cook), Brandon Hurst (Bell), Douglas Walton (Pearson), Sammy Stein (Abelson), Neville Clark (Lt. Hawkins), Paul Hanson (Jock Mackay).

A strange and fascinating film, John Ford's THE LOST PATROL gives a sense of impending doom from frame to frame, but is nevertheless an absorbing adventure drama. The story concerns a British cavalry patrol in the Mesopotamian desert during WW I. A single shot rings out and their leader, an officer, falls dead from his horse, his face buried in the sand. With him goes the knowledge of their mission's purpose and even the direction in which the patrol is traveling. The unnamed sergeant (Victor McLaglen) who takes over finds nothing in the officer's map case to indicate where they are, and tells his men that the officer kept everything in his head. He leads the group to an oasis, but the men find themselves under occasional sniper fire from the Arabs who have surrounded them and lie in wait, out of sight in the stretching dunes. The soldiers—except for the sergeant—never see the Arabs, and this insidious enemy takes on an almost mythic character as, one by one, the British are picked off until only the sergeant, Morelli (Wallace Ford), and Sanders (Boris Karloff) are left, desperately trying to stay alive. Shot on location in the desert around Yuma, Arizona, THE LOST PATROL is a much superior remake of a like-titled 1929 British silent film that featured Agnew McMaster in Karloff's role and Cyril McLaglen, Victor's brother, as the sergeant.

p, Cliff Reid; d, John Ford; w, Dudley Nichols and Garrett Fort, based on the novel *Patrol* by Philip MacDonald; ed, Paul Weatherwax; ph, Harold Wenstrom; m, Max Steiner.

(PR:C MPAA:NR)

LOVE AND ANARCHY***

(1973, It.) 108m Peppercorn-Wormser c (FILM D'AMORE E D'ANARCHIA)

Giancarlo Giannini (Tunin), Mariangela Melato (Salome), Lina Polito (Tripolina), Eros Pagni (Spatoletti), Pina Cei (Madame Aida), Elena Fiore (Donna Carmela).

Lina Wertmuller's film treats the two subjects most dear to her—the relationships between the male and female of the species, and the power struggle between opposing political factions. LOVE AND ANARCHY opens with a wonderful visual prolog, a montage sequence of photographs of Mussolini that sets the film's historic mood. The scene then shifts to the Italian countryside, where Tunin (Giancarlo Giannini), a humble, unattractive farmer, meets an aging anarchist on his way to Rome to assassinate Mussolini. Soon afterwards the anarchist is captured and killed, but not before the seed of revolutionary change has been planted in Tunin's otherwise thick skull. Tunin arrives at a Roman brothel to meet Salome (Mariangela Melato), a vulgar but likable whore who has managed to extract information on Mussolini's itinerary from some of her more talkative Fascist clients. Together, she and Tunin plot their upcoming assassination attempt, but in the meantime Tunin falls in love with Tripolina (Lina Polito), a working-class prostitute who also lives in the brothel. Much of LOVE AND ANARCHY's success stems from Wertmuller's unlikely hero, Tunin. A shy, diminutive, unhealthy-looking commoner, he seems a most unlikely candidate to assassinate an immensely powerful world leader, and since we know that Mussolini was not assassinated, we know that Tunin will fail. Wertmuller shows the elements that force him to become an anarchist—not the usual political convictions, but a naive romanticism that cannot help but falter when confronted by reality. Though LOVE AND ANARCHY is an insightful and complex look at the manner in which political situations affect the romantic, the film is too filled with Wertmuller's Felliniesque excesses (her grotesque vision of brothel life fast becomes annoying) to be totally effective. (In Italian; English subtitles.)

p, Herbert R. Steinmann and Billy Baxter; d, Lina Wertmuller; w, Lina Wertmuller; ed, Franco Fraticelli; ph, Giuseppe Rotunno, Technicolor; m, Nino Rota.

(PR:O MPAA:R)

LOVE AND DEATH***½

(1975) 85m UA c

Woody Allen (Boris Dimitrovich Grushenko), Diane Keaton (Sonja), Georges Adet (Old Nehamkin), Frank Adu (Drill Sergeant), Edmond Ardisson (Priest), Feodor Atkine (Mikhail), Albert Augier (Waiter), Yves Barsacq (Rimsky), Lloyd Battista (Don Francisco), Jack Berard (Gen. Lecoq), Eva Bertrand (Woman in Hygiene Class), George Birt (Doctor), Yves Brainville (Andre), Henry Czamiak (Ivan Grusenko), Despo Diamantidou (Mother), Luce Fabiole (Grandmother), Florian (Uncle Nikolai), Alfred Lutter III (Young Boris).

Woody Allen takes on Russia and just about all its great writers—not to mention Eisenstein, Kierkegaard, and Bob Hope—in this comedy set roughly at the same time as Tolstoy's similarly named *War and Peace*. The plot defies description, but involves the aristocratic yet typically nebbish-ish Boris (Allen), who is impressed into the Russian army during the Napoleonic Wars. Boris and his distant (both emotionally and genetically) cousin Sonja (Diane Keaton) eventually set out (a la Tolstoy's Pierre) to assassinate Napoleon; along the way, the not-so-perfect couple have hilarious philosophical dialogs and numerous comedic adventures in their DR. ZHIVAGO-like hegira across the frozen wastes. The laughs come fast and furious in this film shot in Hungary and France, so if you miss or don't appreciate one joke or allusion, you're likely to pick up on the next. Hailed as one of Allen's best at the time of its release, LOVE AND DEATH's scattershot mix of silly gags and highbrow satire seems much weaker in retrospect—Allen's next film was his breakthrough work, ANNIE HALL.

p, Charles H. Joffe; d, Woody Allen; w, Woody Allen; ed,

Ron Kalish and Ralph Rosenblum; ph, Ghislain Cloquet, Deluxe Color; m, Sergei Prokofiev.

(PR:A-C MPAA:PG)

LOVE IN GERMANY, A**½

(1984, Fr./Ger.) 110m CCC Filmkunst-GAU-TF 1 F.P. Stand Art/Triumph c (UN AMOUR EN ALLEMAGNE; EINE LIEBE IN DEUTSCHLAND)

Hanna Schygulla *(Paulina Kropp)*, Marie-Christine Barrault *(Maria Wyler)*, Armin Mueller-Stahl *(Mayer)*, Elisabeth Trissenaar *(Elsbeth Schnittgens)*, Daniel Olbrychski *(Wiktorczyk)*, Piotr Lysak *(Stanislaw Zasada)*, Gerard Desarthe *(Karl Wyler)*, Bernhard Wicki *(Dr. Borg)*, Ralf Wolter *(Schultze)*, Otto Sander *(Narrator)*.

Hanna Schygulla stars as Paulina Kropp, a German shopkeeper in the village of Brombach during WW II. Her husband away at war, she falls in love with Stanislaw (Piotr Lysak), a Polish laborer—thereby disregarding the official ban on relationships between Germans and prisoners of war. The lovers go to great lengths to keep their romance secret, but are discovered by a snoopy neighbor, Maria Wyler (Marie-Christine Barrault), who wants to take over Paulina's shop. To escape the gossipmongers and the threat of discovery by the Nazis, Paulina tries to visit her husband in Bavaria; however, after intercepting one of Paulina's letters to Stanislaw, the Nazis finally learn of the affair and apprehend the Pole. Officials in Brombach attempt to Aryanize Stanislaw, out of respect for Paulina and in order to save her from a charge of criminal misconduct. Intercut with the wartime story is that of a modern-day search by a mysterious stranger who, with his 16-year-old son in tow, tries to discover what really happened between Paulina and Stanislaw. Based on a nonfiction best-seller that documented the actual case on which the film is based (including the Germans' embarrassing failure to Aryanize the Pole and their botched attempt to execute him in a quarry), A LOVE IN GERMANY seems less concerned with the love of the title than with the political climate and its anti-Nazi message. Andrzej Wajda, who has turned out some of cinema's most provocative political statements, does so again here. The politics, tend to obscure the love story, but this is undoubtedly what Wajda intended. (In German and Polish; English subtitles.)

p, Arthur Brauner; d, Andrzej Wajda; w, Andrzej Wajda, Boleslaw Michalek, and Agnieszka Holland, based on the book by Rolf Hochhuth; ed, Halina Prugar-Ketling; ph, Igor Luther; m, Michel Legrand.

(PR:O MPAA:R)

M

MAC ARTHUR***½

(1977) 128m UNIV c

Gregory Peck *(Gen. Douglas MacArthur)*, Ed Flanders *(President Truman)*, Dan O'Herlihy *(President Roosevelt)*, Ivan Bonar *(Gen. Sutherland)*, Ward Costello *(Gen. George Marshall)*, Nicolas Coster *(Col. Huff)*, Marj Dusay *(Mrs. MacArthur)*, Art Fleming *(The Secretary)*, Russell D. Johnson *(Adm. King)*, Sandy Kenyon *(Gen. Wainwright)*, Robert Mandan *(Rep. Martin)*, Addison Powell *(Adm. Chester Nimitz)*, G.D. Spradlin *(Gen. Eichelberger)*, Kenneth Tobey *(Adm. "Bull" Halsey)*.

General of the Army Douglas MacArthur was not a modest man, but he was charismatic, dashing, eloquent, and arguably the most brilliant military strategist of WW II. Gregory Peck captures all those qualities in his magnificent portrayal of the man who symbolized the spirited refusal to accept defeat in the Pacific. Using MacArthur's speech to an assembly of West Point cadets as a framing device, the film traces his illustrious and stormy career, from his retreat from the Philippines and famous promised return, through the success of his controversial island-hopping strategy (bypassing Japanese strongholds and cutting off their supply lines), onto his success as the military governor of a ruined but rebuilding Japan, and finally to his explosive conflict with President Harry Truman over the conduct of the Korean War, which led to the general's retirement. MacARTHUR is an enormous undertaking of a subject much too big to encompass in a single film, and the slices of MacArthur's life sometimes appear disjointed. But Peck is memorable and believable in one of his best parts, capturing the general's eccentricities, vanities, and heroism, and, while the film lacks the panache of PATTON, it presents a more introspective look at one of this century's most celebrated warriors. At the time of the film's release, critics found little of the exceptional in MacARTHUR, but Peck's forceful performance and director Joseph Sargent's honest effort to tell an unwieldy story later compelled many to acknowledge the film as a superior production.

p, Frank McCarthy; d, Joseph Sargent; w, Hal Barwood and Matthew Robbins; ed, George Jay Nicholson; ph, Mario Tosi, Technicolor; m, Jerry Goldsmith.

(PR:A MPAA:PG)

MAC ARTHUR'S CHILDREN***

(1985, Jap.) 120m Herald Ace/Orion Classics bw-c

Takaya Yamauchi *(Ryuta Ashigara)*, Yoshiyuki Omori *(Saburo Masaki)*, Shiori Sakura *(Mume Hatano)*, Masako Natsume *(Komako Nakai)*, Shuji Otaki *(Tadao Ashigara)*, Haruko Kato *(Haru Ashigara)*, Ken Watanabe *(Tetsuo Nakai)*, Naomi Chiaki *(Miyo)*.

An attempt to bring about an understanding of how the Japanese reacted to their humiliating defeat in WW II, MAC ARTHUR'S CHILDREN deals with the problem on a microcosmic level, concentrating on a small, remote island called Awaji Shima rather than on the whole country. Set in the days just following the defeat, the film portrays events through the eyes of children, particularly Ryuta Ashigara (Takaya Yamauchi), a young boy whose father was killed in battle and who is being raised by his grandfather, the local police chief. Ryuta's best friend, the rebellious Saburo (Yoshiyuki Omori), refuses to accept national dishonor and instead threatens to run away to become a gangster, or *baraketsu*. Although the children cannot fully comprehend what has happened to their country, they see the changes in the people around them. Then come the Americans, bringing candy bars and gum, baseball, and Glenn Miller. They easily win over the children, but simultaneously litter Japanese culture with their own unconscious imperialism. As with fellow Japanese director Nagisa Oshima, Masahiro Shinoda's talents blossomed in the 1960s, his subjects pertaining chiefly to the passions of youth. Here, Shinoda places these passions in a historical context and a highly westernized narrative style, but unfortunately comes up with a mannered film lacking the power one might expect from a depiction of the clash of pre- and postwar Japanese cultures. (In Japanese; English subtitles.)

p, You-No-Kai and Masato Hara; d, Masahiro Shinoda; w, Takeshi Tamura, based on the novel by Yu Aku; ed, Sachiko Yamaji; ph, Kazuo Miyagawa; m, Shinichiro Ikebe and Glenn Miller.

(PR:C MPAA:PG)

MALTA STORY***

(1954, Brit.) 103m British Film Makers/UA bw

Alec Guinness *(Peter Ross)*, Jack Hawkins *(Air Commanding Officer)*, Anthony Steel *(Bartlett)*, Muriel Pavlow *(Maria)*, Flora Robson *(Melita)*, Renee Asherson *(Joan)*, Ralph Truman *(Banks)*, Reginald Tate *(Payne)*, Hugh Burden *(Eden)*, Nigel Stock *(Giuseppe)*, Harold Siddons *(Matthews)*.

Blending real newsreel footage with the affecting personal tales at its center, this fine British action film tells the story of the heroic defense of Malta during WW II. Alec Guinness delivers a strong performance as Peter Ross, an archaeologist-turned-reconnaissance pilot pressed into service during a stopover on the embattled island. Deeply touched by the spirit of its indomitable people, he becomes part of the British effort to defend the island fortress against the fascist onslaught, and, in the process, falls in love with Maria (Muriel Pavlow), a pretty Maltese woman. Ross risks (and eventually loses) his life on flights that provide valuable information about German and Italian strategy, while the film's main subplot concerns the struggle by Maria's mother (Flora Robson) to understand her son, who not only isn't a patriot but, ultimately, is revealed to be a collaborator with the enemy.

p, Peter de Sarigny; d, Brian Desmond Hurst; w, William Fairchild, Nigel Balchin, Thorold Dickinson, and Peter de Sarigny; ed, Michael Gordon; ph, Robert Krasker; m, William Alwyn.

(PR:A-C MPAA:NR)

MARATHON MAN****

(1976) 125m PAR c

Dustin Hoffman *(Babe Levy)*, Laurence Olivier *(Szell)*, Roy Scheider *(Doc Levy)*, William Devane *(Janeway)*, Marthe Keller *(Elsa)*, Fritz Weaver *(Prof. Biesenthal)*, Richard Bright *(Karl)*, Marc Lawrence *(Erhard)*, Allen Joseph *(Babe's Father)*, Tito Goya *(Melendez)*, Ben Dova *(Szell's Brother)*, James Wing Woo *(Chen)*, Lotta Andor-Palfi *(Old Lady on 47th Street)*.

A truly harrowing film, MARATHON MAN is a clever series of accidents that produce a nightmare thriller with an unrelenting attack on the viewer's nerves. Babe Levy (Dustin Hoffman), a Columbia University graduate student who runs whenever possible, dreaming of the Olympic marathon, is haunted by the memory of his father's suicide, brought about by the McCarthy witchhunts. Babe's brother, Doc (Roy Scheider), an American secret agent, helps sneak Szell (Laurence Olivier), an old Nazi, into the US from South America. Szell's brother, who has watched over a fortune in jewels taken from Jewish concentration camp victims, has died, and Szell has come to New York to collect the booty. After killing Doc, Szell uses the tools of his dentist's trade to torture Babe to get information the student doesn't possess. Putting his marathon training to use, Babe escapes Szell, and eventually the pursuer becomes the pursued. Hoffman is excellent as the crazed Szell's victim and Olivier is the essence of evil, his sadistic acts so expertly enacted that the film has a deeply disturbing quality. John Schlesinger's direction is highly stylized and more than effective, jammed with action and offering unforgettably terrifying scenes. Scheider is good as the errant older brother, and William Devane is his usual tricky self as the double-dealing intelligence chief. William Goldman's script, based on his novel, is literate and full of surprises.

p, Robert Evans and Sidney Beckerman; d, John Schlesinger; w, William Goldman, based on his novel; ed, Jim Clark; ph, Conrad Hall, Metrocolor; m, Michael Small.

(PR:O MPAA:R)

MARCH OR DIE***

(1977, Brit.) 107m ITC-Associated General/COL c

Gene Hackman *(Maj. William Sherman Foster)*, Terence Hill *(Marco Segrain)*, Max von Sydow *(Francois Marneau)*, Catherine Deneuve *(Simone Picard)*, Ian Holm *(El Krim)*, Rufus *(Sgt. Triand)*, Jack O'Halloran *(Ivan)*, Marcel Bozzuffi *(Lt. Fontaine)*, Andre Penvern *("Top Hat" Francois Gilbert)*, Paul Sherman *(Fred Hastings)*, Vernon Dobtcheff *(Mean Corporal)*, Marne Maitland *(Leon)*, Gigi Bonds *(Andre)*.

The French Foreign Legion has been the subject of countless films, some realistic, some romantic, some outright ridiculous. This one is a little bit of each. Set at the end of WW I, it follows the contingent of Legionnaires commanded by Maj. William Sherman Foster (Gene Hackman), an American kicked out of West Point, as it travels to Morocco to act as escort for an archaeological expedition headed by Louvre curator Marneau (Max von Sydow). Among the new recruits assigned to the dangerous mission are Marco (Terence Hill), a cat burglar fleeing arrest; Ivan (Jack O'Halloran), a onetime Imperial Guardsman for the Russian Court; Hastings (Paul Sherman), an aristocrat seeking adventure; and "Top Hat" (Andre Penvern), a talented musician. Although they survive brutal desert training under the sadistic Lt. Fontaine (Marcel Bozzuffi) and a romantic triangle involving Maj. Foster, Marco, and Simone (Catherine Deneuve), whose archaeologist father was lost on a previous expedition, the Legionnaires' biggest challenge comes from El Krim (Ian Holm), a vicious Arab leader who is determined to unite his people to expel foreigners from their land. The blood-drenched final battle leaves few Legionnaire survivors, but even after this awful defeat their "Marche ou Creve" spirit (which provides the film's title) lives on. This hardboiled movie, replete with excessive violence, offers a compelling performance by Hackman and a fascinating one from Hill as the weird but courageous burglar-turned-soldier. Although Dick Richards' direction is uneven, Oscar-winning cinematographer John Alcott (BARRY LYNDON) makes the most of the exotic Sahara Desert locations, and on the whole MARCH OR DIE is a well-made, offbeat, and interesting offering that occasionally confuses gratuitous bloodletting for realistic drama.

p, Dick Richards and Jerry Bruckheimer; d, Dick Richards; w, David Zelag Goodman, based on a story by David Zelag Goodman and Dick Richards; ed, John C. Howard, Stanford C. Allen, and O. Nicholas Brown; ph, John Alcott, Technicolor; m, Maurice Jarre.

(PR:C-O MPAA:PG)

MARRIAGE OF MARIA BRAUN, THE****

(1979, Ger.) 120m Albatros-Trio-Westdeutscher Rundfunk-Filmverlag der Autoren/New Yorker c (DIE EHE DER MARIA BRAUN)

Hanna Schygulla *(Maria Braun)*, Klaus Lowitsch *(Hermann Braun)*, Ivan Desny *(Oswald)*, Gottfried John *(Willi)*, Gisela Uhlen *(Mother)*, Gunter Lamprecht *(Hans)*, Hark Bohm *(Senkenberg)*, George Byrd *(Bill)*, Elisabeth Trissenaar *(Betti)*, Rainer Werner Fassbinder *(Peddler)*.

The first in Rainer Werner Fassbinder's trilogy about women in post-WW II Germany (followed by VERONIKA VOSS and LOLA), this was also the film that solidified Fassbinder's reputation abroad and in Germany. In the opening sequence, a German city is being torn apart by Allied bombs while Maria (Hanna Schygulla) and her soldier fiance, Hermann Braun (Klaus Lowitsch), are getting married. Immediately afterwards, the new husband is sent to the Russian front, leaving Maria with her mother and sister, impoverished and waiting for her husband, visiting the train station every day with the hope of hearing news about him. After receiving word that he has died, Maria takes work as a barmaid in a cafe that caters to American soldiers. There she meets Bill (George Byrd), a hefty black soldier who, despite the fact the they can barely converse, becomes her lover. Just when she has nearly forgotten about her husband, however, the starving and emasculated Hermann turns up while Maria and Bill are beginning to make love. The highly stylized, deliberate structure of THE MARRIAGE OF MARIA BRAUN owes much to such Douglas Sirk 1950s Hollywood melodramas as IMITATION OF LIFE and WRITTEN ON THE WIND. For both Sirk and Fassbinder, the director remains distanced from the heart-wrenching dramatics of the story in order to comment on certain societal ills, but Fassbinder is the further removed from his material—a product of the alienation prominent in a postwar Germany striving to rebuild itself into an industrial power, yet failing to account for the human bonds that make a society healthy. The effect is one of helplessness; we can only watch as the beautiful, young Maria Braun places herself in an emotional vacuum. Schygulla is quite powerful in perhaps the best role of her career, remaining cold and aloof, yet evoking a strong sense of pity. Though THE MARRIAGE OF MARIA BRAUN is not always an easy film to understand, the stark atmosphere, icy performances, and poignant revelations make it one of the most important films to emerge from Germany in the 1970s, and one of Fassbinder's best. (In German; English subtitles.)

p, Michael Fengler; d, Rainer Werner Fassbinder; w, Peter Marthesheimer, Pia Frohlich, and Rainer Werner Fassbinder, based on an idea by Rainer Werner Fassbinder; ed, Juliane Lorenz and Franz Walsch [Rainer Werner Fassbinder]; ph, Michael Ballhaus, Fujicolor; m, Peer Raben.

(PR:O MPAA:R)

M*A*S*H****

(1970) 116m Aspen/FOX c

Donald Sutherland *(Hawkeye Pierce)*, Elliott Gould *(Trapper John McIntyre)*, Tom Skerritt *(Duke Forrest)*, Sally Kellerman *(Maj. Hot Lips Houlihan)*, Robert Duvall *(Maj. Frank Burns)*, Jo Ann Pflug *(Lt. Dish)*, Rene Auberjonois *(Dago Red)*, Roger Bowen *(Col. Henry Blake)*, Gary Burghoff *(Radar O'Reilly)*, David Arkin *(Sgt. Major Vollmer)*, Fred Williamson *(Spearchucker)*, Michael Murphy *(Me Lay)*.

Set during the Korean War but made at the height of the war in Vietnam, Robert Altman's exceptional antiwar comedy-drama follows the fortunes of a MASH (Mobile Army Surgical Hospital) unit. Working from Richard Hooker's novel, screenwriter Ring Lardner, Jr., amassed a wacky corps of characters who would become even more familiar to fans of the popular, long-running TV series spawned by the film. Hawkeye Pierce (Donald Sutherland), Trapper John (Elliott Gould), and Duke Forrest (Tom Skerritt) are the martini-swilling, prank-playing, but compassionate and capable battlefield surgeons who make life miserable for chief nurse Hot Lips Houlihan (Sally Kellerman) and fellow surgeon Maj. Frank Burns (Robert Duvall), a by-the-book prig. Among the terrible trio's shenanigans are the broadcast of a Burns-Houlihan lovemaking session over the camp public address system (which becomes a character itself, offering one silly announcement after another) and the collapse of the women's shower to reveal the naked Maj. Houlihan. At the root of all this foolishness, however, is the attempt to mitigate the otherwise overwhelming bleakness of the war, to distract the doctors and nurses from the terrible waste of life they witness. The film's climactic football game, one of Hollywood's funniest (featuring a number of onetime pro players), pits the MASH unit against a crack team brought in by a general who has been investigating the unit. Clever camera setups, Altman's patented overlapping dialog, wonderful sight gags and situations, and universally fine ensemble performances combine to make this one the most enjoyable war-themed films ever. What makes M*A*S*H so extraordinary, however, is that beyond its hilarious antics and rich characters, the film offers a poignant portrait of the madness of war.

p, Ingo Preminger; d, Robert Altman; w, Ring Lardner, Jr., based on the novel by Richard Hooker [Dr. H. Richard Hornberger, William Heinz]; ed, Danford B. Greene; ph, Harold E. Stine, Panavision, Deluxe Color; m, Johnny Mandel.

(PR:C-O   MPAA:R)

MASSACRE IN ROME***

(1973, It.) 103m CHAM/NG c (RAPPRESAGLIA)

Richard Burton *(Col. Kappler)*, Marcello Mastroianni *(Don Antonelli)*, Leo McKern *(Gen. Kurt Maelzer)*, John Steiner *(Col. Dollmann)*, Delia Boccardo *(Elena)*, Renzo Montagnani *(Police Chief Caruso)*, Giancarlo Prete *(Paolo)*, Robert Harris *(Fr. Pancrazio)*.

This compelling war drama is based on the controversial book *Death in Rome*, which suggested that Pope Pius XII was aware of Hitler's plan to kill 10 Italians for every German lost in a partisan attack, then either feigned ignorance of the edict or could do nothing about it. Col. Kappler (Richard Burton) is a devoted Nazi who believes in Hitler with all his heart, but is caught between his duty and his love for Rome when he is ordered to execute 330 Italians in retaliation for the death of 33 Germans. Although Kappler would prefer not to carry out the orders, his alcoholic superior, Gen. Kurt Maelzer (Leo McKern), is determined to see them through. Standing defiant is Don Antonelli (Marcello Mastroianni), a Vatican priest who chooses to die with the partisans rather than continue to act as a liaison between the Romans and Germans. Filmed in a documentary style and featuring some superb performances, MASSACRE IN ROME is an effective retelling of this infamous slaughter, which took place on March 24, 1944, in the Ardeatine Caves outside of Rome.

p, Carlo Ponti; d, George P. Cosmatos; w, George P. Cosmatos and Robert Katz, based on his book *Death in Rome*; ed, Francoise Bonnot and Roberto Silvi; ph, Marcello Gatti, Technicolor; m, Ennio Morricone.

(PR:C   MPAA:PG)

MASTER RACE, THE**½

(1944) 96m RKO bw

George Coulouris *(Von Beck)*, Stanley Ridges *(Phil Carson)*, Osa Massen *(Helena)*, Carl Esmond *(Andrei)*, Nancy Gates *(Nina)*, Morris Carnovsky *(Old Man Bartoc)*, Lloyd Bridges *(Frank)*, Eric Feldary *(Altmeier)*, Helen Beverly *(Mrs. Varin)*, Gavin Muir *(William Forsythe)*, Paul Guilfoyle *(Katry)*, Richard Nugent *(Sgt. O'Farrell)*, Louis Donath *(Schmidt)*, Herbert Rudley *(John)*, Jason Robards, Sr. *(Jacob Weiner)*, Merrill Roden *(George Rudan)*.

This end-of-the-war cautionary tale stars George Coulouris as von Beck, a zealous Nazi officer who, at the close of WW II, is ordered to infiltrate a small Belgian town, there to sow hatred and dissension among its citizens in preparation for the coming Fourth Reich, which will someday rise from the ashes of the near-defeated Germany. Released towards the end of WW II, this was Hollywood's attempt to warn the world that the events leading to the war could easily be repeated. Though it did fairly well at the box office, the film was not nearly as successful as the same production team's HITLER'S CHILDREN of the previous year, viewers perhaps tiring of screen portrayals of Nazis. The sets depicting a bombarded northern European town were the same as those used for THE HUNCHBACK OF NOTRE DAME (1939), in which they served as medieval Paris.

p, Robert Golden; d, Herbert Biberman and Madeleine Dmytryk; w, Herbert Biberman, Anne Froelick, and Rowland Leigh, based on a story by Biberman; ed, Ernie Leadley; ph, Russell Metty; m, Roy Webb.

(PR:A   MPAA:NR)

MEN, THE***½

(1950) 85m Kramer/UA bw (AKA: BATTLE STRIPE)

Marlon Brando *(Ken)*, Teresa Wright *(Ellen)*, Everett Sloane *(Dr. Brock)*, Jack Webb *(Norm)*, Richard Erdman *(Leo)*, Arthur Jurado *(Angel)*, Virginia Farmer *(Nurse Robbins)*, Dorothy Tree *(Ellen's Mother)*, Howard St. John *(Ellen's Father)*, Nita Hunter *(Dolores)*, Patricia Joiner *(Laverne)*, John Miller *(Mr. Doolin)*, Cliff Clark *(Dr. Kameran)*, Ray Mitchell *(Thompson)*, Pete Simon *(Mullin)*, Paul Peltz *(Hopkins)*, Tom Gillick *(Fine)*.

This was Marlon Brando's film debut and, as such, set standards not only for his fellow actors but for himself. Brando gives a tremendous performance as Ken, a WW II veteran who has been left a paraplegic as a result of a sniper's bullet in the lower back. In the hospital, Ken is angry, resentful, and uncooperative with his doctors and nurses. His girl friend, Ellen (Teresa Wright), visits him but the embittered Ken turns her away. Dr. Brock (Everett Sloane) slowly breaks through Ken's mental wall, however, convincing him to begin his exercise program, through which Ken strengthens his upper torso, later learning to expertly manipulate his wheelchair and to drive a specially equipped auto. Ellen will not give up on him and soon Ken agrees to marry her, but despite the progress he has made, the vet is still consumed with doubt, anger, and self-pity. Producer Stanley Kramer earlier produced such message-filled films as CHAMPION and HOME OF THE BRAVE, the first concerning the corruption of the blood sport of prizefighting, the second dealing with racism and bigotry. Here Kramer, aided by the steady direction of Fred Zinnemann, studies the adjustment of severely wounded men with little hope of complete recovery. Zinnemann rarely steps over the line into mawkishness or bathos, and Carl Foreman's witty, sensitive script was the reason Brando agreed to step off the stage to appear in this film. Brando worked hard at his role, actually moving into a 32-

bed ward with real paraplegics and observing their day-to-day agonies, research that resulted in a finely nuanced performance.

p, Stanley Kramer; d, Fred Zinnemann; w, Carl Foreman; ed, Harry Gerstad; ph, Robert de Grasse; m, Dimitri Tiomkin.

(PR:C   MPAA:NR)

MEN IN WAR****

(1957) 104m Security/UA bw

Robert Ryan *(Lt. Benson)*, Aldo Ray *(Montana)*, Robert Keith *(Colonel)*, Philip Pine *(Riordan)*, Vic Morrow *(Zwickley)*, Nehemiah Persoff *(Lewis)*, James Edwards *(Killian)*, L.Q. Jones *(Sam Davis)*, Adam Kennedy *(Maslow)*, Scott Marlowe *(Meredith)*, Walter Kelley *(Ackerman)*, Robert Normand *(Christensen)*, Anthony Ray *(Penelli)*, Michael Miller *(Lynch)*, Victor Sen Yung *(Korean Sniper)*, Race Gentry *(Haines)*.

Brilliantly directed by Anthony Mann, MEN IN WAR was the veteran filmmaker's only modern war film and is also one of his best. Set during the Korean War, Mann's film paints a hellish portrait of the insanity of combat as seen through the eyes of the common foot soldier. Robert Ryan is superb as Lt. Benson, the tough, grizzled commander with orders to march his weary patrol to Hill 465, where they will join their battalion and take the hill. Aldo Ray is Montana, a sergeant from another company whose job is to squire his shell-shocked colonel (Robert Keith) back to a field hospital for treatment. His weapons' carrier wrecked, Benson commandeers Montana's jeep—with the catatonic colonel strapped inside—to carry ammo and other equipment to help his stranded battalion. Montana is adamantly against this, as he is determined to get his colonel, the only fellow soldier who matters to him, to the hospital. Benson's duty, however, is to his men and he will not let Montana stand in his way. The men make their way through hostile territory amidst several skirmishes, losing several of their number along the way, and eventually get to Benson's battalion, only to discover that most of its members are dead and the North Koreans occupy the hill. Left with only a handful of men, Benson follows his orders and tries to retake the hill. A truly unique war film, MEN IN WAR rejects many of the narrative and character stereotypes common in the genre (there are no easily identifiable "types" such as the green recruit or the bookworm here; nor are there any touching conversations about life after the war; nor propagandizing over the war's just cause—it simply *is*). MEN IN WAR is just what its title implies: a gritty, harrowing, and totally deglamorized view of combat. As in his masterful westerns featuring Jimmy Stewart, Mann pits his heroes and villains against a massive, rugged, and unforgiving landscape. The enemy is mostly unseen, leaving the soldiers to struggle against the alien and hostile surroundings. Using a variety of unusual (especially for the period) cinematic techniques, including extreme close-ups, off-screen sounds, and dislocating jump-cuts, Mann creates one of film's most memorable and affecting visions of the hell of war, driving home the futility of it all.

p, Sidney Harmon; d, Anthony Mann; w, Philip Yordan, based on the novel *Combat* by Van Van Praag; ed, Richard C. Meyer; ph, Ernest Haller; m, Elmer Bernstein.

(PR:A-C   MPAA:NR)

MEPHISTO****

(1981, Ger.) 144m Mafilm-Durniok/Cinegate-Analysis c

Klaus Maria Brandauer *(Hendrik Hofgen)*, Krystyna Janda *(Barbara Bruckner)*, Ildiko Bansagi *(Nicoletta Von Niebuhr)*, Karin Boyd *(Juliette Martens)*, Rolf Hoppe *(The General)*, Christine Harbort *(Lotte Lindenthal)*, Gyorgy Cserhalmi *(Hans Miklas)*, Christiane Graskoff *(Cesar Von Muck)*.

The winner of 1982's Academy Award for Best Foreign-Language Film, MEPHISTO is an inspired update of the Faust legend with a tour-de-force performance by Klaus Maria Brandauer. Critically acclaimed stage actor Hendrik Hofgen (Brandauer) tires of the "entertaining" theatrical forms and attempts something more revolutionary, more Brechtian. Despite his ground-breaking ideas, he does not rise to fame—they cannot even spell his name correctly on posters. Desperate, Hendrik sells his soul, not to the Devil, but to the Nazis—his desire for fame more urgent than his hatred of the oppressor. It is only later, after he is indebted to the Third Reich, that he realizes his mistake. Based on a novel by Klaus Mann (son of Thomas), exquisitely photographed, MEPHISTO bubbles over with the energy of Brandauer's bravura performance, which quickly attracted the attention of Hollywood. Brandauer and director Istvan Szabo would team again to make COLONEL REDL and HANUSSEN. Unfortunately, the videotape version is atrociously dubbed from German into English, making Brandauer sound like some suburban dinner theater actor.

p, Manfred Durniok; d, Istvan Szabo; w, Istvan Szabo and Peter Dobai, based on the novel by Klaus Mann; ed, Zsuzsa Csekany; ph, Lajos Koltai, Eastmancolor; m, Zdenko Tamassy.

(PR:O   MPAA:NR)

MERRY CHRISTMAS, MR. LAWRENCE****

(1983, Jap./Brit.) 124m Recorded Picture-Cineventure TV, Asahi-Oshima/UNIV c

David Bowie *(Jack Celliers)*, Tom Conti *(Col. John Lawrence)*, Ryuichi Sakamoto *(Capt. Yoni)*, Takeshi *(Sgt. Hara)*, Jack Thompson *(Hicksley-Ellis)*, Johnny Okura *(Kanemoto)*, Alistair Browning *(DeJong)*, James Malcolm *(Celliers' Brother)*, Chris Brown *(Celliers, Age 12)*.

Japanese director Nagisa Oshima's first film in English stars Tom Conti as the title character, a British colonel in a Japanese-run POW camp during WW II. Col. Lawrence is an astute observer of cultural codes among both his fellow Britishers and his Japanese captors, and even forms a sort of friendship with one Japanese officer (Takeshi). He is also witness to the strange dynamics between new camp commandant Yoni (Ryuichi Sakamoto) and new prisoner Jack Celliers (David Bowie), an intrepid soldier Lawrence served with in Libya. Yoni is fascinated by Celliers, and plans to make him the prisoners' CO, replacing Hicksley-Ellis (Jack Thompson), whose Britishisms Yoni construes as signs of weakness. When Yoni calls for Hicksley-Ellis' execution, however, Celliers performs an act that upsets and exposes the film's precarious balance of national codes, personal relationships, and individual psychologies. Oshima's ambitious film is not without faults, but these are overshadowed by its emotional power. Many of the characters' actions and impulses are contradictory or not overtly explained, but answers can generally be found buried in Oshima's complex story (the Yoni-Celliers relationship, which needs greater development, is a notable exception). Fine performances of Conti, Takeshi (brilliant in his first dramatic role), Sakamoto (a Japanese pop star in his film acting debut, he also contributes the memorable score), and Bowie enhance this provocative film.

p, Jeremy Thomas; d, Nagisa Oshima; w, Nagisa Oshima and Paul Mayersberg, based on the novel *The Seed And The Sower* by Laurens Van Der Post; ed, Tomoyo Oshima; ph, Toichiro Narushima, Eastmancolor; m, Ryuichi Sakamoto.

(PR:O MPAA:R)

MIDWAY**

(1976) 132m UNIV c (GB: BATTLE OF MIDWAY, THE)

Charlton Heston *(Capt. Matt Garth)*, Henry Fonda *(Adm. Chester W. Nimitz)*, James Coburn *(Capt. Vinton Maddox)*, Glenn Ford *(Rear Adm. Raymond A. Spruance)*, Hal Holbrook *(Comdr. Joseph Rochefort)*, Toshiro Mifune *(Adm. Isoroku Yamamoto)*, Robert Mitchum *(Adm. William F. Halsey)*, Cliff Robertson *(Comdr. Carl Jessop)*, Robert Wagner *(Lt. Comdr. Ernest L. Blake)*, Robert Webber *(Rear Adm. Frank J. "Jack" Fletcher)*, Ed Nelson *(Adm. Harry Pearson)*, James Shigeta *(Vice Adm. Chuichi Nagumo)*, Christina Kokubo *(Haruko Sakura)*, Monte Markham *(Comdr. Max Leslie)*, Edward Albert *(Lt. Tom Garth)*, Dabney Coleman *(Capt. Murray Arnold)*.

Despite a crowded cast of famous actors, this WW II adventure falls flat because of its claustrophobic sets, cliched dialog, and hackneyed story. MIDWAY's best action sequence is the bombing run on Tokyo during the opening credits, which is lifted wholly from the black-and-white film THIRTY SECONDS OVER TOKYO, tinted in red for insertion in this color production. The overlong story concerns events leading up to and including the Battle of Midway (fought in June 1942), when planes from US carriers utterly destroyed a Japanese invasion fleet, sinking four enemy carriers. A corny subplot deals with Capt. Matt Garth (Charlton Heston), whose ensign son, Tom (Edward Albert, in a ludicrous casting choice), wants to marry a Hawaiian woman of Japanese descent. Henry Fonda does an admirable job in the role of the stoic Adm. Chester W. Nimitz and Glenn Ford is above average as Rear Adm. Raymond Spruance, the man who led the American carriers to victory. The film is bloated with cameo appearances, though all of the actors are worth watching, if even for just a few minutes. Hal Holbrook is probably the most likable as the unorthodox Navy officer who breaks the Japanese code; Robert Mitchum appears in only two scenes, as the sickly Adm. Halsey; and Toshiro Mifune, dubbed in English by announcer Paul Frees, gets some mileage out of his role. The battle scenes were very obviously shot in miniature, and the film's big draw—the "Sensurround" sound system—provided nothing more than exaggerated battle noises that annoyed audiences instead of enhancing the production. Not surprisingly, the effect is lost on videocassette.

p, Walter Mirisch; d, Jack Smight; w, Donald S. Sanford; ed, Robert Swink and Frank J. Urioste; ph, Harry Stradling, Jr., Sensurround, Panavision, Technicolor; m, John Williams.

(PR:A MPAA:PG)

MIRACLE OF THE WHITE STALLIONS**

(1963) 117m Disney/BV c (AKA: FLIGHT OF THE WHITE STALLIONS, THE)

Robert Taylor *(Col. Podhajsky)*, Lilli Palmer *(Verena Podhajsky)*, Curt Jurgens *(Gen. Tellheim)*, Eddie Albert *(Rider Otto)*, James Franciscus *(Maj. Hoffman)*, John Larch *(Gen. Patton)*, Brigitte Horney *(Countess Arco-Valley)*, Philip Abbott *(Col. Reed)*, Douglas Fowley *(US General)*, Charles Regnier *(Gen. Stryker)*, Fritz Wepper *(Rider Hans)*, Gunther Haenel *(Groom Sascha)*.

Loosely based in fact, this slow-moving Disney film is an uninspired treatment of an inspiring story—the preservation of the famed Lipizzan horses at the end of WW II. Returning to the screen after a three-year absence, Robert Taylor delivers a lackluster performance as Col. Podhajsky, the head of Vienna's Spanish Riding School. Worried about the fate of his magnificent white horses as the Allies approach the Austrian capital, Podhajsky persuades a German general (well played by Curt Jurgens) to bend the definition of "art treasures" to allow him to transport the horses out of harm's way. Because the mares and stallions are separated, however, Podhajsky fears that the breed may die out, but after the Allies occupy the city, he arranges an impressive demonstration of the Lipizzans' talents for Gen. Patton (John Larch), who sees to it that the stallions are returned safely to Vienna from Czechoslovakia. Suffering from a script that doesn't seem to know whether its target audience is kids or adults, THE MIRACLE OF THE WHITE STALLIONS captures the fancy of neither, though the grace and beauty of the horses is undeniable.

p, Walt Disney and Peter V. Herald; d, Arthur Hiller; w, A.J. Carothers, based on the book *The Dancing White Stallions of Vienna* by Col. Alois Podhajsky; ed, Alfred Srp and Cotton Warburton; ph, Gunther Anders, Technicolor; m, Paul Smith.

(PR:AA MPAA:NR)

MISFIT BRIGADE, THE**
(1988) 101m Panorama-Manley/Trans World c (AKA: WHEELS OF TERROR)

Bruce Davison *(Porta)*, David Patrick Kelly *(The Legionnaire)*, Don W. Moffett *(Capt. von Barring)*, Jay O. Sanders *(Tiny)*, Keith Szarabajka *("Old Man")*, Oliver Reed *(The General)*, David Carradine *(Col. Von Weisshagen)*, Slavko Stimac *(Sven)*, Andrija Maricic *(Stege)*, Boris Komnenic *(Bauer)*, Bane Vidakovic *(Muller)*, Irena Prosen *(The Madam)*, Svetlana

In 1943 the Nazi government, desperate for soldiers, began raiding prisons for recruits. THE MISFIT BRIGADE recounts the exploits of a brigade of such ex-cons, attached to a Panzer division. Their crimes range from bigamy to desertion to Marxism, and none is much enamored of Hitler, but they find fighting preferable to prison and enjoy boozing, brawling, and generally raising hell until Col. von Weisshagen (David Carradine) sends them to the Russian front, then assigns them to blow up a train in the Russian village of Dankau. To their objection that this is a suicide mission, the colonel promises they will be permanently transferred from the front and given long leaves if they succeed, and they head off for Dankau, where, eventually, they do the job. Back in Germany, at an airbase ceremony where they and von Weisshagen are to be honored for their feat by a general (Oliver Reed), they find that von Weisshagen is set to renege on his pledge. As Allied fighters strafe the base, the two officers head for a plane to fly them out—but their pilot is gone, and they find themselves surrounded by the armed members of the brigade at the fadeout. Though the brigade's assignment is supposed to be a suicide mission, there's no sense of tension or danger and it all seems pretty easy; the cast, however, is excellent. David Patrick Kelly, Bruce Davison, Jay O. Sanders, and the other "misfits" are all properly cynical; Carradine is terrific as the arrogant colonel. Director Gordon Hessler previously specialized in martial arts films.

p, Just Betzer and Benni Korzen; d, Gordon Hessler; w, Nelson Gidding, based on the novel *Wheels of Terror* by Sven Hassel; ed, Bob Gordon; ph, George Nikolic, Eastmancolor; m, Ole Hoyer.

(PR:O   MPAA:R)

MISSING****
(1982) 122m Polygram/UNIV c

Jack Lemmon *(Ed Horman)*, Sissy Spacek *(Beth Horman)*, Melanie Mayron *(Terry Simon)*, John Shea *(Charles Horman)*, Charles Cioffi *(Capt. Ray Tower)*, David Clennon *(Consul Phil Putnam)*, Richard Venture *(US Ambassador)*, Jerry Hardin *(Col. Sean Patrick)*, Richard Bradford *(Carter Babcock)*, Joe Regalbuto *(Frank Teruggi)*, Keith Szarabajka *(David Holloway)*, Janice Rule *(Kate Newman)*.

With MISSING, Costa-Gavras (Z; STATE OF SEIGE; THE CONFESSION), one of cinema's most political filmmakers, turned his attention to the alleged US involvement in the coup that led to the death of socialist Chilean president Salvador Allende in 1973. Based on Thomas Hauser's *The Execution of Charles Horman*, Costa-Gavras' first Hollywood-produced film presents an only slightly fictionalized account of the disappearance of American expatriate writer Charles Horman (John Shea) in Santiago (though neither the city nor Chile are ever mentioned) just after a military coup. His wife, Beth (Sissy Spacek), and his conservative father, Ed (Jack Lemmon), who has traveled from the US, become a political odd couple as they search for Charles, growing closer as they run into the official stonewalling of American embassy and Chilean authorities who insist there is no trace of Charles. In the course of their private investigation, the formerly flag-waving Ed becomes convinced that his own government has not only precipitated the military coup but sanctioned the execution of his son, who observed US involvement in the overthrow while visiting a coastal town. Costa-Gavras pulled so few punches in this powerful, provocative thriller that then-Secretary of State Alexander Haig felt compelled to issue categorical denials of the film's allegations. Few films fuse the personal and the political as successfully as MISSING does, and Lemmon and Spacek bring tremendous feeling and verisimilitude to their portrayals. Lemmon, in particular, is excellent as the middle-of-the-road American who comes to realize that his own prosperity is predicated on US covert meddling in the affairs of other nations. Though Costa-Gavras clearly has a political axe to grind, he manages to do so without haranguing the viewer, keeping the film's focus on his characters and masterfully building tension as the story moves toward its stinging resolution.

p, Edward Lewis and Mildred Lewis; d, Costa-Gavras; w, Donald Stewart and Costa-Gavras, based on *The Execution of Charles Horman* by Thomas Hauser; ed, Francoise Bonnot; ph, Ricardo Aronovich, Technicolor; m, Vangelis.

(PR:A-C   MPAA:PG)

MISSING IN ACTION**
(1984) 101m Cannon c

Chuck Norris *(Braddock)*, M. Emmet Walsh *(Tuck)*, David Tress *(Sen. Porter)*, Lenore Kasdorf *(Ann)*, James Hong *(Gen. Tran)*, Ernie Ortega *(Vinh)*, Pierrino Mascarino *(Jacques)*, E. Erich Anderson *(Masucci)*, Joseph Carberry *(Carter)*, Avi Kleinberger *(Dalton)*, Willy Williams *(Randall)*.

Braddock (Chuck Norris) is an American officer who spent seven years in a North Vietnamese POW camp, then escaped. After the war, Braddock accompanies a government investigation team that goes to Ho Chi Minh City to check out reports of Americans still held prisoner. He gets the evidence he needs, then travels to Thailand, where he meets Tuck (M. Emmet Walsh), an old Army buddy turned black market kingpin, and together they launch a mission deep into the jungle to free the American POWs and shoot up a lot of Communists. This is the film that opened the floodgates of Vietnam revisionism carried to its macho extreme in RAMBO: FIRST BLOOD PART II (1985)—if America couldn't win the war, it can at least make films in which we get even. As an action picture, MISSING IN ACTION works fairly well. Norris is a worthy hero, shooting and kicking oriental enemies right and left, and the film is

MISSING IN ACTION 2—THE BEGINNING—

blessed with production values that make it quite watchable. A major success at the box office, the film spawned an equally successful prequel, MISSING IN ACTION 2—THE BEGINNING (1985), shot at the same time and released only four months after MISSING IN ACTION, and yet another sequel, the less successful BRADDOCK: MISSING IN ACTION 3.

p, Menahem Golan and Yoram Globus; d, Joseph Zito; w, James Bruner, based on a story by John Crowther, Lance Hool, from characters created by Arthur Silver, Larry Levinson, Steve Bing; ed, Joel Goodman and Daniel Loewenthal; ph, Joao Fernandes, Metrocolor; m, Jay Chattaway.

(PR:O MPAA:R)

MISSING IN ACTION 2—THE BEGINNING**
(1985) 96m Cannon c

Chuck Norris (Col. Braddock), Soon-Teck Oh (Col. Yin), Steven Williams (Nester), Bennett Ohta (Col. Ho), Cosie Costa (Mazilli), Joe Michael Terry (Opelka), John Wesley (Franklin), David Chung (Dou Chou), Prof. Toru Tanaka (Lao), Christopher Cary (Emerson), Dean Ferrandini (Kittle), Pierre Issot (Francois).

This prequel to the phenomenally successful MISSING IN ACTION tells the story of Braddock's (Chuck Norris) original confinement by the North Vietnamese and his ultimate escape. While supervising the helicopter evacuation of a reconnaissance team deep behind Communist lines, Braddock is shot down in his chopper and captured along with a number of his elite team. Ten years later the war is long over, but the men are still being held by the sadistic Col. Yin (Soon-Teck Oh), whose driving motivation in all the atrocities he commits is to force Braddock to sign a confession of war crimes. On the side, Yin is involved with French drug smuggler (Pierre Issot) and forces his prisoners to grow and process opium. Any prisoner who tries to escape is shot or impaled on booby traps in the jungle. After suffering many horrors, Braddock escapes—but doesn't run, as he systematically sets about arming himself and prepares to go back to do battle. Though certainly not a profound statement about America's involvement in Southeast Asia, MISSING IN ACTION 2 is, nevertheless, an adequate action film, more akin to CAMP ON BLOOD ISLAND than to APOCALYPSE NOW or even THE BRIDGE ON THE RIVER KWAI. Norris, acceptably rugged and intransigent, makes a serviceable hero, but Soon-Teck Oh's insane but clever commander steals the show. Shot on location on St. Kitt's in the Caribbean at the same time as the original installment, MISSING IN ACTION 2 joined its predecessor in mopping up at the box office.

p, Menahem Golan and Yoram Globus; d, Lance Hool; w, Arthur Silver, Larry Levinson, and Steve Bing; ed, Mark Conte and Marcus Manton; ph, Jorge Stahl, TVC Color; m, Brian May.

(PR:O MPAA:R)

MISSION BATANGAS*½
(1968) 100m Batangas-Diba/Manson c

Dennis Weaver (Chip Corbett), Vera Miles (Joan Barnes), Keith Larsen (Col. Turner).

Chip Corbett (Dennis Weaver), a self-interested American pilot, crash-lands on Corregidor while the Japanese invasion of the Philippines is in full swing and becomes involved in an attempt to prevent the invaders from getting hold of the Filipino government's gold stock. After failing to transfer the bullion from a barge to a waiting US submarine, Turner (Keith Larsen, who also produced and directed the film), an American colonel, and Joan Barnes (Vera Miles), a missionary nurse, persuade Corbett to bomb and sink the barge, sending the gold to the safe haven of the ocean bottom until the war is over. The problem is getting to a plane; accompanied by courageous Filipino fighters, the threesome makes a dangerous journey through the jungle, and though neither Barnes nor Turner survives, Corbett accepts the Filipino struggle as his own and makes it into the air. Filmed on location in the Philippines and originally released in 1969, MISSION BATANGAS received new life as a New World videocassette in 1985, though one wonders why anyone felt the need to dust off this less-than-involving actioner.

p, Keith Larsen; d, Keith Larsen; w, Lew Antonio, based on a story by Larsen; ed, Tony Di Marco and George Schrader; ph, Herbert Theis, Technicolor.

(PR:A MPAA:NR)

MISTER ROBERTS***½
(1955) 123m Orange/WB c

Henry Fonda (Lt. Doug Roberts), James Cagney (Captain), Jack Lemmon (Ens. Frank Thurlowe Pulver), William Powell (Doc), Ward Bond (CPO Dowdy), Betsy Palmer (Lt. Ann Girard), Phil Carey (Mannion), Nick Adams (Reber), Harry Carey, Jr. (Stefanowski), Ken Curtis (Dolan), Perry Lopez (Rodrigues), Pat Wayne (Bookser).

The movie version of one of the most beloved American stage plays is wholly entertaining, with wonderful performances from the entire cast—notably Henry Fonda (who created the title role) and Jack Lemmon (who won a Best Supporting Actor Oscar for his work)—but the story behind the film is a turbulent one, the production going through three directors (John Ford, Mervyn LeRoy, and Josh Logan) before its completion. In the Pacific, during WW II, we meet Lt. Roberts (Fonda), the cargo officer of the USS Reluctant, a toothpaste and toilet paper supply ship aimlessly sailing the South Pacific. Roberts feels that the war is passing him by and he yearns to be a part of it. His captain (James Cagney) is a megalomaniac who is forever distressing his crew with his asinine orders and who dotes on a small palm tree sitting outside his quarters, lavishing more attention and compassion on the plant than he does his own men. Roberts, normally a calm and kind man, is driven to outrage by the insensitive captain and acts as a buffer between him and the restless crew. While Roberts takes the brunt of the captain's wrath, the young and immature Ens. Pulver (Jack Lemmon) does his part by constantly pulling pranks on the captain in hopes of driving him mad. With Roberts growing more desperate for a transfer—a request that must be approved by the captain—the captain has the troublesome lieutenant right where he wants him and continues to make life miserable for the crew at Roberts' expense. Fonda had abandoned Hollywood for the Broadway stage, and studio bosses felt his marquee value was dubious, despite the fact that he had created the role of Mr. Roberts onstage. Producer Leland Hayward wanted either Marlon Brando or William Holden to play Roberts, but director Ford insisted that Fonda be given the part. Unfortunately, it wasn't long before Ford and Fonda clashed, mostly because Fonda had some fixed ideas as to how to play Roberts, having done it so many times before. The dispute grew heated and led to Ford's assaulting Fonda, causing a rift between them that never healed, despite the director's attempts to apologize. Shortly thereafter, Ford suffered a gallbladder attack and was hospitalized. Having completed only the exterior scenes, Ford was replaced by Warners veteran LeRoy, who finished the picture. Later, playwright and screenwriter Logan (who also directed the Broadway original) was brought in to direct some additional scenes. The resulting effort is a bit of a mess, with Ford's scenes instantly recognizable by his distinctive style (actor Ward Bond's removing his work glove to handle a letter from Roberts at the climax is a definite "Fordian" bit of business), while LeRoy's scenes—mostly interiors—suffer from static, stagy direction. (The exact nature of Logan's contributions have never been made crystal clear, but some sources credit him with some of the comedic scenes, such as the making of the bootleg scotch and Pulver's blowing up the laundry.) Luckily, the sparkling script and terrific cast make up for the schizophrenic cinematic treatment and the film is, overall, a success. MR. ROBERTS was shot aboard the USS Hewell at the South Pacific island of Midway before moving to Kaneoke Bay in Hawaii for the final filming.

p, Leland Hayward; d, John Ford, Mervyn LeRoy, and Joshua Logan; w, Joshua Logan and Frank S. Nugent, based on the play by Joshua Logan and Thomas Heggen and the novel by Heggen; ed, Jack Murray; ph, Winton C. Hoch, CinemaScope, WarnerColor; m, Franz Waxman.

(PR:A   MPAA:NR)

MR. WINKLE GOES TO WAR**

(1944) 80m COL bw (GB: ARMS AND THE WOMAN)

Edward G. Robinson *(Wilbert George Winkle)*, Ruth Warrick *(Amy Winkle)*, Ted Donaldson *(Barry)*, Bob Haymes *(Jack Pettigrew)*, Richard Lane *(Sgt. "Alphabet")*, Robert Armstrong *(Joe Tinker)*, Richard Gaines *(Ralph Wescott)*, Walter Baldwin *(Plummer)*, Art Smith *(McDavid)*, Ann Shoemaker *(Martha Pettigrew)*, George Tyne [Buddy Yarus] *(Johnson)*, Bernadene Hayes *(Gladys)*, Robert Mitchum *(Corporal)*.

Not really the war comedy its title leads one to expect, MR. WINKLE GOES TO WAR stars Edward G. Robinson as Wilbert Winkle, who, after working for 15 years as a bank clerk, gives up his job and sets up a repair shop next to his home, much to the consternation of his wife, Amy (Ruth Warrick), who tosses him out of the house. In short order, however, 44-year-old Wilbert receives a call from Uncle Sam and, though he expects to be turned away at the induction center, soon finds himself in uniform, survives basic training, and is sent into combat against the Japanese. Not only does he make it through the war—unlike a pair of his "mature" comrades in arms (Robert Armstrong and Richard Lane)—but Wilbert also distinguishes himself in battle, repairing a stalled bulldozer, then using it to attack an enemy position. A hero's welcome awaits Wilbert's return, but he is much more interested in getting back to his shop and Amy. Released at the height of WW II, MR. WINKLE GOES TO WAR has its humorous moments, but for the most part this is rather serious stuff, reasonably well performed, though it's not easy to accept tough guy Robinson as so mild-mannered a character.

p, Jack Moss; d, Alfred E. Green; w, Waldo Salt, George Corey, and Louis Solomon, based on the novel by Theodore Pratt; ed, Richard Fantl; ph, Joseph Walker; m, Carmen Dragon and Paul Sawtell.

(PR:A   MPAA:NR)

MORITURI***

(1965) 128m Arcola-Colony/FOX bw (AKA: SABOTEUR: CODE NAME MORITURI, THE)

Marlon Brando *(Robert Crain)*, Yul Brynner *(Capt. Mueller)*, Janet Margolin *(Esther)*, Trevor Howard *(Col. Statter)*, Martin Benrath *(Kruse)*, Hans Christian Blech *(Donkeyman)*, Wally Cox *(Dr. Ambach)*, Max Haufler *(Branner)*, Rainer Penkert *(Milkereit)*, William Redfield *(Baldwin)*, Oscar Beregi *(Admiral)*.

Capt. Mueller (Yul Brynner) is a German seaman assigned in WW II to deliver a cargo of much-needed rubber from Japan to occupied France. Though the politically neutral Mueller feels the assignment is foolish, he is overruled, and the ship—partly crewed by political prisoners of the Nazi government—prepares for the voyage, a mission fervently supported by Mueller's first officer, Kruse (Martin Benrath). Robert Crain (Marlon Brando) is a wealthy deserter from the German army now living in India under the guise of a Swiss national. He is approached by Col. Statter (Trevor Howard), a British intelligence man, who threatens Crain with exposure unless he goes undercover for the British war effort. Crain is assigned to pose as an SS observer aboard Mueller's ship, where he can be instrumental in helping the British capture the vessel. Crain undertakes the mission, leaving Statter with the salutation *morituri te salutant*, a phrase once used by Roman gladiators that means "we who are about to die salute you." Brando and Brynner both give strong performances, complementing each other's role like two sides of a coin, and MORITURI is a handsome film, photographed in black and white to often stunning effect by Conrad Hall. Unfortunately, the work as a whole is not what it could have been, a victim (like so many other films) of various misunderstandings and indif-

MOROCCO—

ferences. Bernhard Wicki, a German director working for the first time in Hollywood, found himself face to face with the conglomerate powers of the California movie business, which insisted on tight schedules and budgets, a restraint the meticulous director found unbearable. Despite the problems the studio created over money and budgets, producer Aaron Rosenberg did manage to get hold of an authentic merchant vessel from circa 1938 to serve as Brynner's ship. The 540-foot Scottish ship was found docked in Yokohama harbor and subsequently chartered to California, where the film was to be shot. Eighty thousand dollars were put into the creation of an authentic looking Japanese submarine, a remarkable replica built entirely of plywood. MORITURI was inspired by the fictionalized memoirs of a partly Jewish German who was stationed as a naval attache in Tokyo during WW II. When his heritage was discovered by authorities, he was returned to Germany on a freighter similar to that portrayed here and sent to the Russian front as part of his punishment.

p, Aaron Rosenberg; d, Bernhard Wicki; w, Daniel Taradash, based on the novel by Werne Joerg Luedecke; ed, Joseph Silver; ph, Conrad Hall; m, Jerry Goldsmith.

(PR:C   MPAA:NR)

MOROCCO****

(1930) 90m PAR bw

Gary Cooper *(Tom Brown)*, Marlene Dietrich *(Amy Jolly)*, Adolphe Menjou *(Le Bessier)*, Ullrich Haupt *(Adjutant Caesar)*, Juliette Compton *(Anna Dolores)*, Francis McDonald *(Cpl. Tatoche)*, Albert Conti *(Col. Quinnevieres)*, Eve Southern *(Mme. Caesar)*, Michael Visaroff *(Barratire)*, Paul Porcasi *(Lo Tinto)*.

Marlene Dietrich's first American film was this stylish, poetic, and atmospheric tale of love during wartime, directed by the brilliant Josef von Sternberg. Amy Jolly (Dietrich), a German singer, arrives in North Africa and is soon hired as the lead act in a cabaret frequented by members of the Foreign Legion. She is pursued by Le Bessier (Adolphe Menjou), a worldly gentleman, but finds herself attracted to Tom Brown (Gary Cooper), the handsome Legionnaire she secretly invites to her room. When Tom does visit her, he shocks her with his indifference and leaves; it seems Amy has never been refused by any man. Tom is sent off on a dangerous mission, but fails to return to the desert city, deciding instead to remain in his desert outpost. Fearing that he has been killed or wounded, Amy searches for him or news of his condition. When she finally locates him, in a cheap bar with a local woman, he explains that he is again being shipped out on another mission. Refusing to let her man leave again without her, Amy, along with a group of women who are wholly devoted to the Legionnaires, follows Tom into the desert. An intelligent story of devotion, MOROCCO is slim on plot but heavy on atmosphere. The movie exists solely to give Sternberg the opportunity to create a poetic world of his own, peopled with characters (specifically Dietrich) and situations that do not exist in the real world, especially in a Moroccan desert city. Although MOROCCO is set during wartime and is populated with members of the Foreign Legion, Sternberg is concerned with a different legion—"a foreign legion of woman," in Sternberg's words, as devoted to their men as the men are to the military. Includes the Dietrich number "What Am I Bid for My Apples?" by Leo Robin and Karl Hajos.

p, Hector Turnbull; d, Joseph von Sternberg; w, Jules Furthman, based on the novel *Amy Jolly* by Benno Vigny; ed, Sam Winston; ph, Lee Garmes and Lucien Ballard; m, Karl Hajos.

(PR:C   MPAA:NR)

MOUSE THAT ROARED, THE****

(1959, Brit.) 83m Open Road/COL c

Peter Sellers *(Tully Bascombe/Grand Duchess Gloriana XII/Prime Minister Count Mountjoy)*, Jean Seberg *(Helen)*, David Kossoff *(Prof. Kokintz)*, William Hartnell *(Will)*, Timothy Bateson *(Roger)*, MacDonald Parke *(Snippet)*, Monty Landis *(Cobbley)*, Leo McKern *(Benter)*, Harold Kasket *(Pedro)*, Colin Gordon *(BBC Announcer)*, George Margo *(O'Hara)*, Robin Gatehouse *(Mulligan)*, Mavis Villiers *(Telephone Operator)*.

THE MOUSE THAT ROARED is the outlandish, sidesplitting tale of the fortunes of the Duchy of Grand Fenwick, a mythical land on the verge of bankruptcy because its one export, a fine wine, has been copied and undercut by a US company. Grand Fenwick's prime minister (Peter Sellers) and female monarch (Sellers again) cook up a scheme to solve the problem: they will declare war on the States, lose immediately, then get back in the black with all the aid that the US usually bestows upon its beaten foes. They send out an "army" of 20, clad in armor and carrying bows and arrows, led by Tully Bascombe (Sellers once more). Of course, the arrival of these ragtag warriors in New York leads to a series of very funny situations, including the group's inadvertent acquisition of the "Q-bomb," a weapon that makes them a genuine threat. In the meantime, Bascombe meets and falls in love with Helen (Jean Seberg), the daughter of a scientist. Besides the wonderful Sellers, there are fine performances from all, especially Leo McKern as the pompous leader of Grand Fenwick's "loyal opposition." An inferior sequel, MOUSE ON THE MOON (1963), was directed by Richard Lester.

p, Jon Pennington and Walter Shenson; d, Jack Arnold; w, Roger MacDougall and Stanley Mann, based on the novel *The Wrath of the Grapes* by Leonard Wibberley; ed, Raymond Poulton; ph, John Wilcox, Eastmancolor; m, Edwin Astley.

(PR:AAA   MPAA:NR)

MRS. MINIVER*****

(1942) 134m MGM bw

Greer Garson *(Kay Miniver)*, Walter Pidgeon *(Clem Miniver)*, Teresa Wright *(Carol Beldon)*, Dame May Whitty *(Lady Beldon)*, Henry Travers *(Mr. Ballard)*, Reginald Owen *(Foley)*, Henry Wilcoxon *(Vicar)*, Richard Ney *(Vin Miniver)*,

Clare Sandars *(Judy Miniver)*, Christopher Severn *(Toby Miniver)*, Brenda Forbes *(Gladys, the Housemaid)*, Rhys Williams *(Horace Perkins)*, Marie De Becker *(Ada, the Cook)*, Helmut Dantine *(German Flier)*, Mary Field *(Miss Spriggins)*, Tom Conway *(Man)*.

A visually stunning and emotionally rich vision of a country at war, MRS. MINIVER tells of the British people's will to survive the German bombing raids and fight to the end for their own human dignity. Director William Wyler achieves his goal by concentrating on the inhabitants of the country village of Belham, especially the middle-class Miniver family—Kay Miniver (Greer Garson), husband Clem (Walter Pidgeon), eldest son Vin (Richard Ney) and younger children Toby and Judy (Christopher Severn and Clare Sandars). As the country slips into war, Vin falls in love with Carol (Teresa Wright), the teenage daughter of village matriarch Lady Beldon (Dame May Whitty). As romance grows and the village prepares for its annual flower-growing competition, German bombs begin to decimate the once-peaceful countryside and a downed German aviator seeks refuge with the Minivers. Villagers die, the Miniver home is bombed, and the church is reduced to rubble, but the people's spirit is strengthened when the vicar (Henry Wilcoxon) delivers a powerful speech, concluding: "This is not only a war of soldiers in uniform. It is a war of the people—of all people, and it must be fought not only on the battlefield, but in the cities and in the villages, in the factories and on the farms, in the home and in the heart of every man, woman, and child who loves freedom." When Winston Churchill saw the film, he maintained that MRS. MINIVER would prove more valuable than the combined efforts of six divisions. At Oscar time, MRS. MINIVER was named Best Picture; statuettes were also given to Garson (Actress); Wyler (Director); Wright (Supporting Actress); Joseph Ruttenberg (Cinematography); Arthur Wimperis, George Froeschel, James Hilton, and Claudine West (Screenplay); and producer Sidney Franklin (the Irving G. Thalberg Memorial Award). Only Pidgeon lost out, the votes in the Best Actor category going to James Cagney for his performance in YANKEE DOODLE DANDY.

p, Sidney Franklin; d, William Wyler; w, Arthur Wimperis, George Froeschel, James Hilton, and Claudine West, based on the novel by Jan Struther; ed, Harold F. Kress; ph, Joseph Ruttenberg; m, Herbert Stothart.

(PR:A   MPAA:NR)

MURPHY'S WAR**½

(1971, Brit.) 106m Yates-Deeley-London Screenplays/PAR c

Peter O'Toole *(Murphy)*, Sian Phillips *(Dr. Hayden)*, Philippe Noiret *(Louis Brezan)*, Horst Janson *(Kapitan Lauchs)*, John Hallam *(Lt. Ellis)*, Ingo Mogendorf *(Lt. Voght)*.

This unsatisfying war adventure is worth watching only for the central performances of Peter O'Toole as Murphy, an Irish seaman with a vendetta against a German U-boat; Sian Phillips (O'Toole's real-life wife at the time) as Hayden, a doctor who nurses Murphy back to health; and Philippe Noiret as the French engineer who saves Murphy's life. In the final days of WW II, Murphy is a member of the crew of an armed British merchant ship that is sunk off the coast of Venezuela by a German U-boat. The seamen who survive the initial attack, floundering helplessly in the water, are mercilessly machine-gunned to death by the U-boat's commander, but Murphy survives and eventually winds up at a remote mission along the banks of the Orinoco. There, he learns that the U-boat is hiding upriver, camouflaged and quietly awaiting the signing of the Armistice. Murphy, however is bent on revenge, and plans to carry out his personal vendetta against the vessel, even after the war has ended. Though little more than a third-rate AFRICAN QUEEN, MURPHY'S WAR does boast some exciting action scenes and a picturesque South American locale. Unfortunately, the script drags, and the film sputters along like Murphy's dilapidated warplane. What promises to be an effective relationship between Murphy and Dr. Hayden, a la Bogart and Hepburn, is quickly overshadowed by Murphy's slide into madness and his senseless vendetta, while the supposed antiwar message of the picture gets oddly obscured as Murphy wages war for personal reasons *after* the Armistice is signed—a curious warping of pacifist sentiments, especially in a film made during the Vietnam years.

p, Michael Deeley; d, Peter Yates; w, Stirling Silliphant, based on the novel by Max Catto; ed, Frank P. Keller and John Glen; ph, Douglas Slocombe, Panavision, Eastmancolor; m, John Barry and Ken Thorne.

(PR:C-O   MPAA:GP)

MY NAME IS IVAN****

(1962, USSR) 97m Mosfilm/Sig Shore bw (IVANOVO DETSTVO; AKA: IVAN'S CHILDHOOD, THE YOUNGEST SPY)

Kolya Burlyayev *(Ivan)*, Valentin Zubkov *(Capt. Kholin)*, Ye. Zharikov *(Lt. Galtsev)*, S. Krylov *(Cpl. Katasonych)*, N. Grinko *(Col. Gryaznov)*, D. Milyutenko *(Old Man)*, V. Malyavina *(Masha)*, I. Tarkovsky *(Ivan's Mother)*.

This first feature from Soviet director Andrei Tarkovsky, an intense cinematic poem about war and childhood, presents the most horrific account of war's ravaging effect on a child's innocence since Roberto Rossellini's GERMANY, YEAR ZERO. Like Rossellini's Edmund, Tarkovsky's Ivan (Kolya Burlyayev) is a 12-year-old man/boy who has known little else but war—war that has forced him to become an adult and (in the irony of the actual translated title) robbed him of his childhood. When first seen, Ivan might be assumed to be an average youngster, till he is shown trekking, neck-deep, through a murky swamp. This swamp is at the enemy's front line, to which Ivan, a member of a WW II Russian military intelligence unit, has been sent to gather information on troop movements. Ivan has only a cause and a country: his town has been overrun by the Germans, his father murdered, his mother shot and killed, his sister blown apart by a bomb. Although his superiors are pleased with his efforts, they protectively transfer him to the rear, but Ivan rebels at this and is allowed to go on one more mission. Much more than a war film about a young boy, MY

NAME IS IVAN is a pure film experience. Tarkovsky fills the frame with beautiful images composed in extreme high, low, or tilted angles; uses an unpredictable editing style that alternates between rapid, jarring cuts and carefully composed long takes; employs a stark black-and-white contrast, which often turns natural scenery into abstract imagery; and constructs a soundtrack that is as inventive as his visuals. Complementing Tarkovsky's vision is the performance of Burlyayev, whose face expresses both determination and tenderness. Highly praised upon its release—it won awards at the Venice Film Festival for Best Film, Director, and Actor—MY NAME IS IVAN has found a new audience with the rising international recognition of Tarkovsky. The videocassette is in Russian with English subtitles, though the subtitles are often out of frame.

d, Andrei Tarkovsky; w, Vladimir Osipovich Bogomolov, Mikhail Papava, and E. Smirnov, based on the short story "Ivan" by Vladimir Osipovich Bogomolov; ed, L. Feyginova; ph, Vadim Yusov; m, Vyacheslav Ovchinnikov.

(PR:O MPAA:NR)

N

NAKED AND THE DEAD, THE*½

(1958) 131m RKO-Gregjac/WB c

Aldo Ray (Croft), Cliff Robertson (Hearn), Raymond Massey (Gen. Cummings), Lili St. Cyr (Lily), William Campbell (Brown), Barbara Nichols (Mildred), Richard Jaeckel (Gallagher), James Best (Ridges), Joey Bishop (Roth), Jerry Paris (Goldstein), Robert Gist (Red), L.Q. Jones (Wilson), Casey Adams (Dalleson).

The Naked and the Dead, thought by many to be the finest novel written about WW II, is disappointingly truncated and toned down in this (still violent) adaptation, which steamrolls Norman Mailer's dark depiction of the horrors of war into just another WW II film. Mailer's doomed dogfaces, killed one by one as they participate in the taking of a small Pacific island, are transformed into a standard WW II "melting pot" platoon, much to the film's detriment. Cliff Robertson plays the admirable Lt. Hearn, Raymond Massey is his close-minded superior, Aldo Ray a brutal sergeant. Although none of their performances are particulary distinguished, the supporting players—including Joey Bishop, L.Q. Jones, Jerry Paris, and Richard Jaeckel—turn in much more solid work, and the film does offer a number of excellent combat scenes.

p, Paul Gregory; d, Raoul Walsh; w, Denis Sanders and Terry Sanders, based on the novel by Norman Mailer; ed, Arthur P. Schmidt; ph, Joseph LaShelle, WarnerScope, Technicolor; m, Bernard Herrmann.

(PR:O MPAA:NR)

NAPOLEON***

(1955, Fr.) 115m Filmsonor-CLM-Francinex/Cinedis c

Jean Pierre Aumont (Renault de Saint-Jean d'Angely), Jeanne Boitel (Mme. de Dino), Pierre Brasseur (Barras), Gianna-Maria Canale (Pauline Borghese), Daniel Gelin (Bonaparte), Raymond Pellegrin (Napoleon), Danielle Darrieux (Eleonore Denuelle), Sacha Guitry (Talleyrand), Michele Morgan (Josephine de Beauharnais), Dany Robin (Desiree Clary), Erich von Stroheim (Beethoven), Orson Welles (Hudson Lowe), Jean Gabin (Marshal Lannes), Jean Marais (Count de Montholon), Yves Montand (Marshal Lefebvre), Patachou (Mme. Sans-Gene), Micheline Presle (Hortense de Beauharnais), Maria Schell (Marie-Louis d'Autriche).

The life, loves, and military campaigns of Napoleon are brought to the screen in this opus from French stage and screen director-writer-actor Sacha Guitry. Not the masterpiece that Abel Gance's silent NAPOLEON is, Guitry's retelling is just that—Guitry, as Talleyrand, telling his friends about various episodes in Napoleon's life. Guitry re-creates the period with the help of legendary art director Eugene Lourie and a cast that includes two of the cinema's greatest directors—Orson Welles (as Sir Hudson Lowe) and Erich von Stroheim (as Beethoven, whose "Eroica" symphony is said to have been originally dedicated to Napoleon). As expected, most of the highlights of Napoleon's career are here—the campaigns of Italy, Austria, and Egypt; his rise to emperor; his return from Elba and the Battle of Waterloo; and his involvement with both Josephine and Desiree (affairs fictionalized in the 1954 Marlon Brando film DESIREE). Originally released at 190 minutes, the videocassette version has been reduced to 115 minutes and dubbed into English.

d, Sacha Guitry; w, Sacha Guitry; ed, Raymond Lamy; ph, Pierre Montazel, Eastmancolor; m, Jean Francaix.

(PR:A MPAA:NR)

NICHOLAS AND ALEXANDRA***½

(1971, Brit.) 183m Horizon/COL c

Michael Jayston (Nicholas II), Janet Suzman (Alexandra), Roderic Noble (Alexis), Ania Marson (Olga), Lynne Frederick (Tatiana), Candace Glendenning (Marie), Fiona Fullerton (Anastasia), Harry Andrews (Grand Duke Nicholas), Irene Worth (The Queen Mother), Tom Baker (Rasputin), Jack Hawkins (Count Fredericks), Laurence Olivier (Count Witte), Eric Porter (Stolypin), Michael Redgrave (Sazonov), Michael Bryant (Lenin), Brian Cox (Trotsky), James Hazeldine (Stalin), Curt Jurgens (German Consul Sklarz).

This lavish, overlong production chronicles the downfall of the last Russian czar, Nicholas II (Michael Jayston), and his wife, Alexandra (Janet Suzman). The film concentrates on their troubled family life, especially the affliction of their only son, Alexis (Roderic Noble), with hemophilia. Nicholas' preoccupation with this tragedy influences state decisions and increases his disengagement from his starving people, while Alexandra falls completely under the influence of the profligate peasant monk Rasputin (Tom

Baker), believing that his mystic powers can heal her son. Rasputin's power increases in the Imperial Court despite Nicholas' weak efforts to maintain authority; meanwhile, hundreds are slaughtered at the Winter Palace, fueling Lenin (Michael Bryant) and Trotsky's (Brian Cox) crusade to overthrow "Bloody Nicholas." As the tide of assassination and unrest rises, an ill-prepared Russia suffers terrible losses in WW I, setting the stage for revolution in 1917 and the execution of the deposed czar and family in July 1918. While it remains a treat for the eyes, NICHOLAS AND ALEXANDRA suffers from the filmmakers' attempts to tell too much. Its overview of more than two decades of tumultuous, epochal history develops few of its famous figures beyond caricature (although Baker, of "Dr. Who" fame, plays Rasputin with flamboyance and verve), and the failure to bring Nicholas and Alexandra to life—despite the script's intimate and sympathetic treatment of the pair—is especially critical. Shot on location in Spain and Yugoslavia, the film won Oscars for Best Art Direction, Set Decoration, and Costumes.

p, Sam Spiegel; d, Franklin J. Schaffner; w, James Goldman and Edward Bond, based on a book by Robert K. Massie; ed, Ernest Walter; ph, Freddie Young, Panavision, Eastmancolor; m, Richard Rodney Bennett.

(PR:C MPAA:GP)

NIGHT OF THE GENERALS, THE***

(1967, Brit./Fr.) 148m Horizon-Filmsonor/COL c (LA NUIT DE GENERAUX)

Peter O'Toole *(Gen. Tanz)*, Omar Sharif *(Maj. Grau)*, Tom Courtenay *(Cpl. Hartmann)*, Donald Pleasence *(Gen. Kahlenberge)*, Joanna Pettet *(Ulrike von Seidlitz-Gabler)*, Philippe Noiret *(Inspector Morand)*, Charles Gray *(Gen. von Seidlitz-Gabler)*, Coral Browne *(Eleanore von Seidlitz-Gabler)*, John Gregson *(Col. Sandauer)*, Nigel Stock *(Otto)*, Christopher Plummer *(Field Marshal Rommel)*, Juliette Greco *(Juliette)*.

Set against the backdrop of WW II, this hit-and-miss mystery, told in flashback, begins in Warsaw in 1942 with the murder of a prostitute who doubles as an agent for German intelligence. The prime suspects are three German generals—Tanz (Peter O'Toole), Kahlenberge (Donald Pleasence), and von Seidlitz-Gabler (Charles Gray)—but when the investigating officer, Maj. Grau (Omar Sharif), becomes too determined in his pursuit of the culprit, he is transferred. Two years later in Paris, another prostitute is killed. Again Grau is on hand, but when he confronts the psychotic Tanz, who is clearly the murderer, the general frames his driver, Cpl. Hartmann (Tom Courtenay), and then kills Grau, claiming the major was involved in an unsuccessful attempt to assassinate Hitler. Many years later, at a neo-Nazi rally, Tanz, the honored guest, recently released from a long prison stay for his war crimes, is confronted by the Paris detective (Philippe Noiret) who helped Grau with his 1944 murder investigation. What's more, the Frenchman has brought along Hartmann, who has identified the former general as the killer. THE NIGHT OF THE GENERALS is not entirely successful in its attempt to parallel individual killings with the sanctioned mass murder of war, chiefly because of its frequently confusing multiple flashback structure and a less than effective performance by O'Toole. Still, most of the other performances are strong and the film does offer a few terrific moments, including the dramatic confrontation between Grau and Tanz.

p, Sam Spiegel; d, Anatole Litvak; w, Joseph Kessel and Paul Dehn, based on the books *Die Nacht der Generale* by Hans Helmut Kirst and *The Wary Transgressor* by James Hadley Chase; ed, Alan Osbiston; ph, Henri Decae, Panavision, Technicolor; m, Maurice Jarre.

(PR:O MPAA:NR)

NIGHT OF THE SHOOTING STARS, THE***

(1982, It.) 106m RAI Radiotelevisione-Ager CinematograficaPremier/UA c (GB: NIGHT OF SAN LORENZO, THE)

Omero Antonutti *(Galvano)*, Margarita Lozano *(Concetta)*, Claudio Bigagli *(Corrado)*, Massimo Bonetti *(Nicole)*, Norma Martelli *(Ivana)*, Enrica Maria Modugno *(Mara)*, Sabina Vannucchi *(Rosanna)*.

On the night of San Lorenzo (a magical evening during which Europeans believe wishes may become fulfilled), a shooting star darts across the sky, sending a grown woman into a recollection of her childhood. As the star passes her window, she relates the events that took place in her small town during the last days of WW II: With the advancing Allies pushing the last remnants of the German army out of Italy, the Nazis enact sick and desperate revenge on the Italian civilians, staging vicious attacks on the old men, women, and children left in the villages. The members of the small town of San Miniato are divided in their opinions as to whether to remain in their village and risk dealing with the Germans, or to attempt traveling across the back roads, dodging attacks from sadistic Blackshirts, in an effort to meet the advancing Allies. One group made up of various segments of the town's population sets out on the journey, with all the old prohibitions breaking down as the people pull together in an effort to survive. An elderly peasant man with natural leadership ability is chosen to guide the group to safety. Despite a few voices of dissent, the old man brings ingenuity to his assignment and keeps the group's spirits up by showing a humane concern for all and encouraging them to watch out for one another. During the journey, he develops a romantic relationship with an aristocratic woman who has always admired him, but could never let him know because of their difference in class. Once he has guided the group out of danger, however, the townspeople immediately resume the societal roles that previously divided them. The Taviani brothers, who previously gained international attention with 1977 Cannes Film Festival Golden Palm winner PADRE PADRONE, approached this film in much the same way—using an imaginative combination of events and showing them as remembered by the narrator as she reminisces about the magical moments of her childhood—and came up with a dazzling, immensely popular film that

NIGHT PORTER, THE—

earned them the Special Jury Prize at Cannes. (In Italian; English subtitles.)

p, Giuliani G. De Negri; d, Paolo Taviani and Vittorio Taviani; w, Vittorio Taviani, Paolo Taviani, Giuliani G. De Negri, and Tonino Guerra; ed, Roberto Perpignani; ph, Franco di Giacomo, Agfacolor; m, Nicola Piovani.

(PR:O MPAA:R)

NIGHT PORTER, THE**½

(1974, It./US) 117m Edwards-Esae De Simone/AE c (IL PORTIERE DI NOTTE)

Dirk Bogarde *(Max)*, Charlotte Rampling *(Lucia)*, Philippe Leroy *(Klaus)*, Gabriele Ferzetti *(Hans)*, Giuseppe Addobbati *(Stumm)*, Isa Miranda *(Countess Stein)*, Nino Bignamini *(Adolph)*, Marino Mase *(Atherton)*, Amedeo Amodio *(Bert)*, Piero Vida *(Day Porter)*.

Filmmaker Liliana Cavani visited a Nazi concentration camp after WW II and interviewed a woman who had been involved in a sado-masochistic relationship with a guard, then made her story the basis for this powerful, sometimes ponderous film starring Dirk Bogarde as Max, the night porter in a Viennese hotel in 1958. Max's duties go far beyond the usual for a man in his position, since the hotel guests—former Nazis—and the proprietress enjoy being sadistically "dealt with" by the night porter, an ex-storm trooper. All believe they have managed to eliminate any witnesses to their war crimes, and though Max himself is about to go on trial, he too thinks he's safe, until Lucia (Charlotte Rampling) and her husband check in. Max recognizes Lucia as a former concentration camp prisoner of whom he took photographs while pretending to be a physician. That's not all, however; the picture flashes forward and back to show past episodes of rape, sodomy, and torture between Max and Lucia—episodes Lucia apparently enjoyed. Max and Lucia rekindle their strange love, but the other hotel residents are determined to stop them. A strange and unforgettable picture that questions deeply the psyches of torturers and tortured, THE NIGHT PORTER presents its psychoanalytically provocative material without exploitation, but the subject was apparently too strong for most audiences and the film never caught fire with the public. (In English.)

p, Robert Gordon Edwards; d, Liliana Cavani; w, Liliana Cavani and Italo Moscati, based on a story by Liliana Cavani, Barbara Alberti, Amedeo Pagani; ed, Franco Arcalli; ph, Alfio Contini, Technicolor; m, Daniele Paris.

(PR:O MPAA:R)

NIGHT TRAIN TO MUNICH*****

(1940, Brit.) 90m GAU/FOX bw (GB: GESTAPO; NIGHT TRAIN)

Margaret Lockwood *(Anna Bomasch)*, Rex Harrison *(Gus Bennett)*, Paul von Hernreid [Paul Henreid] *(Karl Marsen)*, Basil Radford *(Charters)*, Naunton Wayne *(Caldicott)*, James Harcourt *(Axel Bomasch)*, Felix Aylmer *(Dr. Federicks)*, Wyndham Goldie *(Dryton)*, Roland Culver *(Roberts)*, Eliot Makeham *(Schwab)*, Raymond Huntley *(Kampenfeldt)*, Austin Trevor *(Capt. Prada)*.

One of the finest spy films ever, NIGHT TRAIN TO MUNICH reflects the immense talents of its brilliant director, Carol Reed, and of scripters Frank Launder and Sydney Gilliat. After Hitler's conquest of Czechoslovakia, Anna Bomasch (Margaret Lockwood) is arrested. Her father, Axel (James Harcourt), who possesses technical information the Nazis want, has fled to England, but Anna is interred in a concentration camp. There, she meets Karl Marsen (Paul Henreid), with whom she also manages to escape to England, and in London she contacts music hall performer Gus Bennett (Rex Harrison)—who is actually a British secret agent—to get in touch with her father. In short order the Bomasches, duped by Marsen—who is himself a Gestapo plant—are taken to Germany, where the Nazis threaten Anna to secure Axel's cooperation. Bennett follows, infiltrates the Naval Ministry in Berlin, and discovers that the Bomasches are on the night train to Munich. With the help of two comedic cricketers played by Naunton Wayne and Basil Radford (who performed the same service in Alfred Hitchcock's THE LADY VANISHES), Bennett boards the train and is able to free father and daughter, leading to the trio's final flight to Switzerland, with Marsen and the SS in hot pursuit. Though action-packed with one harrowing scene after another, the film is not broadly played, and Reed employs subtlety over bravado. Its portrayal of the Germans, too, is fairly balanced, without the propagandistic characterizations that would mark films made later in the war. Harrison is perfect as the daring, suave British spy; Lockwood is fine as his love interest; and Henried is appropriately subtle as the deceiving Marsen in this gripping, razor-edged melodrama that mounts to a stunning climax.

p, Edward Black; d, Carol Reed; w, Sydney Gilliat and Frank Launder, based on a story by Gordon Wellesley; ed, R.E. Dearing; ph, Otto Kanturek.

(PR:A MPAA:NR)

NIGHTWARS**

(1988) 88m Action Intl. c

Brian O'Connor *(Trent Matthews)*, Dan Haggerty *(Dr. Campbell)*, Cameron Smith *(Jim Lowry)*, Steve Horton, Chet Hood, Jill Foor, Mike Hickam, David Ott, Kimberley Casey.

A sort of A NIGHTMARE ON ELM STREET 3 meets PLATOON, NIGHTWARS concerns Trent Matthews (Brian O'Connor) and Jim Lowry (Cameron Smith), Vietnam vets who suffer from nightmares that propel them back into the jungle. Racked with guilt for having left a buddy behind, the duo relive the horror every night, then awake to find that the wounds they suffer in their dreams have actually appeared on their bodies. They turn to vet-turned-psychiatrist Dr. Campbell (Dan Haggerty) for help; not surprisingly, he doesn't believe their stories and sedates them—*making* them sleep. When some nightmare machine-gun fire kills Trent's wife, however, the shrink finally takes heed. Determined to end the terror, Trent and Jim don their uniforms and arm themselves to do battle with their demons in dreamland.

p, Fritz Matthews; d, David A. Prior; w, David A. Prior; ed, Reinhard Schreiner; ph, Stephen Ashley Blake; m, Tim James, Steve McClintick, and Mark Mancina.

(PR:O MPAA:R)

1941**½

(1979) 118m UNIV-COL-A-Team/UNIV c

Dan Aykroyd *(Sgt. Tree)*, Ned Beatty *(Ward Douglas)*, John Belushi *(Wild Bill Kelso)*, Lorraine Gary *(Joan Douglas)*, Murray Hamilton *(Claude)*, Christopher Lee *(Von Kleinschmidt)*, Tim Matheson *(Birkhead)*, Toshiro Mifune *(Comdr. Mitamura)*, Warren Oates *(Maddox)*, Robert Stack *(Gen. Stilwell)*, Treat Williams *(Sitarski)*, Nancy Allen *(Donna)*, John Candy *(Foley)*, Elisha Cook, Jr. *(Patron)*, Patti LuPone *(Lydia Hedberg)*, Penny Marshall *(Miss Fitzroy)*, Slim Pickens *(Hollis Wood)*, Lionel Stander *(Scioli)*, Dub Taylor *(Malcomb)*.

A massive, spectacular, all-star, notoriously big-budgeted slapstick comedy in the IT'S A MAD, MAD, MAD, MAD WORLD vein, 1941 is loaded with slam-bang sight gags and action, but comedy isn't director Steven Spielberg's forte and the movie isn't nearly as funny as it could have been. Taken from an inspired script by Robert Zemeckis (future director of BACK TO THE FUTURE and WHO FRAMED ROGER RABBIT), Bob Gale, and John Milius, 1941 is very loosely based on a real event that came to be known as the "Great Los Angeles Air Raid" and occurred on February 26, 1942, as mass hysteria broke out in southern California after a Japanese submarine was spotted off Santa Barbara. With the date changed to December 13, 1941, and the event turned into a situation ripe for broad comedy by the screenwriters, the story juggles as many as seven different story lines simultaneously and features dozens of characters. After the bombing of Pearl Harbor, Gen. Stilwell (Robert Stack) is appointed commander of the West Coast and ordered to repel any Japanese invasion. Tanks are placed in downtown Los Angeles; anti-aircraft guns are deployed on the rooftops of buildings; along the beaches, 40mm cannon are positioned, one of them placed outside the seaside home of Ward Douglas (Ned Beatty), a patriotic private citizen. When Comdr. Mitamura's (Toshiro Mifune) submarine is spotted surfacing off Santa Barbara, all hell breaks loose in LA, as gung-ho fighter pilot Wild Bill Kelso (John Belushi), an Army tank crew (with the likes of Dan Aykroyd and John Candy aboard), and a bevy of private citizens rise to Hollywood's defense. Star-studded and loaded with millions of dollars worth of state-of-the-art special effects (Hollywood Blvd. was re-created in miniature), 1941 is hilarious at times, but not consistently so. Spielberg admitted that his grasp of subtle comedic timing was tenuous at best, so the director opted to assault the viewer with one spectacular gag after another, presented at a breathless pace. The result is merely numbing, and with the exception of a few genuinely eye-opening scenes, most of 1941 is remarkable only for its fiscal decadence. While the all-star cast of young comedians perform familiar shtick (Belushi's Kelso is just a retread of his Bluto from ANIMAL HOUSE), the funniest moments come from such veteran character actors as Slim Pickens, Warren Oates, Beatty, Murray Hamilton, Christopher Lee, Mifune, Elisha Cook, Lionel Stander, and Dub Taylor. Spielberg's expensive pyrotechnics may dazzle the easily impressed, but the lasting memories of 1941 are of the smaller moments, as when Mifune's Japanese commander and Lee's Nazi observer bicker aboard the submarine, when Pickens is captured by an enemy who doesn't know what to make of him, and when Stack, as Gen. Stilwell, sits awestruck and misty-eyed watching DUMBO in a theater.

p, Buzz Feitshans; d, Steven Spielberg; w, Robert Zemeckis and Bob Gale, based on a story by Robert Zemeckis, Bob Gale, John Milius; ed, Michael Kahn; ph, William A. Fraker, Panavision 70, Metrocolor; m, John Williams.

(PR:C-O MPAA:PG)

NO DEAD HEROES zero

(1987) 86m Cineventures-Maharaj-Miller c

Max Thayer *(Lt. Ric Sanders)*, John Dresden *(Capt. Harry Cotter)*, Toni Nero *(Barbara Perez)*, Nick Nicholson *(Ivan Dimanovitch)*, Mike Monty *(Frank Baylor)*, Dave Anderson *(Gen. Craig)*.

MISSING IN ACTION meets THE MANCHURIAN CANDIDATE in this poorly conceived and abysmally executed espionage drama. When a secret mission to free a CIA agent from a North Vietnamese POW camp collapses, Capt. Harry Cotter (John Dresden) helps Lt. Ric Sanders (Max Thayer) board the evacuation helicopter but is forced to remain behind himself. Ten years later, after being programmed to kill in Moscow (a tiny microchip implanted in his brain), Cotter is sent to the States to eliminate Sanders' and his own family, then dispatched to Central America to assassinate the Pope. Sanders is given special training by the CIA and sent to track down Cotter, whom he catches up with in El Salvador. There Sanders, aided by a beautiful double agent (Toni Nero), has to battle with Cotter, his sadistic Russian controller (Nick Nicholson), and a collection of "rebels." There may have been some potential in the story, but the strictly amateur-hour production values undermine whatever serious content might have been intended by such florid dialog as: "We are the watchdogs of the world; if we go to sleep, the Communists will steal our freedoms like thieves in the night." People don't even die interestingly in this film, tipping over like felled trees.

p, J.C. Miller; d, J.C. Miller; w, J.C. Miller and Arthur N. Gelfield; ed, Edgar Vine; ph, Freddie C. Grant; m, Marita M. Wellman.

(PR:O MPAA:NR)

NO DRUMS, NO BUGLES**½

(1971) 85m Cinerama Releasing Corp. c

Martin Sheen *(Ashby Gatrell)*, Davey Davidson *(Callie*

NORTH STAR, THE—

Gatrell), Rod McCary *(Lieutenant)*, Denine Terry *(Sarah)*, Carmen Costi, Ray Marsh, Frank Stubock, Bob Wagner, Edward Underwood *(Foxhunters)*.

Martin Sheen gives a strong, sensitive performance as Ashby Gatrell, a Virginian who refuses to face the possibility of looking down a gunsight at friends or relatives during the Civil War. Instead, he hides out in a cave for the duration of the war, living a primitive existence, occasionally learning news of the war and his family from the conversations of passersby he monitors from hiding. Novelist-turned-director Clyde Ware's camera records Ashby's rustic life with much style, using the West Virginia locations nicely, and his well-paced story is never compromised by effusive sentimentality. In the final analysis, however, it is Sheen's wholly believable performance that carries the film.

p, Clyde Ware; d, Clyde Ware; w, Clyde Ware; ed, David Bretherton and Richard Halsey; ph, Richard McCarthy and Parker Bartlett, Techniscope, Technicolor; m, Lyle Ritz.

(PR:A   MPAA:G)

NORTH STAR, THE**½

(1943) 105m Goldwyn/RKO bw (AKA: ARMORED ATTACK!)

Anne Baxter *(Marina)*, Farley Granger *(Damian)*, Jane Withers *(Claudia)*, Eric Roberts *(Grisha)*, Dana Andrews *(Kolya)*, Walter Brennan *(Karp)*, Dean Jagger *(Rodion)*, Ann Harding *(Sophia)*, Carl Benton Reid *(Boris)*, Ann Carter *(Olga)*, Walter Huston *(Dr. Kurin)*, Erich von Stroheim *(Dr. Otto von Harden)*, Paul Guilfoyle *(Iakin)*.

During WW II, President Franklin Delano Roosevelt called upon Hollywood to pay tribute to America's valiant Russian allies, and Samuel Goldwyn Studios (of which Roosevelt's son James was then president) was the first to heed the call. Playwright Lillian Hellman was enlisted to write the script, Lewis Milestone directed, and gifted cinematographer James Wong Howe took care of the cameras for this story of a Ukrainian farm collective, the North Star, and the gallant reaction of its people (including Walter Huston, Anne Baxter, Farley Granger, and Dana Andrews) when the Germans invade. With the invader's arrival, some of the villagers take to the hills to become guerrillas, while others torch stocks that would be of value to the enemy. Under the direction of Dr. Otto von Harden (Erich von Stroheim), who claims only to be carrying out his orders, the Germans forcibly take blood from the children of the North Star for transfusions for wounded soldiers. In time, however, the guerrillas attack and, despite heavy losses, rout the Germans. While certainly competent and reasonably entertaining, the film does come off a bit obviously as propaganda, and even at the time of its release Red-baiters were more than willing to take its Soviet advocacy to task. Moreover, at the height of the McCarthy witch-hunts in the 1950s, the filmmakers were called before the House Un-American Activities Committee to explain their reasons for making the film. Then, in 1957, 22 minutes were cut from the film, including most of the character development and every mention of the word "comrade." A spokesman from NTA,

the company that released this politically corrected version under the title ARMORED ATTACK! noted that "the only thing we couldn't take out was Dana Andrews running around in a damn Soviet uniform."

p, William Cameron Menzies; d, Lewis Milestone; w, Lillian Hellman, based on her story; ed, Daniel Mandell; ph, James Wong Howe; m, Aaron Copland.

(PR:A-C   MPAA:NR)

NORTHERN PURSUIT***

(1943) 94m WB bw

Errol Flynn *(Steve Wagner)*, Julie Bishop *(Laura McBain)*, Helmut Dantine *(Col. von Keller)*, John Ridgely *(Jim Austin)*, Gene Lockhart *(Ernst)*, Tom Tully *(Inspector Barnett)*, Bernard Nedell *(Dagor)*, Warren Douglas *(Sergeant)*, Monte Blue *(Jean)*, Alec Craig *(Angus McBain)*, Carl Harbaugh *(Radio Operator)*, John Forsythe, Robert Kent *(Soldiers)*, Richard Allord *(Preisser)*, Jay Silverheels

Set in Canada, this compelling WW II actioner presents the dashing Errol Flynn in the role of a traitor . . . or at least that's what he appears to be through much of the film. When Steve Wagner (Flynn), a Mountie with German-born parents, learns that the man he has rescued is a German spy, he reveals his sympathies for the Fatherland and sets out to help Col. von Keller (Helmut Dantine) complete his mission. The German remains skeptical, however, and demands that Wagner bring along girl friend Laura McBain (Julie Bishop) as a kind of hostage. Wagner then proceeds to lead von Keller and several other German agents to the site of their rendezvous with a bomber that will strike select targets they have identified. But with the mission on the brink of successful completion, what better time for Wagner to show his true colors? Flynn, who had been rejected by every branch of the military because of a multitude of physical problems, collapsed during the making of this fast-paced film, the result of a bout with tuberculosis. NORTHERN PURSUIT, for all its comic book heroics, is nevertheless entertaining and expertly directed by action helmsman Raoul Walsh. The great swashbuckler Flynn had lost none of his dash, Bishop is alluring, and Dantine is properly repulsive as the heavy.

p, Jack Chertok; d, Raoul Walsh; w, Frank Gruber and Alvah Bessie, based on the story "Five Thousand Trojan Horses" by Leslie T. White; ed, Jack Killifer; ph, Sid Hickox; m, Adolph Deutsch.

(PR:A   MPAA:NR)

NURSE EDITH CAVELL***

(1939) 95m Imperadio/RKO bw

Anna Neagle *(Nurse Edith Cavell)*, Edna May Oliver *(Countess de Mavon)*, George Sanders *(Capt. Heinrichs)*, May Robson *(Mme. Rappard)*, ZaSu Pitts *(Mme. Moulin)*, H.B. Warner *(Mr. Gibson)*, Sophie Stewart *(Sister Watkins)*, Mary Howard *(Nurse O'Brien)*, Robert Coote *(Bungey)*, Martin Kosleck *(Pierre)*.

WAR MOVIES

Released only days after the start of WW II, British producer-director Herbert Wilcox's remake of his own 1928 silent is a poignant biography with a strong antiwar message. Anna Neagle plays nurse Edith Cavell, who works in a hospital in German-occupied Brussels where casualties from both sides of WW I are treated. However, nurse Cavell and several other capable women (ZaSu Pitts, Edna May Oliver, May Robson) also operate an underground network that helps escaped POWs make their way to safety in Holland—that is until the Germans learn of her activity and execute the courageous nurse for espionage. Uncompromising in its portrait of the ravages of war, NURSE EDITH CAVELL is much less interested in pointing an accusing finger at the Germans than it is in indicting war itself.

p, Herbert Wilcox; d, Herbert Wilcox; w, Michael Hogan, based on the novel *Dawn* by Capt. Reginald Berkeley; ed, Elmo Williams; ph, F.A. Young and Joseph H. August.

(PR:A MPAA:NR)

O

OBJECTIVE, BURMA!****

(1945) 142m WB bw

Errol Flynn *(Maj. Nelson)*, James Brown *(Sgt. Treacy)*, William Prince *(Lt. Jacobs)*, George Tobias *(Gabby Gordon)*, Henry Hull *(Mark Williams)*, Warner Anderson *(Col. Carter)*, John Alvin *(Hogan)*, Mark Stevens *(Lt. Barker)*, Richard Erdman *(Nebraska Hooper)*, Anthony Caruso *(Miggleori)*, Hugh Beaumont *(Capt. Hennessey)*, John Whitney *(Negulesco)*, Joel Allen *(Brophy)*, George Tyne [Buddy Yarus] *(Soapy)*, Rod Redwing *(Sgt. Chattu)*, William Hudson *(Hollis)*, Lester Matthews *(Maj. Fitzpatrick)*.

This is one of the finest WW II films made during the war, and Errol Flynn, discarding his usual impudent and pranksterish style, is terrific as the straightforward and very human leader of 50 American paratroops who drop behind enemy lines to destroy a Japanese radar station. The commandos complete their mission successfully, but while waiting to rendezvous with the rescue planes they are attacked by a force of Japanese and have to fight their way out of the Burmese jungle on foot. Flynn gives one of his most convincing and powerful performances, and Raoul Walsh's direction is nothing less than excellent, with the great action director maintaining a harrowing pace, providing a wealth of interesting military detail, and delivering one thrilling scene after another. Alvah Bessie, who would later become one of the "Hollywood Ten" writers indicted by HUAC, provided the engrossing story, marked by its relative lack of patriotic speechifying and some marvelously entertaining banter between the experienced commandos. Exceptional, too, is the dynamic, masterful score by Franz Waxman, which fits the mood and menace of the mysterious jungle and incorporates the sounds of wild animals and exotic birds. James Wong Howe's splendid photography, with its naturalistic lighting, lends a great deal of authenticity to the jungle scenes, especially when one considers that the film was shot almost entirely on the "Lucky" Baldwin Santa Anita ranch outside Pasadena. The film received rave reviews and heavy box-office support in the US, but when OBJECTIVE, BURMA! was released in England, the British press exploded, claiming that the film minimized the efforts of the British in Burma by giving the impression that an American commando team liberated the area by themselves. The film was banned in Britain until 1952, when prints were reissued with a prolog extolling the British contribution to the campaign.

p, Jerry Wald; d, Raoul Walsh; w, Ranald MacDougall and Lester Cole, based on a story by Alvah Bessie; ed, George Amy; ph, James Wong Howe; m, Franz Waxman.

(PR:A MPAA:NR)

ODD ANGRY SHOT, THE**½

(1979, Aus.) 90m Samson/Roadshow c

Graham Kennedy *(Harry)*, John Hargreaves *(Bung)*, John Jarratt *(Bill)*, Bryan Brown *(Rogers)*, Graeme Blundell *(Dawson)*, Richard Moir *(Medic)*, Ian Gilmour *(Scott)*, John Allen *(Lt. Golonka)*, Brandon Burke *(Isaacs)*, Graham Rouse *(Cook)*.

An Australian film about that country's involvement in the Vietnam War, THE ODD ANGRY SHOT centers on a group of Aussie volunteers in the Special Air Service, an elite fighting unit. These men view the war as if they were competitive athletes looking forward to a sporting contest, until things become violent and bloody. Director Tom Jeffrey goes to great pains to convey a detailed sense of the sights and sounds of the fighting, both on the front lines and behind them. He is aided by the evocative lensing of Don McAlpine, who worked as a cameraman in Vietnam during the war, and by the US Department of Defense, which provided the necessary military hardware. But Jeffrey's real emphasis is on the way his soldiers react to the chaos that surrounds them, and he manages to wrench comedy from their attempts to survive in one piece. Graham Kennedy, in particular, is persuasive as a career soldier who becomes disillusioned with the army life he had embraced to escape the pressures of civilian existence.

p, Tom Jeffrey and Sue Milliken; d, Tom Jeffrey; ed, Brian Kavanagh; ph, Don McAlpine, Eastmancolor; m, Michael Carlos.

(PR:C MPAA:NR)

ODESSA FILE, THE***½

(1974, Brit./Ger.) 128m Domino-Oceanic/COL c

Jon Voight *(Peter Miller)*, Maximilian Schell *(Eduard Roschmann)*, Maria Schell *(Frau Miller)*, Mary Tamm *(Sigi)*, Derek Jacobi *(Klaus Wenzer)*, Peter Jeffrey *(David Porath)*, Klaus Lowitsch *(Gustav MacKensen)*, Kurt Meisel *(Alfred Oster)*, Hannes Messemer *(Gen. Glucks)*, Garfield Morgan *(Israeli General)*, Shmuel Rodensky *(Simon Wiesenthal)*,

OFF LIMITS—

Ernst Schroder *(Werner Deilman)*, Gunter Strack *(Police Official Kunik)*, Noel Willman *(Franz Bayer)*, Martin Brandt *(Marx)*.

Set in 1963, this fine, fast-paced, edge-of-the-seat international thriller revolves around the efforts of Peter Miller (Jon Voight), a reporter and son of a WW II German soldier, to track down some old SS men who mysteriously vanished after the war. Miller comes across the diary of a death camp survivor, and after reading the chilling narrative begins his search for Eduard Roschmann (Maximilian Schell), a Nazi who has gone into hiding. The investigation is sidetracked by members of the Odessa, a secret group of former Nazis who realize that Miller poses a threat to their existence and send a hit man after him; however, with the help of Israeli intelligence and lots of makeup, Miller assumes a new identity and infiltrates the Odessa en route to a plot-twisted finale. Maria Schell, cast as the mother of Voight's character, is actually only 12 years older than Voight, but her cameo performance is so strong that one never notices, and Voight's Miller is another in his gallery of superior portraits. Producer John Woolf and cowriter Kenneth Ross collaborated on another adaptation of a Frederick Forsyth novel, the excellent DAY OF THE JACKAL, and though this time around their film is a bit too long and very convoluted, it's a rewarding experience if one concentrates on the subtleties.

p, John Woolf; d, Ronald Neame; w, George Markstein and Kenneth Ross, based on the novel by Frederick Forsyth; ed, Ralph Kemplen; ph, Oswald Morris, Panavision, Eastmancolor; m, Andrew Lloyd Webber.

(PR:C MPAA:PG)

OFF LIMITS**

(1988) 102m FOX c (AKA: SAIGON)

Willem Dafoe *(Buck McGriff)*, Gregory Hines *(Albaby Perkins)*, Fred Ward *(Sgt. Benjamin Dix)*, Amanda Pays *(Nicole)*, Kay Tong Lim *(Lime Green)*, Scott Glenn *(Col. Dexter Armstrong)*, David Alan Grier *(Rogers)*, Keith David *(Maurice)*, Raymond O'Connor *(Staff Sgt. Flowers)*, Richard Brooks *(Preacher)*, Thuy Ann Luu *(Lanh)*, Richard Lee Reed *(Col. Sparks)*, Woody Brown *(Co-Pilot)*, Kenneth Siu *(Ploughboy)*, Viladda Vanadurongwan *(Sister Agnes)*, Norah Elizabeth Cazaux *(Mother Superior)*.

Combining the traditional whodunit with the Vietnam film subgenre, OFF LIMITS might have been an interesting reflection on the American presence in Southeast Asia; sadly, it is merely an annoyingly obvious murder mystery. Set in Saigon, 1968, OFF LIMITS stars Willem Dafoe and Gregory Hines as Buck McGriff and Albaby Perkins, plainclothes investigators with the Criminal Investigations Department (CID) of the Military Police. Ugly Americans who care little for Vietnam or its people, the two are assigned to solve the murders of six Vietnamese prostitutes with Amerasian children. Reporting to their immediate superior, Dix (Fred Ward), they hunt the killer—suspected to be a high-ranking US military man—along the way encountering antagonistic Vietnamese police chief Lime Green (Kay Tong Lim); beautiful French nun Nicole (Amanda Pays); and Col. Armstrong (Scott Glenn), whose kinky wanderings through Saigon incriminate him. Leaving a predictable trail of bodies behind them and decoyed by the usual red herrings, the sleuths finally get their man. Slickly directed by Christopher Crowe, OFF LIMITS presents Saigon (actually Bangkok) as a nighttime vision, hung ubiquitously with neon lights in a cliched visual style. The daytime scenes aren't much better, though Crowe does pack tension into a confrontation between the CID men and a crowd of hostile Vietnamese—until a US helicopter suddenly (and silently) appears in the middle of downtown Saigon to rescue the Americans. The film is full of such preposterous moments; however, Hines is terrific as the high-strung Perkins, and Ward and Glenn are also fine. PLATOON veteran Dafoe, on the other hand, seems more intent on getting the hell out of Southeast Asia than on giving a convincing performance. OFF LIMITS' view of the US presence in Vietnam as irredeemably corrupt lends it some interest, but the theme is lost in the machinations of the unsatisfying plot.

p, Alan Barnette; d, Christopher Crowe; w, Christopher Crowe and Jack Thibeau; ed, Douglas Ibold; ph, David Gribble, Deluxe Color; m, James Newton Howard.

(PR:O MPAA:R)

OFFICER AND A GENTLEMAN, AN***

(1982) 126m Lorimar/PAR c

Richard Gere *(Zack Mayo)*, Debra Winger *(Paula Pokrifki)*, David Keith *(Sid Worley)*, Robert Loggia *(Byron Mayo)*, Lisa Blount *(Lynette Pomeroy)*, Lisa Eilbacher *(Casey Seeger)*, Louis Gossett, Jr. *(Sgt. Emil Foley)*, Tony Plana *(Emiliano Della Serra)*, Harold Sylvester *(Perryman)*.

Lou Gossett, Jr., won a much-deserved Best Supporting Actor Oscar for his stellar portrayal of a drill instructor in this story of determination and love set against the backdrop of a Naval Aviation Officer Candidate School. Richard Gere plays Zack Mayo, a would-be flyer with a tough-luck background who, like his classmates, must survive the rigors of training under draconian Marine sergeant Emil Foley (Gossett) before moving on to flight school. Sgt. Foley singles out Zack for special derision, and though he pushes his charge to the limit, the feisty Zack refuses to give up, eventually tangling with the DI in martial-arts battle. Meanwhile, Zack and classmate Sid Worley (David Keith), the film's tragic figure, become involved with a couple of local girls, millworkers Paula Pokrifki (Debra Winger, who received a Best Actress nomination for her fine performance) and Lynette Pomeroy (Lisa Blount). Paula becomes convinced that Zack is like all the other officer candidates who do their training, take advantage of local women, and then disappear forever once they've earned their white uniform. The film's fairy tale ending proves her wrong, however. Douglas Day Stewart's Oscar-nominated screenplay is generally involving (if a little overheated), but it is ultimately compromised by its sexism, particularly in the finale, which leaves Paula with only one hope for happiness—to be carried off by a dashing knight. Nonetheless, the performances are uniformly strong, with Gere offering some of his best work—though it pales in comparison with Gossett's tour de force as the tough, principled Sgt. Foley, which he patterned after real-life Army DI Bill Dower (familiar to some from his appearances in Miller Lite commercials). The film's memorable theme song, "Up Where We Belong" (sung by Joe Cocker and Jennifer Warnes), also won an Academy Award.

p, Martin Elfand; d, Taylor Hackford; w, Douglas Day Stewart; ed, Peter Zinner; ph, Donald Thorin, Metrocolor; m, Jack Nitzsche.

(PR:O MPAA:R)

ON THE BEACH**½

(1959) 133m Kramer/UA bw

Gregory Peck *(Dwight Towers)*, Ava Gardner *(Moira Davidson)*, Fred Astaire *(Julian Osborn)*, Anthony Perkins *(Peter Holmes)*, Donna Anderson *(Mary Holmes)*, John Tate *(Adm. Bridie)*, Lola Brooks *(Lt. Hosgood)*, John Meillon *(Swain)*, Lou Vernon *(Davidson)*, Guy Doleman *(Farrel)*, Ken Wayne *(Benson)*.

Based on Nevil Shute's popular novel, this flawed but moving end-of-the-world drama is set in Australia in 1964, after nuclear war has eliminated life in the northern hemisphere. While the folks down under await the nuclear fallout that will eventually kill them, the US *Sawfish*, a submarine commanded by Dwight Towers (Gregory Peck), ventures to California, only to learn that the radio signal still being transmitted from San Diego is being produced by a soda bottle—everyone at home is dead (dramatically reenforced by some extraordinary shots of a deserted San Francisco). Back in Australia, the principal characters deal with their imminent deaths in their own way: scientist Julian Osborn (Fred Astaire) enters and wins an auto race, then asphyxiates himself; Australian naval officer Peter Holmes (Anthony Perkins) and his wife, Mary (Donna Anderson), take their child's life, then their own; good-time girl Moira Davidson (Ava Gardner) tries to drink her fears away, then falls for Towers, who eventually returns with his crew to the US to die at home. Produced and directed by Stanley Kramer, this unremittingly bleak message film was intended to have a big impact and premiered simultaneously in 18 cities on all seven continents. And though it occasionally goes over the top with its melodrama and lacks some technical credibility, given the wisdom of scientific hindsight, ON THE BEACH remains a powerful, well-acted, deftly photographed film in the tradition of THE WORLD, THE FLESH AND THE DEVIL (1959); FAIL SAFE (1964); DR. STRANGELOVE (1964); and TESTAMENT (1983). Its effective use of "Waltzing Matilda" also contributed to making that most Australian of songs a hit in the US.

p, Stanley Kramer; d, Stanley Kramer; w, John Paxton and James Lee Barrett, based on the novel by Nevil Shute; ed, Frederic Knudtson; ph, Giuseppe Rotunno and Daniel L. Fapp; m, Ernest Gold.

(PR:O MPAA:NR)

ONE OF OUR AIRCRAFT IS MISSING***½

(1942, Brit.) 90m BN-Archers/UA bw

Godfrey Tearle *(Sir George Corbett)*, Eric Portman *(Tom Earnshaw)*, Hugh Williams *(Frank Shelley)*, Bernard Miles *(Geoff Hickman)*, Hugh Burden *(John Glyn Haggard)*, Emrys Jones *(Bob Ashley)*, Googie Withers *(Jo de Vries)*, Pamela Brown *(Else Meertens)*, Joyce Redman *(Jet van Dieren)*, Hay Petrie *(Burgomeister)*, Arnold Marle *(Pieter Sluys)*, Robert Helpmann *(De Jong)*, Peter Ustinov *(Priest)*, Michael Powell *(Dispatching Officer)*.

During WW II, squadrons of heavy Wellington bombers take off from Britain at dusk and cross the English Channel for a raid on Stuttgart. On the return flight, six crewmen on one plane are forced to bail out over German-occupied Holland. Some Dutch children help them evade a German patrol; then, disguised, they are aided by an underground network that enables them to reach the coast and to return to Britain in a small boat. Almost immediately after being reunited with their squadron they are back in the air, flying even more dangerous missions into Germany. The second Michael Powell-Emeric Pressburger collaboration (the first on which Pressburger was codirector), this film does not reach the heights of their previous, similarly plotted picture, THE 49TH PARALLEL. The best sequences are the opening ones, precisely detailing the raid as the men concentrate on their duties, adjusting instruments while their planes shake under the anti-aircraft fire all around them. The performances—of the stiff-upper-lip variety—are all good, especially Godfrey Tearle's as the aircraft commander, Googie Withers' as an important link in the chain of rescuers, and Scottish character actor Hay Petrie's as an apoplectic burgomeister. The film's worth as a propaganda piece was considerable, but too many long-winded speeches about people uniting to fight the Germans date the film somewhat now.

p, Michael Powell and Emeric Pressburger; d, Michael Powell and Emeric Pressburger; w, Michael Powell and Emeric Pressburger; ed, David Lean; ph, Ronald Neame.

(PR:A MPAA:NR)

ONE THAT GOT AWAY, THE**½

(1958, Brit.) 111m Rank bw

Hardy Kruger *(Franz von Werra)*, Colin Gordon *(Army Interrogator)*, Michael Goodliffe *(RAF Interrogator)*, Terence Alexander *(RAF Intelligence Officer)*, Jack Gwillim *(Commandant Grizedale)*, Andrew Faulds *(Lt. Grizedale)*, Julian Somers *(Booking Clerk)*, Alec McCowen *(Duty Officer Hucknall)*.

Set in the early days of WW II, this is the true story of Franz von Werra (Hardy Kruger), a German Luftwaffe pilot who was captured by the British during the Battle of Britain and made a prisoner of war. Self-assured and confident, the brash flyer brags to his captors that he'll escape within six months. He makes two unsuccessful attempts while in England, then is transported to Canada. On a train to Montreal, he escapes and heads toward the US (neutral at the time), and eventually makes his way to Mexico,

ONLY WAY, THE—

where he begins his slow journey back to Germany. This was the breakthrough film for young German actor Kruger, who was already a star on the Continent, but not in Britain or the US. Under veteran helmer Roy Ward Baker's solid direction, Kruger makes a surprisingly sympathetic "enemy" protagonist, and one can't help but root for the brave and determined young German in his escape attempt.

p, Julian Wintle; d, Roy Baker; w, Howard Clewes, based on a novel by Kendal Burt, James Leasor; ed, Sidney Hayers; ph, Eric Cross; m, Hubert Clifford.

(PR:A MPAA:NR)

ONLY WAY, THE***

(1970, Panama/Den./US) 98m Hemisphere/Laterna/UMC c

Ove Sprogoe *(Petersen)*, Jane Seymour, Martin Potter

An intelligent low-budget entry set in Denmark during WW II, THE ONLY WAY concerns the Nazi round-up of Danish Jews, many of whom saw themselves more as Danes than Jews. When the occupying Germans decide to export them to the concentration camps, a typical local, Petersen (Ove Sprogoe) acts bravely, not out of heroism but out of a duty to humanity. He helps organize a secret exodus from Denmark, making possible the safe passage to Sweden of some 7,000 potential Nazi victims in just a few days' time. Based on an actual incident, the film unfolds along predictable lines, but the ensemble acting and particularly Sprogoe's quiet, anchoring performance create something extraordinary.

d, Bent Christensen; w, Bent Christensen, Leif Panduro, and John Gould; ph, Henning Kristiansen, Eastmancolor; m, Carl Davis.

(PR:A MPAA:G)

OPEN CITY*****

(1945, It.) 105m Excelsa/Mayer-Burstyn bw (ROMA, CITTA APERTA; AKA: ROME, OPEN CITY)

Anna Magnani *(Pina)*, Aldo Fabrizi *(Don Pietro Pellegrini)*, Marcello Pagliero *(Giorgio Manfredi)*, Maria Michi *(Marina)*, Harry Feist *(Maj. Bergmann)*, Francesco Grandjacquet *(Francesco)*, Giovanna Galletti *(Ingrid)*.

One of the most important achievements in the history of cinema, OPEN CITY is the first great fusion of documentary and melodrama. Filmed on the streets, without the use of sound recorders (dialog was dubbed in later), during the months just after the Allies liberated Italy from the grip of Fascism, the film has the appearance of a documentary. The actors, except for Anna Magnani (then a sometime dance-hall girl), were all nonprofessionals. The backgrounds were not constructions on a Cinecitta lot, but actual apartments, shops, and streets—a change for those used to sets and costumes. Set in Rome, 1943-44, the story brings together two enemy forces—the Communists and the Catholics—and unites them in the fight for their country's liberation. Manfredi (Marcello Pagliero) is a Resistance leader wanted by the Germans who must deliver some money to his compatriots. Hiding out in the apartment block of Francesco (Francesco Grandjacquet) and his pregnant fiancee, Pina (Magnani), Manfredi plans to let a Catholic priest, Don Pietro (Aldo Fabrizi), make the delivery. When their building is raided, Francesco is arrested and hauled away. Pino chases after him, screaming, and is gunned down in the middle of the street. Manfredi takes refuge in the apartment of his mistress, Marina (Maria Michi), a lesbian drug addict who, unknown to him, is an informant whose drug supplier is a female Gestapo agent (Giovanna Galleti). As excellent as OPEN CITY is, it has often been criticized for its black-and-white division of characters into Good and Evil, and the emotional manipulation of Renzo Rossellini's score as well as its use of comic devices—these attributes apparently weakening the objective aims of Neo-Realist cinema. Director Roberto Rossellini, however, cannot be criticized for stirring emotions rather than intellect, since objectivity is not possible here. In OPEN CITY one can see, above all else, the honesty and morality of Rossellini's direction, and, while his result may not wholly comply with the accepted definition of Neo-Realism, his intent—to bring reality to the screen—most certainly does. Most videotape copies offer prints of mediocre quality and often unreadable (Italian into English) subtitles.

p, Roberto Rossellini; d, Roberto Rossellini; w, Sergio Amidei, Federico Fellini, and Roberto Rossellini, based on a story by Sergio Amidei, Alberto Consiglio; ph, Ubaldo Arata; m, Renzo Rossellini.

(PR:O MPAA:NR)

OPERATION AMSTERDAM**

(1960, Brit.) 105m RANK/FOX bw

Peter Finch *(Jan Smit)*, Eva Bartok *(Anna)*, Tony Britton *(Maj. Dillon)*, Alexander Knox *(Walter Keyser)*, Malcolm Keen *(Johann Smit)*, Christopher Rhodes *(Alex)*, Tim Turner *(Lieutenant)*, John Horsley *(Comdr. Bowerman)*.

Set in 1940, OPERATION AMSTERDAM tells the true story of the removal of $10 million worth of industrial diamonds from the title city just before the Nazi occupation. Jan Smit (Peter Finch), diamond expert Walter Keyser (Alexander Knox), British officer Maj. Dillon (Tony Britton), and Dutch contact Anna (Eva Bartok) are the foursome who must get the diamonds out, having just 14 hours to catch a boat to England while avoiding local fifth columnists and outwitting the Germans. Although the film does contain a few exciting action sequences, the rest of OPERATION AMSTERDAM is fairly tedious and padded with far too much travelog footage of picturesque European locations. Finch contributes an interesting performance, but the rest of the cast is rather unremarkable.

p, Maurice Cowan; d, Michael McCarthy; w, Michael McCarthy and John Eldridge, based on *Adventure in Dia-*

monds by David E. Walker; ed, Arthur Stevens; ph, Reginald Wyer; m, Philip Green.

(PR:A MPAA:NR)

OPERATION CIA*½

(1965) 90m Hei-Ra-Matt/AA bw (AKA: LAST MESSAGE FROM SAIGON)

Burt Reynolds *(Mark Andrews)*, Kieu Chinh *(Kim-chinh)*, Danielle Aubry *(Denise)*, John Hoyt *(Wells)*, Cyril Collick *(Withers)*, Vic Diaz *(Prof. Yen)*, Bill Catching *(Frank Decker)*, Marsh Thomson *(Stacey)*.

Burt Reynolds is Mark Andrews, a CIA agent sent to Saigon during the Vietnam War to investigate a fellow agent's murder. While snooping, Andrews stumbles onto a plot to kill the US ambassador. With the help of friendly female contact Kim-chinh (Kieu Chinh), he escapes from terrorist kidnaper Prof. Yen (Vic Diaz) and tries to prevent the ambassador's murder by a French double agent (Danielle Aubry). The only point of interest in this tepid espionage actioner (aside from the glimpse of early Reynolds) is that some of the footage was actually shot in Saigon just as the American presence began to intensify. But even with authentic locations, the story is just too stock to maintain much interest. Dully directed by Christian Nyby, OPERATION CIA is further evidence for film *auteurists* that "producer" Howard Hawks really directed the excellent science-fiction film THE THING (1951) and gave his protege Nyby the credit.

p, Peer J. Oppenheimer; d, Christian Nyby; w, Bill S. Ballinger and Peer J. Oppenheimer, based on a story by Oppenheimer; ed, Joseph Gluck and George Watters; ph, Richard Moore; m, Paul Dunlap.

(PR:A MPAA:NR)

OPERATION PETTICOAT***½

(1959) 124m Granarte/UNIV c

Cary Grant *(Adm. Matt Sherman)*, Tony Curtis *(Lt. Nick Holden)*, Joan O'Brien *(Lt. Dolores Crandall)*, Dina Merrill *(Lt. Barbara Duran)*, Arthur O'Connell *(Sam Tostin)*, Gene Evans *(Molumphrey)*, Richard Sargent *(Stovall)*, Virginia Gregg *(Maj. Edna Hayward)*, Robert F. Simon *(Capt. J.B. Henderson)*, Robert Gist *(Watson)*, Gavin MacLeod *(Ernest Hunkle)*, George Dunn *(Prophet)*, Dick Crockett *(Harmon)*, Madlyn Rhue *(Lt. Claire Reid)*, Marion Ross *(Lt. Ruth Colfax)*, Clarence Lung *(Ramon)*, Frankie Darro *(Dooley)*.

After the end of WW II, Adm. Matt Sherman (Cary Grant) reads over his log from the USS *Sea Tiger*, the submarine he captains. Sherman is about to turn over the command of the sub to Lt. Nick Holden (Tony Curtis), who is assigned to squire it until it is destroyed and replaced by a nuclear vessel. The movie unwinds in flashback as Sherman recalls some of the events in the sub's life—particularly how that life was renewed when he became determined to raise the *Sea Tiger* in the wake of an attack in Manila Bay. It's December 1941 and, with help from Holden, who secures the supplies and gear to help restore the badly damaged sub, Sherman and his crew take to the waters. Along the way, they are joined by five stranded nurses, a couple of Filipino families, and a goat. The sailors ferry them out of harm's way, especially enjoying the presence of the nurses—a chesty bunch who always seem to be passing the hot young sailors in the sub's very narrow corridors. They also paint the sub pink. There's not much story to speak of, and the jokes are more than a bit sexist, but the gags are bright and Blake Edwards' direction adroit enough to make OPERATION PETTICOAT an enjoyable time. A TV series was later attempted, but never came close to the energy of the movie.

p, Robert Arthur; d, Blake Edwards; w, Stanley Shapiro and Maurice Richlin, based on a story by Paul King, Joseph Stone; ed, Ted J. Kent and Frank Gross; ph, Russell Harlan and Clifford Stine, Eastmancolor; m, David Rose.

(PR:A MPAA:NR)

OUTPOST IN MOROCCO**

(1949) 92m UA bw

George Raft *(Capt. Paul Gerard)*, Marie Windsor *(Cara)*, Akim Tamiroff *(Lt. Glysko)*, John Litel *(Col. Pascal)*, Eduard Franz *(Emir of Bel-Rashad)*, Erno Verebes *(Bamboule)*, Crane Whitley *(Caid Osman)*, Damian O'Flynn *(Commandant Fronval)*.

A poor man's version of THE LIVES OF A BENGAL LANCER, OUTPOST IN MOROCCO tells the story of a desert fighter assigned to put down a tribal rebellion among the Arabs. The mission of this French Legionnaire, Capt. Paul Gerard (George Raft), gets detoured, however, when he falls in love with Cara (Marie Windsor), the daughter of rebel leader Emir of Bel-Rashad (Eduard Franz). Hardly a credible story, made less credible by some cardboard characterizations. Veteran character actor Akim Tamiroff, who plays Gerard's subordinate, also appeared in the vastly superior LIVES OF A BENGAL LANCER as the friendly Emir.

p, Samuel Bischoff and Joseph N. Ermolieff; d, Robert Florey; w, Charles Grayson and Paul de Sainte-Colombe, based on the story by Ermolieff; ed, George Arthur; ph, Lucien Andriot; m, Michel Michelet.

(PR:A MPAA:NR)

PQ

PAISAN*****

(1948, It.) 120m Organization Films International-Foreign Film/Mayer-Burstyn bw (PAISA)

Carmela Sazio *(Carmela)*, Robert Van Loon *(Joe from Jersey)*, Alfonsino Pasca *(Boy)*, Maria Michi *(Francesca)*,

PASSAGE TO MARSEILLE—

Renzo Avanzo (Massimo), Harriet White (Harriet), Dots M. Johnson (Black MP), Bill Tubbs (Capt. Bill Martin), Dale Edmonds (Dale), Gar Moore (Fred).

PAISAN is one of those rare segmented films that never loses steam as it moves through six chronologically ordered sequences beginning with the Allied invasion of Sicily in 1943 and concluding with liberation in 1945. In addition to moving across time, the film transports the viewer throughout Italy—from Sicily to Naples to Rome to Florence to Romagna to Po—each episode observing a slice of regional life. A film unlike any other the world had seen, PAISAN is OPEN CITY without the melodrama, though, despite its re-created scenes from life, it is anything but a flat, uninvolving newsreel. It is instead a portrait of life during wartime filled with humor, pathos, adventure, romance, tension, and warmth that are as tangible in the film as they are in the real world. Perhaps the straightforward nature of Roberto Rossellini's portrayal of the events is best reflected in the Naples segment: a young boy meets a drunken GI who is on the verge of passing out, but before he nods off, the boy warns him, "If you fall asleep, I'll steal your boots." The GI falls asleep and the boy steals his boots. PAISAN is a film about truth—truth stated and truth observed. Collaborating on the script was future director Federico Fellini, who was at the time also employed as Rossellini's full-time assistant. (In Italian; English subtitles.)

p, Roberto Rossellini, Rod E. Geiger, and Mario Conti; d, Roberto Rossellini; w, Sergio Amidei, Federico Fellini, Roberto Rossellini, and Annalena Limentani, based on stories by Victor Haines, Marcello Pagliero, Sergio Amidei, Federico Fellini, Roberto Rossellini, Klaus Mann, Vasco Pratolini; ed, Eraldo Da Roma; ph, Otello Martelli; m, Renzo Rossellini.

(PR:C MPAA:NR)

PASSAGE TO MARSEILLE***½

(1944) 110m WB bw

Humphrey Bogart (Matrac), Claude Rains (Capt. Freycinet), Michele Morgan (Paula), Philip Dorn (Renault), Sydney Greenstreet (Maj. Duval), Peter Lorre (Marius), George Tobias (Petit), Victor Francen (Capt. Patain Malo), Helmut Dantine (Garou), John Loder (Manning), Konstantin Shayne (1st Mate), Monte Blue (2nd Mate), Corinna Mura (Singer), Eduardo Ciannelli (Chief Engineer), Vladimir Sokoloff (Grandpere), Charles La Torre (Lt. Lenoir), Hans Conried (Jourdain), Mark Stevens (Lt. Hastings), Louis Mercier (Engineer).

With adventurer Humphrey Bogart as his lead, director Michael Curtiz here offers a slam-bang action film, one with a tricky plot whose narrative unfolds through a complicated series of flashbacks-within-flashbacks and flash forwards, but that is nevertheless exciting and absorbing all the way. A group of prisoners who have escaped the dreaded prison at Cayenne in French Guiana are picked up by a passing French freighter, commanded by Malo (Victor Francen), who is loyal to Free France but who hides his sympathies from the fascistic Maj. Duval (Sydney Greenstreet), a French officer sympathetic to the Vichy government. The rescued men claim they are survivors of a torpedoed ship, but eventually their true identities are learned. They are Matrac (Bogart), a French journalist who opposed the Nazi takeover of his country from within, and his criminal comrades Marius (Peter Lorre), Garou (Helmut Dantine), Renault (Philip Dorn), and Petit (George Tobias). All are loyal to the Free French, and when Maj. Duval plans to turn the ship over to the Vichy government, Matrac and his comrades fight to keep the ship from the clutches of the collaborators. Although Curtiz draws superb performances from his great cast, many of whom (Bogart, Lorre, Greenstreet, Dantine, Claude Rains, Corinna Mura, and Louis Mercier) appeared in Warner Bros. recent smash hit CASABLANCA (1942), the story is more than a little confusing, because of the unwieldy flashbacks used to tell the tale. Yet the great action director packs the film with marvelous adventure and exciting scenes, not to mention stirring patriotism. Warners attempted to time PASSAGE TO MARSEILLE's release to coincide with what the studio thought would be the invasion of southern France, but when this failed to take place the film was distributed without an international news event to boost the production (as had been the case with CASABLANCA, released just after American troops landed in Africa and Allied leaders met in that African city for top-level conferences). James Wong Howe's gritty photography helps set the mood and Max Steiner's music dynamically establishes patriotic fervor.

p, Hal B. Wallis; d, Michael Curtiz; w, Casey Robinson and Jack Moffitt, based on the novel Men Without a Country by Charles Nordhoff, James Norman Hall; ed, Owen Marks; ph, James Wong Howe; m, Max Steiner.

(PR:A MPAA:NR)

PATHS OF GLORY*****

(1957) 86m Bryna/UA bw

Kirk Douglas (Col. Dax), Ralph Meeker (Cpl. Paris), Adolphe Menjou (Gen. Broulard), George Macready (Gen. Mireau), Wayne Morris (Lt. Roget), Richard Anderson (Maj. Saint-Auban), Joseph Turkel (Pvt. Arnoud), Timothy Carey (Pvt. Ferol), Peter Capell (Col. Judge), Susanne Christian (The German Girl), Bert Freed (Sgt. Boulanger), Emile Meyer (Priest), Kem Dibbs (Pvt. LeJeune), Jerry Hausner (Pvt. Meyer), Frederic Bell (Shell-Shocked Soldier).

Beyond all doubt this is one of the greatest antiwar films ever made, a jarring, utterly harrowing masterpiece from Stanley Kubrick that ranks with Lewis Milestone's 1930 epic ALL QUIET ON THE WESTERN FRONT in its power. Col. Dax (Kirk Douglas) is the commander of the battle-decimated 701st Infantry Regiment of the French Army, dug in along the Western Front in a brutally stalemated war. It is 1916, and the Allies have been struggling to overcome an equally determined German war machine for two years. Dax's hope that his regiment will be relieved from front-line duty is destroyed when corps commander Gen. Broulard (Adolphe Menjou) orders Gen. Mireau (George Macready), the divisional general in charge, to make an all-out attack against an impregnable German position nicknamed "The Ant Hill." The battle scenes showing the suicidal attack on the Ant Hill are devastating and brutally authentic, the barrage through which Dax leads his men (Kubrick's cameras moving almost dreamily through the battle) a hurricane of death that comes closer to the real thing than any other dramatization. Kubrick's condemnation of war is overwhelming—but PATHS OF GLORY is also a document of human courage, compassion, and the white-heat will that insists upon survival despite the efforts of tyrants to wipe out others' lives, to vanquish principle, honesty, and the greatness of human spirit. This is a director's film: Kubrick profiles naked power with a visual excitement seldom seen on the screen, his presence always felt but never interfering with the astounding traveling shots through the trenches—where the troops cringe in claustrophobic terror—and through the expansive ballrooms and headquarters, where the generals dally, in contrast to their men.

p, James B. Harris; d, Stanley Kubrick; w, Stanley Kubrick, Calder Willingham, and Jim Thompson, based on the novel by Humphrey Cobb; ed, Eva Kroll; ph, George Krause; m, Gerald Fried.

(PR:C MPAA:NR)

PATTON*****

(1970) 170m FOX c (AKA: PATTON: A SALUTE TO A REBEL; GB: PATTON—LUST FOR GLORY)

George C. Scott *(Gen. George S. Patton, Jr.)*, Karl Malden *(Gen. Omar N. Bradley)*, Michael Bales *(Field Marshal Sir Bernard Law Montgomery)*, Edward Binns *(Maj. Gen. Walter Bedell Smith)*, Lawrence Dobkin *(Col. Bell)*, John Doucette *(Maj. Gen. Lucian K. Truscott)*, James Edwards *(Sgt. Meeks)*, Frank Latimore *(Lt. Col. Davenport)*, Richard Muench *(Col. Gen. Jodl)*, Morgan Paull *(Capt. Jenson)*, Siegfried Rauch *(Capt. Steiger)*, Paul Stevens *(Lt. Col. Codman)*, Michael Strong *(Brig. Gen. Carver)*, Karl Michael Vogler *(Field Marshal Erwin Rommel)*, Lowell Thomas *(Newsreel Narrator)*.

This WW II spectacle is immense but George C. Scott's virtuoso performance looms larger than any of its battles. Scott simply *is* George S. Patton, Jr.—insensitive to his men's plight on some occasions, gentle as a loving father on others—providing one of the most acute and dynamic biographical portrayals ever seen. Beginning with a classic six-minute speech by Patton about the fighting spirit of Americans that is worth the entire film, PATTON traces the legendary WW II exploits of "Old Blood and Guts" from his defeat of Rommel's Afrika Korps at El Guettar to the invasion of Sicily, during which he disobeys orders and beats rival Field Marshal Montgomery (Michael Bates) to Messina, on to his loss of command for slapping a battle-fatigued soldier because he has been hospitalized but has no wounds. Then, after sitting out D-Day as a decoy, Patton is given command of the Third Army, winning one mighty battle after another with his armored troops and eventually speeding to the rescue of the encircled 101st Airborne Division at Bastogne, ending Hitler's last great counteroffensive in the Battle of the Bulge. Following the war, Patton is sent into involuntary retirement after his highly vocal criticism of the Soviet Union, and the film ends with his farewell to his faithful staff. Scott is nothing less than amazing as the controversial general, capturing his multidimensional character with subtle undertones and rich extravagance, and won an Academy Award (which he refused) for his performance. Wonderful support comes from Karl Malden as Gen. Omar Bradley, Edward Binns as Maj. Gen. Walter Bedell Smith, John Doucette as Maj. Gen. Lucian K. Truscott, and Bates as Montgomery. Franklin J. Schaffner's direction is majestic and his handling of complex battles is masterful; shot in 70-millimeter Dimension 150, these broad, impersonal spectacles have a macabre beauty that removes the viewer from the brutalities of modern warfare. Fox hoped to duplicate the success of its black-and-white blockbuster, THE LONGEST DAY, by spending a fortune on this incredible film, which was shot on location in England, Spain, Morocco, and Greece.

p, Frank McCarthy and Frank Caffey; d, Franklin J. Schaffner; w, Francis Ford Coppola and Edmund H. North, based on the books *Patton: Ordeal and Triumph* by Ladislas Farago and *A Soldier's Story* by Gen. Omar N. Bradley; ed, Hugh S. Fowler; ph, Fred Koenekamp, Dimension 150, CinemaScope, Deluxe Color; m, Jerry Goldsmith.

(PR:C MPAA:PG)

PAWNBROKER, THE****

(1965) 114m Landau-Unger-Pawnbroker/Landau Releasing Organization-AA-AIP bw

Rod Steiger *(Sol Nazerman)*, Geraldine Fitzgerald *(Marilyn Birchfield)*, Brock Peters *(Rodriguez)*, Jaime Sanchez *(Jesus Ortiz)*, Thelma Oliver *(Ortiz' Girl)*, Marketa Kimbrell *(Tessie)*, Baruch Lumet *(Mendel)*, Juano Hernandez *(Mr. Smith)*, Linda Geiser *(Ruth Nazerman)*, Nancy R. Pollock *(Bertha)*, Raymond St. Jacques *(Tangee)*, John McCurry *(Buck)*, Eusebia Cosme *(Mrs. Ortiz)*, Warren Finnerty *(Savarese)*.

Although there have been numerous films about the post-Vietnam era and the war's psychological aftereffects on the soldier returning home, very few pictures have dealt with the similar predicament of those who lived through WW II (or WW I, for that matter). THE PAWNBROKER, one of the seminal American films of the 1960s, focuses on Sol Nazerman (Rod Steiger), a middle-aged concentration camp survivor who lost his entire family to the Nazis and now runs a pawnshop in Harlem. That he remained alive is a source of bewilderment and pain; he has lost faith in God and man, emotionless and totally removed from the world that surrounds his run-down shop. Shop assistant Jesus Ortiz (Jaime Sanchez) and social worker Marilyn Birchfield (Geraldine Fitzgerald) try to get through Sol's icy exterior, but to no avail. Instead, Sol becomes increasingly cruel and offensive. Meanwhile, he conducts an affair with Tessie (Marketa Kimbrell), a fellow camp survivor whose husband was a victim of Nazi atrocities. Directed by Sidney Lumet in a gritty, raw style that was fashionable at the time, THE PAWNBROKER is memorable today for its innovative (if gimmicky) use of flashbacks—in this case quick cuts lasting only a fraction of a second—to represent the disturbing, unrelenting flashes of Sol's memory. Also unforgettable is Steiger's towering performance as the volatile survivor, a powder keg of hateful remembrances.

p, Roger Lewis and Philip Langner; d, Sidney Lumet; w, David Friedkin and Morton Fine, based on the novel by Edward Lewis Wallant; ed, Ralph Rosenblum; ph, Boris Kaufman; m, Quincy Jones.

(PR:C MPAA:NR)

PEDESTRIAN, THE***½

(1974, Ger.) 97m Cinerama c (DER FUSSGANGER)

Gustav Rudolf Sellner *(Heinz Alfred Giese)*, Ruth Hausmeister *(Inge Maria Giese)*, Maximilian Schell *(Andreas Giese)*, Manuel Sellner *(Hubert Giese)*, Elsa Wagner *(Elsa Giese)*, Dagmar Hirtz *(Elke Giese)*, Michael Weinert *(Michael Giese)*, Peter Hall *(Rudolf Hartmann)*, Alexander May *(Alexander Markowitz)*, Christian Kohlund *(Erwin Gotz)*, Franz Seitz *(Dr. Karl Peters)*, Gertrud Bald *(Henriette Markowitz)*, Walter Kohut *(Dr. Rolf Meineke)*, Margarethe Schell von Noe *(Frau Buchmann)*, Fani Fotinou *(Greek Woman)*, Gaddi Ben-Artzi *(Greek Man)*, Walter von Varndal *(Dr. Kratzer)*, Peggy Ashcroft *(Lady Gray)*.

A powerful and revealing film about death, guilt, and Germany's involvement in wartime atrocities, THE PEDESTRIAN focuses on an aging industrialist, Heinz Alfred Giese (Gustav Rudolf Sellner), who prefers not to remember the events of WW II. In fact, he prefers to be involved with life as little as possible. Since the death of his son Andreas (Maximilian Schell) in an auto accident in which Giese was driving (resulting in the loss of his license, hence the title), his whole life has centered around his grandson, Hubert (Manuel Sellner). Although Giese would rather forget his past, Alexander Markowitz (Alexander May), the senior editor of a newspaper, begins a probe into Giese's involvement in the massacre of a Greek village. With the help of two witnesses—a survivor of the attack (Fani Fotinou) and a former German soldier (Walter von Varndal)—Markowitz discovers that Giese was involved in the massacre and could have prevented it had he tried. When the story is printed, Giese becomes the target of moral outrage and violence. This strong indictment of his generation's complacency is especially damning because its villain is not a monster but a well-respected businessman and a loving grandfather. Produced, directed, and written by Maximilian Schell, THE PEDESTRIAN received an Oscar nomination for Best Foreign-Language Film. The videocassette is dubbed in English.

p, Maximilian Schell and Zev Braun; d, Maximilian Schell; w, Maximilian Schell; ed, Dagmar Hirtz; ph, Wolfgang Treu and Klaus Koenig, Eastmancolor; m, Manos Hadjidakis.

(PR:C MPAA:PG)

PIMPERNEL SMITH***½

(1942, Brit.) 100m BN/UA bw (AKA: MISTER V)

Leslie Howard *(Prof. Horatio Smith)*, Francis L. Sullivan *(Gen. von Graum)*, Mary Morris *(Ludmilla Koslowski)*, Hugh McDermott *(David Maxwell)*, Raymond Huntley *(Marx)*, Manning Whiley *(Bertie Gregson)*, Peter Gawthorne *(Sidimir Koslowski)*, Allan Jeayes *(Dr. Beckendorf)*, Dennis Arundell *(Hoffman)*, Philip Friend *(Spencer)*, Lawrence Kitchen *(Clarence Elstead)*.

Leslie Howard more or less reprises his most famous swashbuckling role, that of THE SCARLET PIMPERNEL, as that tale of disguise and rescue is transplanted from Paris during the Reign of Terror to Germany under the Nazis. Prof. Horatio Smith (Howard), an absent-minded professor of archaeology, is supposedly involved in the search for Aryan artifacts near Switzerland, but secretly he runs refugees over the border to safety while disguising himself in a bewildering variety of get-ups. Meanwhile, Gen. von Graum (Francis L. Sullivan), a corpulent Gestapo officer, sets out to stop the elusive "Pimpernel." Eventually Smith's students figure out what their professor is up to and help him smuggle a large group of persecuted scientists across the border. Smith then goes back one more time, all the way to Berlin, to free Ludmilla Koslowski (Mary Morris), a young woman being held by the Gestapo. This was Howard's first solo directorial effort (he codirected PYGMALION earlier) and he does a creditable job, keeping the film moving with the right mixture of action and suave, stiff-upper-lip heroism; however, his relaxed acting and immensely likable screen presence are what carry the film.

p, Leslie Howard; d, Leslie Howard; w, Anatole de Grunwald, Roland Pertwee, and Ian Dalrymple, based on a story by A.G. MacDonnell, Wolfgang Wilhelm; ed, Douglas Myers; ph, Jack Hildyard and Mutz Greenbaum; m, John Greenwood.

(PR:A MPAA:NR)

PLATOON****

(1986) 111m Hemdale/Orion c

Tom Berenger *(Sgt. Barnes)*, Willem Dafoe *(Sgt. Elias)*, Charlie Sheen *(Chris)*, Forest Whitaker *(Big Harold)*, Francesco Quinn *(Rhah)*, John C. McGinley *(Sgt. O'Neill)*, Richard Edson *(Sal)*, Kevin Dillon *(Bunny)*, Reggie Johnson *(Junior)*, Keith David *(King)*, Johnny Depp *(Lerner)*, David Neidorf *(Tex)*, Mark Moses *(Lt. Wolfe)*, Chris Pedersen *(Crawford)*, Oliver Stone *(Officer in Bunker)*.

Chris (Charlie Sheen), a green recruit and child of privilege who dropped out of college and enlisted, finds himself in Vietnam as a member of a platoon divided against itself. On one side is Sgt. Barnes (Tom Berenger), a horribly scarred veteran of several tours of duty who believes in total war—a morally corrupt, remorseless killing machine. The men who follow him seek clear-cut solutions to the complicated realities they face. On the other side is veteran sergeant Elias (Willem Dafoe), who, though equally skilled in the ways of death, still retains some semblance of humanity and attempts to impose a sense of compassion and responsibility on his men. Chris is caught between the two men in what he describes as a "battle for possession of my soul." PLATOON is a shattering experience. Writer-director Stone, a Vietnam veteran, used his first-hand knowledge to create what will surely be viewed as one of the most realistic war films ever made. PLATOON's success lies in the mass of detail Stone brings to the screen, bombarding the senses with vivid sights and sounds that have the feel of actual experience. Stone captures the heat, the dampness, the bugs, the jungle rot, and, most important, the confusion and fear experienced by the average soldier. The men in PLATOON do perform heroic acts on occasion, but the heroism isn't motivated by love of country or idealism—it is motivated by pure terror, by desperation, by a desire to end the madness one way or another. Never before in a war film has stark terror among soldiers been such a tangible, motivating force. There is nothing appealing in Stone's war; it doesn't have a "recruitment flavor." However, while PLATOON has no equal when it comes to capturing the reality of men in combat, it falters when Stone attempts to apply greater meaning to his vision. As he proved in his equally excellent SALVADOR, Stone is a master at building intense situations, but he is a less than subtle screenwriter. Although Stone claims to have known sergeants like Barnes and Elias while serving in Vietnam, the film's metaphysical battle between the forces of good and evil as represented by the two men is heavy-handed, as is Sheen's totally unnecessary voice-over narration in the form of letters to Chris' grandmother. Stone dilutes the power of his own visuals by inserting the fairly vapid narration to drive his points home. On an incredibly low budget of $6.5 million, Stone brought his cast and crew to the Philippines and shot PLATOON in a swift 54 days. To everyone's surprise, the film was a massive hit with the critics and the public, grossing over $127,551,000 (as of this writing) and winning Best Picture, Best Director, Best Editing, and Best Sound Academy Awards. What makes PLATOON an important film is the starkly realistic portrayal of men at war. Those mindless minions who thrilled to the cartoonish exploits of RAMBO; MISSING IN ACTION; or TOP GUN should see PLATOON and be jolted back to the reality of the hardship, suffering, and death that is war.

p, Arnold Kopelson; d, Oliver Stone; w, Oliver Stone; ed, Claire Simpson; ph, Robert Richardson, CFI Color; m, Samuel Barber.

(PR:O MPAA:R)

PLATOON LEADER**

(1988) 100m Breton/Cannon c

Michael Dudikoff *(Lt. Jeff Knight)*, Robert F. Lyons *(Sgt. Michael McNamara)*, Michael De Lorenzo *(Pvt. Raymond Bacera)*, Rich Fitts *(Robert Hayes)*, Jesse Dabson *(Joshua Parker)*, Brian Libby *(Roach)*.

While some recent Vietnam films superbly show the ambivalence and dislocation American troops felt in Southeast Asia, others have more modestly aimed just to be entertaining. PLATOON LEADER is in the latter class, pale in comparison to PLATOON or APOCALYPSE NOW, but—considered in the context of the entire war film genre—not bad, either. Jeff Knight (Michael Dudikoff) is the title character, a young lieutenant fresh from the States. Stationed at a small firebase, he is at first the butt of jokes from his battle-hardened men, but, under the tutelage of Sgt. McNamara (Robert F. Lyons), he soon learns the ropes and leads daily patrols into the bush, captured in some effective scenes. When it is learned that the Viet Cong are preparing a major attack on the base and the village it protects, Knight leads a preemptive strike against the enemy, but a breakdown of communications causes the attack's failure, with McNamara wounded and the village left in flames—its inhabitants dead or scattered, the firebase without a purpose. Despite its pandering title (changed from NAM after the success of PLATOON) and no-name cast, PLATOON LEADER is fairly watchable. Aaron Norris' direction shows some improvement over his debut in brother Chuck's BRADDOCK: MISSING IN ACTION III, Dudikoff has just the right square-jawed sincerity as the young officer trying to make his training jibe with the reality of combat, and Lyons' performance as the savvy sergeant is in the finest tradition of this rather cliched character.

p, Harry Alan Towers; d, Aaron Norris; w, Rick Marx, Andrew Deutsch, David Walker, and Peter Welbeck [Harry Alan Towers], based on the book by James R. McDonough; ed, Michael J. Duthie; ph, Arthur Wooster, Rank color; m, George S. Clinton.

(PR:O MPAA:R)

PLENTY***

(1985) 125m FOX c

Meryl Streep *(Susan Traherne)*, Charles Dance *(Raymond Brock)*, Tracey Ullman *(Alice Park)*, John Gielgud *(Sir Leonard Darwin)*, Sting *(Mick)*, Ian McKellen *(Sir Andrew Charleson)*, Sam Neill *(Lazar)*, Burt Kwouk *(Mr. Aung)*, Pik Sen Lim *(Mme. Aung)*.

Adapted by playwright-director David Hare (A Map of the World; WEATHERBY) from his own play, PLENTY follows the fortunes of Englishwoman Susan Traherne (Meryl Streep) from her thrilling days as a courier behind the lines in Occupied France through the boredom she experiences in her postwar life. During the war, in France, she has a brief but passionate affair with a dashing young British agent called "Lazar" (Sam Neill), and when she returns to England after the outbreak of peace, she is unable to forget him. Taking a stab at bohemian life, she becomes involved in a calculated relationship with Mick (Sting), a working-class gent she's decided will make a suitable father for her child. When they fail to produce a baby, however, Susan drops Mick and eventually marries Raymond Brock (Charles Dance), a patient, polished foreign service officer she follows around the globe. But the life of a diplomat's wife is hardly satisfying for the increasingly frustrated and neurotic Susan, and her cruelty to her husband worsens as the years pass. On its face, director Fred Schepisi's film concerns a woman whose warped person-

PORK CHOP HILL—

ality becomes less rational and more malicious as she realizes she will never recapture the excitement of her life during wartime; however, Hare's well-crafted screenplay also uses Susan as a symbol of the squandered hopes for a better postwar Britain. Middle-class Susan and working-class Mick's inability to produce a child is symbolic of postwar Labor governments' failure to eliminate class division and inequity from British society, even in a time of economic "plenty." Intriguing and generally overlooked, PLENTY works on both levels. Employing yet another flawless accent, Streep delivers an excellent, restrained but edgy performance, well supported by Dance, Sting, and Tracey Ullman, playing her best friend.

p, Edward R. Pressman and Joseph Papp; d, Fred Schepisi; w, David Hare, based on the play by Hare; ed, Peter Honess; ph, Ian Baker, Panavision, Technicolor; m, Bruce Smeaton.

(PR:O MPAA:R)

PORK CHOP HILL****
(1959) 97m Melville/UA bw

Gregory Peck *(Lt. Clemons)*, Harry Guardino *(Forstman)*, Rip Torn *(Lt. Russell)*, George Peppard *(Fedderson)*, James Edwards *(Cpl. Jurgens)*, Bob Steele *(Kern)*, Woody Strode *(Franklin)*, George Shibata *(Lt. Ohashi)*, Norman Fell *(Sgt. Coleman)*, Robert Blake *(Velie)*, Biff Elliot *(Bowen)*, Barry Atwater *(Davis)*, Martin Landau *(Marshall)*, Bert Remsen *(Lt. Cummings)*, Kevin Hagen *(Cpl. Kissell)*, Harry Dean Stanton *(MacFarland)*.

A grim, harrowing film detailing a single brutal Korean War battle, PORK CHOP HILL was directed by veteran helmsman Lewis Milestone and is the third entry in his informal trilogy devoted to 20th-century military conflict (ALL QUIET ON THE WESTERN FRONT [1930] was set during WW I, and A WALK IN THE SUN [1945] during WW II). Gregory Peck plays the commander of an Army company that is ordered to take Pork Chop Ridge, an inconsequential tactical objective. Compounding the seeming pointlessness of the assignment are the Panmunjom peace talks, which the troops believe may end the war at any minute, so that they are reluctant to participate in what may be its final battle. PORK CHOP HILL is an ode to the common American infantryman, soldiers who manage to retain their honor and dignity despite being ordered into an insane action by a top brass unwilling to lose face to the enemy, even though the conflict's end appears imminent. Peck is outstanding as the resolute but compassionate commander, and Rip Torn, Harry Guardino, Woody Strode, James Edwards (veteran of Sam Fuller's excellent Korean War film THE STEEL HELMET), and Robert Blake provide solid support. Moreover, Milestone employs his considerable technical skills to create an authentic and memorable cinematic experience, projecting a grim realistic air that captures the forlorn atmosphere of the meaningless mission. Sam Leavitt's photography is topnotch and depicts this heroic battle in such stark detail that the viewer can almost smell the acrid fumes of cordite and taste the dust blown from the dead ridge. This powerful movie and HAM-

BURGER HILL (1987), which deals similarly with an assault during the Vietnam War, would make a very interesting double bill.

p, Sy Bartlett; d, Lewis Milestone; w, James R. Webb, based on a story by S.L.A. Marshall; ed, George Boemler; ph, Sam Leavitt; m, Leonard Rosenman.

(PR:C MPAA:NR)

P.O.W. THE ESCAPE**
(1986) 90m Golan-Globus/Cannon c

David Carradine *(Col. Cooper)*, Charles R. Floyd *(Sparks)*, Mako *(Capt. Vinh)*, Steve James *(Johnson)*, Phil Brock *(Adams)*, Daniel Demorest *(Thomas)*, Tony Pierce *(Waite)*, Steve Freedman *(Scott)*, James Acheson *(McCoy)*, Rudy Daniels *(Gen. Morgan)*.

Every war develops its own cinema, and the Vietnam movies show no sign of slowing up, arriving in every form—from the big-budget, star-studded spectacular (APOCALYPSE NOW; FULL METAL JACKET) to B-movie fodder (P.O.W. THE ESCAPE). The film opens as Col. Cooper (David Carradine) leads a mission to rescue POWs from a secret camp in the last days of the war. The mission is botched, and Cooper ends up a prisoner himself. Commanding the camp is Capt. Vinh (Mako), who has a trunk full of gold bullion and another filled with watches and trinkets he has stolen from prisoners. With the war coming to an end, Vinh is eager to get to the US with his loot, and he proposes a deal to Cooper in which they will travel to Saigon, each the respective prisoner of the other—depending on where they are—until they reach the South Vietnamese capital. Cooper refuses to cooperate unless all the men are included, and eventually Vinh agrees, but their escape route is fraught with danger, greed, and betrayal. Coming in an obscure fourth in the Vietnam-prisoner-rescue mission sweepstakes (after RAMBO: FIRST BLOOD II, the Chuck Norris MISSING IN ACTION films, and the Gene Hackman starrer UNCOMMON VALOR), P.O.W. THE ESCAPE has a few things going for it most of the others don't: it takes place during the war, so we don't have any of those one-man armies invading sovereign nations in time of peace; it has a fairly interesting performance by Carradine; and the film is technically quite good, making the most of obviously limited funds to create a passable Vietnam out of the Philippines.

p, Menahem Golan and Yoram Globus; d, Gideon Amir; w, Jeremy Lipp, James Bruner, Malcolm Barbour, and John Langley, based on a story by Avi Kleinberger, Gideon Amir; ed, Marcus Manton; ph, Yechiel Ne'eman, TVC Color; m, David Storrs.

(PR:O MPAA:R)

POWER PLAY**
(1978, Brit./Can.) 109m Magnum International-Cowry/Robert Cooper c

Peter O'Toole *(Col. Zeller)*, David Hemmings *(Col. Narriman)*, Donald Pleasence *(Blair)*, Barry Morse *(Jean Rous-*

seau), Jon Granik (Raymond Kasai), Marcella Saint-Amant (Mrs. Rousseau), George Touliatos (Barrientos), Chuck Shamata (Hillsman), Gary Reineke (Aramco), Harvey Atkin (Anwar), August Schellenberg (Minh), Eli Rill (Dominique), Dick Cavett (Himself).

A coup d'etat in some unnamed country is the backdrop for this confusing action tale, which is heavy on the blood pellets and gunplay. Col. Narriman (David Hemmings) leads a coup d'etat against a violent and corrupt dictatorship, but in doing so causes more blood to flow in the name of liberty than was shed under the tyrannical regime. Col. Zeller (Peter O'Toole) is a tank commander who becomes part of the insurrection only to double-cross the conspirators in the end, ordering the death of Narriman. The picture gives a vivid depiction of brutality in a politically unstable government (Donald Pleasence heads the torturers) and addresses the moral ambiguities concerning the effect of revolt.

p, Christopher Dalton; d, Martyn Burke; w, Martyn Burke, based on a novel by Edward N. Luttwak; ed, John Victor-Smith; ph, Ousama Rawi.

(PR:C MPAA:NR)

PRAYER FOR THE DYING, A**

(1987) 104m Goldwyn c

Mickey Rourke (Martin Fallon), Alan Bates (Jack Meehan), Bob Hoskins (Fr. Da Costa), Sammi Davis (Anna), Christopher Fulford (Billy), Liam Neeson (Liam Docherty), Alison Doody (Siobhan Donovan), Camille Coduri (Jenny), Ian Bartholomew, Mark Lambert

Pared down to its basics, A PRAYER FOR THE DYING is a film about moral self-examination, addressing the dilemma "to kill or not to kill." It's an honest attempt to understand the morality of murder, but sinks, however unintentionally, into campiness and treacly melodrama. As the film opens, Martin Fallon (Mickey Rourke, in an excellent, chameleonic performance) and two fellow IRA terrorists accidentally blow up a school bus instead of a British military transport. Fallon's pals escape, but Fallon, who is devastated by the incident, turns his back on the Cause and escapes to London, where he hopes to find safe passage to the US. Instead, the IRA and the British police tail him, forcing him to depend on a ruthless gangster, Jack Meehan (Alan Bates), for a passport. Riddled with production problems (the initial director, Franc Roddam, left the project, citing irreparable script problems), A PRAYER FOR THE DYING fails on nearly all counts. Rourke, who later disowned the film, directed a personal attack at studio head Sam Goldwyn, Jr.: "I was making a small movie that I hoped would make things clearer about what's going on [in Northern Ireland]. He wanted to turn it into a big commercial extravaganza-type thing." The film that resulted corresponds to neither of these visions.

p, Peter Snell; d, Mike Hodges; w, Edmund Ward and Martin Lynch; ed, Peter Boyle; ph, Mike Garfath; m, Bill Conti.

(PR:C-O MPAA:R)

PRIVATE BENJAMIN**½

(1980) 109m WB c

Goldie Hawn (Judy Benjamin), Eileen Brennan (Capt. Doreen Lewis), Armand Assante (Henri Tremont), Robert Webber (Col. Clay Thornbush), Sam Wanamaker (Teddy Benjamin), Barbara Barrie (Harriet Benjamin), Mary Kay Place (Pvt. Mary Lou Glass), Harry Dean Stanton (Sgt. Jim Ballard), Albert Brooks (Yale Goodman), Alan Oppenheimer (Rabbi), Gretchen Wyler (Aunt Kissy), Sally Kirkland (Helga), Maxine Stuart (Aunt Betty).

Goldie Hawn brings that old standby, the service comedy, into the 1980s in this funny tale of a Jewish American Princess who decides to be all that she can be in the all-new Army. After her second husband (wonderfully played by Albert Brooks) dies while they are making love, Judy Benjamin (Hawn) enlists in the Army, much to the chagrin of her well-to-do parents (Sam Wanamaker and Barbara Barrie). The reality of Army life under demanding CO Capt. Doreen Lewis (Eileen Brennan) turns out to be a far cry from Judy's expectation of her own room to decorate and the opportunity to visit exciting locales, and laughs aplenty are provided by the pampered Judy's reactions to rigorous training exercises, her interactions with her superiors, and a not-quite-successful love affair with a French physician (Armand Assante) while on duty in Europe. Nancy Meyers, Charles Shyer, and Harvey Miller's Oscar-nominated script offers Hawn ample opportunity to strut her patented comedic stuff, and she makes the most of the strong material, providing many funny moments in a performance that earned her an Academy Award nomination as Best Actress. Brennan, as her lesbian-leaning commanding officer, received a Best Supporting Actress nod from the Academy, and Robert Webber (as the unit commander) and Mary Kay Place (as Judy's sidekick) also provide strong support.

p, Nancy Meyers, Charles Shyer, and Harvey Miller; d, Howard Zieff; w, Nancy Meyers, Charles Shyer, and Harvey Miller; ed, Sheldon Kahn; ph, David M. Walsh, Technicolor; m, Bill Conti.

(PR:O MPAA:R)

PRIVATES ON PARADE*

(1984, Brit.) 96m HandMade/Orion Classics c

John Cleese (Maj. Giles Flack), Dennis Quilley (Acting Capt. Terri Dennis), Michael Elphick (Sgt. Maj. Reg Drummond), Nicola Pagett (Acting Lt. Sylvia Morgan), Bruce Payne (Flight Sgt. Kevin Artwright), Joe Melia (Sgt. Len Bonny), David Bamber (Sgt. Charles Bishop), Simon Jones (Sgt. Eric Young-Love), Patrick Pearson (Sgt. Steven Flowers), Phil Tan (Lee), Vincent Wong (Cheng), John Standing (Capt. Sholto Savory), John Quayle (Capt. Henry Cox), Brigitte Kahn (Mrs. Reg).

Although Peter Nichols' "Privates on Parade" was a hit with audiences and critics during its run in London's West End in 1977, this Michael Blakemore-directed film adaptation leaves much to be desired, turning the story into a sniggering homophobic farce with wildly varying shifts of tone.

PT 109—

John Cleese takes on the role of Maj. Giles Flack, the uptight commander of the British military's Song and Dance Unit, Southeast Asia (SADUSEA—"Sad, you see"), stationed near Singapore in 1948. Dennis Quilley provides the film's only real bright spot as Capt. Terri Dennis, the gay revue director who guides the troupe through a variety of female impersonations. The picture spends most of its time on "drag" humor; however, it also offers a subplot involving Sgt. Maj. Reg Drummond (Michael Elphick), an unrepentant creep who not only impregnates the company's sole female member and then pawns her off on another innocent soldier, but also provides local insurgents with ammunition and information, leading to a bloody confrontation that inexplicably moves the film away from its comic base.

p, Simon Relph; d, Michael Blakemore; w, Peter Nichols, based on his play; ed, Jim Clark; ph, Ian Wilson; m, Dennis King.

(PR:O MPAA:R)

PT 109***

(1963) 140m WB c

Cliff Robertson (Lt.[j.g.] John F. Kennedy), Ty Hardin (Ens. Leonard J. Thom), James Gregory (Comdr. C.R. Ritchie), Robert Culp (Ens. "Barney" Ross), Grant Williams (Lt. Alvin Cluster), Lew Gallo (Yeoman Rogers), Errol John (Benjamin Kevu), Michael Pate (Lt. Reginald Evans), Robert Blake ("Bucky" Harris), William Douglas (Gerard E. Zinser).

Almost 20 years before matinee idol Ronald Reagan became the president of the United States, the then-incumbent president, John F. Kennedy, was transformed into a matinee idol by this naval adventure film, which recreates his thrilling WW II heroics. Under the command of Lt. (j.g.) Kennedy (Cliff Robertson), the battle-toughened crew of PT 109 participates in a daring rescue of Marines from the island of Choiseul. Later, their speedy but susceptible craft is rammed by a Japanese destroyer and split in two, forcing the crew to swim to the relative safety of a not-so-nearby island. One of the sailors is too badly hurt to swim, however, so Kennedy carries him; later, Kennedy makes a perilous journey to an island when an Australian who monitors Japanese activity (Michael Pate) radios for help. While he makes no attempt to imitate Kennedy's distinctive accent and speech pattern, Robertson delivers a believable, if less than charismatic, portrayal of The Man Who Would Be President, though Richard L. Breen, Howard Sheehan, and Vincent X. Flaherty's adaptation of Robert J. Donovan's book leaves him no choice but to do some unnatural speechifying on occasion. The long section during which Kennedy and crew (including Ty Hardin, Robert Culp, and James Gregory) get to know each other is slow going, but the action scenes are generally worth the wait.

p, Bryan Foy; d, Leslie H. Martinson; w, Richard L. Breen, Howard Sheehan, and Vincent X. Flaherty; ed, Folmar Blangsted; ph, Robert Surtees, Panavision, Technicolor; m, William Lava and David Buttolph.

(PR:A MPAA:NR)

PURPLE HEART, THE***

(1944) 99m FOX bw

Dana Andrews (Capt. Harvey Ross), Richard Conte (Lt. Angelo Canelli), Farley Granger (Sgt. Howard Clinton), Kevin O'Shea (Sgt. Jan Skvoznik), Donald Barry (Lt. Peter Vincent), Trudy Marshall (Mrs. Ross), Sam Levene (Lt. Wayne Greenbaum), Charles Russell (Lt. Kenneth Bayforth), John Craven (Sgt. Martin Stoner), Tala Birell (Johanna Hartwig), Richard Loo (Gen. Mitsubi), Peter Chong (Mitsuru Toyama), Gregory Gay (Peter Voshenksy), Torben Meyer (Karl Kappel).

Wildly overrated at the time of its release, THE PURPLE HEART has not aged well, and viewers today may have trouble with its leering racism, overwrought patriotic speechifying, and terribly bombastic musical score. The story concerns two bomber crews captured by the Japanese after the 1942 air raid against Tokyo. Capt. Harvey Ross (Dana Andrews) is the ranking American officer of the eight bomber crew members who are imprisoned in Japan and brought to trial, not as prisoners of war, but as war criminals. The false charge against them is that they purposely dropped bombs on schools, hospitals, and other nonmilitary targets. When none of the Americans will admit to such atrocities, they are taken from their cells one by one and tortured by Gen. Mitsubi (Richard Loo), the sadistic military intelligence officer, not so much to gain confessions but so that their Japanese interrogators can learn the base from which the bombers flew. The bombers, unbeknownst to the Japanese, launched their planes from the US carrier *Hornet* while at sea—a secret the men must keep from the enemy no matter what. Directed by veteran helmsman Lewis Milestone, who seems to have shed the pacifism he so movingly extolled in ALL QUIET ON THE WESTERN FRONT (1930), THE PURPLE HEART was based on an actual kangaroo trial conducted by the Japanese in which some American pilots were condemned as war criminals and later beheaded. Although based on fact and obviously designed as propaganda to fuel patriotic fervor at the height of WW II, the film is a bit hard to take now because of the overt racism embodied by Loo, who specialized in the sort of devious, sneering, buck-toothed portrayals of the Japanese common in those days. Racism aside, the film is not without cinematic interest. Milestone brings his trademark visual style to the proceedings, especially in the courtroom scenes, in which the camera constantly prowls through the space. Cinematographer Arthur Miller's use of light and shadow is almost expressionistic, and is especially effective as the prisoners are led down the long hallway from their cells to the courtroom. The filmic highlight occurs when news comes that Corregidor has fallen to the Japanese and Milestone conveys the triumph of the enemy through an impressive Eisensteinian montage.

p, Darryl F. Zanuck; d, Lewis Milestone; w, Jerry Cady,

based on a story by Melville Crossman [Darryl F. Zanuck]; ed, Douglas Biggs; ph, Arthur Miller; m, Alfred Newman.

(PR:A MPAA:NR)

PURPLE HEARTS**

(1984) 115m Ladd/WB c

Ken Wahl *(Don Jardian)*, Cheryl Ladd *(Deborah Solomon)*, Stephen Lee *(Wizard)*, Annie McEnroe *(Hallaway)*, Paul McCrane *(Brenner)*, Cyril O'Reilly *(Zuma)*, David Harris *(Hanes)*, Hillary Bailey *(Jill)*, Lee Ermey *(Gunny)*, Drew Snyder *(Lt. Col. Larimore)*, Lane Smith *(Comdr. Markel)*, James Whitmore, Jr. *(Bwana)*.

In the days before his hit television series "Wiseguy," actor Ken Wahl was just another pretty face struggling through forgettable dreck like this. Here he's Don Jardian, a young doctor in Vietnam counting the moments until he can flee Southeast Asia and hustle back to the US, where he can open his own practice and make lots of money. When he meets Deborah Solomon (the unlikely Cheryl Ladd), a nurse who believes in the war and in what she's doing, he falls in love with her, but Deborah keeps him at arm's length because she can't bear the thought that anyone would become a doctor for any other reason than to heal. Her devotion to duty soon inspires him, and their love affair flourishes amid the horror of war. True love never runs smoothly, however, and neither does this movie. So little is made of the Vietnam setting that this story could have been set during the Spanish-American War, and with lead players as bland as Wahl and Ladd, the 115-minute running time seems interminable.

p, Sidney J. Furie; d, Sidney J. Furie; w, Rick Natkin and Sidney J. Furie; ed, George Grenville; ph, Jan Kiesser, Panavision, Technicolor; m, Robert Folk.

(PR:C-O MPAA:R)

PURSUIT OF THE GRAF SPEE, THE***

(1957, Brit.) 106m RANK c (AKA: GRAF SPEE; GB: BATTLE OF THE RIVER PLATE, THE)

John Gregson *(Capt. F.S. Bell, Exeter)*, Anthony Quayle *(Comdr. Henry Harwood, Ajax)*, Peter Finch *(Capt. Hans Langsdorff, Admiral Graf Spee)*, Ian Hunter *(Capt. Woodhouse, Ajax)*, Jack Gwillim *(Capt. Parry, Achilles)*, Bernard Lee *(Capt. Patrick Dove, Africa Shell)*, Lionel Murton *(Mike Fowler, American Radio Commentator)*, Anthony Bushell *(Mr. Millington-Drake, British Minister)*, Peter Illing *(Dr. Auani, Uruguayan Foreign Minister)*, Michael Goodliffe *(Capt. McCall, British Naval Attache)*, Patrick MacNee *(Lt. Comdr. Medley, Comdr. Harwood's Aide)*, Christopher Lee *(Manola, Cantina Manager)*, Anthony Newley *(Ralph, Merchant Seaman)*, David Farrar *(Narrator)*.

The penultimate Powell-Pressburger collaboration, THE PURSUIT OF THE GRAF SPEE (as it is known to US audiences) is a workmanlike filmization of an actual WW II naval battle between Great Britain and Germany. Much feared by the Allies in the waters of the south Atlantic is the swift German raider the Admiral Graf Spee, the pride of the German naval forces, captained by the intelligent and humanistic Capt. Hans Langsdorff (Peter Finch). Having sunk a number of Allied ships, the Graf Spee is discovered near the eastern shore of the River Plate between Argentina and Uruguay. Although vastly outpowered, three British vessels—the Ajax, the Exeter, and the Achilles—pursue the raider into the neutral Uruguayan port of Montevideo, where, through trickery and diplomatic bluffing, British intelligence convinces Lansdorff that he is about to be attacked by a huge naval force. The film is adroitly directed by Powell and Pressburger, though the concentration is on the vessels, rather than the men aboard them.

p, Michael Powell and Emeric Pressburger; d, Michael Powell and Emeric Pressburger; w, Michael Powell and Emeric Pressburger; ed, Reginald Mills; ph, Christopher Challis, VistaVision, Technicolor; m, Brian Easdale.

(PR:A MPAA:NR)

R

RAID ON ROMMEL*

(1971) 99m UNIV c

Richard Burton *(Capt. Alec Foster)*, John Colicos *(Sgt. Maj. Al MacKenzie)*, Clinton Greyn *(Maj. Tarkington)*, Wolfgang Preiss *(Gen. Erwin Rommel)*, Danielle De Metz *(Vivi)*, Karl Otto Alberty *(Capt. Heinz Schroeder)*, Christopher Cary *(Conscientious Objector)*, John Orchard *(Garth)*, Brook Williams *(Sgt. Joe Reilly)*, Greg Mullavey *(Pvt. Peter Brown)*.

The hopelessly inconsistent Richard Burton once again wanders aimlessly through a project beneath his talents in RAID ON ROMMEL. This time he plays British commando Capt. Alec Foster, stationed in North Africa during WW II, who leads a group of commandos on a mission to get behind the German lines and destroy their big guns so that the Brits can attack. To do this, Foster and company allow themselves to be captured and interred in a POW camp, making it a fairly simple matter to escape and blow up the artillery. Dully directed by veteran helmsman Henry Hathaway in the twilight of his career, RAID ON ROMMEL is a would-be desert epic that lifts exciting footage from the vastly superior TOBRUK (1967). Unfortunately, these pilfered action scenes are far and away the most interesting part of the movie, and if you've seen TOBRUK, you've already seen the best that RAID ON ROMMEL has to offer.

p, Harry Tatelman; d, Henry Hathaway; w, Richard Bluel; ed, Gene Palmer; ph, Earl Rath, Technicolor; m, Hal Mooney.

(PR:C MPAA:GP)

RAMBO: FIRST BLOOD, PART II—

RAMBO: FIRST BLOOD, PART II zero

(1985) 92m Anabasis/Tri-Star c

Sylvester Stallone *(John Rambo)*, Richard Crenna *(Trautman)*, Charles Napier *(Murdock)*, Steven Berkoff *(Podovsky)*, Julia Nickson *(Co Bao)*, George Kee Cheung *(Tay)*, Andy Wood *(Banks)*, Martin Kove *(Ericson)*.

This big-budget action film is yet another chapter in the canonization of muscle-bound Sylvester Stallone, who has made a career of selling himself as "America's Hero" by playing the same two characters, Rocky and Rambo, over and over. RAMBO, the sequel to his surprisingly successful FIRST BLOOD, was the pinnacle of what has come to be known as the Vietnam War fantasy film—movies that feature a small band of heroic American commandos reentering Vietnam and winning decisive battles UNCOMMON VALOR and the Chuck Norris MISSING IN ACTION films were among the most popular). After venting his anger against the "system" by single-handedly destroying an entire American town, vet John Rambo (Stallone) is offered a chance to get out of prison if he will accept an assignment to covertly return to Vietnam and obtain evidence that will prove that American POWs are still being held. Of course Rambo accepts the proposal, and after parachuting into Vietnam, he hooks up with Co Bao (Julia Nickson), a beautiful Vietnamese freedom fighter who serves as his guide. Rambo locates a camp chock full of American POWs, then battles both Vietnamese Communists and their evil Soviet advisors to free his countrymen. The image of the sweaty, muscular super-hero, with gunbelts draped over his bulging biceps, caught on big with the public, and a rash of Rambo toys, games, posters, clothing, and even a children's cartoon show (though children should be kept away from this film) hit the market with a vengeance. All-in-all, it's a pretty offensive film, especially to the Americans who fought in Vietnam.

p, Buzz Feitshans; d, George P. Cosmatos; w, Sylvester Stallone and James Cameron, based on a story by Kevin Jarre and characters by David Morrell; ed, Mark Goldblatt and Mark Helfrich; ph, Jack Cardiff, Panavision, Technicolor; m, Jerry Goldsmith.

(PR:O MPAA:R)

RAMBO III*½

(1988) 101m Carolco/Tri-Star c

Sylvester Stallone *(John Rambo)*, Richard Crenna *(Col. Trautman)*, Marc de Jonge *(Col. Zaysen)*, Kurtwood Smith *(Griggs)*, Spiros Focas *(Masoud)*, Sasson Gabai *(Mousa)*, Doudi Shoua *(Hamid)*, Randy Raney *(Gen. Kourov)*, Marcus Gilbert *(Tomask)*, Alon Abutbul *(Nissem)*, Mahmoud Assadollahi *(Rahim)*, Yosef Shiloah *(Khalid)*, Harold Diamond *(Stick Fighter)*, Shaby Ben-Aroya *(Uri)*, Marciano Shoshi *(Afghan Girl)*.

Reportedly the most expensive film ever made ($63 million, not including Sylvester Stallone's $20 million salary), RAMBO III begins in Thailand, where John Rambo's (Stallone) only friend, Col. Trautman (Richard Crenna), tracks him down and invites him to join a covert mission in Afghanistan to deliver Stinger missiles to the *mujahedeen* combating the Soviet invasion there. Mumbling that his "war is over," Rambo declines. When Trautman is caught by the Soviets, however, the warrior can't let the capture of his only friend slide by unanswered, and he launches a one-man invasion of Afghanistan to rescue Trautman, hooking up with the Afghan rebels in the process. The film soon becomes one long series of huge explosions as—using his trusty knife, bow-with-exploding-arrows, and whatever weapons he picks up along the way—Rambo wipes out scores of Russians in an effort to rescue his buddy and to defeat his nemesis, evil Soviet commander Zaysen (Marc de Jonge). Released in the same month that Soviet troops began to leave Afghanistan, RAMBO III became an instant Gorbachev-era anachronism, its absurd heroics appearing more cartoonish than ever. With an unusually troubled production history in which many of its crew, from the director to the still photographer, were fired—mainly due to "differences" with cowriter Stallone—the film is, moreover, so rudimentary in concept and presentation that it actually manages to be boring during its lengthy scenes of mass mayhem. Less offensive than its predecessor, RAMBO III is still a mindless and uninspired effort.

p, Buzz Feitshans; d, Peter MacDonald; w, Sylvester Stallone and Sheldon Lettich, based on characters created by David Morrell; ed, James Symons, Andrew London, O. Nicholas Brown, and Edward Warschilka; ph, John Stanier, Technicolor; m, Jerry Goldsmith.

(PR:O MPAA:R)

RAN*****

(1985, Jap./Fr.) 160m Herald Ace-Nippon Herald-Greenwich/Orion c

Tatsuya Nakadai *(Lord Hidetora Ichimonji)*, Akira Terao *(Tarotakatora Ichimonji)*, Jinpachi Nezu *(Jiromasatora Ichimonji)*, Daisuke Ryu *(Saburonaotora Ichimonji)*, Mieko Harada *(Lady Kaede)*, Yoshiko Miyazaki *(Lady Sue)*, Kazuo Kato *(Ikoma)*, Masayuki Yui *(Tango)*, Peter *(Kyoami)*.

At age 75, Akira Kurosawa, Japan's greatest living director, created one more magnificent work that will surely stand the test of time. In RAN, Kurosawa turned to Shakespeare for inspiration—as he had in THRONE OF BLOOD nearly 30 years before—and chose to film a Japanese adaptation of "King Lear." Set in 16th-century Japan, RAN (the Japanese character for fury, revolt, and madness—chaos) begins as Hidetora Ichimonji (Tatsuya Nakadai), an aging warlord who has acquired power through 50 years of ruthless bloodshed, announces his intention to divide his kingdom among his three sons, each of whom will live at one of three outlying castles. While the elder sons thank him for the honor, the youngest calls his father senile and mad, noting—prophetically—that it will only be a matter of time until the ambitious brothers begin battling for possession of the whole domain. In the process, Hidetora and his kingdom are consigned to a tragic and spectacular end. Kurosawa wanted desperately to make RAN for more than

10 years before, on the strength of KAGEMUSHA's success, he was finally able to obtain funding for this, the most expensive film ever made in Japan (though the $11-million budget is small by Hollywood standards). Partly shot at two of that country's most revered landmarks (the ancient castles at Himeji and Kumamoto; the third castle was constructed of plastic and wood on the slopes of Mount Fuji), RAN is a visually stunning epic, containing some of the most beautiful, colorful, breathtaking imagery ever committed to celluloid. As he grew older, Kurosawa began to shoot his films in a more traditionally Japanese style (static takes, little camera movement, no flamboyant editing). Here, especially in the battle scenes, he adopts a detached, impassive camera, heightening the tragedy by giving the audience a godlike, but powerless, perspective on all the madness and folly unfolding on-screen. At the same time, Kurosawa infuses the film with deep human emotion, aided by uniformly superb performances. The work of a mature artist in complete control of his medium, RAN is a true cinematic masterwork of sight, sound, intelligence, and—most importantly—passion. (In Japanese; English subtitles.)

p, Masato Hara and Serge Silberman; d, Akira Kurosawa; w, Akira Kurosawa, Hideo Oguni, and Masato Ide, based on *King Lear* by William Shakespeare; ed, Akira Kurosawa; ph, Takao Saito, Masaharu Ueda, and Asakazu Nakai; m, Toru Takemitsu.

(PR:O MPAA:R)

RAZOR'S EDGE, THE****

(1946) 146m FOX bw

Tyrone Power *(Larry Darrell)*, Gene Tierney *(Isabel Bradley)*, John Payne *(Gray Maturin)*, Anne Baxter *(Sophie Nelson)*, Clifton Webb *(Elliott Templeton)*, Herbert Marshall *(Somerset Maugham)*, Lucile Watson *(Mrs. Louise Bradley)*, Frank Latimore *(Bob MacDonald)*, Elsa Lanchester *(Miss Keith)*, Fritz Kortner *(Kosti)*, John Wengraf *(Joseph)*.

Larry Darrell (Tyrone Power) is an idealistic youth, a former WW I pilot whose experiences in battle have caused him to question the moral values and the very fiber of his society. Returning to Chicago, Larry disturbs his high-society fiancee, Isabel (Gene Tierney), with his inexplicable urge to seek out the real meaning of life. He balks at the thought of joining the social *creme de la creme*, and instead embarks on a quest to find intellectual and spiritual freedom, journeying to Paris and Nepal, where he finds an elderly Hindu mystic who brings peace to his troubled mind and spirit. Ten years later, Larry is reunited with Isabel and his former friends, all of whom have undergone various degrees of suffering—physically, emotionally, and financially. More melodrama and romance than war film, THE RAZOR'S EDGE—based on the classic novel by Somerset Maugham—depicts a generation of people affected by war, by the senselessness of battlefield deaths and war's constant reminders of mortality. The film examines the possible futility of life, including the certain futility of war, and provides an intelligent and thoughtful counterpoint to the many films that celebrate glory in battle.

p, Darryl F. Zanuck; d, Edmund Goulding; w, Lamar Trotti, based on the novel by W. Somerset Maugham; ed, J. Watson Webb; ph, Arthur Miller; m, Alfred Newman.

(PR:C MPAA:NR)

RAZOR'S EDGE, THE***

(1984) 128m Colgems/COL c

Bill Murray *(Larry Darrell)*, Theresa Russell *(Sophie)*, Catherine Hicks *(Isabel)*, Denholm Elliott *(Elliott Templeton)*, James Keach *(Gray Maturin)*, Peter Vaughan *(MacKenzie)*, Brian Doyle-Murray *(Piedmont)*, Stephen Davies *(Malcolm)*, Saeed Jaffrey *(Raaz)*, Faith Brook *(Louisa Bradley)*, Andre Maranne *(Joseph)*, Bruce Boa *(Henry Maturin)*.

Bill Murray takes the lead role of Larry Darrell (played by Tyrone Power in the 1946 original adaptation of Somerset Maugham's tale), an upper-class lad who isn't ready to settle down into marriage, home, and job. Instead, he wants to travel, read, and learn about life—to find the path to salvation. He breaks off his engagement to Isabel (Catherine Hicks), says farewell to friends Gray (James Keach) and Sophie (Theresa Russell), and shortly thereafter finds himself in the trenches of WW I. After the death of a fellow soldier (played by Murray's actual brother Brian Doyle-Murray), Larry moves on to India in search of religious enlightenment. Living atop the Himalayas and discovering his own spirituality with the help of Raaz (Saeed Jaffrey), Larry continues to grow, although he is warned that "the path to salvation is narrow, and it's as difficult to walk as the razor's edge." Next, he travels to Paris and is reunited with Isabel, who has since married Gray, and Sophie, who is now a drug-addicted, drunken prostitute. While not as compelling as its 1946 predecessor (John Byrum's direction is unfocused and Murray's acting is somewhere between complex and goofy) this version of *The Razor's Edge*, with a script cowritten by Murray, still manages to make a potent statement about the effect of war; for Larry, the experience of death and suffering proves the catalyst that sets him on his journey of self-discovery. The film was a pet project of Murray's, and went before the cameras only because of the actor's bartering power. His selling point to Columbia executives was simple—he would do GHOSTBUSTERS only if they let him do THE RAZOR'S EDGE.

p, Robert P. Marcucci and Harry Benn; d, John Byrum; w, John Byrum and Bill Murray, based on the novel by W. Somerset Maugham; ed, Peter Boyle; ph, Peter Hannan; m, Jack Nitzsche.

(PR:C-O MPAA:PG-13)

REASON TO LIVE, A REASON TO DIE, A*½

(1974, It./Fr./Ger./Sp.) 92m Heritage-Sancropsiap-Terza-Europrodis-Corona-Atlantida/ K Tel c (UNA RAGIONE PER VIVERE E UNA PER MORIRE; AKA: MASSACRE AT FORT HOLMAN)

James Coburn *(Col. Pembroke)*, Telly Savalas *(Maj. Ward)*, Bud Spencer [Carlo Pedersoli] *(Eli Sampson)*, Ralph Good-

REBEL—

win (Sgt. Brent), Joseph Mitchell (Maj. Ballard), William Spofford (Ted Wendel), Guy Ranson (Will Fernandez), Joe Pollini (Half-breed), Allan Leroy (Confederate Sergeant), Robert Burton (Donald MacIvers).

A subpar spaghetti western from Italian director Tonino Valerii, this film borrows heavily from such diverse sources as Jean Renoir's GRAND ILLUSION (1936), Robert Aldrich's THE DIRTY DOZEN (1967), Sam Peckinpah's THE WILD BUNCH (1969), and Sergio Leone's DUCK, YOU SUCKER! (1971). During the Civil War, we meet Yankee commander Col. Pembroke (James Coburn), who inexplicably turns over his fort to Confederate forces led by Maj. Ward (Telly Savalas, doing Eric von Stroheim) without putting up a fight. Facing court martial, Pembroke decides to redeem himself by organizing a group of soldiers sentenced to death and leading them on a raid to get the fort back. Although director Valerii emulates and parodies the aforementioned directors, he is *not* in their league, and the film is a fairly tedious effort with only the charms of Coburn, Savalas, and veteran spaghetti western star Bud Spencer [Carlo Pedersoli] to recommend it.

p, Michael Billingsley; d, Tonino Valerii; w, Tonino Valerii and Ernesto Gastaldi; m, Riz Ortolani.

(PR:A   MPAA:PG)

REBEL*½

(1985, Aus.) 91m Village Roadshow/Vestron c

Matt Dillon (Rebel), Debbie Byrne (Kathy McLeod), Bryan Brown (Tiger Kelly), Bill Hunter (Browning), Ray Barrett (Bubbles), Julie Nihill (Joycie), John O'May (Bernie), Kim Deacon (Hazel), Sheree da Costa (Barbara).

A lavish, big-budget musical wartime drama set in Australia, REBEL is an example of the kind of film they—fortunately—just don't make anymore. Kathy McLeod (Debbie Byrne) is an entertainer in a small Quonset hut saloon that stages amazing production numbers (they could shame Busby Berkeley) for the benefit of Allied troops returning from battle with the Japanese. One night she hosts a small party at her flat, where the guests include a young Marine sergeant (Matt Dillon) just back from Guadalcanal. He immediately sets his sights on Kathy (whose husband is off fighting), dogging her and feigning illness to remain in her apartment, and eventually she begins to open her heart to him. After her husband is ever so conveniently killed, the marine reveals himself to be a deserter sick of the senselessness of war. A shallow exercise, REBEL fails chiefly because of Dillon's ridiculous character—though supposedly some kind of hero at Guadalcanal, he seems little more than a dim-witted and manipulative heel. The film does have an undeniable visual flair, but, from the overly lavish production numbers to the marine's stylish battle flashbacks, it hardly seems appropriate to the material. One of the few signs of wartime austerity are the silk stockings purchased on the black market; and oh, those stockings!—director Michael Jenkins has a lingerie fetish not to be believed. The film was originally to star Olivia Newton-John, who refused the role—luckily, since REBEL opened to universal indifference.

p, Phillip Emanuel; d, Michael Jenkins; w, Michael Jenkins and Bob Herbert, based on the play "No Names. . .No Packdrill" by Herbert; ed, Michael Honey; ph, Peter James, Panavision, Eastmancolor; m, Chris Neal.

(PR:O   MPAA:R)

REBEL LOVE*½

(1986) 80m Raven Cliff/Troma Team c

Jamie Rose (Columbine Cromwell), Terence Knox (Hightower/McHugh), Fran Ryan (Granny Plug), Carl Spurlock (Yankee Sergeant), Rick Waln (Yankee Corporal), Larry Larson (Aaron Cromwell), Charles Hill (Rebel Captain), Harry Howell (Gen. Clarence Mason), Thom Gossom, Jr. (Pompeii, a Slave), Jimmy Rosser (Unfriendly Farmer).

A well-intentioned but nonetheless amateurish romance set near the Indiana-Kentucky border during the Civil War, REBEL LOVE concerns Hightower (Terence Knox), an actor who is hired to work as a spy for the Confederates. In the meantime, Columbine Cromwell (Jamie Rose), a war widow, spends her days listening to stories of past romances told by local merchant Granny Plug (Fran Ryan), an aging tramp who has been married nine times. When Columbine opens her front door to find Hightower unconscious, the spy—disguising himself as an Irish stove repairman named McHugh—is nursed back to health by the lovelorn woman. Their idyllic existence is shaken, however, when a troop of Union soldiers come looking for Hightower and, in the process, reveal to Columbine her lover's true identity. A low-budget entry filmed entirely in Alabama, REBEL LOVE is an attempt to reproduce the passions of a Harlequin romance, with a little bit of the Civil War tossed in for color. The performances (save Ryan's) are merely passable (Knox) or thoroughly unconvincing (Rose), and the Civil War backdrop is just that—a one-dimensional setting serving only to differentiate this love story from countless others just as trite.

p, John Quenelle; d, Milton Bagby, Jr.; w, Milton Bagby, Jr.; ed, Mellena Bridges; ph, Joseph A. Whigham, Panavision, TVC Color; m, Bobby Horton.

(PR:C-O   MPAA:NR)

RED BADGE OF COURAGE, THE*****

(1951) 69m MGM bw

Audie Murphy (Henry Fleming), Bill Mauldin (Tom Wilson), Douglas Dick (Lieutenant), Royal Dano (Tattered Man), John Dierkes (Jim Conlin), Arthur Hunnicutt (Bill Porter), Andy Devine (Fat Soldier), Robert Easton Burke [Robert Easton] (Thompson), Smith Ballew (Captain), Glenn Strange (Colonel), Dan White (Sergeant), Frank McGraw (Captain), Tim Durant (General), James Whitmore (Narrator).

John Huston always insisted that this Civil War battle picture examining the fine line between cowardice and bravery *could have been* his greatest film, and certainly it is among the director's best despite the tampering of studio executives. Audie Murphy, the most decorated hero of

WW II, is Henry Fleming, a youth who joins the Union army and grows restless waiting for the orders that will take him into battle. When news finally comes that his unit is to join others for an impending battle, he turns braggart. But faced with the enemy, Henry runs in terror, only to confront his fear later and return to his unit for another battle. Huston's direction is vivid in every scene; however, the film's battle sequences are its most impressive element. In more pensive moments, THE RED BADGE OF COURAGE is a moving study of Americans fighting Americans, and the reluctance many of them bring to this awful task. Much of the credit for the overall visual effect of the film goes to cameraman Harold Rosson, who lends it a gritty hardscrabble feel, marvelously capturing the period. Huston left the production immediately after its completion to fly across the world to make THE AFRICAN QUEEN, leaving his film in the hands of studio chiefs who cut it as they saw fit, removing much of the director's questioning of the necessity of warfare (unacceptable during the Cold War), adding narration by James Whitmore, and reducing the running time to a scant 69 minutes. When the film didn't play well with premiere audiences, MGM sent it out without fanfare, offering it as a second feature on double bills—hardly a way to recoup production costs. Audiences failed to identify with the film's grim realism and its mostly unknown cast, and the well-known Crane story wasn't enough of a draw to insure box-office success. Huston maintained that the movie as he filmed it was one of his favorites, and in the 1970s an attempt was made to revive the uncut version, but to Huston's knowledge a print of his original cut no longer existed and the idea was dropped.

p, Gottfried Reinhardt; d, John Huston; w, John Huston and Albert Band, based on the novel by Stephen Crane; ed, Ben Lewis; ph, Harold Rosson; m, Bronislau Kaper.

(PR:C   MPAA:NR)

RED DAWN*

(1984) 100m MGM/UA c

Patrick Swayze *(Jed)*, C. Thomas Howell *(Robert)*, Lea Thompson *(Erica)*, Charlie Sheen *(Matt)*, Darren Dalton *(Daryl)*, Jennifer Grey *(Toni)*, Brad Savage *(Danny)*, Doug Toby *(Aardvark)*, Ben Johnson *(Mason)*, Harry Dean Stanton *(Mr. Eckert)*, Ron O'Neal *(Bella)*, William Smith *(Strelnikov)*, Vladek Sheybal *(Bratchenko)*, Powers Boothe *(Andy)*, Frank McRae *(Mr. Teasdale)*, Roy Jenson *(Mr. Morris)*, Lane Smith *(Mayor Bates)*.

Yet another infantile right-wing fantasy from writer-director John Milius, this cinematic embodiment of the paranoid delusions of militarists, survivalists, and television evangelists is definitely a film for the Reagan era. It's as if the clock has turned back to the mid-1950s, when short subjects like RED NIGHTMARE (in which a man wakes up one morning to find his small American town taken over by Communists) and COMMUNISM AT OUR DOOR were presented to scare the daylights out of the complacent public. After an unconvincing explanation of the origins of a conventional war between the US and the USSR, RED DAWN begins as students in a small town in the Northwest watch in amazement as Russian and Cuban troops parachute in and open fire. A few clever kids (Patrick Swayze, C. Thomas Howell, Lea Thompson, Charlie Sheen, Darren Dalton, Jennifer Grey, and Brad Savage) jump in a pickup truck and hightail it to the general store, stocking up on food, weapons, and ammo. Then they head for the mountains, where they stage guerrilla operations on par with those undertaken in the Soviet-Afghan war. Meanwhile, after token resistance from the adults, the Commies install an occupation government—the Soviet commander, Strelnikov (William Smith), putting a Cuban, Bella (Ron O'Neal), in charge. The male American adults are then rounded up and held in a drive-in theater-cum-reeducation camp, where their sadistic Soviet captors force them to watch Russian director Sergei Eisenstein's 1938 classic ALEXANDER NEVSKY (needless to say, this sequence is unintentionally hilarious). Back in town, Communist propaganda springs up everywhere, and dreaded breadlines begin to form. In the mountains, the teenagers have some success ambushing armed columns of the invasion force, aided by a recluse (Ben Johnson) and a downed fighter pilot (Powers Boothe). The rumination of an adolescent sensibility—wholly lacking in plausibility, character development, or social observation—RED DAWN would be much more offensive if it weren't so darn silly. Badly paced and poorly executed, the film even fails as an action movie. Unintentional laughter erupts in nearly every scene, and the characters are so cliched and broadly sketched that there are no surprises at all. The cast struggles to make the material believable, with Harry Dean Stanton scoring the only memorable moment as the imprisoned father of one of the boys, but RED DAWN is simply too simplistic and inept to be taken seriously.

p, Buzz Feitshans and Barry Beckerman; d, John Milius; w, Kevin Reynolds and John Milius, based on the novel by Reynolds; ed, Thom Noble; ph, Ric Waite, Metrocolor; m, Basil Poledouris.

(PR:O   MPAA:PG-13)

REDS***½

(1981) 200m PAR c

Warren Beatty *(John Reed)*, Diane Keaton *(Louise Bryant)*, Edward Herrmann *(Max Eastman)*, Jerzy Kosinski *(Grigory Zinoviev)*, Jack Nicholson *(Eugene O'Neill)*, Paul Sorvino *(Louis Fraina)*, Maureen Stapleton *(Emma Goldman)*, Nicolas Coster *(Paul Trullinger)*, M. Emmet Walsh *(Speaker at the Liberal Club)*, Ian Wolfe *(Mr. Partlow)*, Bessie Love *(Mrs. Partlow)*, MacIntyre Dixon *(Carl Walters)*, Pat Starr *(Helen Walters)*, Eleanor D. Wilson *(Mrs. Reed)*, Max Wright *(Floyd Dell)*, George Plimpton *(Horace Whigham)*, Gene Hackman *(Pete Van Wherry)*.

Produced, directed, and cowritten by Warren Beatty, who also stars as radical journalist John Reed, REDS is a sprawling yet highly personal epic. Focusing on Reed's tempestuous relationship with feminist Louise Bryant (Diane Keaton), the $45-million production also encompasses a capsule history of the American Left in the early 20th century, and depicts the Bolshevik Revolution, which

RETURN OF THE SOLDIER, THE—

Reed chronicled in *Ten Days That Shook the World*. Punctuated by the reminiscences of a number of Reed's real-life contemporaries—shot in stark black and white and unidentified, though they include Rebecca West, Henry Miller, and Hamilton Fish—the three-hour-plus marathon shifts the action among a variety of American locales and from the States to the Soviet Union. Among the larger-than-life figures given the personal treatment are Louise's one-time lover Eugene O'Neill (Jack Nicholson), Emma Goldman (magnificently played by Maureen Stapleton, who won a Best Supporting Actress Oscar for her work), Communist party chief Grigory Zinoviev (novelist Jerzy Kosinski), and Max Eastman (Edward Herrmann). Beatty, who won the Academy Award for Best Director and was nominated as Best Actor, has created a film of DOCTOR ZHIVAGO-like scope and majesty, yet REDS succeeds best in smallest moments, when focusing on the interaction between its carefully drawn characters. Keaton fails to bring the necessary depth to her portrayal and relies too much on her well-known quirky film persona, but Beatty gives a highly nuanced, appropriately energized performance, and the supporting players are uniformly excellent. The film's chief attribute, however, is also one of its major flaws, for in presenting an up-close-and-personal look at the lives of its famous figures—particularly Reed and Bryant's love affair and marriage—the world-shaking events whose depiction lend the film its uniqueness are sometimes given short shrift. Nonetheless, the brilliantly designed and photographed REDS is a beautiful, passionate film, both in its stunningly re-created action scenes and in its quietest moments.

p, Warren Beatty; d, Warren Beatty; w, Warren Beatty and Trevor Griffiths; ed, Dede Allen and Craig McKay; ph, Vittorio Storaro, Technicolor; m, Stephen Sondheim and Dave Grusin.

(PR:C-O MPAA:PG)

RETURN OF THE SOLDIER, THE***½
(1983, Brit.) 102m Brent Walker-Barry R. Cooper-Skreba/FOX c

Julie Christie *(Kitty)*, Glenda Jackson *(Margaret)*, Ann-Margret *(Jenny)*, Alan Bates *(Chris)*, Ian Holm *(Ernest)*, Frank Finlay *(William)*, Jeremy Kemp *(Frank)*, Hilary Mason *(Ward)*, John Sharp *(Pearson)*, Elizabeth Edmunds *(Emery)*, Valerie Whittington *(Beatrice)*, Patsy Byrne *(Mrs. Plummer)*, Robert Keegan *(Chauffeur)*, Amanda Grinling *(Alexandra)*, Edward De Souza *(Edward)*, Michael Cochrane *(Stephen)*, Vickery Turner *(Jessica)*.

Chris (Alan Bates) is a shell-shocked British WW II vet who returns home with no memory of his marriage to Kitty (Julie Christie), a snobbish woman who comes to represent his dissatisfaction with life. Seeing the opportunity finally to win Chris after years of yearning, old maid Jenny (Ann-Margret) tries to fulfill her unrequited love, but soon finds herself competing for his affections with Margaret (Glenda Jackson), his childhood flame. Chris, however, finds all of these emotional entanglements difficult to deal with, so he retreats into the past. It's a somewhat slow-moving film, but one filled with touching, genuine performances from a fine cast.

p, Ann Skinner and Simon Relph; d, Alan Bridges; w, Hugh Whitemore, based on the novel by Rebecca West; ed, Laurence Mery Clark; ph, Stephen Goldblatt, Technicolor; m, Richard Rodney Bennett.

(PR:C MPAA:NR)

REVOLT OF JOB, THE***½
(1984, Hung./Ger.) 98m Mafilm Tarsulas-Starfilm-ZDFMacropus-Hungarian Television/Teleculture c (JOB LAZADASA)

Ferenc Zenthe *(Job)*, Hedi Temessy *(Roza)*, Gabor Feher *(Lacko)*, Peter Rudolf *(Jani)*, Leticia Caro *(Ilka)*.

Set in a small East Hungarian farming village in 1943, THE REVOLT OF JOB stars Ferenc Zenthe and Hedi Temessy as Job and Roza, an elderly Jewish couple who have outlived all their children. Wishing for an heir, the couple schemes with an adoption center to gain custody of a seven-year-old Christian boy, Lacko (Gabor Feher), by trading two calves for him. Lacko is at first rebellious and cannot be reached by his loving "parents," choosing instead to play with a dog he has befriended, but eventually he warms to Job and Roza. All the while, the advance of Hitler's troops threatens Job and Roza's safety, and the couple prepare for the worst, arranging for a Gentile family to take care of their bewildered, now-loving adopted son while teaching him all they can about their own, endangered culture. Wisely concentrating its examination of religious and historical themes in a simple, small story, THE REVOLT OF JOB is a moving and intelligent film. As told from the boy's point of view, the film is dependent on Feher's performance as Lacko, and, thankfully, he is superb in his debut role. The script and direction by Imre Gyongyossy and Barna Kabay are fine, but it is the young star—selected from more than 4,000 hopefuls by the filmmakers—who remains the film's brightest point. The film received a Best Foreign-Language Film Oscar nomination. (In Hungarian; English subtitles.)

d, Imre Gyongyossy and Barna Kabay; w, Imre Gyongyossy, Barna Kabay, and Katalin Petenyi; ed, Katalin Petenyi; ph, Gabor Szabo, Eastmancolor; m, Zoltan Jeny.

(PR:O MPAA:NR)

REVOLUTION**
(1985, Brit./Norway) 125m Goldcrest-Viking/WB c

Al Pacino *(Tom Dobb)*, Donald Sutherland *(Sgt. Maj. Peasy)*, Nastassja Kinski *(Daisy McConnahay)*, Joan Plowright *(Mrs.McConnahay)*, Dave King *(Mr. McConnahay)*, Steven Berkoff *(Sgt. Jones)*, John Wells *(Corty)*, Annie Lennox *(Liberty Woman)*, Dexter Fletcher *(Ned Dobb)*, Sid Owen *(Young Ned)*, Richard O'Brien *(Lord Hampton)*, Eric Milota *(Merle)*, Felicity Dean *(Betsy)*, Jo Anna Lee *(Amy)*.

A beautifully photographed but emotionally uninvolving

story of the American Revolution, REVOLUTION, instead of concentrating on the conflict's major players, follows the lives of a handful of everyday people. Tom Dobb (Al Pacino) is a Scottish immigrant (and as much of a caricature as Pacino's Cuban refugee in SCARFACE) driven to fight when his son is captured and tortured by Sgt. Maj. Peasy (Donald Sutherland), a sadistic British officer. Where there is war and suffering in movies, there also is romance and, in REVOLUTION, it comes in the form of Daisy McConnahay (Nastassja Kinski), a patrician who turns her back on Mom and Dad to take up with the rebels. Naturally, Tom and Daisy are separated, only to be happily reunited after the war. Hugh Hudson had previously proven himself a rather capable director with CHARIOTS OF FIRE and GREYSTOKE, but here the thoughtfulness and subtlety of those previous pictures is reduced to lifelessness. The film makes a noble attempt to present history in a realistic, nonheroic light, but Hudson is done in by a dull script and some ludicrous (curiously *un*realistic) casting (Pacino as a Scot, Sutherland as a Brit, and Kinski as an American). It is no surprise that REVOLUTION died a quick death at the box office—filmgoers want their history bigger than life, and rejected Hudson's attempt to put it all in realistic perspective.

p, Irwin Winkler; d, Hugh Hudson; w, Robert Dillon; ed, Stuart Baird; ph, Bernard Lutic, System 35 Widescreen, Technicolor; m, John Corigliano.

(PR:C   MPAA:PG)

RICHARD III*****

(1956, Brit.) 158m LFP-Big Ben/Lopert c

Laurence Olivier *(King Richard III)*, Ralph Richardson *(Buckingham)*, Claire Bloom *(Lady Anne)*, John Gielgud *(Clarence)*, Sir Cedric Hardwicke *(King Edward IV)*, Mary Kerridge *(Queen Elizabeth)*, Pamela Brown *(Jane Shore)*, Alec Clunes *(Hastings)*, Stanley Baker *(Henry Tudor)*, Michael Gough *(Dighton)*, Laurence Naismith *(Stanley)*, Norman Wooland *(Catesby)*, Helen Haye *(Duchess of York)*, John Laurie *(Lovel)*, Esmond Knight *(Ratcliffe)*, Nicholas Hannen *(Archbishop of Canterbury)*, John Phillips *(Norfolk)*.

This was Laurence Olivier's third Shakespeare film—the first two were HENRY V and HAMLET, the latter earning him an Oscar—and RICHARD III is arguably the best of the three. The picture begins with the coronation of Edward IV (Cedric Hardwicke), in a scene borrowed from the end of "Henry IV, Part III," with Richard (Olivier) watching jealously in the background. Edward is soon drowned in a vat of wine and Richard is the king, engaging in a series of back-stabbings and duplicities that eventually bring him to the Battle of Bosworth, where he is unseated from his steed, screams "A horse, a horse! My kingdom for a horse!" and is then set upon by the minions of Henry Tudor (Stanley Baker). This scene was the first shot (in Spain), and the picture began dangerously when Olivier was accidentally pierced by a bolt from the film's stunt archer that was supposed to hit the protected horse (an animal that had been trained to fall and play dead on command). Olivier continued the scene until a natural break in the action was called for, then asked for medical aid. It took three hours each day to put the complex makeup—the same prosthetics he wore on stage, including a false nose, hunched back, false hand, and black pageboy wig—on Olivier, who, with screenwriter Alan Dent, added to Shakespeare's story the two monks who act as a silent Greek chorus as they view the intrigues. RICHARD III was not a hit when it came out in England, so the producers made a unique deal for the US and premiered it on NBC television for the sum of $500,000 (in later years it was re-released to resounding success, and has been the most financially rewarding of Olivier's Shakespeare films). Olivier and Alexander Korda had hoped to film a version of "Macbeth," with Vivien Leigh as Lady MacBeth, but Korda died a year after RICHARD III was made and lack of interest in the project caused it to be tabled. The British Film Academy gave RICHARD III Best British Film, Best Film, and Best Actor awards, totally overlooking the superior photography by Otto Heller and the sets by Roger Furse and Carmen Dillon. Olivier was nominated for a Best Actor Academy Award, but lost to Yul Brynner for THE KING AND I.

p, Laurence Olivier; d, Laurence Olivier and Anthony Bushell; w, Alan Dent, Laurence Olivier, Colley Cibber, and David Garrick, based on the play by William Shakespeare; ed, Helga Cranston; ph, Otto Heller, VistaVision, Technicolor; m, Sir William Walton.

(PR:A-C   MPAA:NR)

RIDDLE OF THE SANDS, THE**

(1979, Brit.) 102m RANK c

Michael York *(Charles Carruthers)*, Jenny Agutter *(Clara Dollman)*, Simon MacCorkindale *(Arthur Davies)*, Alan Badel *(Dollman)*, Jurgen Andersen *(Von Bruning)*, Olga Lowe *(Frau Dollman)*, Hans Meyer *(Grimm)*, Michael Sheard *(Bohme)*, Wolf Kahler *(The Kaiser)*, Ronald Markham *(Withers)*.

British yachtsman Arthur Davies (Simon MacCorkindale) is sailing along the northern coast of Germany, circa 1901, when he encounters German sea captain Dollmann (Alan Badel), who, it is later discovered, is actually a renegade British naval officer. His suspicions aroused, Davies calls on his old college chum Charles Carruthers (Michael York), and together they uncover the Kaiser's secret plan to invade England. The film is based on the 1903 Erskine Childers novel considered by many to be the forerunner of the modern espionage thriller; however, there are no thrills in this film adaptation, full of implausible situations and long sections in which nothing really seems to be happening. MacCorkindale and York are adequate but given very little to do; the exceptional Jenny Agutter may be familiar to fans of Nicholas Roeg's WALKABOUT. The film does have some fine photography and interesting visual compositions.

p, Drummond Challis; d, Tony Maylam; w, Tony Maylam and John Bailey, based on the novel by Erskine Childers;

RIO GRANDE—

ed, Peter Hollywood; ph, Christopher Challis, Panavision, EastmanColor; m, Howard Blake.

(PR:C MPAA:NR)

RIO GRANDE*****

(1950) 105m Argosy Pictures/REP bw

John Wayne *(Lt. Col. Kirby Yorke)*, Maureen O'Hara *(Mrs. Kathleen Yorke)*, Ben Johnson *(Trooper Tyree)*, Claude Jarman, Jr. *(Trooper Jeff Yorke)*, Harry Carey, Jr. *(Trooper Daniel "Sandy" Boone)*, Chill Wills *(Dr. Wilkins)*, J. Carrol Naish *(Gen. Philip Sheridan)*, Victor McLaglen *(Sgt. Maj. Quincannon)*, Grant Withers *(Deputy Marshal)*, Peter Ortiz *(Capt. St. Jacques)*, Gaylord "Steve" Pendleton *(Capt. Prescott)*, Sons of the Pioneers

This fine portrait of the US Cavalry was the third in John Ford's magnificent trilogy about the troopers of the Old West, following FORT APACHE (1948) and SHE WORE A YELLOW RIBBON (1949). Lt. Col. Kirby Yorke (John Wayne) is a tough commanding officer at a remote cavalry post whose hard edge is softened when his only son, Jeff (Claude Jarman, Jr.), reports for duty. After dropping out of West Point, the shamed Jeff has enlisted in the Cavalry and now wants to prove himself to his father. Kirby is cool toward the boy, promising no favoritism, and explains what Army life is really about: "Put out of your mind any romantic ideas that it's a way of glory. It's a life of suffering and hardship, an uncompromising devotion to your oath and your duty." Jeff is taken under the wings of fun-loving troopers Tyree (Ben Johnson) and Boone (Harry Carey, Jr.), who keep an eye on the young man, and the arrival of Kathleen Yorke (Maureen O'Hara), Kirby's estranged wife and Jeff's mother, adds some tension to the scene. She is determined to buy back Jeff's enlistment, and in the process rekindles Kirby's love for her. An excellent post-Civil War tale with romance (Wayne and O'Hara), humor (Johnson, Carey, and Victor McLaglen), and music (a few tunes by the Sons of the Pioneers), RIO GRANDE is one of Ford's great achievements. As in FORT APACHE and SHE WORE A YELLOW RIBBON, Ford creates a powerful portrait of the wild, remote Southwest during the Indian wars, presenting the traditions and exploits of the old cavalry in very realistic terms, showing them in action as tired, dirty, wounded men performing their assignments in pain and discomfort and emphasizing the real glory of these soldiers as typified by their leader Kirby. The director's camera angles, broadly encompassing whole lines of riding cavalrymen, accentuate their prosaic nobility and dedication to taming the frontier. Much of the score nicely supports the story, indicating the cavalrymen's Irish background and sentimentality, especially in the inclusion of the fine Sons of the Pioneers song "I'll Take You Home Again, Kathleen."

p, John Ford and Merian C. Cooper; d, John Ford; w, James Kevin McGuinness, based on the story "Mission with No Record" by James Warner Bellah; ed, Jack Murray; ph, Bert Glennon; m, Victor Young.

(PR:A MPAA:NR)

ROLLING THUNDER***

(1977) 99m AIP c

William Devane *(Maj. Charles Rane)*, Tommy Lee Jones *(Johnny Vohden)*, Lisa Richards *(Janet)*, Dabney Coleman *(Maxwell)*, James Best *(Texan)*, Cassie Yates *(Candy)*, Lawrason Driscoll *(Clif)*, Jordan Gerler *(Mark)*, Luke Askew *(Slim)*, James Victor *(Lopez)*, Jane Abbott *(Sister)*.

Hot on the successful heels of TAXI DRIVER came a new film penned by its prolific screenwriter (soon to be director), Paul Schrader, and shot on a shoestring by director John Flynn in Texas. ROLLING THUNDER stars William Devane (in a superb performance) as Maj. Charles Rane, a Vietnam POW who, after years in captivity, is returned home along with cellmate Johnny Vohden (Tommy Lee Jones). Rane is given a hero's welcome by his little Texas town and presented with a small fortune in silver dollars—one for each day he was a prisoner. While all this attention is heartwarming, Rane has also come home to a wife who no longer loves him, a son who doesn't remember him, and a society that doesn't understand him. Emotionally deadened by his wartime experiences ("You learn to love the pain," the vet ominously tells his wife's lover), Rane only comes alive when he seeks vengeance after his wife and son are killed by thieves who invade their home to steal the silver coins. These thieves try to torture information out of Rane by shoving his hand down a garbage disposal, but he refuses to break—a macho display that is the cause of his family's deaths. Fitted with a hook to replace his mangled hand, Rane, with the help of his former comrade Johnny, goes to Mexico in search of the killers. While ROLLING THUNDER suffers from what has become Schrader's predictable obsession with ritual and gunplay, Devane and Jones overpower the material with their nuanced, sensitive portrayals of men who have lost their souls in another land. The scenes of their attempted readjustment are unforgettable, especially those in which the obviously tormented Johnny rots away in the bosom of his stiflingly polite family, who refuse to discuss the war with him.

p, Norman T. Herman; d, John Flynn; w, Paul Schrader and Heywood Gould; ed, Frank P. Keller; ph, Jordan Cronenweth, Deluxe Color; m, Barry DeVorzon.

(PR:O MPAA:R)

RUN SILENT, RUN DEEP***

(1958) 93m Hecht-Hill-Lancaster/UA bw

Clark Gable *(Comdr. Richardson)*, Burt Lancaster *(Lt. Jim Bledsoe)*, Jack Warden *(Mueller)*, Brad Dexter *(Cartwright)*, Don Rickles *(Ruby)*, Nick Cravat *(Russo)*, Joe Maross *(Kohler)*, Mary LaRoche *(Laura)*, Eddie Foy III *(Larto)*, Rudy Bond *(Cullen)*, H.M. Wynant *(Hendrix)*, John Bryant *(Beckman)*, Ken Lynch *(Frank)*, Joel Fluellen *(Bragg)*, Jimmie Bates *(Jessie)*, John Gibson *(Capt. Blunt)*.

After his lucrative teaming with Gary Cooper in VERA CRUZ (1954), Burt Lancaster and his partners, Harold Hecht and James Hill, decided to pair the rising young star with the fading but still popular Clark Gable. Gable plays Comdr. Richardson, the only survivor when the submarine he commands is sunk by a Japanese destroyer dubbed "Bongo Pete." Back at Pearl Harbor, he is given command of another submarine, the *Nerka*, but on it he encounters much dissension. Lt. Bledsoe (Lancaster), the sub's executive officer, is upset because he expected to get the command, and the crew refuses to trust a commander who is the sole survivor of a sunken vessel. Richardson battles frequently with Bledsoe, who is just short of mutinous, and drills the crew repeatedly in a tricky maneuver designed to torpedo "Bongo Pete" head on, an operation Richardson calls the "down the throat shot." Ordered to stay well clear of Japan's dangerous Bongo Straits, the obsessed commander disobeys and pursues the destroyer. Gable, two years and three films away from death, is plainly too old for his role, but he makes the most of it with a very good performance. The entire film, in fact, is one of the better submarine dramas ever made, tense and claustrophobic, with a minimum of dalliances back at the base (in defiance of the Hollywood dictum that no movie without a love interest can succeed). On the set, things were rather tense, with Lancaster and his two partners arguing over the script, while Gable worried about what was going to happen to his character when the dust settled. Although reasonably successful at the box office, RUN SILENT, RUN DEEP was ultimately overshadowed by another film that put an old star and a new star in a submarine, OPERATION PETTICOAT (1959), with Cary Grant and Tony Curtis.

p, Harold Hecht; d, Robert Wise; w, John Gay, based on the novel by Comdr. Edward L. Beach; ed, George Boemler; m, Franz Waxman.

(PR:A-C MPAA:NR)

S

SABOTEUR****

(1942) 108m UNIV bw

Priscilla Lane *(Patricia Martin)*, Robert Cummings *(Barry Kane)*, Otto Kruger *(Charles Tobin)*, Alan Baxter *(Freeman)*, Clem Bevans *(Neilson)*, Norman Lloyd *(Frank Fry)*, Alma Kruger *(Mrs. Henrietta Sutton)*, Vaughan Glaser *(Phillip Martin)*, Dorothy Peterson *(Mrs. Mason)*, Ian Wolfe *(Robert, the Butler)*, Frances Carson *(Society Woman)*, Murray Alper *(Mac, the Deputy Driver)*, Kathryn Adams *(Young Mother)*, Pedro de Cordoba *(Bones, the Human Skeleton)*, Billy Curtis *("Major," the Midget)*, Marie LeDeaux *(Tatania, the Fat Woman)*, Alfred Hitchcock *(Deaf and Dumb Man Outside Drug Store)*.

This film, Hitchcock's first contribution to wartime American propaganda, is as polished and suspenseful as any the great director would make. A forerunner to NORTH BY NORTHWEST, SABOTEUR tells a similar story of an innocent man accused of murder and chasing a bunch of insidious spies across the country. Barry Kane (Robert Cummings) is a simple factory worker in an airplane plant whose best friend is killed in a fire. It turns out the extinguisher Kane handed him was filled with gasoline, engulfing his friend in flames before burning the whole factory. An investigation points to Kane as the saboteur, forcing him to flee across the country to find the real fifth columnist. Along the way he meets Pat Martin (Priscilla Lane), the only one who believes his story. SABOTEUR is no doubt best remembered for its harrowing Statue of Liberty (actually a Universal backlot) finale, in which Cummings chases his man to the Lady's torch. Hitchcock had originally hoped to cast Gary Cooper and Barbara Stanwyck in the leads, with Harry Carey, Sr., in the role of master spy Charles Tobin.

p, Frank Lloyd and Jack H. Skirball; d, Alfred Hitchcock; w, Peter Viertel, Joan Harrison, and Dorothy Parker, based on an original story by Alfred Hitchcock; ed, Otto Ludwig; ph, Joseph Valentine; m, Charles Previn and Frank Skinner.

(PR:A MPAA:NR)

SAHARA****

(1943) 97m COL bw

Humphrey Bogart *(Sgt. Joe Gunn)*, Bruce Bennett [Herman Brix] *(Waco Hoyt)*, Lloyd Bridges *(Fred Clarkson)*, Rex Ingram *(Sgt. Tambul)*, J. Carrol Naish *(Giuseppe)*, Dan Duryea *(Jimmy Doyle)*, Richard Nugent *(Capt. Jason Halliday)*, Patrick O'Moore *(Ozzie Bates)*, Louis Mercier *(Jean Leroux)*, Carl Harbord *(Marty Williams)*, Guy Kingsford *(Peter Stegman)*, Kurt Kreuger *(Capt. Von Schletow)*, John Wengraf *(Maj. Von Falken)*, Hans Schumm *(Sgt. Krause)*.

One of the most exciting and entertaining propaganda films to come out of WW II, SAHARA features Humphrey Bogart as Sgt. Joe Gunn, an American tank commander who, along with his crew (Bruce Bennett and Dan Duryea), is separated from his unit just after the fall of Tobruk. As the tank, nicknamed "Lulubelle," slowly makes its way through the desert, Sgt. Gunn and his crew pick up a number of stragglers: several British soldiers (Patrick O'Moore, Lloyd Bridges, Richard Nugent, Carl Harbord), a Sudanese corporal (Rex Ingram) with an Italian prisoner (J. Carrol Naish) in tow, a Free Frenchman (Louis Mercier), a South African volunteer (Guy Kingsford), and a downed Nazi pilot (Kurt Kreuger). As the small rag-tag unit advances, the search for an oasis becomes their primary mission; however, they soon discover that a large German force in the area has the same objective. Blessed with a great cast and smart direction by Zoltan Korda, SAHARA remains one of the most appealing films of WW II. Although the constant speechifying, especially by Naish's repentant Italian, may strike some as passe and overbearing, the basic humanity of the entire affair is a pleasant change from the xenophobic posturing found in most films of the era. Sadly, scriptwriter John Howard Lawson's humane outlook would come back to haunt him when, in the 1950s, he became one of the Hollywood Ten. However, when McCarthyite government officials tried to pressure Columbia Pictures boss Harry Cohn into firing Lawson, he refused, much to his credit.

SALUTE JOHN CITIZEN—

p, Harry Joe Brown; d, Zoltan Korda; w, John Howard Lawson, Zoltan Korda, and James O'Hanlon, based on a story by Philip MacDonald from an incident in the film THE THIRTEEN [USSR]; ed, Charles Nelson; ph, Rudolf Mate; m, Miklos Rozsa.

(PR:A MPAA:NR)

SALUTE JOHN CITIZEN***
(1942, Brit.) 96m BN/Anglo-American bw

Edward Rigby *(Mr. Bunting)*, Mabel Constanduros *(Mrs. Bunting)*, Stanley Holloway *(Oskey)*, George Robey *(Corder)*, Jimmy Hanley *(Ernest Bunting)*, Henry Hallett *(Mr. Bickerton)*, Christine Silver *(Mrs. Bickerton)*, Eric Micklewood *(Chris Bunting)*, Peggy Cummins *(Julie Bunting)*, Stewart Rome *(Col. Saunders)*.

A wartime drama from Britain's most prolific film director, Maurice Elvey, SALUTE JOHN CITIZEN centers around the family headed by patriarch Mr. Bunting (Edward Rigby), an elderly store clerk who loses his job after nearly 50 years of company service. With the coming of WW II, Bunting is rehired in his former position, though little else in his life is positive. The London blitz destroys everything in sight, and one of his sons, Chris (Eric Micklewood), is killed. In the wake of this destruction, his other son, Ernest (Jimmy Hanley) is converted from pacifism to the war effort. Though clearly a propaganda piece, SALUTE JOHN CITIZEN is a nice little film—a simple telling of a modest family's attempts to cope with ongoing conflict that recalls MRS. MINIVER.

p, Wallace Orton; d, Maurice Elvey; w, Elizabeth Baron and Clemence Dane, based on the novels *Mr. Bunting* and *Mr. Bunting at War* by Robert Greenwood; ph, James Wilson.

(PR:A MPAA:NR)

SALVADOR****
(1986, Brit.) 123m Hemdale c

James Woods *(Richard Boyle)*, James Belushi *(Dr. Rock)*, Michael Murphy *(Ambassador Thomas Kelly)*, John Savage *(John Cassady)*, Elpedia Carrillo *(Maria)*, Tony Plana *(Maj. Max)*, Colby Chester *(Jack Morgan)*, Cynthia Gibb *(Cathy Moore)*, Will MacMillian *(Col. Hyde)*, Valerie Wildman *(Pauline Axelrod)*, Jose Carlos Ruiz *(Archbishop Romero)*, Jorge Luke *(Col. Julio Figueroa)*, Juan Fernandez *(Army Lieutenant)*, Salvador Sanchez *(Human Rights Leader)*, Rosario Zuniga *(His Assistant)*, Martin Fuentes *(Maria's Brother)*, Gary Farr *(Australian Reporter)*, Gilles Milinaire *(French Reporter)*.

The first, and, so far, only major film about the war in El Salvador, this Oliver Stone effort is as good as his Oscar-winning Vietnam film PLATOON (1986) but never received the recognition it deserved from critics or the public. Although there have been other major films dealing with conflict in Latin America (Chile in MISSING, and Nicaragua in UNDER FIRE), none has conveyed the chaos, tension, and fear within the region as vividly as this movie. Based on the experiences of real-life journalist Richard Boyle, the film begins in 1980 as the unemployed veteran reporter (played brilliantly by James Woods) heads down to El Salvador with his buddy, Dr. Rock (James Belushi), an out-of-work disc jockey. Promising drink, drugs, and an endless supply of inexpensive virginal whores, Boyle cons his friend into coming to a place where he can make some quick money covering a "little guerrilla war." Once they cross the border, however, things begin to get dangerous as the country is embroiled in a devastating civil war. A scant plot synopsis cannot fully convey the vivid events that explode in every frame of SALVADOR. Not only does director Stone successfully convey the turmoil and horror of life in El Salvador, he also shows us the rebirth of the conscience of a cynical, self-absorbed journalist whose problems pale in comparison with the atrocities suffered by the Salvadoran people, for whom he genuinely cares. Woods is superb as the journalist who recovers his lost humanity, and it is a tribute to his considerable skills as an actor that he is able to engage the viewer throughout the film with his basically repugnant character. While Woods' character is one of the most challenging and fascinating to hit the screen in some time, it is Stone's vivid portrayal of El Salvador that gives the film its disturbing tone. The power of the film lies in its simple-but-detailed portrayal of the chaotic events of 1980-81. Stone successfully conveys the confusion, terror, senselessness, and despair felt by Salvadorans, while jaded Americans—government, military, and press—blithely ignore the realities. Stone's camera is like a photojournalist, always on the move, running, swirling, probing, trying to "get close to the truth" of the tragic reality that is El Salvador.

p, Gerald Green and Oliver Stone; d, Oliver Stone; w, Oliver Stone and Richard Boyle; ed, Claire Simpson; ph, Robert Richardson; m, Georges Delerue.

(PR:O MPAA:R)

SALZBURG CONNECTION, THE*
(1972) 93m FOX c

Barry Newman *(William Mathison)*, Anna Karina *(Anna Bryant)*, Klaus Maria Brandauer *(Johann Kronsteiner)*, Karen Jensen *(Elissa Lang)*, Joe Maross *(Chuck)*, Wolfgang Preiss *(Felix Zauner)*, Helmut Schmid *(Grell)*, Udo Kier *(Anton)*, Michael Haussermann *(Lev Benedescu)*, Whit Bissell *(Newhart)*, Elisabeth Felchner *(Trudi Seidl)*, Alf Beinell *(Anton's Companion)*.

Helen MacInnes has been served rather poorly by Hollywood, whose film adaptations of her excellent espionage thrillers have been mediocre at best. THE SALZBURG CONNECTION, however, is the absolute worst. William Mathison (Barry Newman), an American lawyer vacationing in Salzburg, unwittingly becomes involved with a plethora of international secret agents—all of whom want to get their hands on a chest containing a list of Nazi collaborators and war criminals. As agents from the US, USSR, China, and neo-Nazi organizations fight among themselves for possession of the list, William finds time to romance beautiful widow Anna Bryant (Anna Karina), whose husband was killed as an innocent participant in the debacle. Unfortunately, her brother, Johann (Klaus Maria Brandauer), is one of the neo-Nazis after the coveted list. Solid performances from Karina and Brandauer help save this otherwise confusing thriller, most of whose problems stem from the direction of Lee H. Katzin. Katzin even fails to bring a sense of excitement to a car chase here, despite the fact that he previously directed LE MANS (1971), a film about the Grand Prix.

p, Ingo Preminger; d, Lee H. Katzin; w, Oscar Millard, based on the novel by Helen MacInnes; ed, John M. Woodcock; ph, Wolfgang Treu, Deluxe Color; m, Lionel Newman.

(PR:C MPAA:PG)

SAND PEBBLES, THE****

(1966) 195m Argyle-Solar Productions/FOX c

Steve McQueen *(Jake Holman)*, Richard Attenborough *(Frenchy Burgoyne)*, Richard Crenna *(Capt. Collins)*, Candice Bergen *(Shirley Eckert)*, Marayat Andriane [Emmanuelle Arsan] *(Maily)*, Mako *(Po-han)*, Larry Gates *(Jameson)*, Charles Robinson *(Ens. Bordelles)*, Simon Oakland *(Stawski)*, Ford Rainey *(Harris)*, Joseph Turkel *(Bronson)*, Gavin MacLeod *(Crosley)*, Joe di Reda *(Shanahan)*, Richard Loo *(Maj. Chin)*, Barney Phillips *(Chief Franks)*, Gus Trikonis *(Restorff)*.

A powerful and spectacular film, featuring Steve McQueen at his finest and director Robert Wise at his most persuasive, THE SAND PEBBLES is the panoramic story of a US Navy gunboat cruising China's Yangtze River in 1926 amidst nationalist rebellion led by Chiang Kai-Shek. In an Oscar-nominated performance, McQueen plays Jake Holman, the lone wolf sailor who keeps the cranky engines of the USS *San Pablo* running while Collins (Richard Crenna), its captain, negotiates tricky political waters. Ordered to remain neutral in the Chinese conflict despite the abuse heaped on them, the crew, who call themselves the "Sand Pebbles," become restive. When Chinese authorities, anxious to create an international incident, frame Jake for the murder of the Chinese wife of a dead shipmate (Richard Attenborough), Collins refuses to hand over the engineer, though the crew is reluctant to back him up. However, when US Marines land in Shanghai, the Sand Pebbles are finally given a chance to fight back, the gunboat battling its way through a blockade to evacuate American missionaries Jameson (Larry Gates), who resents the US involvement in Chinese affairs, and Shirley Eckert (Candice Bergen), with whom Jake has fallen in love. The final rescue, like the rest of this long but involving film, is carefully unfolded by Wise, building in intensity towards a heroic but tragic conclusion. Beautifully photographed (by Joseph MacDonald) and designed, THE SAND PEBBLES earned Academy Award nominations for Best Picture, Art Direction, Color Cinematography, Editing, Musical Score and Sound. Mako (nominated for Best Supporting Actor for his portrayal of Jake's Chinese assistant), Crenna, Attenborough, and Bergen are all excellent, but McQueen (who actually learned how to run the engines of the 150-foot gunboat replica built for the $12-million film) steals the show. Released in 1966, THE SAND PEBBLES offered parallels to the controversial US involvement then taking place in Vietnam. Although it has undergone several edits, THE SAND PEBBLES is available on videocassette at its original 195-minute running time.

p, Robert Wise; d, Robert Wise; w, Robert W. Anderson, based on the novel by Richard McKenna; ed, William Reynolds; ph, Joseph MacDonald, Panavision, Deluxe Color; m, Jerry Goldsmith.

(PR:C-O MPAA:M)

SANDS OF IWO JIMA****

(1949) 110m REP bw

John Wayne *(Sgt. John M. Stryker)*, John Agar *(Pfc. Peter Conway)*, Adele Mara *(Allison Bromley)*, Forrest Tucker *(Pfc. Al Thomas)*, Wally Cassell *(Pfc. Benny Regazzi)*, James Brown *(Pfc. Charlie Bass)*, Richard Webb *(Pfc. Shipley)*, Arthur Franz *(Cpl. Robert Dunne/Narrator)*, Julie Bishop *(Mary)*, James Holden *(Pfc. Soames)*, Peter Coe *(Pfc. Hellenpolis)*, Richard Jaeckel *(Pfc. Frank Flynn)*, Bill Murphy *(Pfc. Eddie Flynn)*, George Tyne [Buddy Yarus] *(Pfc. Harris)*, Hal Fieberling [Hal Baylor] *(Pvt. "Ski" Choynski)*, Martin Milner *(Pvt. Mike McHugh)*, Pfc. Rene A. Gagnon, Pfc. Ira H. Hayes, PM 3/C John H. Bradley.

Unlike John Wayne's many WW II films in which he single-handedly destroys whole Japanese battalions, SANDS OF IWO JIMA presents him as a believable, vulnerable human being. Sgt. John M. Stryker (Wayne), a battle-toughened Marine, prepares a group of recruits for combat, driving them hard without worrying about making friends, although he is hurt when Pfc. Peter Conway (John Agar) hopes aloud that his newborn son won't be anything like Stryker. Later, in combat on Tarawa, Stryker's men grow furious with him when he refuses to rescue a Marine who has been separated from the squad, because to do so would give away their position. After Tarawa, they go to Hawaii for some R & R, where Stryker shows his heart of gold to a young mother forced into prostitution. The Marines' biggest test comes on Iwo Jima, and Stryker's men perform magnificently as they inch their way up Mt. Suribachi, but their leader is killed and Conway, now his disciple, must try to fill Stryker's big shoes. This is one of Wayne's finest performances, earning him an Oscar nomination. Directed with marvelous restraint by old hand Allan Dwan, SANDS OF IWO JIMA features appearances by three of the Marines who actually participated in the famous flag-raising on Mt. Suribachi—Ira Hayes, Rene Gagnon, and John Bradley.

p, Edmund Grainger; d, Allan Dwan; w, Harry Brown and James Edward Grant, based on a story by Brown; ed, Richard L. Van Enger; ph, Reggie Lanning; m, Victor Young.

(PR:C MPAA:NR)

SAYONARA****

(1957) 147m Goetz-Pennebaker/WB c

Marlon Brando *(Maj. Lloyd Gruver)*, Ricardo Montalban *(Nakamura)*, Red Buttons *(Joe Kelly)*, Patricia Owens *(Eileen Webster)*, Martha Scott *(Mrs. Webster)*, James Garner *(Capt. Mike Bailey)*, Miiko Taka *(Hana-ogi)*, Miyoshi Umeki *(Katsumi)*, Kent Smith *(Gen. Webster)*, Douglas Watson *(Col. Craford)*, Reiko Kuba *(Fumiko-san)*, Soo Young *(Teruko-san)*, Harlan Warde *(Consul)*, Shochiku Kagekidan Girls Revue

This beautifully photographed and often moving story of racial prejudice features Marlon Brando as Lloyd Gruver, an Army major reassigned to a Japanese air base in the midst of the Korean conflict. In Japan, Gruver sees the US military's racism against the Japanese, which goes so far as to forbid servicemen from marrying Japanese women. Although at first indifferent to the situation, Gruver is forced to take a stand when his buddy Joe Kelly (Red Buttons) falls in love with a local woman, Katsumi (Miyoshi Umeki), and becomes determined to marry her, going over the heads of the military high command and petitioning Congress for permission. Sticking by his comrade, Gruver risks the wrath of his superiors when he agrees to be Kelly's best man at the ceremony. What's more, Gruver himself falls in love with a beautiful Japanese dancer, Hana-ogi (Miiko Taka), and finds himself in the same predicament as Kelly. SAYONARA is a sensitive work, sparing neither Americans nor Japanese in condemning prejudice. This updating of the "Madame Butterfly" theme is a powerful, well-told story, with a statement on racism that remains timeless. It was certainly topical: when filming began, in 1956, more than 10,000 American servicemen had defied extant regulations and married Japanese women (as the novel's author, James A. Michener, had done earlier). The film received 10 Academy Award nominations, including Best Picture, Best Director, Best Actor, Best Cinematography, Best Screenplay, and Best Editing. Oscars went to the film for Sound, Art Direction, and Set Decoration, as well as to Buttons and Umeki for their supporting performances.

p, William Goetz; d, Joshua Logan; w, Paul Osborn, based on the novel by James A. Michener; ed, Arthur P. Schmidt and Philip W. Anderson; ph, Ellsworth Fredricks, Technirama, Technicolor; m, Franz Waxman.

(PR:A MPAA:NR)

SEA HAWK, THE*****

(1940) 126m WB bw

Errol Flynn *(Capt. Geoffrey Thorpe)*, Brenda Marshall *(Donna Maria Alvarez de Cordoba)*, Claude Rains *(Don Jose Alvarez de Cordoba)*, Flora Robson *(Queen Elizabeth)*, Donald Crisp *(Sir John Burleson)*, Henry Daniell *(Lord Wolfingham)*, Alan Hale *(Carl Pitt)*, Una O'Connor *(Martha)*, William Lundigan *(Danny Logan)*, James Stephenson *(Abbott)*, J.M. Kerrigan *(Eli Matson)*, Gilbert Roland *(Capt. Lopez)*, Julien Mitchell *(Oliver Scott)*, David Bruce *(Martin Burke)*.

Audiences anxiously awaited this wonderful swashbuckling film starring the inimitable Errol Flynn, who became a star five years earlier in the similar CAPTAIN BLOOD. Everything worked here, thanks to Warner Bros.' great facilities and the superior talents of director Michael Curtiz, cinematographer Sol Polito, composer Erich Wolfgang Korngold, Flynn, and a cast of character actors hard to match in any era. As the film opens, Spain's King Philip II (Montagu Love) instructs his advisors to devise a plan to conquer England and continental Europe. To placate England's Queen Elizabeth (Flora Robson), he sends Don Jose Alvarez de Cordoba (Claude Rains), his crafty ambassador, to soothe the Virgin Queen's fears and disguise Spain's intentions. En route, the Spanish galleon carrying Don Jose and his niece, Donna Maria (Brenda Marshall), is sunk by a British ship commanded by Geoffrey Thorpe (Flynn). The dashing captain takes the indignant ambassador and Maria on board, bringing them safely to England. Despite his fine manners, Thorpe is a dedicated "Sea Hawk," one of a half-dozen British sea captains who foresee war and have been raiding Spanish coastal forts and seizing Philip's treasures to fund a British fleet, all with Elizabeth's unofficial approval. Although Thorpe's gallantry soon wins over Maria, Don Jose intrigues to capture him in Panama, where Spanish forces waylay the Englishman. Ambushed, Thorpe and the surviving members of his crew are sentenced to serve as galley slaves on a Spanish ship. Never fear, however, for Thorpe fights his way out of captivity, foiling a plot against Elizabeth by Lord Wolfingham (Henry Daniell) with some exciting swordplay and alerting her to Philip's plans for his armada, and wins the love of Maria and the undying gratitude of his queen. Warners lavished a then-staggering $1.7 million on THE SEA HAWK, with gorgeous results. The 31-year-old Flynn, at the peak of his spectacular career, is magnificent in his swashbuckling role; Marshall was never more radiant; Rains is deliciously evil; and Robson makes a wonderfully witty and intelligent Elizabeth.

p, Jack L. Warner, Hal B. Wallis, and Henry Blanke; d, Michael Curtiz; w, Howard Koch and Seton I. Miller; ed, George Amy; ph, Sol Polito; m, Erich Wolfgang Korngold.

(PR:A MPAA:NR)

SEA SHALL NOT HAVE THEM, THE***

(1955, Brit.) 91m UA bw

Michael Redgrave *(Air Commodore Waltby)*, Dirk Bogarde *(Flight Sgt. Mackay)*, Anthony Steel *(Flying Officer Treherne)*, Nigel Patrick *(Flight Sgt. Slingsby)*, Bonar Colleano *(Sgt. Kirby)*, James Kenney *(Cpl. Skinner)*, Sydney Tafler *(Capt. Robb)*, Ian Whittaker *(Air Crewman Milliken)*, George Rose *(Tebbitt)*, Victor Maddern *(Gus Westover)*, Michael Ripper *(Botterill)*, Glyn Houston *(Knox)*, Jack Taylor *(Robinson)*, Michael Balfour *(Dray)*, Jack Watling *(Flying Officer Harding)*, Paul Carpenter *(Lt. Pat Boyle)*.

This saga of men against the sea takes place in 1944, as a Hudson aircraft is shot down while flying over the North Sea. On board is Air Commodore Waltby (Michael Redgrave), who possesses secret documents that could bring about an end to Germany's air raids on London. Waltby survives, adrift in a dinghy, along with Flight Sgt. Mackay (Dirk Bogarde), Sgt. Kirby (Bonar Colleano), and Flying Officer Harding (Jack Watling). The Air-Sea Rescue Unit sweeps into action under the command of Flying Officer Treherne (Anthony Steel) and his second-in-command, Flight Sgt. Slingsby (Nigel Patrick), who battle foul weather and enemy attacks before finally pulling the drifters from the middle of an ocean minefield.

p, Daniel M. Angel; d, Lewis Gilbert; w, Lewis Gilbert and Vernon Harris, based on the novel by John Harris; ed, Russell Lloyd; ph, Stephen Dade; m, Malcolm Arnold.

(PR:A-C MPAA:NR)

SEA WOLVES, THE***

(1980, Brit.) 120m Lorimar/PAR c

Gregory Peck *(Col. Lewis Pugh)*, Roger Moore *(Capt. Gavin Stewart)*, David Niven *(Col. Bill Grice)*, Trevor Howard *(Jack Cartwright)*, Barbara Kellermann *(Mrs. Cromwell)*, Patrick Macnee *(Maj. Yogi Crossley)*, Patrick Allen *(Colin MacKenzie)*, Bernard Archard *(Underhill)*, Martin Benson *(Montero)*, Faith Brook *(Doris Grice)*, Allan Cuthbertson *(Melborne)*, Kenneth Griffith *(Wilton)*, Donald Houston *(Hilliard)*, Wolf Kahler *(Trompeta)*.

This attempt to capture the spirit of the classic wartime adventures is only moderately successful, "a geriatric GUNS OF NAVARONE," as film critic Vincent Canby described it. Based on an actual WW II incident, THE SEA WOLVES concerns a clandestine operation of 1943 involving the Calcutta Light Horse, a regiment of aging war volunteers who previously saw service in the Boer War of 1900. Their mission, under the command of Col. Lewis Pugh (Gregory Peck, with a passable English accent), is to explode three German ships docked in the neutral Indian port of Marmagoa, at the time part of the Portuguese colony of Goa. The warships are known to be supplying German U-boats with information on Allied shipping schedules. With the usual amount of intrigue, the old fighters—including the likes of Roger Moore, David Niven, Trevor Howard, and Patrick Macnee—hit their destined target. THE SEA WOLVES is nothing special, though it is a well-crafted picture, worthy of comparison with the war adventures of the 1940s and 50s. The film is dedicated to Earl Mountbatten, an honorary commander of the Calcutta Light Horse, who fell victim to an IRA bomb in August 1979.

p, Euan Lloyd; d, Andrew V. McLaglen; w, Reginald Rose, based on the novel *The Boarding Party* by James Leasor; ed, John Glen; ph, Tony Imi, Eastmancolor; m, Roy Budd.

(PR:A MPAA:PG)

SECRET WAR OF HARRY FRIGG, THE**½

(1968) 110m Albion/UNIV c

Paul Newman *(Harry Frigg)*, Sylva Koscina *(Countess di Montefiore)*, Andrew Duggan *(Gen. Armstrong)*, Tom Bosley *(Gen. Pennypacker)*, John Williams *(Gen. May-*
hew), Charles D. Gray *(Gen. Cox-Roberts)*, Vito Scotti *(Col. Ferrucci)*, Jacques Roux *(Gen. Rochambeau)*, Werner Peters *(Maj. Von Steignitz)*, James Gregory *(Gen. Homer Prentiss)*, Buck Henry *(Stockade Commandant)*.

Often lambasted by the critics for his comedic work, Paul Newman was somewhat more successful in this uneven WW II comedy, playing Harry Frigg, a private whose ability to break out of Army stockades earns him a special assignment and a temporary promotion to major general. Five Allied generals (Tom Bosley, Andrew Duggan, Charles D. Gray, Jacques Roux, and John Williams) are being held in a villa by the Italians under the not-so-watchful eye of Col. Ferrucci (Vito Scotti), and Harry is sent to engineer their escape. He drags his feet, though, when he becomes involved with the beautiful owner of the villa (Sylva Koscina), and the escape is delayed further because the generals don't want to disrupt Ferrucci's promotion ceremonies. Then, Italy surrenders and the Germans take possession of the prisoners, but Harry is more than up to this new challenge. Although Newman's performance here is unquestionably of the hit-and-miss variety, he does manage to generate more than a few laughs with his glib delivery of some very funny lines by screenwriters Frank Tarloff and Peter Stone, including his "cheece und craggers" greeting upon encountering the generals while dressed in a German uniform.

p, Hal E. Chester; d, Jack Smight; w, Peter Stone and Frank Tarloff, based on a story by Tarloff; ed, J. Terry Williams; ph, Russell Metty, Techniscope, Technicolor; m, Carlo Rustichelli.

(PR:A-C MPAA:NR)

SERGEANT YORK*****

(1941) 134m WB bw

Gary Cooper *(Alvin C. York)*, Walter Brennan *(Pastor Rosier Pile)*, Joan Leslie *(Gracie Williams)*, George Tobias *(Michael T. "Pusher" Ross)*, Stanley Ridges *(Maj. Buxton)*, Margaret Wycherly *(Mother York)*, Ward Bond *(Ike Botkin)*, Noah Beery, Jr. *(Buck Lipscomb)*, June Lockhart *(Rose York)*, Dickie Moore *(George York)*, Clem Bevans *(Zeke)*, Howard Da Silva *(Lem)*, Charles Trowbridge *(Cordell Hull)*, Harvey Stephens *(Capt. Danforth)*, David Bruce *(Bert Thomas)*, Elisha Cook, Jr. *(Piano Player)*.

Gary Cooper won his first Oscar for his brilliant portrayal here of WW I hero Alvin C. York, who single-handedly captured 132 German soldiers during the Meuse-Argonne offensive and became one of America's most decorated and beloved heroes. Beginning in 1916, Howard Hawks' masterfully directed film follows the man from the hills of East Tennessee as he falls in love with Gracie Williams (Joan Leslie) and struggles to hold onto his land. When lightni..g strikes his rifle, York views it a sign from God and, becoming a pacifist, tries to avoid service in WW I. Eventually he does fight in France, however, and the rest is spectacular military history. Hawks brings the life of this incredible hero to the screen with forceful integrity, and Cooper is wonderful as the country fellow who gets religion and holds onto it, even through the nightmare of war.

SEVEN DAYS IN MAY—

Technically, the film is faultless, with Hawks keeping his cameras fluid and employing Sol Polito's magnificent photographic skills at every turn. Jesse Lasky, who saw York in the 1919 Armistice Day Parade, spent years trying to convince the modest Tennessean to allow his story to be filmed, finally winning York's approval provided that the proceeds go to charity and that Gary Cooper play him. At first Cooper refused, but he changed his mind after visiting York. Warner Bros. had hoped to have Michael Curtiz direct SERGEANT YORK, but Cooper wouldn't work with him, and when several others couldn't take the job, Hawks was hired, to the lasting pleasure of all who see this magnificent film.

p, Jesse L. Lasky and Hal B. Wallis; d, Howard Hawks; w, Abem Finkel, Harry Chandlee, Howard Koch, and John Huston, based on *War Diary of Sergeant York* by Sam K. Cowan, *Sergeant York and His People* by Cowan, and *Sergeant York—Last of the Long Hunters* by Tom Skeyhill; ed, William Holmes; ph, Sol Polito and Arthur Edeson, war sequences; m, Max Steiner.

(PR:A MPAA:NR)

SEVEN DAYS IN MAY****

(1964) 120m Seven Arts-Joel/PAR bw

Burt Lancaster *(Gen. James M. Scott)*, Kirk Douglas *(Col. Martin "Jiggs" Casey)*, Fredric March *(President Jordan Lyman)*, Ava Gardner *(Eleanor Holbrook)*, Edmond O'Brien *(Sen. Raymond Clark)*, Martin Balsam *(Paul Girard)*, George Macready *(Christopher Todd)*, Whit Bissell *(Sen. Prentice)*, Hugh Marlowe *(Harold McPherson)*, Bart Burns *(Arthur Corwin)*, Richard Anderson *(Col. Murdock)*, John Houseman *(Adm. Barnswell)*.

The surprising revelations of the Iran-Contra scandal have given new meaning to this gripping, well-acted political thriller based on Charles Waldo Bailey II and Fletcher Knebel's 1962 best-seller. SEVEN DAYS IN MAY begins as the President of the United States, Jordan Lyman (Fredric March), signs a nuclear disarmament treaty with the Soviets, outraging the military establishment, particularly Gen. James M. Scott (Burt Lancaster), head of the Joint Chiefs of Staff, who conspires with other Joint Chiefs to stage a coup d'etat. His aide, Marine Col. "Jiggs" Casey (Kirk Douglas), stumbles onto evidence of the plot, including a secret Air Force base, and approaches the president. With only days left before the coup is to take place, Lyman swings into action, but trusted friends Sen. Raymond Clark (Edmond O'Brien) and Paul Girard (Martin Balsam), whom the president has sent to secure the proof needed to expose Scott and his cohorts, are captured and killed in a plane crash, respectively. Armed with incriminating letters from Scott's former mistress (Ava Gardner), Lyman confronts the general, and though the president cannot bring himself to use blackmail he eventually triumphs over Scott. Filmed in stark black and white, unraveling its complicated plot at a rapid clip, this exciting film from John Frankenheimer, the director of the similarly taut THE MANCHURIAN CANDIDATE, packs a grim warning about the military's potential abuse of power. Douglas, who, like Lancaster and March, contributes an outstanding performance, initiated the project after reading galleys of the novel. Given the enthusiastic cooperation of the Kennedy administration (though not of the Pentagon, whom the filmmakers understandably never approached), SEVEN DAYS IN MAY smacks of realism, from its skillfully realized sets to its wholly believable supporting performances by O'Brien, Balsam, and John Houseman. Sure to keep you on the edge of your seat.

p, Edward Lewis; d, John Frankenheimer; w, Rod Serling, based on the novel by Fletcher Knebel, Charles Waldo Bailey II; ed, Ferris Webster; ph, Ellsworth Fredricks; m, Jerry Goldsmith.

(PR:C MPAA:NR)

SHE WORE A YELLOW RIBBON****

(1949) 103m Argosy/RKO c

John Wayne *(Capt. Nathan Brittles)*, Joanne Dru *(Olivia Dandridge)*, John Agar *(Lt. Flint Cohill)*, Ben Johnson *(Sgt. Tyree)*, Harry Carey, Jr. *(Lt. Ross Pennell)*, Victor McLaglen *(Sgt. Quincannon)*, Mildred Natwick *(Mrs. Abby Allshard)*, George O'Brien *(Maj. Mack Allshard)*, Arthur Shields *(Dr. O'Laughlin)*, Francis Ford *(Barman)*, Harry Woods *(Karl Rynders)*, Chief John Big Tree *(Pony That Walks)*, Noble Johnson *(Red Shirt)*, Cliff Lyons *(Trooper Cliff)*.

The second of John Ford's "Cavalry Trilogy" features John Wayne at his best and boasts some incredible, Oscar-winning Technicolor photography of Monument Valley. Capt. Nathan Brittles (Wayne) is a career officer in the US Cavalry marking the final days before his forced retirement from the service. In the wake of the massacre of Custer and the Seventh Cavalry, the local Indians are becoming agitated, and, worse, confident. Brittles is assigned to escort two women (Joanne Dru and Mildred Natwick) from the fort to the stagecoach stop at Sudrow's Wells, but the Indians are on the warpath and there is little chance now to evacuate the women from the area. Wayne gives one of the finest performances of his career here, in the first serious role Ford gave him. (Wayne later said of Ford, "Jack never respected me as an actor until I made RED RIVER.") As Capt. Brittles—the character a full generation older than the actor—Wayne is at his most human, a man who has made the Army his whole life, even sacrificing the lives of his family to its service, and now having to watch his Army career end on a note of failure. The passing of time is the film's recurring theme, suggested as Brittles arrives late with his troops, is forced to retire because of his age, leaves a dance to speak to his dead wife; even the inscription on the watch the troopers give him, "Lest we forget," plays on this theme of time lost and recalled. Ford's main inspiration for the film's scenic look was the western paintings of Frederic Remington. On the set, the director clashed with cinematographer Winton Hoch, a technical perfectionist who would endlessly fiddle with his camera while the cast baked in the sun. One day in the desert, when a line of threatening clouds darkened the horizon, indicating a thunderstorm, Hoch started to pack up his equipment. Ford ordered him to continue shooting, and

Hoch did so, but filed an official protest with his union. The shot that emerged, a fantastic purple sky with jagged streaks of lightning reaching toward earth in the distance, was breathtaking and helped Hoch win an Oscar for his work on the film. After decades of terribly washed-out color prints of SHE WORE A YELLOW RIBBON, the film has recently been restored to its original glory and may soon be available on home video in pristine condition.

p, John Ford and Merian C. Cooper; d, John Ford; w, Frank S. Nugent and Laurence Stallings, based on the stories "War Party" and "The Big Hunt" by James Warner Bellah; ed, Jack Murray; ph, Winton C. Hoch and Charles P. Boyle, Technicolor; m, Richard Hageman.

(PR:A   MPAA:NR)

SHENANDOAH***½

(1965) 105m UNIV c

James Stewart *(Charlie Anderson)*, Doug McClure *(Sam)*, Glenn Corbett *(Jacob Anderson)*, Patrick Wayne *(James Anderson)*, Rosemary Forsyth *(Jannie Anderson)*, Philip Alford *(Boy Anderson)*, Katharine Ross *(Ann Anderson)*, Charles Robinson *(Nathan Anderson)*, James McMullan *(John Anderson)*, Tim McIntire *(Henry Anderson)*, Paul Fix *(Dr. Tom Witherspoon)*, Denver Pyle *(Pastor Bjoerling)*, James Best *(Carter)*, George Kennedy *(Col. Fairchild)*, Warren Oates *(Billy Packer)*, Strother Martin *(Engineer)*, Harry Carey, Jr. *(Jenkins)*, Bob Steele *(Union Guard with Beard)*.

An offbeat performance from James Stewart as Virginia farmer Charlie Anderson makes SHENANDOAH an involving and entertaining look at one family's attempt to deal with the Civil War. A prosperous farmer with six sons and one daughter, Charlie is a widower whose wife died during the birth of Boy (Philip Alford). Charlie, who is opposed to slavery, tries to maintain a neutral stance in the conflict between North and South; however, a number of events threaten to change his pacifist leanings: 16-year-old Boy is captured by Union soldiers; Confederate son-in-law Sam (Doug McClure) is called to duty; son James (Patrick Wayne) and his wife, Ann (Katharine Ross), are murdered by Confederate looters; and another son, Jacob (Glenn Corbett), is killed by a Confederate guardsman. Andrew V. McLaglen's excellent direction and carefully crafted battle scenes successfully combine with one of the best supporting casts you're likely to find outside of a John Ford film, including Harry Carey, Jr., Warren Oates, Strother Martin, Denver Pyle, George Kennedy, Paul Fix, and Bob Steele.

p, Robert Arthur; d, Andrew V. McLaglen; w, James Lee Barrett; ed, Otho Lovering; ph, William Clothier, Technicolor; m, Frank Skinner.

(PR:C   MPAA:NR)

SHERLOCK HOLMES AND THE SECRET WEAPON***

(1942) 68m UNIV bw

Basil Rathbone *(Sherlock Holmes)*, Nigel Bruce *(Dr. John H. Watson)*, Kaaren Verne *(Charlotte Eberli)*, Lionel Atwill *(Prof. Moriarty)*, William Post, Jr. *(Dr. Franz Tobel)*, Dennis Hoey *(Inspector Lestrade)*, Harry Woods *(Man)*, George Burr MacAnnan *(Gottfried)*, Paul Fix *(Mueller)*, Holmes Herbert *(Sir Reginald Bailey)*, Mary Gordon *(Mrs. Hudson)*, Henry Victor *(Frederick Hoffner)*, Harold de Becker *(Peg Leg)*, Harry Cording *(Jack Brady)*.

Holmes (Basil Rathbone) disguises himself as an old Swiss bookseller, a villainous waterfront lascar, and a bearded scientist in an attempt to keep his archenemy, Prof. Moriarty (Lionel Atwill), from the newly developed bombsight the English hope to use on Hitler. Moriarty pops up just when everyone thought him to be long dead, and he's working for the Nazis, having little concern for his native country. In one confrontation between Holmes and his nemesis, the former is strapped to a table and tortured by having his blood taken from his veins, drop by drop. This was the first of 11 in the Holmes series to be directed by Roy William Neill, who kept everything at a swift pace, including the dialog.

p, Howard Benedict; d, Roy William Neill; w, Edward T. Lowe, W. Scott Darling, and Edmund L. Hartmann, based on the Sir Arthur Conan Doyle story "The Dancing Men"; ed, Otto Ludwig; ph, Lester White; m, Frank Skinner.

(PR:A   MPAA:NR)

SHOP ON MAIN STREET, THE****

(1966, Czech.) 128m Barrandov/Prominent bw (OBCH OD NA KORZE; AKA: SHOP ON HIGH STREET, THE)

Jozef Kroner *(Tono Brtko)*, Ida Kaminska *(Rosalie Lautmann)*, Hana Slivkova *(Evelina Brtko)*, Frantisek Zvarik *(Marcus Kolkotsky)*, Helena Zvarikov *(Rose Kolkotsky)*, Martin Holly *(Imro Kuchar)*, Martin Gregory *(Katz)*.

One of the best-known, most highly praised Eastern European films of the 1960s, THE SHOP ON MAIN STREET is a profoundly moving tragicomedy set against a WW II backdrop of racial hatred and fascism. Tono Brtko (Jozef Kroner) seemingly walks through life without any guiding morals or principles. He is content just to get by, do some carpentry work, and soak his feet—though his domineering wife, Evelina (Hana Slivkova), who longs for a more comfortable existence, tries to force him into more financially lucrative endeavors, like working for her fascist brother-in-law, Marcus (Frantisek Zvarik). One evening, Marcus and Evelina's sister, Rose (Helena Zvarikov), pay an unexpected visit, bringing food, wine, and gifts that thrill Evelina but leave her husband indifferent. Marcus also brings news that Tono has been appointed Aryan comptroller of a Jewish button shop, a job that will bring money and status. The next day, Tono visits the shop, informing the aged, frail, and rheumatic proprietress, Rozalie (Ida Kaminska), that he is now in charge of the business, although Rozalie is too deaf to understand and too blind to read his authorization. Only later does Tono learn that the shop is completely bankrupt, and that the old woman is supported by her fellow Jewish merchants. Having no other choice, he agrees to the charade of working as Rozalie's assistant, and forms a strong friendship with her that transcends racial, religious, and political divisions.

SHOUT AT THE DEVIL—

Codirected by Jan Kadar and Elmar Klos, THE SHOP ON MAIN STREET is a relatively straightforward narrative, without the stylistic virtuosity of so many other films by young Eastern European filmmakers. What the film lacks in style, however, it makes up for in craftsmanship, intelligence, and universality. Mixing a comic tone with a tragic subject, it enforces the view that the greatest, most inhumane of tragedies can strike anyone, anywhere, at any time. It received a Best Foreign-Language Film Oscar in 1965 and a Best Actress nomination for Kaminska in 1966. (In Czech; English subtitles.)

p, Ladislav Hanus, Jaromir Lukas, and Jordan Balurov; d, Jan Kadar and Elmar Klos; w, Jan Kadar, Elmar Klos, and Ladislav Grossman, based on the story "Obchod No Korze" by Grossman; ed, Jaromir Janacek and Diana Heringova; ph, Vladimir Novotny; m, Zdenek Liska.

(PR:C-O MPAA:NR)

SHOUT AT THE DEVIL**½
(1976, Brit.) 128m AIP c

Lee Marvin (Flynn), Roger Moore (Sebastian), Barbara Parkins (Rosa), Ian Holm (Mohammed), Rene Kolldehoff (Commissioner Fleischer), Horst Janson (Kyller), Karl Michael Vogler (Von Kleine), Gernot Endemann (Braun), Maurice Denham (Mr. Smythe), Jean Kent (Mrs. Smythe), Heather Wright (Cynthia), Bernard Horsfall (Capt. Joyce).

A WW I German cruiser is hidden away for repairs in Southeast Africa; Sebastian (Roger Moore), a witty Englishman, and Flynn (Lee Marvin), a hard-drinking Irish-American, want to blow it up and show the Germans a thing or two. Assisting the pair is Sebastian's wife, Rosa (Barbara Parkins), who is determined to avenge the Germans' murder of her child. Like many of the big-star, big-budget action movies of the 1970s, SHOUT AT THE DEVIL does have its moments (particularly the action sequences), but for the most part it's an overlong study of two caricatures—the proper Englishman and the sauced Irishman. There's even a very macho brawl between the two to point up their differences and the male myths they respectively represent. Moore's character has a certain James Bond-style machismo, no surprise when one considers that director Peter Hunt made his debut with the George Lazenby Bond film ON HER MAJESTY'S SECRET SERVICE before going on to film two non-Bond adventure films with future 007 Moore (both based on Wilbur Smith novels), GOLD and SHOUT AT THE DEVIL. Originally released at 147 minutes, but mercifully reduced to its present length for its US release.

p, Michael Klinger; d, Peter Hunt; w, Wilbur Smith, Stanley Price, and Alastair Reid, based on the novel by Smith; ed, Michael Duthie; ph, Michael Reed, Panavision, Technicolor; m, Maurice Jarre.

(PR:C MPAA:PG)

SKY BANDITS*
(1986, Brit.) 93m London Front/Galaxy Int. c (AKA: GUNBUS)

Scott McGinnis (Barney), Jeff Osterhage (Luke), Ronald Lacey (Fritz), Miles Anderson (Bannock), Valerie Steffen (Yvette), Ingrid Held (Mitsou), Keith Buckley (Comdr. von Schlussel), Terrence Harvey (Col. Canning), Ten Maynard (Big Jake).

SKY BANDITS tells the story of two clownish bank robbers in the waning days of the Old West, Luke (Jeff Osterhage) and Barney (Scott McGinnis). When the law finally catches up with them, they must choose between prison and the Army, and before you can say "The War to End All Wars" Biff and Skippy (or whatever their names are) are in the trenches in France. They manage to join a British fighter squadron commanded by Bannock (Miles Anderson), whose sole objective is to down a massive German dirigible that regularly wreaks havoc over the Allied lines. The fliers always bear the brunt of their actions, and every landing is a crash, though the planes are constantly put together in ever more outlandish fashion by resident aeronautical genius Fritz (Ronald Lacey), a Briton who has had his head shaken in so many crash landings that he speaks with a German accent. Naturally, the boys pick up flying in no time, eventually becoming the only ones who can stop the zeppelin's predations. The leads are wooden and the script inane, but the flying scenes are hilarious, with unlikely looking bags of canvas, string, and cannibalized parts lumbering down the runway. The real star, though, is the gargantuan dirigible; a fantastic airship so big that the top disappears in the clouds when it is tied to the ground. A first feature from Zoran Perisic, an Oscar-winning special effects whiz from SUPERMAN, SKY BANDITS cost some $18 million and quickly disappeared from sight.

p, Richard Herland; d, Zoran Perisic; w, Thom Keyes; ed, Peter Tanner; ph, David Watkin, Rank Color; m, Alfie Kabiljo.

(PR:A-C MPAA:PG13)

SLAUGHTERHOUSE-FIVE**½
(1972) 104m UNIV-Vandas/UNIV c

Michael Sacks (Billy Pilgrim), Ron Leibman (Paul Lazzaro), Eugene Roche (Edgar Derby), Sharon Gans (Valencia Marble Pilgrim), Valerie Perrine (Montana Wildhack), Roberts Blossom (Wild Bob Cody), Sorrell Booke (Lionel Merble), Kevin Conway (Weary), Gary Waynesmith (Stanley), John Dehner (Rumford), Perry King (Robert Pilgrim), Holly Near (Barbara), Richard Schaal (Campbell).

George Roy Hill's bold adaptation of Kurt Vonnegut's popular novel focuses on the weird but seldom wonderful exploits of Billy Pilgrim (Michael Sacks), a middle-aged optometrist who bounces back and forth from one stage of his life to another. Intercut are his devastating WW II experiences as a POW in Dresden, where he lives through the Allies' disastrous bombing of the city; his postwar nervous breakdown; his marriage to the obese Valencia (Sharon Gans); the raising of a daughter who grows up just like her mother and a son who goes from hippie to Green Beret; and Billy's future stay on the planet Tralfamadore, where he and beautiful adult film star Montana Wildhack (Valerie Perrine) are closely observed by the Tralfamadorians. Able to survive calamity after calamity by blind luck, Billy finally is killed by a former comrade in arms (Ron Leibman) who blames him for the death of a friend, then it's back to Tralfamadore. Vonnegut's wildly shifting narrative and provocative theme—that life consists of a continuum of random moments—are given an adept cinematic treatment by Hill, who effectively translates both the serious and the satirical elements of the novel to the screen. Gans, Leibman, and Eugene Roche, as Billy's wartime companion, turn in fine performances, but Perrine and Sacks, making their film debuts, rightfully dominate the proceedings.

p, Paul Monash; d, George Roy Hill; w, Stephen Geller, based on the novel *Slaughterhouse-Five or the Children's Crusade* by Kurt Vonnegut, Jr.; ed, Dede Allen; ph, Miroslav Ondricek, Technicolor; m, Glenn Gould, from the works of Johann Sebastian Bach.

(PR:O   MPAA:R)

SNOW TREASURE**

(1968) 95m Sagittarius/AA c

James Franciscus *(Lt. Kalasch)*, Ilona Rodgers *(Bente Nielsen)*, Paul Austad *(Peter Lundstrom)*, Raoul Oyen *(Victor Lundstrom)*, Randi Borch *(Inger Lundstrom)*, Tor Stokke *(Lars Lundstrom)*, Wilfred Breistrand *(Capt. Kantzeler)*.

A stilted and unexciting WW II children's adventure tale, SNOW TREASURE concerns some Norwegian youngsters who smuggle some gold in their backpacks to a boat manned by the Norwegian underground. Peter (Paul Austad), a 12-year-old villager who watches as the booty is hidden away in a snowy cave during the early days of the Nazi invasion of Norway, devises a plan with his friends to smuggle it to the hideout of his Uncle Victor (Raoul Oyen), a member of the Resistance. Billed above the title is James Franciscus, who has a relatively small role as a German soldier who discovers the Norwegians' game, but offers assistance instead of reporting it back to the authorities. More enjoyable for youngsters than adults, SNOW TREASURE will, at the very least, give its young viewers some sense of history.

p, Irving Jacoby; d, Irving Jacoby; w, Irving Jacoby and Peter Hansen, based on the novel by Marie McSwigan; ed, Ralph Sheldon; ph, Sverre Bergli, Eastmancolor; m, Egil Monn-Iversen.

(PR:A   MPAA:NR)

SOLDIER BLUE*

(1970) 112m c

Candice Bergen *(Cresta Marybelle Lee)*, Peter Strauss *(Pvt. Honus Gant)*, Donald Pleasence *(Isaac Q. Cumber)*, Bob Carraway *(Lt. John McNair)*, Jorge Rivero *(Spotted Wolf)*, Dana Elcar *(Capt. Battles)*, John Anderson *(Col. Iverson)*, Martin West *(Lt. Spingarn)*, Jorge Russek *(Running Fox)*, Marco Antonio Arzate *(Kiowa Brave)*, Ron Fletcher *(Lt. Mitchell)*.

Using the US Cavalry's Indian wars as a ham-handed analogy for America's then-current morass in Vietnam, SOLDIER BLUE is a misguided, confused, film that re-creates Cavalry atrocities in leering, bloody detail. Cresta Maybelle Lee (Candice Bergen), a white woman who once lived with the Cheyenne, and Pvt. Honus Gant (Peter Strauss), the only survivors of an Indian attack on his Cavalry detachment, struggle to make their way back to the safety of an Army outpost, falling in love in the process of their perilous journey. When the Cavalry prepares to enact brutal revenge on the Cheyenne, Cresta tries to warn the Indians, but is unable to prevent the awful slaughter. In addition to being annoyingly simpleminded (especially the filmmakers' attempt to draw a parallel between the 1864 Sand Creek Massacre and the My Lai incident), SOLDIER BLUE suffers from an absolutely awful performance from Bergen as the strident Indian lover, and Strauss is simply bland. A much more successful attempt at using the past to comment on the present is Arthur Penn's considerably more complex LITTLE BIG MAN (1970).

p, Gabriel Katzka and Harold Loeb; d, Ralph Nelson; w, John Gay, based on the novel *Arrow in the Sun* by Theodore V. Olsen; ed, Alex Beaton; ph, Robert Hauser and Arthur J. Ornitz, Panavision, Technicolor; m, Roy Budd.

(PR:O   MPAA:PG)

SOLDIER OF ORANGE***½

(1979, Neth.) 165m RANK/International Picture Show c

Rutger Hauer *(Erik)*, Jeroen Krabbe *(Gus)*, Peter Faber *(Will)*, Derek De Lint *(Alex)*, Eddy Habbema *(Robby)*, Lex Van Delden *(Nico)*, Edward Fox *(Col. Rafelli)*.

Carefully crafted by veteran Dutch director Paul Verhoeven (ROBOCOP; THE FOURTH MAN), this WW II drama details the effects of Nazi occupation on a group of Dutch students. Erik (Rutger Hauer) is at first hesitant to join the resistance effort, but after escaping to England he becomes deeply involved, courageously transporting supplies to his comrades in Holland. After the war, he returns home to find that most of his fellow students and resistance fighters have been killed, including onetime student leader Gus (Jeroen Krabbe), while others have come through the war barely affected. An exceptional character study, SOLDIER OF ORANGE is also beautifully photographed by Peter De Bont—the shots of Hauer on the supply boat's windy prow as he travels between Britain and Holland linger long after the film is over. Verhoeven would again work with Krabbe and screenwriter Gerard Soeteman in his haunting THE FOURTH MAN. (In Dutch; English subtitles.)

p, Rob Houwer; d, Paul Verhoeven; w, Paul Verhoeven, Gerard Soeteman, and Kees Holierhoek, based on the autobiography of Erik Hazelhoff Roelfzema; ed, Jane

SOLDIER'S REVENGE—

Speer; ph, Peter De Bont and Jost Vacano, Eastmancolor; m, Rogier Van Otterloo.

(PR:O MPAA:R)

SOLDIER'S REVENGE*½
(1986) 88m Continental c

John Savage *(Frank Morgan)*, Maria Socas *(Baetriz)*, Edgardo Moreira *(Ricardo)*, Frank Cane *(Gomez)*, Paul Lambert *(Gen. Burns)*, Sebastian Larrie *(Tiny)*, George Wellurtz *(Sheriff)*, Jack Arndt *(Realtor)*, Albert Uris *(Carlos)*, Brian McKlunn *(Uncle Benjamin)*, Fiona Keyne *(Amy)*.

Frank Morgan (John Savage) is a Vietnam veteran who turned against the war after he was shot down and saw the carnage wreaked by bombs dropped from his plane. Later, he told a magazine about the unsavory secret operations in which he participated and was branded a traitor by many in his Texas home town. After the death of his mother, he returns home to clear up her affairs and sell the farm, continually harassed by the locals even though he is simply trying to mind his own business. Meanwhile, a plane full of weapons for a Central American revolution puts down at the local airstrip for repairs. The pilot quits, leaving Baetriz (Maria Socas), who is accompanying the load because her father has been kidnaped by the revolutionaries, who have demanded the arms as ransom. Baetriz persuades Morgan to help her and the two become embroiled in the revolution. Released in the same year that gave us one of the most intelligent films made about the conflicts in Central America—SALVADOR—SOLDIER'S REVENGE is a idiotic fantasy for pacifists who still like to see trucks blown up, with Savage wandering through the film offering near-pointless narration and facing down overwhelming odds every few minutes. No mention is made of the politics of revolution; we just get Savage whining about how no one can win a war. Shot in the US and Argentina in 1984, the film appeared on videocassette without ever gracing a theater screen in the US.

p, J.C. Crespo; d, David Worth; w, Lee Stull and David Worth, based on a story by Eduard Sarlui; ed, Raja Gosnell; ph, Leonardo Solis and Stephen Sealy; m, Don Great and Gary Rist.

(PR:C MPAA:NR)

SOME KIND OF HERO***
(1982) 97m PAR c

Richard Pryor *(Eddie Keller)*, Margot Kidder *(Toni)*, Ray Sharkey *(Vinnie)*, Ronny Cox *(Col. Powers)*, Lynne Moody *(Lisa)*, Olivia Cole *(Jesse)*, Paul Benjamin *(Leon)*, David Adams *(The Kid)*, Martin Azarow *(Tank)*, Shelly Batt *(Olivia)*, Susan Berlin *(Jeanette)*, Tim Thomerson *(Cal)*.

Although much was lost from the title James Kirkwood novel in its transition from the printed page to the screen (despite the author's collaboration on the screenplay), Richard Pryor's assured tragicomic performance is so engaging that this otherwise forgettable film is not only worth watching, but often compelling. Pryor plays Eddie Keller, an Army conscript who spends five years in a North Vietnamese POW camp, cleverly getting the best of his captors, but ultimately signing a statement denouncing US involvement in Indochina so that his fellow prisoner and friend, Vinnie (Ray Sharkey), will be given proper medical treatment. That denunciation catches up with Eddie when he returns home and is denied his back pay because of it. Moreover, he learns upon his return that his wife has taken up with another man, his business is bankrupt, and his mother has been institutionalized. Hitting bottom, Eddie finally finds comfort in his relationship with Toni (Margot Kidder), the archetypal prostitute with a heart of gold, but not before turning to crime.

p, Howard W. Koch; d, Michael Pressman; w, James Kirkwood and Robert Boris, based on the novel by Kirkwood; ed, Christopher Greenbury; ph, King Baggot, Movielab Color; m, Patrick Williams.

(PR:O MPAA:R)

SOUTHERN COMFORT****
(1981) 100m Phoenix-Cinema Group FOX c

Keith Carradine *(Spencer)*, Powers Boothe *(Hardin)*, Fred Ward *(Reece)*, Franklyn Seales *(Simms)*, T.K. Carter *(Cribbs)*, Lewis Smith *(Stuckey)*, Les Lannom *(Casper)*, Peter Coyote *(Poole)*, Carlos Brown *(Bowden)*.

Arguably writer-director Walter Hill's best film to date, SOUTHERN COMFORT works both as a pure action film and as a extremely effective allegory for America's involvement in Vietnam. Vaguely reminiscent of John Boorman's DELIVERANCE, the film follows a group of National Guardsmen on maneuvers in the swamps of Louisiana. These weekend warriors, ill-equipped for their task, prefer joking around and bickering to taking their service seriously. While out in the country, they "borrow" some canoes from local Cajuns, and soon find themselves pursued by the angry backwoodsmen. When one idiotic Guardsman (Lewis Smith) makes the mistake of shooting blanks at the Cajuns, the enraged locals return the fire with real bullets, killing Poole (Peter Coyote), the detachment's commander and the only real soldier in the bunch. A deadly battle then ensues as the Guardsmen attempt to get out of the swamp before more blood is shed. Unfamiliar with the terrain and extremely disorganized, the soldiers become easy marks and are picked off one by one. Tautly directed by Hill, superbly shot by Andrew Lazlo, and boasting an excellent score by Ry Cooder that incorporates authentic Cajun music (long before THE BIG EASY made it popular), SOUTHERN COMFORT is a gripping, atmospheric, and ultimately disturbing film. Without straining to make his points, Hill evokes the American struggle in Southeast Asia by pitting a group of naive, directionless recruits sent to unfamiliar terrain against enigmatic *foreign* guerrillas. The director doesn't limit himself to mere allegory, however; he also continues to explore some of his own favorite themes. As he did in HARD TIMES; THE DRIVER; THE WARRIORS; THE LONG RIDERS; 48 HRS.; and RED HEAT, Hill considers the tensions that result when very different men are thrown together in extreme situations. In the process, he also delivers one hell of a good action film.

p, David Giler; d, Walter Hill; w, Michael Kane, Walter Hill, and David Giler; ed, Freeman Davies; ph, Andrew Laszlo, Deluxe Color; m, Ry Cooder.

(PR:O   MPAA:R)

SPARTACUS****
(1960) 196m Bryna/UNIV c

Kirk Douglas *(Spartacus)*, Laurence Olivier *(Marcus Licinius Crassus)*, Tony Curtis *(Antoninus)*, Jean Simmons *(Varinia)*, Charles Laughton *(Gracchus)*, Peter Ustinov *(Lentulus Batiatus)*, John Gavin *(Julius Caesar)*, Nina Foch *(Helena Glabrus)*, Herbert Lom *(Tigranes)*, John Ireland *(Crixus)*, John Dall *(Glabrus)*, Charles McGraw *(Marcellus)*, Joanna Barnes *(Claudia Marius)*, Woody Strode *(Draba)*, Harold J. Stone *(David)*, Peter Brocco *(Ramon)*, Paul Lambert *(Gannicus)*, Robert Wilke *(Guard Captain)*, Nick Dennis *(Dionysius)*.

Although this is the only one of Stanley Kubrick's pictures over which he did not have complete control (he was brought in by Kirk Douglas to direct when Anthony Mann was fired after the first week of shooting), SPARTACUS is still a remarkable epic—one of the greatest tales of the ancient world ever to hit the screen. It tells the true story of a slave rebellion that panicked Rome for more than two years circa 73 BC, though some historical facts have been Hollywoodized (including Spartacus' demise—he was hacked to death in battle, not crucified). Spartacus (Douglas) is a rebellious Libyan slave purchased by Lentulus Batiatus (Peter Ustinov), the proprietor of a school for gladiators. Like his fellow trainees, he is rigorously trained in fighting skills in order to be profitably peddled to Roman coliseum owners. Discovering in himself and his fellow gladiators a spark of human dignity, Spartacus helps to lead a revolt and organize an army of slaves that will descend on Rome and liberate all oppressed men from the tyrannical rule of the patricians, specifically Marcus Crassus (Laurence Olivier). Also playing parts in this battle between free will and oppression are Gracchus (Charles Laughton), a senator engaged in a political power struggle with Crassus; Varinia (Jean Simmons), the beautiful slave and wife of Spartacus whom Crassus previously arranged to purchase; and young Julius Caesar (John Gavin), a student of Gracchus who later allies himself with Crassus. More visually restrained than usual with Kubrick (the Technirama equipment made camera movement difficult), SPARTACUS instead concentrates on the choreography of characters within the frame, most notably in the preparation of the massive final battle scene, as the various Roman military units position themselves like pieces on some gigantic chessboard. Although a television viewing of the film is rather uneventful (missing is the scope of the horizon and much of Kubrick's careful composition), SPARTACUS today remains a stirring, intelligent comment on the spirit of revolt.

p, Edward Lewis; d, Stanley Kubrick and Anthony Mann, uncredited; w, Dalton Trumbo, based on the novel by Howard Fast; ed, Robert Lawrence, Robert Schulte, and Fred Chulack; ph, Russell Metty and Clifford Stine, Super Technirama-70, Technicolor; m, Alex North.

(PR:C   MPAA:NR)

SPITFIRE***½
(1943, Brit.) 90m Misbourne-British Aviation/RKO bw
(GB: FIRST OF THE FEW, THE)

Leslie Howard *(R.J. Mitchell)*, David Niven *(Geoffrey Crisp)*, Rosamund John *(Diana Mitchell)*, Roland Culver *(Comdr. Bride)*, Annie Firth *(Miss Harper)*, David Horne *(Higgins)*, John H. Roberts *(Sir Robert MacLean)*, Derrick de Marney *(S/L Jefferson)*, Rosalyn Boulter *(Mabel Livesey)*, Tonie Edgar Bruce *(Lady Houston)*, Gordon MacLeod *(Maj. Buchan)*, Erik Freund *(Willi Messerschmidt)*.

Leslie Howard, who also produced and directed here, made his last screen appearance in this above-average biography with a strong propaganda message. Howard plays R.J. Mitchell, who designed the Spitfire fighter plane, the weapon that would foil Hitler's plans to invade England after gaining air superiority. The film opens as a squadron of fighter pilots sits at a base, awaiting the next wave of German planes. Squadron leader Geoffrey Crisp (David Niven) begins to tell the men about his close friend Mitchell, the designer of their craft, and the details of the origin of the Spitfire are related in a lengthy flashback that makes up most of the film's running time. This was Howard's last film before he was shot out of the sky by the Luftwaffe while returning from a semi-secret diplomatic mission in Lisbon. (There are rumors that the Germans knew Churchill was to be attending a meeting in Casablanca and that Howard's plane was used as a decoy.) Niven was actually detached from the service to appear in SPITFIRE, and his smooth performance is probably the best in the film. Howard's direction is assured and keeps the story from getting bogged down in its message. The score, by "serious" composer William Walton, is superb.

p, Leslie Howard, George King, John Stafford, and Adrian Brunel; d, Leslie Howard; w, Anatole de Grunwald and Miles Malleson, based on a story by Henry C. James, Kay Strueby; ed, Douglas Myers; ph, Georges Perinal; m, Sir William Walton.

(PR:A   MPAA:NR)

SPY IN BLACK, THE***
(1939, Brit.) 77m Harefield/COL bw (AKA: U-BOAT 29)

Conrad Veidt *(Capt. Hardt)*, Valerie Hobson *(Joan)*, Sebastian Shaw *(Comdr. Davis Blacklock)*, Marius Goring *(Lt. Schuster)*, June Duprez *(Anne Burnett)*, Athole Stewart *(Rev. Hector Matthews)*, Agnes Lauchlan *(Mrs. Matthews)*, Helen Haye *(Mrs. Sedley)*, Cyril Raymond *(Rev. John Harris)*, Hay Petrie *(Chief Engineer)*, Grant Sutherland *(Bob Bratt)*.

Released in the US under the not-so-catchy title U-BOAT 29, this Michael Powell espionage picture takes place during WW I. Conrad Veidt plays German submarine com-

STAGE DOOR CANTEEN—

mander Capt. Hardt, who is cruising off the coast of England when he gets word that he is to proceed forthwith to the northern Orkney Islands and rendezvous with a female agent who will give him further instructions. He meets Joan (Valerie Hobson), a schoolteacher in the employ of the Kaiser, only to learn in time that she and her cohort, British naval officer Blacklock (Sebastian Shaw), are triple agents. Veidt is sensational in one of his many German roles, the most memorable being CASABLANCA's Maj. Strasser.

p, Irving Asher; d, Michael Powell; w, Emeric Pressburger and Roland Pertwee, based on the novel by J. Storer Clouston; ed, William Hornbeck and Hugh Stewart; ph, Bernard Browne; m, Miklos Rozsa.

(PR:A MPAA:NR)

STAGE DOOR CANTEEN****

(1943) 132m UA bw

Cheryl Walker *(Eileen)*, William Terry *(Ed "Dakota" Smith)*, Marjorie Riordan *(Jean Rule)*, Lon McCallister *("California")*, Margaret Early *(Ella Sue)*, Michael Harrison [Sunset Carson] *("Texas")*, Judith Anderson, Tallulah Bankhead, Ralph Bellamy, Edgar Bergen and Charlie McCarthy, Ray Bolger, Katharine Cornell, Jane Darwell, Dorothy Fields, Gracie Fields, Lynn Fontanne, Helen Hayes, Katharine Hepburn, George Jessel, Gertrude Lawrence, Gypsy Rose Lee, Alfred Lunt, Harpo Marx, Elsa Maxwell, Yehudi Menuhin, Ethel Merman, Paul Muni, Merle Oberon, George Raft, Ethel Waters, Johnny Weissmuller, Dame May Whitty, Ed Wynn *(Stage Door Canteen Stars)*, Count Basie and His Band, Xavier Cugat and His Orchestra with Lina, Benny Goodman and His Orchestra with Peggy, Kay Kyser and His Band, Freddy Martin and His Orchestra, Guy Lombardo and His Orchestra *(Themselves)*.

In this boy-meets-canteen-girl story set in a Stage Door Canteen in Manhattan, three enlisted men on a one-day pass in New York fall in love with three young hostesses at the canteen. The story is nothing special, but the cast is: everybody who was anybody at the time, from Katharine Hepburn to Johnny Weissmuller to Gypsy Rose Lee to violinist Yehudi Menuhin, makes an appearance. The American Theatre Wing operated Stage Door Canteens in several cities, with a flagship location on West 44th Street in Manhattan. The stars donated their time and 90 percent of the profits from this hit movie went back to the Theatre Wing to help defray the expenses for the canteens, which were an oasis for young service personnel on brief leave from WW II duty.

p, Sol Lesser; d, Frank Borzage; w, Delmer Daves; ed, Hal Kern; ph, Harry J. Wild; m, Freddie Rich.

(PR:A MPAA:NR)

STALAG 17*****

(1953) 120m PAR bw

William Holden *(Sefton)*, Don Taylor *(Lt. Dunbar)*, Otto Preminger *(Oberst Von Scherbach)*, Robert Strauss *("Animal" Stosh)*, Harvey Lembeck *(Harry)*, Richard Erdman *(Hoffy)*, Peter Graves *(Price)*, Neville Brand *(Duke)*, Sig Rumann *(Schultz)*, Michael Moore *(Manfredi)*, Peter Baldwin *(Johnson)*, Robinson Stone *(Joey)*, Robert Shawley *(Blondie)*, William Pierson *(Marko)*, Gil Stratton, Jr. *(Cookie/Narrator)*, Jay Lawrence *(Bagradian)*.

Made just eight years after the end of WW II, writer-director Billy Wilder's classic black comedy tells it like it was in a German POW camp, and nobody tells it better than William Holden, who won an Oscar for his portrayal of Sefton, the glib loner whose scams and scheming make life in Stalag 17 bearable for him but incur the wrath of his fellow POWs. Still, they willingly participate in the games and attractions (like observing female Russian prisoners through a telescope) he operates for fun and profit. When two prisoners are killed while trying to escape, the Americans come to believe an informer is in their midst, and suspicion falls on Sefton. Later, after the camp's sadistic commandant, Von Scherbach (well played by director Otto Preminger), learns how newcomer Dunbar (Don Taylor) managed to blow up a train, the POWs are certain Sefton is the rat and make life miserable for him. He, in turn, sets about discovering the real informer, then tricks him into revealing himself before Sefton and Dunbar (whom the prisoners have hidden in the water tower) escape. Unlike in previous POW films, Wilder and cowriter Edwin Blum's script, based on the play by Donald Bevan and Edmund Trzcinski, presents the prisoners not as paragons of patriotic virtue but as real, self-interested, bored soldiers just trying to survive. Holden is magnificent as the heel-turned-hero, but STALAG 17 is full of wonderful, well-directed performances, including Sig Rumann as the barracks guard (the prototype for John Banner's Sgt. Schultz on "Hogan's Heroes," the long-running TV series inspired by the film); Gil Stratton, Jr., as Sefton's gopher; Harvey Lembeck and Robert Strauss as the barracks clowns; and real-life war hero Neville Brand. Peppered with Wilder's distinctive sardonic wit, STALAG 17 is one of the most enjoyable and engrossing films ever made about WW II and was justly a hit with the critics and at the box office.

p, Billy Wilder; d, Billy Wilder; w, Billy Wilder and Edwin Blum, based on the play by Donald Bevan, Edmund Trzcinski; ed, Doane Harrison and George Tomasini; ph, Ernest Laszlo; m, Franz Waxman.

(PR:C MPAA:NR)

START THE REVOLUTION WITHOUT ME***

(1970) 90m Norbud/WB c

Gene Wilder *(Claude Coupe/Philippe DeSisi)*, Donald Sutherland *(Charles Coupe/Pierre DeSisi)*, Hugh Griffith *(King Louis XVI)*, Jack MacGowran *(Jacques Cabriolet)*, Billie Whitelaw *(Queen Marie Atoinette)*, Victor Spinetti *(Duke d'Escargot)*, Orson Welles *(Narrator)*, Helen Fraser *(Mimi Montage)*, Ewa Aulin *(Christina)*, Harry Fowler *(Marcel)*.

This often hysterical farce starts like a house afire, then simply burns down. In 18th-century France, two sets of twin boys are born to different families—one aristocratic, one peasant—then confused by the attending physician. Determined to be at least half-right, the doctor switches one child in each pair. Time passes and the privileged boys, Pierre (Donald Sutherland) and Philippe (Gene Wilder), grow into arrogant scoundrels, renowned for their willingness to run their rapiers through anyone who opposes them. When revolution appears imminent, King Louis XVI (Hugh Griffith) calls on the noble swordsmen to help quell the rebels. Disguised as ordinary citizens, Pierre and Philippe go to Paris, where they are confused with the other set of brothers, Charles and Claude (Sutherland and Wilder, again), doltish peasants who have joined the rebellious forces. While very funny throughout most of its running time, the picture eventually, almost inevitably, disintegrates into a "how the heck are we going to end this?" conclusion, not unlike BLAZING SADDLES' cop-out finale. Sutherland and Wilder are delightful, but it is Griffith as Louis XVI who steals the movie, and the palace ball scene, wherein he dresses as a chicken, is unforgettably funny. Indeed, what works best here are the sight gags, the funniest of which involves "The Man in the Iron Mask," who, when his armored suit is hit by a bullet, turns and runs in the opposite direction like a penny arcade shooting-gallery figure.

p, Bud Yorkin; d, Bud Yorkin; w, Fred Freeman and Lawrence J. Cohen, based on the story "Two Times Two" by Freeman; ed, Ferris Webster; ph, Jean Tournier, Technicolor; m, John Addison.

(PR:C-O MPAA:PG)

STEEL CLAW, THE**

(1961) 96m Ponderey/WB c

George Montgomery (Capt. John Larsen), Charito Luna (Lolita), Mario Barri (Santana), Paul Sorensen (Frank Powers), Amelia De La Rama (Christina), Carmen Austin (Rosa), Ben Perez (Dolph Rodriguez), John MacGloan (Commander), Joe Sison (Himself).

THE STEEL CLAW was the first of four films shot in the Philippines in which rugged Hollywood star George Montgomery served as writer, director, producer, and actor. This time out he plays Capt. John Larsen of the USMC, a fighter tried and true who is stationed in Manila during WW II and about to be discharged after losing a hand in an accident. Undaunted, he has himself fitted for a "steel claw" and, with a guerrilla squad of Filipinos, sets out on a suicide mission inside Japanese lines to rescue Gen. Frank Powers (Paul Sorensen). After a show of bravery and derring-do, Larsen frees Powers, only to learn that the man he saved is a cowardly impostor who assumed the dead general's identity in order to receive special treatment from his captors.

p, George Montgomery; d, George Montgomery; w, George Montgomery, Ferde Grofe, Jr., and Malvin Wald; ed, Jack Murray; ph, Manuel Rojas, Technicolor; m, Harry Zimmerman.

(PR:A MPAA:NR)

STRANGER, THE****

(1946) 95m International Pictures/RKO bw

Edward G. Robinson (Wilson), Loretta Young (Mary Longstreet), Orson Welles (Prof. Charles Rankin/Franz Kindler), Philip Merivale (Judge Longstreet), Richard Long (Noah Longstreet), Byron Keith (Dr. Jeff Lawrence), Billy House (Potter), Konstantin Shayne (Konrad Meinike), Martha Wentworth (Sara), Isabel O'Madigan (Mrs. Lawrence), Pietro Sasso (Mr. Peabody).

After having made three commercial disasters in a row (THE MAGNIFICENT AMBERSONS; JOURNEY INTO FEAR; and IT'S ALL TRUE), Orson Welles was badly in need of a hit that would right him in the eyes of Hollywood. The result was THE STRANGER, the most restrained and conventional of Welles' films, but still a thrilling entertainment. Set shortly after WW II, the film casts Edward G. Robinson as Wilson, a Nazi hunter assigned the task of finding the infamous Franz Kindler, one of the architects of the genocide of the Jews. Wilson traces Kindler to the sleepy college town of Hartford, Connecticut, where he comes to suspect that Prof. Charles Rankin (Welles) is actually Kindler hiding behind a new identity. Although Rankin does a fine job of casting doubt on Wilson's suspicions, the latter's dogged pursuit of the truth wins out and Kindler is exposed. In THE STRANGER, Welles gives us one of the cinema's most realistic and chilling portrayals of a Nazi. His Franz Kindler is not a cartoon character in uniform spouting propaganda and clicking his heels, but an arrogant, cynical, amoral, and wholly self-confident creature who believes that he is superior to anyone he meets—evil incarnate. Robinson is also quite good as the hunter determined to catch his prey. Technically, as one expects with Welles, the film is superb. THE STRANGER is not as wildly creative as his other films, but all the Welles trademarks are present, including superior lighting, inventive camera angles, strong transitions, and characters silhouetted in darkness.

p, S.P. Eagle [Sam Spiegel]; d, Orson Welles; w, Anthony Veiller, John Huston, uncredited, and Orson Welles, based on the story by Victor Trivas, Decla Dunning; ed, Ernest Nims; ph, Russell Metty; m, Bronislau Kaper.

(PR:C MPAA:NR)

STREAMERS**½

(1983) 118m UA Classics c

Matthew Modine (Billy), Michael Wright (Carlyle), Mitchell Lichtenstein (Richie), David Alan Grier (Roger), Guy Boyd (Rooney), George Dzundza (Cokes), Albert Macklin (Martin), B.J. Cleveland (Pfc. Bush), Bill Allen (Lt. Townsend), Paul Lazar (MP Lieutenant), Phil Ward (MP Sgt. Kilick), Terry McIlvain (Orderly), Todd Savell (MP Sgt. Savio), Mark Fickert (Dr. Banes).

Director Robert Altman was once heralded as being on the cutting edge of the American cinema with films like M*A*S*H (1970); THE LONG GOODBYE (1973); and NASHVILLE (1975). In the 1980s, however, he has seemed more interested in the stage than the screen, and

SUNDOWN—

the vast majority of his films have been movie versions of popular or critically acclaimed plays such as "Secret Honor," "Come Back to the 5 and Dime Jimmy Dean, Jimmy Dean," and "Fool for Love." STREAMERS is no exception. Based on a play by David Rabe, it is set in an Army barracks circa 1965, as a group of young soldiers awaits assignment to Vietnam. The draftees come from a variety of class, racial, and sexual backgrounds and include two blacks, a country boy, and a Yale-educated homosexual; all of them are confronted by two brutal sergeants, veterans of the Korean War. Sexual and racial tensions build as the men await their transfer orders in the claustrophobic barracks, and eventually shocking violence erupts. Although Rabe's use of the barracks as a microcosm of the explosive emotions and issues coming to a head in America just before the Vietnam War is at times obvious, the play was an excruciatingly intense experience on stage. As filmed by Altman, however, STREAMERS becomes a distanced and rather static affair that feels more stagebound than the director's other stage-to-screen projects. While there is little of cinematic interest in the film, the performances Altman elicits from his cast—especially from Matthew Modine, Michael Wright, and George Dzundza—are superb. The odd title is Army slang for a paratrooper whose chute has been engaged but failed to open.

p, Robert Altman and Nick J. Mileti; d, Robert Altman; w, David Rabe, based on his play; ed, Norman Smith; ph, Pierre Mignot, Movielab Color.

(PR:O MPAA:R)

SUNDOWN**½

(1941) 90m UA bw

Gene Tierney *(Zia)*, Bruce Cabot *(Capt. Bill Crawford)*, George Sanders *(Maj. Coombes)*, Sir Cedric Hardwicke *(Bishop Coombes)*, Harry Carey *(Dewey)*, Joseph Calleia *(Pallini)*, Reginald Gardiner *(Lt. Turner)*, Carl Esmond *(Kuypens)*, Marc Lawrence *(Hammud)*, Jeni Le Gon *(Miriami)*, Emmett Smith *(Kipsang)*, Dorothy Dandridge *(Kipsang's Bride)*, Gilbert Emery *(Ashburton)*, Prince Modupe *(Miriami's Sweetheart)*.

In Africa at the onset of WW II, the Germans try to get the local tribes to rebel against the British colonials. Capt. Bill Crawford (Bruce Cabot) is a local commissioner who, with the help of military man Maj. Coombes (George Sanders), discovers the German plot to run guns to the natives; Zia (Gene Tierney) is the adopted daughter of an Arab who now runs some trading caravans and trading posts. Zia agrees to help the British and joins Kuypens (Carl Esmond), the local undercover Nazi chief, in order to find out more about his plans. Despite some thrilling action sequences, this is little more than a standard B-western plot with an exotic setting and touches of British imperialism, with a bit of wartime patriotism thrown in for good measure. The Nazis are evil personified, the British all that is good in the world. Henry Hathaway's direction is to the point, the cast does a good job with the material, and

some fine photography makes good use of the sets and locations.

p, Walter Wanger; d, Henry Hathaway; w, Barre Lyndon and Charles G. Booth, based on a story by Lyndon; ed, Dorothy Spencer; ph, Charles Lang; m, Miklos Rozsa.

(PR:A MPAA:NR)

SUPERNATURALS, THE**

(1987) 80m Republic Ent. c

Maxwell Caulfield *(Lt. Ray Ellis)*, Nichelle Nichols *(Sgt. Leona Hawkins)*, Talia Balsam *(Pvt. Angela Lejune)*, Bradford Bancroft *(Pvt. Tom Weir)*, LeVar Burton *(Pvt. Michael Osgood)*, Bobby Di Cicco *(Pvt. Tim Cort)*, Margaret Shendal *(Melanie)*, James Kirkwood *(Captain)*, Scott Jacoby *(Pvt. Chris Mendez)*, Richard Pachorek *(Pvt. Ralph Sedgewick)*, John Zarchen *(Pvt. Julius Engel)*, Chad Sheets *(Jeremy)*.

Tough Sgt. Leona Hawkins (Nichelle Nichols) leads a group of Army trainees on a survival mission through the Alabama woodlands, where they have a number of strange experiences. Lt. Ray Ellis (Maxwell Caulfield) sees a ghostly woman appear and disappear; Pvt. Tim Cort (Bobby Di Cicco) finds a human skull; unexplained winds and scorched earth baffle the recruits; and an underground bunker is discovered. Then a series of unexplained murders occur, with the unseen attackers terrorizing the recruits' bivouac. When a deep fog descends on the camp, the recruits are at their most vulnerable. Only then do they see their attackers—skeletal Confederate soldiers who have risen from their graves to continue their Civil War battles. Lacking the excessive gore, gratuitous nudity, amateurish acting, and tepid direction upon which many recent horror entries have thrived, THE SUPERNATURALS (despite its nondescript title) proves to be an entertaining time if one can ignore the ridiculous premise. Displaying professional technical qualities, the film also boasts some superb performances from Caulfield (GREASE II and ELECTRIC DREAMS), LeVar Burton (of the TV miniseries "Roots"), Di Cicco (THE PHILADELPHIA EXPERIMENT and SPLASH), Nichols (STAR TREK IV), Talia Balsam, and Bradford Bancroft. Director Armand Mastroianni has great success in his decision to keep the Confederate attackers out of sight for most of the picture: the greatest fear comes from the unseen attacker. The film's strength lies in its solid characterizations and a fairly concise script.

p, Michael S. Murphey and Joel Soisson; d, Armand Mastroianni; w, Michael S. Murphey and Joel Soisson; ph, Peter Collister; m, Robert O. Ragland.

(PR:O MPAA:R)

SWING SHIFT**½

(1984) 100m WB c

Goldie Hawn *(Kay Walsh)*, Kurt Russell *(Lucky Lockhart)*, Christine Lahti *(Hazel Zanussi)*, Fred Ward *(Biscuits Toohey)*, Ed Harris *(Jack Walsh)*, Sudie Bond *(Annie)*, Holly Hunter *(Jeannie Sherman)*, Patty Maloney *(Laverne)*, Lisa

Pelikan *(Violet Mulligan)*, Susan Peretz *(Edith Castle)*, Joey Aresco *(Johnny Bonnano)*, Morris "Tex" Biggs *(Clarence)*, Reid Cruikshanks *(Spike)*, Roger Corman *(Mr. MacBride)*.

This latter-day look at "Rosie the Riveter" stars Goldie Hawn as Kay Walsh, whose husband, Jack (Ed Harris), is sent off to fight in WW II. Kay goes to work at an aircraft factory, where she meets Lucky (Kurt Russell), whose heart problem has kept him out of uniform. They begin an affair; meanwhile, Kay develops a close friendship with her "loose" (i.e., emancipated) neighbor, Hazel (Christine Lahti). When Jack comes home on furlough, he discovers Kay's infidelity and goes back to war with a broken heart. In turn, Lucky, feeling rejected, sleeps with the lonely Hazel, upsetting relations among the three civilians. Later, Jack returns from the war and reunites with Kay, who reconciles with Hazel. SWING SHIFT's view of adultery isn't very palatable—since Jack is at least as likable, if not more, than Lucky and seems to have a "good" marriage with Kay—and many castigated the film for using wartime hardships to justify Kay's affair and tarnish the patriotic image of the homefront "Rosies." A fairer assessment suggests that director Jonathan Demme's characteristic generosity towards his characters and refusal to make absolute moral judgments is a strong point, while the feminist subtext adds freshness to the story. The dullness of Kay and Lucky's romance, however, does damage the film, and may be the result of friction between Demme and Hawn, who reportedly had another director brought in to shoot new scenes that conventionalized the love triangle and downplayed Lahti's Hazel. Lahti nonetheless gives by far the film's best performance, and was justly nominated for a Best Supporting Actress Oscar. Released at 113, 100, and 99 minutes, the film is on videocassette at 100 minutes.

p, Jerry Bick; d, Jonathan Demme; w, Rob Morton; ed, Craig McKay; ph, Tak Fujimoto, Technicolor; m, Patrick Williams.

(PR:A-C   MPAA:PG)

T

TAPS***

(1981) 119m FOX c

George C. Scott *(Gen. Harlan Bache)*, Timothy Hutton *(Brian Moreland)*, Ronny Cox *(Col. Kerby)*, Sean Penn *(Alex Dwyer)*, Tom Cruise *(David Shawn)*, Brendan Ward *(Charlie Auden)*, Evan Handler *(Edward West)*, John P. Navin, Jr. *(Derek Mellott)*, Billy Van Zandt *(Bug)*, Giancarlo Esposito *(J.C. Pierce)*, Donald Kimmell *(Billy Harris)*, Tim Wahrer *(John Cooper)*, Tim Riley *(Hulk)*, Jeff Rochlin *(Shovel)*, Rusty Jacobs *(Rusty)*, Wayne Tippett *(M. Sgt. Kevin Moreland)*, Jess Osuna *(Dean Ferris)*.

This gripping but sometimes overwrought drama shows what happens when a military school becomes a military zone. Gen. Harlan Bache (George C. Scott, top-billed in little more than a cameo) runs the military academy, which is in danger of being closed because a greedy real estate combine wants to knock down the ivy-covered, tradition-laden buildings and build luxury condominiums on the valuable property. The deal is made, but when the real estaters try to move in and shut the place down prior to razing the structures, the students revolt. Led by Moreland (Timothy Hutton), the boys unite in a fighting force that will demonstrate all they've learned, and, taking over the armory, which is filled with weaponry and live ammunition, they keep the invaders at bay. The Army is called in to quell this student revolt, but the boys continue to fight and real bullets begin flying. Although Hutton was the hot property when the film was produced, his younger costars, Sean Penn and Tom Cruise, stole the film and became superstars in their own right. Unfortunately, director Harold Becker moves the film along at a snail's pace, giving the audience too much time to ponder holes in the plot and weakening the tension-filled climax by delaying it too long.

p, Stanley R. Jaffe and Howard B. Jaffe; d, Harold Becker; w, Darryl Ponicsan, Robert Mark Kamen, and James Lineberger, based on the novel *Father Sky* by Devery Freeman; ed, Maury Winetrobe; ph, Owen Roizman, DeLuxe Color; m, Maurice Jarre.

(PR:C   MPAA:PG)

TARAS BULBA*½

(1962) 123m Hecht-Curtleigh/UA c

Tony Curtis *(Andrei Bulba)*, Yul Brynner *(Taras Bulba)*, Christine Kaufmann *(Natalia Dubrov)*, Sam Wanamaker *(Filipenko)*, Brad Dexter *(Shilo)*, Guy Rolfe *(Prince Grigory)*, Perry Lopez *(Ostap Bulba)*, George Macready *(Governor)*, Ilka Windish *(Sophia Bulba)*, Vladimir Sokoloff *(Old Stepan)*, Vladimir Irman *(Grisha Kubenko)*, Daniel Ocko *(Ivan Mykola)*, Abraham Sofaer *(Abbot)*, Mickey Finn *(Korzh)*, Richard Rust *(Capt. Alex)*, Ron Weyand *(Tymoshevsky)*, Vitina Marcus *(Gypsy Princess)*, Chuck Hayward *(Dolotov)*, Syl Lamont *(Kimon Kandor)*, Ellen Davalos *(Zina)*, Marvin Goux *(Brother Bartholomew)*.

This is a poor adaptation of Gogol's classic novel, featuring Yul Brynner as the legendary Cossack leader Taras Bulba. Betrayed by the Polish army circa 1550, the Cossack and his men are forced to flee across the Russian steppes. Later, Taras raises two sons, who follow in their father's footsteps. Andrei (Tony Curtis), however, falls in love with a Polish noblewoman (Christine Kaufmann), a romance that leads to a violent confrontation between father and son. TARAS BULBA seemed doomed to fail from the start. First, producer Harold Hecht wanted to cut costs, so he filmed this tale of 16th-century Cossacks in Argentina. The local gauchos, who played the hundreds of soldiers, did more fighting to get on camera than they did on-screen. Moreover, Curtis was again the victim of poor casting, his character became ludicrous due to his heavy Brooklyn accent. To make matters worse, the actor's personal life went awry when he fell for his costar, 17-year-old

TASTE OF HELL, A—

Kaufmann, causing his wife, Janet Leigh, to go home—a repentant Curtis giving chase and causing some delays. Veteran hack director J. Lee Thompson brings his typically bland style to the affair, and while the battle scenes are less than spectacular, his handling of the actors is even worse. The only bright spot here is Franz Waxman's Oscar-nominated musical score, which builds up a thematic scheme as the various Cossack tribes ride and come together for the climactic battle.

p, Harold Hecht; d, J. Lee Thompson; w, Waldo Salt and Karl Tunberg, based on the story by Nikolai Gogol; ed, William Reynolds, Gene Milford, Eda Warren, Ace Blangsted, and Folmar Blangsted; ph, Joseph MacDonald, Panavision, Eastmancolor; m, Franz Waxman.

(PR:A MPAA:NR)

TASTE OF HELL, A*

(1973) 90m Boxoffice International c

John Garwood (Barry Mann), Lisa Lorena (Maria), William Smith (Jack Lowell), Vic Diaz (Maj. Kuramoto), Lloyd Kino (Capt. Seiko), Angel Buenaventura (Tomas).

This low-budget WW II story, set in the Philippines, follows the exploits of American Army officers Barry Mann (John Garwood) and Jack Lowell (William Smith), who find themselves trapped behind enemy lines. Caught by the Japanese, the Americans surrender, only to be machine-gunned by a vicious Japanese officer. Mann is shot in the leg, but despite his injury vows vengeance and joins forces with a Filipino guerrilla troop determined to defeat the invaders. A substandard actioner, A TASTE OF HELL went straight to home video in the US.

p, John Garwood; d, Neil Yarema and Basil Bradbury; w, Neil Yarema; ph, Fred Conde, Movielab Color; m, Nester Robles.

(PR:C MPAA:PG)

TESTAMENT***

(1983) 90m Entertainment Events-American Playhouse/PAR c

Jane Alexander (Carol Wetherly), William Devane (Tom Wetherly), Ross Harris (Brad Wetherly), Roxana Zal (Mary Liz Wetherly), Lukas Haas (Scottie Wetherly), Philip Anglim (Hollis), Lilia Skala (Fania), Leon Ames (Henry Abhart), Lurene Tuttle (Rosemary Abhart), Rebecca De Mornay (Cathy Pitkin), Kevin Costner (Phil Pitkin), Mako (Mike), Mico Olmos (Larry), Gerry Murillo (Hiroshi).

Set in a small town in northern California, this flawed but moving film begins by establishing the pattern of everyday life for an average American family, then rips it apart by introducing the nightmare of nuclear war. Tom and Carol Wetherly (William Devane and Jane Alexander), the loving parents of three children (Lukas Haas, Ross Harris, and Roxana Zal), joke, bicker, and make love, until one day Tom doesn't come home from work because of the outbreak of nuclear war. Thereafter, the film shows the effects of the fallout, both physical and psychological, on the little town and particularly the Wetherlys. As living conditions deteriorate, looting begins, and people start dying—including two of the Wetherly children—Carol and her surviving son search for solace in the past, stirring their memories with home movies of happier times. Ultimately, they even find the will to go on into the bleak future. Less sensationalistic than the similar TV movie "The Day After," TESTAMENT patiently draws us into the pre-holocaust lives of the Wetherly family, making them real for us, so that when the family is destroyed by the horror of nuclear war their pain and loss are tangible. Unfortunately, at more than a few junctures in the film, first-time director Lynne Littman lays on the sentiment and symbolism a little thickly, and some may find the pre-disaster section of TESTAMENT slow going, but the acting is undeniably strong—particulary Alexander's heartfelt performance, which earned her a Best Actress Oscar nomination.

p, Jonathan Bernstein and Lynne Littman; d, Lynne Littman; w, John Sacret Young, based on the story "The Last Testament" by Carol Amen; ed, Suzanne Pettit; ph, Steven Poster, CFI Color; m, James Horner.

(PR:A MPAA:PG)

THAT HAMILTON WOMAN**½

(1941) 128m UA bw (GB: LADY HAMILTON)

Vivien Leigh (Emma Hart Hamilton), Laurence Olivier (Lord Horatio Nelson), Alan Mowbray (Sir William Hamilton), Sara Allgood (Mrs. Cadogan-Lyon), Gladys Cooper (Lady Nelson), Henry Wilcoxon (Capt. Hardy), Heather Angel (Street Girl), Halliwell Hobbes (Rev. Nelson), Gilbert Emery (Lord Spencer), Miles Mander (Lord Keith), Ronald Sinclair (Josiah), Luis Alberni (King of Naples), Norma Drury (Queen of Naples), Juliette Compton (Lady Spencer), Olaf Hytten (Gavin), Guy Kingsford (Capt. Troubridge).

A drunken crone (played by Vivien Leigh), jailed on charges of theft and assault, begins to tell the story of her life to a cellmate, and the tale of THAT HAMILTON WOMAN unfolds in flashback. In 1786, young Emma Hart (Leigh) arrives at the court of Naples, expecting to wed the British ambassador's nephew. He proves a rascal, but Emma's joie de vivre soon attracts the ambassador himself, Sir William Hamilton (Alan Mowbray), and she eventually becomes his bride. Seven years later, British naval hero Lord Nelson (Laurence Olivier) arrives in Naples, seeking the king's aid in the war against Napoleon, and the rest, as they say, is history—or at least producer-director Alexander Korda's version of such. The film traces the growth in Naples of Emma and Nelson's love (to which her husband turns a blind eye, though tongues wag back home) and their return to England, where the lovers set up house, although Nelson's wife refuses to divorce him. The war goes badly, and Emma persuades Nelson to return to his command, leading to his mortal wounding in the victory at Trafalgar, which in turn begins her slide into decrepitude. Despite the marquee pull of newlyweds Olivier and Leigh (she fresh from GONE WITH THE WIND), THAT HAMILTON WOMAN was not the hit its makers hoped it would be—though it reportedly *was* Winston Churchill's favorite movie. Korda, shooting in the US with little money, was forced to film quickly, without the lavish sets that were his specialty, and the script's "tastefulness"—which downplays Nelson's sensuality and alters facts in making Emma pay for her sins later in the classic Hollywood style—while pleasing to 1941 censors and strengthening its propaganda value for then-embattled Britain, also lowers the level of excitement. For a more accurate account, see the Glenda Jackson-Peter Finch THE NELSON AFFAIR (1973).

p, Alexander Korda; d, Alexander Korda; w, Walter Reisch and R.C. Sherriff; ed, William Hornbeck; ph, Rudolph Mate; m, Miklos Rozsa.

(PR:A MPAA:NR)

THEY DIED WITH THEIR BOOTS ON****

(1942) 140m WB bw

Errol Flynn *(George Armstrong Custer)*, Olivia de Havilland *(Elizabeth Bacon Custer)*, Arthur Kennedy *(Ned Sharp)*, Charles Grapewin *(California Joe)*, Gene Lockhart *(Samuel Bacon)*, Anthony Quinn *(Crazy Horse)*, Stanley Ridges *(Maj. Romolus Taipe)*, John Litel *(Gen. Phil Sheridan)*, Walter Hampden *(Sen. Sharp)*, Sydney Greenstreet *(Gen. Winfield Scott)*, Regis Toomey *(Fitzhugh Lee)*, Hattie McDaniel *(Callie)*, G.P. Huntley, Jr. *(Lt. Butler)*, Frank Wilcox *(Capt. Webb)*, Joseph Sawyer *(Sgt. Doolittle)*, Minor Watson *(Sen. Smith)*, Gig Young *(Lt. Roberts)*.

If one can ignore the blatantly fictitious nature of this Hollywood "biography" of the still-controversial George Armstrong Custer, THEY DIED WITH THEIR BOOTS ON is a wholly entertaining movie, fueled by Raoul Walsh's direction and Errol Flynn's energetic performance. The film follows Custer (Flynn) from his youth as a West Point cadet to his service in the Civil War and finally to his days with the Seventh Cavalry, which ended with the massacre at Little Big Horn on June 25, 1876. Walsh creates a rousing film, its pace as fast as the many cavalry charges the dashing Custer leads. Unfortunately, the picture does not adhere to the facts and, in many instances, strays far afield to keep Custer's legend intact, going so far as to invest the cavalry commander with impassioned sympathy for the plight of the Indians! Though historically inaccurate, THEY DIED WITH THEIR BOOTS ON still provides sprawling, exciting epic action, with huge masses of men moved in the Civil War scenes, and particularly in the final battle against the Indians, with great skill by Walsh. Walsh used more than 1,000 extras, with mostly Filipinos doubling for the Sioux because, not surprisingly, only 16 real Sioux from the reservation at South Dakota's Fort Yates answered the casting call (the rest, presumably, refusing to insult the memories of their ancestors). Dozens of stuntmen were injured in horse falls, so many that the studio had to set up a field hospital at the location site to handle the daily injuries, with doctors and nurses—and veterinarians—attending the scores of riders and horses hobbling in for treatment after battle scenes. Indeed, three stuntmen died during the filming of this wild actioner: one from a broken neck, another from a heart attack, and, in the most bizarre and gruesome death, one impaled on his own sword—which was real at his own insistence. Despite the film's wanton distortion of history, THEY DIED WITH THEIR BOOTS ON did paint a fairly sympathetic portrait of the Indians. Director Walsh later stated: "Most westerns had depicted the Indian as a painted, vicious savage. In THEY DIED WITH THEIR BOOTS ON I tried to show him as an individual who only turned violent when his rights as defined by treaty were violated by white men."

p, Hal B. Wallis; d, Raoul Walsh; w, Wally Kline and Aeneas MacKenzie; ed, William Holmes; ph, Bert Glennon; m, Max Steiner.

(PR:A MPAA:NR)

THEY WERE EXPENDABLE****

(1945) 135m MGM bw

Robert Montgomery *(Lt. John Brickley)*, John Wayne *(Lt. J.G. "Rusty" Ryan)*, Donna Reed *(2nd Lt. Sandy Davyss)*, Jack Holt *(Gen. Martin)*, Ward Bond *("Boots" Mulcahey)*, Marshall Thompson *(Ens. Snake Gardner)*, Paul Langton *(Ens. Andy Andrews)*, Leon Ames *(Maj. James Morton)*, Arthur Walsh *(Seaman Jones)*, Donald Curtis *(Lt. J.G. "Shorty" Long)*, Cameron Mitchell *(Ens. George Cross)*, Jeff York *(Ens. "Lefty" Tony Aiken)*, Murray Alper *("Slug" Mahan)*, Harry Tenbrook *("Cookie" Squarehead Larsen)*, Jack Pennick *("Doc")*, J. Alex Havier *(Benny Lacoco)*, Charles Trowbridge *(Adm. Blackwell)*, Bruce Kellogg *(Lt. Elder Tompkins)*, Louis Jean Heydt *(Capt. Ohio Carter)*, Robert Barrat *(Gen. Douglas MacArthur)*, Russell Simpson *(Dad Knowland)*.

In direct contrast to the flag-waving, jingoistic propaganda films typical of Hollywood during WW II, John Ford's THEY WERE EXPENDABLE is a somber and moving account of America's defeat in the Philippines early in the war. Filming this grim failure, Ford beautifully and poetically captures the heroism and bravery of the men and women who fought there—and does so without impassioned speechifying or gushing patriotism. Instead, Ford commemorates the quiet and uncomplaining devotion to duty, the will to serve, and the nobility of sacrifice of those left in an untenable situation. Based on the exploits of Lt. John Bulkeley, commander of Motor Torpedo Boat Squadron No. 3 (the predecessor of the Navy PT boat force), the film follows the coolly professional lieutenant (Robert Montgomery, in one of his best performances), renamed "Brickley" for the film, and his hot-headed executive officer, Lt. J.G. "Rusty" Ryan (John Wayne), as they struggle to get the Navy to accept the PT boats as a valuable new tool in the war effort. The top commanders, however, see no use for the unit and relegate Brickley and crew to running messages and ferrying supplies. As Bataan and Corregidor fall to the Japanese, however, the PT unit proves itself valuable by sinking many enemy ships, although the effort proves too little too late. Japan emerges triumphant and the American brass is forced to leave their troops stranded before the enemy and to flee to Australia, where they will regroup and plan their return. From the time Ford shot THEY WERE

THIRTY SECONDS OVER TOKYO—

EXPENDABLE to the day he died, the director was ambivalent about the film, his opinion of the work alternating between disapproval and satisfaction. This may have been largely due to the fact that he was pressured into making THEY WERE EXPENDABLE soon after having seen action himself in the South Pacific as a documentary filmmaker for the Navy. Capt. Ford had lost 13 men in his unit and the making of this film no doubt stirred painful memories for the director, memories he may have preferred to ignore when asked to discuss his films later in life. Despite Ford's ambivalence, THEY WERE EXPENDABLE is one of the greatest films to come out of WW II, a lasting and poignant tribute to those who go in harm's way.

p, John Ford; d, John Ford and (uncredited) Robert Montgomery; w, Frank W. Wead, based on the book by William L. White; ed, Frank E. Hull and Douglass Biggs; ph, Joseph H. August; m, Herbert Stothart.

(PR:A MPAA:NR)

THIRTY SECONDS OVER TOKYO***½
(1944) 138m MGM bw

Spencer Tracy *(Lt. Col. James H. Doolittle)*, Van Johnson *(Capt. Ted W. Lawson)*, Robert Walker *(David Thatcher)*, Phyllis Thaxter *(Ellen Jones Lawson)*, Tim Murdock *(Dean Davenport)*, Scott McKay *(Davey Jones)*, Gordon McDonald *(Bob Clever)*, Don DeFore *(Charles McClure)*, Robert Mitchum *(Bob Gray)*, John R. Reilly *(Shorty Manch)*, Horace McNally [Stephen McNally] *(Doc White)*, Donald Curtis *(Lt. Randall)*, Louis Jean Heydt *(Lt. Miller)*, William Phillips *(Don Smith)*, Douglas Cowan *(Brick Holstrom)*, Paul Langton *(Capt. Ski York)*, Leon Ames *(Lt. Jurika)*, Benson Fong *(Young Chung)*.

In 1942, 131 days after the Japanese bombing of Pearl Harbor, an American force retaliated, bombing the major Japanese cities of Tokyo and Yokohama. This picture, a quasi-documentary re-creation of that event, was authored by one of the survivors of the raid, Ted Lawson (played here by Van Johnson). Since land bases near the target are unavailable—and in-flight refueling techniques undeveloped—a dangerous, untried tactic must be employed for the top-secret mission: for the first time in history, twin-engine bombers are to take off from the deck of an aircraft carrier. Because the planes are too large to land on a carrier deck, after the attack they must continue on to mainland China—occupied by the Japanese—and then make their way to Allied-held territory as best they can. Weeks of preparation and training take place before the aircraft and their crews are finally loaded aboard the USS *Hornet*. Following a final shipboard briefing by mission leader Lt. Col. Jimmmy Doolittle (Spencer Tracy), the fliers man their twin-engine Mitchell bombers and are catapulted from the flight deck. The remainder of the film follows the adventures of Lawson's crew only. A well-made war film, THIRTY SECONDS OVER TOKYO was sufficiently accurate to prompt all the real-life principals to approve the use of their names in the picture. Screenwriter Dalton Trumbo wisely elected not to attempt to alter the limited perspective of Lawson's memoir by including more of the details of the famous raid. In the actual event, all 16 participating bombers made it to China, although three men died in crashes and eleven others were captured by the Japanese, who executed three of them. Although top-billed, Tracy's appearance here is basically a cameo, with Johnson the real star of the film. Popular with both critics and the public, THIRTY SECONDS OVER TOKYO received an Oscar for Best Special Effects.

p, Sam Zimbalist; d, Mervyn LeRoy; w, Dalton Trumbo, based on the book by Capt. Ted W. Lawson, Robert Considine; ed, Frank Sullivan; ph, Harold Rosson and Robert Surtees; m, Herbert Stothart.

(PR:A MPAA:NR)

THIS ABOVE ALL***
(1942) 110m FOX bw

Tyrone Power *(Clive Briggs)*, Joan Fontaine *(Prudence Cathaway)*, Thomas Mitchell *(Monty)*, Henry Stephenson *(Gen. Cathaway)*, Nigel Bruce *(Ramsbottom)*, Gladys Cooper *(Iris)*, Philip Merivale *(Dr. Roger Cathaway)*, Queenie Leonard *(Violet Worthing)*.

Prudence Cathaway (Joan Fontaine), daughter of a wealthy London surgeon of great repute, goes beneath her social station and volunteers for the WAAFs instead of entering the service as an officer, because she wants to go in at the bottom and attend training camp as a private. While in training, she gets fixed up with Clive Briggs (Tyrone Power), who is not in the service. Briggs, who was wounded at Dunkirk and placed on recuperation status, is a bitter young man from the working class who feels that the upper crust rules England and that saving their lives is hardly worth losing his. Briggs has no idea that Prudence is an aristocrat when they begin dating and, despite their vastly different backgrounds, she finds herself attracted to him. When the time for Clive to return to duty arrives, he goes AWOL and is branded a deserter, leaving Prudence to persuade him that England, despite its class conflicts, is worth fighting for. Adapted from a popular novel, THIS ABOVE ALL begins as an interesting look at heightened English class-consciousness during the war, but then disintegrates (as did the novel) into an unbelievable and treacly climax that violates the integrity of Power's character. The performances, however, are admirable, Fontaine having just received her Oscar for SUSPICION and Power finally beginning to be taken seriously as an actor. The film won an Oscar for Art/Set Decoration, and was nominated for Cinematography, Editing, and Best Sound.

p, Darryl F. Zanuck; d, Anatole Litvak; w, R.C. Sherriff, based on the novel by Eric Knight; ed, Walter Thompson; ph, Arthur Miller; m, Alfred Newman.

(PR:A MPAA:NR)

THIS IS THE ARMY***
(1943) 120m WB c

Irving Berlin *(Himself)*, George Murphy *(Jerry Jones)*, Joan Leslie *(Eileen Dibble)*, George Tobias *(Maxie Stoloff)*, Alan

Hale *(Sgt. McGee)*, Charles Butterworth *(Eddie Dibble)*, Rosemary DeCamp *(Ethel)*, Dolores Costello *(Mrs. Davidson)*, Una Merkel *(Rose Dibble)*, Stanley Ridges *(Maj. Davidson)*, Ruth Donnelly *(Mrs. O'Brien)*, Dorothy Peterson *(Mrs. Nelson)*, Kate Smith *(Herself)*, Frances Langford *(Cafe Singer)*, Gertrude Niesen *(Singer)*, Ronald Reagan *(Johnny Jones)*, Joe Louis *(Himself)*.

This star-studded musical salute to the American soldier is filled with Irving Berlin's songs and morale-boosting patriotism. Taken from Berlin's stage play, which opened July 4, 1942, THIS IS THE ARMY also adapts portions of Berlin's earlier musical "Yip Yip Yaphank." Jerry Jones (George Murphy, later a California senator) is a big-time Broadway star who, at the beginning of WW I, is drafted into the service and given the job of putting on a big show. He does his bit and, when the show ends, cast and crew go off to fight in Europe. Years pass and Jerry is now a producer with a son, Johnny (Ronald Reagan, who joined Murphy in rising through California politics), who is drafted in WW II and given the same job as his father. Johnny writes a terrific show *and* marries sweetheart Eileen Dibble (Joan Leslie). The show tours the country and at the final performance, before the boys go to war, Irving Berlin (as himself) comes onstage in Washington to sing. The plot is just barely enough to hang the musical numbers on, but it's the tunes that count. Berlin used his clout to get the Army to lend him more than 300 soldiers for the stage show, promising to donate more than a million dollars from the show's receipts to a relief fund for the families the boys left behind.

p, Jack L. Warner and Hal B. Wallis; d, Michael Curtiz; w, Casey Robinson and Claude Binyon, based on the play by Irving Berlin; ed, George Amy; ph, Bert Glennon and Sol Polito, Technicolor.

(PR:AA MPAA:NR)

THIS LAND IS MINE***½

(1943) 103m RKO bw

Charles Laughton *(Arthur Lory)*, Maureen O'Hara *(Louise Martin)*, George Sanders *(George Lambert)*, Walter Slezak *(Maj. Erich von Keller)*, Kent Smith *(Paul Martin)*, Una O'Connor *(Mrs. Emma Lory)*, Philip Merivale *(Prof. Sorel)*, Thurston Hall *(Mayor Henry Manville)*, George Coulouris *(Prosecuting Attorney)*, Nancy Gates *(Julie Grant)*, Ivan Simpson *(Judge)*, John Donat *(Edmund Lorraine)*, Frank Alten *(Lt. Schwartz)*.

Set "somewhere in Europe" (clearly Jean Renoir's French homeland), THIS LAND IS MINE stars Charles Laughton as a cowardly schoolteacher, Arthur Lory, who whimpers during air raids and can only be comforted by his overly possessive mother (Una O'Connor). Arthur chooses to keep a low profile and go about his business unnoticed until his mentor, Prof. Sorel (Philip Merivale), lights a patriotic spark in him. Aware of his cowardice, he turns to fellow schoolteacher Louise Martin (Maureen O'Hara), who is sympathetic both to his fears and to the cause of the Resistance, of which her brother Paul (Kent Smith) is an active member who throws bombs at German officers. As much as he tries to remain neutral, Arthur finds himself increasingly sympathetic to the Resistance movement. Although some consider THIS LAND IS MINE preachy and overly talky, it must be praised for its understanding of humanity. Instead of painting the Germans as mighty evildoers and the French as innocent victims, Renoir took a more daring and honest approach, implicating the French as being partly responsible for the Occupation, when many citizens collaborated with the Nazis to ensure that they would remain immune from punishment and that their orderly lives would not be shattered by the invaders. Renoir avoided propagandistic cliches and took into consideration human nature; human nature, however, is not what people look for in war heroes and patriotic messages. Although long considered a propaganda film, THIS LAND IS MINE is more correctly seen as anti-propagandistic. There is no black and white, no good or evil. There is only grey, and, in that grey area, an understanding of the frailty of human nature.

p, Jean Renoir and Dudley Nichols; d, Jean Renoir; w, Dudley Nichols; ed, Frederic Knudtson; ph, Frank Redman; m, Lothar Perl.

(PR:A MPAA:NR)

THRONE OF BLOOD****

(1961, Jap.) 110m Brandon Films bw (KUMONOSUJO, KUMONOSU-DJO; AKA: COBWEB CASTLE; THE CASTLE OF THE SPIDER'S WEB)

Toshiro Mifune *(Taketoki Washizu)*, Isuzu Yamada *(Asaji)*, Takashi Shimura *(Noriyasu Odagura)*, Minoru Chiaki *(Yoshaki Miki)*, Akira Kubo *(Yoshiteru)*, Takamaru Sasaki *(Kuniharu Tsuzuki)*, Yoichi Tachikawa *(Kunimaru)*, Chieko Naniwa *(Witch)*.

A truly remarkable film combining beauty and terror to produce a mood of haunting power, THRONE OF BLOOD was the brilliant fulfillment of Japanese master Akira Kurosawa's longtime ambition to bring Shakespeare's "Macbeth" to Japanese audiences. Kurosawa set the story in feudal Japan, and the transposition of cultures is surprisingly successful, with all the plot elements intact. After putting down a mutinous rebellion for their lord, warriors Taketoki Washizu (Toshiro Mifune) and Yoshaki Miki (Minoru Chiaki) are called to the main castle for an audience. Riding through the dense and foggy forest that protects the warlord's castle, they encounter a mysterious old woman bathed in white light and mist. When questioned, the woman prophesies that Washizu will be given command of a castle and soon become warlord, but his reign will be brief and his throne will be occupied by his friend's son thereafter. When it appears her predictions are coming true, Washizu grows increasingly corrupted by his own ambitions. THRONE OF BLOOD is filled with unforgettable, haunting imagery. Departing from his usual (very Western) fluid camera style and fast-paced editing, Kurosawa borrowed here from the conventions of Noh theater. While the visuals are gorgeous, the compositions are static and stagy, concentrating on the emotional moment as it seems to hang in the air—unaltered by editing or camera movement. The visual (and acting) styles work marvelously with the material, although the film is somewhat cold and detached, containing little of the exhilarating passion found in Kurosawa's other work. (In Japanese; English subtitles.)

p, Akira Kurosawa and Sojiro Motoki; d, Akira Kurosawa; w, Hideo Oguni, Shinobu Hashimoto, Ryuzo Kikushima, and Akira Kurosawa, based on the play "Macbeth" by William Shakespeare; ed, Akira Kurosawa; ph, Asaichi Nakai, Tohoscope; m, Masaru Sato.

(PR:O MPAA:NR)

TIN DRUM, THE***½

(1979, Ger./Fr./Yugo./Pol.) 142m Artemis-Hallelujah Argos/NW c (DIE BLECHTROMMEL)

David Bennent *(Oskar Matzerath)*, Mario Adorf *(Alfred Matzerath)*, Angela Winkler *(Agnes Matzerath)*, Daniel Olbrychski *(Jan Bronski)*, Katharina Thalbach *(Maria)*, Charles Aznavour *(Sigismund Markus)*, Heinz Bennent *(Greff)*, Andrea Ferreol *(Lina Greff)*.

Winner of the Academy Award for Best Foreign-Language Film and cowinner (along with APOCALYPSE NOW) of the top prize at the Cannes Film Festival, this adaptation of the Gunter Grass novel combines surreal imagery and straightforward storytelling. Oskar (David Bennent), born to a German rural family in the 1920s, becomes disgusted with the behavior of adults and decides, on his third birthday, not to grow any more, preferring instead to beat his tin drum (a birthday present) and shatter glass with his shrill scream. As he "ages," little Oskar continues to observe the hypocritical behavior of adults, beating out a constant tattoo on his tin drum to control the world around him. His small stature also makes for a very peculiar relationship with a teenage girl, Maria (Katharina Thalbach), who is also mistress to a much older, and bigger, man. THE TIN DRUM is a disturbing film, rich with black humor, that takes a decidedly bitter and horrific look at the German people. Director Volker Schlondorff frames a piercing study of the origins of the German nightmare and the rise of Naziism through national complacency. Only Oskar, in his singularly demented way, is the voice of reason, proclaiming, "Once there was a credulous people who believed in Santa Claus, but Santa Claus turned out to be the gas man." The film is often difficult to watch and downright frightening, especially due to the haunting face of 12-year-old actor Bennent. (In German; English subtitles.)

p, Franz Seitz and Anatole Dauman; d, Volker Schlondorff; w, Franz Seitz, Volker Schlondorff, Jean-Claude Carriere, and Gunter Grass, based on the novel by Grass; ed, Suzanne Baron; ph, Igor Luther, Eastmancolor; m, Friedrich Meyer and Maurice Jarre.

(PR:O MPAA:R)

TIME OF DESTINY, A*

(1988) 118m Nelson-Alive/COL c

William Hurt *(Martin Larraneta)*, Timothy Hutton *(Jack McKenna)*, Melissa Leo *(Josie Larraneta)*, Francisco Rabal *(Jorge Larraneta)*, Concha Hidalgo *(Sebastiana Larraneta)*, Stockard Channing *(Margaret Larraneta)*, Megan Follows *(Irene Larraneta)*, Frederick Coffin *(Ed)*, Kelly Pacheco *(Young Josie Larraneta)*, John O'Leary *(Father Basil)*, Justin Gocke *(Young Martin Larraneta)*, John Thatcher *(Young George)*.

Despite the starring presence of Timothy Hutton and William Hurt, A TIME OF DESTINY is a disappointingly overblown melodrama. Beginning at a battlefront in WW II Italy, where American soldiers Martin and Jack (Hurt and Hutton, respectively) seem closer than brothers, the story flashes back to San Diego. There, Basque immigrant Jorge (Francisco Rabal) heads a family that includes his wife (Concha Hidalgo), married daughter Margaret (Stockard Channing), and adored daughter Josie (Melissa Leo), whose relationship with GI Jack he has forbidden. The couple elopes, but Jorge coaxes Josie from her honeymoon bed and into his car during a driving rainstorm, with Jack in pursuit, leading to an accident. Josie survives, but her father drowns. Jorge's outcast son, Martin, vows to gain vengeance on Jack, whom he blames for the death of the father who never loved or trusted him, and finagles to be transferred overseas with Jack's unit, seemingly planning to do him in during battle; instead, the two become bosom buddies and save each other's lives. On the eve of their return to the US, however, Martin tells his brother-in-law just who he really is, promising to kill him if he tries to return to Josie, leading eventually to a climactic, VERTIGO-derived fight to the finish between the two men in the bell tower of the church where Jack and Josie are about to renew their vows. Writer-director Gregory Nava and writer-producer Anna Thomas (makers of EL NORTE) intend the film to make a grand statement about love, vengeance, and fate, but A TIME OF DESTINY instead meanders to an end that has less to do with destiny than predictability. With the exception of the excellent Channing, none of the characters are sympathetic enough to be involving. Hutton and Leo's personalities are so underdeveloped that it never becomes clear just exactly what makes them love each other so damn much; Hurt is less one-dimensional, but the psychological motivation provided for his strangely driven character is forced, his off-the-wall performance brave but unconvincing. All of which is a shame, since Nava does provide some stunning camerawork and memorable images that transcend his script's limitations—most notably in the opening shot, the point-of-view journey of a shell through the barrel of an artillery piece, into airborne trajectory, and ultimately to explosive impact.

p, Anna Thomas; d, Gregory Nava; w, Gregory Nava and Anna Thomas; ed, Betsy Blankett; ph, James Glennon, DeLuxe Color; m, Ennio Morricone.

(PR:C MPAA:PG-13)

TIME TO LOVE AND A TIME TO DIE, A****

(1958) 133m UNIV c

John Gavin *(Ernest Graeber)*, Lilo Pulver *(Elizabeth Kruse)*,

Jock Mahoney *(Immerman)*, Don DeFore *(Boettcher)*, Keenan Wynn *(Reuter)*, Erich Maria Remarque *(Pohlmann)*, Dieter Borsche *(Capt. Rahe)*, Thayer David *(Oscar Binding)*, Charles Regnier *(Joseph)*, Dorothea Wieck *(Frau Lieser)*, Kurt Meisel *(Heini)*, Agnes Windeck *(Frau Witte)*, Clancy Cooper *(Sauer)*, Klaus Kinski *(Gestapo Lieutenant)*, Alice Treff *(Frau Langer)*, Jim Hutton *(Hirschland)*, Wolf Harnisch *(Sgt. Muecke)*.

This sad, romantic account of two lovers who spend three innocent weeks together in a bombed-out section of Germany before being driven apart by WW II concerns Ernest Graeber (John Gavin), a German soldier on the Russian front who, after fighting for two years, is allowed a furlough. Upon his return home, however, he learns that his town has been reduced to rubble by steady bombing. His search for news of his parents' whereabouts leads him to the home of the family physician, Dr. Kruse, an opponent of the Nazis who has been hauled off by the Gestapo. There he meets Kruse's daughter, Elizabeth (Lilo Pulver), a sweet but cynical young woman with pessimistic views of the future. Both hoping to find their parents, Ernest and Elizabeth fall in love, though their romantic interludes are spoiled by the reality of air-raid sirens and the deadly whistling of bombs. They marry, but have little hope of living out their idyllic young dreams of love, for Ernest must report back to the Russian front or face the wrath of the Gestapo. The most honest and personal film from Douglas Sirk (WRITTEN ON THE WIND; IMITATION OF LIFE), a Danish-born director who spent his early years in Germany and began his filmmaking career (as Detlef Sierck) under the constraints of Nazi rule, the aptly titled A TIME TO LOVE AND A TIME TO DIE is not an apology for Germany's actions in WW II, but a complex and realistic portrayal in which Sirk refuses to paint every German soldier as a barbarian. Instead he portrays them as men—some strong, some weak, but all partially implicated in their country's atrocities. Beautifully photographed by Russell Metty (the CinemaScope framing is unforgivably absent from the videocassette) amidst some of Germany's ruins and featuring some excellent performances, including the adorable Pulver as Elizabeth, Keenan Wynn as a high-class lieutenant, and Thayer David as a former schoolmate of Ernest's turned decadent Nazi, the film is based on a novel by Erich Maria Remarque (ALL QUIET ON THE WESTERN FRONT), who also has a small role as Ernest's former teacher.

p, Robert Arthur; d, Douglas Sirk; w, Orin Jannings, based on the novel *A Time to Live and a Time to Die* by Erich Maria Remarque; ed, Ted J. Kent; ph, Russell Metty, Cinema-Scope, Eastmancolor; m, Miklos Rozsa.

(PR:A-C   MPAA:NR)

TO BE OR NOT TO BE*****

(1942) 99m UA bw

Carole Lombard *(Maria Tura)*, Jack Benny *(Joseph Tura)*, Robert Stack *(Lt. Stanislav Sobinski)*, Felix Bressart *(Greenberg)*, Lionel Atwill *(Rawitch)*, Stanley Ridges *(Prof. Alexander Siletsky)*, Sig Rumann *(Col. Ehrhardt)*, Tom Dugan *(Bronski)*, Charles Halton *(Dobosh)*, Peter Caldwell *(Wilhelm Kunze)*, Helmut Dantine, Otto Reichow *(Copilots)*, Miles Mander *(Maj. Cunningham)*, Henry Victor *(Capt. Schultz)*, Maude Eburne *(Anna the Maid)*, Halliwell Hobbes *(Gen. Armstrong)*.

A masterpiece of satire and one of the more controversial films of its day, TO BE OR NOT TO BE is a brilliant example of how comedy can be as effective in raising social and political awareness as a serious propaganda film, while still providing great entertainment. The film begins in Poland, 1939, where Joseph Tura (Jack Benny), a tremendously vain Polish actor, and his wife, Maria (Carole Lombard), a national institution in Warsaw, are starring in an anti-Nazi stage play that subsequently is censored and replaced with a production of "Hamlet." Maria has taken a fancy to a young Polish fighter pilot, Sobinski (Robert Stack), who is called to duty when Germany invades Poland. In England, he and his fellow pilots in the Polish squadron of the RAF bid farewell to their much-loved mentor, Prof. Siletsky (Stanley Ridges), who confides to them that he is on a secret mission to Warsaw. Sobinski, however, begins to suspect that Siletsky is a spy and flies to Warsaw to stop him from keeping an appointment with Nazi colonel Ehrhardt (Sig Rumann)—an appointment that will destroy the Warsaw underground. There, Sobinski enlists the aid and special talents of the Tura's theater group to save and protect the Resistance. A satire built around a rather complex spy plot and directed with genius by Ernst Lubitsch, TO BE OR NOT TO BE lampoons the Nazis and paints the Poles as brave patriots fighting for their land, for whom Hamlet's question "To be or not to be" takes on national implications. Released in 1942, in the midst of America's involvement in WW II, the film drew a great deal of criticism from people who felt that Lubitsch, a German (though he left long before Hitler's rise) was somehow making fun of the Poles. TO BE OR NOT TO BE is also remembered as the last screen appearance for the lovely Lombard, who, just after the film's completion, was killed in a plane crash while on her way to Hollywood for a war bonds spot on Benny's radio show.

p, Ernst Lubitsch; d, Ernst Lubitsch; w, Edwin Justus Mayer, based on a story by Ernst Lubitsch, Melchior Lengyel; ed, Dorothy Spencer; ph, Rudolph Mate; m, Miklos Rozsa.

(PR:A   MPAA:NR)

TO BE OR NOT TO BE**½

(1983) 108m Brooksfilms/FOX c

Mel Brooks *(Frederick Bronski)*, Anne Bancroft *(Anna Bronski)*, Tim Matheson *(Lt. Andre Sobinski)*, Charles Durning *(Col. Erhardt)*, Jose Ferrer *(Prof. Siletski)*, Christopher Lloyd *(Capt. Schultz)*, James Haake *(Sasha)*, Scamp *(Mutki)*, George Gaynes *(Ravitch)*, George Wyner *(Ratkowski)*, Jack Riley *(Dobish)*, Lewis J. Stadlen *(Lupinski)*, Ronny Graham *(Sondheim)*, Estelle Reiner *(Gruba)*, Zale Kessler *(Bieler)*, Earl Boen *(Dr. Boyarski)*, Roy Goldman *(Hitler)*.

Mel Brooks and his real-life wife, Anne Bancroft, starred

TO HELL AND BACK—

for the first time together in the husband-and-wife roles previously played by Jack Benny and Carole Lombard. The plot is much the same as in the Ernst Lubitsch original, with everything played for laughs and Brooks at his funniest in impersonations of Nazis, particularly a witty rendition of Hitler (whom Brooks apparently lives to lampoon). What's missing is the social relevance of the 1942 original, released in the midst of Germany's occupation of Poland. That version still holds up today, because of the brilliance of Lubitsch's direction—the magnificent "touch" he had with everything inside the film frame. It should go without saying that Alan Johnson, who directed here, is no Lubitsch.

p, Mel Brooks; d, Alan Johnson; w, Thomas Meehan and Ronny Graham, based on the film written by Ernst Lubitsch and Melchior Lengyel; ed, Alan Balsam; ph, Gerald Hirschfeld, Deluxe Color; m, John Morris.

(PR:C MPAA:PG)

TO HELL AND BACK**½

(1955) 106m UNIV c

Audie Murphy *(Himself)*, Marshall Thompson *(Johnson)*, Jack Kelly *(Kerrigan)*, Charles Drake *(Brandon)*, Paul Picerni *(Valentino)*, Gregg Palmer *(Lt. Manning)*, David Janssen *(Lt. Lee)*, Richard Castle *(Kovak)*, Paul Langton *(Col. Howe)*, Bruce Cowling *(Capt. Marks)*, Julian Upton *(Steiner)*, Denver Pyle *(Thompson)*, Felix Noriego *(Swope)*, Brett Halsey *(Saunders)*, Susan Kohner *(Maria)*.

Audie Murphy was America's most decorated soldier of WW II, winning more than 20 medals, including the Congressional Medal of Honor, while fighting in North Africa, Italy, France, Germany, and Austria—all before the age of 19. These accomplishments brought Murphy to the attention of Hollywood, and he starred in a number of B westerns throughout the late 1940s and early 1950s. A marginal actor at best, Murphy spent several years doing quickie oaters, until he was given a shot at the big time in John Huston's THE RED BADGE OF COURAGE (1951). Finally, in 1955, Murphy starred as himself in the film adaptation of his own best-selling autobiography, *To Hell and Back*. Given a big-budget, Technicolor, CinemaScope presentation, the film traces Murphy from his hard-working origins as the son of Texas sharecroppers to his rejection by both the Marines and Navy for being too young. Eventually Murphy is accepted by the Army, proving to be a courageous natural leader, rising through the ranks to lieutenant and company commander, killing some 240 of the enemy in the process. The script is loaded with cliches and the direction lackluster, but despite such flaws there is a certain amount of interest in watching the rather awkward Murphy re-create some of the most dramatic events of his life. In the 1960s, Murphy suffered several personal and career setbacks, including problems with alcohol and drugs, and a charge of attempted murder stemming from a barroom brawl. In 1971 he was killed in a small plane crash along with five others.

p, Aaron Rosenberg; d, Jesse Hibbs; w, Gil Doud, based on the book by Audie Murphy; ed, Edward Curtiss; ph, Maury Gertsman, CinemaScope, Technicolor.

(PR:A-C MPAA:NR)

TOBRUK**½

(1966) 107m Gibraltar/UNIV c

Rock Hudson *(Maj. Donald Craig)*, George Peppard *(Capt. Kurt Bergman)*, Nigel Green *(Col. John Harker)*, Guy Stockwell *(Lt. Max Mohnfeld)*, Jack Watson *(Sgt.-Maj. Tyne)*, Norman Rossington *(Alfie)*, Percy Herbert *(Dolan)*, Liam Redmond *(Henry Portman)*, Heidy Hunt *(Cheryl Portman)*, Leo Gordon *(Sgt. Krug)*, Robert Wolders *(Cpl. Bruckner)*, Anthony Ashdown *(Lt. Boyden)*.

This action-filled WW II drama places Maj. Donald Craig (Rock Hudson) in command of a small special force whose mission is to cross the Libyan desert and destroy the fuel depot at Tobruk, thus slowing the advance of Rommel's Afrika Korps on the Suez Canal. The detachment of 90 men is made up of German-born Jews and British commandos; the former pose as Nazis, the latter as prisoners of war being transported through Axis territory. En route, the brave column cunningly outwits German and Italian contingents, and also discovers a traitor in their midst. Competently directed by the uneven Arthur Hiller, this well-paced and frequently exciting effort nearly overcomes the deficiencies of its script, written by Leo V. Gordon, who is also featured in a small role. Yuma, Arizona, and El Centro, California, stood in for the North African desert. The scenes of mass mayhem and destruction in TOBRUK were borrowed to generate the only moments of interest in the execrable Richard Burton desert opus RAID ON ROMMEL (1971).

p, Gene Corman; d, Arthur Hiller; w, Leo V. Gordon; ed, Robert C. Jones; ph, Russell Harlan and Nelson Tyler, Techniscope, Technicolor; m, Bronislau Kaper.

(PR:A MPAA:NR)

TOO LATE THE HERO***

(1970) 133m ABC-Palomar Associates and Aldrich/Cinerama c (AKA: SUICIDE RUN)

Michael Caine *(Pvt. Tosh Hearne)*, Cliff Robertson *(Lt. Lawson)*, Ian Bannen *(Pvt. Thornton)*, Harry Andrews *(Lt. Col. Thompson)*, Denholm Elliott *(Capt. Hornsby)*, Ronald Fraser *(Pvt. Campbell)*, Lance Percival *(Cpl. McLean)*, Percy Herbert *(Sgt. Johnstone)*, Henry Fonda *(Capt. Nolan)*, Ken Takakura *(Maj. Yamaguchi)*.

Director Robert Aldrich's vain attempt to repeat the box-office bonanza of his 1967 hit THE DIRTY DOZEN comes off only adequately. Shot on location in the Philippines with an all-star cast, TOO LATE THE HERO tells a tale of bravery and cowardice among dissimilar men. It's the nadir of WW II, and the Japanese are ensconced on an island in the New Hebrides where they have an observation base and are able to watch shipping in the area and order air strikes. The Allies' problem is how to get them out of there. Lt. Lawson (Cliff Robertson) is a gold-bricking US Navy lieutenant who is doing his best to stay out of harm's way. Because he can speak Japanese, Lawson is recruited—against his will—to be part of what may be a suicide mission to knock out the Japanese outpost, and is ordered by his immediate boss, Capt. Nolan (Henry Fonda, in a pretitle cameo of just a few lines), into the thick of things. The leader of the Brits is Capt. Hornsby (Denholm Elliott), a wishy-washy type who shows few signs of intelligence, and while Cockney private Tosh Hearne (Michael Caine) doesn't like Lawson, he does share the American's belief that Hornsby is ill-suited for command. With this unlikely band of heroes assembled, the soldiers make their way to the Japanese encampment to complete their mission. Although it contains many of the same elements as THE DIRTY DOZEN and boasts a good cast, TOO LATE THE HERO finds veteran action director Aldrich resting on his laurels, delivering a rather bland retread of past success.

p, Robert Aldrich; d, Robert Aldrich; w, Robert Aldrich and Lukas Heller, based on a story by Robert Aldrich, Robert Sherman; ed, Michael Luciano; ph, Joseph Biroc, Metrocolor; m, Gerald Fried.

(PR:C MPAA:GP)

TOP GUN**

(1986) 110m Paramount Pictures c

Tom Cruise *(Lt. Pete Mitchell)*, Anthony Edwards *(Lt. Nick Bradshaw)*, Kelly McGillis *(Charlotte Blackwood)*, Tom Skerritt *(Comdr. Mike Metcalf)*, Val Kilmer *(Tom Kasanzky)*, Michael Ironside *(Dick Wetherly)*, Rick Rossovich *(Ron Kerner)*, Barry Tubb *(Henry Ruth)*, Whip Hubley *(Rick Neven)*, Clarence Gilyard, Jr. *(Evan Gough)*, Tim Robbins *(Sam Wills)*, John Stockwell *(Cougar)*, James Tolkan *(Stinger)*, Meg Ryan *(Carole)*.

This paean to hotshot Navy fighter pilots and high technology attracted mass audiences despite its familiar plot and characters so vapid they vanish from memory as soon as the house lights come up. Young fighter pilot Lt. Pete Mitchell (Tom Cruise), nicknamed "Maverick" for his individualistic flying style, is sent to Miramar Naval Air Station, near San Diego, for advanced fighter training. There he trains with the best pilots from other squadrons, flying against instructors and firing electronic missiles tracked by computer. The best student from each class wins the prized "Top Gun" award, and the privilege of remaining at Miramar as an instructor. Maverick's chief competition is Tom Kasanzky (Val Kilmer), nicknamed "Ice," and eventually an international incident arises that allows the pilots to prove themselves. In an unlikely subplot, Maverick has an affair with Charlotte Blackwood (Kelly McGillis), a civilian expert on the physics of high-speed jet performance. What TOP GUN contributes to the genre is an increased emphasis on military hardware and an almost homoerotic attraction for male bodies, mostly sweaty ones. In the final analysis, though, everything that happens on the ground is extraneous to the real heart of the film, the flying sequences. Much praised, the airborne footage seamlessly intercuts live action shots of planes with special effects models. But for all the skill of their execution, the flying scenes are often confusing, rarely giving any idea of where the planes are in relation to one another. Jets streak by and pilots spin their heads around yelling, "Where'd he go? Where'd he go?" until the beepers aboard their planes tell them they've been shot down. The producers of TOP GUN went to the Navy with the project and received complete cooperation after certain changes were made in the plot. In fact, five different types of planes were made available to the filmmakers, in addition to a variety of other services ranging from technical advisors to air-sea rescue operations. Taxpayers, however, didn't bankroll TOP GUN; the filmmakers received a bill for $1.1 million from the Navy. The armed forces are not always so cooperative, however, as the makers of IRON EAGLE; PLATOON; and HEARTBREAK RIDGE found out when, for a variety of reasons, the Department of Defense refused to help them with their films. The Navy received yet another dividend for its trouble when enlistment soared after the film—one of the slickest ever made—became a hit. Ultimately, TOP GUN is a facile movie in which Americans kill Russians with impunity—proving their inherent superiority—and Tom Cruise gets the girl.

p, Don Simpson and Jerry Bruckheimer; d, Tony Scott; w, Jim Cash and Jack Epps, Jr.; ed, Billy Weber and Chris Lebenzon; ph, Jeffrey Kimball, Metrocolor; m, Harold Faltermeyer.

(PR:A-C MPAA:PG)

TORA! TORA! TORA!**

(1970, US/Jap.) 143m FOX c

Martin Balsam *(Adm. Husband E. Kimmel)*, Soh Yamamura *(Adm. Isoroku Yamamoto)*, Jason Robards, Jr. *(Gen. Walter C. Short)*, Joseph Cotten *(Henry L. Stimson)*, Tatsuya Mihashi *(Comdr. Minoru Genda)*, E.G. Marshall *(Lt. Col. Rufus S. Bratton)*, Takahiro Tamura *(Lt. Comdr. Fuchida)*, James Whitmore *(Adm. William F. Halsey)*, Eijiro Tono *(Adm. Chuichi Nagumo)*, Wesley Addy *(Lt. Comdr. Alvin D. Kramer)*, Shogo Shimada *(Ambassador Kichisaburo Nomura)*, Frank Aletter *(Lt. Comdr. Thomas)*, Koreya Senda *(Prince Fumimaro Konoye)*, Leon Ames *(Frank Knox)*, Junya Usami *(Adm. Zengo Yoshida)*, Richard Anderson *(Capt. John Earle)*, Kazuo Kitamura *(Foreign Minister Yosuke Matuoka)*, Keith Andes *(Gen. George C. Marshall)*, Edward Andrews *(Adm. Harold R. Stark)*, Neville Brand *(Lt. Kaminsky)*, Asao Uchida *(Gen. Hideki Tojo)*.

The Japanese sneak attack that plunged the US into WW II is lavishly and fairly accurately, if not enthrallingly, brought to the screen in this Japanese-US coproduction. The strategies of the Japanese high command as they prepare to further their expansionist aims by destroying the main American naval base in the Pacific are contrasted with the normal peacetime business of US government and military brass, with only a few individuals suspicious that the Japanese aren't sincere in their desire to negotiate. The film climaxes with the Pearl Harbor attack itself, re-created on the actual locations with the kind of detail that only millions of Hollywood dollars can buy. The first half of this movie, as the Japanese plot and Americans

TRAIN, THE—

scratch their heads in apprehension, is static, boring, and 79 minutes long, the duration of many better movies. This is followed by 65 more minutes that largely comprise the actual attack—which, once it finally comes, is spectacular, involving dozens of planes refurbished to look like Japanese fighters, dive bombers, and torpedo planes. But despite all the grand spectacle, even the attack, as unimaginatively staged by Richard Fleischer, begins to bore after a while. How many times can one see planes swoop down and drop bombs on ships without it getting tedious? The film was the result of years of negotiation between Japanese and American investors. In the end, two different films were made; a Japanese film showing the Japanese side, and an American film doing the same for the US point of view. The two films were then edited together in two different versions, one for each nation. Initially, 20th Century Fox hired the great Japanese director Akira Kurosawa (THE SEVEN SAMURAI) to direct the Japanese sequences, telling him that Englishman David Lean (LAWRENCE OF ARABIA) was to direct the American sequences. As it turned out, Lean was never involved with the film and Kurosawa shot only for a few weeks, chafing under the tight controls imposed on him by the studio. The unhappy Kurosawa purposely got himself fired from the picture, and was replaced by Toshio Masuda and Kinji Fukasaku, two unremarkable directors of Japanese genre pictures equal in stature to Hollywood hack Fleischer. It all ended up costing over $25 million and failed miserably at the box office in the US, but was a great success in Japan, although it still took several years before the studio made back its money (partly by selling the battle footage to other filmmakers, some of it appearing in MIDWAY, 1976, and in MACARTHUR, 1977).

p, Elmo Williams; d, Richard Fleischer, US, Toshio Masuda, and Kinji Fukasaku, Japan; w, Larry Forrester, Hideo Oguni, and Ryuzo Kikushima, based on the book by Gordon W. Prange and *The Broken Seal* by Ladislas Farago; ed, James E. Newcom, Pembroke J. Herring, and Inoue Chikaya; ph, Charles F. Wheeler, Shinsaku Himeda, Masamichi Sato, and Osami Furuya, Panavision, Deluxe Color; m, Jerry Goldsmith.

(PR:C MPAA:G)

TRAIN, THE****

(1965, Fr./It./US) 140m Les Productions Artistes-Ariane Dear/UA bw

Burt Lancaster *(Labiche)*, Paul Scofield *(Col. von Waldheim)*, Jeanne Moreau *(Christine)*, Michel Simon *(Papa Boule)*, Suzanne Flon *(Miss Villard)*, Wolfgang Preiss *(Herren)*, Richard Munch *(Von Lubitz)*, Albert Remy *(Didont)*, Charles Millot *(Pesquet)*, Jacques Marin *(Jacques)*, Paul Bonifas *(Spinet)*, Jean Bouchaud *(Schmidt)*, Donald O'Brien *(Schwartz)*, Jean-Pierre Zola *(Octave)*, Art Brauss *(Pilzer)*, Jean-Claude Bercq *(Major)*, Howard Vernon *(Dietrich)*, Bernard La Jarrige *(Bernard)*.

A superior WW II film that provides plenty of edge-of-the-seat thrills, THE TRAIN also poses a rather serious philosophical question: Is the preservation of art worth a human life? Set in France in the summer of 1944, with the Germans in retreat, the film begins as a German colonel, von Waldheim (Paul Scofield), is ordered to transport the collection of the Jeu de Paume Museum—including numerous masterpieces—by train to the Fatherland. The curator of the museum gets word of the plan to the Resistance and they persuade Labiche (Burt Lancaster), a railway inspector, to try to save the priceless works of art. THE TRAIN was originally to have been helmed by Arthur Penn, but during the first two weeks of shooting the director had some severe disagreements with Lancaster and producer Jules Bricken and left the production. Lancaster then called in John Frankenheimer, whom he had just worked with on SEVEN DAYS IN MAY (they had also collaborated on THE YOUNG SAVAGES and THE BIRDMAN OF ALCATRAZ). The film was shot entirely on location in France, and Frankenheimer employed a number of cameras shooting simultaneously so that the action with the trains would be captured from several different angles with as few takes as possible. His camera placement perfectly captures the massive trains (no models or miniatures were used) from every conceivable perspective and their movement is directly contrasted with the chess game played by Labiche and von Waldheim. The acting in the film is superb, with Scofield taking top honors as the obsessed German general, though veteran French character actor Michel Simon nearly steals the film as a determined old engineer.

p, Jules Bricken; d, John Frankenheimer; w, Franklin Coen, Frank Davis, Walter Bernstein, and Albert Husson, based on the novel *Le Front de l'Art* by Rose Valland; ed, David Bretherton and Gabriel Rongier; ph, Jean Tournier and Walter Wottitz; m, Maurice Jarre.

(PR:C MPAA:NR)

TRANSPORT FROM PARADISE***

(1967, Czech.) 94m Barrandov Ceskoslovensky/Impact bw (TRANSPORT Z RAJE)

Zdenek Stepanek *(Lowenbach)*, Cestmir Randa *(Marmulstaub)*, Ilja Prachar *(Moric Herz)*, Jaroslav Rauser *(Von Holler)*, Jiri Vrstala *(Binde)*, Ladislav Pesek *(Roubicek)*, Walter Taub *(Spiegel)*.

Set during WW II in the Terezin Ghetto, the name given to the concentration camp Theresienstadt, this award-winning Czech film details the devastating brutality of the Nazis against the Jewish population. Unlike the Nazi death camps, the Terezin Ghetto was a model camp in southeast Germany to which Jews from many countries were sent. Created as proof that the Nazis were treating their prisoners humanely, the "town" had banks, shops, and a local administrative board. In TRANSPORT FROM PARADISE, as the Nazis receive word that the International Red Cross will be inspecting the prison camp, the authorities even make a film to illustrate just how wonderful life is there. But underneath the decorative posters are others that read, in a variety of languages, "Death to Fascism." As pleasant as the Nazis try to make the camp, there is always the fear among the inmates of being shipped to another, and when the chairman of the Council of Jewish Elders is requested to authorize a transport to another camp equipped with gas chambers, he refuses to sign the order. The Germans simply get rid of him and find someone else who will comply. A group is rounded up—without realizing where they are headed, they actually save places on the train for loved ones and finally, in the haunting final scene, board the transport and go on to death. A grim, sad reminder of an unforgettable human ordeal, TRANSPORT FROM PARADISE reveals the savagery that can exist behind a mask of humanity. Zbynek Brynych's direction stresses the herding of masses, generally of all European Jews in Europe as they are sent to Terezin and particularly of the group (and their numbered suitcases piled high against a wall) who are shipped off in the film to the death camp. Brynych underlines the Nazi masquerade by using an upbeat musical score. (In Czech, German, and French; English subtitles.)

d, Zbynek Brynych; w, Arnost Lustig and Zbynek Brynych; ed, Miroslav Hajek; ph, Jan Curik; m, Jiri Sternwald.

(PR:A MPAA:NR)

TUNES OF GLORY***½
(1960, Brit.) 106m HM/Lopert c

Alec Guinness (Lt. Col. Jock Sinclair), John Mills (Lt. Col. Basil Barrow), Dennis Price (Maj. Charlie Scott), Susannah York (Morag Sinclair), John Fraser (Cpl. Piper Fraser), Allan Cuthbertson (Capt. Eric Simpson), Kay Walsh (Mary), John MacKenzie (Pony Major), Gordon Jackson (Capt. Jimmy Cairns), Duncan MacRae (Pipe Maj. MacLean).

A powerful and highly effective tale of military life during peacetime, TUNES OF GLORY follows two very different officers in a Scottish Highland regiment. Director Ronald Neame and the producers cast against type in giving the suave Alec Guinness the role of crude, up-from-the-ranks Lt. Col. Jock Sinclair, who had bravely led his troops to victory at El Alamein, while John Mills must convince the audience that he is Lt. Col. Basil Barrow, an Oxbridge type who is all spit, polish, and protocol. Sinclair is the interim commander of the 200-year-old unit, a man of war with little interest in commanding a peacetime unit, which suffers from a lack of discipline in the ranks. Rules are easily bent; dress rehearsals are not taken seriously. Enter military man Barrow, sent to replace Sinclair. Devoted to restoring the faded glory of the regiment, he demands respect from everyone and ruffles many feathers, though some who served under Sinclair, appreciating Jock's personal bravery and abilities but hating his boorish ways, flock to Barrow in the hope that he will bring back their former days of glory. When Sinclair faces a possible court martial (he punches out a young corporal who is courting his daughter [Susannah York]) and asks for a second chance, Barrow, against his better judgment, relents and lets Sinclair off, an action that deeply affects both men and sends them off to a grim and unexpected conclusion. Mills and Guinness are the center of the movie and it's a tossup as to which is "better," though Mills won the Best Actor Award at the 1960 Venice Film Festival. The film is all acting and character, nicely accented by the Scottish bagpipe music of Malcolm Arnold.

p, Colin Lesslie; d, Ronald Neame; w, James Kennaway, based on his novel; ed, Anne V. Coates; ph, Arthur Ibbetson, Technicolor; m, Malcolm Arnold.

(PR:C MPAA:NR)

TWELVE O'CLOCK HIGH*****
(1949) 132m FOX bw

Gregory Peck (Gen. Frank Savage), Hugh Marlowe (Lt. Col. Ben Gately), Gary Merrill (Col. Keith Davenport), Dean Jagger (Maj. Harvey Stovall), Millard Mitchell (Gen. Pritchard), Robert Arthur (Sgt. McIllhenny), Paul Stewart (Capt. "Doc" Kaiser), John Kellogg (Maj. Cobb), Robert Patten (Lt. Bishop), Lee MacGregor (Lt. Zimmerman), Sam Edwards (Birdwell), John Zilly (Sgt. Ernie), William Short (Lt. Pettinghill), Richard Anderson (Lt. McKessen).

Gregory Peck is excellent in this Henry King-directed drama about the physical and emotion stress that results from giving the "maximum effort" day after day. The films opens obscurely and hauntingly as a bald, bespectacled man, Harvey Stovall (Dean Jagger), wanders through postwar England, arriving at the edge of a former American air base, now overgrown with weeds. As the onetime major looks into the sky, his memory takes over; bomber squadrons return from the daylight missions in Germany. The 918th Bomber Group is under the command of Col. Keith Davenport (Gary Merrill), a likable leader who operates as a friend to his men. However, it is Col. Davenport's identification with his men—boys really—that leads to his downfall. Overly concerned with their health and well-being (after a seemingly endless succession of dangerous bombing missions, the squadron is a jumble of wounds and jangled nerves), the colonel is unable to meet the demands of his superiors, Gen. Pritchard (Millard Mitchell) and Gen. Frank Savage (Peck). Davenport is relieved of his duties and replaced by Gen. Savage, a callous martinet who tries to whip the men back into shape, immediately cutting back on three-day passes, closing the local bar, demanding that he be saluted and that everyone be properly uniformed. Most of the pilots put in for a transfer; however, one confused but heroic young pilot, Lt. Bishop (Bob Patten), rallies them. Moved by his pilot's show of unity, Savage becomes increasingly friendly, identifying with the men even more than his predecessors have. One of the first films to take a complex look at the heroism of WW II, TWELVE O'CLOCK HIGH is not afraid to make its heroes vulnerable. Four years after the war's end, audiences no longer needed the blatant propaganda that filled wartime screens. Instead, Savage's character (based on the real-life nervous breakdown of Air Corps Maj. Gen. Frank A. Armstrong) is entirely human—a man with real emotions, fears, and inadequacies. Peck's flawless portrayal of Gen. Savage earned an Academy Award nomination, but the film's pivotal performance is Jagger's as Maj. Stovall, and he deservedly won a Best Supporting Actor Oscar. The alter ego of director King, Stovall is an introspective, older military man; friend and assistant to both Davenport and

TWILIGHT'S LAST GLEAMING—

Savage, he has lived through one world war and now holds together the frayed ends of the 918th Bomber Group. In addition to the fine acting, TWELVE O'CLOCK HIGH features some gorgeous camerawork by Leon Shamroy and one of the most horrifying aerial attack sequences ever put on film. Judging from this picture alone, the subsequent devaluation of King's work is a gross injustice.

p, Darryl F. Zanuck; d, Henry King; w, Sy Bartlett and Beirne Lay, Jr., based on the novel by Bartlett, Lay; ed, Barbara McLean; ph, Leon Shamroy; m, Alfred Newman.

(PR:C   MPAA:NR)

TWILIGHT'S LAST GLEAMING***½
(1977, US/Ger.) 146m Geria-Lorimar-Bavaria/AA c

Burt Lancaster (Lawrence Dell), Richard Widmark (Martin MacKenzie), Charles Durning (President Stevens), Melvyn Douglas (Zachariah Guthrie), Paul Winfield (Willis Powell), Burt Young (Augie Garvas), Joseph Cotten (Arthur Renfrew), Roscoe Lee Browne (James Forrest), Gerald S. O'Loughlin (Brig. Gen. Michael O'Rourke), Richard Jaeckel (Capt. Stanford Towne), William Marshall (Attorney Gen. William Klinger), Charles Aidman (Col. Bernstein), Leif Erickson (CIA Director Ralph Whittaker), Charles McGraw (Gen. Peter Crane), William Smith (Hoxey).

A flawed but nonetheless highly exciting political thriller, TWILIGHT'S LAST GLEAMING has some deeply disturbing things to say about the powers that be in America. The action begins in 1981 (the near future for this 1977 release) and centers on former US Air Force general Lawrence Dell (Burt Lancaster), a Vietnam veteran who served five years as a POW. Upon his return, Dell became a vocal advocate of disclosing the truth behind US involvement in Southeast Asia in the hope that a post-Watergate America would forgive its government and have renewed faith its leaders. Because of his radical stance, however, Dell is eventually sent to prison on trumped up manslaughter charges. Still determined, he recruits three inmates (Paul Winfield, Burt Young, and William Smith) to help him escape and take over a nearby SAC base that he helped design. Once in control of the base, Dell demands that the president (Charles Durning) reveal the truth about the Vietnam War to the American people by reading National Security Council document No. 9759 on national television. If these demands are not met, Dell promises to send the nine Titan missiles to their targets in the Soviet Union. TWILIGHT'S LAST GLEAMING is a stunning indictment of the arrogance of America's decision makers and the lengths to which they will go to maintain "business as usual." At the same time it also dramatizes the danger of our unthinking faith in technology. Tellingly, it comes as a deep shock to the military that their usually reliable machines and detailed procedures seem to have gone haywire on the day of the siege, leaving them powerless to stop Dell. Though a bit slow at the outset and suffering from some occasional lapses of logic, Robert Aldrich's film—shot in Germany with no cooperation from the US military—is a fascinating, tension-filled effort. Lancaster contributes a fine performance as the righteous, populist general, and Durning is superb as the president who comes to share Lancaster's high hopes. Further, Aldrich uses some remarkable split-screen techniques that add to the film's tension and speed up the complicated expository passages. Despite some flaws, TWILIGHT'S LAST GLEAMING is a gripping drama that will have you on the edge of your seat until the bitter end.

p, Merv Adelson; d, Robert Aldrich; w, Ronald M. Cohen and Edward Huebsch, based on the novel *Viper Three* by Walter Wager; ed, Michael Luciano and Maury Weintrobe; ph, Robert Hauser, Technicolor; m, Jerry Goldsmith.

(PR:O   MPAA:R)

TWO WOMEN****
(1960, It./Fr.) 105m C.C. Champion-Les Films Marceau-Cocinor-S.G.C./EM bw (LA CIOCIARA)

Sophia Loren (Cesira), Jean-Paul Belmondo (Michele), Eleanora Brown (Rosetta), Raf Vallone (Giovanni), Renato Salvatori (Florindo), Carlo Ninchi (Michele's Father), Andrea Checchi (Fascist).

Sophia Loren won a Best Actress Oscar—the first to a non-American actress in a foreign-language film—for this Vittorio De Sica film, adapted by screenwriter Cesare Zavattini from an Alberto Moravia novel. Loren plays Cesira, a young widow in 1943 Italy who leaves her grocery store in San Lorenzo in the hands of her sometime lover (Raf Vallone), fleeing Allied bombing with her teenage daughter, Rosetta (Eleanora Brown), to return to her native village. There, after an arduous journey, she meets Michele (Jean-Paul Belmondo), the intellectual son of a local farmer with whom Rosetta falls in love, though he falls for her lovely mother. As the town grows increasingly besieged by bombing and shortages, Michele is forced to guide some fleeing Germans on an escape route, while Cesira and Rosetta go back to Rome for safety. Along the way, mother and daughter suffer a tragedy that changes both their lives forever, despite Cesira's best efforts to protect her child from the ravages of war. Loren also won the Best Actress Award at Cannes and the same honor from the British Film Academy; more important, she demonstrated in this film that she was a mature actress with talent to match her looks. De Sica (who also won an Oscar for the film) and Zavattini's previous collaborations included SHOESHINE; THE BICYCLE THIEF; and UMBERTO D, and while TWO WOMEN doesn't match the greatness or simplicity of those Neo-Realist masterworks, it remains a remarkably moving, humane vision of individual struggle in an inhumane world. (In Italian; English subtitles.)

p, Carlo Ponti; d, Vittorio De Sica; w, Cesare Zavattini and Vittorio De Sica, based on the novel by Alberto Moravia; ed, Adriana Novelli; ph, Gabor Pogany and Mario Capriotti, CinemaScope; m, Armando Trovajoli.

(PR:C-O   MPAA:NR)

UV

UGLY AMERICAN, THE**½

(1963) 120m UNIV c

Marlon Brando *(Harrison Carter MacWhite)*, Eiji Okada *(Deong)*, Sandra Church *(Marion MacWhite)*, Pat Hingle *(Homer Atkins)*, Arthur Hill *(Grainger)*, Jocelyn Brando *(Emma Atkins)*, Kukrit Pramoj *(Prime Minister Kwen Sai)*, Judson Pratt *(Joe Bing)*, Reiko Sato *(Rachani)*, George Shibata *(Munsang)*, Judson Laire *(Sen. Brenner)*, Philip Ober *(Sears)*, Stefan Schnabel *(Andrei Krupitzyn)*, Pock Rock Ann *(Col. Chee)*.

An obviously sincere, but nonetheless simplistic critique of American foreign policy in Southeast Asia, THE UGLY AMERICAN quickly squanders whatever interest it may hold due to its didactic script and dull direction. Set in the fictional Asian nation of Sarkhan, the film follows American ambassador Harrison Carter MacWhite (a somewhat silly-looking Marlon Brando, sporting the thinnest of mustaches), a powerful newspaper publisher who is sent to Sarkhan to oversee the construction of the "Freedom Road," an international highway financed by the US. Sarkhan, however, is engulfed in civil war, and construction of the road is constantly threatened by communist rebels. MacWhite, who has trouble understanding the aims of the communists, is shocked to discover that his former comrade-in-arms, Deong (Eiji Okada), is now the leader of the rebels. Through his association with Deong, MacWhite becomes aware of the reality of "Yankee imperialism" and begins to realize that the US "can't hope to win the Cold War unless we remember what we're for as well as what we're against." Although well-intentioned, THE UGLY AMERICAN simply isn't a very good film. Part of the problem is that producer-director George Englund, a friend of star Brando, isn't much of a director, and as a result the film is static and ponderous. Brando once again turns in an interesting performance, but as demonstrated in many of his films of this period, one good performance does not a good film make. Brando's costar, Japanese actor Eiji Okada, is best known for his performance in Alain Resnais' HIROSHIMA, MON AMOUR (1959).

p, George Englund; d, George Englund; w, Stewart Stern, based on the novel by William J. Lederer, Eugene Burdick; ed, Ted J. Kent; ph, Clifford Stine, Eastmancolor; m, Frank Skinner.

(PR:A-C MPAA:NR)

ULZANA'S RAID****

(1972) 103m UNIV c

Burt Lancaster *(McIntosh)*, Bruce Davison *(Lt. Garnett DeBuin)*, Jorge Luke *(Ke-Ni-Tay)*, Richard Jaeckel *(Sergeant)*, Joaquin Martinez *(Ulzana)*, Lloyd Bochner *(Capt. Gates)*, Karl Swenson *(Rukeyser)*, Douglas Watson *(Maj. Cartwright)*, Dran Hamilton *(Mrs. Riordan)*, John Pearce *(Corporal)*, Gladys Holland *(Mrs. Rukeyser)*, Margaret Fairchild *(Mrs. Ginsford)*, Aimee Eccles *(McIntosh's Indian Woman)*, Richard Bull *(Ginsford)*, Otto Reichow *(Steegmeyer)*.

One of the greatest films made by director Robert Aldrich (who has been unjustly overlooked by the vast majority of critics), ULZANA'S RAID isn't really a war film per se, but within its traditional western format, Aldrich and screenwriter Alan Sharp transform the material into a effective and damning allegory of America's involvement in Vietnam. Set in Arizona during the late 1880s, the film centers on McIntosh (Burt Lancaster), a hard-riding scout who accompanies idealistic, young Lt. Garnett DeBuin (Bruce Davison) in his pursuit of a group of rapacious renegade Apaches led by Ulzana (Joaquin Martinez). On the trail it becomes apparent that McIntosh and DeBuin hold radically different views of Ulzana's actions—the scout is cold and cynical, while DeBuin's Christian morality is incensed by the Apache atrocities. As the film progresses it poses a complex series of questions about the nature of heroism, racism, and American imperialism. However, as an allegorical indictment of the Vietnam War, ULZANA'S RAID avoids the preachy stance of similarly themed westerns like SOLDIER BLUE (1970), benefitting from Aldrich's stark, violent treatment of Sharp's (NIGHT MOVES, 1975) well-developed script. Regrettably, this challenging film was much abused by its studio and several different versions were circulated, including a European cut containing alternative takes and slightly altered scene construction (most noticeable in the film's opening section). This was the third time the by-then-crusty Lancaster and director Aldrich had worked together, after a lapse of 18 years (their previous collaborations, APACHE and VERA CRUZ, were both released in 1954), and they would soon team again on TWILIGHT'S LAST GLEAMING (1977).

p, Carter De Haven; d, Robert Aldrich; w, Alan Sharp; ed, Michael Luciano; ph, Joseph Biroc, Technicolor; m, Frank DeVol.

(PR:O MPAA:R)

UNBEARABLE LIGHTNESS OF BEING, THE**½

(1988) 171m Orion c

Daniel Day-Lewis *(Tomas)*, Juliette Binoche *(Tereza)*, Lena Olin *(Sabina)*, Derek de Lint *(Franz)*, Erland Josephson *(The Ambassador)*, Pavel Landovsky *(Pavel)*, Donald Moffat *(Chief Surgeon)*, Daniel Olbrychski *(Interior Ministry Official)*, Stellan Skarsgard *(The Engineer)*, Tomek Bork *(Jiri)*, Bruce Myers *(Czech Editor)*.

Phil Kaufman's film version of Milan Kundera's acclaimed novel opens in Prague shortly before the Soviet invasion of 1968, where Tomas (Daniel Day-Lewis), a brilliant playboy surgeon, lives a "light" existence free of commitment. Tomas falls in love with the shy, provincial Tereza (Juliette Binoche), eventually marrying her, although he continues to womanize, especially with the similarly free and easy Sabina (Lena Olin), defending his adultery by insisting that sex and love are not the same thing. When the Soviet

UNCOMMON VALOR—

tanks roll into Prague, Sabina flees to Geneva, but Tomas and Tereza stay behind—she snapping pictures of the clampdown, riots, demonstrations, and violence. Eventually they, too, head for Geneva, and Tomas resumes his liaison with Sabina, until Tereza decides to return to Czechoslovakia and he follows her home. There, they sustain the weight of Soviet influence fairly easily, until authorities discover that Tomas once wrote an anti-Communist article. Though Thomas, typically, wrote the piece on a whim, he refuses to renounce it and suffers professionally; in the meantime, he continues to philander and Tereza continues to try to understand his philosophy of sex versus love. With its distinguished international cast and crew, volatile historical backdrop, and numerous erotic, "adult" scenes, all filtered through the eye of American director Kaufman (THE RIGHT STUFF), THE UNBEARABLE LIGHTNESS OF BEING is the perfect European art film for American audiences who thirst for movies that are "intellectual" but not so much so that they can't understand them. Unfortunately, for all its credentials and the virtuoso performances of its three leads, this lengthy film doesn't add up to much, failing to explore its themes—love and hedonism, freedom and commitment (political and sexual)—in depth, floating haphazardly from scene to scene without emotional or intellectual development. Shot in Geneva and Lyon, France (the latter town standing in for Prague, where Kundera's work is banned), the film places greater stress on the actual events of the 1968 Soviet invasion than does its original, incorporating real black-and-white footage of the time with simulated shots featuring Binoche and Day-Lewis.

p, Saul Zaentz; d, Philip Kaufman; w, Jean-Claude Carriere and Philip Kaufman, based on the novel by Milan Kundera; ed, Walter Murch; ph, Sven Nykvist, Technicolor; m, Mark Adler, Keith Richards, and Leos Janacek.

(PR:O MPAA:R)

UNCOMMON VALOR**

(1983) 105m PAR c

Gene Hackman *(Col. Rhodes)*, Robert Stack *(MacGregor)*, Fred Ward *(Wilkes)*, Reb Brown *(Blaster)*, Randall "Tex" Cobb *(Sailor)*, Patrick Swayze *(Scott)*, Harold Sylvester *(Johnson)*, Tim Thomerson *(Charts)*, Alice Lau *(Lai Fun)*, Kwan Hi Lim *(Jiang)*, Gail Strickland *(Mrs. Helen Rhodes)*, Kelly Yunkermann *(Paul MacGregor)*, Todd Allen *(Frank Rhodes)*.

One of the first "Let's go back and rescue our boys still trapped in 'Nam" movies, UNCOMMON VALOR stars Gene Hackman as Col. Rhodes, a retired Army officer and Vietnam vet who comes to believe that his son, listed as missing in action over Laos 10 years before, is still alive and being held as a POW. With financial support from a gung-ho oil tycoon (Robert Stack), Rhodes gathers a group of veterans, subjects them to a period of intensive training, and leads them back into the jungles in hopes of finding his son. A typically nuanced performance from Hackman, beautiful photography by Stephen Burum (RUMBLE FISH) and Ric Waite (THE LONG RIDERS), and some effective action direction from Ted Kotcheff (FIRST BLOOD) make this watchable, but the jingoist wish-fulfillment inherent in the material is ultimately disturbing. Coproducer John Milius carries this kind of right-wing propaganda even farther in his anti-Red, pro-survivalist RED DAWN (1984).

p, John Milius and Buzz Feitshans; d, Ted Kotcheff; w, Joe Gayton; ed, Mark Melnick; ph, Stephen H. Burum and Ric Waite, Movielab Color; m, James Horner.

(PR:O MPAA:R)

UNDER FIRE***½

(1983) 127m Lion's Gate/Orion c

Nick Nolte *(Russell Price)*, Ed Harris *(Oates)*, Gene Hackman *(Alex Grazier)*, Joanna Cassidy *(Claire)*, Alma Martinez *(Isela)*, Holly Palance *(Journalist)*, Oswaldo Doria *(Boy Photographer)*, Fernando Elizondo *(Businessman)*, Hamilton Camp *(Regis Seydor)*, Jean-Louis Trintignant *(Jazy)*, Richard Masur *(Hub Kittle)*, Eric Valdez *(Time Stringer)*, Rene Enriquez *(Somoza)*.

Flawed but still fascinating, UNDER FIRE looks at the Nicaraguan revolution through the eyes of Russell Price (Nick Nolte), an American photojournalist who uses his camera to distance himself from reality ("I take pictures. I don't take sides"). In Managua, Price's noncommittal attitude is put to the test by the startling contrast between the high life enjoyed by the supporters of President Anastasio Somoza (Rene Enriquez) and the reality experienced by most Nicaraguans. The American begins to realize that the plush Hotel Continental, home of the press corps, is an obscene imperialist outpost that distances the reporters from the people they are supposed to be covering. None of this, however, is news to Claire (Joanna Cassidy), a National Public Radio reporter, and under her influence Price eventually becomes actively involved with the revolutionaries, faking a picture of a slain leader so that it will appear that he is still alive. The sensational photo brings network news anchor Alex Grazier (Gene Hackman) to Managua, where he is shot and killed by one of Somoza's National Guardsmen (mirroring the horrifying true-life murder of ABC correspondent Bill Stewart by Somoza's troops in 1979—an event that was captured on videotape and shown to a shocked American audience). Price records the whole incident on film and his pictures create worldwide outrage that helps sound the death knell for Somoza's government. Nolte gives one of his best performances as the photographer who suddenly finds himself looking past what he sees in the viewfinder in this insightful look at revolution and the world of journalism. Director Roger Spottiswoode, who edited a number of Sam Peckinpah movies, succeeds brilliantly in creating the chaotic last days of Somoza's government while at the same time incisively evaluating the moral dilemma faced by war correspondents. Where the film falters, however, is screenwriter Ron Shelton's (BULL DURHAM) overly simplistic view of both Somoza and the Sandinistas. Shown to be the white knights riding to the rescue of the oppressed masses, the Sandinistas are given almost embarrassingly reverent treatment, with no hint of the ideological divisions, confusion, and suffering that would follow their takeover (problems at least hinted at in Oliver Stone's remarkable SALVADOR, 1986).

p, Jonathan Taplin; d, Roger Spottiswoode; w, Ron Shelton and Clayton Frohman, based on a story by Frohman; ed, John Bloom; ph, John Alcott, Technicolor; m, Jerry Goldsmith.

(PR:O   MPAA:R)

UP IN ARMS****

(1944) 106m Goldwyn/RKO c

Danny Kaye (Danny Weems), Constance Dowling (Mary Morgan), Dinah Shore (Virginia Merrill), Dana Andrews (Joe Nelson), Louis Calhern (Col. Ashley), George Mathews (Blackie), Benny Baker (Butterball), Elisha Cook, Jr. (Info Jones), Lyle Talbot (Sgt. Gelsey), Walter Catlett (Maj. Brock), George Meeker (Ashley's Aide), Richard Powers [Tom Keene] (Captain), Margaret Dumont (Mrs. Willoughby).

Danny Kaye made his film debut in this boisterous Samuel Goldwyn-produced musical comedy as Danny Weems, a hypochondriac drafted into the Army during WW II. Danny's best pal, Joe Nelson (Dana Andrews), is also called to do his patriotic duty, and romantic complications abound when it comes time for them to say their goodbyes. You see, Danny loves Mary Morgan (Constance Dowling), but Mary loves Joe, and her friend, Virginia Merrill (Dinah Shore), is ga-ga over Danny. When the women, who've joined the WACs, see off the ship that is transporting the fellas to active duty in the Pacific, they accidentally get stuck on board, and hilarity ensues as Danny tries to keep Mary (as a nurse, Virginia has an easier time explaining her presence) hidden from his commanding officer (Louis Calhern). After Mary is discovered, Danny is tossed in the brig when the ship arrives at its destination, only to be taken prisoner during a Japanese raid. Later, however, he proves himself to be a real hero when he leads a big escape. Kaye's superb comic timing, perfected in the Catskill Mountains resorts and on various nightclub stages, serves him well as he dominates the movie in every scene. He and Shore get ample opportunity to show off their voices, including her singing of the Oscar-nominated "Now I Know" (Harold Arlen, Ted Koehler), and his rendition of "Melody in 4-F" from Cole Porter's musical "Let's Face It." The film also boasts excellent choreography, superb sets, and fine costumes.

p, Samuel Goldwyn; d, Elliott Nugent; w, Don Hartman, Allen Boretz, and Robert Pirosh, based on the play "The Nervous Wreck" by Owen Davis; ed, Daniel Mandell and James Newcom; ph, Ray Rennahan, Technicolor; m, Ray Heindorf.

(PR:AA   MPAA:NR)

VICTORY**

(1981) 117m Victory-Lorimar/PAR c (GB: ESCAPE TO VICTORY)

Sylvester Stallone (Robert Hatch), Michael Caine (John Colby), Pele (Luis Fernandez), Bobby Moore (Terry Brady), Osvaldo Ardiles (Carlos Rey), Paul Van Himst (Michel Fileu), Kazimierz Deyna (Paul Wolchek), Hallvar Thorensen (Gunnar Hilsson), Mike Summerbee (Sid Harmor), Co Prins (Pieter Van Beck), Russell Osman (Doug Clure), John Wark (Arthur Hayes), Soren Linsted (Erik Borge), Kevin O'Calloghan (Tony Lewis), Max von Sydow (Maj. Karl Von Steiner), Amidou (Andre).

Part THE GREAT ESCAPE, part standard underdog-comes-from-behind sports movie, John Huston's VICTORY limps along unimaginatively for its first three-quarters, but hits full stride in the final half-hour, brilliantly staged soccer sequence that provides the film's climax. The setting is a WW II POW camp, where Maj. Karl Von Steiner (Max von Sydow), a onetime member of the German national soccer team, spots John Colby (Michael Caine), a former English international player, among the Allied prisoners. The major persuades Colby to put together a team to play a "friendly" match against a German team, but with the intervention of the Nazi propaganda machine, the contest escalates into a confrontation between the German national team and an all-star squad of Allied prisoners to be played in Colombes Stadium in Paris. While the prisoners prepare for the match, Hatch (Sylvester Stallone), their American trainer, escapes, meets with the French Resistance to plan a halftime escape from the stadium, then reluctantly allows himself to be recaptured. Before 50,000 spectators and a worldwide radio audience, the Germans, aided by a biased referee, take a commanding 4-1 lead into the locker room at halftime, but instead of making good their escape, the Allies return to the field determined to win, despite the fact that the inexperienced Hatch is in goal. All of which leads to the well-shot, tightly edited, and, yes, exciting finale that features some extraordinary play by a number of real-life soccer stars, including Brazilian great Pele; Bobby Moore, captain of England's 1966 World Cup champions; and Argentine superstar Osvaldo Ardiles. Alternately hokey and inspiring, the climactic game, which features the crowd chanting victoire and bursting into "La Marseillaise," is unquestionably VICTORY's highlight, and good enough reason to sit through the rest of the film.

p, Freddie Fields; d, John Huston; w, Evan Jones and Yabo Yablonsky, based on a story by Yabo Yablonsky, Djordje Milicevic, Jeff Maguire; ed, Roberto Silvi; ph, Gerry Fisher, Panavision, Metrocolor; m, Bill Conti.

(PR:A-C   MPAA:PG)

VON RYAN'S EXPRESS***½

(1965) 117m P-R Productions/FOX c

Frank Sinatra (Col. Joseph L. Ryan), Trevor Howard (Maj. Eric Fincham), Raffaela Carra (Gabriella), Brad Dexter (Sgt. Bostick), Sergio Fantoni (Capt. Oriani), John Leyton

VOYAGE OF THE DAMNED—

(Orde), Edward Mulhare (Constanzo), Wolfgang Preiss (Maj. von Klemment), James Brolin (Pvt. Ames), John Van Dreelen (Col. Gortz), Adolfo Celi (Battaglia), Michael Goodliffe (Capt. Stein), Ivan Triesault (Von Kleist).

Frank Sinatra stars in this implausible but relatively engaging WW II POW escape film, playing Col. Joseph Ryan, a downed US Army Air Corps pilot who leads 600 British and American prisoners in a dramatic escape through Italy aboard a commandeered train. Aided by some of their Italian jailers, who are anxious to jump sides as the 1943 Allied invasion gets under way, the POWs take over a train, and with some of their number masquerading as Germans guards set off for neutral Switzerland. Initially called "von" Ryan by the other prisoners, who thought him too accommodating to the enemy, the American colonel proves his courage over and over again as the train makes its way to freedom, fending off attacking Messerschmitts and narrowly escaping a pursuing German troop train. Sinatra is convincing as the gutsy American officer who engineers the escape but is dealt a cruel blow by fate, and Trevor Howard gives a strong performance as the British major he replaces as ranking prisoner, but there isn't much else that's believable in VON RYAN'S EXPRESS. Nonetheless, Mark Robson's film is packed with action and occasionally technically impressive, especially in the duel between the train and the German planes that attack it in the mountains of northern Italy. If it's realism you're after, look elsewhere; but if you enjoy straightforward wartime thrills (or films with particularly stupid German soldiers), VON RYAN'S EXPRESS is just the ticket.

p, Saul David; d, Mark Robson; w, Wendell Mayes and Joseph Landon, based on the novel by David Westheimer; ed, Dorothy Spencer; ph, William Daniels, CinemaScope, Deluxe Color; m, Jerry Goldsmith.

(PR:C MPAA:NR)

VOYAGE OF THE DAMNED*½

(1976, Brit.) 134m Associated General/AE c

Faye Dunaway (Denise Kreisler), Max von Sydow (Capt. Schroeder), Oskar Werner (Dr. Kreisler), Malcolm McDowell (Max Gunter), Orson Welles (Estedes), James Mason (Remos), Lee Grant (Lillian Rosen), Ben Gazzara (Morris Troper), Katharine Ross (Mira Hauser), Luther Adler (Prof. Weiler), Paul Koslo (Aaron Pozner), Michael Constantine (Clasing), Nehemiah Persoff (Mr. Hauser), Jose Ferrer (Benitez), Fernando Rey (Cuban President), Lynne Frederick (Anna Rosen), Maria Schell (Mrs. Hauser), Helmut Griem (Otto Schiendick), Victor Spinetti (Dr. Strauss), Julie Harris (Alice Feinchild), Janet Suzman (Leni Strauss), Wendy Hiller (Rebecca Weiler), Sam Wanamaker (Carl Rosen), Denholm Elliott (Adm. Wilhelm Canaris).

This long, star-studded film, based on a shocking true story, seeks to involve too many characters in various interrelated vignettes. Directed with a well-meaning but heavy hand by Stuart Rosenberg (SAVE THE TIGER), VOYAGE OF THE DAMNED takes place in 1939, as a group of Jews are expelled from Nazi Germany and loaded on a ship bound for Havana, where the Germans correctly expect them to be denied haven. The whole thing is a publicity stunt for the Nazis, who want to prove that no country will accept the people they seek to annihilate. Turned away by Cuba, the ship—skippered by non-Nazi Schroeder (Max von Sydow)—must sail back to Germany and to certain death for the passengers, who include the sophisticated Kreislers (Faye Dunaway and Oskar Werner); an elderly professor and his wife (Luther Adler and Wendy Hiller); and the Hausers (Nehemiah Persoff and Maria Schell), who look forward to reuniting with their daughter (Katharine Ross), a hooker in Havana. Also in Cuba are industrialist Estedes (Orson Welles); Remos (James Mason), a sympathetic minister; local bureaucrat Benitez (Jose Ferrer); and Morris Troper (Ben Gazzara), who heads a Jewish agency. The film cuts quickly among all the above (and a few more) to puzzling or dull effect, playing like the TV miniseries it was originally slated to be. The huge cast seems to share in the sense of confusion and, sadly, what should be a moving treatment of an important story merely falls flat.

p, Robert Fryer; d, Stuart Rosenberg; w, Steve Shagan and David Butler, based on the book by Max Morgan-Witts, Gordon Thomas; ed, Tom Priestley; ph, Billy Williams, Eastmancolor; m, Lalo Schifrin.

(PR:A-C MPAA:PG)

W

WACKIEST SHIP IN THE ARMY, THE**½

(1961) 99m COL c

Jack Lemmon (Lt. Rip Crandall), Ricky Nelson (Ens. Tommy Hanson), John Lund (Comdr. Vandewater), Chips Rafferty (Patterson), Tom Tully (Capt. McClung), Joby Baker (Josh Davidson), Warren Berlinger (Sparks), Patricia Driscoll (Maggie), Mike Kellin (Chief Mate MacCarthy), Richard Anderson (Lt. Foster).

Without Jack Lemmon's engaging performance there would be little to recommend in this standard service comedy; with it THE WACKIEST SHIP IN THE ARMY is diverting if unexceptional entertainment. During WW II, Lt. Rip Crandall (Lemmon) is given command of the USS Echo—a run-down ship with the archetypal inexperienced, motley crew—then assigned to deliver an Australian observer to a Japanese-held island. After doing his best to whip his crew into shape, Crandall, with the help of his inexperienced second in command, Ens. Tommy Hanson (Ricky Nelson), steers the Echo through enemy waters disguised as a native vessel, and after a series of thrilling but mostly humorous adventures, manages to learn the whereabouts of the Japanese fleet. This slight premise is primarily an excuse to exploit the comic genius of Lemmon; placed in a seemingly hopeless situation (as he is in so many of his more successful roles), he goes through his chores with a look of exasperation and confusion, his boundless energy preventing the film from sliding into the tedium the script otherwise seems to have promised. When not providing the film's love interest (with Patricia Driscoll) or acting wet behind the ears, Nelson "hits the high C's"—as the film's advertising proclaimed—offering his rendition of "Do You Know What It Means to Miss New Orleans" (Louis Alter, Eddie De Lange), introduced by Billie Holiday in NEW ORLEANS (1947). Warren Berlinger and Mike Kellin also contribute fine supporting performances to this film that later served as the inspiration for a short-lived TV series.

p, Fred Kohlmar; d, Richard Murphy; w, Richard Murphy, Herbert Margolis, and William Raynor, based on a story by Herbert Carlson; ed, Charles Nelson; ph, Charles Lawton, CinemaScope, Eastmancolor; m, George Duning.

(PR:A MPAA:NR)

WAKE ISLAND****

(1942) 78m PAR bw

Brian Donlevy *(Maj. Caton)*, MacDonald Carey *(Lt. Cameron)*, Robert Preston *(Joe Doyle)*, William Bendix *(Smacksie Randall)*, Albert Dekker *(Shad McClosky)*, Walter Abel *(Comdr. Roberts)*, Mikhail Rasumny *(Probenzky)*, Don Castle *(Pvt. Cunkel)*, Rod Cameron *(Capt. Lewis)*, Bill Goodwin *(Sergeant)*, Barbara Britton *(Sally Cameron)*, Damian O'Flynn *(Capt. Patrick)*, Frank Albertson *(Johnny Rudd)*, Phillip Terry *(Pvt. Warren)*, Philip Van Zandt *(Cpl. Goebbels)*, Keith Richards *(Sparks Wilcox)*.

The heroic but doomed defense of Wake Island against the Japanese in the opening days of WW II provided the basis for this slightly fictionalized, immensely popular flag waver that garnered several Academy Award nominations. A perfect example of Hollywood's contribution to the war effort, the film demonstrated that even in defeat there was victory, and provided needed inspiration for a nation reeling from loss after loss at the hands of the Japanese. Hunkered down in foxholes and machine gun nests, the courageous Marine defenders of the island, under the command of the determined Maj. Caton (Brian Donlevy), refuse to bend to the assault of countless Japanese troops. For two weeks they hold on, but with no help coming and ammunition running low, they are doomed and know it. Still, they refuse to give up, and in the end, Maj. Caton, Joe Doyle (Robert Preston), Lt. Cameron (MacDonald Carey), Smacksie Randall (William Bendix), and the other brave Marines go down in a blaze of glory. All the performers are good, particularly Donlevy, brilliantly evoking calm in the face of overwhelming odds, and Bendix, who earned a Best Supporting Actor Oscar nomination. The film was widely shown to soldiers at training camps all over the country, and reportedly never failed to rouse cheers. Shot on location on the shores of the Salton Sea in the California desert, the film was also nominated for Best Picture, Best Director, and Best Original Screenplay.

p, Joseph Sistrom; d, John Farrow; w, W.R. Burnett and Frank Butler; ed, LeRoy Stone; ph, Theodor Sparkuhl; m, David Buttolph.

(PR:A MPAA:NR)

WALK IN THE SUN, A***½

(1945) 117m FOX bw (GB: SALERNO BEACHHEAD)

Dana Andrews *(Sgt. Tyne)*, Richard Conte *(Rivera)*, John Ireland *(Windy)*, George Tyne [Buddy Yarus] *(Friedman)*, Lloyd Bridges *(Sgt. Ward)*, Sterling Holloway *(McWilliams)*, Herbert Rudley *(Sgt. Porter)*, Norman Lloyd *(Archimbeau)*, Steve Brodie *(Judson)*, Huntz Hall *(Carraway)*, James Cardwell *(Sgt. Hoskins)*, Chris Drake *(Rankin)*, Richard Benedict *(Tranella)*, George Offerman, Jr. *(Tinker)*.

One of the better films to emerge from the final days of WW II, A WALK IN THE SUN is the story of one infantry platoon, covering one morning, from the time they hit the beach at Salerno until they reach and capture their objective, a farmhouse six miles inland. Before they even get ashore things begin to go badly, and the green lieutenant in command is killed. A sergeant takes over for a time, but the stress proves too great and he cracks. The men encounter a German armored car for which they set up an ambush, raining it with grenades, then continue on their mission with natural leader Sgt. Tyne (Dana Andrews) now in command. Eventually, the soldiers reach their objective, but the situation appears suicidal, and Sgt. Tyne must devise some way to complete the mission with a minimum loss of life. Throughout the film, as it follows the men in battle, the soundtrack picks up their chatty conversations and private thoughts. They think about their place in the great scheme of the war, about their fear of being killed, and about the hard, dirty, tedious, and dangerous job of being a front-line foot soldier. A languorous sense of resignation holds sway over all: weary, hard-bitten, and somewhat cynical, they are there to do a job, and although they don't even understand what part they play in the big picture, they do it anyway, even at the cost of their lives. Although director Lewis Milestone seemed to have put the pacifism of his ALL QUIET ON THE WESTERN FRONT (1930) on hold for the duration of WW II, A WALK IN THE SUN mostly avoids the patriotic posing and outright racism (indeed, the enemy is never given a face here) of his previous THE PURPLE HEART (1944) and instead concentrates on the rugged day-to-day existence of the common foot soldier. While the film is consistently engaging, some of the narrative devices Milestone employs, such as the voice-over narration and the occasional off-screen singing of a somewhat sappy folk song dedicated to foot soldiers, now seem more of an intrusion on the visuals than a complement.

p, Lewis Milestone; d, Lewis Milestone; w, Robert Rossen, based on a story by Harry Brown; ed, Duncan Mansfield; ph, Russell Harlan; m, Freddie Rich.

(PR:A MPAA:NR)

WALKER***

(1987) 95m Edward R. Pressman-Incine/UNIV-Northern Dist. Partners c

Ed Harris *(William Walker)*, Richard Masur *(Ephraim Squier)*, Rene Auberjonois *(Maj. Siegfried Henningson)*, Keith Szarabajka *(Timothy Crocker)*, Sy Richardson *(Capt.*

Hornsby), Xander Berkeley (Bryon Cole), John Diehl (Stebbins), Peter Boyle (Commodore Cornelius Vanderbilt), Marlee Matlin (Ellen Martin), Alfonso Arau (Raousset), Pedro Armendariz, Jr. (Munoz), Gerrit Graham (Norvell Walker), William O'Leary (James Walker), Alan Bolt (Don Domingo), Miguel Sandoval (Parker French).

Reviled by the vast majority of American film critics, this distinctly odd, at times confused, but nonetheless wildly creative and compelling political cartoon from SID AND NANCY director Alex Cox is far from a total washout. An agitprop treatise on the United States' ongoing military intrusions into Nicaragua (invasions and occupations in 1855, 1912, and 1926, and the current US-funded contra war), Cox's film examines the problem by dramatizing the career of William Walker, a bizarre historical figure who has been all but forgotten in the US, but who continues to serve as a vivid symbol of Yankee oppression for the people of Central America. Instead of presenting WALKER in generic historical epic fashion, hoping the audience would make the connection between the events of 1855 and 1987 unaided, Cox and screenwriter Rudy Wurlitzer provide a strange hodgepodge of past and present, inserting such anachronisms as modern slang, a computer, a Mercedes-Benz, a Zippo lighter, *Time*, *Newsweek*, and *People* magazines, and even a helicopter during key moments in the film. The result is a truly unique movie universe where all history takes place in a discontinuous time warp. The film follows Walker (played with a manic intensity by Ed Harris) as he decides to bring democracy to the heathens in Nicaragua. Assembling a rag-tag group of mercenaries (58 in all) whom he calls "The Immortals," Walker invades Nicaragua with the support of that country's Liberal party, defeats the army, sets up a puppet government, and eventually assumes the presidency, only to have his own men and sponsor, Cornelius Vanderbilt (Peter Boyle), turn on him. WALKER has dismayed critics on both ends of the political spectrum and at all points in between, with the Right dismissing it as hopelessly biased, vulgar, incoherent, and dishonest propaganda; while the Left's hackles were raised because Cox didn't used this golden opportunity to present their anti-*contra* views in a sanitized manner promoting "political correctness" while offending no one. Granted, some of these charges are valid, but what makes WALKER so fascinating is its total refusal to play by anyone's rules—cinematic or political. As unconventional as Cox's film is, it still succeeds in painting an interesting psychological portrait of William Walker, presenting him as a man whose fervent belief in the justice of his mission blinds him to his perversion of his own dearly held ideals. Cox is both intrigued and repelled by this moral arrogance and his lyrical treatment of violence, a la Peckinpah, may be an attempt to convey the seductive power of such righteousness. WALKER is not for all tastes, but a fascinating film nonetheless.

p, Lorenzo O'Brien and Angel Flores Marini; d, Alex Cox; w, Rudy Wurlitzer; ed, Carlos Puente Ortega and Alex Cox; ph, David Bridges; m, Joe Strummer.

(PR:O MPAA:R)

WANNSEE CONFERENCE, THE***

(1987, Ger./Aust.) 87m Infafilm GmbH-Austrian Television-ORFBavarian Broadcasting/Rearguard c (DIE WANNSEEKONFERENZ)

Robert Artzorn (Hofmann), Friedrich Beckhaus (Muller), Gerd Bockmann (Adolf Eichmann), Jochen Busse (Leibbrandt), Hans W. Bussinger (Luther), Harald Dietl (Meyer, Gauleiter for the Occupied Eastern Territories), Peter Fitz (Dr. Wilhelm Stuckart, Interior Minister), Reinhard Glemnitz (Buhler), Dieter Groest (Neumann), Martin Luttge (Dr. Rudolf Lange, Commander of the Gestapo in Latvia), Dietrich Mattausch (Reinhard Heydrich, Chief of the Security Police), Gerd Rigauer (Schongarth), Franz Rudnick (Kritzinger, Reich Chancellery Representative), Gunter Sporrle (Gerhard Klopfer), Rainer Steffen (Friesler, Justice Minister).

This is a startling re-creation of one of the most infamous events in history—the gathering of 14 Nazi officials on Jan. 20, 1942, in the Berlin suburb of Wannsee to discuss the "final solution," or the extermination of some 11 million Jews. Like the meeting, the film lasts 85 minutes and takes place almost entirely in the conference room. Organized by Reinhard Heydrich, chief of the Nazi security police and secret service, the conference was held at the request of Adolf Hitler and Hermann Goering in order to secure and coordinate the cooperation of key figures in the Nazi hierarchy to carry out the operation. Already devoted to the Nazi ideology, the conferees did not discuss the project's morality, only the most efficient means of achieving their goal, and the film follows their casual, at times petty discussion of genocide. Made for German and Austrian TV, THE WANNSEE CONFERENCE is not an exact re-creation, since no Wannsee transcript exists (only minutes and other archival material, including conferee Adolf Eichmann's recollections of the meeting). Screenwriter Paul Mommertz and director Heinz Schirk reconstructed dialog and characters through research, then, without providing additional historical background, replayed the meeting in real time to eerie effect. The entire scene takes on an absurd quality, a "banality of evil," as if the participants were discussing marketing strategy for a new product line. The camera wanders the room dispassionately, while the convincing performances nearly fool the audience into thinking the real event is unfolding before their eyes—although some have alleged that the film reshapes certain historical events—and the result is undeniably chilling. (In German; English subtitles.)

p, Manfred Korytowski; d, Heinz Schirk; w, Paul Mommertz; ed, Ursula Mollinger; ph, Horst Schier.

(PR:A-C MPAA:NR)

WAR AND PEACE***

(1956, It./US) 208m Ponti-DD/PAR c

Audrey Hepburn (Natasha Rostov), Henry Fonda (Pierre Bezukhov), Mel Ferrer (Prince Andrei Bolkonsky), Vittorio Gassman (Anatole Kuragin), John Mills (Platon Karatayev), Herbert Lom (Napoleon), Oscar Homolka (Gen. Mikhail

Kutuzov), Anita Ekberg *(Helene Kuragin)*, Helmut Dantine *(Dolokhov)*, Barry Jones *(Count Ilya Rostov)*, Maria Ferrero *(Mary Bolkonsky)*, Milly Vitale *(Lise)*, Jeremy Brett *(Nicholas Rostov)*, Lea Seidl *(Countess Rostov)*, Wilfred Lawson *(Prince Nicholai Bolkonsky)*, Sean Barrett *(Petya Rostov)*, Tullio Carminati *(Prince Vasili Kuragin)*, May Britt *(Sonya Rostov)*.

King Vidor's version of Tolstoy's great novel seems insufficient at more than three hours, and fared ill both with the critics and at the box office, but does deliver the spectacular visuals expected of historical epics. As Napoleon (Herbert Lom) prepares to invade Russia, the gentle, awkward, intellectual Pierre Bezukhov (Henry Fonda) falls in undeclared love with young Natasha Rostov (Audrey Hepburn). Soon afterwards, his father dies—making Pierre the wealthy new Count Bezukhov and a desirable marriage prospect—and he marries the luscious, adulterous Helene (Anita Ekberg). Meanwhile, his dear friend, the haughty, gloomy Prince Andrei (Mel Ferrer), an aide to Gen. Kutuzov (Oscar Homolka), returns home from battle after being wounded. Depressed after his wife's death in childbirth, Andrei rediscovers the joy of life when he, too, falls in love with Natasha, and she with him—the two having been introduced by Pierre, who battles his own spiritual malaise after the failure of his loveless marriage. Andrei returns to the front and is wounded again, this time critically, in the disastrous Russian defeat at Borodino; Pierre observes the carnage in horror and vows to assassinate Napoleon, but is captured and held prisoner when the French occupy Moscow. When all looks darkest, however, the Russian winter sets in, and after much hardship, the French are routed, Pierre is reunited with Natasha, and the love that was hinted at in the opening scenes finally comes to fruition. Lovers of Tolstoy's work are likely to be frustrated by this somewhat static film, which, inevitably, omits a great deal of his characterization, plotting, philosophy, and historical analysis—while on the other hand playing up the Pierre-Natasha romance. The performances are similarly limited, though Hepburn charmingly captures the gamine radiance of the young Natasha and Fonda (who felt he was miscast) effectively communicates Pierre's integrity. Cinematographers Jack Cardiff and Aldo Tonti contribute the film's most stunning work, as does Mario Soldati, who directed the battle scenes.

p, Dino De Laurentiis; d, King Vidor; w, Bridget Boland, Robert Westerby, King Vidor, Mario Camerini, Ennio De Concini, Ivo Perilli, and Irwin Shaw, based on the novel by Leo Tolstoy; ed, Stuart Gilmore and Leo Cattozzo; ph, Jack Cardiff and Aldo Tonti, VistaVision, Technicolor; m, Nino Rota.

(PR:A-C   MPAA:NR)

WAR AND PEACE***

(1967, USSR) 373m Mosfilm/CD c (VOINA I MIR)

Lyudmila Savelyeva *(Natasha Rostova)*, Sergei Bondarchuk *(Pierre Bezukhov)*, Vyacheslav Tikhonov *(Andrey Bolkonskiy)*, Viktor Stanitsyn *(Ilya Andreyevich Rostov)*, Kira Golovko *(Countess Rostova)*, Oleg Tabakov *(Nikolay Rostov)*.

If King Vidor's version of *War and Peace* suffered from its Hollywood-style simplification of Tolstoy's tale, Soviet director Sergei Bondarchuk's WAR AND PEACE may be *too* painstaking in its faithfulness to the novel. Originally released in the USSR in four parts totalling almost nine hours, made on what Russian sources estimated as $100 million, the film—cut to 380 minutes for its US and video release—is most successful in its epic battle scenes (the battle of Borodino runs nearly an hour), which stunningly portray the scope and inhumanity of war, and in its equally staggering, lavishly re-created visions of the Russian aristocracy's glamor and wealth, most notably the ball at which Andrei (Vyacheslav Tikhonov) meets Natasha (Ludmilla Savelyeva). (Bondarchuk himself plays Pierre.) In between the spectacles, however, are some failures of dramatic finesse and pacing—particularly Bondarchuk's over-reliance on narration and interior monolog to convey the complexity of Tolstoy's characters—flaws compounded for English-speaking viewers by the affectless quality of the dubbing. Nonetheless, Bondarchuk's film, which won a Best Foreign Film Academy Award, is certainly the definitive movie version of *War and Peace* (it has also been serialized faithfully for British television), memorably impressive in its scope and ambition. (Dubbed in English.)

p, Sergei Bondarchuk; d, Sergei Bondarchuk; w, Sergei Bondarchuk and Vasiliy Solovyov, based on the novel by Leo Tolstoy; ed, Tatyana Likhachyova; ph, Anatoliy Petritskiy, Sovscope 70, Sovcolor; m, Vyacheslav Ovchinnikov.

(PR:A-C   MPAA:NR)

WAR LOVER, THE***

(1962, US/Brit.) 105m COL bw

Steve McQueen *(Buzz Rickson)*, Robert Wagner *(Ed Bolland)*, Shirley Ann Field *(Daphne Caldwell)*, Gary Cockrell *(Lynch)*, Michael Crawford *(Junior Sailen)*, Bill Edwards *(Brindt)*, Chuck Julian *(Lamb)*, Robert Easton *(Handown)*, Al Waxman *(Prien)*, Tom Busby *(Farr)*, George Sperdakos *(Bragliani)*, Bob Kanter *(Haverstraw)*, Jerry Stovin *(Emmet)*, Ed Bishop *(Vogt)*.

Buzz Rickson (Steve McQueen), an American bomber pilot stationed in Britain during WW II, revels in combat and has no compunction about killing. His crew members, including copilot Ed Bolland (Robert Wagner), are dismayed by Rickson's zeal, but they all respect his flying ability. Trouble brews between Rickson and Bolland, however, when the copilot takes up with an Englishwoman (Shirley Ann Field) whom Rickson is determined to add to his list of conquests, though she sees through the pilot's facade of bravado, realizing he is incapable of a mature relationship. With the rivalry between the fliers at its peak, they are called upon to undertake an especially dangerous mission over Germany that tests their skills to the limit. Based on a novel by John Hersey, THE WAR LOVER probes the psychopathic, childish, and suicidal impulses that lurk beneath Rickson's veneer of heroism. Howard Koch's script does a fine job balancing moral questions and character study

WAR LOVER, THE—

with WW II action, but falters when it comes to the romance. McQueen contributes a nicely nuanced performance, making his rather despicable character real and likable, and Wagner is also surprisingly good in what could have been a grating and thankless role. While indulging his passion for auto racing during lulls in the shooting, McQueen was nearly badly injured when his car spun out on a wet track. Although the only injury he received was a split lip, the stitches used to close it were noticeable enough that director Philip Leacock let McQueen do all his cockpit scenes with an oxygen mask on to cover the scar. The plane used for THE WAR LOVER was one of less than half a dozen B-17s still in serviceable condition, and it appeared in several other films, including TWELVE O'CLOCK HIGH.

p, Arthur Hornblow, Jr.; d, Philip Leacock; w, Howard Koch, based on the novel by John Hersey; ed, Gordon Hales; ph, Bob Huke; m, Richard Addinsell.

(PR:C MPAA:NR)

WARGAMES***

(1983) 113m MGM/UA c

Matthew Broderick *(David)*, Dabney Coleman *(McKittrick)*, John Wood *(Falken)*, Ally Sheedy *(Jennifer)*, Barry Corbin *(Gen. Beringer)*, Juanin Clay *(Pat Healy)*, Kent Williams *(Cabot)*, Dennis Lipscomb *(Watson)*, Joe Dorsey *(Conley)*, Irving Metzman *(Richter)*, Michael Ensign *(Beringer's Aide)*, William Bogert *(Mr. Lightman)*, Susan Davis *(Mrs. Lightman)*, James Tolkan *(Wigan)*, David Clover *(Stockman)*.

Slick and suspenseful, but a little heavy-handed, John Badham's WARGAMES tells the story of a high-school hacker, David (Matthew Broderick), who manages to tap into WOPR, the Pentagon's top defense computer. Thinking he's discovered a great new video game, "Global Thermonuclear War," David innocently brings the US and the Soviet Union to the brink of WW III. Convinced that the Soviets have launched an assault, the computer prepares for a retaliatory strike, and when the military's top minds can't set it straight, it's up to young David to teach WOPR that the only way to win this "strange game" is not to play. Featuring some strong performances from a cast that includes Dabney Coleman and Ally Sheedy, convincing re-creations of defense technology, and nicely modulated tension, WARGAMES is a generally effective message film.

p, Harold Schneider; d, John Badham; w, Lawrence Lasker and Walter F. Parkes; ed, Tom Rolf; ph, William A. Fraker, Metrocolor; m, Arthur B. Rubinstein.

(PR:A MPAA:PG)

WARKILL**½

(1968, US/Phil.) 100m Balut-Centaur/UNIV c

George Montgomery *(Col. John Hannegan)*, Tom Drake *(Phil Sutton)*, Conrad Parham *(Pedring)*, Eddie Infante *(Dr. Fernandez)*, Henry Duval *(Willy)*, Paul Edwards, Jr. *(Mike Harris)*, Bruno Punzalan *(Maj. Hashiri)*, David Michael *(Sgt. Johnson)*.

Set in the Philippines near the end of WW II, WARKILL tells the story of John Hannegan (George Montgomery), the hardened, animalistic American colonel who leads a band of Filipino guerrillas in attacks against Japanese troops, and Phil Sutton (Tom Drake), the journalist who has lionized Hannegan without having met him. When Sutton decides finally to cover the hero in the flesh, he is shocked by his subject's brutal take-no-prisoners tactics. His repulsion lessens, however, when he witnesses atrocities committed by the Japanese, then joins Hannegan on a raid in which the colonel dies bravely just before reinforcements arrive to fend off the enemy. Afterwards, Sutton decides to keep what he knows about Hannegan's methods secret, preserving his heroic image. This violent film will please action fans who can overlook its hedging on the ethical conflict between its American protagonists—which becomes more difficult when one considers that this WW II story filmed in the Philippines was released in 1968, deep into the Vietnam War.

p, Ferde Grofe, Jr.; d, Ferde Grofe, Jr.; w, Ferde Grofe, Jr.; ed, Phillip Innes; ph, Remegio Uoung, Deluxe Color; m, Gene Kauer and Douglas Lackey.

(PR:O MPAA:NR)

WATCH ON THE RHINE****

(1943) 114m WB bw

Bette Davis *(Sara Muller)*, Paul Lukas *(Kurt Muller)*, Geraldine Fitzgerald *(Marthe de Brancovis)*, Lucile Watson *(Fanny Farrelly)*, Beulah Bondi *(Anise)*, George Coulouris *(Teck de Brancovis)*, Donald Woods *(David Farrelly)*, Henry Daniell *(Phili von Ramme)*, Donald Buka *(Joshua Muller)*, Eric Roberts *(Bodo Muller)*, Janis Wilson *(Babette Muller)*, Helmut Dantine *(Young Man)*, Mary Young *(Mrs. Mellie Sewell)*, Kurt Katch *(Herr Blecher)*, Erwin Kalser *(Dr. Klauber)*.

Lillian Hellman's respected play was adapted for film by Hellman and Dashiell Hammett, her longtime companion, and helmed by Herman Shumlin, who directed the stage original and cast some of its players here. The resulting powerful drama was nominated for Best Picture, Script, and Supporting Actress (Lucile Watson) Oscars, while Paul Lukas, repeating his stage role, won as Best Actor. Kurt and Sara Muller (Lukas and Bette Davis), refugees from Nazi Germany, arrive with their children after a long absence to visit Sara's mother (Watson) in her Washington, DC, home. Already there are Teck de Brancovis (George Coulouris), a Rumanian count, and his American wife (Geraldine Fitzgerald). The Mullers plan to stay in the US only until Kurt's health improves; then he will return to his "business" abroad, the exact nature of which is unclear. When the count, who socializes at the German embassy, hears of the Gestapo's unsuccessful attempts to crack an underground resistance group, he suspects that Kurt may be one of them and offers to spy on him, then in turn tries to blackmail Kurt, who is forced to kill him and flee. At film's end, months have passed with no news of Kurt, whose son announces his intention to go to Europe and fight the fascists himself. One of the first American films to present the philosophy—rather than just the warmongering—of fascism as a danger, WATCH ON THE RHINE is expertly directed, avoiding the static pitfalls of so many play adaptations. Davis (in a fairly small role, though top-billed) tones down her usual fireworks here to good effect.

p, Hal B. Wallis; d, Herman Shumlin; w, Dashiell Hammett and Lillian Hellman, based on the play by Hellman; ed, Rudi Fehr; ph, Merritt Gerstad and Hal Mohr; m, Max Steiner.

(PR:A MPAA:NR)

WE DIVE AT DAWN***½

(1943, Brit.) 98m Gainsborough/GFD bw

Eric Portman *(James Hobson)*, John Mills *(Lt. Freddie Taylor)*, Reginald Purdell *(CPO Dicky Dabbs)*, Niall MacGinnis *(PO Mike Corrigan)*, Joan Hopkins *(Ethel Dabbs)*, Josephine Wilson *(Alice Hobson)*, Louis Bradfield *(Lt. Brace)*, Ronald Millar *(Lt. Johnson)*, Jack Watling *(Lt. Gordon)*, Caven Watson *(CPO Duncan)*, Leslie Weston *(Tug Wilson)*, Norman Williams *(Canada)*.

This well-done wartime British entry, directed by Anthony Asquith, follows the crew of the submarine *Sea Tiger* as they proceed from a week of shore leave at home to a dangerous mission to sink the German battleship *Brandenberg*. The sub's commander, Lt. Taylor (John Mills), directs *Sea Tiger* through a mine field so it can get a shot off at the German warship, but circumstances prevent the Britons from knowing whether they have managed to sink their target (they have). After avoiding German pursuit, the submarine runs out of fuel, but a tanker is discovered in a Danish port, and the Brits and the local resistance manage to hold off the Germans long enough to complete refueling. Then it's back to England, where seaman Hobson (Eric Portman) finds his estranged wife waiting for him. This above-average submarine movie manages to avoid most of the cliches of the genre, generates more than a little tension, and offers universally strong performances. Mills prepared for his role by riding a submarine down the river Clyde, and was struck by the youthfulness of the crew—the captain was only 21 and his first officer all of 19. When the submarine crash-dived, Mills recalled in his autobiography *(Up in the Clouds, Gentlemen Please)*, "The ship then seemed to stand on her nose and I felt her speeding like an arrow towards the sea bed; charts and crockery went flying in all directions; I hung onto a rail near the periscope trying to look heroic and totally unconcerned; the only thing that concerned me was the fact that I was sure my face had turned a pale shade of pea-green."

p, Edward Black; d, Anthony Asquith; w, J.B. Williams, Val Valentine, and Frank Launder (uncredited); ed, R.E. Dearing; ph, Jack Cox.

(PR:A MPAA:NR)

WHAT PRICE GLORY?****

(1952) 111m FOX c

James Cagney *(Capt. Flagg)*, Corinne Calvet *(Charmaine)*, Dan Dailey *(Sgt. Quirt)*, William Demarest *(Cpl. Kiper)*, Craig Hill *(Lt. Aldrich)*, Robert Wagner *(Lewisohn)*, Marisa Pavan *(Nicole Bouchard)*, Casey Adams [Max Showalter] *(Lt. Moore)*, James Gleason *(Gen. Cokely)*, Wally Vernon *(Lipinsky)*, Henri Letondal *(Cognac Pete)*.

A rare misfire from director John Ford, this is a remake of director Raoul Walsh's classic 1926 film version of Maxwell Anderson and Laurence Stallings' popular stage play. The story is a familiar one: It is WW I, and Capt. Flagg (James Cagney) and Sgt. Quirt (Dan Dailey) are stationed in France, assigned to take a company of old men and young boys from a small French village into the brutal reality of the war in the trenches. In addition to battling German forces, Flagg and Quirt must fight one another for the attentions of Charmaine (Corinne Calvet), the pretty daughter of a French innkeeper. Although studio chiefs wanted Ford to make this new version of WHAT PRICE GLORY? a musical, the director more or less ignored their orders (there are a few musical numbers at the beginning) and concentrated instead on the broad humor of the material, urging Cagney and Dailey to chew up the scenery. While the performances from the leads are entertaining, the resulting film—on a purely visual level—is more than a little weird, with Ford making interesting use of the highly artificial sets and color schemes that were designed for a musical, then stripped of their *raison d'etre*. The effect is dreamlike and slightly surreal, but, because of Ford's apparent lack of interest in the material, the movie never rises above the level of a fascinating failure.

p, Sol C. Siegel; d, John Ford; w, Phoebe Ephron and Henry Ephron, based on the play by Maxwell Anderson, Laurence Stallings; ed, Dorothy Spencer; ph, Joseph MacDonald, Technicolor; m, Alfred Newman.

(PR:C MPAA:NR)

WHERE EAGLES DARE***½

(1968, Brit.) 155m Winkast/MGM c

Richard Burton *(John Smith)*, Clint Eastwood *(Lt. Morris Schaffer)*, Mary Ure *(Mary Ellison)*, Patrick Wymark *(Col. Turner)*, Michael Hordern *(Vice Adm. Rolland)*, Donald Houston *(Christiansen)*, Peter Barkworth *(Berkeley)*, Robert Beatty *(Cartwright Jones)*, William Squire *(Thomas)*, Derren Nesbitt *(Maj. von Hapen)*, Anton Diffring *(Col. Kramer)*, Brook Williams *(Sgt. Harrod)*, Neil McCarthy *(MacPherson)*.

A high-powered, big-budget WW II espionage thriller, WHERE EAGLES DARE follows an elite group of Allied commandos, led by John Smith (Richard Burton) and assigned to rescue an American general being held captive by the Nazis in a castle high in the Bavarian Alps. Ably assisted by a young American lieutenant, Morris Schaffer (Clint Eastwood), Smith and his crew of six don German uniforms and parachute into enemy territory. One of their number is found dead after landing, and Smith begins to suspect that one of his men is a double agent. He meets up with a pair of Allied agents, Mary Ellison (Mary Ure) and Heidi (Ingrid Pitt), and they manage to infiltrate the castle, which is accessible only by a tramway. An exciting picture with much derring-do and adventure, WHERE EAGLES

WHICH WAY TO THE FRONT?—

DARE is also a lengthy film, though there is more than enough action to keep it moving along. Of course, it's all a bit hard to credit (especially since the Germans can't seem to hit anything with their machine guns), but that's part of the fun. Burton, in a switch from the heavy dramatic roles that made his famous, is excellent as an action hero, but Eastwood is the one who makes it all worthwhile. If it's explosions, gunplay, and wartime treachery that you like, WHERE EAGLES DARE delivers.

p, Elliott Kastner; d, Brian G. Hutton; w, Alistair MacLean; ed, John Jympson; ph, Arthur Ibbetson, Panavision 70, Metrocolor; m, Ron Goodwin.

(PR:C MPAA:M)

WHICH WAY TO THE FRONT?*½
(1970) 96m WB c

Jerry Lewis *(Brendan Byers III)*, Jan Murray *(Sid Hackle)*, Willie Davis *(Lincoln)*, John Wood *(Finkel)*, Steve Franken *(Peter Bland)*, Dack Rambo *(Terry Love)*, Paul Winchell *(Schroeder)*, Sidney Miller *(Adolf Hitler)*, Robert Middleton *(Colonico)*, Kaye Ballard *(Mayor's Wife)*, Harold J. Stone *(Gen. Luther Buck)*.

This misfired Jerry Lewis effort (some would argue passionately that *all* of Lewis' work is a misfire) is one of the last films the comedian directed. Lewis plays Brendan Byers III, a multimillionaire whose greatest desire is to do something to help the US effort in WW II, but who has been declared unfit for service. Desperate to aid the cause, the millionaire assembles his own little army and undertakes to enter the war on the Allied side. The ragtag group sails to Italy to embark upon this goal, coming up with a plan to kidnap a high-ranking Nazi officer. To do this, Byers takes over the Nazi's identity, getting himself into trouble when the Allied forces come marching into town. This film lets Lewis try his hand at playing a Nazi to comic effect, something done much more effectively by Charlie Chaplin in THE GREAT DICTATOR at a more fitting time in the course of world events. There is one enjoyable bit of humor supplied by Sidney Miller as Hitler, but it's wasted in the overall scheme of things. While this film has its champions, they are few and far between.

p, Jerry Lewis; d, Jerry Lewis; w, Gerald Gardner and Dee Caruso, based on a story by Gardner, Caruso, and Richard Miller; ed, Russel Wiles; ph, W. Wallace Kelley, Technicolor; m, Louis Y. Brown.

(PR:A MPAA:G)

WHITE GHOST**
(1988) 93m White Ghost/Gibraltar c

William Katt *(Steve Shepard)*, Rosalind Chao *(Thi Hau)*, Martin Hewitt *(Waco)*, Wayne Crawford *(Capt. Walker)*, Reb Brown *(Maj. Cross)*, Raymond Ma *(Camp Commander)*.

A 1988 straight-to-video release, WHITE GHOST stars William Katt as ex-US intelligence officer Steve Shepard, who still wages war against the Vietnamese in 1985, 15 years after surviving the jungle massacre of his Special Forces squad. Listed as missing in action but actually hiding out in the jungle with only the beautiful, pregnant Thi Hau (Rosalind Chao) for company, Shepard wages a one-man guerilla war on the Vietnamese soldiers who patrol the area, wearing Kabuki-style makeup that gives rise to the nickname that provides the film's title. A squad of American soldiers, led by Walker (Wayne Crawford), the White Ghost's former Green Beret nemesis, is sent to Vietnam to rescue the loose cannon, but once there it turns out Walker secretly would rather put his old enemy out of action for good. After the standard barbarous tortures (by the Vietnamese), incredible heroics (by the Americans), and pyrotechnics a la Rambo and Braddock, the nefarious Walker gets his just desserts and the White Ghost gets to go home at last.

p, Jay Davidson and William Fay; d, B.J. Davis; w, Gary Thompson; ed, Ettie Feldman; ph, Hans Kuhle, Kodak color; m, Parmer Fuller.

(PR:C MPAA:R)

WHO'LL STOP THE RAIN?***½
(1978) 125m UA c

Nick Nolte *(Ray Hicks)*, Tuesday Weld *(Marge Converse)*, Michael Moriarty *(John Converse)*, Anthony Zerbe *(Antheil)*, Richard Masur *(Danskin)*, Ray Sharkey *(Smitty)*, Gail Strickland *(Chairman)*, Charles Haid *(Eddy)*, David O. Opatoshu *(Bender)*.

An effective film adaptation of Robert Stone's excellent novel *Dog Soldiers*, WHO'LL STOP THE RAIN? begins in Vietnam and follows jaded, cynical, and bitter photojournalist John Converse (Michael Moriarty) as he arranges to smuggle a large shipment of Asian heroin into the US. To assist him, Converse enlists Vietnam vet Ray Hicks (Nick Nolte). Once a Marine, now working for the Merchant Marine, Hicks can easily smuggle the heroin out of Vietnam and into the docks at Oakland, California, where he is to hook up with Converse's wife, Marge (Tuesday Weld), and await Converse's return to the states. Unfortunately, Antheil (Anthony Zerbe), a corrupt federal drug enforcement agent, has gotten wind of the shipment and sent two of his men (Richard Masur and Ray Sharkey) to kill Marge and Hicks and confiscate the heroin for his own purposes. Fueled by excellent performances from the entire cast—with Nolte a definite standout—WHO'LL STOP THE RAIN? is a gripping action film that also illustrates the bitter disillusionment of Americans who witnessed the corruption, confusion, and moral chaos of the country's leadership during the Vietnam era. Smartly directed by Karel Reisz (a Czech-born Englishman), whose previous feature was the memorable THE GAMBLER (1974) with James Caan, the film boasts fine photography by Richard H. Kline and an unforgettable climax in the surreal ruins of an abandoned hippie commune.

p, Herb Jaffe and Gabriel Katzka; d, Karel Reisz; w, Judith Rascoe and Robert Stone, based on the novel *Dog Sol-*

diers by Robert Stone; ed, John Bloom; ph, Richard H. Kline; m, Laurence Rosenthal.

(PR:C MPAA:R)

WILD GEESE, THE**

(1978, Brit.) 132m AA c

Richard Burton *(Col. Allen Faulkner)*, Roger Moore *(Shawn Flynn)*, Richard Harris *(Rafer Janders)*, Hardy Kruger *(Pieter Coetzee)*, Stewart Granger *(Sir Edward Matherson)*, Jack Watson *(Sandy Young)*, Winston Ntshona *(President Limbani)*, John Kani *(Jesse)*, Kenneth Griffith *(Witty)*, Frank Finlay *(The Priest)*, Barry Foster *(Balfour)*, Jeff Corey *(Mr. Martin)*, Ronald Fraser *(Jock)*.

This adventure film offers no surprises and tries to get by on an all-star cast, although most of the stars are a bit long in the tooth to be taken seriously in their roles as battle-hardened soldiers of fortune. Richard Burton plays Col. Allen Faulkner, the leader of a force of mercenaries who invade an African nation intent on rescuing a former president of that country and putting him back in office so that British industrialists can return to business as usual. The first third of the picture has Burton rounding up the necessary men (Roger Moore, Richard Harris, and Hardy Kruger among them) for the mission, followed by an intense training period. Veteran hack Andrew V. McLaglen fails to inject much excitement into the proceedings and falls back on some substandard Sam Peckinpah-style slow-motion bloodletting.

p, Euan Lloyd; d, Andrew V. McLaglen; w, Reginald Rose, based on the novel by Daniel Carney; ed, John Glen; ph, Jack Hildyard, Eastmancolor; m, Roy Budd.

(PR:O MPAA:R)

WILD GEESE II*½

(1985, Brit.) 125m Frontier/UNIV c

Scott Glenn *(John Haddad)*, Barbara Carrera *(Kathy Lukas)*, Edward Fox *(Alex Faulkner)*, Laurence Olivier *(Rudolf Hess)*, Robert Webber *(Robert McCann)*, Robert Freitag *(Heinrich Stroebling)*, Kenneth Haigh *(Col. Reed-Henry)*, Stratford Johns *(Mustapha El Ali)*, Derek Thompson *(Hourigan)*, John Terry *(Michael Lukas)*, Ingrid Pitt *(Hooker)*, Malcolm Jamieson *(Pierre)*, David Lumsden *(Joseph)*, Frederick Warder *(Jamil)*, Paul Antrim *(Sgt. Maj. Murphy)*.

The picture begins with a dedication to Richard Burton, who starred in the first WILD GEESE seven years before and was supposed to star in this one. Edward Fox was brought in as a replacement and introduced as Burton's younger but equally adroit brother. The plot is dumb and the script is dumber, but the actors go about matters with such complete sincerity that they almost manage to bring it off. John Haddad (Scott Glenn) is a mercenary, hired by a TV company to pull off one of the most incredible kidnapings of all time, namely the snatch of Rudolf Hess from his four-decade-long solitary confinement in Spandau prison. Kathy (Barbara Carrera) and Michael Lukas (John Terry) are a brother-sister act who work for the TV company and play a part in the caper, which has something to do with getting Hess (played by Laurence Olivier in yet another one of his German jobs, including Dr. Szell in MARATHON MAN and a Nazi hunter in THE BOYS FROM BRAZIL) finally to divulge the secrets he's been keeping all these years. As in any caper movie, a great deal of time is spent assembling the team, going over the plot, carefully casing the area, etc. Delete that and this is a short movie. The film boasts more hardware than the Hammacher-Schlemmer catalog, fetishistically fixating on items like noise-suppressed machine guns, machine pistols, and quick-release knives. Since none of the four countries—the US, USSR, Britain, and France—overseeing Spandau would give permission for any shooting having to do with Hess (who was later to die in the prison), Spandau, or even an area close to the jail, the filming was done at an old jail in the Tegel section of Berlin.

p, Euan Lloyd; d, Peter Hunt; w, Reginald Rose, based on the novel *The Square Circle* by Daniel Carney; ed, Keith Palmer; ph, Michael Reed, Technicolor; m, Roy Budd.

(PR:O MPAA:R)

WIND AND THE LION, THE***½

(1975) 119m MGM/UA c

Sean Connery *(Mulay el Raisuli)*, Candice Bergen *(Eden Pedecaris)*, Brian Keith *(Theodore Roosevelt)*, John Huston *(John Hay)*, Geoffrey Lewis *(Gummere)*, Steve Kanaly *(Capt. Jerome)*, Vladek Sheybal *(The Bashaw)*, Nadim Sawalha *(Sherif of Wazan)*, Roy Jenson *(Adm. Chadwick)*, Deborah Baxter *(Alice Roosevelt)*, Jack Cooley *(Quentin Roosevelt)*, Chris Aller *(Kermit Roosevelt)*, Simon Harrison *(William Pedecaris)*, Polly Gottesman *(Jennifer Pedecaris)*, Antoine St. John *(Von Roerkel)*, Luis Barboo *(Gayaan the Terrible)*.

A stirring, if grossly inaccurate, look at the dawn of US interventionism, THE WIND AND THE LION features Brian Keith as a Teddy Roosevelt determined to establish his presidential identity, having come to office after the death of William McKinley. When a rebellious Arab chieftain, Mulay el Raisuli (Sean Connery), seizes an American woman, Eden Pedecaris (Candice Bergen), and her children, Roosevelt prepares to send in the Marines. At the same time, the Germans land in North Africa in force, looking for a way to turn the situation to their advantage. The chieftain and Eden talk a great deal of philosophy and the Arab ruler begins to take on heroic stature in the eyes of her son. Eventually, under pressure from Roosevelt, Raisuli releases his hostages to the Marines and is immediately arrested and imprisoned by the Germans. The Marines are none too happy about this development—since Roosevelt had promised Raisuli his freedom if he released his prisoners—so they march into the town (in a scene almost directly stolen from THE WILD BUNCH) and shoot it out with the Germans. THE WIND AND THE LION is certainly jingoistic to a fault, and its portrayal of the various factions is little above the cartoon level, but thanks to marvelous performances by Keith and Connery, the film works as a

WOODEN HORSE, THE—

maker of myths. The real facts of the incident were not so grand: Raisuli, a brigand chief, kidnaped Ion Perdicaris, a balding, overweight businessman who bore no resemblance to the lovely Bergen, to embarrass the Sultan of Morocco, who was already having troubles with the US. Perdicaris was freed after only a couple of days, but before his release was made public, the Republican party, looking for a rallying issue, announced that a telegram had been sent to the kidnaper saying, "Perdicaris alive or Raisuli dead." No troops were landed. No one was killed. But historical truth isn't what's important here; heroes and myth are the currency of this film, and it delivers two heroes in admirable fashion.

p, Herb Jaffe; d, John Milius; w, John Milius; ed, Robert L. Wolfe; ph, Billy Williams, Panavision, Metrocolor; m, Jerry Goldsmith.

(PR:C MPAA:PG)

WOODEN HORSE, THE***½

(1951, Brit.) 101m BL-Wessex/BL-Snader bw

Leo Genn *(Peter)*, David Tomlinson *(Phil)*, Anthony Steel *(John)*, David Greene *(Bennett)*, Peter Burton *(Nigel)*, Patrick Waddington *(Senior British Officer)*, Michael Goodliffe *(Robbie)*, Anthony Dawson *(Pomfret)*, Bryan Forbes *(Paul)*, Franz Schaftheitlin *(Commandant)*, Hans Meyer *(Charles)*, Jacques Brunius *(Andre)*, Peter Finch *(The Australian)*, Dan Cunningham *(David)*, Russell Waters *("Wings" Cameron)*.

One of the cleverest escapes of WW II was pulled off by British prisoners in 1943, and this film tells their story. Pondering a method of escaping their camp, POWs Peter (Leo Genn), John (Anthony Steel), and Phil (David Tomlinson) hit upon a brilliant scheme. They construct a boxlike vaulting horse, which is daily brought out to the yard for a few hours of exercise by their fellow internees. Inside the horse, however, are one and sometimes two men who start a tunnel from underneath the horse, then cover it up at the end of each day's vaulting. After months of digging and close calls, the tunnel is ready. Three men remain inside it until after dark, then break through the last few feet of ground to the surface beyond the fence. Peter and John travel together and are eventually spirited by the Danish underground to Sweden, where they rejoin Phil. This was the first of the British POW films and set the subgenre's style, in which Stalag life takes on the character of a British public school, a rigorous discipline and hierarchy in which the Germans function as "rather nasty prefects, who exist simply to be tricked and humiliated," as one critic put it. THE WOODEN HORSE subscribes to this trivialization of what was really a horrible, degrading experience, but as an adventure the film is more than successful—suspenseful and fast-paced, with all the leads well done in suitably stiff-upper-lip style.

p, Ian Dalrymple; d, Jack Lee; w, Eric Williams, based on his book; ed, John Seabourne, Sr. and Peter Seabourne; ph, C. Pennington-Richards; m, Clifton Parker.

(PR:A MPAA:NR)

XYZ

YANK IN THE R.A.F., A***

(1941) 98m FOX bw

Tyrone Power *(Tim Baker)*, Betty Grable *(Carol Brown)*, John Sutton *(Wing Comdr. Morley)*, Reginald Gardiner *(Roger Pillby)*, Donald Stuart *(Cpl. Harry Baker)*, John Wilde *(Graves)*, Richard Fraser *(Thorndyke)*, Morton Lowry *(Squadron Leader)*, Ralph Byrd *(Al Bennett)*, Denis Green *(Redmond)*.

Tyrone Power stars here, in one of his most successful films, as Tim Baker, a brash American pilot (he easily could have been the model for TOP GUN's Tom Cruise) ferrying planes to Canada as part of the US' WW II "Cash-and-Carry" policy to arm Britain while maintaining neutrality. In Canada, he agrees to fly planes across the Atlantic. During a London air raid he meets an old girl friend, Carol Brown (Betty Grable), who is now working at a nightclub and volunteering daily for the war effort and who wants nothing to do with Tim, criticizing his ambivalence about the war. To impress her, he joins the RAF and is forced to go through flight school again, a routine that bores him silly, while finding competition for Carol in the person of his wing commander (John Sutton). The air battles, some taken from actual footage shot in combat over Europe, are seamlessly cut into the film, as is footage of the Dunkirk evacuation, with a huge reenactment of the battle staged on a beach in northern California. The film was a great success and helped prepare isolationist America for its upcoming role in the war.

p, Darryl F. Zanuck; d, Henry King; w, Darrell Ware and Karl Tunberg, based on a story by Melville Crossman [Darryl F. Zanuck]; ed, Barbara McLean; ph, Leon Shamroy and Ronald Neame.

(PR:A MPAA:NR)

YEAR OF LIVING DANGEROUSLY, THE***½

(1982, Aus.) 115m MGM c

Mel Gibson *(Guy Hamilton)*, Sigourney Weaver *(Jill Bryant)*, Linda Hunt *(Billy Kwan)*, Michael Murphy *(Pete Curtis)*, Bembol Roco *(Kumar)*, Domingo Landicho *(Hortono)*, Noel Ferrier *(Wally O'Sullivan)*, Paul Sonkkila *(Kevin Condon)*.

Ambitious, gripping, and stylish, THE YEAR OF LIVING DANGEROUSLY falters in its attempts to be thriller, romance, and political tract and to encompass director Peter Weir's penchant for mysticism all at once. Still, it's an excellent film, set in Indonesia, 1965, as Australian reporter Guy Hamilton (Mel Gibson) arrives in Jakarta. His photographer, Billy Kwan (Linda Hunt), a Chinese-Australian dwarf, shows him the ropes, introducing him to the city's poverty and corruption and to various contacts, including Jill Bryant (Sigourney Weaver), an embassy attache with whom Guy begins a romance. When Jill secures information of the planned Communist coup against President Sukarno and urges Guy to leave, he betrays her confidence and files a major story—for which she is the obvious source. Billy, previously a fence-sitter, now comes out against Sukarno, feeling that he has betrayed Indonesia in much the same way as Guy betrayed Jill (whom Billy also loves), and is killed as he protests Sukarno's rule. As revolt and reaction explode on all sides, Guy races to catch the last plane out of the country, reuniting with Jill at the end. Weir is only partly successful in attempting to link his various themes symbolically with images of Indonesian shadow puppetry and Billy's advice to "look at the shadows, not at the puppets," but the director indisputably made the right move in his risky casting of the tiny, gravel-voiced Hunt to play Billy Kwan, winning her a Best Supporting Actress Oscar and a New York Film Critic's Award. The film's hot, humid, seedy ambience is nearly palpable, enhancing this fascinating story of Sukarno's downfall.

p, James McElroy; d, Peter Weir; w, David Williamson, Peter Weir, and C.J. Koch, based on the novel by Koch; ed, Bill Anderson; ph, Russell Boyd, Panavision, Metrocolor; m, Maurice Jarre.

(PR:C   MPAA:PG)

YOUNG LIONS, THE***½

(1958) 167m FOX bw

Marlon Brando *(Christian Diestl)*, Montgomery Clift *(Noah Ackerman)*, Dean Martin *(Michael Whiteacre)*, Hope Lange *(Hope Plowman)*, Barbara Rush *(Margaret Freemantle)*, May Britt *(Gretchen Hardenberg)*, Maximilian Schell *(Capt. Hardenberg)*, Dora Doll *(Simone)*, Lee Van Cleef *(Sgt. Rickett)*, Liliane Montevecchi *(Francoise)*, Parley Baer *(Brant)*, Arthur Franz *(Lt. Green)*, Hal Baylor *(Pvt. Burnecker)*, John Alderson *(Cpl. Kraus)*.

A somewhat bloated adaptation of Irwin Shaw's sprawling WW II novel, THE YOUNG LIONS follows three soldiers—one German, two American—from the time of their enlistment until the end of the war. Christian Diestl (Marlon Brando) is an idealistic young German who believes in Hitler and becomes a lieutenant in the Wehrmacht. As he makes his way from the occupation of Paris to duty in Rommel's Afrika Korps and then back into Europe, Diestl becomes disillusioned and embittered over Nazi brutality and comes to hate his uniform and everything it represents. Meanwhile, in the US, a young Jew, Noah Ackerman (Montgomery Clift), and a popular singer, Michael Whiteacre (Dean Martin), meet as draftees and become fast friends. Although patriotic and dedicated, Ackerman becomes the victim of the Army's anti-Semitism, and is forced to fight his fellow Americans before ever facing the Germans. As the years go by, the fates of Ackerman, Whiteacre, and Diestl grow closer, until they eventually intersect outside a concentration camp. Great departures were made in the script from Shaw's original story, mostly in the character of the German, Diestl. In the book, he is an unredeemed Nazi to the last, and in the final confrontation kills the Jewish soldier, then is killed by the other American.

It was largely Brando who made the German a sympathetic character, arguing that Shaw had written his book in the immediate, angry aftermath of the war, although Shaw later told the actor that he wouldn't have changed his opinions even if he had written the book 10 years later. Although Edward Dmytryk's direction was never more than workmanlike and the film is bit overlong and draggy at times, it does contain a pair of worthwhile performances: Brando and Clift.

p, Al Lichtman; d, Edward Dmytryk; w, Edward Anhalt, based on the novel by Irwin Shaw; ed, Dorothy Spencer; ph, Joseph MacDonald, CinemaScope; m, Hugo Friedhofer.

(PR:C   MPAA:NR)

ZULU*****

(1964, Brit.) 135m Diamond/EM c

Stanley Baker *(Lt. John Chard)*, Jack Hawkins *(Rev. Otto Witt)*, Ulla Jacobsson *(Margareta Witt)*, James Booth *(Pvt. Henry Hook)*, Michael Caine *(Lt. Gonville Bromhead)*, Nigel Green *(Color Sgt. Bourne)*, Ivor Emmanuel *(Pvt. Owen)*, Paul Daneman *(Sgt. Maxfield)*, Glynn Edwards *(Cpl. Allen)*, Neil McCarthy *(Pvt. Thomas)*, David Kernan *(Pvt. Hitch)*, Gary Bond *(Pvt. Cole)*, Patrick Magee *(Surgeon Reynolds)*, Dafydd Havard *(Gunner Howarth)*, Richard Burton *(Narrator)*.

Set in 1879 in Natal, this magnificently staged, brilliantly acted film tells the story of the heroic defense by overwhelmingly outnumbered British troops of the tiny outpost Rorke's Drift. Having been warned by a pacifist missionary (Jack Hawkins) that a British army contingent has been massacred by Zulu warriors, Lt. John Chard (Stanley Baker, the film's producer) orders his troops to dig in, despite the pleas of Lt. Gonville Bromhead (Michael Caine), the blueblood second-in-command who wants to abandon the post and who feels that he, rather than Chard (an engineer), should be in charge. Rather than fleeing, however, the courageous Brits withstand attack after attack, night and day, from 4,000 Zulus, and eventually triumph through a combination of ingenuity, determination, and luck. This amazing film is devastatingly accurate in its depiction of the Rorke's Drift action, and is superbly directed by Cy Endfield, whose battle scenes are some of the most terrifying ever committed to film. Producer Baker, however, had a difficult time getting his Zulu extras to cooperate on the location shoot in Natal. None had ever seen a motion picture, and he couldn't make the chiefs understand what he wanted to do. Finally, Baker had an old western starring Gene Autry flown in and showed it to the Zulus, who, grasping the fictional game at hand, later cooperated and lent the battle scenes tremendous power. ZULU is dramatically narrated by Richard Burton, who points out that of the 1,344 Victoria Crosses awarded since 1856, 11 were given to the defenders at Rorke's Drift, an all-time record for one engagement.

p, Stanley Baker and Cy Endfield; d, Cy Endfield; w, John Prebble and Cy Endfield, based on a story by Prebble; ed,

ZULU DAWN—

John Jympson; ph, Stephen Dade, Technirama, Technicolor; m, John Barry.

(PR:C MPAA:NR)

ZULU DAWN***

(1980, Brit.) 117m Samarkand-Lamitas/WB c

Burt Lancaster *(Col. Durnford)*, Peter O'Toole *(Lord Chelmsford)*, Simon Ward *(William Vereker)*, John Mills *(Sir Bartle Frere)*, Nigel Davenport *(Col. Hamilton-Brown)*, Michael Jayston *(Col. Crealock)*, Ronald Lacey *(Norris Newman)*, Denholm Elliott *(Lt. Col. Pulleine)*, Freddie Jones *(Bishop Colenso)*, Christopher Cazenove *(Lt. Coghill)*, Ronald Pickup *(Lt. Harford)*, Donald Pickering *(Maj. Russell)*, Anna Calder-Marshall *(Fanny Colenso)*, James Faulkner *(Lt. Melvill)*, Peter Vaughan *(Quartermaster Sergeant)*, Graham Armitage *(Capt. Shepstone)*, Bob Hoskins *(Sgt. Maj. Williams)*.

Fifteen years after the release of ZULU—Cy Enfield's masterful re-creation of the 1879 battle of Rorke's Drift in which Stanley Baker and Michael Caine lead the heroic stand by a vastly outnumbered contingent of British soldiers against thousands of Zulu warriors—the British film industry offered this prequel. ZULU DAWN documents the circumstances leading up to that confrontation, focusing on the increasing tensions between British colonial officials and the Zulus, and culminates with the extermination of 1,500 British soldiers at the battle of Isandhlwana, which occurred only hours before the events depicted in ZULU began. Peter O'Toole plays Lord Chelmsford, the commander of British forces in Natal, and Burt Lancaster is Col. Durnford, the one-armed hero who leads his men to their deaths when their column is attacked and annihilated by Zulu forces that outnumber them 16 to 1. That attack, as well as the scenes of the marching British and the Zulus preparing to descend on them, are impressively staged and shot. Yet while ZULU DAWN succeeds in painting these events on a broad canvas, it lacks the interpersonal conflicts that made ZULU so fascinating, and ultimately this film, penned by Enfield but directed by Douglas Hickox, is a far cry from that classic war film.

p, Nate Kohn; d, Douglas Hickox; w, Cy Endfield and Anthony Storey, based on a story by Endfield; ed, Malcolm Cooke; ph, Ousama Rawi, Panavision, Technicolor; m, Elmer Bernstein.

(PR:C-O MPAA:PG)

ALTERNATE TITLE INDEX

Listed below are alternate, foreign, and Great Britain titles of films, followed by the title under which the film is listed in this volume.

A
ANXIOUS YEARS, THE
  (SEE: DARK JOURNEY)
ARMORED ATTACK!
  (SEE: NORTH STAR, THE)
ARMS AND THE WOMAN
  (SEE: MR. WINKLE GOES TO WAR)
AUSTERLITZ (SEE: BATTLE OF AUSTERLITZ, THE)

B
BATTLE FOR ANZIO, THE
  (SEE: ANZIO)
BATTLE OF MIDWAY, THE
  (SEE: MIDWAY)
BATTLE OF THE RIVER PLATE, THE (SEE: PURSUIT OF THE GRAF SPEE, THE)
BATTLE STRIPE (SEE: MEN, THE)
BIRUMANO TATEGOTO
  (SEE: HARP OF BURMA)
BITKA NA NERETVI
  (SEE: BATTLE OF NERETVA)
BURNING HEARTS
  (SEE: KOLBERG)

C
CAMPANADAS A MEDIANOCHE
  (SEE: CHIMES AT MIDNIGHT)
CARRINGTON V.C. (SEE: COURT MARTIAL)
CASTLE OF THE SPIDER'S WEB
  (SEE: THRONE OF BLOOD)
COBWEB CASTLE
  (SEE: THRONE OF BLOOD)
COLONEL BLIMP (SEE: LIFE AND DEATH OF COLONEL BLIMP, THE)
COMRADESHIP
  (SEE: KAMERADSCHAFT)
CUBAN REBEL GIRLS
  (SEE: ASSAULT OF THE REBEL GIRLS)

D
DA DUNKERQUE ALLA VITTORIA (SEE: FROM HELL TO VICTORY)
DAS BOOT (SEE: BOAT, THE)
DEMANTY NOCI
  (SEE: DIAMONDS OF THE NIGHT)
DER FANGSCHUSS (SEE: COUP DE GRACE)
DER FUSSGANGER
  (SEE: PEDESTRIAN, THE)
DIE BLECHTROMMEL (SEE: TIN DRUM, THE)
DIE EHE DER MARIA BRAUN
  (SEE: MARRIAGE OF MARIA BRAUN, THE)
DIE VIER IM JEEP (SEE: FOUR IN A JEEP)
DIE WANNSEEKONFERENZ
  (SEE: WANNSEE CONFERENCE, THE)
DOUBLE, THE
  (SEE: KAGEMUSHA)
DRUM, THE (SEE: DRUMS)

E
EINE LIEBE IN DEUTSCHLAND
  (SEE: LOVE IN GERMANY, A)
ESCAPE OF THE AMETHYST
  (SEE: BATTLE HELL)
ESCAPE TO VICTORY
  (SEE: VICTORY)

F
FALSTAFF (SEE: CHIMES AT MIDNIGHT)
FILM D'AMORE E D'ANARCHIA
  (SEE: LOVE AND ANARCHY)
FIRST OF THE FEW, THE
  (SEE: SPITFIRE)
FLIGHT OF THE WHITE STALLIONS, THE
  (SEE: MIRACLE OF THE WHITE STALLIONS)

G
GERMANIA, ANNO ZERO
  (SEE: GERMANY, YEAR ZERO)
GESTAPO (SEE: NIGHT TRAIN TO MUNICH)
GIFT HORSE, THE (SEE: GLORY AT SEA)
GOTTERDAMERRUNG
  (SEE: DAMNED, THE)
GRAF SPEE (SEE: PURSUIT OF THE GRAF SPEE, THE)
GUNBUS (SEE: SKY BANDITS)

H
HARP OF BURMA (SEE: BURMESE HARP, THE)
HMS DEFIANT (SEE: DAMN THE DEFIANT!)
HUNTER OF THE APOCALYPSE, THE (SEE: LAST HUNTER, THE)

I
IL BUONO, IL BRUTTO, IL CATTIVO (SEE: GOOD, THE BAD, AND THE UGLY, THE)
IL GENERALE DELLA ROVERE
  (SEE: GENERALE DELLA ROVERE)
IL GIARDINO DEL FINZI-CONTINI
  (SEE: GARDEN OF THE FINZI-CONTINIS, THE)
IL PORTIERE DI NOTTE
  (SEE: NIGHT PORTER, THE)
INVADERS, THE (SEE: 49TH PARALLEL)
IVAN GROZNYI (SEE: IVAN THE TERRIBLE, PARTS I & II)
IVAN'S CHILDHOOD, THE YOUNGEST SPY (SEE: MY NAME IS IVAN)

J
JIGOKUMEN (SEE: GATE OF HELL)
JOB LAZADASA (SEE: REVOLT OF JOB, THE)

K
KUMONOSUJO, KUMONOSU-DJO
  (SEE: THRONE OF BLOOD)

L
LA CADUTA DEGLI DEI
  (SEE: DAMNED, THE)
LA CHAMBRE VERTE
  (SEE: GREEN ROOM, THE)
LA CIOCIARA (SEE: TWO WOMEN)
LA DALLE ARDENNE ALL INFERNO (SEE: DIRTY HEROES)
LA GRANDE ILLUSION
  (SEE: GRAND ILLUSION)
LA KERMESSE HEROIQUE
  (SEE: CARNIVAL IN FLANDERS)

LA NUIT DE GENERAUX
(SEE: NIGHT OF THE
GENERALS, THE)
LA VICTOIRE EN CHANTANT
(SEE: BLACK AND WHITE IN
COLOR)
LADY HAMILTON (SEE: THAT
HAMILTON WOMAN)
LAST MESSAGE FROM SAIGON
(SEE: OPERATION CIA)
LE CAPORAL EPINGLE
(SEE: ELUSIVE CORPORAL,
THE)
LE DERNIER METRO
(SEE: LAST METRO, THE)
LES JEUX INTERDIT
(SEE: FORBIDDEN GAMES)
LETYAT ZHURAVLI
(SEE: CRANES ARE FLYING,
THE)
LONG RIDE, THE
(SEE: BRADY'S ESCAPE)

M

MASK OF FURY (SEE: FIRST
YANK INTO TOKYO)
MASSACRE AT FORT HOLMAN
(SEE: REASON TO LIVE, A
REASON TO DIE, A)
MISTER V (SEE: PIMPERNEL
SMITH)

N

NIGHT OF SAN LORENZO, THE
(SEE: NIGHT OF THE
SHOOTING STARS, THE)
NIGHT TRAIN (SEE: NIGHT
TRAIN TO MUNICH)
NINGEN NO JOKEN
(SEE: HUMAN CONDITION,
THE)
NO GREATER LOVE
(SEE: HUMAN CONDITION,
THE)
NO HABRA MAS PENAS NI
OLVIDO (SEE: FUNNY, DIRTY
LITTLE WAR, A)
NOBI (SEE: FIRES ON THE
PLAIN)

O

OBCH OD NA KORZE
(SEE: SHOP ON MAIN STREET,
THE)
OBERST REDL (SEE: COLONEL
REDL)
OMAR MUKHTAR (SEE: LION OF
THE DESERT)
ONE-MAN MUTINY
(SEE: COURT-MARTIAL OF
BILLY MITCHELL, THE)

P

PAISA (SEE: PAISAN)
PATTON—LUST FOR GLORY
(SEE: PATTON)
PATTON: A SALUTE TO A REBEL
(SEE: PATTON)
POPIOL Y DIAMENT
(SEE: ASHES AND DIAMONDS)

Q

QUEIMADA! (SEE: BURN)

R

RAPPRESAGLIA
(SEE: MASSACRE IN ROME)
REDL EZREDES (SEE: COLONEL
REDL)
ROAD TO ETERNITY
(SEE: HUMAN CONDITION,
THE)
ROME, OPEN CITY (SEE: OPEN
CITY)
ROMMEL—DESERT FOX
(SEE: DESERT FOX, THE)
ROOKIES (SEE: BUCK PRIVATES)

S

SABOTEUR: CODE NAME
MORITURI, THE
(SEE: MORITURI)
SAIGON (SEE: OFF LIMITS)
SALERNO BEACHHEAD
(SEE: WALK IN THE SUN, A)
SHADOW WARRIOR, THE
(SEE: KAGEMUSHA)
SHOP ON HIGH STREET, THE
(SEE: SHOP ON MAIN STREET,
THE)

SIXTH OF JUNE, THE
(SEE: D-DAY, THE SIXTH OF
JUNE)
SOLDIER'S PRAYER, A
(SEE: HUMAN CONDITION,
THE)
SOLDIERS, THE (SEE: LES
CARABINIERS)
SUICIDE RUN (SEE: TOO LATE
THE HERO)

T

TARTU (SEE: ADVENTURES OF
TARTU, THE)
THEY LOVED LIFE (SEE: KANAL)
TO BE A MAN (SEE: CRY OF
BATTLE)
TRANSPORT Z RAJE
(SEE: TRANSPORT FROM
PARADISE)

U

U-BOAT 29 (SEE: SPY IN BLACK,
THE)
UN AMOUR EN ALLEMAGNE
(SEE: LOVE IN GERMANY, A)
UNA RAGIONE PER VIVERE E
UNA PER MORIRE
(SEE: REASON TO LIVE, A
REASON TO DIE, A)

V

VOINA I MIR (SEE: WAR AND
PEACE)

W

WAY AHEAD, THE
(SEE: IMMORTAL BATTALION,
THE)
WHEELS OF TERROR
(SEE: MISFIT BRIGADE, THE)
WHO DARES WIN (SEE: FINAL
OPTION, THE)

Y

YANGTSE INCIDENT
(SEE: BATTLE HELL)
YOUNG INVADERS
(SEE: DARBY'S RANGERS)

INDEX

Individuals listed in this index are grouped by function as follows:

Actors (major players only)
Cinematographers
Directors
Editors
Music Composers
Producers
Screenwriters
Source Authors (authors of the original material upon which a film is based)

Individual names are followed by an alphabetical listing of the films in which the individual was involved.

ACTORS

Abbott, Bud
BUCK PRIVATES

Agar, John
SANDS OF IWO JIMA

Alexander, Jane
TESTAMENT

Allen, Woody
BANANAS
LOVE AND DEATH

Andress, Ursula
BLUE MAX, THE

Andrews, Anthony
HANNA'S WAR

Andrews, Dana
BEST YEARS OF OUR LIVES, THE
PURPLE HEART, THE
WALK IN THE SUN, A

Angel, Heather
LAST OF THE MOHICANS, THE

Ann-Margret
LAST REMAKE OF BEAU GESTE, THE
RETURN OF THE SOLDIER, THE

Arkin, Alan
CATCH-22

Astaire, Fred
ON THE BEACH

Attenborough, Richard
GLORY AT SEA

Aumont, Jean Pierre
NAPOLEON

Aykroyd, Dan
1941

Ayres, Lew
ALL QUIET ON THE WESTERN FRONT

Baker, Stanley
ZULU

Bale, Christian
EMPIRE OF THE SUN

Balsam, Martin
CATCH-22
TORA! TORA! TORA!

Bancroft, Anne
HINDENBURG, THE
TO BE OR NOT TO BE

Bankhead, Tallulah
LIFEBOAT

Bannen, Ian
HOPE AND GLORY
TOO LATE THE HERO

Barnes, Binnie
LAST OF THE MOHICANS, THE

Barrat, Robert
LAST OF THE MOHICANS, THE

Basehart, Richard
HITLER

Bates, Alan
KING OF HEARTS
PRAYER FOR THE DYING, A
RETURN OF THE SOLDIER, THE

Bauer, Steven
BEAST, THE

Baxter, Anne
NORTH STAR, THE

Beatty, Ned
1941

Beatty, Warren
REDS

Belushi, James
SALVADOR

Belushi, John
1941

Bendix, William
LIFEBOAT

Benny, Jack
TO BE OR NOT TO BE

Berenger, Tom
DOGS OF WAR, THE
PLATOON

Bergen, Candice
SAND PEBBLES, THE
SOLDIER BLUE
WIND AND THE LION, THE

Berger, Helmut
GARDEN OF THE FINZI-CONTINIS, THE

Berger, Senta
CAST A GIANT SHADOW

Bergman, Ingrid
CASABLANCA
INN OF THE SIXTH HAPPINESS, THE

Beymer, Richard
DIARY OF ANNE FRANK, THE

Binoche, Juliette
UNBEARABLE LIGHTNESS OF BEING, THE

Birma, Serafima
IVAN THE TERRIBLE, PARTS I & II

Bloom, Claire
ALEXANDER THE GREAT
BUCCANEER, THE
RICHARD III

Bogarde, Dirk
BRIDGE TOO FAR, A
DAMN THE DEFIANT!
DAMNED, THE
NIGHT PORTER, THE
SEA SHALL NOT HAVE THEM, THE

Bogart, Humphrey
AFRICAN QUEEN, THE
CASABLANCA
PASSAGE TO MARSEILLE
SAHARA

Borgnine, Ernest
DIRTY DOZEN, THE

Bottoms, Timothy
JOHNNY GOT HIS GUN

Bowie, David
MERRY CHRISTMAS, MR. LAWRENCE

Boyer, Charles
BUCCANEER, THE
FOUR HORSEMEN OF THE APOCALYPSE, THE

Brandauer, Klaus Maria
COLONEL REDL
MEPHISTO
SALZBURG CONNECTION, THE

Brando, Marlon
APOCALYPSE NOW
BURN
DESIREE
MEN, THE

ACTORS

MORITURI
SAYONARA
UGLY AMERICAN, THE
YOUNG LIONS, THE

Brazzi, Rossano
AUSTERLITZ

Brennan, Walter
SERGEANT YORK

Bridges, Lloyd
SAHARA

Broderick, Matthew
BILOXI BLUES
WARGAMES

Bronson, Charles
DIRTY DOZEN, THE
GREAT ESCAPE, THE

Brooks, Mel
TO BE OR NOT TO BE

Brown, Bryan
BREAKER MORANT
REBEL

Brynner, Yul
BATTLE OF NERETVA
BUCCANEER, THE
MORITURI
TARAS BULBA

Buchholz, Horst
CODE NAME: EMERALD

Buckler, Hugh
LAST OF THE MOHICANS, THE

Burstyn, Ellen
HANNA'S WAR

Burton, Richard
ALEXANDER THE GREAT
DESERT RATS, THE
MASSACRE IN ROME
RAID ON ROMMEL
WHERE EAGLES DARE
WILD GEESE, THE

Buttons, Red
SAYONARA

Caan, James
BRIDGE TOO FAR, A
GARDENS OF STONE

Cabot, Bruce
LAST OF THE MOHICANS, THE

Cage, Nicolas
BIRDY

Cagney, James
BLOOD ON THE SUN
MISTER ROBERTS
WHAT PRICE GLORY?

Caine, Michael
BATTLE OF BRITAIN, THE
BRIDGE TOO FAR, A
EAGLE HAS LANDED, THE
TOO LATE THE HERO
VICTORY
ZULU

Cardinale, Claudia
AUSTERLITZ

Carmet, Jean
BLACK AND WHITE IN COLOR

Caron, Leslie
FATHER GOOSE

Carradine, David
P.O.W. THE ESCAPE

Carradine, Keith
DUELLISTS, THE
SOUTHERN COMFORT

Cassavetes, John
BRASS TARGET

Cassel, Jean-Pierre
ELUSIVE CORPORAL, THE

Cassidy, Joanna
UNDER FIRE

Cazale, John
DEER HUNTER, THE

Chandler, Jeff
AWAY ALL BOATS

Chaplin, Charles
GREAT DICTATOR, THE

Cherkassov, Nikolai
ALEXANDER NEVSKY
IVAN THE TERRIBLE, PARTS I & II

Christie, Julie
DOCTOR ZHIVAGO
RETURN OF THE SOLDIER, THE

Cleese, John
PRIVATES ON PARADE

Clift, Montgomery
FROM HERE TO ETERNITY
JUDGMENT AT NUREMBERG
YOUNG LIONS, THE

Cobb, Lee J.
FOUR HORSEMEN OF THE
APOCALYPSE, THE

Coburn, James
CROSS OF IRON
GREAT ESCAPE, THE
MIDWAY
REASON TO LIVE, A REASON TO DIE, A

Colbert, Claudette
DRUMS ALONG THE MOHAWK

Coleman, Dabney
WARGAMES

Connery, Sean
BRIDGE TOO FAR, A
CUBA
WIND AND THE LION, THE

Conte, Richard
PURPLE HEART, THE

Cooper, Gary
BEAU GESTE
CLOAK AND DAGGER
COURT-MARTIAL OF BILLY MITCHELL, THE
DISTANT DRUMS
FAREWELL TO ARMS, A
LIVES OF A BENGAL LANCER
MOROCCO

SERGEANT YORK

Costello, Lou
BUCK PRIVATES

Cotten, Joseph
TORA! TORA! TORA!

Courtenay, Tom
DOCTOR ZHIVAGO
NIGHT OF THE GENERALS, THE

Coward, Noel
IN WHICH WE SERVE

Craig, James
DRUMS IN THE DEEP SOUTH

Crenna, Richard
FIRST BLOOD
RAMBO III

Cross, Ben
ASSISI UNDERGROUND, THE

Cruise, Tom
TOP GUN

Cummings, Robert
SABOTEUR

Curtis, Tony
OPERATION PETTICOAT
TARAS BULBA

Dafoe, Willem
OFF LIMITS
PLATOON

Dance, Charles
PLENTY

Danner, Blythe
GREAT SANTINI, THE

Dantine, Helmut
NORTHERN PURSUIT

Davis, Bette
WATCH ON THE RHINE

Davis, Judy
FINAL OPTION, THE

Davis, Nancy
HELLCATS OF THE NAVY

Davis, Sammi
HOPE AND GLORY

Day, Laraine
FOREIGN CORRESPONDENT

Day-Lewis, Daniel
UNBEARABLE LIGHTNESS OF BEING, THE

de Havilland, Olivia
CHARGE OF THE LIGHT BRIGADE, THE
GONE WITH THE WIND
THEY DIED WITH THEIR BOOTS ON

De Lint, Derek
ASSAULT, THE

De Niro, Robert
DEER HUNTER, THE

De Sica, Vittorio
GENERALE DELLA ROVERE

Delon, Alain
LOST COMMAND, THE

ACTORS

Deneuve, Catherine
LAST METRO, THE
MARCH OR DIE

Depardieu, Gerard
DANTON
LAST METRO, THE

Dern, Bruce
COMING HOME

Devane, William
ROLLING THUNDER

Dickinson, Angie
CAST A GIANT SHADOW

Dietrich, Marlene
JUDGMENT AT NUREMBERG
MOROCCO

Dillon, Matt
REBEL

Donat, Robert
ADVENTURES OF TARTU, THE
INN OF THE SIXTH HAPPINESS, THE

Donlevy, Brian
BEAU GESTE
WAKE ISLAND

Douglas, Kirk
CAST A GIANT SHADOW
FINAL COUNTDOWN, THE
IN HARM'S WAY
PATHS OF GLORY
SEVEN DAYS IN MAY
SPARTACUS

Dru, Joanne
SHE WORE A YELLOW RIBBON

Dudikoff, Michael
PLATOON LEADER

Dunaway, Faye
LITTLE BIG MAN
VOYAGE OF THE DAMNED

Dunne, Irene
GUY NAMED JOE, A

Duvall, Robert
APOCALYPSE NOW
EAGLE HAS LANDED, THE
GREAT SANTINI, THE
M*A*S*H

Dzundza, George
BEAST, THE

Eastwood, Clint
FIREFOX
FRANCIS IN THE NAVY
GOOD, THE BAD, AND THE UGLY, THE
HEARTBREAK RIDGE
KELLY'S HEROES
WHERE EAGLES DARE

Elliott, Denholm
CRUEL SEA, THE

Fairbanks, Jr., Douglas
GUNGA DIN

Falk, Peter
ANZIO

Farrar, David
FRIEDA

Ferrer, Jose
COCKLESHELL HEROES, THE

Ferrer, Mel
WAR AND PEACE

Field, Sally
HEROES

Finch, Peter
OPERATION AMSTERDAM
PURSUIT OF THE GRAF SPEE, THE

Finney, Albert
DUELLISTS, THE

Fitzgerald, Geraldine
PAWNBROKER, THE
WATCH ON THE RHINE

Flynn, Errol
AGAINST ALL FLAGS
ASSAULT OF THE REBEL GIRLS
CHARGE OF THE LIGHT BRIGADE, THE
DAWN PATROL, THE
DESPERATE JOURNEY
EDGE OF DARKNESS
KIM
NORTHERN PURSUIT
OBJECTIVE, BURMA!
SEA HAWK, THE
THEY DIED WITH THEIR BOOTS ON

Fonda, Henry
BATTLE OF THE BULGE
DRUMS ALONG THE MOHAWK
FAIL SAFE
FORT APACHE
IMMORTAL SERGEANT, THE
LONGEST DAY, THE
MIDWAY
MISTER ROBERTS
WAR AND PEACE

Fonda, Jane
COMING HOME

Ford, Glenn
FOUR HORSEMEN OF THE APOCALYPSE, THE
MIDWAY

Ford, Harrison
FORCE 10 FROM NAVARONE
HEROES

Fossey, Brigitte
FORBIDDEN GAMES

Foster, Preston
GUADALCANAL DIARY

Fox, Edward
WILD GEESE II

Franciscus, James
SNOW TREASURE

Gabin, Jean
GRAND ILLUSION

Gable, Clark
GONE WITH THE WIND
RUN SILENT, RUN DEEP

Gardner, Ava
55 DAYS AT PEKING
ON THE BEACH
SEVEN DAYS IN MAY

Garfield, John
DESTINATION TOKYO

Garland, Judy
JUDGMENT AT NUREMBERG

Garner, James
DARBY'S RANGERS
GREAT ESCAPE, THE

Garson, Greer
MRS. MINIVER

Gavin, John
TIME TO LOVE AND A TIME TO DIE, A

Gazzara, Ben
BRIDGE AT REMAGEN, THE

Genn, Leo
WOODEN HORSE, THE

Gere, Richard
OFFICER AND A GENTLEMAN, AN

Giannini, Giancarlo
LOVE AND ANARCHY

Gibson, Mel
GALLIPOLI
YEAR OF LIVING DANGEROUSLY, THE

Gielgud, John
RICHARD III

Glenn, Scott
KEEP, THE
WILD GEESE II

Gossett, Jr., Louis
IRON EAGLE
IRON EAGLE II

Gould, Elliott
M*A*S*H

Grable, Betty
YANK IN THE R.A.F., A

Granger, Farley
NORTH STAR, THE

Grant, Cary
DESTINATION TOKYO
FATHER GOOSE
GUNGA DIN
OPERATION PETTICOAT

Greenstreet, Sydney
CASABLANCA
PASSAGE TO MARSEILLE

Grey, Joel
CABARET

Guinness, Alec
BRIDGE ON THE RIVER KWAI, THE
CROMWELL
DAMN THE DEFIANT!
HITLER: THE LAST TEN DAYS
LAWRENCE OF ARABIA
MALTA STORY
TUNES OF GLORY

Hackman, Gene
BAT 21
MARCH OR DIE

ACTORS

UNCOMMON VALOR
UNDER FIRE

Hanks, Tom
EVERY TIME WE SAY GOODBYE

Hardwicke, Sir Cedric
DESERT FOX, THE
RICHARD III

Hardy, Oliver
FLYING DEUCES, THE
GREAT GUNS

Harris, Ed
CODE NAME: EMERALD
WALKER

Harris, Julie
HIDING PLACE, THE

Harris, Richard
CROMWELL
WILD GEESE, THE

Harrison, Rex
NIGHT TRAIN

Harvey, Laurence
ALAMO, THE

Hauer, Rutger
FLESH AND BLOOD
SOLDIER OF ORANGE

Hawkins, Jack
CRUEL SEA, THE
MALTA STORY
ZULU

Hawn, Goldie
PRIVATE BENJAMIN
SWING SHIFT

Hayden, Sterling
BATTLE TAXI
DR. STRANGELOVE: OR HOW I LEARNED TO STOP WORRYING AND LOVE THE BOMB
FLAT TOP

Hayes, Helen
FAREWELL TO ARMS, A

Hayward, Susan
CONQUEROR, THE
FIGHTING SEABEES, THE

Heflin, Van
BATTLE CRY
CRY OF BATTLE

Hemmings, David
POWER PLAY

Henreid, Paul
CASABLANCA
FOUR HORSEMEN OF THE APOCALYPSE, THE

Hepburn, Audrey
WAR AND PEACE

Hepburn, Katharine
AFRICAN QUEEN, THE
DRAGON SEED

Heston, Charlton
55 DAYS AT PEKING
BUCCANEER, THE
EL CID

MIDWAY

Hines, Gregory
OFF LIMITS

Hobson, Valerie
ADVENTURES OF TARTU, THE
DRUMS

Hodiak, John
DRAGONFLY SQUADRON

Hoffman, Dustin
LITTLE BIG MAN
MARATHON MAN

Holden, William
ALVAREZ KELLY
BRIDGE ON THE RIVER KWAI, THE
BRIDGES AT TOKO-RI, THE
HORSE SOLDIERS, THE
STALAG 17

Holt, Tim
HITLER'S CHILDREN

Hoskins, Bob
PRAYER FOR THE DYING, A

Howard, Leslie
49TH PARALLEL
GONE WITH THE WIND
PIMPERNEL SMITH
SPITFIRE

Howard, Trevor
BATTLE OF BRITAIN, THE
COCKLESHELL HEROES, THE
FATHER GOOSE
GLORY AT SEA
MORITURI
SEA WOLVES, THE
VON RYAN'S EXPRESS

Hudson, Rock
TOBRUK

Hunt, Linda
ELENI
YEAR OF LIVING DANGEROUSLY, THE

Hunter, Jeffrey
HELL TO ETERNITY

Hurt, William
TIME OF DESTINY, A

Huston, Anjelica
GARDENS OF STONE

Huston, Walter
DRAGON SEED
EDGE OF DARKNESS

Hutton, Timothy
TAPS
TIME OF DESTINY, A

Ives, Burl
ENSIGN PULVER

Jackson, Glenda
RETURN OF THE SOLDIER, THE

Janssen, David
HELL TO ETERNITY

Jayston, Michael
NICHOLAS AND ALEXANDRA

Johns, Glynis
ADVENTURES OF TARTU, THE

FRIEDA

Johnson, Van
GO FOR BROKE
GUY NAMED JOE, A
THIRTY SECONDS OVER TOKYO

Jones, James Earl
GARDENS OF STONE

Jones, Tommy Lee
ROLLING THUNDER

Jurgens, Curt
BATTLE OF NERETVA
DIRTY HEROES
INN OF THE SIXTH HAPPINESS, THE
MIRACLE OF THE WHITE STALLIONS

Kaminska, Ida
SHOP ON MAIN STREET, THE

Karloff, Boris
LOST PATROL, THE

Kaye, Danny
UP IN ARMS

Keaton, Diane
LITTLE DRUMMER GIRL, THE
LOVE AND DEATH
REDS

Keitel, Harvey
DUELLISTS, THE

Keith, David
LORDS OF DISCIPLINE, THE

Kellerman, Sally
M*A*S*H

Kelly, Grace
BRIDGES AT TOKO-RI, THE

Kerr, Deborah
FROM HERE TO ETERNITY
LIFE AND DEATH OF COLONEL BLIMP, THE

Kinski, Klaus
LITTLE DRUMMER GIRL, THE

Kinski, Nastassja
REVOLUTION

Kruger, Hardy
BATTLE OF NERETVA
ONE THAT GOT AWAY, THE

Kruger, Otto
SABOTEUR

Kyo, Machiko
GATE OF HELL

Ladd, Alan
DEEP SIX, THE

Ladd, Cheryl
PURPLE HEARTS

Lancaster, Burt
FROM HERE TO ETERNITY
GO TELL THE SPARTANS
JUDGMENT AT NUREMBERG
RUN SILENT, RUN DEEP
SEVEN DAYS IN MAY
TRAIN, THE
TWILIGHT'S LAST GLEAMING
ULZANA'S RAID
ZULU DAWN

ACTORS

Lane, Priscilla
SABOTEUR

Laughton, Charles
THIS LAND IS MINE

Laurel, Stan
FLYING DEUCES, THE
GREAT GUNS

Le Mat, Paul
HANOI HILTON, THE

Leigh, Jennifer Jason
FLESH AND BLOOD

Leigh, Vivien
DARK JOURNEY
FIRE OVER ENGLAND
GONE WITH THE WIND
THAT HAMILTON WOMAN

Leighton, Margaret
COURT MARTIAL

Lemmon, Jack
MISSING
MISTER ROBERTS
WACKIEST SHIP IN THE ARMY, THE

Lennon, John
HOW I WON THE WAR

Lewis, Jerry
WHICH WAY TO THE FRONT?

Lindfors, Viveca
FOUR IN A JEEP

Lithgow, John
DISTANT THUNDER

Livesey, Roger
LIFE AND DEATH OF COLONEL BLIMP, THE

Lombard, Carole
TO BE OR NOT TO BE

Loren, Sophia
BRASS TARGET
EL CID
TWO WOMEN

Lorre, Peter
PASSAGE TO MARSEILLE

Loy, Myrna
BEST YEARS OF OUR LIVES, THE

Lukas, Paul
WATCH ON THE RHINE

Luppi, Federico
FUNNY, DIRTY LITTLE WAR, A

Lynch, John
CAL

Macchio, Ralph
DISTANT THUNDER

Madison, Guy
DRUMS IN THE DEEP SOUTH

Magnani, Anna
OPEN CITY

Maharis, George
LAST DAY OF THE WAR, THE

Makepeace, Chris
CAPTIVE HEARTS

Malden, Karl
PATTON

Malkovich, John
ELENI
EMPIRE OF THE SUN

Manesse, Gaspard
AU REVOIR LES ENFANTS

March, Fredric
ALEXANDER THE GREAT
BEST YEARS OF OUR LIVES, THE
BRIDGES AT TOKO-RI, THE

Martin, Dean
YOUNG LIONS, THE

Martin, Jean
BATTLE OF ALGIERS, THE

Marvin, Lee
BIG RED ONE, THE
DELTA FORCE, THE
DIRTY DOZEN, THE
SHOUT AT THE DEVIL

Marx, Chico
DUCK SOUP

Marx, Groucho
DUCK SOUP

Marx, Harpo
DUCK SOUP

Marx, Zeppo
DUCK SOUP

Mason, James
ASSISI UNDERGROUND, THE
BLUE MAX, THE
BOYS FROM BRAZIL, THE
CROSS OF IRON
DESERT FOX, THE

Mason, Marsha
HEARTBREAK RIDGE

Massey, Raymond
49TH PARALLEL
DESPERATE JOURNEY
DRUMS
FIRE OVER ENGLAND

Mastroianni, Marcello
MASSACRE IN ROME

Matthau, Walter
ENSIGN PULVER
FAIL SAFE

McAnally, Ray
CAL

McCrea, Joel
FOREIGN CORRESPONDENT

McGillis, Kelly
TOP GUN

McGlynn, Sr., Frank
LAST OF THE MOHICANS, THE

McLaglen, Victor
CALL OUT THE MARINES
GUNGA DIN
LOST PATROL, THE

McQueen, Steve
GREAT ESCAPE, THE
SAND PEBBLES, THE

WAR LOVER, THE

Meeker, Ralph
FOUR IN A JEEP

Melato, Mariangela
LOVE AND ANARCHY

Menjou, Adolphe
PATHS OF GLORY

Mifune, Toshiro
MIDWAY
THRONE OF BLOOD

Miles, Sarah
HOPE AND GLORY

Milland, Ray
BEAU GESTE

Mills, John
COLDITZ STORY, THE
IN WHICH WE SERVE
TUNES OF GLORY
WE DIVE AT DAWN

Minnelli, Liza
CABARET

Mirren, Helen
CAL

Mitchum, Robert
ANZIO
LONGEST DAY, THE

Modine, Matthew
BIRDY
FULL METAL JACKET
STREAMERS

Montgomery, George
STEEL CLAW, THE
WARKILL

Montgomery, Robert
THEY WERE EXPENDABLE

Moore, Dudley
BEST DEFENSE

Moore, Roger
ESCAPE TO ATHENA
SEA WOLVES, THE
WILD GEESE, THE

Moreau, Jeanne
CHIMES AT MIDNIGHT

Moriarty, Michael
HANOI HILTON, THE

Morita, Noriyuki [Pat]
CAPTIVE HEARTS

Morley, Robert
CROMWELL

Muni, Paul
COMMANDOS STRIKE AT DAWN, THE

Murphy, Audie
RED BADGE OF COURAGE, THE
TO HELL AND BACK

Murphy, Eddie
BEST DEFENSE

Murphy, George
THIS IS THE ARMY

Murray, Bill
RAZOR'S EDGE, THE

ACTORS

Naish, J. Carrol
BEHIND THE RISING SUN
SAHARA

Neagle, Anna
NURSE EDITH CAVELL

Neal, Patricia
IN HARM'S WAY

Neal, Tom
BEHIND THE RISING SUN
FIRST YANK INTO TOKYO

Nelligan, Kate
ELENI
EYE OF THE NEEDLE

Newhart, Bob
CATCH-22

Newman, Barry
SALZBURG CONNECTION, THE

Newman, Paul
SECRET WAR OF HARRY FRIGG, THE

Ngor, Haing S.
KILLING FIELDS, THE

Nicholson, Jack
REDS

Niven, David
55 DAYS AT PEKING
COURT MARTIAL
DAWN PATROL, THE
ESCAPE TO ATHENA
GUNS OF NAVARONE, THE
IMMORTAL BATTALION, THE
SEA WOLVES, THE
SPITFIRE

Nolan, Lloyd
GUADALCANAL DIARY

Nolte, Nick
FAREWELL TO THE KING
UNDER FIRE
WHO'LL STOP THE RAIN?

Norris, Chuck
BRADDOCK: MISSING IN ACTION III
DELTA FORCE, THE
INVASION U.S.A.
MISSING IN ACTION
MISSING IN ACTION 2—THE BEGINNING

O'Brien, Pat
BOMBARDIER

O'Connor, Donald
FRANCIS IN THE NAVY

O'Hara, Maureen
AGAINST ALL FLAGS
IMMORTAL SERGEANT, THE
RIO GRANDE
THIS LAND IS MINE

O'Herlihy, Dan
FAIL SAFE

O'Toole, Peter
LAWRENCE OF ARABIA
MURPHY'S WAR
NIGHT OF THE GENERALS, THE
POWER PLAY
ZULU DAWN

Oberon, Merle
BERLIN EXPRESS

Okada, Eiji
HIROSHIMA, MON AMOUR

Olin, Lena
UNBEARABLE LIGHTNESS OF BEING, THE

Olivier, Laurence
49TH PARALLEL
BATTLE OF BRITAIN, THE
BOYS FROM BRAZIL, THE
FIRE OVER ENGLAND
HENRY V
MARATHON MAN
RICHARD III
SPARTACUS
THAT HAMILTON WOMAN
WILD GEESE II

Pacino, Al
REVOLUTION

Palmer, Lilli
CLOAK AND DAGGER
MIRACLE OF THE WHITE STALLIONS

Papas, Irene
ASSISI UNDERGROUND, THE

Patric, Jason
BEAST, THE

Peck, Gregory
BEHOLD A PALE HORSE
BOYS FROM BRAZIL, THE
DAYS OF GLORY
GUNS OF NAVARONE, THE
MAC ARTHUR
ON THE BEACH
PORK CHOP HILL
SEA WOLVES, THE
TWELVE O'CLOCK HIGH

Peppard, George
BLUE MAX, THE
FROM HELL TO VICTORY

Perkins, Anthony
ON THE BEACH

Perkins, Millie
DIARY OF ANNE FRANK, THE

Pidgeon, Walter
MRS. MINIVER

Pleasence, Donald
GREAT ESCAPE, THE
HANNA'S WAR
NIGHT OF THE GENERALS, THE
POWER PLAY

Powell, Dick
CORNERED

Power, Tyrone
RAZOR'S EDGE, THE
THIS ABOVE ALL
YANK IN THE R.A.F., A

Preston, Robert
BEAU GESTE

Prochnow, Jurgen
BOAT, THE

Pryor, Richard
SOME KIND OF HERO

Quayle, Anthony
PURSUIT OF THE GRAF SPEE, THE

Quinn, Anthony
AGAINST ALL FLAGS
BACK TO BATAAN
BEHOLD A PALE HORSE
GUNS OF NAVARONE, THE
LAWRENCE OF ARABIA
LION OF THE DESERT
LOST COMMAND, THE

Raft, George
OUTPOST IN MOROCCO

Rains, Claude
CASABLANCA
PASSAGE TO MARSEILLE
SEA HAWK, THE

Rampling, Charlotte
NIGHT PORTER, THE

Rathbone, Basil
DAWN PATROL, THE
SHERLOCK HOLMES AND THE SECRET WEAPON

Ray, Aldo
BATTLE CRY
NAKED AND THE DEAD, THE

Reagan, Ronald
DESPERATE JOURNEY
HELLCATS OF THE NAVY
THIS IS THE ARMY

Redgrave, Michael
DAM BUSTERS, THE
SEA SHALL NOT HAVE THEM, THE

Reed, Philip
LAST OF THE MOHICANS, THE

Reynolds, Burt
OPERATION CIA

Richardson, Ralph
FOUR FEATHERS, THE
RICHARD III

Ridgely, John
AIR FORCE

Riva, Emmanuelle
HIROSHIMA, MON AMOUR

Robards, Jr., Jason
TORA! TORA! TORA!

Robertson, Cliff
NAKED AND THE DEAD, THE
PT 109
TOO LATE THE HERO

Robertson, Willard
LAST OF THE MOHICANS, THE

Robinson, Edward G.
MR. WINKLE GOES TO WAR
STRANGER, THE

Robson, Flora
FIRE OVER ENGLAND

Rosay, Francoise
CARNIVAL IN FLANDERS

ACTORS

Rourke, Mickey
PRAYER FOR THE DYING, A

Russell, Kurt
SWING SHIFT

Ryan, Robert
ANZIO
BATTLE OF THE BULGE
BERLIN EXPRESS
FLYING LEATHERNECKS
LONGEST DAY, THE
MEN IN WAR

Saadi, Yacef
BATTLE OF ALGIERS, THE

Sanda, Dominique
GARDEN OF THE FINZI-CONTINIS, THE

Sanders, George
ACTION IN ARABIA

Savage, John
BRADY'S ESCAPE
DEER HUNTER, THE
SOLDIER'S REVENGE

Savalas, Telly
ESCAPE TO ATHENA
KELLY'S HEROES

Schell, Maximilian
ASSISI UNDERGROUND, THE
CROSS OF IRON
JUDGMENT AT NUREMBERG
ODESSA FILE, THE

Schildkraut, Joseph
DIARY OF ANNE FRANK, THE

Schygulla, Hanna
LOVE IN GERMANY, A
MARRIAGE OF MARIA BRAUN, THE

Scofield, Paul
TRAIN, THE

Scott, George C.
DR. STRANGELOVE: OR HOW I LEARNED TO STOP WORRYING AND LOVE THE BOMB
HINDENBURG, THE
PATTON
TAPS

Scott, Randolph
BOMBARDIER
GUNG HO!
LAST OF THE MOHICANS, THE

Segal, George
BRIDGE AT REMAGEN, THE
KING RAT
LOST COMMAND, THE

Sellers, Peter
DR. STRANGELOVE: OR HOW I LEARNED TO STOP WORRYING AND LOVE THE BOMB
MOUSE THAT ROARED, THE

Sharif, Omar
BEHOLD A PALE HORSE
DOCTOR ZHIVAGO
NIGHT OF THE GENERALS, THE

Shaw, Robert
BATTLE OF THE BULGE
FORCE 10 FROM NAVARONE

Shaw, Stan
BOYS IN COMPANY C, THE

Sheen, Charlie
PLATOON

Sheen, Martin
APOCALYPSE NOW
FINAL COUNTDOWN, THE
NO DRUMS, NO BUGLES

Sheridan, Ann
EDGE OF DARKNESS

Simmons, Jean
DESIREE
SPARTACUS

Sinatra, Frank
FROM HERE TO ETERNITY
VON RYAN'S EXPRESS

Slezak, Walter
LIFEBOAT

Spacek, Sissy
MISSING

Stallone, Sylvester
FIRST BLOOD
RAMBO III
RAMBO: FIRST BLOOD, PART II
VICTORY

Stanton, Will
LAST OF THE MOHICANS, THE

Steiger, Rod
COURT-MARTIAL OF BILLY MITCHELL, THE
LONGEST DAY, THE
PAWNBROKER, THE

Stewart, James
SHENANDOAH

Stockwell, Dean
KIM

Streep, Meryl
DEER HUNTER, THE
PLENTY

Sutherland, Donald
EAGLE HAS LANDED, THE
EYE OF THE NEEDLE
M*A*S*H
REVOLUTION
START THE REVOLUTION WITHOUT ME

Suzman, Janet
NICHOLAS AND ALEXANDRA

Swayze, Patrick
RED DAWN

Sweeney, D.B.
GARDENS OF STONE

Tamiroff, Akim
OUTPOST IN MOROCCO

Taylor, Robert
BATAAN
D-DAY, THE SIXTH OF JUNE
MIRACLE OF THE WHITE STALLIONS

Temple, Shirley
FORT APACHE

Tierney, Gene
RAZOR'S EDGE, THE
SUNDOWN

Todd, Richard
BATTLE HELL
D-DAY, THE SIXTH OF JUNE
DAM BUSTERS, THE

Tone, Franchot
LIVES OF A BENGAL LANCER

Tracy, Spencer
GUY NAMED JOE, A
JUDGMENT AT NUREMBERG
THIRTY SECONDS OVER TOKYO

Truffaut, Francois
GREEN ROOM, THE

Ustinov, Peter
LAST REMAKE OF BEAU GESTE, THE

Van Cleef, Lee
GOOD, THE BAD, AND THE UGLY, THE

Vaughn, Robert
BRIDGE AT REMAGEN, THE

Veidt, Conrad
DARK JOURNEY
SPY IN BLACK, THE

Voight, Jon
COMING HOME
ODESSA FILE, THE

von Stroheim, Erich
CRIMSON ROMANCE
GRAND ILLUSION

Von Sydow, Max
CODE NAME: EMERALD
MARCH OR DIE
VOYAGE OF THE DAMNED

von Trotta, Margarethe
COUP DE GRACE

Wagner, Robert
WAR LOVER, THE

Wahl, Ken
PURPLE HEARTS

Walken, Christopher
BILOXI BLUES
DEADLINE
DEER HUNTER, THE
DOGS OF WAR, THE

Walker, Jr., Robert
ANGKOR-CAMBODIA EXPRESS
ENSIGN PULVER

Walker, Robert
THIRTY SECONDS OVER TOKYO

Wallach, Eli
GOOD, THE BAD, AND THE UGLY, THE

Waterston, Sam
KILLING FIELDS, THE

Wayne, John
ALAMO, THE
BACK TO BATAAN
CONQUEROR, THE
FIGHTING SEABEES, THE

CINEMATOGRAPHERS

FLYING LEATHERNECKS
FLYING TIGERS
FORT APACHE
GREEN BERETS, THE
HORSE SOLDIERS, THE
IN HARM'S WAY
LONGEST DAY, THE
RIO GRANDE
SANDS OF IWO JIMA
SHE WORE A YELLOW RIBBON
THEY WERE EXPENDABLE

Weaver, Dennis
MISSION BATANGAS

Weaver, Sigourney
YEAR OF LIVING DANGEROUSLY, THE

Webb, Jack
D.I., THE

Weld, Tuesday
WHO'LL STOP THE RAIN?

Welles, Orson
CHIMES AT MIDNIGHT
STRANGER, THE
VOYAGE OF THE DAMNED

Whitaker, Forest
GOOD MORNING, VIETNAM

Widmark, Richard
ALAMO, THE
ALVAREZ KELLY
DESTINATION GOBI
FINAL OPTION, THE
JUDGMENT AT NUREMBERG
TWILIGHT'S LAST GLEAMING

Wilcoxon, Henry
LAST OF THE MOHICANS, THE

Wilder, Gene
START THE REVOLUTION WITHOUT ME

Williams, Robin
GOOD MORNING, VIETNAM

Winger, Debra
OFFICER AND A GENTLEMAN, AN

Winkler, Henry
HEROES

Winters, Shelley
DIARY OF ANNE FRANK, THE

Woods, James
SALVADOR

Woodward, Edward
BREAKER MORANT

Wright, Teresa
BEST YEARS OF OUR LIVES, THE
MEN, THE

York, Michael
LAST REMAKE OF BEAU GESTE, THE
RIDDLE OF THE SANDS, THE

Young, Gig
AIR FORCE

Young, Loretta
STRANGER, THE

CINEMATOGRAPHERS

Agostini, Claude
BLACK AND WHITE IN COLOR

Alcaine, Jose Luis
FROM HELL TO VICTORY

Alcott, John
MARCH OR DIE
UNDER FIRE

Alekan, Henri
AUSTERLITZ

Allwork, Peter
EAGLE HAS LANDED, THE

Almendros, Nestor
GREEN ROOM, THE
LAST METRO, THE

Alphen, Jean-Paul
LA MARSEILLAISE

Anders, Gunther
MIRACLE OF THE WHITE STALLIONS

Andriot, Lucien
OUTPOST IN MOROCCO

Arata, Ubaldo
OPEN CITY

Arnold, Peter
COUP DE GRACE

Aronovich, Ricardo
MISSING

August, Joseph H.
GUNGA DIN
NURSE EDITH CAVELL
THEY WERE EXPENDABLE

Baberske, Robert
KAMERADSCHAFT

Badal, Jean
BEHOLD A PALE HORSE

Baggot, King
SOME KIND OF HERO

Baker, Ian
PLENTY

Ballard, Lucien
BERLIN EXPRESS
DESERT RATS, THE
MOROCCO

Ballhaus, Michael
MARRIAGE OF MARIA BRAUN, THE

Bartlett, Parker
NO DRUMS, NO BUGLES

Berenger, Manuel
55 DAYS AT PEKING

Bergamini, Gianni
DIRTY HEROES

Bergli, Sverre
SNOW TREASURE

Berna, Emil
FOUR IN A JEEP

Berta, Renato
AU REVOIR LES ENFANTS

Biroc, Joseph
HITLER
TOO LATE THE HERO
ULZANA'S RAID

Blake, Stephen Ashley
NIGHTWARS

Bode, Ralf D.
DISTANT THUNDER

Borradaile, Osmond
DRUMS
FOUR FEATHERS, THE

Bourgoin, Jean
LONGEST DAY, THE

Bourgoin, Jean-Serge
LA MARSEILLAISE

Boyd, Russell
GALLIPOLI
YEAR OF LIVING DANGEROUSLY, THE

Boyle, Charles P.
SHE WORE A YELLOW RIBBON

Bradford, William
FIGHTING SEABEES, THE

Brenner, Jules
JOHNNY GOT HIS GUN

Bridges, David
WALKER

Brodine, Norbert
DESERT FOX, THE

Browne, Bernard
SPY IN BLACK, THE

Burgess, Don
DEATH BEFORE DISHONOR

Burum, Stephen H.
UNCOMMON VALOR

Butler, Bill
BILOXI BLUES

Capriotti, Mario
TWO WOMEN

Cardiff, Jack
AFRICAN QUEEN, THE
DIARY OF ANNE FRANK, THE
DOGS OF WAR, THE
FOUR FEATHERS, THE
LIFE AND DEATH OF COLONEL BLIMP, THE
RAMBO: FIRST BLOOD, PART II
WAR AND PEACE

Carlini, Carlo
GENERALE DELLA ROVERE

Caso, Alan
84 CHARLIE MOPIC

Challis, Christopher
DAMN THE DEFIANT!
DRUMS
FORCE 10 FROM NAVARONE
PURSUIT OF THE GRAF SPEE, THE
RIDDLE OF THE SANDS, THE

Clarke, Charles
DESTINATION GOBI
GUADALCANAL DIARY

CINEMATOGRAPHERS

Cloquet, Ghislain
LOVE AND DEATH

Clothier, William
ALAMO, THE
DARBY'S RANGERS
HORSE SOLDIERS, THE
SHENANDOAH

Collister, Peter
SUPERNATURALS, THE

Colman, Edward
D.I., THE

Conde, Fred
TASTE OF HELL, A

Contini, Alfio
NIGHT PORTER, THE

Coquillon, John
CROSS OF IRON

Cortez, Stanley
BRIDGE AT REMAGEN, THE

Costikyan, Andrew M.
BANANAS

Coutard, Raoul
LES CARABINIERS

Cox, Jack
WE DIVE AT DAWN

Cox, John J.
ADVENTURES OF TARTU, THE

Cronenweth, Jordan
GARDENS OF STONE
ROLLING THUNDER

Cross, Eric
ONE THAT GOT AWAY, THE

Curik, Jan
TRANSPORT FROM PARADISE

Dade, Stephen
SEA SHALL NOT HAVE THEM, THE
ZULU

Daniels, William
AWAY ALL BOATS
VON RYAN'S EXPRESS

Davanzati, Roberto Forges
ANGKOR-CAMBODIA EXPRESS

Daviau, Allen
EMPIRE OF THE SUN

De Bont, Jan
FLESH AND BLOOD

De Bont, Peter
SOLDIER OF ORANGE

de Grasse, Robert
CLAY PIGEON, THE
HOME OF THE BRAVE
MEN, THE

De Santis, Pasquale
DAMNED, THE

De Vinna, Clyde
IMMORTAL SERGEANT, THE

Decae, Henri
BOYS FROM BRAZIL, THE
NIGHT OF THE GENERALS, THE

Delli Colli, Tonino
GOOD, THE BAD, AND THE UGLY, THE

di Giacomo, Franco
NIGHT OF THE SHOOTING STARS, THE

Dickinson, Desmond
BLACK TENT, THE
COURT MARTIAL

Dines, Gordon
COLDITZ STORY, THE
CRUEL SEA, THE
FRIEDA

Dostie, Alain
IRON EAGLE II

Douarinou, Alain
LA MARSEILLAISE

Dyer, Elmer
AIR FORCE

Edeson, Arthur
ALL QUIET ON THE WESTERN FRONT
CASABLANCA
SERGEANT YORK

Fapp, Daniel L.
GREAT ESCAPE, THE
ON THE BEACH

Fernandes, Joao
BRADDOCK: MISSING IN ACTION III
INVASION U.S.A.
MISSING IN ACTION

Figueroa, Gabriel
KELLY'S HEROES

Fisher, Gerry
LAST REMAKE OF BEAU GESTE, THE
VICTORY

Folsey, George
GUY NAMED JOE, A

Fraker, William A.
1941
WARGAMES

Francis, Freddie
CODE NAME: EMERALD

Fredricks, Ellsworth
SAYONARA
SEVEN DAYS IN MAY

Freund, Karl
GUY NAMED JOE, A

Freund, (uncredited) Karl
ALL QUIET ON THE WESTERN FRONT

Fujimoto, Tak
SWING SHIFT

Furuya, Osami
TORA! TORA! TORA!

Garfath, Mike
PRAYER FOR THE DYING, A

Garmes, Lee
D-DAY, THE SIXTH OF JUNE
GONE WITH THE WIND
MOROCCO

Garroni, Romolo
LAST DAY OF THE WAR, THE

Gatti, Marcello
BATTLE OF ALGIERS, THE
BURN
MASSACRE IN ROME

Gaudio, Tony
DAWN PATROL, THE
DAYS OF GLORY

Gerstad, Merritt
WATCH ON THE RHINE

Gertsman, Maury
TO HELL AND BACK

Gibbs, Gerald
HILL 24 DOESN'T ANSWER

Glennon, Bert
DESPERATE JOURNEY
DESTINATION TOKYO
DRUMS ALONG THE MOHAWK
RIO GRANDE
THEY DIED WITH THEIR BOOTS ON
THIS IS THE ARMY

Glennon, James
TIME OF DESTINY, A

Godar, Godfrey A.
BOYS IN COMPANY C, THE

Goldblatt, Stephen
RETURN OF THE SOLDIER, THE

Grant, Freddie C.
NO DEAD HEROES

Green, Guy
IMMORTAL BATTALION, THE

Green, Jack N.
HEARTBREAK RIDGE

Greenbaum, Mutz
PIMPERNEL SMITH

Greenberg, Adam
BIG RED ONE, THE
IRON EAGLE

Gribble, David
OFF LIMITS

Griggs, Loyal
BRIDGES AT TOKO-RI, THE
BUCCANEER, THE
IN HARM'S WAY

Guarnieri, Ennio
GARDEN OF THE FINZI-CONTINIS, THE
HITLER: THE LAST TEN DAYS

Guffey, Burnett
FROM HERE TO ETERNITY
HELL TO ETERNITY
KING RAT

Gurfinkel, David
DELTA FORCE, THE

Guthrie, Carl
FRANCIS IN THE NAVY

Hall, Conrad
MARATHON MAN
MORITURI

Haller, Ernest
GONE WITH THE WIND
MEN IN WAR

CINEMATOGRAPHERS

Hannan, Peter
RAZOR'S EDGE, THE

Harlan, Russell
OPERATION PETTICOAT
TOBRUK
WALK IN THE SUN, A

Harris, John
HOPE AND GLORY

Hauser, Robert
SOLDIER BLUE
TWILIGHT'S LAST GLEAMING

Heller, Otto
RICHARD III

Hickox, Sid
BATTLE CRY
DISTANT DRUMS
EDGE OF DARKNESS
NORTHERN PURSUIT

Hildyard, Jack
55 DAYS AT PEKING
BATTLE OF THE BULGE
BRIDGE ON THE RIVER KWAI, THE
HENRY V
LION OF THE DESERT
PIMPERNEL SMITH
WILD GEESE, THE

Hillier, Erwin
DAM BUSTERS, THE

Himeda, Shinsaku
TORA! TORA! TORA!

Hirschfeld, Gerald
FAIL SAFE
TO BE OR NOT TO BE

Hoch, Winton C.
GREEN BERETS, THE
MISTER ROBERTS
SHE WORE A YELLOW RIBBON

Howe, James Wong
AIR FORCE
FIRE OVER ENGLAND
NORTH STAR, THE
OBJECTIVE, BURMA!
PASSAGE TO MARSEILLE

Huke, Bob
BATTLE OF BRITAIN, THE
WAR LOVER, THE

Hume, Alan
EYE OF THE NEEDLE

Hunt, J. Roy
ACTION IN ARABIA
CALL OUT THE MARINES

Ibbetson, Arthur
TUNES OF GLORY
WHERE EAGLES DARE

Imi, Tony
BRASS TARGET
SEA WOLVES, THE

Irwin, Mark
BAT 21
HANOI HILTON, THE

James, Peter
REBEL

Juillard, Robert
FORBIDDEN GAMES
GERMANY, YEAR ZERO

Kanturek, Otto
NIGHT TRAIN

Kaufman, Boris
PAWNBROKER, THE

Kelley, W. Wallace
WHICH WAY TO THE FRONT?

Kemper, Victor J.
FINAL COUNTDOWN, THE

Kiesser, Jan
PURPLE HEARTS

Kimball, Jeffrey
TOP GUN

Kline, Richard H.
WHO'LL STOP THE RAIN?

Kobayashi, Setsuo
FIRES ON THE PLAIN

Koenekamp, Fred
PATTON

Koenig, Klaus
PEDESTRIAN, THE

Koltai, Lajos
COLONEL REDL
MEPHISTO

Krasker, Robert
ALEXANDER THE GREAT
DRUMS
EL CID
HENRY V
MALTA STORY

Krasner, Milton
BUCK PRIVATES
DESIREE
FOUR HORSEMEN OF THE APOCALYPSE, THE
GUNG HO!

Krause, George
PATHS OF GLORY

Kristiansen, Henning
ONLY WAY, THE

Kucera, Jaroslav
DIAMONDS OF THE NIGHT

Kuhle, Hans
WHITE GHOST

L'Homme, Pierre
KING OF HEARTS

Lanci, Giuseppe
EVERY TIME WE SAY GOODBYE

Lang, Charles
FAREWELL TO ARMS, A
LIVES OF A BENGAL LANCER
SUNDOWN

Lang, Jr., Charles
FATHER GOOSE

Lanning, Reggie
SANDS OF IWO JIMA

LaShelle, Joseph
CONQUEROR, THE
NAKED AND THE DEAD, THE

Laszlo, Andrew
FIRST BLOOD
SOUTHERN COMFORT

Laszlo, Ernest
JUDGMENT AT NUREMBERG
STALAG 17

Lawton, Charles
ENSIGN PULVER
WACKIEST SHIP IN THE ARMY, THE

Leavitt, Sam
COURT-MARTIAL OF BILLY MITCHELL, THE
PORK CHOP HILL

Leclerc, Georges
ELUSIVE CORPORAL, THE

Linden, Lionel
DRUMS IN THE DEEP SOUTH

Lipman, Jerzy
KANAL

Lippman, Irving
HELLCATS OF THE NAVY

Lloyd, Art
FLYING DEUCES, THE

Louis, J.
LA MARSEILLAISE

Luther, Igor
COUP DE GRACE
DANTON
LOVE IN GERMANY, A
TIN DRUM, THE

Lutic, Bernard
REVOLUTION

McAlpine, Don
BREAKER MORANT
DON'T CRY, IT'S ONLY THUNDER
ODD ANGRY SHOT, THE

McCarthy, Richard
NO DRUMS, NO BUGLES

MacDonald, Joseph
ALVAREZ KELLY
SAND PEBBLES, THE
TARAS BULBA
WHAT PRICE GLORY?
YOUNG LIONS, THE

MacDonald, Peter
HAMBURGER HILL

MacWilliams, Glen
GREAT GUNS
LIFEBOAT

Maillols, Jean-Marie
LA MARSEILLAISE

Marta, Jack
FLYING TIGERS

Martelli, Otello
PAISAN

Mate, Rudolf
SAHARA

Mate, Rudolph
FOREIGN CORRESPONDENT
THAT HAMILTON WOMAN

CINEMATOGRAPHERS

TO BE OR NOT TO BE

Matras, Christian
GRAND ILLUSION

Mauch, Thomas
DEADLINE

Meheux, Phil
FINAL OPTION, THE

Mellor, William C.
COMMANDOS STRIKE AT DAWN, THE
DIARY OF ANNE FRANK, THE

Menges, Chris
KILLING FIELDS, THE

Metty, Russell
AGAINST ALL FLAGS
BEHIND THE RISING SUN
HITLER'S CHILDREN
MASTER RACE, THE
SECRET WAR OF HARRY FRIGG, THE
SPARTACUS
STRANGER, THE
TIME TO LOVE AND A TIME TO DIE, A

Mignot, Pierre
STREAMERS

Miller, Arthur
IMMORTAL SERGEANT, THE
PURPLE HEART, THE
RAZOR'S EDGE, THE
THIS ABOVE ALL

Miller, Ernest
CRIMSON ROMANCE

Milsome, Douglas
BEAST, THE
FULL METAL JACKET

Miyagawa, Kazuo
KAGEMUSHA
MACARTHUR'S CHILDREN

Miyajima, Yoshio
HUMAN CONDITION, THE

Mohr, Hal
WATCH ON THE RHINE

Montazel, Pierre
NAPOLEON

Moore, Richard
OPERATION CIA

Moore, Ted
COCKLESHELL HEROES, THE

Morris, Oswald
GUNS OF NAVARONE, THE
ODESSA FILE, THE

Moskvin, Andrei
IVAN THE TERRIBLE, PARTS I & II

Musuraca, Nicholas
BACK TO BATAAN
BOMBARDIER
CALL OUT THE MARINES

Nakai, Asaichi
KAGEMUSHA
THRONE OF BLOOD

Nakai, Asakazu
RAN

Nannuzzi, Armando
DAMNED, THE

Narushima, Toichiro
MERRY CHRISTMAS, MR. LAWRENCE

Ne'eman, Yechiel
P.O.W. THE ESCAPE

Neame, Ronald
IN WHICH WE SERVE
ONE OF OUR AIRCRAFT IS MISSING
YANK IN THE R.A.F., A

Neumann, Harry
DRAGONFLY SQUADRON
FLAT TOP

Nikolic, George
MISFIT BRIGADE, THE

Novotny, Vladimir
SHOP ON MAIN STREET, THE

Nykvist, Sven
UNBEARABLE LIGHTNESS OF BEING, THE

Ondricek, Miroslav
SLAUGHTERHOUSE-FIVE

Ornitz, Arthur J.
SOLDIER BLUE

Pallottini, Riccardo
LAST HUNTER, THE

Pennington-Richards, C.
WOODEN HORSE, THE

Perinal, Georges
DARK JOURNEY
DRUMS
FOUR FEATHERS, THE
LIFE AND DEATH OF COLONEL BLIMP, THE
SPITFIRE

Persin, Henri
LONGEST DAY, THE

Peterman, Don
BEST DEFENSE

Petritskiy, Anatoliy
WAR AND PEACE

Pike, Melvin
DR. STRANGELOVE: OR HOW I LEARNED TO STOP WORRYING AND LOVE THE BOMB

Pinter, Tomislav
BATTLE OF NERETVA

Planck, Robert
LAST OF THE MOHICANS, THE

Pogany, Gabor
TWO WOMEN

Polito, Sol
CHARGE OF THE LIGHT BRIGADE, THE
CLOAK AND DAGGER
SEA HAWK, THE
SERGEANT YORK
THIS IS THE ARMY

Poster, Steven
TESTAMENT

Ragalyi, Elemer
HANNA'S WAR

Ragayli, Elemer
BRADY'S ESCAPE

Rath, Earl
RAID ON ROMMEL

Rawi, Ousama
POWER PLAY
ZULU DAWN

Redman, Frank
THIS LAND IS MINE

Reed, Michael
HIDING PLACE, THE
SHOUT AT THE DEVIL
WILD GEESE II

Reed, Paul
GOING HOME

Rennahan, Ray
DRUMS ALONG THE MOHAWK
UP IN ARMS

Richard, Edmond
CHIMES AT MIDNIGHT

Richardson, Robert
PLATOON
SALVADOR

Richmond, Tony
EAGLE HAS LANDED, THE

Roizman, Owen
TAPS

Rojas, Manuel
STEEL CLAW, THE

Rosson, Harold
RED BADGE OF COURAGE, THE
THIRTY SECONDS OVER TOKYO

Rotunno, Giuseppe
ANZIO
ASSISI UNDERGROUND, THE
LOVE AND ANARCHY
ON THE BEACH

Rousselot, Philippe
HOPE AND GLORY

Ruban, Al
DAVID

Ruttenberg, Joseph
MRS. MINIVER

Sacdalan, Felipe
CRY OF BATTLE
HOT BOX, THE

Saito, Takao
KAGEMUSHA
RAN

Salomon, Amnon
DEADLINE

Sato, Masamichi
TORA! TORA! TORA!

Scaife, Edward
DIRTY DOZEN, THE

Schier, Horst
WANNSEE CONFERENCE, THE

CINEMATOGRAPHERS

Schoedsack, Ernest
LIVES OF A BENGAL LANCER

Sealy, Stephen
SOLDIER'S REVENGE

Seitz, John
DEEP SIX, THE

Semler, Dean
FAREWELL TO THE KING

Seresin, Michael
BIRDY

Shamroy, Leon
TWELVE O'CLOCK HIGH
YANK IN THE R.A.F., A

Sharpe, Henry
DUCK SOUP

Sigel, Tom
LATINO

Skall, William V.
KIM

Slocombe, Douglas
BLUE MAX, THE
MURPHY'S WAR

Snyder, William
CONQUEROR, THE
FLYING LEATHERNECKS

Solis, Leonardo
FUNNY, DIRTY LITTLE WAR, A
SOLDIER'S REVENGE

Sova, Peter
GOOD MORNING, VIETNAM

Sparkuhl, Theodor
BEAU GESTE
BLOOD ON THE SUN
WAKE ISLAND

Stahl, Jorge
MISSING IN ACTION 2—THE
BEGINNING

Stanier, John
RAMBO III

Stanley, Frank
HEROES

Stengler, Mack
JUNGLE PATROL

Stine, Clifford
OPERATION PETTICOAT
SPARTACUS
UGLY AMERICAN, THE

Stine, Harold E.
M*A*S*H

Storaro, Vittorio
APOCALYPSE NOW
REDS

Stout, Archie
BEAU GESTE
FORT APACHE

Stradling, Harry
CARNIVAL IN FLANDERS
DARK JOURNEY

Stradling, Jr., Harry
GO TELL THE SPARTANS

LITTLE BIG MAN
MIDWAY

Struss, Karl
GREAT DICTATOR, THE

Sugiyama, Kohei
GATE OF HELL

Surtees, Bruce
FIREFOX

Surtees, Robert
HINDENBURG, THE
LOST COMMAND, THE
PT 109
THIRTY SECONDS OVER TOKYO

Szabo, Gabor
REVOLT OF JOB, THE

Tabary, Guy
LONGEST DAY, THE

Takahashi, Michio
HIROSHIMA, MON AMOUR

Taylor, Gil
ESCAPE TO ATHENA

Theis, Herbert
MISSION BATANGAS

Thomson, Alex
KEEP, THE

Thorin, Donald
OFFICER AND A GENTLEMAN, AN

Tidy, Frank
DUELLISTS, THE

Tisse, Edward
ALEXANDER NEVSKY
IVAN THE TERRIBLE, PARTS I & II

Toland, Gregg
BEST YEARS OF OUR LIVES, THE

Tonti, Aldo
CAST A GIANT SHADOW
WAR AND PEACE

Tosi, Mario
MAC ARTHUR

Totheroh, Roland
GREAT DICTATOR, THE

Tournier, Jean
START THE REVOLUTION WITHOUT
ME
TRAIN, THE

Tover, Leo
CONQUEROR, THE

Treu, Wolfgang
LITTLE DRUMMER GIRL, THE
PEDESTRIAN, THE
SALZBURG CONNECTION, THE

Tufano, Brian
LORDS OF DISCIPLINE, THE

Tyler, Nelson
TOBRUK

Ueda, Masaharu
RAN

Ueda, Shoji
KAGEMUSHA

Unsworth, Geoffrey
BRIDGE TOO FAR, A
CABARET
CROMWELL
DRUMS

Uoung, Remegio
WARKILL

Urussevsky, Sergei
CRANES ARE FLYING, THE

Vacano, Jost
BOAT, THE
SOLDIER OF ORANGE

Valentine, Joseph
SABOTEUR

Vamos, Thomas
CAPTIVE HEARTS

van de Sande, Theo
ASSAULT, THE

Vierny, Sacha
HIROSHIMA, MON AMOUR

Vogel, Paul C.
GO FOR BROKE

Wagner, Fritz Arno
KAMERADSCHAFT

Wagner, Sidney
BATAAN
DRAGON SEED

Waite, Ric
RED DAWN
UNCOMMON VALOR

Walker, Joseph
MR. WINKLE GOES TO WAR

Walsh, David M.
PRIVATE BENJAMIN

Watkin, David
CATCH-22
CUBA
HOW I WON THE WAR
SKY BANDITS

Waxman, Harry
GLORY AT SEA

Wenstrom, Harold
LOST PATROL, THE

Wexler, Haskell
COMING HOME

Wheeler, Charles F.
TORA! TORA! TORA!

Whigham, Joseph A.
REBEL LOVE

White, Lester
SHERLOCK HOLMES AND THE
SECRET WEAPON

Wilcox, John
COCKLESHELL HEROES, THE
MOUSE THAT ROARED, THE

Wild, Harry J.
CONQUEROR, THE
CORNERED
FIRST YANK INTO TOKYO
STAGE DOOR CANTEEN

Williams, Billy
ELENI
VOYAGE OF THE DAMNED
WIND AND THE LION, THE

Wilson, Ian
PRIVATES ON PARADE

Wilson, James
SALUTE JOHN CITIZEN

Wojcik, Jerzy
ASHES AND DIAMONDS

Woolsey, Ralph
GREAT SANTINI, THE

Wooster, Arthur
PLATOON LEADER

Worth, Lothrop B.
BATTLE TAXI

Wottitz, Walter
LONGEST DAY, THE
TRAIN, THE

Wyer, Reginald
OPERATION AMSTERDAM

Yokoyama, Minoru
HARP OF BURMA

Young, F.A.
LAWRENCE OF ARABIA
NURSE EDITH CAVELL

Young, Freddie
49TH PARALLEL
BATTLE OF BRITAIN, THE
DOCTOR ZHIVAGO
INN OF THE SIXTH HAPPINESS, THE
NICHOLAS AND ALEXANDRA

Yusov, Vadim
MY NAME IS IVAN

Zielinski, Jerzy
CAL

Zsigmond, Vilmos
DEER HUNTER, THE

DIRECTORS

Akkad, Moustapha
LION OF THE DESERT

Aldrich, Robert
DIRTY DOZEN, THE
TOO LATE THE HERO
TWILIGHT'S LAST GLEAMING
ULZANA'S RAID

Allen, Woody
BANANAS
LOVE AND DEATH

Almond, Paul
CAPTIVE HEARTS

Altman, Robert
M*A*S*H
STREAMERS

Amir, Gideon
P.O.W. THE ESCAPE

Anderson, Michael
BATTLE HELL
DAM BUSTERS, THE

Annakin, Ken
BATTLE OF THE BULGE
LONGEST DAY, THE

Annaud, Jean-Jacques
BLACK AND WHITE IN COLOR

Arnold, Jack
MOUSE THAT ROARED, THE

Ashby, Hal
COMING HOME

Asquith, Anthony
COURT MARTIAL
WE DIVE AT DAWN

Attenborough, Richard
BRIDGE TOO FAR, A

Badham, John
WARGAMES

Bagby, Jr., Milton
REBEL LOVE

Baker, Roy
ONE THAT GOT AWAY, THE

Banks, Monty
GREAT GUNS

Bardem, Juan Antonio
LAST DAY OF THE WAR, THE

Beatty, Warren
REDS

Beck, Reginald
HENRY V

Becker, Harold
TAPS

Bennett, Compton
GLORY AT SEA

Beresford, Bruce
BREAKER MORANT

Biberman, Herbert
MASTER RACE, THE

Blakemore, Michael
PRIVATES ON PARADE

Bondarchuk, Sergei
WAR AND PEACE

Boorman, John
HOPE AND GLORY

Borzage, Frank
FAREWELL TO ARMS, A
STAGE DOOR CANTEEN

Bradbury, Basil
TASTE OF HELL, A

Bridges, Alan
RETURN OF THE SOLDIER, THE

Brynych, Zbynek
TRANSPORT FROM PARADISE

Bucquet, Harold S.
ADVENTURES OF TARTU, THE
DRAGON SEED

Bulajic, Veljko
BATTLE OF NERETVA

Burke, Martyn
POWER PLAY

Bushell, Anthony
RICHARD III

Byrum, John
RAZOR'S EDGE, THE

Carlino, Lewis John
GREAT SANTINI, THE

Cavani, Liliana
NIGHT PORTER, THE

Chaplin, Charles
GREAT DICTATOR, THE

Chetwynd, Lionel
HANOI HILTON, THE

Christensen, Bent
ONLY WAY, THE

Chukhrai, Grigori
BALLAD OF A SOLDIER

Cimino, Michael
DEER HUNTER, THE

Clement, Rene
FORBIDDEN GAMES

Collier, James F.
HIDING PLACE, THE

Conway, Jack
DRAGON SEED

Coppola, Francis Ford
APOCALYPSE NOW
GARDENS OF STONE

Cosmatos, George P.
MASSACRE IN ROME
RAMBO: FIRST BLOOD, PART II

Cosmatos, George Pan
ESCAPE TO ATHENA

Costa-Gavras
MISSING

Coward, Noel
IN WHICH WE SERVE

Cox, Alex
WALKER

Crowe, Christopher
OFF LIMITS

Cukor, George
GONE WITH THE WIND

Curtiz, Michael
CASABLANCA
CHARGE OF THE LIGHT BRIGADE, THE
PASSAGE TO MARSEILLE
SEA HAWK, THE
THIS IS THE ARMY

Daves, Delmer
DESTINATION TOKYO

Davis, B.J.
WHITE GHOST

Dawson [Antonio Margheriti], Anthony M.
LAST HUNTER, THE

de Broca, Philippe
KING OF HEARTS

DIRECTORS

De Concini, Ennio
HITLER: THE LAST TEN DAYS

De Martino, Alberto
DIRTY HEROES

De Sica, Vittorio
GARDEN OF THE FINZI-CONTINIS, THE
TWO WOMEN

Dearden, Basil
FRIEDA

Demme, Jonathan
SWING SHIFT

Dickinson, Thorold
HILL 24 DOESN'T ANSWER

Dmytryk, Edward
ALVAREZ KELLY
ANZIO
BACK TO BATAAN
BEHIND THE RISING SUN
CORNERED
HITLER'S CHILDREN
YOUNG LIONS, THE

Dmytryk, Madeleine
MASTER RACE, THE

Douglas, Gordon
FIRST YANK INTO TOKYO

Duncan, Patrick
84 CHARLIE MOPIC

Dwan, Allan
SANDS OF IWO JIMA

Eastwood, Clint
FIREFOX
HEARTBREAK RIDGE

Edwards, Blake
OPERATION PETTICOAT

Eisenstein, Sergei
ALEXANDER NEVSKY
IVAN THE TERRIBLE, PARTS I & II

Elvey, Maurice
SALUTE JOHN CITIZEN

Endfield, Cy
ZULU

Englund, George
UGLY AMERICAN, THE

Enright, Ray
GUNG HO!

Farrow, John
COMMANDOS STRIKE AT DAWN, THE
WAKE ISLAND

Fassbinder, Rainer Werner
MARRIAGE OF MARIA BRAUN, THE

Feldman, Marty
LAST REMAKE OF BEAU GESTE, THE

Ferrer, Jose
COCKLESHELL HEROES, THE

Feyder, Jacques
CARNIVAL IN FLANDERS

Fleischer, Richard
CLAY PIGEON, THE
TORA! TORA! TORA!

Fleming, Victor
GONE WITH THE WIND
GUY NAMED JOE, A

Florey, Robert
OUTPOST IN MOROCCO

Flynn, John
ROLLING THUNDER

Forbes, Bryan
KING RAT

Ford, John
DRUMS ALONG THE MOHAWK
FORT APACHE
HORSE SOLDIERS, THE
LOST PATROL, THE
MISTER ROBERTS
RIO GRANDE
SHE WORE A YELLOW RIBBON
THEY WERE EXPENDABLE
WHAT PRICE GLORY?

Fosse, Bob
CABARET

Frankenheimer, John
SEVEN DAYS IN MAY
TRAIN, THE

Franklin, Sidney
GONE WITH THE WIND

Frend, Charles
CRUEL SEA, THE

Fukasaku, Kinji
TORA! TORA! TORA!

Fuller, Samuel
BIG RED ONE, THE

Furie, Sidney J.
BOYS IN COMPANY C, THE
IRON EAGLE
IRON EAGLE II
PURPLE HEARTS

Gabor, Pal
BRADY'S ESCAPE

Gance, Abel
AUSTERLITZ

Garnett, Tay
BATAAN

Gilbert, Lewis
DAMN THE DEFIANT!
SEA SHALL NOT HAVE THEM, THE

Godard, Jean-Luc
LES CARABINIERS

Golan, Menahem
DELTA FORCE, THE
HANNA'S WAR

Goulding, Edmund
DAWN PATROL, THE
RAZOR'S EDGE, THE

Green, Alfred E.
MR. WINKLE GOES TO WAR

Grofe, Jr., Ferde
WARKILL

Guillermin, John
BLUE MAX, THE
BRIDGE AT REMAGEN, THE

Guitry, Sacha
NAPOLEON

Gutman, Nathaniel
DEADLINE

Gyongyossy, Imre
REVOLT OF JOB, THE

Hackford, Taylor
OFFICER AND A GENTLEMAN, AN

Hamilton, Guy
BATTLE OF BRITAIN, THE
COLDITZ STORY, THE
FORCE 10 FROM NAVARONE

Hamilton, William
CALL OUT THE MARINES

Harlan, Veit
KOLBERG

Hathaway, Henry
DESERT FOX, THE
LIVES OF A BENGAL LANCER
RAID ON ROMMEL
SUNDOWN

Hawks, Howard
AIR FORCE
SERGEANT YORK

Heisler, Stuart
HITLER

Hessler, Gordon
MISFIT BRIGADE, THE

Hibbs, Jesse
TO HELL AND BACK

Hickox, Douglas
ZULU DAWN

Hill, George Roy
LITTLE DRUMMER GIRL, THE
SLAUGHTERHOUSE-FIVE

Hill, Walter
SOUTHERN COMFORT

Hiller, Arthur
MIRACLE OF THE WHITE STALLIONS
TOBRUK

Hitchcock, Alfred
FOREIGN CORRESPONDENT
LIFEBOAT
SABOTEUR

Hodges, Mike
PRAYER FOR THE DYING, A

Hool, Lance
MISSING IN ACTION 2—THE BEGINNING

Hough, John
BRASS TARGET

Howard, David
CRIMSON ROMANCE

Howard, Leslie
PIMPERNEL SMITH
SPITFIRE

Howard, William K.
FIRE OVER ENGLAND

Hudson, Hugh
REVOLUTION

DIRECTORS

Hughes, Ken
CROMWELL

Hunt, Peter
SHOUT AT THE DEVIL
WILD GEESE II

Hurst, Brian Desmond
BLACK TENT, THE
MALTA STORY

Huston, John
AFRICAN QUEEN, THE
RED BADGE OF COURAGE, THE
VICTORY

Hutton, Brian G.
KELLY'S HEROES
WHERE EAGLES DARE

Huyck, Willard
BEST DEFENSE

Ichikawa, Kon
FIRES ON THE PLAIN
HARP OF BURMA

Irvin, John
DOGS OF WAR, THE
HAMBURGER HILL

Jacoby, Irving
SNOW TREASURE

Jeffrey, Tom
ODD ANGRY SHOT, THE

Jenkins, Michael
REBEL

Joffe, Roland
KILLING FIELDS, THE

Johnson, Alan
TO BE OR NOT TO BE

Juran [Nathan Hertz], Nathan
HELLCATS OF THE NAVY

Kabay, Barna
REVOLT OF JOB, THE

Kadar, Jan
SHOP ON MAIN STREET, THE

Kagan, Jeremy Paul
HEROES

Kalatozov, Mikhail
CRANES ARE FLYING, THE

Karlson, Phil
HELL TO ETERNITY

Katzin, Lee H.
SALZBURG CONNECTION, THE

Kaufman, Philip
UNBEARABLE LIGHTNESS OF
BEING, THE

Kellogg, Ray
GREEN BERETS, THE

King, Henry
TWELVE O'CLOCK HIGH
YANK IN THE R.A.F., A

Kinugasa, Teinosuke
GATE OF HELL

Kitiparaporn, Lek
ANGKOR-CAMBODIA EXPRESS

Klos, Elmar
SHOP ON MAIN STREET, THE

Kobayashi, Masaki
HUMAN CONDITION, THE

Korda, Alexander
THAT HAMILTON WOMAN

Korda, Zoltan
DRUMS
FOUR FEATHERS, THE
SAHARA

Koster, Henry
D-DAY, THE SIXTH OF JUNE
DESIREE

Kotcheff, Ted
FIRST BLOOD
UNCOMMON VALOR

Kramer, Stanley
JUDGMENT AT NUREMBERG
ON THE BEACH

Kubrick, Stanley
DR. STRANGELOVE: OR HOW I
LEARNED TO STOP WORRYING AND
LOVE THE BOMB
FULL METAL JACKET
PATHS OF GLORY
SPARTACUS

Kurosawa, Akira
KAGEMUSHA
RAN
THRONE OF BLOOD

Lang, Fritz
CLOAK AND DAGGER

Larsen, Keith
MISSION BATANGAS

Leacock, Philip
WAR LOVER, THE

Lean, David
BRIDGE ON THE RIVER KWAI, THE
DOCTOR ZHIVAGO
IN WHICH WE SERVE
LAWRENCE OF ARABIA

Lee, Jack
WOODEN HORSE, THE

Leonard, Terry J.
DEATH BEFORE DISHONOR

Leone, Sergio
GOOD, THE BAD, AND THE UGLY, THE

Lerner, Irving
CRY OF BATTLE

LeRoy, Mervyn
MISTER ROBERTS
THIRTY SECONDS OVER TOKYO

Lester, Richard
CUBA
HOW I WON THE WAR

Levinson, Barry
GOOD MORNING, VIETNAM

Lewis, Jerry
WHICH WAY TO THE FRONT?

Lilienthal, Peter
DAVID

Lindtberg, Leopold
FOUR IN A JEEP

Littman, Lynne
TESTAMENT

Litvak, Anatole
NIGHT OF THE GENERALS, THE
THIS ABOVE ALL

Lloyd, Frank
BLOOD ON THE SUN

Logan, Joshua
ENSIGN PULVER
SAYONARA

Lubin, Arthur
BUCK PRIVATES
FRANCIS IN THE NAVY

Lubitsch, Ernst
TO BE OR NOT TO BE

Ludwig, Edward
FIGHTING SEABEES, THE

Lumet, Sidney
FAIL SAFE
PAWNBROKER, THE

Lydecker, Howard
FIGHTING SEABEES, THE

McCarey, Leo
DUCK SOUP

McCarthy, Michael
OPERATION AMSTERDAM

MacDonald, Peter
RAMBO III

McLaglen, Andrew V.
SEA WOLVES, THE
SHENANDOAH
WILD GEESE, THE

Mahon, Barry
ASSAULT OF THE REBEL GIRLS

Malle, Louis
AU REVOIR LES ENFANTS

Mann, Anthony
EL CID
MEN IN WAR
SPARTACUS

Mann, Michael
KEEP, THE

Markle, Peter
BAT 21

Marquand, Richard
EYE OF THE NEEDLE

Martinson, Leslie H.
PT 109

Marton, Andrew
LONGEST DAY, THE

Mastroianni, Armand
SUPERNATURALS, THE

Masuda, Toshio
TORA! TORA! TORA!

WAR MOVIES

DIRECTORS

Mate, Rudolph
DEEP SIX, THE

Maylam, Tony
RIDDLE OF THE SANDS, THE

Menzies, William Cameron
DRUMS IN THE DEEP SOUTH
GONE WITH THE WIND

Milestone [Umberto Lenzi], Hank
FROM HELL TO VICTORY

Milestone, Lewis
ALL QUIET ON THE WESTERN FRONT
EDGE OF DARKNESS
NORTH STAR, THE
PORK CHOP HILL
PURPLE HEART, THE
WALK IN THE SUN, A

Milius, John
FAREWELL TO THE KING
RED DAWN
WIND AND THE LION, THE

Miller, David
FLYING TIGERS

Miller, J.C.
NO DEAD HEROES

Minnelli, Vincente
FOUR HORSEMEN OF THE
APOCALYPSE, THE

Mizrahi, Moshe
EVERY TIME WE SAY GOODBYE

Moguy, Leonide
ACTION IN ARABIA

Montgomery, George
STEEL CLAW, THE

Montgomery, Robert
THEY WERE EXPENDABLE

Murphy, Richard
WACKIEST SHIP IN THE ARMY, THE

Nava, Gregory
TIME OF DESTINY, A

Neame, Ronald
ODESSA FILE, THE
TUNES OF GLORY

Neill, Roy William
SHERLOCK HOLMES AND THE
SECRET WEAPON

Nelson, Ralph
FATHER GOOSE
SOLDIER BLUE

Nemec, Jan
DIAMONDS OF THE NIGHT

Newman, Joe
JUNGLE PATROL

Nichols, Mike
BILOXI BLUES
CATCH-22

Norris, Aaron
BRADDOCK: MISSING IN ACTION III
PLATOON LEADER

Nugent, Elliott
UP IN ARMS

Nyby, Christian
OPERATION CIA

O'Connor, Pat
CAL

Olivera, Hector
FUNNY, DIRTY LITTLE WAR, A

Olivier, Laurence
HENRY V
RICHARD III

Oshima, Nagisa
MERRY CHRISTMAS, MR. LAWRENCE

Oswald, Gerd
LONGEST DAY, THE

Pabst, G.W.
KAMERADSCHAFT

Parker, Alan
BIRDY

Peckinpah, Sam
CROSS OF IRON

Penn, Arthur
LITTLE BIG MAN

Perisic, Zoran
SKY BANDITS

Petersen, Wolfgang
BOAT, THE

Pevney, Joseph
AWAY ALL BOATS

Pirosh, Robert
GO FOR BROKE

Pontecorvo, Gillo
BATTLE OF ALGIERS, THE
BURN

Post, Ted
GO TELL THE SPARTANS

Powell, Dick
CONQUEROR, THE

Powell, Michael
49TH PARALLEL
LIFE AND DEATH OF COLONEL
BLIMP, THE
ONE OF OUR AIRCRAFT IS MISSING
PURSUIT OF THE GRAF SPEE, THE
SPY IN BLACK, THE

Preminger, Otto
COURT-MARTIAL OF BILLY
MITCHELL, THE
IN HARM'S WAY

Pressburger, Emeric
ONE OF OUR AIRCRAFT IS MISSING
PURSUIT OF THE GRAF SPEE, THE

Pressman, Michael
SOME KIND OF HERO

Prior, David A.
NIGHTWARS

Quinn, Anthony
BUCCANEER, THE

Rademakers, Fons
ASSAULT, THE

Ramati, Alexander
ASSISI UNDERGROUND, THE

Ray, Nicholas
55 DAYS AT PEKING
FLYING LEATHERNECKS

Reed, Carol
IMMORTAL BATTALION, THE
NIGHT TRAIN

Reisz, Karel
WHO'LL STOP THE RAIN?

Renoir, Jean
ELUSIVE CORPORAL, THE
GRAND ILLUSION
LA MARSEILLAISE
THIS LAND IS MINE

Resnais, Alain
HIROSHIMA, MON AMOUR

Reynolds, Kevin
BEAST, THE

Richards, Dick
MARCH OR DIE

Robson, Mark
BRIDGES AT TOKO-RI, THE
HOME OF THE BRAVE
INN OF THE SIXTH HAPPINESS, THE
LOST COMMAND, THE
VON RYAN'S EXPRESS

Roddam, Franc
LORDS OF DISCIPLINE, THE

Rosenberg, Stuart
VOYAGE OF THE DAMNED

Rosenthal, Rick
DISTANT THUNDER

Rossellini, Roberto
GENERALE DELLA ROVERE
GERMANY, YEAR ZERO
OPEN CITY
PAISAN

Rossen, Robert
ALEXANDER THE GREAT

Ryan, Frank
CALL OUT THE MARINES

Ryan, Terry
GOING HOME

Sanger, Jonathan
CODE NAME: EMERALD

Sargent, Joseph
MAC ARTHUR

Saville, Victor
DARK JOURNEY
KIM

Schaffner, Franklin J.
BOYS FROM BRAZIL, THE
NICHOLAS AND ALEXANDRA
PATTON

Schell, Maximilian
PEDESTRIAN, THE

Schepisi, Fred
PLENTY

Schirk, Heinz
WANNSEE CONFERENCE, THE

Schlesinger, John
MARATHON MAN

Schlondorff, Volker
COUP DE GRACE
TIN DRUM, THE

Scott, Ridley
DUELLISTS, THE

Scott, Tony
TOP GUN

Seiler, Lewis
GUADALCANAL DIARY

Seitz, George B.
LAST OF THE MOHICANS, THE

Selander, Lesley
DRAGONFLY SQUADRON
FLAT TOP

Sharp, Ian
FINAL OPTION, THE

Shavelson, Melville
CAST A GIANT SHADOW

Sherman, George
AGAINST ALL FLAGS

Shinoda, Masahiro
MACARTHUR'S CHILDREN

Shumlin, Herman
WATCH ON THE RHINE

Sirk, Douglas
TIME TO LOVE AND A TIME TO DIE, A

Smight, Jack
MIDWAY
SECRET WAR OF HARRY FRIGG, THE

Spielberg, Steven
1941
EMPIRE OF THE SUN

Spottiswoode, Roger
UNDER FIRE

Stahl, John
IMMORTAL SERGEANT, THE

Stevens, George
DIARY OF ANNE FRANK, THE
GUNGA DIN

Stone, Oliver
PLATOON
SALVADOR

Strock, Herbert L.
BATTLE TAXI

Sturges, John
EAGLE HAS LANDED, THE
GREAT ESCAPE, THE

Sutherland, A. Edward
FLYING DEUCES, THE

Szabo, Istvan
COLONEL REDL
MEPHISTO

Tarkovsky, Andrei
MY NAME IS IVAN

Taviani, Paolo
NIGHT OF THE SHOOTING STARS, THE

Taviani, Vittorio
NIGHT OF THE SHOOTING STARS, THE

Taylor, Don
FINAL COUNTDOWN, THE

Thompson, J. Lee
GUNS OF NAVARONE, THE
TARAS BULBA

Tourneur, Jacques
BERLIN EXPRESS
DAYS OF GLORY

Truffaut, Francois
GREEN ROOM, THE
LAST METRO, THE

Trumbo, Dalton
JOHNNY GOT HIS GUN

Valerii, Tonino
REASON TO LIVE, A REASON TO DIE, A

Vassillev, D.I.
ALEXANDER NEVSKY

Verhoeven, Paul
FLESH AND BLOOD
SOLDIER OF ORANGE

Vidor, King
WAR AND PEACE

Viola, Joe
HOT BOX, THE

Visconti, Luchino
DAMNED, THE

von Sternberg, Joseph
MOROCCO

Wajda, Andrzej
ASHES AND DIAMONDS
DANTON
KANAL
LOVE IN GERMANY, A

Wallace, Richard
BOMBARDIER

Walsh, Raoul
BATTLE CRY
DESPERATE JOURNEY
DISTANT DRUMS
NAKED AND THE DEAD, THE
NORTHERN PURSUIT
OBJECTIVE, BURMA!
THEY DIED WITH THEIR BOOTS ON

Ware, Clyde
NO DRUMS, NO BUGLES

Wayne, John
ALAMO, THE
GREEN BERETS, THE

Webb, Jack
D.I., THE

Weir, Peter
GALLIPOLI
YEAR OF LIVING DANGEROUSLY, THE

Welles, Orson
CHIMES AT MIDNIGHT
STRANGER, THE

Wellman, William A.
BEAU GESTE
DARBY'S RANGERS

EDITORS

Werner, Peter
DON'T CRY, IT'S ONLY THUNDER

Wertmuller, Lina
LOVE AND ANARCHY

Wexler, Haskell
LATINO

Wicki, Bernhard
LONGEST DAY, THE
MORITURI

Wilcox, Herbert
NURSE EDITH CAVELL

Wilder, Billy
STALAG 17

Wise, Robert
DESERT RATS, THE
DESTINATION GOBI
HINDENBURG, THE
RUN SILENT, RUN DEEP
SAND PEBBLES, THE

Wood, Sam
GONE WITH THE WIND

Worth, David
SOLDIER'S REVENGE

Wyler, William
BEST YEARS OF OUR LIVES, THE
MRS. MINIVER

Yarema, Neil
TASTE OF HELL, A

Yates, Peter
ELENI
MURPHY'S WAR

Yorkin, Bud
START THE REVOLUTION WITHOUT ME

Zieff, Howard
PRIVATE BENJAMIN

Zinnemann, Fred
BEHOLD A PALE HORSE
FROM HERE TO ETERNITY
MEN, THE

Zito, Joseph
INVASION U.S.A.
MISSING IN ACTION

EDITORS

Adams, Edgar
ALL QUIET ON THE WESTERN FRONT

Alabiso, Eugenio
GOOD, THE BAD, AND THE UGLY, THE

Allen, Dede
LITTLE BIG MAN
REDS
SLAUGHTERHOUSE-FIVE

Allen, Fred
GUADALCANAL DIARY

Allen, Stanford C.
MARCH OR DIE

Amy, George
AIR FORCE

WAR MOVIES

EDITORS

CHARGE OF THE LIGHT BRIGADE, THE
OBJECTIVE, BURMA!
SEA HAWK, THE
THIS IS THE ARMY

Anderson, Bill
YEAR OF LIVING DANGEROUSLY, THE

Anderson, Philip W.
SAYONARA

Anderson, William
BREAKER MORANT
GALLIPOLI

Arcalli, Franco
NIGHT PORTER, THE

Arthur, George
OUTPOST IN MOROCCO

Austin, William
FLAT TOP

Azar, Leonide
AUSTERLITZ

Baird, Stuart
REVOLUTION

Balsam, Alan
TO BE OR NOT TO BE

Baragli, Nino
GOOD, THE BAD, AND THE UGLY, THE

Barcelon, Ben
HOT BOX, THE

Baron, Suzanne
TIN DRUM, THE

Barraque, Martine
LAST METRO, THE

Barraque-Curie, Martine
GREEN ROOM, THE

Barton, Sean
EYE OF THE NEEDLE

Bates, Bert
BATTLE OF BRITAIN, THE
CAST A GIANT SHADOW

Bauchens, Anne
COMMANDOS STRIKE AT DAWN, THE

Beaton, Alex
SOLDIER BLUE

Beck, Reginald
HENRY V

Beetley, Samuel E.
CLAY PIGEON, THE
LONGEST DAY, THE

Benedict, Max
BLUE MAX, THE

Benson, James
BOYS IN COMPANY C, THE

Berman, Henry
GUNGA DIN

Berman, Michael
BOYS IN COMPANY C, THE

Best, Richard
DAM BUSTERS, THE

Biggs, Douglas
PURPLE HEART, THE

Biggs, Douglass
THEY WERE EXPENDABLE

Bjenjas, Vojislav
BATTLE OF NERETVA

Blangsted, Ace
TARAS BULBA

Blangsted, Folmar
COURT-MARTIAL OF BILLY MITCHELL, THE
DISTANT DRUMS
PT 109
TARAS BULBA

Blankett, Betsy
TIME OF DESTINY, A

Bloom, John
UNDER FIRE
WHO'LL STOP THE RAIN?

Blum, Robert
FOUR IN A JEEP

Boemler, George
KIM
PORK CHOP HILL
RUN SILENT, RUN DEEP

Bonnot, Francoise
BLACK AND WHITE IN COLOR
MASSACRE IN ROME
MISSING

Bornstein, Ken
BRADDOCK: MISSING IN ACTION III

Boyle, Peter
BEAST, THE
PRAYER FOR THE DYING, A
RAZOR'S EDGE, THE

Bradsell, Michael
CAL

Bretherton, David
CABARET
NO DRUMS, NO BUGLES
TRAIN, THE

Bridges, Mellena
REBEL LOVE

Brillouin, Jacques
CARNIVAL IN FLANDERS

Brotherton, David
DIARY OF ANNE FRANK, THE

Brown, O. Nicholas
MARCH OR DIE
RAMBO III

Burns, Mark
EVERY TIME WE SAY GOODBYE

Cahn, Philip
BUCK PRIVATES

Cambern, Donn
HINDENBURG, THE

Carruth, Milton
ALL QUIET ON THE WESTERN FRONT
FRANCIS IN THE NAVY
GUNG HO!

Cartwright, William
BRIDGE AT REMAGEN, THE

Castro, Emmanuelle
AU REVOIR LES ENFANTS

Cattozzo, Leo
WAR AND PEACE

Cavagna, Cesare
GENERALE DELLA ROVERE

Chapman, Joan
FIRST BLOOD

Chasney, Jasmine
HIROSHIMA, MON AMOUR

Chegwidden, Ann
HIDING PLACE, THE

Chikaya, Inoue
TORA! TORA! TORA!

Chulack, Fred
SPARTACUS

Clark, James B.
DESERT FOX, THE
IMMORTAL SERGEANT, THE

Clark, Jim
KILLING FIELDS, THE
LAST REMAKE OF BEAU GESTE, THE
MARATHON MAN
PRIVATES ON PARADE

Clark, Laurence Mery
RETURN OF THE SOLDIER, THE

Coates, Anne V.
EAGLE HAS LANDED, THE
FAREWELL TO THE KING
LAWRENCE OF ARABIA
TUNES OF GLORY

Colangeli, Otello
DIRTY HEROES

Colpi, Henri
COUP DE GRACE
HIROSHIMA, MON AMOUR

Connor, Kevin
HITLER: THE LAST TEN DAYS

Conte, Mark
MISSING IN ACTION 2—THE BEGINNING

Cooke, Malcolm
ZULU DAWN

Copelan, Jodie
BATTLE TAXI

Cornelius, Henry
DRUMS
FOUR FEATHERS, THE

Cox, Alex
WALKER

Cox, Joel
HEARTBREAK RIDGE

Crafford, Ian
HOPE AND GLORY

Cranston, Helga
RICHARD III

Csakany, Zsuzsa
COLONEL REDL

EDITORS

Csekany, Zsuzsa
MEPHISTO

Curtiss, Edward
TO HELL AND BACK

Da Roma, Eraldo
GERMANY, YEAR ZERO
PAISAN

Dalva, Robert
LATINO

Davies, Freeman
SOUTHERN COMFORT

Dawson, Ralph
DAWN PATROL, THE

Dearing, R.E.
NIGHT TRAIN
WE DIVE AT DAWN

DeGaetano, Al
GREAT GUNS

Dennis, Jack
FLYING DEUCES, THE
LAST OF THE MOHICANS, THE

Dennis, John
FIRE OVER ENGLAND

Di Marco, Tony
MISSION BATANGAS

Dickinson, Joanna
HILL 24 DOESN'T ANSWER

Dickinson, Thorold
HILL 24 DOESN'T ANSWER

Dorn, Anette
COUP DE GRACE

Dornisch, William P.
JOHNNY GOT HIS GUN

Drought, Doris
CRIMSON ROMANCE

Duthie, Michael
ASSISI UNDERGROUND, THE
SHOUT AT THE DEVIL

Duthie, Michael J.
BRADDOCK: MISSING IN ACTION III
PLATOON LEADER

Dwyre, Roger
FORBIDDEN GAMES

Ellis, Michael
LORDS OF DISCIPLINE, THE

Ellis, Mike
CROSS OF IRON

Fantl, Richard
MR. WINKLE GOES TO WAR

Fay, Marston
BACK TO BATAAN

Fazan, Adrienne
FOUR HORSEMEN OF THE APOCALYPSE, THE

Fehr, Rudi
DESPERATE JOURNEY
WATCH ON THE RHINE

Feldman, Ettie
WHITE GHOST

Feyginova, L.
MY NAME IS IVAN

Fields, Verna
CRY OF BATTLE

Ford, Robert
CONQUEROR, THE

Fowler, Hugh S.
IN HARM'S WAY
PATTON

Fraticelli, Franco
LOVE AND ANARCHY

Fritch, Robert
DESTINATION GOBI

Fujii, Hiroaki
FIRES ON THE PLAIN

Gallitti, Alberto
ANZIO

Gay, Norman
BRADY'S ESCAPE

Gerstad, Harry
HOME OF THE BRAVE
MEN, THE

Gibbs, Anthony
BRIDGE TOO FAR, A

Gibbs, Antony
DOGS OF WAR, THE

Gilmore, Stuart
ALAMO, THE
WAR AND PEACE

Glen, John
MURPHY'S WAR
SEA WOLVES, THE
WILD GEESE, THE

Gluck, Joseph
OPERATION CIA

Goldblatt, Mark
RAMBO: FIRST BLOOD, PART II

Goodman, Joel
MISSING IN ACTION

Goodyear, Morris
ANGKOR-CAMBODIA EXPRESS

Gordon, Bob
MISFIT BRIGADE, THE

Gordon, Michael
MALTA STORY

Gosnell, Raja
SOLDIER'S REVENGE

Greenbury, Christopher
SOME KIND OF HERO

Greene, Danford B.
M*A*S*H

Grenville, George
IRON EAGLE
PURPLE HEARTS

Gross, Frank
AGAINST ALL FLAGS
OPERATION PETTICOAT

Gross, Roland
DEEP SIX, THE

Grover, John
FINAL OPTION, THE

Guillemot, Agnes
LES CARABINIERS

Hajek, Miroslav
DIAMONDS OF THE NIGHT
TRANSPORT FROM PARADISE

Hales, Gordon
WAR LOVER, THE

Halsey, Richard
NO DRUMS, NO BUGLES

Hambling, Gerry
BIRDY

Hannemann, Walter
BLOOD ON THE SUN
DRAGONFLY SQUADRON
HITLER

Harrison, Doane
STALAG 17

Harvey, Anthony
DR. STRANGELOVE: OR HOW I LEARNED TO STOP WORRYING AND LOVE THE BOMB

Hayers, Sidney
ONE THAT GOT AWAY, THE

Heermance, Richard
DRUMS IN THE DEEP SOUTH

Helfrich, Mark
RAMBO: FIRST BLOOD, PART II

Heringova, Diana
SHOP ON MAIN STREET, THE

Herring, Pembroke J.
TORA! TORA! TORA!

Hirtz, Dagmar
PEDESTRIAN, THE

Hoagland, Ellsworth
LIVES OF A BENGAL LANCER

Hoare, Lionel
DARK JOURNEY

Hoenig, Dov
KEEP, THE

Hollywood, Peter
RIDDLE OF THE SANDS, THE

Holmes, William
SERGEANT YORK
THEY DIED WITH THEIR BOOTS ON

Honess, Peter
PLENTY

Honey, Michael
REBEL

Hornbeck, William
DARK JOURNEY
DRUMS
FOUR FEATHERS, THE
SPY IN BLACK, THE
THAT HAMILTON WOMAN

Howard, John C.
MARCH OR DIE

Huguet, Marthe
LA MARSEILLAISE

WAR MOVIES 191

EDITORS

Hull, Frank E.
THEY WERE EXPENDABLE

Hunt, Peter
DAMN THE DEFIANT!

Hunter, Martin
FULL METAL JACKET

Ibold, Douglas
OFF LIMITS

Ichikawa, Kon
FIRES ON THE PLAIN

Innes, Phillip
WARKILL

Jager, Siegrun
DAVID

Jakubowicz, Alain
DELTA FORCE, THE
HANNA'S WAR

Janacek, Jaromir
SHOP ON MAIN STREET, THE

Javet, Francoise
KING OF HEARTS

Jones, Robert C.
TOBRUK

Jordan, Bert
JUNGLE PATROL

Jympson, John
KELLY'S HEROES
WHERE EAGLES DARE
ZULU

Kahn, Michael
1941
EMPIRE OF THE SUN

Kahn, Sheldon
PRIVATE BENJAMIN

Kalish, Ron
BANANAS
LOVE AND DEATH

Karmento, Eva
BRADY'S ESCAPE

Kavanagh, Brian
ODD ANGRY SHOT, THE

Keller, Frank P.
MURPHY'S WAR
ROLLING THUNDER

Kemplen, Ralph
AFRICAN QUEEN, THE
COURT MARTIAL
ESCAPE TO ATHENA
ODESSA FILE, THE

Kempler, Ralph
ALEXANDER THE GREAT

Kennedy, Patrick
HEROES

Kent, Ted J.
AWAY ALL BOATS
FATHER GOOSE
OPERATION PETTICOAT
TIME TO LOVE AND A TIME TO DIE, A
UGLY AMERICAN, THE

Kern, Hal
STAGE DOOR CANTEEN

Kern, Hal C.
GONE WITH THE WIND

Killifer, Jack
NORTHERN PURSUIT

Knudtson, Frederic
JUDGMENT AT NUREMBERG
ON THE BEACH
THIS LAND IS MINE

Kress, Harold F.
ALVAREZ KELLY
DRAGON SEED
MRS. MINIVER

Kroll, Eva
PATHS OF GLORY

Kruydenburg, Tim
GOING HOME

Kurosawa, Akira
RAN
THRONE OF BLOOD

Lakshmanan, Lila
LES CARABINIERS

Lamb, Irene
EAGLE HAS LANDED, THE

Lambert, Robert K.
FINAL COUNTDOWN, THE

Lamy, Raymond
NAPOLEON

Lane, David
BRASS TARGET

Lawrence, Robert
55 DAYS AT PEKING
EL CID
SPARTACUS

Lawson, Tony
CROSS OF IRON

Leadley, Ernie
MASTER RACE, THE

Lean, David
49TH PARALLEL
IN WHICH WE SERVE
ONE OF OUR AIRCRAFT IS MISSING

Lebenzon, Chris
TOP GUN

Leeds, Robert M.
D.I., THE

Lenny, Bill
CROMWELL

Lewis, Ben
FOUR HORSEMEN OF THE APOCALYPSE, THE
RED BADGE OF COURAGE, THE

Lichtig, Renee
ELUSIVE CORPORAL, THE

Likhachyova, Tatyana
WAR AND PEACE

Linder, Stewart
CODE NAME: EMERALD

Linder, Stu
GOOD MORNING, VIETNAM

Linthorst, Kees
ASSAULT, THE

Livingston, Roy V.
HELL TO ETERNITY

Lloyd, Russell
SEA SHALL NOT HAVE THEM, THE

Lockert, John
GUNGA DIN

Loewenthal, Daniel
INVASION U.S.A.
MISSING IN ACTION

London, Andrew
RAMBO III

Lopez, Eduardo
FUNNY, DIRTY LITTLE WAR, A

Lorenz, Juliane
MARRIAGE OF MARIA BRAUN, THE

Lovejoy, Raymond
ELENI

Lovering, Otho
FAREWELL TO ARMS, A
FOREIGN CORRESPONDENT
GREEN BERETS, THE
SHENANDOAH

Luciano, Michael
DIRTY DOZEN, THE
TOO LATE THE HERO
TWILIGHT'S LAST GLEAMING
ULZANA'S RAID

Ludwig, Otto
SABOTEUR
SHERLOCK HOLMES AND THE SECRET WEAPON

Luhovy, Yurij
CAPTIVE HEARTS

Lyon, William
FROM HERE TO ETERNITY

McDonell, Fergus
IMMORTAL BATTALION, THE

Mace, William
D-DAY, THE SIXTH OF JUNE
DIARY OF ANNE FRANK, THE

McKay, Craig
REDS
SWING SHIFT

McLean, Barbara
DESERT RATS, THE
TWELVE O'CLOCK HIGH
YANK IN THE R.A.F., A

Macrorie, Alma
BRIDGES AT TOKO-RI, THE

Malkin, Barry
GARDENS OF STONE

Mandell, Daniel
BEST YEARS OF OUR LIVES, THE
NORTH STAR, THE
UP IN ARMS

Mansfield, Duncan
WALK IN THE SUN, A

WAR MOVIES

EDITORS

Manton, Marcus
MISSING IN ACTION 2—THE BEGINNING
P.O.W. THE ESCAPE

Marks, Owen
CASABLANCA
DARBY'S RANGERS
PASSAGE TO MARSEILLE

Marks, Richard
APOCALYPSE NOW

Marshek, Archie
BUCCANEER, THE

Marstella, Kenneth
CONQUEROR, THE

Martin, Jr., Philip
FIRST YANK INTO TOKYO

Martin, Yvonne
AUSTERLITZ

Mastroianni, Ruggero
DAMNED, THE

Mayhew, Peter
COLDITZ STORY, THE

Melnick, Mark
UNCOMMON VALOR

Meyer, Richard C.
MEN IN WAR

Milford, Gene
TARAS BULBA

Mills, Reginald
PURSUIT OF THE GRAF SPEE, THE

Mirkovich, Steve
DEATH BEFORE DISHONOR

Mollinger, Ursula
WANNSEE CONFERENCE, THE

Montanari, Anna Maria
GENERALE DELLA ROVERE

Moore, Millie
GO TELL THE SPARTANS

Moriani, Alberto
LAST HUNTER, THE

Morra, Mario
BATTLE OF ALGIERS, THE
BURN

Muller, Fritz
CHIMES AT MIDNIGHT

Murch, Walter
UNBEARABLE LIGHTNESS OF BEING, THE

Murray, Jack
FORT APACHE
HORSE SOLDIERS, THE
MISTER ROBERTS
RIO GRANDE
SHE WORE A YELLOW RIBBON
STEEL CLAW, THE

Myers, Douglas
PIMPERNEL SMITH
SPITFIRE

Myers, Thelma
IN WHICH WE SERVE

Nawrocka, Halina
ASHES AND DIAMONDS
KANAL

Nelson, Charles
SAHARA
WACKIEST SHIP IN THE ARMY, THE

Newcom, James
UP IN ARMS

Newcom, James E.
GO FOR BROKE
GONE WITH THE WIND
TORA! TORA! TORA!

Nicholson, George Jay
MAC ARTHUR

Nico, Willard
GREAT DICTATOR, THE

Nikel, Hannes
BOAT, THE

Nims, Ernest
FLYING TIGERS
STRANGER, THE

Noble, Thom
FIRST BLOOD
RED DAWN

Noriega, Joseph
BEHIND THE RISING SUN
CORNERED
DAYS OF GLORY
HITLER'S CHILDREN

Norman, Leslie
FRIEDA

Novelli, Adriana
GARDEN OF THE FINZI-CONTINIS, THE
TWO WOMEN

Nyby, Christian
CLOAK AND DAGGER
DESTINATION TOKYO

O'Meara, C. Timothy
FAREWELL TO THE KING

O'Steen, Sam
BILOXI BLUES
CATCH-22

Ochoa, Margarita
LAST DAY OF THE WAR, THE

Ortega, Carlos Puente
WALKER

Osbiston, Alan
COCKLESHELL HEROES, THE
GUNS OF NAVARONE, THE
NIGHT OF THE GENERALS, THE

Oser, Hans
KAMERADSCHAFT

Oshima, Tomoyo
MERRY CHRISTMAS, MR. LAWRENCE

Palmer, Gene
RAID ON ROMMEL

Palmer, Keith
WILD GEESE II

Parsons, Derek
BATTLE OF THE BULGE

Pattillo, Allan
BOYS IN COMPANY C, THE

Perpignani, Roberto
NIGHT OF THE SHOOTING STARS, THE

Petenyi, Katalin
REVOLT OF JOB, THE

Pettit, Suzanne
TESTAMENT

Pokras, Barbara
DON'T CRY, IT'S ONLY THUNDER

Poulton, Ray
FORCE 10 FROM NAVARONE

Poulton, Raymond
MOUSE THAT ROARED, THE

Powers, Pamela
DUELLISTS, THE

Priestley, Tom
VOYAGE OF THE DAMNED

Prugar-Ketling, Halina
DANTON
LOVE IN GERMANY, A

Przygodda, Peter
DEADLINE

Purvis, Stephen
84 CHARLIE MOPIC

Renoir, Marguerite
GRAND ILLUSION
LA MARSEILLAISE

Reynolds, William
DESIREE
ENSIGN PULVER
LITTLE DRUMMER GIRL, THE
SAND PEBBLES, THE
TARAS BULBA

Rivkin, Stephen E.
BAT 21

Rolf, Tom
WARGAMES

Rongier, Gabriel
TRAIN, THE

Roome, Alfred
BLACK TENT, THE

Rosenblum, Ralph
FAIL SAFE
LOVE AND DEATH
PAWNBROKER, THE

Ruggiero, Gene
CAST A GIANT SHADOW

Sarraute, Anne
HIROSHIMA, MON AMOUR

Savage, Norman
DOCTOR ZHIVAGO

Schenkkan, Ine
FLESH AND BLOOD

Schmidt, Arthur
LAST REMAKE OF BEAU GESTE, THE

Schmidt, Arthur P.
NAKED AND THE DEAD, THE
SAYONARA

EDITORS

Schrader, George
MISSION BATANGAS

Schreiner, Reinhard
NIGHTWARS

Schulte, Robert
SPARTACUS

Scott, Thomas
BEAU GESTE

Seabourne, John
LIFE AND DEATH OF COLONEL BLIMP, THE

Seabourne, Peter
WOODEN HORSE, THE

Seabourne, Sr., John
WOODEN HORSE, THE

Serandrei, Mario
BATTLE OF ALGIERS, THE

Shaw, Penelope
HANOI HILTON, THE

Sheldon, Ralph
SNOW TREASURE

Shirley, John
LION OF THE DESERT

Silver, Joseph
MORITURI

Silvi, Roberto
MASSACRE IN ROME
VICTORY

Simpson, Claire
PLATOON
SALVADOR

Simpson, Robert
DRUMS ALONG THE MOHAWK

Smith, John Victor
CUBA
HOW I WON THE WAR

Smith, Norman
STREAMERS

Snyder, Ray
FRANCIS IN THE NAVY

Spang, Ron
FIREFOX

Speer, Jane
SOLDIER OF ORANGE

Spencer, Dorothy
FOREIGN CORRESPONDENT
LIFEBOAT
LOST COMMAND, THE
SUNDOWN
TO BE OR NOT TO BE
VON RYAN'S EXPRESS
WHAT PRICE GLORY?
YOUNG LIONS, THE

Sperr, Jane
COUP DE GRACE

Srp, Alfred
MIRACLE OF THE WHITE STALLIONS

Stevens, Arthur
OPERATION AMSTERDAM

Stevenson, Houseley
GREAT SANTINI, THE

Stevenson, Michael A.
BEST DEFENSE

Stewart, Hugh
DARK JOURNEY
SPY IN BLACK, THE

Stone, LeRoy
DUCK SOUP
WAKE ISLAND

Sullivan, Frank
GUY NAMED JOE, A
THIRTY SECONDS OVER TOKYO

Swink, Robert
ACTION IN ARABIA
DIARY OF ANNE FRANK, THE
MIDWAY

Swink, Robert E.
BOYS FROM BRAZIL, THE

Symons, James
RAMBO III

Tanner, Peter
CRUEL SEA, THE
HAMBURGER HILL
SKY BANDITS

Taschner, Herbert
CROSS OF IRON

Taylor, Peter
ANZIO
BRIDGE ON THE RIVER KWAI, THE

Thompson, Walter
BEHOLD A PALE HORSE
KING RAT
THIS ABOVE ALL

Thoms, Jerome
HELLCATS OF THE NAVY

Timofeyeva, M.
CRANES ARE FLYING, THE

Todd, Sherman
BERLIN EXPRESS
FLYING LEATHERNECKS

Tomasi, Vincenzo
FROM HELL TO VICTORY

Tomasini, George
IN HARM'S WAY
STALAG 17

Tsujii, Masanori
HARP OF BURMA

Tubor, Morton
BIG RED ONE, THE

Uraoka, Keiichi
HUMAN CONDITION, THE

Urioste, Frank J.
BOYS IN COMPANY C, THE
MIDWAY

Van Enger, Richard
FIGHTING SEABEES, THE

Van Enger, Richard L.
SANDS OF IWO JIMA

Vickrey, Scott
INVASION U.S.A.

Victor-Smith, John
POWER PLAY

Vine, Edgar
NO DEAD HEROES

Virkler, Dennis
DISTANT THUNDER

Wallis, Rit
IRON EAGLE II

Walsch [Fassbinder], Franz
MARRIAGE OF MARIA BRAUN, THE

Walter, Ernest
INN OF THE SIXTH HAPPINESS, THE
NICHOLAS AND ALEXANDRA

Warburton, Cotton
MIRACLE OF THE WHITE STALLIONS

Warren, Eda
TARAS BULBA

Warschilka, Edward
RAMBO III

Warth, Theron
CALL OUT THE MARINES

Watters, George
OPERATION CIA

Weatherwax, Paul
LOST PATROL, THE

Webb, J. Watson
RAZOR'S EDGE, THE

Weber, Billy
TOP GUN

Webster, Ferris
FIREFOX
GREAT ESCAPE, THE
SEVEN DAYS IN MAY
START THE REVOLUTION WITHOUT ME

Weintrobe, Maury
TWILIGHT'S LAST GLEAMING

Weisbart, David
EDGE OF DARKNESS

White, George
BATAAN
HELL TO ETERNITY

Wiles, Russel
WHICH WAY TO THE FRONT?

Williams, Elmo
NURSE EDITH CAVELL

Williams, J. Terry
SECRET WAR OF HARRY FRIGG, THE

Winetrobe, Maury
TAPS

Winston, Sam
MOROCCO

Wise, Robert
BOMBARDIER

Wolfe, Robert L.
WIND AND THE LION, THE

MUSIC COMPOSERS

Wolinsky, Sidney
BEST DEFENSE

Wood, Truman
BLOOD ON THE SUN

Woodcock, John M.
SALZBURG CONNECTION, THE

Woods, Jack
DON'T CRY, IT'S ONLY THUNDER

Yamaji, Sachiko
MACARTHUR'S CHILDREN

Zeigler, William
BATTLE CRY

Zimmerman, Don
COMING HOME

Zinner, Peter
DEER HUNTER, THE
OFFICER AND A GENTLEMAN, AN

MUSIC COMPOSERS

Addinsell, Richard
DARK JOURNEY
FIRE OVER ENGLAND
WAR LOVER, THE

Addison, John
BRIDGE TOO FAR, A
COCKLESHELL HEROES, THE
CODE NAME: EMERALD
START THE REVOLUTION WITHOUT ME

Adler, Mark
UNBEARABLE LIGHTNESS OF BEING, THE

Akutagawa, Yasushi
FIRES ON THE PLAIN
GATE OF HELL

Alwyn, William
BLACK TENT, THE
IMMORTAL BATTALION, THE
MALTA STORY

Amfitheatrof, Daniele
DESERT FOX, THE

Andriessen, Jurriaan
ASSAULT, THE

Arnold, Malcolm
BRIDGE ON THE RIVER KWAI, THE
INN OF THE SIXTH HAPPINESS, THE
SEA SHALL NOT HAVE THEM, THE
TUNES OF GLORY

Aroclaw Radio Quintet
ASHES AND DIAMONDS

Arthuys, Philippe
LES CARABINIERS

Astley, Edwin
MOUSE THAT ROARED, THE

Bach, Johann Sebastian
LA MARSEILLAISE

Bachelet, Pierre
BLACK AND WHITE IN COLOR

Bakaleinikoff, Constantin
DAYS OF GLORY

Bakaleinikoff, Mischa
HELLCATS OF THE NAVY

Barber, Samuel
PLATOON

Barry, John
KING RAT
MURPHY'S WAR
ZULU

Bath, Hubert
ADVENTURES OF TARTU, THE

Ben Haim, Paul
HILL 24 DOESN'T ANSWER

Bennett, Richard Rodney
NICHOLAS AND ALEXANDRA
RETURN OF THE SOLDIER, THE

Bernstein, Elmer
BRIDGE AT REMAGEN, THE
BUCCANEER, THE
CAST A GIANT SHADOW
GREAT ESCAPE, THE
GREAT SANTINI, THE
MEN IN WAR
ZULU DAWN

Beydts, Louis
CARNIVAL IN FLANDERS

Bhatia, Amin
IRON EAGLE II

Blake, Howard
DUELLISTS, THE
LORDS OF DISCIPLINE, THE
RIDDLE OF THE SANDS, THE

Broekman, David
ALL QUIET ON THE WESTERN FRONT

Brown, Louis Y.
WHICH WAY TO THE FRONT?

Budd, Roy
SEA WOLVES, THE
SOLDIER BLUE
WILD GEESE II
WILD GEESE, THE

Burgon, Geoffrey
DOGS OF WAR, THE

Burns, Ralph
CABARET

Buttolph, David
D.I., THE
DEEP SIX, THE
GUADALCANAL DIARY
HORSE SOLDIERS, THE
IMMORTAL SERGEANT, THE
PT 109
WAKE ISLAND

Carlos, Michael
ODD ANGRY SHOT, THE

Chagrin, Francis
COLDITZ STORY, THE

Chattaway, Jay
BRADDOCK: MISSING IN ACTION III
INVASION U.S.A.
MISSING IN ACTION

Chopin, Frederic
COLONEL REDL

Cipriani, Stelvio
ANGKOR-CAMBODIA EXPRESS

Clifford, Hubert
ONE THAT GOT AWAY, THE

Clinton, George S.
PLATOON LEADER

Coates, Eric
DAM BUSTERS, THE

Coleman, Cy
FATHER GOOSE

Colombo, Alberto
GO FOR BROKE

Conti, Bill
PRAYER FOR THE DYING, A
PRIVATE BENJAMIN
VICTORY

Cooder, Ry
SOUTHERN COMFORT

Copland, Aaron
NORTH STAR, THE

Coppola, Carmine
APOCALYPSE NOW
GARDENS OF STONE

Coppola, Francis Ford
APOCALYPSE NOW

Cordell, Frank
CROMWELL

Corigliano, John
REVOLUTION

Coward, Noel
IN WHICH WE SERVE

Cunneen, Phil
BREAKER MORANT

Davis, Carl
ONLY WAY, THE

de l'Isle, Rouget
LA MARSEILLAISE

De Sica, Manuel
GARDEN OF THE FINZI-CONTINIS, THE

Delerue, Georges
BILOXI BLUES
HIROSHIMA, MON AMOUR
KING OF HEARTS
LAST METRO, THE
SALVADOR

Deutsch, Adolph
NORTHERN PURSUIT

DeVol, Frank
DIRTY DOZEN, THE
ULZANA'S RAID

DeVorzon, Barry
ROLLING THUNDER

Doldinger, Klaus
BOAT, THE

Donovan
84 CHARLIE MOPIC

MUSIC COMPOSERS

Dragon, Carmen
MR. WINKLE GOES TO WAR

Duning, George
ENSIGN PULVER
FROM HERE TO ETERNITY
WACKIEST SHIP IN THE ARMY, THE

Dunlap, Paul
OPERATION CIA

Easdale, Brian
PURSUIT OF THE GRAF SPEE, THE

Faltermeyer, Harold
TOP GUN

Fielding, Jerry
JOHNNY GOT HIS GUN

Folk, Robert
PURPLE HEARTS

Francaix, Jean
NAPOLEON

Frankel, Benjamin
BATTLE OF THE BULGE

Fried, Gerald
PATHS OF GLORY
TOO LATE THE HERO

Friedhofer, Hugo
BEST YEARS OF OUR LIVES, THE
LIFEBOAT
YOUNG LIONS, THE

Fuller, Parmer
WHITE GHOST

Fusco, Giovanni
HIROSHIMA, MON AMOUR

Gabriel, Peter
BIRDY

Glass, Philip
HAMBURGER HILL

Gold, Ernest
CROSS OF IRON
JUDGMENT AT NUREMBERG
ON THE BEACH

Goldsmith, Jerry
BLUE MAX, THE
BOYS FROM BRAZIL, THE
FIRST BLOOD
IN HARM'S WAY
MAC ARTHUR
MORITURI
PATTON
RAMBO III
RAMBO: FIRST BLOOD, PART II
SAND PEBBLES, THE
SEVEN DAYS IN MAY
TORA! TORA! TORA!
TWILIGHT'S LAST GLEAMING
UNDER FIRE
VON RYAN'S EXPRESS
WIND AND THE LION, THE

Goodwin, Ron
BATTLE OF BRITAIN, THE
FORCE 10 FROM NAVARONE
WHERE EAGLES DARE

Gould, Glenn
SLAUGHTERHOUSE-FIVE

Gray, Alan
AFRICAN QUEEN, THE

Gray, Allan
LIFE AND DEATH OF COLONEL BLIMP, THE

Great, Don
SOLDIER'S REVENGE

Green, John
ALVAREZ KELLY

Green, Philip
OPERATION AMSTERDAM

Greenwood, John
DRUMS
FRIEDA
PIMPERNEL SMITH

Gretry
LA MARSEILLAISE

Gross, Charles
BRADY'S ESCAPE

Gruenberg, Louise
COMMANDOS STRIKE AT DAWN, THE

Grusin, Dave
LITTLE DRUMMER GIRL, THE
REDS

Hadjidakis, Manos
PEDESTRIAN, THE

Hageman, Richard
FORT APACHE
SHE WORE A YELLOW RIBBON

Hajos, Karl
MOROCCO

Haller, Hermann
FOUR IN A JEEP

Halligan, Dick
GO TELL THE SPARTANS

Hamlisch, Marvin
BANANAS

Hammond, John
LITTLE BIG MAN

Hand, Herman
FAREWELL TO ARMS, A

Harline, Leigh
DESERT RATS, THE
FIRST YANK INTO TOKYO

Harling, W. Franke
FAREWELL TO ARMS, A

Hazard, Richard
HEROES

Heindorf, Ray
UP IN ARMS

Herrmann, Bernard
NAKED AND THE DEAD, THE

Hollander, Frederick
BERLIN EXPRESS

Horner, James
TESTAMENT
UNCOMMON VALOR

Horton, Bobby
REBEL LOVE

Howard, James Newton
OFF LIMITS

Hoyer, Ole
MISFIT BRIGADE, THE

Ifukube, Akira
HARP OF BURMA

Ikebe, Shinichiro
KAGEMUSHA
MACARTHUR'S CHILDREN

Isham, Mark
BEAST, THE

James, Tim
NIGHTWARS

Janacek, Leos
UNBEARABLE LIGHTNESS OF BEING, THE

Jansen, Hans
DEADLINE

Jarre, Maurice
BEHOLD A PALE HORSE
DAMNED, THE
DISTANT THUNDER
DOCTOR ZHIVAGO
DON'T CRY, IT'S ONLY THUNDER
FIREFOX
LAWRENCE OF ARABIA
LION OF THE DESERT
LONGEST DAY, THE
MARCH OR DIE
NIGHT OF THE GENERALS, THE
SHOUT AT THE DEVIL
TAPS
TIN DRUM, THE
TRAIN, THE
YEAR OF LIVING DANGEROUSLY, THE

Jaubert, Maurice
GREEN ROOM, THE

Jeny, Zoltan
REVOLT OF JOB, THE

Johnson, Laurie
DR. STRANGELOVE: OR HOW I LEARNED TO STOP WORRYING AND LOVE THE BOMB

Jones, Quincy
PAWNBROKER, THE

Kabiljo, Alfie
SKY BANDITS

Kaper, Bronislau
BATAAN
RED BADGE OF COURAGE, THE
STRANGER, THE

Kaper, Bronsilau
TOBRUK

Kaplan, Sol
DESTINATION GOBI

Kauer, Gene
WARKILL

Kaun, Bernhard
FAREWELL TO ARMS, A

Kilar, Wojciech
DAVID

MUSIC COMPOSERS

King, Dennis
PRIVATES ON PARADE

Kinoshita, Chuji
HUMAN CONDITION, THE

Kitajima, Osamu
CAPTIVE HEARTS

Knopfler, Mark
CAL

Koproff, Dana
BIG RED ONE, THE

Korngold, Erich Wolfgang
SEA HAWK, THE

Kosma, Joseph
ELUSIVE CORPORAL, THE
GRAND ILLUSION
LA MARSEILLAISE

Krenz, Jan
KANAL

Lackey, Douglas
WARKILL

Lalande
LA MARSEILLAISE

Lange, Arthur
JUNGLE PATROL

Lava, William
PT 109

Lavagnino, Angelo Francesco
CHIMES AT MIDNIGHT

Legrand, Michel
LOVE IN GERMANY, A

Leipold, John
FAREWELL TO ARMS, A

Leopold, John
FLYING DEUCES, THE

Liska, Zdenek
SHOP ON MAIN STREET, THE

Liszt, Franz
COLONEL REDL

Louie, Diane
LATINO

Lucas, Leighton
DAM BUSTERS, THE

McClintick, Steve
NIGHTWARS

Mancina, Mark
NIGHTWARS

Mandel, Johnny
M*A*S*H

Markowitz, Richard
CRY OF BATTLE

Marquardt, Paul
FAREWELL TO ARMS, A

Martin, Peter
HOPE AND GLORY

May, Brian
DEATH BEFORE DISHONOR
GALLIPOLI
MISSING IN ACTION 2—THE BEGINNING

Mead, Abigail
FULL METAL JACKET

Mendoza-Nava, Jaime
BOYS IN COMPANY C, THE

Meyer, Friedrich
TIN DRUM, THE

Micalizzi, Franco
LAST HUNTER, THE

Michelet, Michel
OUTPOST IN MOROCCO

Miller, Glenn
MACARTHUR'S CHILDREN

Monn-Iversen, Egil
SNOW TREASURE

Mooney, Hal
RAID ON ROMMEL

Morricone, Ennio
BATTLE OF ALGIERS, THE
BURN
DIRTY HEROES
GOOD, THE BAD, AND THE UGLY, THE
MASSACRE IN ROME
TIME OF DESTINY, A

Morris, John
LAST REMAKE OF BEAU GESTE, THE
TO BE OR NOT TO BE

Mozart, Wolfgang Amadeus
LA MARSEILLAISE

Murray, Lyn
BRIDGES AT TOKO-RI, THE
D-DAY, THE SIXTH OF JUNE

Myers, Stanley
COUP DE GRACE
DEER HUNTER, THE

Nascimbene, Mario
ALEXANDER THE GREAT

Neal, Chris
REBEL

Newman, Alfred
BEAU GESTE
DIARY OF ANNE FRANK, THE
DRUMS ALONG THE MOHAWK
FOREIGN CORRESPONDENT
GUNGA DIN
PURPLE HEART, THE
RAZOR'S EDGE, THE
THIS ABOVE ALL
TWELVE O'CLOCK HIGH
WHAT PRICE GLORY?

Newman, Emil
JUNGLE PATROL

Newman, Lionel
SALZBURG CONNECTION, THE

Nicolai, Bruno
DIRTY HEROES

Niehaus, Lennie
HEARTBREAK RIDGE

Nitzsche, Jack
HEROES
OFFICER AND A GENTLEMAN, AN
RAZOR'S EDGE, THE

North, Alex
DESIREE
GOOD MORNING, VIETNAM
SPARTACUS

Ocampo, Oscar Cardoza
FUNNY, DIRTY LITTLE WAR, A

Oldfield, Mike
KILLING FIELDS, THE

Ortolani, Riz
ANZIO
FROM HELL TO VICTORY
REASON TO LIVE, A REASON TO DIE, A

Ovchinnikov, Vyacheslav
MY NAME IS IVAN
WAR AND PEACE

Paris, Daniele
NIGHT PORTER, THE

Parker, Clifton
DAMN THE DEFIANT!
WOODEN HORSE, THE

Perl, Lothar
THIS LAND IS MINE

Pezzullo, Franco
LAST DAY OF THE WAR, THE

Piovani, Nicola
NIGHT OF THE SHOOTING STARS, THE

Poledouris, Basil
FAREWELL TO THE KING
FLESH AND BLOOD
IRON EAGLE
RED DAWN

Pontecorvo, Gillo
BATTLE OF ALGIERS, THE

Previn, Andre
FOUR HORSEMEN OF THE APOCALYPSE, THE
KIM

Previn, Charles
SABOTEUR

Prodromides, Jean
DANTON

Prokofiev, Sergei
ALEXANDER NEVSKY
IVAN THE TERRIBLE, PARTS I & II
LOVE AND DEATH

Raben, Peer
MARRIAGE OF MARIA BRAUN, THE

Ragland, Robert O.
SUPERNATURALS, THE

Rainger, Ralph
FAREWELL TO ARMS, A

Rajteric-Kraus, Vladimir
BATTLE OF NERETVA

Rameau, Jean Philippe
LA MARSEILLAISE

Rawsthorne, Alan
CRUEL SEA, THE

Rich, Freddie
STAGE DOOR CANTEEN

MUSIC COMPOSERS

WALK IN THE SUN, A

Richards, Keith
UNBEARABLE LIGHTNESS OF BEING, THE

Rist, Gary
SOLDIER'S REVENGE

Ritz, Lyle
NO DRUMS, NO BUGLES

Robles, Nester
TASTE OF HELL, A

Roder, Milan
LIVES OF A BENGAL LANCER

Rose, David
OPERATION PETTICOAT

Rosenman, Leonard
PORK CHOP HILL

Rosenthal, Laurence
BRASS TARGET
WHO'LL STOP THE RAIN?

Rossellini, Renzo
GENERALE DELLA ROVERE
GERMANY, YEAR ZERO
OPEN CITY
PAISAN

Rota, Nino
LOVE AND ANARCHY
WAR AND PEACE

Rozsa, Miklos
BLOOD ON THE SUN
DRUMS
EL CID
EYE OF THE NEEDLE
FOUR FEATHERS, THE
GREEN BERETS, THE
SAHARA
SPY IN BLACK, THE
SUNDOWN
THAT HAMILTON WOMAN
TIME TO LOVE AND A TIME TO DIE, A
TO BE OR NOT TO BE

Rubinstein, Arthur B.
WARGAMES

Rustichelli, Carlo
SECRET WAR OF HARRY FRIGG, THE

Saint-Saens, Camille
AU REVOIR LES ENFANTS

Sakamoto, Ryuichi
MERRY CHRISTMAS, MR. LAWRENCE

Salter, Hans J.
AGAINST ALL FLAGS
HITLER

Sarde, Philippe
EVERY TIME WE SAY GOODBYE

Sato, Masaru
THRONE OF BLOOD

Sauveplane
LA MARSEILLAISE

Sawtell, Paul
MR. WINKLE GOES TO WAR

Scharf, Walter
FIGHTING SEABEES, THE

Schifrin, Lalo
EAGLE HAS LANDED, THE
ESCAPE TO ATHENA
KELLY'S HEROES
VOYAGE OF THE DAMNED

Schubert, Franz
AU REVOIR LES ENFANTS

Schultze, Norbert
KOLBERG

Schumann, Robert
COLONEL REDL

Scott, John
FINAL COUNTDOWN, THE

Seltzer, Dov
ASSISI UNDERGROUND, THE
HANNA'S WAR

Shire, David
HINDENBURG, THE

Shuken, Leo
FLYING DEUCES, THE

Silvestri, Alan
DELTA FORCE, THE

Siv, Michael
BALLAD OF A SOLDIER

Skiles, Marlin
FLAT TOP

Skinner, Frank
AWAY ALL BOATS
GUNG HO!
SABOTEUR
SHENANDOAH
SHERLOCK HOLMES AND THE SECRET WEAPON
UGLY AMERICAN, THE

Small, Michael
MARATHON MAN

Smeaton, Bruce
ELENI
PLENTY

Smith, Paul
MIRACLE OF THE WHITE STALLIONS

Sondheim, Stephen
REDS

Spoliansky, Mischa
HITLER: THE LAST TEN DAYS

Steiner, Max
BATTLE CRY
CASABLANCA
CHARGE OF THE LIGHT BRIGADE, THE
CLOAK AND DAGGER
DARBY'S RANGERS
DAWN PATROL, THE
DESPERATE JOURNEY
DISTANT DRUMS
GONE WITH THE WIND
LOST PATROL, THE
PASSAGE TO MARSEILLE
SERGEANT YORK
THEY DIED WITH THEIR BOOTS ON
WATCH ON THE RHINE

Sternwald, Jiri
TRANSPORT FROM PARADISE

Stevens, Leith
HELL TO ETERNITY

Storrs, David
P.O.W. THE ESCAPE

Stothart, Herbert
DRAGON SEED
GUY NAMED JOE, A
MRS. MINIVER
THEY WERE EXPENDABLE
THIRTY SECONDS OVER TOKYO

Strauss, Johann
COLONEL REDL

Strummer, Joe
WALKER

Sukman, Harry
BATTLE TAXI

Takemitsu, Toru
RAN

Tamassy, Zdenko
MEPHISTO

Tangerine Dream
KEEP, THE

Thorne, Ken
HOW I WON THE WAR
MURPHY'S WAR

Tiomkin, Dimitri
55 DAYS AT PEKING
COURT-MARTIAL OF BILLY MITCHELL, THE
DRUMS IN THE DEEP SOUTH
GUNS OF NAVARONE, THE
HOME OF THE BRAVE
MEN, THE

Tiomkin, Dmitri
ALAMO, THE

Trovajoli, Armando
TWO WOMEN

Umali, Resti
HOT BOX, THE

Van Otterloo, Rogier
SOLDIER OF ORANGE

Vangelis
MISSING

Vaynberg, Moisei
CRANES ARE FLYING, THE

Walton, Sir William
BATTLE OF BRITAIN, THE
HENRY V
RICHARD III
SPITFIRE

Waxman, Franz
AIR FORCE
DESTINATION TOKYO
EDGE OF DARKNESS
LOST COMMAND, THE
MISTER ROBERTS
OBJECTIVE, BURMA!
RUN SILENT, RUN DEEP
SAYONARA
STALAG 17

PRODUCERS

TARAS BULBA

Webb, Jimmy
HANOI HILTON, THE

Webb, Roy
BACK TO BATAAN
BEHIND THE RISING SUN
BOMBARDIER
CORNERED
FLYING LEATHERNECKS
HITLER'S CHILDREN
MASTER RACE, THE

Webber, Andrew Lloyd
ODESSA FILE, THE

Wellman, Marita M.
NO DEAD HEROES

Williams, John
1941
EMPIRE OF THE SUN
MIDWAY

Williams, Patrick
BEST DEFENSE
CUBA
SOME KIND OF HERO
SWING SHIFT

Williams, Ralph Vaughn
49TH PARALLEL

Willson, Meredith
GREAT DICTATOR, THE

Yepes, Narcisco
FORBIDDEN GAMES

Young, Christopher
BAT 21

Young, Victor
CONQUEROR, THE
FLYING TIGERS
RIO GRANDE
SANDS OF IWO JIMA

Zimmerman, Harry
STEEL CLAW, THE

Zwart, Jacques
DEADLINE

PRODUCERS

Abarbanel, Sam X.
LAST DAY OF THE WAR, THE

Adelson, Merv
TWILIGHT'S LAST GLEAMING

Adler, Buddy
FROM HERE TO ETERNITY
INN OF THE SIXTH HAPPINESS, THE

Adler, Stanislaw
KANAL

Akkad, Moustapha
LION OF THE DESERT

Aldrich, Robert
TOO LATE THE HERO

Allen, Irving
COCKLESHELL HEROES, THE
CROMWELL

Altman, Robert
STREAMERS

Amati, Edmundo
DIRTY HEROES

Angel, Daniel M.
SEA SHALL NOT HAVE THEM, THE

Arthur, Art
BATTLE TAXI

Arthur, Robert
FATHER GOOSE
OPERATION PETTICOAT
SHENANDOAH
TIME TO LOVE AND A TIME TO DIE, A

Asher, Irving
ADVENTURES OF TARTU, THE
SPY IN BLACK, THE

Ayala, Fernando
FUNNY, DIRTY LITTLE WAR, A

Baker, Stanley
ZULU

Balson, Michael
BAT 21

Balurov, Jordan
SHOP ON MAIN STREET, THE

Barnette, Alan
OFF LIMITS

Bartlett, Sy
PORK CHOP HILL

Baxter, Billy
LOVE AND ANARCHY

Beatty, Warren
REDS

Beckerman, Barry
RED DAWN

Beckerman, Sidney
KELLY'S HEROES
MARATHON MAN

Benedict, Howard
CALL OUT THE MARINES
SHERLOCK HOLMES AND THE SECRET WEAPON

Benn, Harry
GOOD MORNING, VIETNAM
RAZOR'S EDGE, THE

Berg, Benjamin
LATINO

Berman, Pandro S.
DRAGON SEED
GUNGA DIN

Bernstein, Jonathan
TESTAMENT

Betzer, Just
MISFIT BRIGADE, THE

Bick, Jerry
SWING SHIFT

Billingsley, Michael
REASON TO LIVE, A REASON TO DIE, A

Bischoff, Samuel
CHARGE OF THE LIGHT BRIGADE, THE
OUTPOST IN MOROCCO

Bittins, Michael
BOAT, THE

Black, Edward
NIGHT TRAIN
WE DIVE AT DAWN

Blanke, Henry
EDGE OF DARKNESS
SEA HAWK, THE

Blaustein, Julian
DESIREE

Blondy, Raymond
GRAND ILLUSION

Boddoh, Allan F.
GO TELL THE SPARTANS

Bondarchuk, Sergei
WAR AND PEACE

Boorman, John
HOPE AND GLORY

Brabourne, John
DAMN THE DEFIANT!

Brackett, Charles
D-DAY, THE SIXTH OF JUNE

Braun, Zev
PEDESTRIAN, THE

Brauner, Arthur
LOVE IN GERMANY, A

Bren, J. Robert
FIRST YANK INTO TOKYO

Brezner, Larry
GOOD MORNING, VIETNAM

Bricken, Jules
TRAIN, THE

Broccoli, Albert R.
COCKLESHELL HEROES, THE

Bronston, Samuel
55 DAYS AT PEKING
EL CID

Brooks, Mel
TO BE OR NOT TO BE

Brown, Harry Joe
SAHARA

Bruckheimer, Jerry
MARCH OR DIE
TOP GUN

Brunel, Adrian
SPITFIRE

Bulajic, Veljko
BATTLE OF NERETVA

Caffey, Frank
PATTON

Cagney, William
BLOOD ON THE SUN

Calley, John
CATCH-22

PRODUCERS

Campbell, Bruce
JOHNNY GOT HIS GUN

Cannold, Mitchell
GO TELL THE SPARTANS

Carabatsos, Jim
HAMBURGER HILL

Carroll, Matt
BREAKER MORANT

Challis, Drummond
RIDDLE OF THE SANDS, THE

Champion, John
DRAGONFLY SQUADRON

Chaplin, Charles
GREAT DICTATOR, THE

Chertok, Jack
NORTHERN PURSUIT

Chester, Hal E.
SECRET WAR OF HARRY FRIGG, THE

Christie, Howard
AGAINST ALL FLAGS
AWAY ALL BOATS

Cimino, Michael
DEER HUNTER, THE

Clark, Robert
DAM BUSTERS, THE

Cohen, Albert J.
FIGHTING SEABEES, THE

Cohn, Arthur
BLACK AND WHITE IN COLOR
GARDEN OF THE FINZI-CONTINIS, THE

Conti, Mario
PAISAN

Cooper, Merian C.
FORT APACHE
RIO GRANDE
SHE WORE A YELLOW RIBBON

Coppola, Francis Ford
APOCALYPSE NOW
GARDENS OF STONE

Corman, Gene
BIG RED ONE, THE
TOBRUK

Couyoumdjian, Gianfranco
LAST HUNTER, THE

Cowan, Lester
COMMANDOS STRIKE AT DAWN, THE

Cowan, Maurice
OPERATION AMSTERDAM

Coward, Noel
IN WHICH WE SERVE

Craig, Stuart
CAL

Crawford, Robert L.
LITTLE DRUMMER GIRL, THE

Crespo, J.C.
SOLDIER'S REVENGE

Dalrymple, Ian
WOODEN HORSE, THE

Dalton, Christopher
POWER PLAY

Dauman, Anatole
TIN DRUM, THE

David, Saul
VON RYAN'S EXPRESS

Davidson, Jay
WHITE GHOST

de Beauregard, Georges
LES CARABINIERS

de Broca, Philippe
KING OF HEARTS

De Haven, Carter
ULZANA'S RAID

De Laurentiis, Dino
ANZIO
WAR AND PEACE

De Negri, Giuliani G.
NIGHT OF THE SHOOTING STARS, THE

de Sarigny, Peter
MALTA STORY

Deeley, Michael
DEER HUNTER, THE
MURPHY'S WAR

deFarla, Walt
DON'T CRY, IT'S ONLY THUNDER

Del Giudice, Filippo
HENRY V

Demme, Jonathan
HOT BOX, THE

DeWaay, Larry
DOGS OF WAR, THE

Dickinson, Thorold
HILL 24 DOESN'T ANSWER

Disney, Walt
MIRACLE OF THE WHITE STALLIONS

Dorfman, Robert
FORBIDDEN GAMES

Douglas, Peter Vincent
FINAL COUNTDOWN, THE

Dryhurst, Michael
HOPE AND GLORY

Durniok, Manfred
COLONEL REDL
MEPHISTO

Eagle [Sam Spiegel], S.P.
AFRICAN QUEEN, THE
STRANGER, THE

Eastwood, Clint
FIREFOX
HEARTBREAK RIDGE

Edwards, Robert Gordon
NIGHT PORTER, THE

Eisenstein, Sergei
IVAN THE TERRIBLE, PARTS I & II

Elfand, Martin
OFFICER AND A GENTLEMAN, AN

Emanuel, Phillip
REBEL

Endfield, Cy
ZULU

Englund, George
UGLY AMERICAN, THE

Ergas, Morris
GENERALE DELLA ROVERE

Ermolieff, Joseph N.
OUTPOST IN MOROCCO

Evans, Robert
MARATHON MAN

Fay, William
WHITE GHOST

Feitshans, Buzz
1941
FIRST BLOOD
RAMBO III
RAMBO: FIRST BLOOD, PART II
RED DAWN
UNCOMMON VALOR

Fellows, Robert
BACK TO BATAAN
BOMBARDIER

Fengler, Michael
MARRIAGE OF MARIA BRAUN, THE

Ferry, Christian
BLUE MAX, THE

Feuer, Cy
CABARET

Fiedler, John
BEAST, THE

Fields, Freddie
VICTORY

Fisher, David
BAT 21

Fisz, S. Benjamin
BATTLE OF BRITAIN, THE

Ford, John
FORT APACHE
RIO GRANDE
SHE WORE A YELLOW RIBBON
THEY WERE EXPENDABLE

Foreman, Carl
GUNS OF NAVARONE, THE

Foster, David
HEROES

Foxwell, Ivan
COLDITZ STORY, THE

Foy, Bryan
GUADALCANAL DIARY
PT 109

Franklin, Sidney
MRS. MINIVER

Friedman, Stephen
EYE OF THE NEEDLE

Frye, Peter
HILL 24 DOESN'T ANSWER

Fryer, Robert
VOYAGE OF THE DAMNED

PRODUCERS

Furie, Sidney J.
PURPLE HEARTS

Gage, Nicholas
ELENI

Garwood, John
TASTE OF HELL, A

Geiger, Rod E.
PAISAN

Geraghty, Maurice
ACTION IN ARABIA

Giler, David
SOUTHERN COMFORT

Gilmore, William S.
LAST REMAKE OF BEAU GESTE, THE

Globus, Yoram
ASSISI UNDERGROUND, THE
BRADDOCK: MISSING IN ACTION III
DELTA FORCE, THE
HANNA'S WAR
HANOI HILTON, THE
INVASION U.S.A.
MISSING IN ACTION
MISSING IN ACTION 2—THE BEGINNING
P.O.W. THE ESCAPE

Goetz, Harry M.
LAST OF THE MOHICANS, THE

Goetz, William
SAYONARA

Golan, Menahem
ASSISI UNDERGROUND, THE
BRADDOCK: MISSING IN ACTION III
DELTA FORCE, THE
HANNA'S WAR
HANOI HILTON, THE
INVASION U.S.A.
MISSING IN ACTION
MISSING IN ACTION 2—THE BEGINNING
P.O.W. THE ESCAPE

Golden, Edward A.
HITLER'S CHILDREN

Golden, Robert
MASTER RACE, THE

Goldwyn, Samuel
BEST YEARS OF OUR LIVES, THE
UP IN ARMS

Gordon, Leon
KIM

Gottlieb, Alex
BUCK PRIVATES

Grainger, Edmund
FLYING LEATHERNECKS
FLYING TIGERS
SANDS OF IWO JIMA

Granet, Bert
BERLIN EXPRESS

Green, Gerald
SALVADOR

Gregory, Paul
NAKED AND THE DEAD, THE

Griffith, Jill
84 CHARLIE MOPIC

Griffith, Raymond
DRUMS ALONG THE MOHAWK

Grimaldi, Alberto
BURN
GOOD, THE BAD, AND THE UGLY, THE

Grofe, Jr., Ferde
WARKILL

Grossberg, Jack
BANANAS

Haggiag, Ever
DAMNED, THE

Halfon, Samy
HIROSHIMA, MON AMOUR

Halmi, Jr., Robert
BRADY'S ESCAPE

Hanus, Ladislav
SHOP ON MAIN STREET, THE

Hara, Masato
MACARTHUR'S CHILDREN
RAN

Harel, Sharon
EVERY TIME WE SAY GOODBYE
IRON EAGLE II

Harmon, Sidney
MEN IN WAR

Harris, James B.
PATHS OF GLORY

Hartwig, Wolf C.
CROSS OF IRON

Hasoya, Tatsuo
HUMAN CONDITION, THE

Hayward, Leland
MISTER ROBERTS

Hecht, Harold
RUN SILENT, RUN DEEP
TARAS BULBA

Hellman, Jerome
COMING HOME

Herald, Peter V.
MIRACLE OF THE WHITE STALLIONS

Herland, Richard
SKY BANDITS

Herman, Norman T.
ROLLING THUNDER

Hornblow, Jr., Arthur
WAR LOVER, THE

Houwer, Rob
SOLDIER OF ORANGE

Howard, Leslie
PIMPERNEL SMITH
SPITFIRE

Hyman, Kenneth
DIRTY DOZEN, THE

Ide, Masato
KAGEMUSHA

Jacks, Robert L.
DESERT RATS, THE

Jacobson, Frank R.
HIDING PLACE, THE

Jacoby, Irving
SNOW TREASURE

Jaffe, Herb
LORDS OF DISCIPLINE, THE
WHO'LL STOP THE RAIN?
WIND AND THE LION, THE

Jaffe, Howard B.
TAPS

Jaffe, Stanley R.
TAPS

Jeffrey, Tom
ODD ANGRY SHOT, THE

Joffe, Charles H.
BANANAS
LOVE AND DEATH

Johnson, Mark
GOOD MORNING, VIETNAM

Johnson, Nunnally
DESERT FOX, THE

Junkersdorf, Eberhard
COUP DE GRACE

Kalatozov, Mikhail
CRANES ARE FLYING, THE

Kastner, Elliott
WHERE EAGLES DARE

Katz, Gloria
BEST DEFENSE

Katzka, Gabriel
KELLY'S HEROES
LORDS OF DISCIPLINE, THE
SOLDIER BLUE
WHO'LL STOP THE RAIN?

Kemeny, John
IRON EAGLE II

Kennedy, Kathleen
EMPIRE OF THE SUN

King, Frank
DRUMS IN THE DEEP SOUTH

King, George
SPITFIRE

King, Maurice
DRUMS IN THE DEEP SOUTH

Kirkwood, Gene
KEEP, THE

Kitiparaporn, Lek
ANGKOR-CAMBODIA EXPRESS

Klinger, Michael
SHOUT AT THE DEVIL

Kobayashi, Masaki
HUMAN CONDITION, THE

Koch, Howard W.
SOME KIND OF HERO

Koch, Jr., Howard W.
KEEP, THE

Kohlmar, Fred
WACKIEST SHIP IN THE ARMY, THE

PRODUCERS

Kohn, Nate
ZULU DAWN

Kopelson, Arnold
PLATOON

Korda, Alexander
DARK JOURNEY
DRUMS
FOUR FEATHERS, THE
THAT HAMILTON WOMAN

Korytowski, Manfred
WANNSEE CONFERENCE, THE

Korzen, Benni
MISFIT BRIGADE, THE

Kotzky, Jacob
EVERY TIME WE SAY GOODBYE
IRON EAGLE II

Kramer, Stanley
HOME OF THE BRAVE
JUDGMENT AT NUREMBERG
MEN, THE
ON THE BEACH

Kubik, Lawrence
DEATH BEFORE DISHONOR

Kubrick, Stanley
DR. STRANGELOVE: OR HOW I LEARNED TO STOP WORRYING AND LOVE THE BOMB
FULL METAL JACKET

Kuri, John A.
CAPTIVE HEARTS

Kurosawa, Akira
KAGEMUSHA
THRONE OF BLOOD

Laemmle, Jr., Carl
ALL QUIET ON THE WESTERN FRONT

Langner, Philip
PAWNBROKER, THE

Larsen, Keith
MISSION BATANGAS

Lasky, Jesse L.
SERGEANT YORK

Lean, David
LAWRENCE OF ARABIA

Lesser, Sol
STAGE DOOR CANTEEN

Lesslie, Colin
TUNES OF GLORY

Lester, Richard
HOW I WON THE WAR

Levin, Irving H.
HELL TO ETERNITY

Levine, Joseph E.
BRIDGE TOO FAR, A

Levine, Nat
CRIMSON ROMANCE

Levine, Richard
BRIDGE TOO FAR, A

Levy, Alfredo
DAMNED, THE

Levy, Michael I.
GARDENS OF STONE

Lewis, Arthur
BRASS TARGET

Lewis, Edward
MISSING
SEVEN DAYS IN MAY
SPARTACUS

Lewis, Jerry
WHICH WAY TO THE FRONT?

Lewis, Mildred
MISSING

Lewis, Roger
PAWNBROKER, THE

Lichtman, Al
YOUNG LIONS, THE

Lighton, Louis D.
LIVES OF A BENGAL LANCER

Littman, Lynne
TESTAMENT

Lloyd, Euan
FINAL OPTION, THE
SEA WOLVES, THE
WILD GEESE II
WILD GEESE, THE

Lloyd, Frank
SABOTEUR

Loeb, Harold
SOLDIER BLUE

Logan, Joshua
ENSIGN PULVER

Lord, Robert
DAWN PATROL, THE

Lovell, Patricia
GALLIPOLI

Lubitsch, Ernst
TO BE OR NOT TO BE

Lucari, Gianni Hecht
GARDEN OF THE FINZI-CONTINIS, THE

Lukas, Jaromir
SHOP ON MAIN STREET, THE

McCarthy, Frank
MAC ARTHUR
PATTON

McElroy, James
YEAR OF LIVING DANGEROUSLY, THE

Macgowan, Kenneth
LIFEBOAT

MacQuitty, William
BLACK TENT, THE

Mahin, John Lee
HORSE SOLDIERS, THE

Mahon, Barry
ASSAULT OF THE REBEL GIRLS

Malle, Louis
AU REVOIR LES ENFANTS

Mankiewicz, Herman
DUCK SOUP

Mann, Anthony
EL CID

Marcucci, Robert P.
RAZOR'S EDGE, THE

Marini, Angel Flores
WALKER

Marshall, Alan
BIRDY

Marshall, Frank
EMPIRE OF THE SUN

Marshall, Ray
GOING HOME

Marx, Joszef
COLONEL REDL

Matthews, Fritz
NIGHTWARS

Menegoz, Margaret
DANTON

Menzies, William Cameron
NORTH STAR, THE

Meyers, Nancy
PRIVATE BENJAMIN

Milestone, Lewis
WALK IN THE SUN, A

Mileti, Nick J.
STREAMERS

Milius, John
UNCOMMON VALOR

Millar, Stuart
LITTLE BIG MAN

Miller, Harvey
PRIVATE BENJAMIN

Miller, J.C.
NO DEAD HEROES

Milliken, Sue
ODD ANGRY SHOT, THE

Mirisch, Walter
FLAT TOP
MIDWAY

Monash, Paul
SLAUGHTERHOUSE-FIVE

Montgomery, George
STEEL CLAW, THE

Morgan, Andre
FAREWELL TO THE KING

Morgan, Andrew
BOYS IN COMPANY C, THE

Morros, Boris
FLYING DEUCES, THE

Moses, Ben
GOOD MORNING, VIETNAM

Moss, Jack
MR. WINKLE GOES TO WAR

Motoki, Sojiro
THRONE OF BLOOD

PRODUCERS

Murphey, Michael S.
SUPERNATURALS, THE

Musu, Antonio
BATTLE OF ALGIERS, THE

Nagata, Masaichi
FIRES ON THE PLAIN
GATE OF HELL

Nasatir, Marcia
HAMBURGER HILL

Nebenzahl, Seymour
KAMERADSCHAFT

Neill, Gary A.
BAT 21

Nichols, Dudley
THIS LAND IS MINE

Niven, Jr., David
EAGLE HAS LANDED, THE
ESCAPE TO ATHENA

Nolin, Michael
84 CHARLIE MOPIC

Norman, Leslie
CRUEL SEA, THE

O'Brien, Lorenzo
WALKER

O'Toole, Stanley
BOYS FROM BRAZIL, THE

Olivier, Laurence
HENRY V
RICHARD III

Oppenheimer, Peer J.
OPERATION CIA

Orton, Wallace
SALUTE JOHN CITIZEN

Papp, Joseph
PLENTY

Pennington, Jon
MOUSE THAT ROARED, THE

Perlberg, William
BRIDGES AT TOKO-RI, THE

Perrin, Jacques
BLACK AND WHITE IN COLOR

Peverall, John
DEER HUNTER, THE

Pick, Mark
ELENI

Piedra, Emiliano
CHIMES AT MIDNIGHT

Pitcher, George
GLORY AT SEA

Pommer, Erich
FIRE OVER ENGLAND

Ponti, Carlo
DOCTOR ZHIVAGO
LES CARABINIERS
MASSACRE IN ROME
TWO WOMEN

Powell, Dick
CONQUEROR, THE

Powell, Michael
49TH PARALLEL
LIFE AND DEATH OF COLONEL BLIMP, THE
ONE OF OUR AIRCRAFT IS MISSING
PURSUIT OF THE GRAF SPEE, THE

Pratt, Charles A.
GREAT SANTINI, THE

Preminger, Ingo
M*A*S*H
SALZBURG CONNECTION, THE

Preminger, Otto
IN HARM'S WAY

Pressburger, Emeric
LIFE AND DEATH OF COLONEL BLIMP, THE
ONE OF OUR AIRCRAFT IS MISSING
PURSUIT OF THE GRAF SPEE, THE

Pressman, Edward R.
PLENTY

Puttnam, David
CAL
DUELLISTS, THE
KILLING FIELDS, THE

Quenelle, John
REBEL LOVE

Rackin, Martin
DARBY'S RANGERS
DEEP SIX, THE
HORSE SOLDIERS, THE

Rademakers, Fons
ASSAULT, THE

Randall, Richard
ANGKOR-CAMBODIA EXPRESS

Ransohoff, Martin
CATCH-22

Reid, Cliff
LOST PATROL, THE

Reinhardt, Gottfried
RED BADGE OF COURAGE, THE

Reinhardt, Wolfgang
HITLER: THE LAST TEN DAYS

Relph, Michael
FRIEDA

Relph, Simon
PRIVATES ON PARADE
RETURN OF THE SOLDIER, THE

Renoir, Jean
THIS LAND IS MINE

Repetto, Luis Osvaldo
FUNNY, DIRTY LITTLE WAR, A

Richards, Dick
MARCH OR DIE

Richards, Martin
BOYS FROM BRAZIL, THE

Riskin, Everett
GUY NAMED JOE, A

Robinson, Casey
DAYS OF GLORY

Robson, Mark
LOST COMMAND, THE

Rohrbach, Gunter
BOAT, THE

Rosenberg, Aaron
MORITURI
TO HELL AND BACK

Rossellini, Roberto
GERMANY, YEAR ZERO
OPEN CITY
PAISAN

Rossen, Robert
ALEXANDER THE GREAT

Rubin, Stanley
DESTINATION GOBI
FRANCIS IN THE NAVY

Ruddy, Albert S.
FAREWELL TO THE KING

Saadi, Yacef
BATTLE OF ALGIERS, THE

Salkind, Alexander
AUSTERLITZ

Saltzman, Harry
BATTLE OF BRITAIN, THE

Samuels, Ron
IRON EAGLE

Schaffel, Robert
DISTANT THUNDER

Schary, Dore
GO FOR BROKE

Schell, Maximilian
PEDESTRIAN, THE

Schlom, Herman
CLAY PIGEON, THE

Schneer, Charles H.
HELLCATS OF THE NAVY

Schneider, Harold
WARGAMES

Scott, Adrian
CORNERED

Seitz, Franz
TIN DRUM, THE

Sellers, Arlene
CUBA

Seltzer, Frank N.
JUNGLE PATROL

Selznick, David O.
GONE WITH THE WIND

Shavelson, Melville
CAST A GIANT SHADOW

Shenson, Walter
MOUSE THAT ROARED, THE

Shyer, Charles
PRIVATE BENJAMIN

Siegel, Sol C.
ALVAREZ KELLY
WHAT PRICE GLORY?

Silagni, Giorgio
BLACK AND WHITE IN COLOR

PRODUCERS

Silberman, Serge
RAN

Simpson, Don
TOP GUN

Sistrom, Joseph
WAKE ISLAND

Skinner, Ann
RETURN OF THE SOLDIER, THE

Skirball, Jack H.
SABOTEUR

Sloan, John R.
FORCE 10 FROM NAVARONE

Small, Edward
LAST OF THE MOHICANS, THE

Snell, Peter
PRAYER FOR THE DYING, A

Soisson, Joel
SUPERNATURALS, THE

Sperling, Milton
BATTLE OF THE BULGE
CLOAK AND DAGGER
COURT-MARTIAL OF BILLY MITCHELL, THE
DISTANT DRUMS

Spiegel, Sam
BRIDGE ON THE RIVER KWAI, THE
LAWRENCE OF ARABIA
NICHOLAS AND ALEXANDRA
NIGHT OF THE GENERALS, THE

Spielberg, Steven
EMPIRE OF THE SUN

Spikings, Barry
DEER HUNTER, THE

Stafford, John
SPITFIRE

Stanley-Evans, Michael
BRIDGE TOO FAR, A

Starger, Martin
CODE NAME: EMERALD

Stark, Ray
BILOXI BLUES

Starr, Irving
BATAAN

Steinberg, Joe
CRY OF BATTLE

Steinmann, Herbert R.
LOVE AND ANARCHY

Stevens, George
DIARY OF ANNE FRANK, THE

Stigwood, Robert
GALLIPOLI

Stone, Oliver
SALVADOR

Straus, E. Charles
HITLER

Sturges, John
GREAT ESCAPE, THE

Sutro, John
49TH PARALLEL

IMMORTAL BATTALION, THE

Takagi, Masayuki
HARP OF BURMA

Taplin, Jonathan
UNDER FIRE

Tatelman, Harry
RAID ON ROMMEL

Thomas, Anna
TIME OF DESTINY, A

Thomas, Jeremy
MERRY CHRISTMAS, MR. LAWRENCE

Tors, Ivan
BATTLE TAXI

Towers, Harry Alan
PLATOON LEADER

Trotti, Lamar
IMMORTAL SERGEANT, THE

Turman, Lawrence
HEROES

Turnbull, Hector
MOROCCO

Unger, Anthony B.
FORCE 10 FROM NAVARONE

Unger, Oliver A.
FORCE 10 FROM NAVARONE

Vanoff, Nick
ELENI

Versluys, Gys
FLESH AND BLOOD

von Vietinghoff, Joachim
DAVID

Vuattoux, Rene G.
ELUSIVE CORPORAL, THE

Wakatsuki, Shigeru
HUMAN CONDITION, THE

Wald, Jerry
DESTINATION TOKYO
OBJECTIVE, BURMA!

Walker, Norman
IMMORTAL BATTALION, THE

Wallis, Hal B.
AIR FORCE
CASABLANCA
DAWN PATROL, THE
DESPERATE JOURNEY
PASSAGE TO MARSEILLE
SEA HAWK, THE
SERGEANT YORK
THEY DIED WITH THEIR BOOTS ON
THIS IS THE ARMY
WATCH ON THE RHINE

Walsh, Raoul
BATTLE CRY

Wanger, Walter
FOREIGN CORRESPONDENT
GUNG HO!
SUNDOWN

Ware, Clyde
NO DRUMS, NO BUGLES

Warner, Jack L.
SEA HAWK, THE
THIS IS THE ARMY

Wayne, John
ALAMO, THE

Wayne, Michael
CAST A GIANT SHADOW
GREEN BERETS, THE

Webb, Jack
D.I., THE

Wechsler, Lazar
FOUR IN A JEEP

Wellman, William A.
BEAU GESTE

Whittaker, W.A.
DAM BUSTERS, THE

Wiener, Jack
ESCAPE TO ATHENA

Wilcox, Herbert
BATTLE HELL
NURSE EDITH CAVELL

Wilcoxon, Henry
BUCCANEER, THE

Wilder, Billy
STALAG 17

Williams, Elmo
TORA! TORA! TORA!

Winer, Jack
EAGLE HAS LANDED, THE

Winitsky, Alex
CUBA

Winkler, Irwin
REVOLUTION

Wintle, Julian
ONE THAT GOT AWAY, THE

Wise, Robert
SAND PEBBLES, THE

Wizan, Joe
IRON EAGLE

Wolper, David L.
BRIDGE AT REMAGEN, THE

Wolters-Alfs, Elisabeth
DEADLINE

Woolf, James
KING RAT

Woolf, John
ODESSA FILE, THE

Wurtzel, Sol M.
GREAT GUNS

Yordan, Philip
BATTLE OF THE BULGE

Yorkin, Bud
START THE REVOLUTION WITHOUT ME

You-No-Kai
MACARTHUR'S CHILDREN

Youngstein, Max E.
FAIL SAFE

SCREENWRITERS

Zaentz, Saul
UNBEARABLE LIGHTNESS OF BEING, THE

Zanuck, Darryl F.
LONGEST DAY, THE
PURPLE HEART, THE
RAZOR'S EDGE, THE
THIS ABOVE ALL
TWELVE O'CLOCK HIGH
YANK IN THE R.A.F., A

Zimbalist, Sam
THIRTY SECONDS OVER TOKYO

Zinnemann, Fred
BEHOLD A PALE HORSE

SCREENWRITERS

Abarbanel, Sam X.
LAST DAY OF THE WAR, THE

Abbott, George
ALL QUIET ON THE WESTERN FRONT

Abdullah, Achmed
LIVES OF A BENGAL LANCER

Ackland, Rodney
49TH PARALLEL

Agee, James
AFRICAN QUEEN, THE

Agotay, Louis
DIRTY HEROES

Aldrich, Robert
TOO LATE THE HERO

Allen, Chris
LAST REMAKE OF BEAU GESTE, THE

Allen, Jay Presson
CABARET

Allen, Woody
BANANAS
LOVE AND DEATH

Ambler, Eric
BATTLE HELL
CRUEL SEA, THE
IMMORTAL BATTALION, THE

Ambrose, David
FINAL COUNTDOWN, THE

Amidei, Sergio
GENERALE DELLA ROVERE
OPEN CITY
PAISAN

Anderson, Maxwell
ALL QUIET ON THE WESTERN FRONT

Anderson, Robert W.
SAND PEBBLES, THE

Anderson, William C.
BAT 21

Andrews, Del
ALL QUIET ON THE WESTERN FRONT

Andrews, Robert D.
BATAAN

Andrzejewski, Jerzy
ASHES AND DIAMONDS

Anhalt, Edward
ESCAPE TO ATHENA
YOUNG LIONS, THE

Annaud, Jean-Jacques
BLACK AND WHITE IN COLOR

Antonio, Lew
MISSION BATANGAS

Appet, Leah
EVERY TIME WE SAY GOODBYE

Ardrey, Robert
FOUR HORSEMEN OF THE APOCALYPSE, THE

Arlorio, Giorgio
BURN
BURN

Arnold, Elliott
ALVAREZ KELLY

Asmodi, Herbert
CROSS OF IRON

Aurenche, Jean
FORBIDDEN GAMES

Badalucco, Nicola
DAMNED, THE

Bagby, Jr., Milton
REBEL LOVE

Bailey, John
RIDDLE OF THE SANDS, THE

Balchin, Nigel
MALTA STORY

Balderston, John
GONE WITH THE WIND
LAST OF THE MOHICANS, THE
LIVES OF A BENGAL LANCER

Ballinger, Bill S.
OPERATION CIA

Band, Albert
RED BADGE OF COURAGE, THE

Barbour, Malcolm
P.O.W. THE ESCAPE

Bardem, Juan Antonio
LAST DAY OF THE WAR, THE

Baron, Elizabeth
SALUTE JOHN CITIZEN

Barrett, James Lee
D.I., THE
GREEN BERETS, THE
ON THE BEACH
SHENANDOAH

Bartlett, Sy
TWELVE O'CLOCK HIGH

Barwood, Hal
MAC ARTHUR

Barzman, Ben
BACK TO BATAAN

Bass, Ronald
CODE NAME: EMERALD
GARDENS OF STONE

Beatty, Warren
REDS

Becker, Jurek
DAVID

Behr, Jack
BIRDY

Benchley, Robert
FOREIGN CORRESPONDENT

Bennett, Charles
FOREIGN CORRESPONDENT

Beresford, Bruce
BREAKER MORANT

Berk, Howard
LAST DAY OF THE WAR, THE

Bernstein, Walter
FAIL SAFE
TRAIN, THE

Bessie, Alvah
NORTHERN PURSUIT

Biberman, Herbert
ACTION IN ARABIA
MASTER RACE, THE

Bing, Steve
MISSING IN ACTION 2—THE BEGINNING

Binyon, Claude
THIS IS THE ARMY

Biro, Lajos
FOUR FEATHERS, THE

Bluel, Richard
RAID ON ROMMEL

Blum, Edwin
STALAG 17

Bogomolov, Vladimir Osipovich
MY NAME IS IVAN

Boland, Bridget
WAR AND PEACE

Bolt, Robert
DOCTOR ZHIVAGO
LAWRENCE OF ARABIA

Bond, Edward
NICHOLAS AND ALEXANDRA

Bondarchuk, Sergei
WAR AND PEACE

Bonicelli, Vittorio
GARDEN OF THE FINZI-CONTINIS, THE

Boorman, John
HOPE AND GLORY

Booth, Charles G.
SUNDOWN

Boretz, Allen
UP IN ARMS

Boretz, Alvin
BRASS TARGET

Boris, Robert
SOME KIND OF HERO

Bost, Pierre
FORBIDDEN GAMES

SCREENWRITERS

Boulanger, Daniel
KING OF HEARTS

Boule, Pierre
BRIDGE ON THE RIVER KWAI, THE

Boyle, Richard
SALVADOR

Braun, Alfred
KOLBERG

Breen, Richard L.
PT 109

Bren, J. Robert
FIRST YANK INTO TOKYO

Breslow, Lou
GREAT GUNS

Brown, Harry
D-DAY, THE SIXTH OF JUNE
DEEP SIX, THE
SANDS OF IWO JIMA

Bruckner, Jutta
COUP DE GRACE

Bruner, James
BRADDOCK: MISSING IN ACTION III
DELTA FORCE, THE
INVASION U.S.A.
MISSING IN ACTION
P.O.W. THE ESCAPE

Brynych, Zbynek
TRANSPORT FROM PARADISE

Bulajic, Stevo
BATTLE OF NERETVA

Bulajic, Veljko
BATTLE OF NERETVA

Burke, Martyn
POWER PLAY

Burnett, W.R.
GREAT ESCAPE, THE
WAKE ISLAND

Busch, Niven
DISTANT DRUMS

Butler, David
VOYAGE OF THE DAMNED

Butler, Frank
WAKE ISLAND

Byrum, John
RAZOR'S EDGE, THE

Cady, Jerry
GUADALCANAL DIARY
PURPLE HEART, THE

Camerini, Mario
WAR AND PEACE

Cameron, James
RAMBO: FIRST BLOOD, PART II

Carabatsos, James
HEROES

Carabatsos, Jim
HAMBURGER HILL

Carlino, Lewis John
GREAT SANTINI, THE

Carothers, A.J.
MIRACLE OF THE WHITE STALLIONS

Carriere, Jean-Claude
DANTON
TIN DRUM, THE
UNBEARABLE LIGHTNESS OF BEING, THE

Carson, Robert
BEAU GESTE

Caruso, Dee
WHICH WAY TO THE FRONT?

Cash, Jim
TOP GUN

Cavani, Liliana
NIGHT PORTER, THE

Champion, John
DRAGONFLY SQUADRON

Chandlee, Harry
SERGEANT YORK

Chaplin, Charles
GREAT DICTATOR, THE

Chapman, Robin
FORCE 10 FROM NAVARONE

Chase, Borden
FIGHTING SEABEES, THE

Chetwynd, Lionel
HANOI HILTON, THE

Christensen, Bent
ONLY WAY, THE

Chukhrai, Grigori
BALLAD OF A SOLDIER

Cibber, Colley
RICHARD III

Clavell, James
GREAT ESCAPE, THE

Clement, Rene
FORBIDDEN GAMES

Clerici, Gianfranco
FROM HELL TO VICTORY

Clewes, Howard
ONE THAT GOT AWAY, THE

Coen, Franklin
ALVAREZ KELLY
TRAIN, THE

Cohen, Lawrence J.
START THE REVOLUTION WITHOUT ME

Cohen, Ronald M.
TWILIGHT'S LAST GLEAMING

Cole, Lester
BLOOD ON THE SUN
OBJECTIVE, BURMA!

Conchon, Georges
BLACK AND WHITE IN COLOR

Coppola, Francis Ford
APOCALYPSE NOW
PATTON

Corey, George
MR. WINKLE GOES TO WAR

Cosmatos, George P.
MASSACRE IN ROME

Cossa, Roberto
FUNNY, DIRTY LITTLE WAR, A

Costa-Gavras
MISSING

Coward, Noel
IN WHICH WE SERVE

Craig, Hal
ANZIO
LION OF THE DESERT

Crowe, Christopher
OFF LIMITS

Crutchley, Roger
ANGKOR-CAMBODIA EXPRESS

Dalrymple, Ian
PIMPERNEL SMITH

Dane, Clemence
FIRE OVER ENGLAND
SALUTE JOHN CITIZEN

Darling, W. Scott
SHERLOCK HOLMES AND THE SECRET WEAPON

Daves, Delmer
DESTINATION TOKYO
STAGE DOOR CANTEEN

Davies, Valentine
BRIDGES AT TOKO-RI, THE

Davis, Frank
TRAIN, THE

Davis, Gerry
FINAL COUNTDOWN, THE

De Concini, Ennio
HITLER: THE LAST TEN DAYS
WAR AND PEACE

de Grunwald, Anatole
PIMPERNEL SMITH
SPITFIRE

De Martino, Alberto
DIRTY HEROES

De Negri, Giuliani G.
NIGHT OF THE SHOOTING STARS, THE

de Sainte-Colombe, Paul
OUTPOST IN MOROCCO

de Sarigny, Peter
MALTA STORY

De Sica, Vittorio
TWO WOMEN

Dehn, Paul
NIGHT OF THE GENERALS, THE

Demme, Jonathan
HOT BOX, THE

Dent, Alan
HENRY V
RICHARD III

Deutsch, Andrew
PLATOON LEADER

SCREENWRITERS

Deutsch, Helen
KIM

DeVore, Gary
DOGS OF WAR, THE

Dickinson, Thorold
MALTA STORY

Dillon, Robert
REVOLUTION

Dobai, Peter
COLONEL REDL
MEPHISTO

Dormann, Genevieve
COUP DE GRACE

Doud, Gil
TO HELL AND BACK

Dreyfus, Mme. Jean-Paul
LA MARSEILLAISE

Dreyfus, N. Martel
LA MARSEILLAISE

Duncan, Patrick
84 CHARLIE MOPIC

Dunne, Philip
LAST OF THE MOHICANS, THE

Duras, Marguerite
HIROSHIMA, MON AMOUR

Durovic, Ratko
BATTLE OF NERETVA

Eisenstein, Sergei
ALEXANDER NEVSKY
IVAN THE TERRIBLE, PARTS I & II

Elders, Kevin
IRON EAGLE
IRON EAGLE II

Eldridge, John
OPERATION AMSTERDAM

Endfield, Cy
ZULU
ZULU DAWN

Ephron, Henry
WHAT PRICE GLORY?

Ephron, Phoebe
WHAT PRICE GLORY?

Epps, Jr., Jack
TOP GUN

Epstein, Julius J.
CASABLANCA
CROSS OF IRON

Epstein, Phillip G.
CASABLANCA

Fabbri, Diego
GENERALE DELLA ROVERE

Fabien, Rachel
EVERY TIME WE SAY GOODBYE

Fairchild, William
GLORY AT SEA
MALTA STORY

Fassbinder, Rainer Werner
MARRIAGE OF MARIA BRAUN, THE

Faulkner (uncredited), William
AIR FORCE

Feibleman, Peter S.
ENSIGN PULVER

Feldman, Marty
LAST REMAKE OF BEAU GESTE, THE

Fellini, Federico
OPEN CITY
PAISAN

Feyder, Jacques
CARNIVAL IN FLANDERS

Fine, Morton
PAWNBROKER, THE

Finkel, Abem
SERGEANT YORK

Fisher, Steve
FLAT TOP

Fisz, S. Benjamin
BATTLE OF BRITAIN, THE

Fitzgerald, F. Scott
GONE WITH THE WIND

Flaherty, Vincent X.
PT 109

Flamini, Vincenzo
DIRTY HEROES

Flynn, Errol
ASSAULT OF THE REBEL GIRLS

Fonvielle, Lloyd
LORDS OF DISCIPLINE, THE

Forbes, Bryan
BLACK TENT, THE
COCKLESHELL HEROES, THE
KING RAT

Foreman, Carl
CLAY PIGEON, THE
GUNS OF NAVARONE, THE
HOME OF THE BRAVE
MEN, THE

Forrester, Larry
TORA! TORA! TORA!

Fort, Garrett
LOST PATROL, THE

Foster, Michael
GONE WITH THE WIND

Foxwell, Ivan
COLDITZ STORY, THE

Frank, Fredric M.
EL CID

Freeman, Devery
FRANCIS IN THE NAVY

Freeman, Everett
DESTINATION GOBI

Freeman, Fred
START THE REVOLUTION WITHOUT ME

Friedkin, David
PAWNBROKER, THE

Froelick, Anne
MASTER RACE, THE

Froeschel, George
MRS. MINIVER

Frohlich, Pia
MARRIAGE OF MARIA BRAUN, THE

Frohman, Clayton
UNDER FIRE

Frye, Peter
HILL 24 DOESN'T ANSWER

Fuller, Samuel
BIG RED ONE, THE

Furie, Sidney J.
BOYS IN COMPANY C, THE
IRON EAGLE
IRON EAGLE II
PURPLE HEARTS

Furthman, Jules
MOROCCO

Fusco, Marie Pia
HITLER: THE LAST TEN DAYS

Gale, Bob
1941

Gamet, Kenneth
FLYING TIGERS

Gance, Abel
AUSTERLITZ

Gardner, Gerald
WHICH WAY TO THE FRONT?

Garrett, Oliver H.P.
FAREWELL TO ARMS, A
GONE WITH THE WIND

Garrick, David
RICHARD III

Gary, Romain
LONGEST DAY, THE

Gasiorowski, Jacek
DANTON

Gastaldi, Ernesto
REASON TO LIVE, A REASON TO DIE, A

Gatliff, John
DEATH BEFORE DISHONOR

Gay, John
FOUR HORSEMEN OF THE APOCALYPSE, THE
RUN SILENT, RUN DEEP
SOLDIER BLUE

Gayton, Joe
UNCOMMON VALOR

Gelfield, Arthur N.
NO DEAD HEROES

Geller, Stephen
SLAUGHTERHOUSE-FIVE

George, Peter
DR. STRANGELOVE: OR HOW I LEARNED TO STOP WORRYING AND LOVE THE BOMB

Gidding, Nelson
HINDENBURG, THE

SCREENWRITERS

LOST COMMAND, THE
MISFIT BRIGADE, THE

Gilbert, Lewis
SEA SHALL NOT HAVE THEM, THE

Giler, David
SOUTHERN COMFORT

Gilliat, Sydney
NIGHT TRAIN

Glazer, Benjamin
FAREWELL TO ARMS, A

Godard, Jean-Luc
LES CARABINIERS

Golan, Menahem
DELTA FORCE, THE
HANNA'S WAR

Goldman, James
NICHOLAS AND ALEXANDRA

Goldman, William
BRIDGE TOO FAR, A
MARATHON MAN

Goodman, David Zelag
MARCH OR DIE

Goodrich, Frances
DIARY OF ANNE FRANK, THE

Gordon, Bernard
55 DAYS AT PEKING
CRY OF BATTLE

Gordon, George
BAT 21

Gordon, Leo V.
TOBRUK

Gordon, Leon
KIM

Gould, Heywood
BOYS FROM BRAZIL, THE
ROLLING THUNDER

Gould, John
ONLY WAY, THE

Graham, Ronny
TO BE OR NOT TO BE

Grant, James Edward
ALAMO, THE
FLYING LEATHERNECKS
SANDS OF IWO JIMA

Grant, John
BUCK PRIVATES

Grass, Gunter
TIN DRUM, THE

Gray, Hugh
DRUMS

Grayson, Charles
OUTPOST IN MOROCCO

Greatorex, Wilfred
BATTLE OF BRITAIN, THE

Griffiths, Trevor
REDS

Grofe, Jr., Ferde
STEEL CLAW, THE
WARKILL

Grossman, Ladislav
SHOP ON MAIN STREET, THE

Gruault, Jean
GREEN ROOM, THE
LES CARABINIERS

Gruber, Frank
NORTHERN PURSUIT

Grumberg, Jean-Claude
LAST METRO, THE

Guerra, Tonino
NIGHT OF THE SHOOTING STARS, THE

Guiol, Fred
GUNGA DIN

Guitry, Sacha
NAPOLEON

Gyongyossy, Imre
REVOLT OF JOB, THE

Hackett, Albert
DIARY OF ANNE FRANK, THE

Hamer, Robert
55 DAYS AT PEKING

Hamilton, Guy
COLDITZ STORY, THE

Hamilton, William
CALL OUT THE MARINES

Hammett, Dashiell
WATCH ON THE RHINE

Hanley, Gerald
BLUE MAX, THE

Hansen, Peter
SNOW TREASURE

Hardy, Jonathan
BREAKER MORANT

Hare, David
PLENTY

Harmon, Sidney
DRUMS IN THE DEEP SOUTH

Harris, Vernon
SEA SHALL NOT HAVE THEM, THE

Harrison, Joan
FOREIGN CORRESPONDENT
SABOTEUR

Hartman, Don
UP IN ARMS

Hartmann, Edmund L.
SHERLOCK HOLMES AND THE SECRET WEAPON

Harwood, Ronald
CROMWELL

Hasford, Gustav
FULL METAL JACKET

Hashimoto, Shinobu
THRONE OF BLOOD

Hastings, Hugh
GLORY AT SEA

Hecht, Ben
GONE WITH THE WIND

Heller, Lukas
DIRTY DOZEN, THE
TOO LATE THE HERO

Hellman, Lillian
NORTH STAR, THE
WATCH ON THE RHINE

Henry, Buck
CATCH-22

Hensler, Paul
DON'T CRY, IT'S ONLY THUNDER

Herbert, Bob
REBEL

Herr, Michael
FULL METAL JACKET

Hill, Walter
SOUTHERN COMFORT

Hilton, James
FOREIGN CORRESPONDENT
MRS. MINIVER

Hoffman, Joseph
AGAINST ALL FLAGS

Hogan, Michael
NURSE EDITH CAVELL

Holben, Lawrence
HIDING PLACE, THE

Holierhoek, Kees
SOLDIER OF ORANGE

Holland, Agnieszka
DANTON
LOVE IN GERMANY, A

Horman, Arthur T.
BUCK PRIVATES
DESPERATE JOURNEY

Howard, Sidney
GONE WITH THE WIND

Hubbard, Lucien
GUNG HO!

Huebsch, Edward
TWILIGHT'S LAST GLEAMING

Hughes, Ken
CROMWELL

Hunter, John
COURT MARTIAL

Hunter, Thomas
FINAL COUNTDOWN, THE

Husson, Albert
TRAIN, THE

Huston, John
AFRICAN QUEEN, THE
RED BADGE OF COURAGE, THE
SERGEANT YORK
STRANGER, THE

Huyck, Willard
BEST DEFENSE

Ide, Masato
KAGEMUSHA
RAN

Inagaki, Koicji
HUMAN CONDITION, THE

SCREENWRITERS

Jacoby, Irving
SNOW TREASURE

Jacoby, Michel
CHARGE OF THE LIGHT BRIGADE, THE

Jannings, Orin
TIME TO LOVE AND A TIME TO DIE, A

Jenkins, Michael
REBEL

Johnson, Nunnally
DESERT FOX, THE
DIRTY DOZEN, THE

Jones, Evan
VICTORY

Jones, Grover
LIVES OF A BENGAL LANCER

Jones, James
LONGEST DAY, THE

Jones, Robert C.
COMING HOME

Kabay, Barna
REVOLT OF JOB, THE

Kadar, Jan
SHOP ON MAIN STREET, THE

Kailan
ANGKOR-CAMBODIA EXPRESS

Kalmar, Bert
DUCK SOUP

Kamen, Robert Mark
TAPS

Kane, Michael
SOUTHERN COMFORT

Karabatsos, James
HEARTBREAK RIDGE

Katz, Gloria
BEST DEFENSE

Katz, Robert
MASSACRE IN ROME

Kaufman, Philip
UNBEARABLE LIGHTNESS OF BEING, THE

Kennaway, James
BATTLE OF BRITAIN, THE
TUNES OF GLORY

Kessel, Joseph
NIGHT OF THE GENERALS, THE

Keyes, Thom
SKY BANDITS

Kikushima, Ryuzo
THRONE OF BLOOD
TORA! TORA! TORA!

Kinugasa, Teinosuke
GATE OF HELL

Kirkwood, James
SOME KIND OF HERO

Kirwan, Patric
DRUMS

Kline, Wally
THEY DIED WITH THEIR BOOTS ON

Klos, Elmar
SHOP ON MAIN STREET, THE

Kneale, Nigel
DAMN THE DEFIANT!

Kobayashi, Masaki
HUMAN CONDITION, THE

Koch, C.J.
YEAR OF LIVING DANGEROUSLY, THE

Koch, Carl
LA MARSEILLAISE

Koch, Howard
CASABLANCA
SEA HAWK, THE
SERGEANT YORK
WAR LOVER, THE

Kolitz, Zvi
HILL 24 DOESN'T ANSWER

Kolpet, Max
GERMANY, YEAR ZERO

Korda, Zoltan
SAHARA

Kozoll, Michael
FIRST BLOOD

Krims, Mildred
CRIMSON ROMANCE

Kroopf, Sandy
BIRDY

Kubik, Lawrence
DEATH BEFORE DISHONOR

Kubrick, Stanley
DR. STRANGELOVE: OR HOW I LEARNED TO STOP WORRYING AND LOVE THE BOMB
FULL METAL JACKET
PATHS OF GLORY

Kuri, John A.
CAPTIVE HEARTS

Kurosawa, Akira
KAGEMUSHA
RAN
THRONE OF BLOOD

Lampel, Peter Martin
KAMERADSCHAFT

Landau, Richard
BACK TO BATAAN

Landon, Joseph
VON RYAN'S EXPRESS

Lang, David
HELLCATS OF THE NAVY

Langdon, Harry
FLYING DEUCES, THE

Langley, John
P.O.W. THE ESCAPE

Lardner, Jr., Ring
CLOAK AND DAGGER
M*A*S*H

Lasker, Alex
FIREFOX

Lasker, Lawrence
WARGAMES

Lasky, Jr., Jesse L.
BUCCANEER, THE

Launder (uncredited), Frank
WE DIVE AT DAWN

Launder, Frank
NIGHT TRAIN

Lavery, Emmett
BEHIND THE RISING SUN
COURT-MARTIAL OF BILLY MITCHELL, THE
HITLER'S CHILDREN

Lawson, John Howard
SAHARA

Lay, Jr., Beirne
TWELVE O'CLOCK HIGH

Lefranc, Guy
ELUSIVE CORPORAL, THE

Leigh, Rowland
CHARGE OF THE LIGHT BRIGADE, THE
MASTER RACE, THE

Lennart, Isobel
INN OF THE SIXTH HAPPINESS, THE

Lenzi, Umberto
FROM HELL TO VICTORY

Leone, Sergio
GOOD, THE BAD, AND THE UGLY, THE

Lettich, Sheldon
RAMBO III

Levien, Sonya
DRUMS ALONG THE MOHAWK

Levinson, Larry
MISSING IN ACTION 2—THE BEGINNING

Levinson, Richard A.
HINDENBURG, THE

Lewis, William W.
BRADY'S ESCAPE

Lilienthal, Peter
DAVID

Limentani, Annalena
PAISAN

Lineberger, James
TAPS

Link, William
HINDENBURG, THE

Lipp, Jeremy
P.O.W. THE ESCAPE

Lizzani, Carlo
GERMANY, YEAR ZERO

Lochte, Richard S.
ESCAPE TO ATHENA

Logan, Joshua
ENSIGN PULVER
MISTER ROBERTS

Lowe, Edward T.
SHERLOCK HOLMES AND THE SECRET WEAPON

SCREENWRITERS

Lustig, Arnost
DIAMONDS OF THE NIGHT
TRANSPORT FROM PARADISE

Lynch, Martin
PRAYER FOR THE DYING, A

Lyndon, Barre
SUNDOWN

MacArthur, Charles
GONE WITH THE WIND

McCarthy, Michael
OPERATION AMSTERDAM

MacDonald, Philip
ACTION IN ARABIA

MacDougall, Ranald
OBJECTIVE, BURMA!

MacDougall, Roger
MOUSE THAT ROARED, THE

McGuinness, James Kevin
RIO GRANDE

MacKenzie, Aeneas
AGAINST ALL FLAGS
FIGHTING SEABEES, THE
THEY DIED WITH THEIR BOOTS ON

McLaverty, Bernard
CAL

MacLean, Alistair
WHERE EAGLES DARE

McNutt, William Slavens
LIVES OF A BENGAL LANCER

MacPhail, Angus
FRIEDA

Mahin, John Lee
ADVENTURES OF TARTU, THE
GONE WITH THE WIND
HORSE SOLDIERS, THE

Maibaum, Richard
COCKLESHELL HEROES, THE

Malko, George
DOGS OF WAR, THE

Malle, Louis
AU REVOIR LES ENFANTS

Malleson, Miles
ADVENTURES OF TARTU, THE
SPITFIRE

Maltz, Albert
CLOAK AND DAGGER
DESTINATION TOKYO

Mandel, Loring
LITTLE DRUMMER GIRL, THE

Mankiewicz, Tom
EAGLE HAS LANDED, THE

Mann, Abby
JUDGMENT AT NUREMBERG

Mann, Michael
KEEP, THE

Mann, Stanley
EYE OF THE NEEDLE
MOUSE THAT ROARED, THE

Marcus, Raymond
HELLCATS OF THE NAVY

Margolis, Herbert
WACKIEST SHIP IN THE ARMY, THE

Markowitz, Mitch
GOOD MORNING, VIETNAM

Markstein, George
ODESSA FILE, THE

Marthesheimer, Peter
MARRIAGE OF MARIA BRAUN, THE

Martin, Troy Kennedy
KELLY'S HEROES

Marx, Rick
PLATOON LEADER

Mastrosimone, William
BEAST, THE

Matsuyama, Zenzo
HUMAN CONDITION, THE

Maugham, Robin
BLACK TENT, THE

Mayer, Edwin Justus
GONE WITH THE WIND
TO BE OR NOT TO BE

Mayersberg, Paul
MERRY CHRISTMAS, MR. LAWRENCE

Mayes, Wendell
GO TELL THE SPARTANS
IN HARM'S WAY
VON RYAN'S EXPRESS

Maylam, Tony
RIDDLE OF THE SANDS, THE

Medford, Harold
BERLIN EXPRESS

Medioli, Enrico
DAMNED, THE

Meehan, Thomas
TO BE OR NOT TO BE

Melson, John
BATTLE OF THE BULGE

Meyers, Nancy
PRIVATE BENJAMIN

Meyjes, (uncredited) Menno
EMPIRE OF THE SUN

Michalek, Boleslaw
DANTON
LOVE IN GERMANY, A

Milius, John
APOCALYPSE NOW
FAREWELL TO THE KING
RED DAWN
WIND AND THE LION, THE

Millar, Ronald
FRIEDA

Millard, Oscar
CONQUEROR, THE
SALZBURG CONNECTION, THE

Miller, Harvey
PRIVATE BENJAMIN

Miller, J.C.
NO DEAD HEROES

Miller, J.P.
BEHOLD A PALE HORSE

Miller, Seton I.
DAWN PATROL, THE
SEA HAWK, THE

Miller, Winston
GONE WITH THE WIND

Milstone, (uncredited) Lewis
ALL QUIET ON THE WESTERN FRONT

Mizrahi, Moshe
EVERY TIME WE SAY GOODBYE

Moffat, Ivan
D-DAY, THE SIXTH OF JUNE
HITLER: THE LAST TEN DAYS

Moffitt, Jack
PASSAGE TO MARSEILLE

Molls, Jose Luis Martinez
FROM HELL TO VICTORY

Mommertz, Paul
WANNSEE CONFERENCE, THE

Montanelli, Indro
GENERALE DELLA ROVERE

Montgomery, George
STEEL CLAW, THE

Moonblood, Q.
FIRST BLOOD

Moore, Daniel
LAST OF THE MOHICANS, THE

Morita, Pat
CAPTIVE HEARTS

Morton, Rob
SWING SHIFT

Moscati, Italo
NIGHT PORTER, THE

Mosk, Bernice
BUCCANEER, THE

Murfin, Jane
DRAGON SEED

Murphey, Michael S.
SUPERNATURALS, THE

Murphy, Richard
DESERT RATS, THE
WACKIEST SHIP IN THE ARMY, THE

Murray, Bill
RAZOR'S EDGE, THE

Natkin, Rick
BOYS IN COMPANY C, THE
PURPLE HEARTS

Nava, Gregory
TIME OF DESTINY, A

Nemec, Jan
DIAMONDS OF THE NIGHT

Neuman, Sam
HITLER

Nichols, Dudley
AIR FORCE
LOST PATROL, THE

SCREENWRITERS

THIS LAND IS MINE
Nichols, Peter
PRIVATES ON PARADE
Nolbandov, Sergei
FIRE OVER ENGLAND
Norris, Chuck
BRADDOCK: MISSING IN ACTION III
INVASION U.S.A.
North, Edmund H.
DAMN THE DEFIANT!
PATTON
Nugent, Frank S.
FORT APACHE
MISTER ROBERTS
SHE WORE A YELLOW RIBBON
O'Hanlon, James
SAHARA
Oguni, Hideo
RAN
THRONE OF BLOOD
TORA! TORA! TORA!
Olivera, Hector
FUNNY, DIRTY LITTLE WAR, A
Olivier, Laurence
HENRY V
RICHARD III
Oppenheimer, Peer J.
OPERATION CIA
Osborn, Paul
SAYONARA
Oshima, Nagisa
MERRY CHRISTMAS, MR. LAWRENCE
Otten, Karl
KAMERADSCHAFT
Panduro, Leif
ONLY WAY, THE
Papava, Mikhail
MY NAME IS IVAN
Parker, Dorothy
SABOTEUR
Parkes, Walter F.
WARGAMES
Pavlenko, Peter
ALEXANDER NEVSKY
Paxton, John
CORNERED
ON THE BEACH
Peled, Hanan
DEADLINE
Perez, Paul
LAST OF THE MOHICANS, THE
Perilli, Ivo
WAR AND PEACE
Perrin, Nat
DUCK SOUP
Pertwee, Roland
PIMPERNEL SMITH
SPY IN BLACK, THE

Petenyi, Katalin
REVOLT OF JOB, THE
Petersen, Wolfgang
BOAT, THE
Pirosh, Robert
GO FOR BROKE
UP IN ARMS
Pirro, Ugo
BATTLE OF NERETVA
GARDEN OF THE FINZI-CONTINIS, THE
Ponicsan, Darryl
TAPS
Pontecorvo, Gillo
BATTLE OF ALGIERS, THE
Pope, Thomas
LORDS OF DISCIPLINE, THE
Powell, Michael
LIFE AND DEATH OF COLONEL BLIMP, THE
ONE OF OUR AIRCRAFT IS MISSING
PURSUIT OF THE GRAF SPEE, THE
Powell, Peter
FINAL COUNTDOWN, THE
Prebble, John
ZULU
Pressburger, Emeric
49TH PARALLEL
LIFE AND DEATH OF COLONEL BLIMP, THE
ONE OF OUR AIRCRAFT IS MISSING
PURSUIT OF THE GRAF SPEE, THE
SPY IN BLACK, THE
Price, Stanley
SHOUT AT THE DEVIL
Prior, David A.
NIGHTWARS
Pursall, David
BLUE MAX, THE
LONGEST DAY, THE
Rabe, David
STREAMERS
Rackin, Martin
DEEP SIX, THE
DISTANT DRUMS
HORSE SOLDIERS, THE
Ramati, Alexander
ASSISI UNDERGROUND, THE
Rascoe, Judith
WHO'LL STOP THE RAIN?
Raynor, William
WACKIEST SHIP IN THE ARMY, THE
Reid, Alastair
SHOUT AT THE DEVIL
Reinhardt, Wolfgang
HITLER: THE LAST TEN DAYS
Reisch, Walter
THAT HAMILTON WOMAN
Renoir, Jean
ELUSIVE CORPORAL, THE
GRAND ILLUSION

LA MARSEILLAISE
Reynolds, Kevin
RED DAWN
Richlin, Maurice
OPERATION PETTICOAT
Robbins, Matthew
MAC ARTHUR
Roberts, Marguerite
DRAGON SEED
Roberts, William
BRIDGE AT REMAGEN, THE
Robinson, Bruce
KILLING FIELDS, THE
Robinson, Casey
DAYS OF GLORY
PASSAGE TO MARSEILLE
THIS IS THE ARMY
Rogers, Charles
FLYING DEUCES, THE
Rogers, Emmet
ADVENTURES OF TARTU, THE
Rose, Mickey
BANANAS
Rose, Reginald
FINAL OPTION, THE
SEA WOLVES, THE
WILD GEESE II
WILD GEESE, THE
Rose, William
GLORY AT SEA
Ross, Kenneth
ODESSA FILE, THE
Rossellini, Roberto
GERMANY, YEAR ZERO
LES CARABINIERS
OPEN CITY
PAISAN
Rossen, Robert
ALEXANDER THE GREAT
EDGE OF DARKNESS
WALK IN THE SUN, A
Rozov, Victor
CRANES ARE FLYING, THE
Ruby, Harry
DUCK SOUP
Ryan, Cornelius
LONGEST DAY, THE
Ryan, Frank
CALL OUT THE MARINES
Sacchetti, Dardano
LAST HUNTER, THE
Sackheim, William
FIRST BLOOD
Salt, Waldo
COMING HOME
MR. WINKLE GOES TO WAR
TARAS BULBA
Sanders, Denis
NAKED AND THE DEAD, THE

SCREENWRITERS

Sanders, Terry
NAKED AND THE DEAD, THE

Sanford, Donald S.
MIDWAY

Schayer, Richard
KIM

Schell, Maximilian
PEDESTRIAN, THE

Schiffman, Suzanne
LAST METRO, THE

Schiller, Alfred
FLYING DEUCES, THE

Schlondorff, Volker
TIN DRUM, THE

Schmidt, Walter Roeber
HELL TO ETERNITY

Schrader, Paul
ROLLING THUNDER

Schroeder, Doris
CRIMSON ROMANCE

Schweizer, Richard
FOUR IN A JEEP

Seddon, Jack
BLUE MAX, THE
LONGEST DAY, THE

Seitz, Franz
TIN DRUM, THE

Selznick, David O.
GONE WITH THE WIND

Serling, Rod
SEVEN DAYS IN MAY

Shagan, Steve
VOYAGE OF THE DAMNED

Shapiro, Stanley
OPERATION PETTICOAT

Sharp, Alan
ULZANA'S RAID

Shavelson, Melville
CAST A GIANT SHADOW

Shaw, Irwin
COMMANDOS STRIKE AT DAWN, THE
WAR AND PEACE

Sheehan, Howard
PT 109

Sheekman, Arthur
DUCK SOUP

Shelton, Ron
UNDER FIRE

Sherdeman, Ted
AWAY ALL BOATS
HELL TO ETERNITY

Sherriff, R.C.
DAM BUSTERS, THE
FOUR FEATHERS, THE
THAT HAMILTON WOMAN
THIS ABOVE ALL

Sherwood, Robert E.
BEST YEARS OF OUR LIVES, THE

Shyer, Charles
PRIVATE BENJAMIN

Silliphant, Stirling
MURPHY'S WAR

Silver, Arthur
MISSING IN ACTION 2—THE BEGINNING

Silvestri, Franco
DIRTY HEROES

Simon, Neil
BILOXI BLUES

Sloane, Allan
HIDING PLACE, THE

Smirnov, E.
MY NAME IS IVAN

Smith, Wilbur
SHOUT AT THE DEVIL

Soeteman, Gerard
ASSAULT, THE
FLESH AND BLOOD
SOLDIER OF ORANGE

Soisson, Joel
SUPERNATURALS, THE

Solinas, Franco
BATTLE OF ALGIERS, THE
BURN

Solomon, Louis
MR. WINKLE GOES TO WAR

Solovyov, Vasiliy
WAR AND PEACE

Southern, Terry
DR. STRANGELOVE: OR HOW I LEARNED TO STOP WORRYING AND LOVE THE BOMB

Spaak, Charles
CARNIVAL IN FLANDERS
GRAND ILLUSION

Spence, Ralph
FLYING DEUCES, THE

Sperling, Milton
BATTLE OF THE BULGE
COURT-MARTIAL OF BILLY MITCHELL, THE

Stallings, Laurence
SHE WORE A YELLOW RIBBON

Stallone, Sylvester
RAMBO III
RAMBO: FIRST BLOOD, PART II

Stawinski, Jerzy Stefan
KANAL

Stern, Stewart
UGLY AMERICAN, THE

Stevens, David
BREAKER MORANT

Stewart, Donald
MISSING

Stewart, Douglas Day
OFFICER AND A GENTLEMAN, AN

Stitzel, Robert L.
DISTANT THUNDER

Stone, Oliver
PLATOON
SALVADOR

Stone, Peter
FATHER GOOSE
SECRET WAR OF HARRY FRIGG, THE

Stone, Robert
WHO'LL STOP THE RAIN?

Stoppard, Tom
EMPIRE OF THE SUN

Storey, Anthony
ZULU DAWN

Straus, E. Charles
HITLER

Stull, Lee
SOLDIER'S REVENGE

Swan, Francis
JUNGLE PATROL

Swerling, Jo
GONE WITH THE WIND
LIFEBOAT

Szabo, Istvan
COLONEL REDL
MEPHISTO

Tamura, Takeshi
MACARTHUR'S CHILDREN

Taradash, Daniel
DESIREE
FROM HERE TO ETERNITY
MORITURI

Tarloff, Frank
FATHER GOOSE
SECRET WAR OF HARRY FRIGG, THE

Taviani, Paolo
NIGHT OF THE SHOOTING STARS, THE

Taviani, Vittorio
NIGHT OF THE SHOOTING STARS, THE

Tesich, Steve
ELENI

Thibeau, Jack
OFF LIMITS

Thomas, Anna
TIME OF DESTINY, A

Thompson, Gary
WHITE GHOST

Thompson, Jim
PATHS OF GLORY

Totheroh, Dan
DAWN PATROL, THE

Trivers, Barry
FLYING TIGERS

Trosper, Guy
DARBY'S RANGERS

Trotti, Lamar
DRUMS ALONG THE MOHAWK
GUADALCANAL DIARY
IMMORTAL SERGEANT, THE
RAZOR'S EDGE, THE

WAR MOVIES

Truffaut, Francois
GREEN ROOM, THE
LAST METRO, THE

Trumbo, Dalton
GUY NAMED JOE, A
JOHNNY GOT HIS GUN
SPARTACUS
THIRTY SECONDS OVER TOKYO

Tunberg, Karl
TARAS BULBA
YANK IN THE R.A.F., A

Twist, John
BOMBARDIER
DEEP SIX, THE

Uris, Leon W.
BATTLE CRY

Ustinov, Peter
IMMORTAL BATTALION, THE

Vajda, Ladislaus
KAMERADSCHAFT

Valentine, Val
WE DIVE AT DAWN

Valerii, Tonino
REASON TO LIVE, A REASON TO DIE, A

Van Druten, John
GONE WITH THE WIND

Vaughn-Hughes, Gerald
DUELLISTS, THE

Veiller, Anthony
STRANGER, THE

Verde, Dino
DIRTY HEROES

Verhoeven, Paul
FLESH AND BLOOD
SOLDIER OF ORANGE

Verucci, Alberto
DIRTY HEROES

Vidor, King
WAR AND PEACE

Viertel, Peter
SABOTEUR

Vincenzoni, Luciano
GOOD, THE BAD, AND THE UGLY, THE

Viola, Joe
HOT BOX, THE

Visconti, Luchino
DAMNED, THE

von Harbou, Thea
KOLBERG

von Trotta, Margarethe
COUP DE GRACE

Wada, Natto
FIRES ON THE PLAIN
HARP OF BURMA

Wajda, Andrzej
ASHES AND DIAMONDS
DANTON
LOVE IN GERMANY, A

Wald, Malvin
BATTLE TAXI
STEEL CLAW, THE

Walker, David
PLATOON LEADER

Ward, Edmund
PRAYER FOR THE DYING, A

Ware, Clyde
NO DRUMS, NO BUGLES

Ware, Darrell
YANK IN THE R.A.F., A

Washburn, Deric
DEER HUNTER, THE

Wead, Frank W.
THEY WERE EXPENDABLE

Webb, James R.
PORK CHOP HILL

Weir, Peter
YEAR OF LIVING DANGEROUSLY, THE

Welbeck [Harry Alan Towers], Peter
PLATOON LEADER

Welles
STRANGER, THE

Welles, Orson
CHIMES AT MIDNIGHT

Wellman, Wendell
FIREFOX

Wertmuller, Lina
LOVE AND ANARCHY

West, Claudine
MRS. MINIVER

Westerby, Robert
WAR AND PEACE

Wexler, Haskell
LATINO

Whitemore, Hugh
RETURN OF THE SOLDIER, THE

Wilder, Billy
STALAG 17

Williams, Eric
WOODEN HORSE, THE

Williams, J.B.
WE DIVE AT DAWN

Williamson, David
GALLIPOLI
YEAR OF LIVING DANGEROUSLY, THE

Willingham, Calder
LITTLE BIG MAN
PATHS OF GLORY

Wilson, Michael
LAWRENCE OF ARABIA

Wimperis, Arthur
DARK JOURNEY
DRUMS
FOUR FEATHERS, THE
MRS. MINIVER

Wood, Charles
CUBA
HOW I WON THE WAR

Worth, David
SOLDIER'S REVENGE

Wurlitzer, Rudy
WALKER

Yablonsky, Yabo
VICTORY

Yarema, Neil
TASTE OF HELL, A

Yates, Richard
BRIDGE AT REMAGEN, THE

Yordan, Philip
55 DAYS AT PEKING
BATTLE OF THE BULGE
DRUMS IN THE DEEP SOUTH
EL CID
MEN IN WAR

Yoshow, Valentin
BALLAD OF A SOLDIER

Young, John Sacret
TESTAMENT

Young, Waldemar
LIVES OF A BENGAL LANCER

Zavattini, Cesare
GARDEN OF THE FINZI-CONTINIS, THE
TWO WOMEN

Zemeckis, Robert
1941

Zieman, Ulla
DAVID

Zimmer, Bernard
CARNIVAL IN FLANDERS

SOURCE WRITERS

Adamson, Hans Christian
HELLCATS OF THE NAVY

Age-Scarpelli
GOOD, THE BAD, AND THE UGLY, THE

Agotay, Louis
DIRTY HEROES

Aku, Yu
MACARTHUR'S CHILDREN

Alberti, Barbara
NIGHT PORTER, THE

Aldrich, Robert
TOO LATE THE HERO

Alison, Joan
CASABLANCA

Altieri, Maj. James
DARBY'S RANGERS

Ambler, Eric
IMMORTAL BATTALION, THE

Amen, Carol
TESTAMENT

Amidei, Sergio
OPEN CITY
PAISAN

SOURCE WRITERS

Amir, Gideon
P.O.W. THE ESCAPE

Anderson, Maxwell
WHAT PRICE GLORY?

Anderson, William C.
BAT 21

Andrzejewski, Jerzy
ASHES AND DIAMONDS

Appel, Benjamin
CRY OF BATTLE

Arthur, Art
BATTLE TAXI

Atwater, Gladys
FIRST YANK INTO TOKYO

Bailey II, Charles Waldo
SEVEN DAYS IN MAY

Ballard, J.G.
EMPIRE OF THE SUN

Barnett, S.H.
FATHER GOOSE

Barrett, James Lee
D.I., THE

Bartlett, Sy
TWELVE O'CLOCK HIGH

Bass, Ronald
CODE NAME: EMERALD

Bassani, Giorgio
GARDEN OF THE FINZI-CONTINIS, THE

Bassett, James
IN HARM'S WAY

Beach, Comdr. Edward L.
RUN SILENT, RUN DEEP

Bellah, James Warner
FORT APACHE
RIO GRANDE
SHE WORE A YELLOW RIBBON

Berger, Thomas
LITTLE BIG MAN

Berk, Howard
LAST DAY OF THE WAR, THE

Berkeley, Capt. Reginald
NURSE EDITH CAVELL

Berkman, Ted
CAST A GIANT SHADOW

Berlin, Irving
THIS IS THE ARMY

Bessie, Alvah
OBJECTIVE, BURMA!

Bessy, Maurice
KING OF HEARTS

Bevan, Donald
STALAG 17

Biberman, Herbert
MASTER RACE, THE

Bing, Steve
BRADDOCK: MISSING IN ACTION III
MISSING IN ACTION

Biro, Lajos
DARK JOURNEY

Bobrick, Sam
LAST REMAKE OF BEAU GESTE, THE

Boehm, David
GUY NAMED JOE, A

Bogomolov, Vladimir Osipovich
MY NAME IS IVAN

Boldt, Gerhard
HITLER: THE LAST TEN DAYS

Boule, Pierre
BRIDGE ON THE RIVER KWAI, THE

Bowers, William
JUNGLE PATROL

Boyer, Francois
FORBIDDEN GAMES

Bradley, Gen. Omar N.
PATTON

Bren, J. Robert
FIRST YANK INTO TOKYO

Brennan, Frederick H.
GUY NAMED JOE, A

Brickhill, Paul
DAM BUSTERS, THE
GREAT ESCAPE, THE

Brophy, John
IMMORTAL SERGEANT, THE

Brown, Harry
SANDS OF IWO JIMA
WALK IN THE SUN, A

Bruner, James
INVASION U.S.A.

Buchheim, Lothar-Guenther
BOAT, THE

Buck, Pearl S.
DRAGON SEED

Burdick, Eugene
FAIL SAFE
UGLY AMERICAN, THE

Burgess, Alan
INN OF THE SIXTH HAPPINESS, THE

Burnett, Murray
CASABLANCA

Burt, Kendal
ONE THAT GOT AWAY, THE

Busch, Niven
DISTANT DRUMS

Carlson, Herbert
WACKIEST SHIP IN THE ARMY, THE

Carney, Daniel
WILD GEESE II
WILD GEESE, THE

Caruso, Dee
WHICH WAY TO THE FRONT?

Catto, Max
MURPHY'S WAR

Cavani, Liliana
NIGHT PORTER, THE

Chase, Borden
FIGHTING SEABEES, THE

Chase, James Hadley
NIGHT OF THE GENERALS, THE

Childers, Erskine
RIDDLE OF THE SANDS, THE

Christie, Campbell
COURT MARTIAL

Christie, Dorothy
COURT MARTIAL

Cimino, Michael
DEER HUNTER, THE

Clavell, James
KING RAT

Clouston, J. Storer
SPY IN BLACK, THE

Cobb, Humphrey
PATHS OF GLORY

Coen, Franklin
ALVAREZ KELLY

Conrad, Joseph
APOCALYPSE NOW
DUELLISTS, THE

Conroy, Pat
GREAT SANTINI, THE
LORDS OF DISCIPLINE, THE

Considine, Robert
THIRTY SECONDS OVER TOKYO

Consiglio, Alberto
OPEN CITY

Cooper, James Fenimore
LAST OF THE MOHICANS, THE

Cosmatos, George Pan
ESCAPE TO ATHENA

Cowan, Sam K.
SERGEANT YORK

Crane, Stephen
RED BADGE OF COURAGE, THE

Crossman [Darryl F. Zanuck], Melville
PURPLE HEART, THE
YANK IN THE R.A.F., A

Crowther, John
MISSING IN ACTION

Davis, Owen
UP IN ARMS

De Martino, Alberto
DIRTY HEROES

Dibner, Martin
DEEP SIX, THE

Dodson, Kenneth M.
AWAY ALL BOATS

Doud, Gil
HELL TO ETERNITY

Dowd, Nancy
COMING HOME

Doyle, Sir Arthur Conan
SHERLOCK HOLMES AND THE SECRET WEAPON

SOURCE WRITERS

Dunning, Decla
STRANGER, THE

Earl, Laurence
BATTLE HELL

Edmonds, Walter D.
DRUMS ALONG THE MOHAWK

Endfield, Cy
ZULU DAWN

Ermolieff, Joseph N.
OUTPOST IN MOROCCO

Farago, Ladislas
PATTON
TORA! TORA! TORA!

Fassbinder, Rainer Werner
MARRIAGE OF MARIA BRAUN, THE

Fast, Howard
SPARTACUS

Faulkner, William
GUNGA DIN

Feldman, Marty
LAST REMAKE OF BEAU GESTE, THE

Fellini, Federico
PAISAN

Fisher, Steve
DESTINATION TOKYO

Flamini, Vincenzo
DIRTY HEROES

Follett, Ken
EYE OF THE NEEDLE

Ford, Corey
CLOAK AND DAGGER

Ford, Daniel
GO TELL THE SPARTANS

Foreman, Carl
BRIDGE ON THE RIVER KWAI, THE
FORCE 10 FROM NAVARONE

Forester, C.S.
AFRICAN QUEEN, THE
COMMANDOS STRIKE AT DAWN, THE

Forsyth, Frederick
DOGS OF WAR, THE
ODESSA FILE, THE

Fort, Garrett
BLOOD ON THE SUN

Frank, Anne
DIARY OF ANNE FRANK, THE

Freeman, Devery
TAPS

Freeman, Fred
START THE REVOLUTION WITHOUT ME

Frohman, Clayton
UNDER FIRE

Gabor, Pal
BRADY'S ESCAPE

Gage, Nicholas
ELENI

Gale, Bob
1941

Gamet, Kenneth
FLYING LEATHERNECKS
FLYING TIGERS

Gardner, Gerald
WHICH WAY TO THE FRONT?

Garfinkle, Louis
DEER HUNTER, THE

Gatliff, John
DEATH BEFORE DISHONOR

George, Peter
DR. STRANGELOVE: OR HOW I LEARNED TO STOP WORRYING AND LOVE THE BOMB

Gibson, Wing Comdr. Guy
DAM BUSTERS, THE

Goff, Ivan
GLORY AT SEA

Gogol, Nikolai
TARAS BULBA

Goldman, William
MARATHON MAN

Gomigawa, Jumpei
HUMAN CONDITION, THE

Goodman, David Zelag
MARCH OR DIE

Gordon, William
BACK TO BATAAN

Grass, Gunter
TIN DRUM, THE

Greenwood, Robert
SALUTE JOHN CITIZEN

Grossbach, Robert
BEST DEFENSE

Grossman, Ladislav
SHOP ON MAIN STREET, THE

Haines, Victor
PAISAN

Hall, James Norman
PASSAGE TO MARSEILLE

Hare, David
PLENTY

Harris, John
SEA SHALL NOT HAVE THEM, THE

Hasford, Gustav
FULL METAL JACKET

Hassel, Sven
MISFIT BRIGADE, THE

Hauser, Thomas
MISSING

Hecht, Ben
CORNERED
GUNGA DIN

Heggen, Thomas
ENSIGN PULVER
MISTER ROBERTS

Heinrich, Willi
CROSS OF IRON

Heller, Joseph
CATCH-22

Hellman, Lillian
NORTH STAR, THE
WATCH ON THE RHINE

Hemingway, Ernest
FAREWELL TO ARMS, A

Herbert, Bob
REBEL

Hersey, John
WAR LOVER, THE

Higgins, Jack
EAGLE HAS LANDED, THE

Higgins, John C.
ADVENTURES OF TARTU, THE

Hirson, Roger
BRIDGE AT REMAGEN, THE

Hitchcock, Alfred
SABOTEUR

Hochhuth, Rolf
LOVE IN GERMANY, A

Hooker, Richard
M*A*S*H

Hool, Lance
MISSING IN ACTION

Horman, Arthur T.
DESPERATE JOURNEY

Hunter, Jack D.
BLUE MAX, THE

Ibanez, Vicente Blasco
FOUR HORSEMEN OF THE APOCALYPSE, THE

Ingster, Boris
CLOAK AND DAGGER

Isherwood, Christopher
CABARET

Jacoby, Michel
CHARGE OF THE LIGHT BRIGADE, THE

James, Henry
GREEN ROOM, THE

James, Henry C.
SPITFIRE

Jarre, Kevin
RAMBO: FIRST BLOOD, PART II

Jones, James
FROM HERE TO ETERNITY

Joppolo, Benjamino
LES CARABINIERS

Kantor, MacKinlay
BEST YEARS OF OUR LIVES, THE

Katz, Robert
MASSACRE IN ROME

Kennaway, James
TUNES OF GLORY

Kikuchi, Kan
GATE OF HELL

King, Paul
OPERATION PETTICOAT

Kipling, Rudyard
GUNGA DIN

SOURCE WRITERS

KIM

Kirkwood, James
SOME KIND OF HERO

Kirst, Hans Helmut
NIGHT OF THE GENERALS, THE

Kleinberger, Avi
P.O.W. THE ESCAPE

Knebel, Fletcher
SEVEN DAYS IN MAY

Knight, Eric
THIS ABOVE ALL

Koch, C.J.
YEAR OF LIVING DANGEROUSLY, THE

Kolitz, Zvi
HILL 24 DOESN'T ANSWER

Konig, Joel
DAVID

Kubik, Lawrence
DEATH BEFORE DISHONOR

Kundera, Milan
UNBEARABLE LIGHTNESS OF BEING, THE

Lamb, Harold
BUCCANEER, THE

Larkin, John
CLOAK AND DAGGER

Larson, Keith
MISSION BATANGAS

Larteguy, Jean
LOST COMMAND, THE

Laurents, Arthur
HOME OF THE BRAVE

Lavery, Emmett
COURT-MARTIAL OF BILLY MITCHELL, THE

Lawrence, T.E.
LAWRENCE OF ARABIA

Lawson, Capt. Ted W.
THIRTY SECONDS OVER TOKYO

Lay, Jr., Beirne
TWELVE O'CLOCK HIGH

Le Carre, John
LITTLE DRUMMER GIRL, THE

Leasor, James
ONE THAT GOT AWAY, THE
SEA WOLVES, THE

Lederer, William J.
UGLY AMERICAN, THE

LeFrancois, Capt. W.S.
GUNG HO!

Lengyel, Melchior
DAYS OF GLORY
TO BE OR NOT TO BE
TO BE OR NOT TO BE

Leone, Sergio
GOOD, THE BAD, AND THE UGLY, THE

Levin, Ira
BOYS FROM BRAZIL, THE

Levinson, Larry
BRADDOCK: MISSING IN ACTION III
MISSING IN ACTION

Lochte, Richard S.
ESCAPE TO ATHENA

Lockwood, Charles A.
HELLCATS OF THE NAVY

Logan, Joshua
ENSIGN PULVER
MISTER ROBERTS

Love, Edmund G.
DESTINATION GOBI

Lowe, Sherman
CRIMSON ROMANCE

Lubitsch, Ernst
TO BE OR NOT TO BE
TO BE OR NOT TO BE

Luedecke, Werne Joerg
MORITURI

Luttwak, Edward N.
POWER PLAY

Lyndon, Barre
SUNDOWN

MacArthur, Charles
GUNGA DIN

MacBain, Alastair
CLOAK AND DAGGER

MacDonald, Philip
LOST PATROL, THE
SAHARA

MacDonnell, A.G.
PIMPERNEL SMITH

McDonough, James R.
PLATOON LEADER

MacInnes, Helen
SALZBURG CONNECTION, THE

McKenna, Richard
SAND PEBBLES, THE

MacKenzie, Aeneas
AGAINST ALL FLAGS
BACK TO BATAAN

McLaverty, Bernard
CAL

MacLean, Alistair
FORCE 10 FROM NAVARONE
GUNS OF NAVARONE, THE

Macpherson, Jeanie
BUCCANEER, THE

McSwigan, Marie
SNOW TREASURE

Maguire, Jeff
VICTORY

Mailer, Norman
NAKED AND THE DEAD, THE

Mann, Klaus
MEPHISTO
PAISAN

Markstein, George
FINAL OPTION, THE

Marshall, S.L.A.
PORK CHOP HILL

Martin, Al
CRIMSON ROMANCE

Mason, A.E.W.
DRUMS
FIRE OVER ENGLAND
FOUR FEATHERS, THE

Massie, Robert K.
NICHOLAS AND ALEXANDRA

Masteroff, Joe
CABARET

Mastrosimone, William
BEAST, THE

Maugham, W. Somerset
RAZOR'S EDGE, THE
RAZOR'S EDGE, THE

Mayer, Edwin Justus
BUCCANEER, THE

Michener, James
BRIDGES AT TOKO-RI, THE
SAYONARA

Milicevic, Djordje
VICTORY

Milius, John
1941

Millar, Ronald
FRIEDA

Miller, Richard
WHICH WAY TO THE FRONT?

Mitchell, Margaret
GONE WITH THE WIND

Mizrahi, Moshe
EVERY TIME WE SAY GOODBYE

Monsarrat, Nicholas
CRUEL SEA, THE

Montanelli, Indro
GENERALE DELLA ROVERE

Mooney, Michael M.
HINDENBURG, THE

Moore, Robin
GREEN BERETS, THE

Moravia, Alberto
TWO WOMEN

Morgan-Witts, Max
VOYAGE OF THE DAMNED

Morrell, David
FIRST BLOOD
RAMBO III
RAMBO: FIRST BLOOD, PART II

Mountbatten, Lord Louis
IN WHICH WE SERVE

Mulisch, Harry
ASSAULT, THE

Murphy, Audie
TO HELL AND BACK

Nathanson, E.M.
DIRTY DOZEN, THE

SOURCE WRITERS

Nichols, Peter
PRIVATES ON PARADE

Noble, Hollister
DRUMS IN THE DEEP SOUTH

Nolan, Frederick
BRASS TARGET

Nordhoff, Charles
PASSAGE TO MARSEILLE

Norris, Aaron
INVASION U.S.A.

Olsen, Theodore V.
SOLDIER BLUE

Ooka, Shohei
FIRES ON THE PLAIN

Oppenheimer, Peer J.
OPERATION CIA

Osborne, John
COLONEL REDL

Pagani, Amedeo
NIGHT PORTER, THE

Pagliero, Marcello
PAISAN

Palgi, Yoel
HANNA'S WAR

Pasternak, Boris
DOCTOR ZHIVAGO

Perret, Jacques
ELUSIVE CORPORAL, THE

Podhajsky, Col. Alois
MIRACLE OF THE WHITE STALLIONS

Pontecorvo, Gillo
BURN

Prange, Gordon W.
TORA! TORA! TORA!

Pratolini, Vasco
PAISAN

Pratt, Theodore
MR. WINKLE GOES TO WAR

Prebble, John
ZULU

Pressburger, Emeric
49TH PARALLEL
BEHOLD A PALE HORSE

Proffitt, Nicholas
GARDENS OF STONE

Przybyszewska, Stanislawa
DANTON

Rabe, David
STREAMERS

Rackin, Martin
BOMBARDIER

Ramati, Alexander
ASSISI UNDERGROUND, THE

Redeker, Quinn K.
DEER HUNTER, THE

Reid, P.R.
COLDITZ STORY, THE

Remarque, Erich Maria
ALL QUIET ON THE WESTERN FRONT
TIME TO LOVE AND A TIME TO DIE, A

Reynolds, Kevin
RED DAWN

Richards, Dick
MARCH OR DIE

Roberts, Ben
GLORY AT SEA

Roelfzema, Erik Hazelhoff
SOLDIER OF ORANGE

Ross, Kenneth
BREAKER MORANT

Rossellini, Roberto
GERMANY, YEAR ZERO
PAISAN

Rozov, Victor
CRANES ARE FLYING, THE

Ryan, Cornelius
BRIDGE TOO FAR, A
LONGEST DAY, THE

Ryan, Patrick
HOW I WON THE WAR

Sarlui, Eduard
SOLDIER'S REVENGE

Saunders, John Monk
DAWN PATROL, THE

Saxon, Lyle
BUCCANEER, THE

Schanberg, Sidney
KILLING FIELDS, THE

Schiffman, Suzanne
LAST METRO, THE

Schoendoerffer, Pierre
FAREWELL TO THE KING

Selinko, Annemarie
DESIREE

Senesh, Hanna
HANNA'S WAR

Shakespeare, William
CHIMES AT MIDNIGHT
HENRY V
RAN
RICHARD III
THRONE OF BLOOD

Shapiro, Lionel
D-DAY, THE SIXTH OF JUNE

Shaw, Irwin
YOUNG LIONS, THE

Sherill, John
HIDING PLACE, THE

Sherman, Robert
TOO LATE THE HERO

Shute, Nevil
ON THE BEACH

Silver, Arthur
BRADDOCK: MISSING IN ACTION III
MISSING IN ACTION

Silvestri, Franco
DIRTY HEROES

Simon, Neil
BILOXI BLUES

Sinclair, Harold
HORSE SOLDIERS, THE

Siodmak, Curt
BERLIN EXPRESS

Skeyhill, Tom
SERGEANT YORK

Smith, Wilbur
SHOUT AT THE DEVIL

Soeteman, Gerard
FLESH AND BLOOD

Soriano, Osvaldo
FUNNY, DIRTY LITTLE WAR, A

Spaak, Charles
CARNIVAL IN FLANDERS

Sperling, Milton
COURT-MARTIAL OF BILLY MITCHELL, THE

Sprague, Chandler
GUY NAMED JOE, A

Stallings, Laurence
WHAT PRICE GLORY?

Stawinski, Jerzy Stefan
KANAL

Steinbeck, John
LIFEBOAT

Stern, David
FRANCIS IN THE NAVY

Stitzel, Robert L.
DISTANT THUNDER

Stone, Joseph
OPERATION PETTICOAT

Stone, Robert
WHO'LL STOP THE RAIN?

Strauss, Richard
CATCH-22

Strueby, Kay
SPITFIRE

Struther, Jan
MRS. MINIVER

Sullivan, C. Gardner
BUCCANEER, THE

Takeyama, Michio
HARP OF BURMA

Tamimi, Sargon
CAPTIVE HEARTS

Tarloff, Frank
SECRET WAR OF HARRY FRIGG, THE

ten Boom, Corrie
HIDING PLACE, THE

Tennyson, Lord Alfred
CHARGE OF THE LIGHT BRIGADE, THE

Thomas, Craig
FIREFOX

WAR MOVIES

217

SOURCE WRITERS

Thomas, Gordon
VOYAGE OF THE DAMNED

Tilsley, Frank
DAMN THE DEFIANT!

Tolstoy, Leo
WAR AND PEACE
WAR AND PEACE

Tregaskis, Richard
GUADALCANAL DIARY

Trivas, Victor
STRANGER, THE

Truffaut, Francois
LAST METRO, THE

Trumbo, Dalton
JOHNNY GOT HIS GUN

Trzcinski, Edmund
STALAG 17

Twist, John
BOMBARDIER

Uris, Leon
BATTLE CRY

Valland, Rose
TRAIN, THE

Van Der Post, Laurens
MERRY CHRISTMAS, MR. LAWRENCE

Van Druten, John
CABARET

Van Praag, Van
MEN IN WAR

Vaughan-Thomas, Wynford
ANZIO

Verde, Dino
DIRTY HEROES

Verucci, Alberto
DIRTY HEROES

Vicenzoni, Luciano
GOOD, THE BAD, AND THE UGLY, THE

Vigny, Benno
MOROCCO

Vonnegut, Jr., Kurt
SLAUGHTERHOUSE-FIVE

Wager, Walter
TWILIGHT'S LAST GLEAMING

Wald, Malvin
BATTLE TAXI

Walker, David E.
OPERATION AMSTERDAM

Wallant, Edward Lewis
PAWNBROKER, THE

Washburn, Deric
DEER HUNTER, THE

Wehle, Deedee
DISTANT THUNDER

Weir, Peter
GALLIPOLI

Wellesley, Gordon
NIGHT TRAIN

West, Rebecca
RETURN OF THE SOLDIER, THE

Westheimer, David
VON RYAN'S EXPRESS

Wexley, John
CORNERED

Wharton, William
BIRDY

Wheeler, Harvey
FAIL SAFE

White, Leslie T.
NORTHERN PURSUIT

White, William L.
THEY WERE EXPENDABLE

Wibberley, Leonard
MOUSE THAT ROARED, THE

Wilhelm, Wolfgang
PIMPERNEL SMITH

Williams, Eric
WOODEN HORSE, THE

Wilson, F. Paul
KEEP, THE

Wilson, Michael
BRIDGE ON THE RIVER KWAI, THE

Woods, William
EDGE OF DARKNESS

Wren, Percival Christopher
BEAU GESTE

Yablonsky, Yabo
VICTORY

Yeats-Brown, Maj. Francis
LIVES OF A BENGAL LANCER

Young, Desmond
DESERT FOX, THE

Young, James R.
BEHIND THE RISING SUN

Yourcenar, Marguerite
COUP DE GRACE

Zemeckis, Robert
1941

Ziemer, Gregor
HITLER'S CHILDREN